Prentice Hall Brief Review

Global History and Geography

Steven Goldberg / Judith Clark DuPré

Ordering Information

Send orders to:
  Pearson
  PO Box 6820
  Chandler, AZ 85246

or call toll free:
  1-800-848-9500
  (8:00 A.M.-6:00 P.M. EST)

or order online:
  k12oasis.pearson.com

School orders:
  k12.oasis.pearson.com

Individual orders:
  pearsonschool.com/nybriefreviews

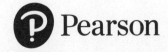

13-digit ISBN 978-0-328-92568-1
10-digit ISBN   0-328-92568-3

1 16

Table of Contents

New York Standards

Standard   Key Idea

4.2

Unit 1 Ancient World: Civilizations and Religions (4000 B.C.–A.D. 500)   1

Unit 1 Standards

1.1	2.1	3.1	4.1	5.1
1.2	2.2	3.2		
1.3	2.3			
1.4	2.4			

Unit 2 Expanding Zones of Exchange (500–1200)   35

Unit 2 Standards

1.1	2.1	3.1	4.1	5.1
1.2	2.2			
1.3	2.3			

Unit 3 Global Interactions (1200–1650)   71

Unit 3 Standards

2.1	3.1	4.1	5.1
2.2			
2.3			

Table of Contents

Unit 7 Standards

1.1	2.1	3.1	4.1	5.1
1.2	2.2			
1.3	2.3			
1.4	2.4			

Unit 8 Standards

1.1	2.1	3.1	4.1	5.1
1.2	2.2		4.2	
	2.3			
	2.4			

About This Book

This book has been written to help you, the student, review your two-year global history and geography course. Its purposes are to:

- Help you focus on the key facts, themes, and concepts that you need to know to succeed on the Regents Examination in global history and geography.
- Allow you to become familiar with the format of the Regents Examination.
- Provide you with the test-taking skills you will need to apply your social studies knowledge to the Regents Examination.

In This Book

In this book, the ninth- and tenth-grade global history and geography curriculum is presented chronologically. In other words, it is presented in time order, from earliest times to the present. Within this organization, there has been a careful attempt to group the material in meaningful eras, or periods of time in which certain types of activity were going on all over the world. For example, Unit 5 covers the period from 1750 through 1914. During this period of more than 160 years, revolutions were occurring all over the world, and nations formed and grew strong.

The book highlights the key themes and concepts that are woven throughout the global history and geography curriculum. Concentrating on themes and concepts will help you organize the global history and geography that you have studied. It will also start you thinking about history in ways that will help you excel on the Regents Examination.

Four Overall Themes

Four overall themes—history; geography; economics; and civics, citizenship, and government—draw these units together. As you review and study, these themes will help you make connections between different times and places. In the side column, several types of help are available.

- **The Big Idea** notes at the beginning of each section organize the section content at a glance. This feature highlights key content in list form.
- **Preparing for the Regents** notes provide questions, explanations, and activities that will give you practice in applying your knowledge to Regents-type questions.
- **Key Themes and Concepts** notes summarize important content and link it to key themes and concepts.

Other sections of this book are also important.

- **Preparing for the Regents** provides instructions and hints for Regents success, using questions like those you will see on the test.
- **Questions for Regents Practice,** found at the end of each unit, will help you figure out your strengths and weaknesses as you practice taking the test.
- **Sample Regents Examinations** also appear at the back of the book.
- **Thematic Review** reviews key content within those themes that the Regents Examination may focus on.

Transition to the new Social Studies Framework

Pearson is committed to supporting the Common Core Standards and the New York State K12 Social Studies Framework. With that in mind, this Brief Review includes new Unit Opener activities for understanding and applying good Social Studies practices. Updated skills notes reinforce Social Studies Practices from the new framework and Common Core skills.

The goal of this book is to help you attain success on the Regents Examination. It will focus your efforts in areas that will pay off on exam day. With this book, you will have the tools to master the material and present it effectively. Best of luck on exam day!

About the Consulting Authors

Steven Goldberg

Steven Goldberg is the District Chairperson of Social Studies for the City School District of New Rochelle. He received his bachelor's degree in history from the University of Rochester, a master's degree in East Asian Studies from Yale University, and an administrative certificate from Teachers' College, Columbia University. He was a Fulbright Fellow to the Netherlands and studied at Sophia University in Tokyo. He is past president of both the New York State Council for the Social Studies and the New York State Social Studies Supervisory Association and has served on the executive board of the Westchester Council of the Social Studies and the National Council for the Social Studies. A consultant to the State Education Department, he has been on numerous Regents Examination committees, as well as the design team for Global History and Geography. In addition, he is a charter member of the Westchester Holocaust Education Center planning committee. He has traveled through Eastern and Western Europe, Japan, Mexico, and Israel.

Judith Clark DuPré

Judith Clark DuPré is a retired social studies teacher from the Fairport School District and current College Supervisor for student teachers at the Ralph C. Wilson School of Education at St. John Fisher College. She received her bachelor's and master's degrees from the State University of New York, Brockport. She is past-president of the Rochester Area Council for the Social Studies, is a member of the New York State Council for the Social Studies, and served on the Advisory Council of the International Studies Program at St. John Fisher College. She has been named to the Who's Who Among America's Teachers and has received the Rochester Area Outstanding High School Social Studies Teacher Award and the New York State Council Distinguished Educator Award. She was a Fulbright Fellow in China and has studied in Germany and Japan. As a consultant to the State Education Department, she has served on numerous Regents Examination Committees and contributed to several curriculum projects in Global Studies and Global History and Geography. She has traveled throughout Western and Eastern Europe, Russia, Southeast Asia, the Middle East, Africa, Australia, and South America.

The Social Studies Standards

Standard 1:
History of the United States and New York

Students will use a variety of intellectual skills to demonstrate their understanding of major ideas, eras, themes, developments, and turning points in the history of the United States and New York.

Standard 2:
World History

Students will use a variety of intellectual skills to demonstrate their understanding of major ideas, eras, themes, developments, and turning points in world history from a variety of perspectives.

Standard 3:
Geography

Students will use a variety of intellectual skills to demonstrate their understanding of the geography of the interdependent world in which we live—local, national, and global—including the distribution of people, places, and environments over Earth's surface.

Standard 4:
Economics

Students will use a variety of intellectual skills to demonstrate their understanding of how the United States and other societies develop economic systems and associated institutions to allocate scarce resources, how major decision-making units function in the United States and other national economies, and how an economy solves the scarcity problem through market and nonmarket economies.

Standard 5:
Civics, Citizenship, and Government

Students will use a variety of intellectual skills to demonstrate their understanding of the necessity for establishing governments; the governmental system of the United States and other nations; the U.S. Constitution; the basic civic values of American constitutional democracy; and the roles, rights, and responsibilities of citizenship, including avenues of participation.

Key Themes and Concepts

Global history and geography can be best understood if it is organized by studying key themes and key concepts that recur in many times and places. Themes and concepts are mental images and classifications that help you to:

- understand important ideas.
- recognize global connections and linkages.
- see similarities and differences among events.
- determine the causes that lead up to events and the effects that result from events.

The Regents Examination uses a number of themes and concepts in constructing questions for the test. They are listed and explained below in four categories: history; geography; economics; and civics, citizenship, and government.

History: Some Key Themes and Concepts

- **Belief Systems** means the established, orderly ways in which groups or individuals look at religious faith or philosophical tenets.
- **Change** is a basic alteration in things, events, and ideas.
- **Choice** means the right or power to select from a range of alternatives.
- **Conflict** is disagreement or opposition between ideas or groups, which may lead to an armed struggle.
- **Culture and Intellectual Life** means the patterns of human behavior that include ideas, beliefs, values, artifacts, and ways of making a living that any society transmits to succeeding generations to meet its fundamental needs. It also includes ways of thinking, studying, and reflecting on ideas and life.
- **Diversity** means understanding and respecting others and oneself, including any similarities or differences in language, gender, socioeconomic class, religion, and other human characteristics and traits.
- **Empathy** means the ability to understand others through identifying in oneself responses similar to the experiences, behaviors, and responses of others.
- **Identity** means awareness of one's own values, attitudes, and capabilities as an individual and as a member of various groups.
- **Imperialism** means the domination by one country of the political and/or economic life of another country or region.
- **Interdependence** means reliance upon others in mutually beneficial interactions and exchanges.
- **Movement of People and Goods** is the exchange of people, ideas, products, technologies, and institutions from one region or civilization to another, a process that has existed throughout history.
- **Nationalism** means a feeling of pride in and devotion to one's country or the desire of a people to control their own government, free from foreign interference or rule.
- **Urbanization** means the movement of people from rural to urban (city) areas.

Key Themes and Concepts

Geography: Some Key Themes and Concepts

The six essential elements of geography follow.

- **The World in Spatial Terms**—Geography studies the relationships among people, places, and environments by mapping information about them in a spatial context.
- **Places and Regions**—The identities and lives of individuals and peoples are rooted in particular places and in those human constructs called regions.
- **Physical Systems**—Physical processes, such as erosion and flooding, shape Earth's surface and interact with plant and animal life to create, sustain, and modify ecosystems.
- **Human Systems**—People are central to geography in that human activities help shape Earth's surface, human settlements and structures are part of Earth's surface, and humans compete for control of Earth's surface.
- **Environment and Society**—Environment means surroundings, including natural elements and elements created by humans. The physical environment is modified by human activities, largely as a consequence of the ways in which human societies value and use Earth's natural resources, and human activities are also influenced by Earth's physical features and processes.
- **The Uses of Geography**—Knowledge of geography enables people to develop an understanding of the relationships between people, places, and environments over time—that is, of Earth as it was, is, and might be.

Economics: Some Key Themes and Concepts

- **Economic Systems** include traditional, command, market, and mixed systems. Each must answer the three basic economic questions: What goods and services are to be produced and in what quantities? How shall these goods and services be produced? For whom shall goods and services be produced?
- **Factors of Production** are human, natural, and capital resources that, when combined, can be converted to various goods and services (for example, land, labor, and capital are used to produce food).
- **Needs and Wants** means those goods and services that are essential, such as food, clothing, and shelter (needs), and those goods and services that people would like to have to improve the quality of their lives, such as education, security, health care, and entertainment (wants).
- **Scarcity** means the conflict between unlimited needs and wants and limited natural and human resources.
- **Science and Technology** means the tools and methods used by people to get what they need and want.

Civics, Citizenship, and Government:
Some Key Themes and Concepts

- **Citizenship** means membership in a community (neighborhood, school, region, state, nation, world) with its accompanying rights, responsibilities, and dispositions.

- **Civic Values** are those important principles that serve as the foundation for our democratic form of government. These values include justice; honesty; self-discipline; due process of law; equality; majority rule with respect for minority rights; and respect of self, others, and property.

- **Decision Making** means the process through which people monitor and influence public and civil life by working with others, clearly articulating ideals and interests, building coalition, seeking consensus, negotiating compromise, and managing conflict.

- **Government** means the formal institutions and processes of a politically organized society with authority to make, enforce, and interpret laws and other binding rules about matters of common interest and concern. Government also refers to the group of people—acting in formal political institutions at national, state, and local levels—who exercise decision-making power or enforce laws and regulations.

- **Human Rights** are those basic political, economic, and social rights to which all human beings are entitled, such as the right to life, liberty, security of person, and a standard of living adequate for the health and well-being of oneself and one's family. Human rights are inalienable and are expressed in various United Nations documents, including the United Nations Charter and the *Universal Declaration of Human Rights*.

- **Justice** means fair, equal, proportional, or appropriate treatment rendered to individuals in interpersonal, societal, or government interactions.

- **Nation-State** means a geographic/political organization that unites people through a common government.

- **Political Systems** include monarchies, dictatorships, and democracies and address certain basic questions of government, such as: What should a government have the power to do? What should a government not have the power to do? A political system also provides for ways in which parts of that system interrelate and combine to perform specific functions of government.

- **Power** is the ability of people to compel or influence the actions of others. Legitimate, or rightful, power is called authority.

This section of the book provides you with strategies for success on the Regents Examination in Global History and Geography. Because you will need to pass the examination in order to graduate from high school, these strategies are important for you to learn and master. They will also help you to succeed in other types of academic work.

Understanding Social Studies

To do well in your study of global history and geography and to pass the Regents Examination, you need to understand three related elements of social studies. On the Regents Examination, you will be asked to demonstrate your mastery of the *factual content* of the global history and geography course, the *concepts* that recur over time, and the *skills* you have mastered.

Specific Factual Content

In a social studies course, you learn about specific historical events and figures. For example, you learn that the French Revolution occurred in 1789 and that Napoleon carried its ideals throughout much of Europe. This is part of the specific content of the global history and geography course you are taking.

Concepts

In social studies courses, you also learn about themes and concepts such as *change and nationalism*. (See "Key Themes and Concepts," which begins on page 2 of this book.) You learn how the French Revolution brought change to France and other lands. You also examine the role that this revolution played in developing and spreading nationalism. In addition, you link developments in France to developments in other places and at different times. You may discuss the similarities and differences in other revolutions, or the types of factors that lead to revolutionary movements. Understanding these connections across place and time is as important as knowing facts about the events themselves.

Skills

In a social studies course, you acquire skills. These skills help you to gather, organize, use, and present information. For example, you learn to interpret various types of documents. Historical documents include maps, graphs, and political cartoons. When you read a circle graph that illustrates class structure and land ownership in France, or when you interpret a political cartoon about Napoleon, you are using social studies skills.

A Glossary of Skill Words

The following is a glossary of skill words that you will see often on the Regents Examination and in other social studies materials. Comprehending these words will help you do well on the Regents Examination.

Analyze to break an idea or concept into parts in order to determine their nature and relationships

Assess to determine the importance, significance, size, or value of

Categorize to place in a class or group; to classify

Classify to arrange in classes or to place in a group according to a system

Compare to state the similarities between two or more examples

Contrast to differentiate; to state the differences between two or more examples

Define to explain what something is or means

Describe to illustrate in words; to tell about

Develop to explain more clearly; to reveal bit by bit

Differentiate to state the difference or differences among two or more examples

Discuss to make observations using facts, reasoning, and argument; to present in some detail

Evaluate to examine and judge the significance, worth, or condition of; to determine the value of

Explain to make plain or understandable; to give reasons for

Generalize to reach a broad conclusion, avoiding specifics, or to base an overall law on particular examples

Hypothesize to present an explanation or an assumption that remains to be proved

Identify to establish the essential character of

Illustrate to make clear or obvious by using examples or comparisons

Incorporate to introduce into or include as a part of something

Infer to conclude or judge from evidence; to draw a conclusion through reasoning

Investigate to research; to inquire into and examine with care

Organize to arrange in a systematic way

Recognize to identify by appearance or characteristics

Restate to say again in a slightly different way

Scrutinize to investigate closely; to examine or inquire into critically

Show to point out; to set forth clearly a position or idea by stating it and giving data that support it

Structure of the Regents Examination

You will have three hours to complete the Regents Examination. The test will include three types of questions.

Multiple-Choice Questions

Together, the multiple-choice questions will account for 55 percent of the points to be earned. There are usually about 50 multiple-choice questions on the Regents Examination. Four possible choices will be provided for each question, only one of which is correct.

Thematic Essay Question

There will be one question of this type on the test. You will be asked to write a thematic essay on a particular topic. Clear and definite directions will be provided to guide you in writing your essay.

Document-Based Question

There will be one multisection document-based question. This question has two major parts. Part A requires that you look at several historical documents and answer one or more questions about each one. Part B requires that you write a clear essay, using evidence from these documents and your knowledge of global history and geography.

You will find examples of all of these types of questions at the end of every unit, in the sample tests, and in the part of the book you are now reading. By working with these examples, you will become familiar with the Regents Examination and build skills for approaching these types of questions. This work will help you get the highest score possible.

Part I: Multiple Choice	50 questions	Approximately 55% of exam grade
Part II: Thematic Essay	1 question based on a specific theme	Approximately 15% of exam grade
Part III: Document-Based Question	Part A: Scaffolding (documents) Part B: Essay	Approximately 15% of exam grade Approximately 15% of exam grade

Strategies for the Regents Examination

The Regents Examination will cover material that you studied in your Global History and Geography course. Some subjects are more likely to appear on the test than others, however. This book will help you review these topics thoroughly.

This book will also teach you how to approach the topics in ways that will help you succeed on all parts of the Regents Examination. Several concepts are especially important.

Understanding the Themes

The test will be built around major themes that recur throughout history. Many themes are listed and defined for you in the Key Themes and Concepts portion of this book. The most common Regents themes are reviewed with examples in the Thematic Review section of this book. As you prepare for the Regents Examination, keep in mind the themes that are most likely to appear on the test. Make sure that you understand these themes and can provide examples of each. Some of the most important themes are listed below.

Belief Systems

Change

Conflict

Culture and Intellectual Life

Diversity

Economic Systems

Geography and the Environment

Imperialism

Interdependence

Justice and Human Rights

Movement of People and Goods (Cultural Diffusion)

Nationalism

Political Systems

Science and Technology

Urbanization

Making Connections Across Place and Time

You will do well on the test if you can make connections among events and developments in different parts of the world and in different time periods. As you study various regions and eras, try to see similarities and differences in events that took place. For example, revolutions occurred in many parts of the world in the 1700s and 1800s. How were these revolutions similar? How were they different? How did earlier revolutions have an impact on later ones? As you review global history and geography, look for patterns and generalizations that hold true across place and time.

Understanding Causes and Impacts

The Regents Examination will also require that you understand the cause-and-effect links between events. As you review major events and turning points, make sure that you understand the factors and conditions that caused them. Then make sure that you can explain the impacts that these events had on later developments.

Practice in Analyzing Documents

This review book provides you with many historical documents, including written documents, maps, tables, charts, graphs, and political cartoons. The multiple-choice and document-based parts of the test will require you to analyze many types of documents. You will be expected to take into account both the source of each document and the author's point of view.

Developing Your Writing Skills

You will earn a higher score on the test if you practice and improve your ability to communicate through writing. Essay-writing skills are required for both the thematic essay and the document-based question. It is most important to write essays that demonstrate a logical plan of organization and include a strong introduction and conclusion.

Multiple-Choice Questions

More than half of the points to be earned on the Regents Examination (55 percent) are earned by answering multiple-choice questions. You will therefore want to get the highest possible score in this section.

Preparing for the Regents

Strategies for Multiple-Choice Questions

Keep several points in mind when you are answering the multiple-choice questions on the Regents Examination.

1. Read the entire question carefully. Read all the choices before you make a decision.
2. Eliminate any choices that you are sure are not true, crossing them out in the test booklet.
3. Remember that in the Regents Examination, there is no penalty for guessing. (This is *not* true of all multiple-choice tests.) Therefore, you should make your best guess at an answer to *every* question.
4. See if there is a key phrase that signals what you should be looking for in the question. Not all questions have such phrases. However, you should be aware of certain signal words and phrases.

Signals for Questions About Cause and Effect: *one effect, one result, is most directly influenced by, have led directly to, have resulted in, a major cause of, are a direct result of*

Signals for Questions That Require an Example: *best illustrates, best reflects, are all examples of, best explains, is an example of*

Signals for Questions That Ask for a Main Idea: *main idea, primarily characterized by, formed the basis for*

Signals for Questions That Ask About Similarities or Differences: *are similar, one similarity, one difference between*

Types of Multiple-Choice Questions

Although you will see many types of multiple-choice questions on the Regents Examination, all fall into one or more of the following general categories.

Unit Content Questions The test will include multiple-choice questions that cover material from each of the eight units in this book.

Cross-Unit Questions Questions that ask you to respond to historical situations or people discussed in several different units will also appear on the test. These questions often ask you to make a deduction that is *valid* (true) about the situations or people, find a *similarity* between them, or identify a *characteristic* that is common to all.

Thematic Questions Some questions will address general social studies themes such as nationalism, imperialism, political systems, or economic systems. These questions often ask you to provide *the best example of* something, explain *how it developed*, or describe *characteristics of* a particular concept or system. The themes that these questions may deal with are listed in the Key Themes and Concepts section of this book and highlighted in the Thematic Review.

Questions Based on Documents Some multiple-choice questions are based on documents. Types of documents that may appear include:

- A short passage
- A map
- A graph
- A table or chart
- A political cartoon

Such document-based questions often ask for the *main idea* of a passage or cartoon. Sometimes they ask you to identify an *accurate statement* or the statement *best supported by the data*. They may also ask you to choose the *valid conclusion* drawn from the document. These types of questions often require both skills in interpreting documents and factual knowledge of global history and geography.

Sample Unit Content Questions

Each of the next two questions tests your knowledge of content from a specific unit of the Global History and Geography course.

1   A negative effect of the partitioning of India in 1947 was that
    (1) foreign rule was reestablished in India
    (2) Hinduism became the only religion practiced in India
    (3) the government policy of nonalignment further divided Indian society
    (4) civil unrest, territorial disputes, and religious conflict continued
        throughout the region

You know from the question that the answer must be an *effect* and that it must be *negative*. Choice 1 cannot be the answer, since British rule ended in 1947. Choice 2 is incorrect because Islam, Sikhism, and other religions besides Hinduism are practiced in India. Choice 3 cannot be correct, since nonalignment was a reaction to the Cold War, not to partition. Choice 4 is the correct answer because the creation of Pakistan and India increased tensions and conflicts between Hindus and Muslims in the region.

2   Which group had the greatest influence on early Russian culture?
    (1) Franks
    (2) Ottoman Turks
    (3) Byzantine empire
    (4) Roman Catholic Church

The important words in this question are *the greatest influence*. The Franks (Choice 1) were a Germanic tribe of the early Middle Ages. They had a strong effect on Western Europe but not on Russia. The Ottoman Turks (Choice 2) had an influence on Russia, but their influence occurred later. The Roman Catholic Church (Choice 4) had little influence because the Orthodox Christian Church was adopted by Russia. The Byzantine empire (Choice 3), however, is the correct answer because it had an enormous impact on early Russia.

Sample Thematic Questions

Each of the next two multiple-choice questions deals with a specific theme or concept.

3   Which aspect of a nation's culture is most directly influenced by the physical
    geography of that nation?
    (1) form of government
    (2) population distribution
    (3) religious beliefs
    (4) social class system

The question involves physical geography and its influence on a nation. The key phrase in the question is *is most directly influenced.* If you understand physical geography, you know that it has a great influence on where people live. For example, people tend to live near sources of water. Large populations live where

Preparing for the Regents

the geography easily allows settlement. The answer to this question would therefore be Choice 2. Geography sometimes influences forms of government (Choice 1), as in the Greek city-states, but it has a more direct influence on population distribution. It has even less influence on religious beliefs (Choice 3) and the social class system (Choice 4).

4   Which quotation best reflects a feeling of nationalism?
     (1) "An eye for an eye and a tooth for a tooth."
     (2) "A person's greatest social obligation is loyalty to the family."
     (3) "For God, King, and Country."
     (4) "Opposition to evil is as much a duty as is cooperation with good."

This question is about nationalism, a theme you need to understand to prepare for the Regents Examination. First, you must know what nationalism is: a feeling of pride in and devotion to one's country. Then you must decide which of the possible answers best expresses that idea. Choice 1 has to do with justice, not nationalism. Choice 2 has to do with social behavior and Choice 4 with moral behavior. Only Choice 3 expresses the idea of devotion to one's nation, so Choice 3 is the correct answer.

Sample Cross-Unit Questions

Each of the next two questions deals with content from two or more units of the Global History and Geography course.

5   One similarity found in the leadership of Peter the Great of Russia, Kemal Atatürk of Turkey, and Jawaharlal Nehru of India is that each leader
     (1) expanded his territory by invading Greece
     (2) borrowed ideas and technology from Western Europe
     (3) supported equal rights for women
     (4) increased the power of religious groups in his nation

Each of these leaders appears in a different unit of this book. Note that this question asks for *one similarity*. This means that the answer must be true for all three leaders. Therefore, if you know that a choice is not true of even one leader, it cannot be the right answer. Choice 1 is not correct because none of the three leaders invaded Greece. Although each of these leaders supported some reforms or societal changes that involved women, none called for equal rights for women, so Choice 3 is incorrect. Peter the Great and Kemal Atatürk actually decreased the power of religious groups in their nations, so Choice 4 cannot be correct. All of these leaders did, however, borrow ideas and technology from the West, making Choice 2 the correct answer.

6   The societies of traditional China, feudal Japan, and czarist Russia were all characterized by
     (1) a rigid class structure
     (2) much interaction with other cultures
     (3) great economic change
     (4) rapidly changing social values

This question also asks you about content from several units of your Global History and Geography course. Familiarity with all three cultures would help you select Choice 1. None of the other choices is characteristic of *any* of the civilizations, so even if you were familiar only with czarist Russia, you would still be able to choose the correct answer (1).

Sample Document-Based Questions

The remaining sample questions are based on historical documents.

Base your answer to question 7 on the map below and on your knowledge of social studies.

African Kingdoms, 1000 B.C.–A.D. 1600

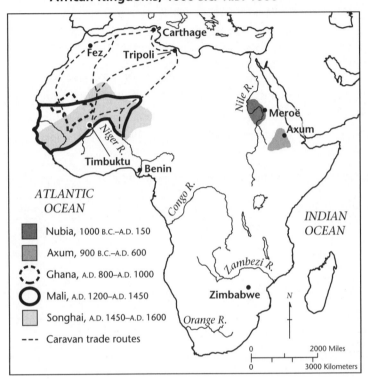

7 Which conclusion regarding early African trade is supported by the information provided by this map?
   (1) The kingdom of Zimbabwe grew rich from trade with Egypt.
   (2) The kingdoms of West Africa traded with the city-states of East Africa.
   (3) The Congo and Zambezi Rivers played an important role in Africa's early trade.
   (4) The West African kingdoms had trading contacts with the cities of the Mediterranean.

The question asks which conclusion can be supported by information provided in the map. Only Choice 4 can be supported by information from the map. Trade routes are shown linking the West African kingdoms with the Mediterranean cities of Carthage and Tripoli. Even if any of the other selections are true, they *are not supported* by evidence in this map. The map provides no information about how rich Zimbabwe was, about trade with East African cities, or about the role of the Congo and Zambezi Rivers.

Base your answer to question 8 on the poem below and on your knowledge of social studies.

> May our country
> Taking what is good
> And rejecting what is bad
> Be not inferior
> to any other
> —Mutsuhito

8   According to this Japanese poem, Mutsuhito believed that Japan should modernize by
(1) completely changing Japanese society
(2) borrowing selectively from other societies
(3) controlling other cultures that were superior
(4) rejecting foreign influence

Here, you are asked to demonstrate understanding of Mutsuhito's poem. Choice 1 is not appropriate because the poem does not indicate whether Mutsuhito favored just a little change or massive change. Choice 3 is incorrect because the poem talks about borrowing from other cultures, not controlling them. Choice 4 is wrong because the poem advises rejection only of "what is bad." Choice 2 correctly summarizes the meaning of the poem.

Base your answer to questions 9 and 10 on the table below and on your knowledge of social studies.

Statistics for Selected Nations of South Asia

Nations	Bangladesh	Malaysia	Myanmar	Pakistan	Thailand
Population Density (per sq mi)	2,294	164	181	440	303
Per Capita Income (dollars)	1,260	10,750	1,120	2,300	7,700
Percentage of Labor Force in Agriculture	65	21	67	47	43
Literacy Rate (percentage)	38	83	83	38	94

9   Which nations have more than half of the labor force engaged in agriculture?
(1) Bangladesh and Myanmar
(2) Pakistan and Bangladesh
(3) Thailand and Malaysia
(4) Myanmar and Thailand

Question 9 asks you to examine one column of the table. Choices 2 and 3 are incorrect because none of those nations have more than 50 percent of the labor force engaged in agriculture. Choice 4 is incorrect because only Myanmar has the appropriate percentage. Choice 1 is correct, listing the two nations with more than half of the labor force in agriculture.

10   Which is a valid conclusion, based on the information in the table?
(1) Bangladesh has the highest per capita income.
(2) Myanmar has the smallest percentage of workers involved in farming.
(3) Malaysia has the highest population density.
(4) Thailand has the highest percentage of children enrolled in school.

For question 10, the correct answer is Choice 4. A high literacy rate (94 percent) indicates that a high percentage of children are learning to read in school. Choice 1 is not true: Bangladesh has nearly the lowest per capita income of the nations shown. Choice 2 is incorrect, since Myanmar has the highest percentage of workers involved in farming. Choice 3 is incorrect because Malaysia actually has the lowest population density, not the highest.

Base your answer to question 11 on the graph below and on your knowledge of social studies.

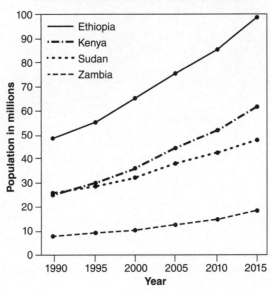

Population Projections for Selected East and Southern African Nations

Source: *The World Bank*

11 Based on the information in the graph, which is a valid conclusion about the populations of East and Southern African nations?
(1) The nation with the largest population in 1990 will have the lowest population in 2015.
(2) Population will rise in all countries, but it will rise fastest in Ethiopia.
(3) Populations will level off in all of these nations after the year 2005.
(4) In 1995, the population of Zambia was approximately 28 million people.

You can rule out Choice 1 because the ranks of the nations changed very little if at all. You can eliminate Choice 3 because one glance at the lines shows all four populations continuing to rise more steeply after 1995. You can rule out Choice 4 by reading the graph and seeing that Zambia's population in 1995 was about 10 million. Choice 2, however, is a valid conclusion to draw from this graph.

Base your answer to question 12 on the cartoon below and on your knowledge of social studies.

THE OLD MAN AND THE SEA

By permission of Rex Babin, *Times Union*, Albany, NY.

12 What is the main idea of the cartoon?
   (1) Cuba's fishing industry is suffering a decline.
   (2) Castro rode the wave of world communism to a successful conclusion.
   (3) Cuba is isolated without Soviet economic support.
   (4) Castro bears responsibility for the failure of communism in Eastern Europe.

Questions on political cartoons require skill in interpreting such cartoons as well as knowledge of global history. When you look at a political cartoon, make sure that you can identify its elements. Many are symbolic. For example, the small boat marked *Cuba* represents the country of Cuba. The figure in it is a caricature of Fidel Castro, the president of Cuba. The carcass of the fish has a hammer and sickle, the national symbol of the former Soviet Union. The image communicates the idea that the Soviet Union is dead.

Choice 1 is incorrect because the cartoon is clearly about political issues, not about the Cuban fishing industry. You can rule out Choice 2 because the figure in the boat does not look happy. Also, you have read that Cuba has experienced difficulty since the fall of communism. Choice 4 is not correct because Castro is feeling the *effects* of change; he was not the *cause*. That leaves only Choice 3, which you know to be true: Cuba has had difficulties without Soviet support.

Base your answer to question 13 on the cartoon below and on your knowledge of social studies.

13 Which conclusion is best supported by the cartoon?
    (1) Imprisonment of political dissidents rarely ends opposition to the government.
    (2) The United Nations supports punishment of acts of civil disobedience.
    (3) Better media coverage would prevent the imprisonment of protesters.
    (4) Mistreatment of political prisoners often results in their acceptance of government policies.

Again, you must first examine the cartoon and analyze its elements. The name *Mandela* and your knowledge of global history tell you that this cartoon shows the time when Nelson Mandela was in prison in South Africa. You notice that Mandela is of normal size when he enters prison in 1962 but has grown greatly by the time he emerges in 1990. His increased size represents his increased world stature during the time of his imprisonment. You can eliminate Choice 2 because it is untrue and because the United Nations is not featured in this cartoon. Choice 3 can be ruled out because media coverage is not shown by the cartoon. Choice 4 is also not supported by the cartoon, since there is no indication that Mandela accepted government policies. Instead, Mandela's changed size indicates that Choice 1 is the answer. Instead of stopping opposition by imprisoning Mandela, the South African government only succeeded in furthering his cause of opposition to apartheid.

Thematic Essay Question

There will be one thematic essay question on the Regents Examination. It will count for approximately 15 percent of the total points you may receive. This section of the exam requires you to understand, interpret, and explain a key social studies theme or concept. In your essay, you should be able to:

- State a main idea in a thesis statement.
- Develop it and add supporting details.
- Summarize it with an effective conclusion.

Basic Characteristics

The directions for thematic essay questions always consist of three parts: a theme, a task, and suggestions.

The Theme This part of the question identifies a broad social studies theme that will be the general topic of your essay. The theme is given more focus by a brief explanatory statement that follows the statement of the theme. (To review the most common themes tested in Regents Examinations, see the Thematic Review section at the end of this book.)

The Task The second part of a thematic essay question is the task. The task section usually has three parts and presents the instructions you will need to write your essay. Generally, you will be asked to define or describe a theme or concept, to give a specific number of examples or results, and then to evaluate the theme or concept in some way. Typical forms of evaluation include describing causes or effects and evaluating positive or negative aspects.

Suggestions The final part of a thematic essay question is the suggestions section. This part lists specific areas that you might choose to discuss in your essay. The suggestions might name people, nations, or civilizations, depending on the topic of the question. These are, of course, only suggestions, and you may choose to write about other examples that are relevant to the essay topic. Often, the suggestions will caution you not to choose the United States as your topic. If this warning is present, pay attention to it. You will not receive full credit for an answer that does not follow the directions.

Strategy for the Thematic Essay Question

Keep the following strategies in mind as you approach a thematic essay question.

1. Read the entire question through first.
2. After you have read the question, begin jotting down any ideas you have.
3. After you have jotted down your initial ideas, begin to make a brief outline. Organization is important in writing a good essay. The outline does not need to be very detailed, but it should include enough information to help you remember all the points that you want to use in the essay. It should also help you to see whether your essay has a logical organization.
4. Use the suggestions to help you recall the importance of the theme in different places and times.
5. Develop your essay logically.
6. Do not merely list facts. Analyze and evaluate the information, and compare or contrast various aspects.
7. Make sure that you provide examples to support your ideas.

8. Make sure that you have completed each of the items listed in the task section.
9. Make sure that your essay has both a strong introduction and a strong conclusion. You cannot get full credit for your essay if either of these elements is missing or weak.

Sample Thematic Essay Questions

The thematic essay questions included throughout this book will provide you with insight into the types of questions you will see on the actual Regents Examination. Below are two sample thematic essay questions. They follow the same format as those that will appear on the actual Regents Examination.

Sample One
Directions
Write a well-organized essay that includes an introduction, several paragraphs addressing the task below, and a conclusion.

Theme: Geography

> Geographic features can positively or negatively affect the development of a nation or region.

Task:

> Select *one* geographic feature from your study of global history.
>
> • Explain how this geographic feature has had an effect on the historical development of *two* nations or regions. Be sure to include specific historical examples in your essay.

You may use any geographic features from your study of global history. Some suggestions you might wish to consider include: river valley, mountain, desert, island, rain forest, and climate. Do not use the United States in your answer.

Sample Two
Directions
Write a well-organized essay that includes an introduction, several paragraphs addressing the task below, and a conclusion.

Theme: Civilization

> Throughout history, great civilizations have existed in various parts of the world. The cultural and intellectual achievements of these civilizations contributed to the advancement of humankind.

Task:

> • Define the term *civilization*.
> • Describe some examples of cultural or intellectual achievements made by past civilizations. Identify each example with the particular civilization that made the contribution.
> • Explain the lasting importance of each of these achievements or contributions to global history.

You may discuss any civilization from your study of global history, except the United States. Some civilizations you might wish to consider include ancient Egypt, classical Rome, the Gupta empire, classical China, or the Muslim golden age.

Thematic Essay Scoring

Knowing how your essay will be scored will help you write it effectively. Essays are scored with point values from 0 to 5. An essay receiving a score of 5 answers the question in a complete, comprehensive manner. You would receive a score of 0 only if you failed to address the theme at all, wrote an essay that was completely illegible, or turned in a blank paper.

The scoring rubric that follows represents the generic criteria on which your essay will be scored.

Generic Scoring Rubric

Thematic Essay

Score of 5:
- Thoroughly develops all aspects of the task evenly and in depth
- Is more analytical than descriptive (analyzes, evaluates, and/or creates information)
- Richly supports the theme with many relevant facts, examples, and details
- Demonstrates a logical and clear plan of organization; includes an introduction and a conclusion that are beyond a restatement of the theme

Score of 4:
- Develops all aspects of the task but may do so somewhat unevenly
- Is both descriptive and analytical (applies, analyzes, evaluates, and/or creates information)
- Supports the theme with relevant facts, examples, and details
- Demonstrates a logical and clear plan of organization; includes an introduction and a conclusion that are beyond a restatement of the theme

Score of 3:
- Develops all aspects of the task with little depth or develops most aspects of the task in some depth
- Is more descriptive than analytical (applies, may analyze, and/or evaluate information)
- Includes some relevant facts, examples, and details; may include some minor inaccuracies
- Demonstrates a satisfactory plan of organization; includes an introduction and a conclusion that may be a restatement of the theme

Score of 2:
- Minimally develops all aspects of the task or develops some aspects of the task in some depth
- Is primarily descriptive; may include faulty, weak, or isolated application or analysis
- Includes few relevant facts, examples, and details; may include some inaccuracies
- Demonstrates a general plan of organization; may lack focus; may contain digressions; may not clearly identify which aspect of the task is being addressed; may lack an introduction and/or a conclusion

Score of 1:

- Minimally develops some aspects of the task
- Is descriptive; may lack understanding, application, or analysis
- Includes few relevant facts, examples, or details; may include inaccuracies
- May demonstrate a weakness in organization; may lack focus; may contain digressions; may not clearly identify which aspect of the task is being addressed; may lack an introduction and/or a conclusion

Score of 0:

- Fails to develop the task or may only refer to the theme in a general way; *OR* includes no relevant facts, examples, or details; *OR* includes only the theme, task, or suggestions as copied from the test booklet; *OR* is illegible; *OR* is a blank paper

Document-Based Question

This type of question presents you with up to eight historical documents on a single subject. The documents may be letters, speeches, or other written records; maps; charts; political cartoons; graphs; or tables.

Basic Characteristics

Questions based on historical documents have several characteristics. The documents provided give information or express viewpoints about a common theme. For space reasons, the samples you will see here and at the end of each unit will include only a few documents. Those on the test, however, may include up to eight documents.

A document-based question always has two parts. Part A requires short answers to specific questions about the documents. Part B requires you to write an essay. The themes for these essays are based on the same social studies themes and concepts as are used for thematic essays. Refer to the sample shown on the following pages as you read this information about document-based questions.

General Directions The question will begin with a set of directions. These directions will tell you what to do for each part of the question.

Historical Context Each question will contain a short statement that defines the historical context for the question. Read this statement carefully. It will help you understand the main topic to be discussed.

Task This statement defines the overall task that you will perform as you examine the documents provided.

Part A: Short Answer In this part of the question, you will be presented with the documents themselves. Documents that are quotations will be enclosed within boxes. The author of the quotation will be clearly identified. Documents may also be maps, charts, or political cartoons. Each document will be followed by one or possibly more questions. The questions will ask you to consider the viewpoint and source of the document. This is important because the author of a document may have a bias or a special motive that makes it difficult to accept his or her words as the whole truth. For example, a person who is trying to persuade soldiers to go into battle will not present the point of view of the opposing side very completely. Skills in interpreting the information in documents are very important.

Part B: Essay The essay portion of the question includes a set of general instructions and repeats the historical context. Pay very close attention to the instructions. Note that they call for a well-organized essay with both an introduction and a conclusion. They require you to use evidence from the documents to support your response. You should not, however, merely repeat the contents of the documents. Be sure also to include specific, related information from your knowledge of global history and geography. You must use additional relevant information that is not found in the documents. Otherwise you will not receive full credit for your essay. For the highest possible score, refer to all of the documents provided in the question, and include additional information from your knowledge of global history.

Strategy for the Document-Based Question

Answering Part A Your first task is to answer each of the questions about the documents. Examine each passage carefully, and look closely at each image. Read the question or questions and then reexamine the documents. Keep in mind the historical context. Recognize the various viewpoints that are being expressed. Finally, write a clear answer to each question.

Answering Part B You can approach this part much as you would a thematic essay, except that you need to consider how to incorporate evidence from the documents provided as well as knowledge from your Global History and Geography course.

You will find it useful to make a brief outline as you did for the thematic essay, showing what you plan to use as a thesis statement, what your supporting facts will be, where you will use various documents for support, and what your conclusion will be.

Take a look at the scoring rubric that follows the sample document-based question. A rubric like this one will be used to score Part B of the document-based question.

To get a high score on the essay portion of the test, do the following:

- Complete all parts of the task thoroughly.
- Provide analysis and interpretation of all or most of the documents supplied in the question. Information from the documents must be included within the body of your essay.
- Include as much related outside information as you can. Relevant outside information is crucial to a high score. Support your essay with related facts, examples, and details.
- Write an essay that is organized clearly and logically. Outlining your essay will help you maintain a clear organization.
- After you have finished writing, check to be sure that you have included a strong introduction and a strong conclusion.

Sample Document-Based Question

The following sample of a document-based question includes three documents. As already noted, a document-based question on the Regents Examination could show up to eight documents. Otherwise, the short-answer questions and essay question in this sample are similar to what you will see on the Regents Examination. For additional practice with questions based on documents, see the Questions for Regents Practice at the end of each unit as well as the sample tests.

Historical Context:

> Throughout history, leaders have had vastly differing viewpoints on whether violence or war is ever justified. Some leaders, for example, have felt that violence is justified for certain purposes. Others have believed that violence against others is never the right choice. These viewpoints have had powerful effects on historical events.

Task: Using information from the documents and your knowledge of global history, answer the questions that follow each document in Part A. Your answers to the questions will help you write the Part B essay, in which you will be asked to

> • Evaluate several viewpoints on whether violence or war is ever justified in order to achieve a desired goal

Part A: Short-Answer

Directions: Analyze the documents and answer the question or questions that follow each document, using the space provided.

Document #1

> *What difference does it make to the dead, the orphans and the homeless, whether the mad destruction is wrought under the name of totalitarianism or the holy name of democracy and liberty?*
>
> — **Mohandas Gandhi, 1948**

1 Does Gandhi think that violence may be justified if the cause is a good one? Explain your answer, referring to the quotation.

_____

_____

_____

_____

_____

_____

Preparing for the Regents

Document #2
The Atomic Bomb

PROBLEM
Should U.S. President Truman use the atomic bomb against Japan?

Reasons FOR	Reasons AGAINST
• It would save American lives. • It would bring a quick end to the war. • It would show the power of the United States to any future enemies.	• It would cause massive destruction. • Once used, it would more likely be used again. • It would release deadly radioactivity.

Decision
Truman orders atomic bomb dropped on Hiroshima and Nagasaki.

RESULTS
• More than 110,000 die. • Japan surrenders.

2 List two reasons why President Truman decided to use atomic bombs against Japan.

_____

_____

_____

_____

_____

3 Describe two reasons why some Americans disagreed with President Truman's decision.

_____

_____

_____

_____

_____

Document #3

> *Brutality is respected. Brutality and physical strength. The plain man in the street respects nothing but brutal strength and ruthlessness—women, too, for that matter, women and children. The people need wholesome fear.*
>
> **— Adolf Hitler, 1936**

4   How did Adolf Hitler justify his inhumanity? Explain your answer, referring to the quotation.

_____

_____

_____

_____

_____

_____

Document #4

> *A government should not mobilize an army out of anger, military leaders should not provoke a war out of wrath. Act when it is beneficial, desist when it is not. Anger can revert to joy, wrath can revert to delight, but a nation destroyed cannot be restored to existence, and the dead cannot be restored to life.*
>
> **— Sun Tzu, *The Art of War*, c. 300 B.C.**

5   Why did Sun Tzu say it is bad to start a war out of anger? Explain your answer, referring to the quotation.

_____

_____

_____

_____

_____

_____

Document #5

> *A revolution is not a dinner party, or writing an essay, or painting a picture or doing embroidery; it cannot be so refined, so leisurely and gentle, so kind, courteous, restrained, and generous. A revolution is an insurrection, an act of violence by which one class overthrows another.*
>
> — **Mao Zedong, leader of the Communist Revolution in China**

6   According to Mao, what means are necessary in order for a revolution to succeed? Explain your answer, referring to the quotation.

_____

_____

_____

_____

_____

Part B

Essay

Directions: Write a well-organized essay that includes an introduction, several paragraphs, and a conclusion. Use evidence from *at least **three*** documents in your essay. Support your response with relevant facts, examples, and details. Include additional outside information.

Historical Context:

Throughout history, leaders have had vastly differing viewpoints on whether violence or war is ever justified. Some leaders, for example, have felt that violence is justified for certain purposes. Others have believed that violence against others is never the right choice. These viewpoints have had powerful effects on historical events.

Task: Using information from the documents and your knowledge of global history and geography, write an essay in which you

> • Evaluate whether violence or war is ever justified in order to achieve a desired goal

Guidelines:

In your essay, be sure to
- Develop all aspects of the task
- Incorporate information from *at least **three*** documents
- Incorporate relevant outside information
- Support the theme with relevant facts, examples, and details
- Use a logical and clear plan of organization, including an introduction and a conclusion that are beyond a restatement of the theme

Document-Based Question Scoring

Knowing how your document-based essay will be scored will help you write it effectively. Like thematic essays, document-based essays are scored with point values from 0 to 5. An essay receiving a score of 5 answers the question in a complete, comprehensive manner. You would receive a score of 0 only if you failed to address the theme at all, wrote an essay that was completely illegible, or turned in a blank paper.

The scoring rubric that follows represents the generic criteria on which your document-based essay will be scored.

Generic Scoring Rubric

Document-Based Question
Score of 5:
- Thoroughly develops all aspects of the task evenly and in depth
- Is more analytical than descriptive (analyzes, evaluates, and/or creates information)
- Incorporates relevant information from *at least* one more than half of the documents
- Incorporates substantial relevant outside information
- Richly supports the theme with many relevant facts, examples, and details
- Demonstrates a logical and clear plan of organization; includes an introduction and a conclusion that are beyond a restatement of the theme

Score of 4:
- Develops all aspects of the task but may do so somewhat unevenly
- Is both descriptive and analytical (applies, analyzes, evaluates, and/or creates information)
- Incorporates relevant information from *at least* half of the documents
- Incorporates relevant outside information
- Supports the theme with relevant facts, examples, and details
- Demonstrates a logical and clear plan of organization; includes an introduction and a conclusion that are beyond a restatement of the theme

Score of 3:
- Develops all aspects of the task with little depth *or* develops most aspects of the task in some depth
- Is more descriptive than analytical (applies, may analyze, and/or evaluates information)
- Incorporates some relevant information from some of the documents
- Incorporates limited relevant outside information
- Includes some relevant facts, examples, and details; may include some minor inaccuracies
- Demonstrates a satisfactory plan of organization; includes an introduction and a conclusion that may be a restatement of the theme

Score of 2:

- Minimally develops all aspects of the task *or* develops some aspects of the task in some depth
- Is primarily descriptive; may include faulty, weak, or isolated application or analysis
- Incorporates limited relevant information from the documents *or* consists primarily of relevant information copied from the documents
- Presents little or no relevant outside information
- Includes few relevant facts, examples, and details; may include some inaccuracies
- Demonstrates a general plan of organization; may lack focus; may contain digressions; may not clearly identify which aspect of the task is being addressed; may lack an introduction and/or a conclusion

Score of 1:

- Minimally develops some aspects of the task
- Is descriptive; may lack understanding, application, or analysis
- Makes vague, unclear references to the documents or consists primarily of relevant and irrelevant information copied from the documents
- Presents no relevant outside information
- Includes few relevant facts, examples, or details; may include inaccuracies
- May demonstrate a weakness in organization; may lack focus; may contain digressions; may not clearly identify which aspect of the task is being addressed; may lack an introduction and/or a conclusion

Score of 0:

- Fails to develop the task or may only refer to the theme in a general way; *OR* includes no relevant facts, examples, or details; *OR* includes only the historical context and/or task as copied from the test booklet; *OR* includes only entire documents copied from the test booklet; *OR* is illegible; *OR* is a blank paper

Preparing for the Regents

A Few Final Words

You have learned a number of strategies to help you prepare for the multiple-choice, thematic essay, and document-based questions on the Regents Examination in Global History and Geography. Try out these strategies on the practice tests included in the book and on the questions at the end of each unit. This practice will help you find out what works best for you and will allow you to become comfortable with the various types of questions found in the Regents Examination. As you practice more, you will also become confident of your ability to do well on the test.

Make sure you are well rested on the day of the examination. If you have devoted serious effort to your study of global history and geography, reviewed the material in this book, and used the many test items provided here for practice, you will be thoroughly prepared for the exam.

Unit 1 Pre-Test

Name _____ **Date** _____

Directions Review the Preparing for the Regents section of this book. Then answer the following questions, drawn from actual Regents examinations. For each statement or question, choose the *number* of the word or expression that, of those given, best completes the statement or answers the question.

1. The Neolithic Revolution was characterized by the
   (1) change from nomadic herding to settled farming
   (2) growth of iron tool-making technology
   (3) migration of early peoples to the Americas
   (4) decline of large empires

2. Why did ancient civilizations develop in valleys of rivers such as the Nile, Indus, Tigris, and Euphrates?
   (1) The river valleys provided a source of fresh water and good farmland.
   (2) The rivers aided in the exploration of new territories.
   (3) The rivers provided power for industries.
   (4) The river valleys provided areas for recreation.

3. Hieroglyphic and cuneiform systems provided the basis for the development of
   (1) subsistence farming
   (2) painting and sculpture
   (3) oral traditions
   (4) recorded history

4. "If a son has struck his father, they shall cut off his hand. If a nobleman has destroyed the eye of a member of the aristocracy, they shall destroy his eye...."
   The idea expressed in this quotation is found in the
   (1) Ten Commandments
   (2) Twelve Tables
   (3) Justinian Code
   (4) Code of Hammurabi

5. Why did the ancient city-states of Athens and Sparta develop different political systems?
   (1) The Byzantine Empire dictated government policies.
   (2) Foreign travelers introduced new philosophies.
   (3) The mountainous topography resulted in the isolation of these city-states.
   (4) For over three centuries, civil wars raged in these city-states.

6. One similarity between the ancient civilizations in Egypt and China is that they developed
   (1) nomadic lifestyles
   (2) monotheistic belief systems
   (3) democratic governments
   (4) written forms of communication

7. One contribution of ancient Roman culture was the development of
   (1) the concept of zero
   (2) the process of making silk
   (3) a republican form of government
   (4) the printing press

8. Which values are most closely associated with the fundamental principles of Buddhism?
   (1) competition and financial success
   (2) maintaining the caste system and providing education for all people
   (3) practicing nonviolence and giving up worldly desires
   (4) self-determination and democracy

Name _____ **Date** _____

9. In China, Confucianism emphasized the idea that

   (1) equality should exist between all members of society
   (2) salvation could be attained by prayer, meditation, and good deeds
   (3) individual goals should be placed ahead of the needs of the group
   (4) harmony could be achieved by the proper behavior of each member of a family or society

10. Christianity, Islam, and Judaism are similar in that they all ask their followers to

    (1) believe in reincarnation
    (2) strive for nirvana
    (3) follow a code of behavior
    (4) practice polytheism

11. One way in which the Han dynasty and the Roman Empire were similar is that both

    (1) governed large areas around the Mediterranean Sea
    (2) created democratic societies in which people elected their government officials
    (3) developed a social system in which great equality existed
    (4) promoted unity and communication by building a strong system of roads

12. Which statement explains a cause rather than an effect of the Bantu migration between 500 B.C. and A.D. 1500?

    (1) Techniques for herding and cultivating were spread to other peoples.
    (2) More than sixty million people now speak a Bantu language.
    (3) Trading cities developed along the coast of east Africa.
    (4) Population increases put pressure on agriculture.

13. The use of the Silk Road in Asia and caravan routes in northern Africa and southwestern Asia encouraged

    (1) self-sufficiency   (3) ethnocentrism
    (2) cultural isolation   (4) cultural diffusion

14. What effect did the geography of ancient Greece have on its early development?

    (1) The mountainous terrain led to the creation of independent city-states.
    (2) A lack of natural seaports limited communication.
    (3) An inland location hindered trade and colonization.
    (4) Abundant natural resources encouraged self-sufficiency.

Unit 2 Pre-Test

Name _____   **Date** _____

Directions Review the Preparing for the Regents section of this book. Then answer the following questions, drawn from actual Regents examinations. For each statement or question, choose the *number* of the word or expression that, of those given, best completes the statement or answers the question.

1. Which factor most influenced a person's social position in early Indian societies?
   (1) education
   (2) birth
   (3) geographic location
   (4) individual achievement

2. One similarity between the Gupta Dynasty (A.D. 320–550) in India and the Tang Dynasty (A.D. 618–907) in China is that each dynasty
   (1) promoted equality for women
   (2) made advances in the arts, sciences, and mathematics
   (3) gained overseas colonies
   (4) developed a representative government

3. What is a major contribution of the Bzyantine Empire to global history?
   (1) preservation of Greek and Roman culture
   (2) construction of the pyramids
   (3) expansion of equal rights
   (4) invention of writing

4. Constantinople became the center of the Byzantine Empire because
   (1) the pope had made it the capital of the Christian world
   (2) it was a religious center for Muslims
   (3) its location made it the crossroads of Europe and Asia
   (4) it was geographically isolated from surrounding empires

5. The Justinian Code is considered a milestone because it
   (1) preserved many ancient Chinese legal decrees in writing
   (2) served as a model for European legal systems
   (3) became the first democratic constitution
   (4) united Muslim and Roman thought

6. An important contribution of the Byzantine Empire to Russia is the establishment in Russia of
   (1) Orthodox Christianity
   (2) representative democracy
   (3) a free-market economy
   (4) a jury system

7. The phrase "from southern Spain, across northern Africa, occupying the Arabian peninsula to Southeast Asia" once described the extent of the
   (1) Aztec Empire   (3) Gupta Empire
   (2) Pax Romana   (4) Muslim world

8. The Golden Age of Muslim culture was best known for its
   (1) attempts to colonize North America
   (2) frequent conflicts between Christians and Jews
   (3) advances in mathematics, science, and medicine
   (4) policies to reduce trade between the Middle East and China

9. The Age of Pericles in Athens, the Gupta Empire in India, and the Tang dynasty in China all experienced a golden age with
   (1) advancements in the principles of democratic governments
   (2) outstanding contributions in the arts and sciences
   (3) the end of foreign domination
   (4) the furthest expansion of their borders

10. During the feudal period in Europe, power and position in society were based on the
    (1) amount of money earned
    (2) level of education achieved
    (3) number of slaves owned
    (4) amount of land possessed

Name _____

Date _____

Base your answer to question 11 on the quotations below and on your knowledge of social studies.

"The pope is the only person whose feet are kissed by all princes. His title is unique in the world. He may depose [remove] emperors." —Pope Gregory VII (11th century)

"An emperor is subject to no one but to God and justice." —Frederick Barbarossa, Holy Roman Emperor (twelfth century)

11. The ideas expressed in these quotations show that during the Middle Ages in Europe

(1) popes gave little attention to political matters

(2) monarchs dominated the Church's leaders

(3) popes and monarchs sometimes challenged the other's authority

(4) monarchs and popes strengthened the role of the Church

12. The Roman Catholic Church during the Middle Ages in Europe can best be described as a church that

(1) favored separation from secular governments

(2) avoided involvement in social and educational matters

(3) was a strong force that divided many people

(4) was a stabilizing influence during a period of weak central governments

13. A major goal of the Christian Church during the Crusades (1096–1291) was to

(1) establish Christianity in Western Europe

(2) capture the Holy Land from Islamic rulers

(3) unite warring Arab peoples

(4) strengthen English dominance in the Arab world

14. The Crusades indirectly contributed to the discovery of the New World by

(1) forcing the religious conversion of the Muslim population

(2) forcing the Turks to flee from Constantinople

(3) stimulating European demand for goods from the East

(4) increasing the power of the feudal lords

15. Many achievements of Islamic civilization reached European society by way of the

(1) Crusades and eastern Mediterranean trading networks

(2) merchant guilds and the Industrial Revolution

(3) Middle Passage and the Columbian Exchange

(4) conquests of the Germanic tribes and trade along the Silk Road

Name _____ **Date** _____

Directions Review the Preparing for the Regents section of this book. Then answer the following questions, drawn from actual Regents examinations. For each statement or question, choose the *number* of the word or expression that, of those given, best completes the statement or answers the question.

1. Which geographic feature contributed most to the concept of cultural diffusion in Japan?
   (1) deposits of fertile soil
   (2) location near the mainland of Asia
   (3) vast mineral resources
   (4) numerous navigable rivers

2. The feudal system in both medieval Europe and early Japan were characterized by
   (1) a decentralized political system
   (2) religious diversity
   (3) an increased emphasis on education
   (4) the development of a wealthy middle class

3. Which factor contributed to the success of the vast empire created by the Mongols?
   (1) avoiding contacts with the West
   (2) paying monetary tribute to local rulers
   (3) employing superior military skills
   (4) converting conquered peoples to Confucianism

4. What was one influence of Mongol rule on the history of Russia?
   (1) Contact with kingdoms in Western Europe greatly increased.
   (2) The Chinese writing system was introduced and adopted.
   (3) Most Russians converted from Orthodox Christianity to Islam.
   (4) Russian leaders adopted the idea of strong, centralized control of the empire.

5. Ibn Battuta and Marco Polo were similar in that both
   (1) ruled over vast empires that included diverse peoples
   (2) produced written records of their extensive travels
   (3) converted thousands of people to Christianity
   (4) fought to free their people from Mongol rule

6. • 1340s—Mongols, merchants, and other travelers carried disease along trade routes west of China.
   • 1346—The plague reached the Black Sea ports of Caffa and Tana.
   • 1347—Italian merchants fled plague-infected Black Sea ports.
   • 1348—The plague became an epidemic in most of Western Europe.

   Which conclusion can be made based on these statements?
   (1) The plague primarily affected China.
   (2) The interaction of people spread the plague.
   (3) Port cities were relatively untouched by the plague.
   (4) The plague started in Western Europe.

7. During the 1400s, the cities of Venice, Constantinople, and Canton achieved prominence because their
   (1) locations were favorable for trade
   (2) pleasant climates led to an increase in population
   (3) democratic governments attracted trade
   (4) military power led to industrialization

8. The introduction of banking, letters of credit, joint stock companies, and guilds contributed to the start of the
   (1) Renaissance
   (2) Agricultural Revolution
   (3) Enlightenment
   (4) Commercial Revolution

9. One way in which the writers of the Renaissance were influenced by the writers of ancient Greece was that the Renaissance writers
   (1) stressed the power of human reason
   (2) promoted the religious doctrines of the Roman Catholic Church
   (3) showed little interest in secular affairs
   (4) produced few new scientific ideas

Name _____   **Date** _____

10. What is meant by Machiavelli's belief that "the end justifies the means"?

   (1) Leaders may use any method to achieve what is best for the state.
   (2) The general public always acts in its own best interest.
   (3) Pleasing all of the people at any given time is possible.
   (4) Leaders must always act for the common good.

11. One major influence the Renaissance had on the Protestant Reformation was that the philosophers of the Renaissance

   (1) supported democratic forms of government
   (2) encouraged a questioning attitude
   (3) stressed the importance of life after death
   (4) denied the existence of God

12. Which action could be considered an effect of the Protestant Reformation?

   (1) posting of the Ninety-five Theses
   (2) decline in the power of the Roman Catholic Church
   (3) sale of indulgences
   (4) end of religious warfare

13. The Magna Carta can be described as a

   (1) journal about English feudal society
   (2) list of feudal rights that limited the power of the English monarchy
   (3) census of all tax-paying nobility in feudal England
   (4) statement of grievances of the middle class in England

14. The West African kingdoms of Ghana, Mali, and Songhai experienced economic prosperity because they all

   (1) controlled vast reserves of oil and gold
   (2) traded with many other nations
   (3) maintained highly structured feudal systems
   (4) solved tribal conflicts within their empires

15. One conclusion that can be reached from the evidence about Mansa Musa rule of Mali is that

   (1) Christianity was a dominant religion in Africa in ancient times
   (2) complex civilizations existed in West Africa, before the arrival of Europeans
   (3) trade was not necessary for a civilization to survive
   (4) the slave trade originated in West Africa

Name _____   **Date** _____

Directions Review the Preparing for the Regents section of this book. Then answer the following questions, drawn from actual Regents examinations. For each statement or question, choose the *number* of the word or expression that, of those given, best completes the statement or answers the question.

1. Inca terrace farming and Aztec floating gardens are examples of
   (1) the ability of civilizations to adapt to their region's physical geography
   (2) slash-and-burn farming techniques
   (3) Mesoamerican art forms symbolizing the importance of agriculture
   (4) colonial economic policies that harmed Latin American civilizations

2. One similarity of the Aztec, Maya, and Inca empires is that they
   (1) developed in fertile river valleys
   (2) maintained democratic political systems
   (3) coexisted peacefully with neighboring empires
   (4) created complex civilizations

3. The ethnocentric attitudes of various Chinese emperors can best be attributed to the
   (1) cultural isolation of China
   (2) failure of other nations to become interested in China
   (3) interest of Chinese scholars in other civilizations
   (4) great cultural diversity within China's borders

4. The fall of the Byzantine Empire to the Ottoman Turks (1453) prompted Spain and Portugal to
   (1) seek new trade routes to East Asia
   (2) extend religious tolerance to Muslim peoples
   (3) reform their political systems
   (4) expand the Catholic Inquisition into the Middle East

5. During the 1500s, technological advances in navigation, naval engineering, and mapmaking contributed directly to the start of the
   (1) Gupta Empire   (3) Age of Exploration
   (2) Mongol Empire   (4) medieval guilds

6. A major reason that the Spanish were able to conquer the peoples of the Americas was the
   (1) military technology of the Spanish conquerors
   (2) inability of the native peoples to adapt to Spanish culture
   (3) enforced slavery of the native peoples by the Spanish
   (4) unified resistance of native peoples to Spanish demands

7. Which statement about the *encomienda* system during the sixteenth and seventeenth centuries is accurate?
   (1) Aztec and Inca civilizations prospered.
   (2) Life expectancy among Native American populations increased.
   (3) Spanish influence declined in its colonies.
   (4) Many Native Americans were forced to labor on large estates.

8. In the 1600s, the interest of Europeans in Africa was based mainly on Europe's need to
   (1) market its surplus agricultural products
   (2) obtain workers for its colonies in the Americas
   (3) establish collective security arrangements
   (4) settle its surplus population on new lands

9. Which statement best explains the increase in the Atlantic slave trade in the 1700s?
   (1) Technological advances in shipping made the slave trade more profitable.
   (2) Converted African slaves worked with Spanish missionaries to conquer the native peoples.
   (3) Many Africans wished to settle in the Americas and paid their own passage.
   (4) As the Europeans developed their American colonies, their need for cheap labor increased.

Name _____

Date _____

10. Which statement describes an impact that the Columbian Exchange had on the lives of Europeans?

   (1) The transfer of new products and ideas encouraged economic growth.

   (2) New diseases were brought to Europe and resulted in massive deaths caused by a plague.

   (3) Native Americans immigrated to Europe and competed with Europeans for jobs.

   (4) Cross-cultural contacts between South America and Asia declined.

11. One principle in the theory of mercantilism is that colonies should be

   (1) granted independence as soon as possible

   (2) considered an economic burden for the colonial power

   (3) encouraged to develop their own industries

   (4) acquired as markets and sources of raw materials

12. The primary goal of most of Europe's absolute monarchs was to

   (1) support political freedom for the new middle classes

   (2) prevent contact with areas beyond Europe's borders

   (3) centralize their political control over their nations

   (4) maintain peaceful relations with neighboring nations

13. One similarity between the rule of Peter the Great of Russia and that of Akbar the Great of India was that both leaders

   (1) implemented strict religious codes of conduct within their nations

   (2) modernized and expanded their empires using ideas from other cultures

   (3) relied on peaceful resolutions of conflicts with neighboring peoples

   (4) introduced democratic ideas into their political systems

14. King Louis XIV of France, Peter the Great of Russia, and Suleiman the Magnificent of the Ottoman Empire were all considered absolute rulers because they

   (1) broke from the Roman Catholic Church

   (2) helped feudal lords build secure castles

   (3) instituted programs that provided more power to their parliaments

   (4) determined government policies without the consent of their people

15. The Magna Carta, the Petition of Right, and the English Bill of Rights were created to

   (1) limit the power of English monarchs

   (2) establish laws protecting the rights of Protestants

   (3) organize England's colonial empire

   (4) abolish the role of Parliament

Unit 5 Pre-Test

Name _____ **Date** _____

Directions Review the Preparing for the Regents section of this book. Then answer the following questions, drawn from actual Regents examinations. For each statement or question, choose the *number* of the word or expression that, of those given, best completes the statement or answers the question.

1. Which statement best describes the effects of the works of Nicolaus Copernicus, Galileo Galilei, Sir Isaac Newton, and Rene Descartes?
   (1) The acceptance of traditional authority was strengthened.
   (2) The scientific method was used to solve problems.
   (3) Funding for education was increased by the English government.
   (4) Interest in Greek and Roman drama was renewed.

2. The Enlightenment philosophers believed that the power of government is derived from
   (1) divine right rulers
   (2) the middle class
   (3) a strong military
   (4) those who are governed

3. "Estates General Meet for First Time in 175 Years"; "National Assembly Issues Declarations of the Rights of Man"; "Reign of Terror Ends; Robespierre Dies"

   Which event in European history is most closely associated with these headlines?
   (1) Puritan Revolution
   (2) Hundred Years' War
   (3) French Revolution
   (4) signing of the Magna Carta

4. Simón Bolívar, José de San Martín, and Toussaint l'Ouverture are important in Latin American history because they were
   (1) twentieth-century caudillos
   (2) leaders of liberation movements
   (3) members of the Organization of American States (OAS)
   (4) winners of the Nobel Peace Prize

5. One of the main purposes of the Congress of Vienna (1814–1815) was to
   (1) promote the unification of Italy
   (2) preserve the German territories gained by Otto von Bismarck
   (3) restore the power of the Holy Roman Empire
   (4) establish a balance of power in Europe after the defeat of Napoleon

6. Which nineteenth-century ideology led to the unification of Germany and of Italy and to the eventual breakup of Austria-Hungary and of the Ottoman Empire?
   (1) imperialism   (3) liberalism
   (2) nationalism   (4) socialism

7. The main cause of the mass starvation in Ireland during the nineteenth century was the
   (1) British blockade of Irish ports
   (2) failure of the potato crop
   (3) war between Protestants and Catholics in northern Ireland
   (4) environmental damage caused by coal mining

8. During the nineteenth century, industrialization in Great Britain differed from industrialization in Japan mainly because Great Britain
   (1) had greater deposits of natural resources
   (2) encountered government resistance to economic growth
   (3) used isolationism to increase its economic power
   (4) duplicated the factory systems used in China

9. Laissez-faire capitalism as attributed to Adam Smith called for
   (1) heavy taxation of manufacturers
   (2) strict government control of the economy
   (3) minimal government involvement in the economy
   (4) government investments in major industries

Name _____   **Date** _____

10. Karl Marx and Friedrich Engels encouraged workers to improve their lives by
    (1) electing union representatives
    (2) participating in local government
    (3) overthrowing the capitalist system
    (4) demanding pensions and disability insurance

11. The needs of the Industrial Revolution in nineteenth-century Europe greatly contributed to the
    (1) growth of overseas empires
    (2) beginning of the triangular trade
    (3) development of international peacekeeping organizations
    (4) promotion of political and economic equality in Asia and Africa

12. The theory of Social Darwinism was sometimes used to justify
    (1) the establishment of communist governments in Asia
    (2) Latin American revolutions in the early nineteenth century
    (3) the independence movement in India
    (4) European imperialism in the late nineteenth century

13. "Take up the White Man's Burden -
    Send forth the best ye breed -
    Go, bind your sons to exile
    To serve your captives' need. . . ."

    —Rudyard Kipling, *The Five Nations* (1903)

    The words of this poem have been used to support the practice of
    (1) imperialism   (3) cultural borrowing
    (2) isolationism   (4) self-determination

14. The Sepoy Rebellion in India and the Boxer Rebellion in China were similar in that both were
    (1) attempts to improve foreign trade
    (2) nonviolent resistance efforts
    (3) revolts against foreign influence
    (4) revolutions against traditional monarchs

15. During the Meiji Restoration, Japan's leaders focused on
    (1) isolating Japan from the influence of foreign ideas
    (2) existing peacefully with their Asian neighbors
    (3) increasing the emperor's power by returning Japan to a feudal political system
    (4) modernizing Japan's economy to compete with western nations

Unit 6 Pre-Test

Name _____   **Date** _____

Directions Review the Preparing for the Regents section of this book. Then answer the following questions, drawn from actual Regents examinations. For each statement or question, choose the *number* of the word or expression that, of those given, best completes the statement or answers the question.

1. The Balkans were referred to as the "Powder Keg of Europe" in the period before World War I because of their
   (1) manufacturing ability
   (2) stockpiles of weapons
   (3) nationalistic rivalries
   (4) economic strength

2. Growing nationalism and militarism in Europe and the creation of secret alliances were
   (1) reasons for the rise of democracy
   (2) causes of World War I
   (3) requirements for economic development
   (4) reasons for the collapse of communism

3. The harsh terms included in the treaties ending World War I have been used to explain the
   (1) Fascist Revolution in Spain
   (2) Bolshevik Revolution in Russia
   (3) rise of Nazism in Germany
   (4) Armenian massacre in Turkey

4. In the 1920s and 1930s, Mustafa Kemal Atatürk changed the Turkish government by
   (1) introducing democratic reforms
   (2) increasing the power of the sultan
   (3) supporting absolutism
   (4) incorporating religious teachings into civil law

5. During the Russian Revolution of 1917, the slogan "peace, bread, and land" appealed to many Russian peasants because this slogan
   (1) called for continued Russian expansion in East Asia
   (2) supported an increase in the power of the Russian czar
   (3) addressed the needs and concerns of the peasants
   (4) promised to return all peasants to serfdom

6. What was the major goal of Joseph Stalin's five-year plans in the Soviet Union?
   (1) encouraging rapid industrialization
   (2) supporting capitalism
   (3) improving literacy rates
   (4) including peasants in the decision-making process

7. Which statement describes one major aspect of a command economy?
   (1) Supply and demand determines what is produced.
   (2) Most economic decisions are made by the government.
   (3) The means of production are controlled by labor unions.
   (4) The economy is mainly agricultural.

8. Which type of political system did V. I. Lenin, Adolf Hitler, and Benito Mussolini establish in their countries?
   (1) constitutional monarchy
   (2) totalitarianism
   (3) representative democracy
   (4) theocracy

9. One characteristic of a totalitarian state is that
   (1) minority groups are granted many civil liberties
   (2) several political parties run the economic system
   (3) citizens are encouraged to criticize the government
   (4) the government controls and censors the media

Name _____ **Date** _____

10. Which global event caused the overall reduction of unemployment between 1914 and 1918?
    (1) the Great Depression
    (2) completion of the Panama Canal
    (3) World War I
    (4) World War II

11. What was a major reason for Adolf Hitler's rise to power?
    (1) provisions of the Treaty of Versailles
    (2) Germany's military support of Poland and France
    (3) strong German economy
    (4) refusal by the League of Nations to admit Germany as a member

12. In Europe during the 1930s, several national leaders, in order to preserve peace at any cost, agreed to the demands of an aggressor. This policy is referred to as
    (1) militarism
    (2) nonalignment
    (3) reparation
    (4) appeasement

13. What was a major reason for Japan's invasion of Manchuria in 1931?
    (1) The province of Manchuria was originally a Japanese territory.
    (2) The government of Japan admired Manchurian technical progress.
    (3) The people of Manchuria favored Japanese control.
    (4) Japan needed the natural resources available in Manchuria.

14. During World War II, which geographic features contributed most to the Soviet Union's defense against the German invasion?
    (1) deposits of many natural resources
    (2) size and climate
    (3) Atlantic ports and rivers
    (4) mountainous territory and desert areas

15. The Holocaust is an example of
    (1) conflict between political parties
    (2) violations of human rights
    (3) limited technological development
    (4) geography's influence on culture

Name _____   **Date** _____

Directions Review the Preparing for the Regents section of this book. Then answer the following questions, drawn from actual Regents examinations. For each statement or question, choose the *number* of the word or expression that, of those given, best completes the statement or answers the question.

1. The formation of the North Atlantic Treaty Organization (NATO), the division of Germany into East Germany and West Germany, and the Korean War were immediate reactions to
   (1) Japanese military aggression in the 1930s
   (2) the rise of German nationalism after World War I
   (3) ethnic conflict and civil war in Africa in the 1950s
   (4) communist expansion after World War II

2. One similarity between the Korean War and the Vietnam War is that both wars were
   (1) resolved through the diplomatic efforts of the United Nations
   (2) fought as a result of differing political ideologies during the Cold War
   (3) fought without foreign influence or assistance
   (4) caused by religious conflicts

3. Which statement best describes India's foreign policy between 1947 and 1990?
   (1) It imitated Great Britain's policies.
   (2) It usually reflected the policies of China.
   (3) It rejected all assistance from communist dictatorships.
   (4) It generally followed a policy of nonalignment.

4. One reason the Chinese Communists were able to gain control of China was primarily due to the support of the
   (1) peasants   (3) foreigners
   (2) landed elite   (4) warlords

5. Which development took place in China under Mao Zedong?
   (1) The family became the dominant force in society.
   (2) The Four Modernizations became the basis for economic reform.
   (3) The people adopted the practice of ancestral worship.
   (4) Communist teachings became required learning in all schools and universities.

6. Since the 1980s, Chinese leaders have tried to improve China's economy by implementing a policy of
   (1) isolationism
   (2) collectivization
   (3) limited free enterprise
   (4) representative government

7. What was one reason that India was divided into two nations in 1947?
   (1) Indian leaders disagreed about India's role in the United Nations.
   (2) Great Britain feared a unified India would be a military threat.
   (3) The Soviet Union insisted that India should have a communist government.
   (4) Differences between the Hindus and the Muslims created religious conflict.

8. One similarity in the actions of Ho Chi Minh and Jomo Kenyatta was that both leaders
   (1) introduced Western ideas to their societies
   (2) established democratic forms of government
   (3) led nationalist movements
   (4) supported separation of church and state

Name _____   **Date** _____

9. Which situation existed under the policy of apartheid in South Africa?

  (1) All people were guaranteed suffrage.
  (2) The black majority held the most political power.
  (3) Society was controlled by the white minority.
  (4) Social inequality was eliminated.

10. What was one factor that contributed to the downfall of apartheid in the Republic of South Africa?

  (1) The African National Congress was outlawed.
  (2) Afrikaners demanded that only they should have ruling power.
  (3) Many foreign countries boycotted South African products.
  (4) President de Klerk and Desmond Tutu were imprisoned.

11. A major source of the dispute between the Israelis and the Palestinians is that each side

  (1) wants to control oil resources in the area
  (2) has historic ties to the same land
  (3) believes in different interpretations of the same religion
  (4) has close military alliances with neighboring countries

12. Since the creation of the Organization of Petroleum Exporting Countries (OPEC), member nations have joined together to

  (1) determine the supply of oil on the world market
  (2) establish a policy of independence in trade
  (3) maintain a low price of oil per barrel
  (4) isolate themselves from the rest of the world

13. Mikhail Gorbachev instituted the policies of glasnost and perestroika to

  (1) reinforce the basic economic principles of communism
  (2) bring the Soviet Union into the European Economic Community
  (3) reform the Soviet Union politically and economically
  (4) gain acceptance for free political elections

14. One way in which Lech Walesa, Mikhail Gorbachev, and Nelson Mandela are similar is that each

  (1) led the people of his nation toward a more democratic government
  (2) fought for power for the black majority over the white minority
  (3) worked to end communism in his country
  (4) refused to participate in the United Nations

15. In Iran, both the Revolution of 1979 and the rise of Islamic fundamentalism have caused

  (1) an increase in women's rights
  (2) tension between traditionalism and modernization to continue
  (3) foreign control of natural resources to expand
  (4) the introduction of a communist form of government

Name _____ **Date** _____

Directions Review the Preparing for the Regents section of this book. Then answer the following questions, drawn from actual Regents examinations. For each statement or question, choose the *number* of the word or expression that, of those given, best completes the statement or answers the question.

1. What is a major reason for the differences in economic prosperity in various areas of the world today?
   (1) an unequal distribution of resources
   (2) the success of nationalist movements
   (3) religious unity between nations
   (4) membership in the United Nations

2. In many of the world's developing nations, improvements in life expectancy and health care have contributed to
   (1) population pressures that limit economic development
   (2) an increased number of epidemics
   (3) a reduction in the need for land reform
   (4) a steady rise in income for all citizens

3. As a society becomes more urbanized and industrialized, it tends to
   (1) develop a more rigid class system
   (2) modify traditional beliefs and customs
   (3) resist cultural diffusion
   (4) depend more on the extended family structure

4. The Green Revolution of the 1960s resulted in
   (1) the destruction of large industrial enterprises
   (2) an increase of food output in many developing nations
   (3) a decrease in world agricultural output
   (4) improvements in human genetic engineering

5. An example of economic interdependence is
   (1) South Africans mining their gold and diamond resources
   (2) the government of France issuing new currency
   (3) Japan selling technological goods to buy Middle Eastern oil
   (4) an Indian subsistence farmer waiting for the rains to water his crops

6. The main purpose of the European Union (EU) and the North American Free Trade Agreement (NAFTA) is to
   (1) reduce the spread of nuclear weapons
   (2) address the problem of international political corruption
   (3) increase educational opportunities for underdeveloped nations
   (4) stimulate economic growth for participating countries

7. Which issue continues to raise concern from the world community regarding the nations of India, Iraq, Pakistan, and North Korea?
   (1) overpopulation
   (2) ethnic cleansing
   (3) desertification
   (4) nuclear proliferation

8. Which environmental issue most concerns Central Africa, the Amazon River Basin, and the Malay Peninsula?
   (1) nuclear contamination
   (2) desertification
   (3) overpopulation
   (4) deforestation

9. • Chernobyl experiences nuclear disaster.
   • Chlorofluorocarbons (CFCs) deplete the ozone layer.
   • Rivers and seas are polluted throughout the world.

   Which conclusion can best be drawn from these statements?
   (1) Modern technology can have serious negative effects.
   (2) Today's environment renews itself.
   (3) Only developing nations have environmental problems.
   (4) Most environmental problems originate in Europe.

Name _____   **Date** _____

10. The late-twentieth-century conflicts in Rwanda, Yugoslavia, and India were similar in that each was caused by the
    (1) deforestation conducted by multinational companies
    (2) collapse of communism
    (3) intervention of United Nations peacekeeping forces
    (4) rivalries between ethnic groups

11. Which statement best describes the impact of the computer on the global economy?
    (1) Countries can increase tariffs on imports.
    (2) Companies now market more products worldwide.
    (3) Wages have risen dramatically for most people in developing nations.
    (4) Prices of oil and other resources have declined worldwide.

12. The reason that the Organization of Petroleum Exporting Countries (OPEC) greatly influences the world today is that it
    (1) commands the loyalty of the worldwide Islamic community
    (2) develops and exports important technology
    (3) controls access to trade routes between the East and West
    (4) manages the oil supply that affects the global economy

Ancient World:
Civilizations and Religions (4000 B.C.–A.D. 500)

Unit Overview

Over the first thousands of years of human existence, people advanced in many different areas. A new era of human development began when humans discovered how to plant crops and domesticate animals. A more settled life and more dependable food sources allowed people to build civilizations with complex political, social, and religious structures. Civilizations began to interact with each other. They shared ideas and technology through such means as trade and conquest. Classical civilizations arose in Africa, Asia, and Europe. These civilizations made contributions to art, architecture, law, government, and other fields. Their achievements continue to affect society today. Ancient civilizations also made an impact on each other and on today's world through the development of powerful belief systems. These belief systems have spread throughout the world and affected cultural development and the course of history.

Using Good Social Studies Practices

Gathering Evidence

Some of the many themes developed in Unit 1 are:

change	movement of people and goods
geography	culture and intellectual life
urbanization	economic systems
political systems	belief systems

Choose one of the themes listed above. As you review Unit 1, gather evidence about how this theme developed from 4000 B.C. to A.D. 500. Include major developments and key turning points having to do with your theme.

Early Peoples and River Civilizations

Section Overview

Scientists believe that humans first appeared over two million years ago. The first humans were wandering hunters and gatherers. They made simple tools and weapons from stone, bone, and wood.

With the development of farming, ancient peoples gave up their nomadic lifestyles and established permanent settlements, which grew over time into civilizations. Early civilizations developed in river valleys. As populations grew, these peoples developed systems of government, social structures, and belief systems. Migration, trade, and warfare helped ideas move from one culture to another.

Key Themes and Concepts

As you review this section, take special note of the following key themes and concepts:

Environment How did the earliest people adapt to their environment?

Urbanization How did the development of agriculture change the way early people lived?

Political Systems What types of government and social structure were created by early civilizations?

Culture and Intellectual Life What contributions did early people make to later civilizations?

Movement of People and Goods How did trade, warfare, and migration spread ideas among early civilizations?

Key People and Terms

Key People and Terms

Place each of the key people and terms into one of these four categories: people, culture, politics, economics.

As you review this section, be sure you understand the significance of these key people and terms:

nomads	polytheistic	empire
cultural diffusion	pharaoh	Code of Hammurabi
Neolithic	Fertile Crescent	Middle Kingdom
technology	ziggurats	dynasty
civilization	cuneiform	

Early Peoples

The first people lived more than two million years ago, in prehistoric times. Prehistory is the time before people invented writing.

Hunters and Gatherers

The earliest people lived during the Old Stone Age, also called the Paleolithic age, which began more than two million years ago. Paleolithic people were **nomads,** or people who moved from place to place, hunting and gathering their food. Their simple social structure consisted of small groups of people who traveled together.

Adapting to Their Environment

Stone Age people adapted to their environment. They made simple tools and weapons, such as digging sticks and spears, from stone, bone, or wood. During Paleolithic times, people developed language, which allowed them to communicate and cooperate during a hunt. Paleolithic people invented clothing made of animal skins. They used fire for warmth as well as for cooking food.

Spiritual Beliefs

Paleolithic people developed some spiritual beliefs. Toward the end of the Old Stone Age, people began burying their dead with care, a practice suggesting that they believed in an afterlife. They buried tools and weapons with their dead.

Migration

Evidence supports the theory that the earliest people lived in East Africa. Their descendants spread to every part of the world. During the Old Stone Age, people migrated north and east into Europe and Asia. After many years, some migrated over a land bridge into North America. Others migrated by boat to islands in the Pacific. Migration led to **cultural diffusion,** or the exchange of ideas, customs, and goods among cultures. Cultural diffusion also occurred through trade and warfare.

The Neolithic Revolution

Environmental changes brought new climate patterns that contributed to the end of the Old Stone Age. Warmer weather allowed plants to grow where, previously, sheets of ice had dominated the landscape.

Around 10,000 B.C., people made two important discoveries. They learned to plant seeds to grow food, and they learned to domesticate animals. These discoveries meant that people no longer had to wander in search of food. They could live in permanent settlements. This change marked the beginning of the New Stone Age, or Neolithic period. Historians call these discoveries the Neolithic Revolution, or the Agricultural Revolution, because farming and domestic animals changed the way people lived.

The Impact of Agriculture

After the Neolithic Revolution, more abundant food helped the population to increase. Humans' lives changed in many ways.

- **Permanent Settlements** People settled together in villages.
- **New Social Classes** When resources were scarce, groups went to war. Chiefs or headmen emerged. Some men gained prestige as warriors and had great power.
- **New Technology** People began to develop technology, or tools and skills they could use to meet their basic needs, such as calendars and plows. Other new technology included the wheel, metal weapons, and metal tools.

These changes paved the way for civilization to emerge.

Note Taking

Reading Skill:
Identify Main Ideas
Make a concept web. Complete the circles with information about Paleolithic people. Add circles if necessary.

Preparing for the Regents

- How did Paleolithic people acquire food from their natural environment?

Key Themes and Concepts

Movement of People and Goods
Three important ways in which cultural diffusion occurs are through migration, trade, and warfare.

Preparing for the Regents

The Neolithic Revolution was one of the great turning points of history. Farming and the domestication of animals changed the way people lived. A dependable source of food allowed villages to grow larger and develop into cities. People who lived in cities developed more complex forms of government and such concepts as division of labor and social classes.

The Rise of Civilization

About 5,000 years ago, the first civilizations began to develop along river valleys. The rich, fertile farmlands of river valleys helped these civilizations to thrive. Most early civilizations were characterized by several basic features:

- Cities
- Central governments
- Traditional economy
- Organized religion
- Social classes
- Art and architecture
- Roads, bridges, and other public works
- System of writing
- Specialized jobs

Cities and Central Government

Cities emerged as farmers cultivated land along river valleys and produced surplus food. Surplus food led to increased population. More systematic leadership than just a headman or council of elders was needed. Governments developed to make sure that enough food was produced and that the city was protected. Rulers also ordered that public works such as roads, bridges, and defensive walls be built.

Traditional Economy

Traditional economies, based primarily on farming, grew up in early civilizations. Skilled craftsworkers made pottery, cloth, and other goods.

Organized Religion

Ancient peoples were **polytheistic,** believing in many gods. Priests and worshipers tried to gain the favor of these gods through complex rituals. They hoped that the gods would ensure plentiful crops and protect their cities.

Job Specialization and Social Classes

People began to specialize in certain jobs because no one person could master all the necessary skills to provide for himself or herself. People became ranked in classes according to their jobs. Priests and nobles were usually at the top of these societies, followed by warriors and merchants, with peasant farmers and slaves at the bottom.

Art and Architecture

Much early art and architecture consisted of temples and palaces, symbols of the power of rulers.

System of Writing

Writing may have first developed in temples, where many types of records were kept. Early writing was picture writing, consisting of simple drawings. Over time the writing became more symbolic.

Egypt

One of the earliest civilizations arose in Egypt about 5,000 years ago.

Geographic Setting

Since most of Egypt is a desert, people settled along the Nile River. The Nile provided water for drinking and for irrigation of crops. Yearly floods soaked the land and left rich deposits of silt that kept the agricultural areas fertile. The river also served as a highway for travel.

Vocabulary Builder

ritual—(RICH oo ul) *n.* a ceremony that is always performed in the same way, in order to mark an important religious or social occasion

Note Taking

Reading Skill:
Identify Supporting Details
Make a table. As you read, record information about Egypt.

Egypt	
Concept	**Main Idea**
Geographic Setting	
Religion	
Government	
Social Structure	

Religion

Egyptians were polytheistic. The sun god Amon-Re was the chief god. Osiris was the god of the Nile. Osiris controlled the annual flood that made the land fertile. The Egyptians also believed in a host of other gods who served specific functions.

The cornerstone of the religious faith of the Egyptians was a belief in life after death. Egyptians prepared their dead for the afterlife through a preservation process called mummification.

Government

The Egyptian ruler was called a **pharaoh.** Egyptians believed that the pharaoh was both a god and a king. In fact, when a pharaoh died, he was buried in a majestic pyramid. The pyramids took years to build and required enormous planning and organization. When the mummies of pharaohs were buried in pyramids, they were surrounded by possessions for use in the afterlife. After the death of a pharaoh, power usually passed to another member of the family. These ruling families were called dynasties.

Social Structure

Egyptian society was divided into classes. The pharaoh held the highest position in society. Next were the priests, who served the gods and goddesses. Third were the nobles, who fought the pharaoh's wars, followed by the craftspeople and merchants. Near the bottom was the biggest group, the peasant farmers. Beneath the peasants were the slaves.

Women had a higher status in Egyptian society than in any other ancient civilization. A woman could own property, enter business deals, and obtain a divorce.

Contributions

The Egyptians made many advances in science and art. The process of mummification helped them learn much about the human body, allowing them to diagnose many illnesses and perform surgery. Egyptians developed a calendar very similar to the one we use today. They also created a system of picture writing called hieroglyphics. Egyptian temples and monuments, as well as the pyramids, have survived thousands of years. Egyptian statues and paintings show daily life, ceremonies, and military victories.

Mesopotamia

Geographic Setting

To the north and east of Egypt, the **Fertile Crescent,** a crescent-shaped region of good farmland created by the Tigris and Euphrates Rivers, stretches from the Persian Gulf to the Mediterranean. The lack of natural barriers in the Fertile Crescent allowed frequent migrations and invasions, while the diversity of the people made it difficult to unite them into a single nation. In this area great civilizations arose, giving the Fertile Crescent the name "the cradle of civilization."

In the eastern end of the Fertile Crescent lies Mesopotamia. There early civilizations developed, along the banks of the Tigris and Euphrates Rivers. This river valley region was called Mesopotamia, from a Greek word meaning "land between the rivers." With few natural barriers, this area became a crossroads where people mingled and shared customs and ideas.

Key Themes and Concepts

Belief Systems
Many early peoples had polytheistic belief systems. The gods were seen as closely tied to the forces of nature, and keeping them happy was essential to agriculture. Therefore, religious leaders became very important in early societies.

Preparing for the Regents

The Egyptians formed a centralized government with the pharaoh as its focus. As in many ancient civilizations, the pharaohs claimed divine support for their rule and eventually claimed that they themselves were gods. This claim was an effective way to maintain power.

Preparing for the Regents

• What geographical features of the Fertile Crescent helped civilization to grow and ideas to spread between cultures?

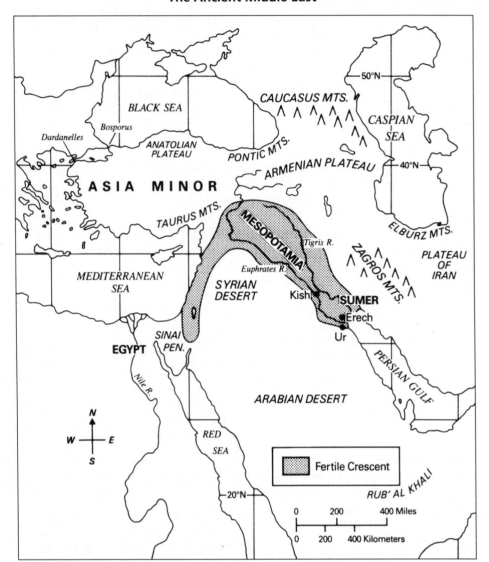

Preparing for the Regents

Practice your map skills by answering the following questions about the map.

1. Which two rivers ran through the Fertile Crescent?

2. Which two river valley civilizations are shown on this map?

Key Themes and Concepts

Technology and Innovation The tools and other technology that a civilization develops tells much about what is important to that culture. Early river valley civilizations developed methods of flood control and irrigation.

Preparing for the Regents

• Compare Sumerian society to Egyptian society. How were they alike? How were they different?

Supporting Details

The Sumerians made many contributions to the world. List three.

The Civilizations of the Fertile Crescent

Sumerians The first civilization in Mesopotamia was Sumer. City-states developed along the Tigris and Euphrates Rivers about 5,000 years ago. The Sumerians were polytheistic and built their cities around pyramid-like structures called **ziggurats.** A ziggurat had steps that people could climb to reach the shrine of that particular city's chief god or goddess. The Sumerians developed irrigation systems, dikes, and canals to provide protection from floods and water for crops. They grew wealthy from trade with places as far away as Egypt and India. Among the contributions the Sumerians made to the world were the first wheeled vehicles, a metal plow, and a 12-month calendar based on the cycles of the moon. Their number system was based on 60, which is the basis for our clocks' minutes and seconds. They also developed **cuneiform,** a wedge-shaped writing formed by pressing a pen-like instrument into clay.

Babylonians The Babylonians established an early **empire,** or groups of states or territories governed by one ruler. Babylon's most powerful ruler, Hammurabi, is best known for his set of laws called the **Code of Hammurabi.** This was the first major collection of laws in history. Although these laws favored higher classes over lower ones, they established standards of justice for all classes. Punishment was harsh, stressing the idea of "an eye for an eye, a tooth for a tooth."

Indus River Valley

Like the civilizations that developed in Mesopotamia and the Nile Valley, Indian civilization evolved in a fertile river valley.

Geographic Setting

The Indian subcontinent is a large, wedge-shaped peninsula that extends southward into the Indian Ocean. This peninsula is surrounded on the north and northwest by huge mountains, which often limited India's contacts with other cultures.

Winds called monsoons bring rain every summer. India depended on monsoons to grow their crops. When there was not enough rain, people could not grow crops. When there was too much, rivers rose to cause deadly floods.

Indus Valley Cities

About 2500 B.C., at about the time when the pyramids were rising in Egypt, the first Indian civilization arose in the Indus River Valley. Archaeologists have found remains of impressive cities, but little is known about the civilization that produced them. However, it is clear that the Indus Valley civilization covered a large area and that its cities were well planned.

The two main cities of this civilization were Harappa and Mohenjo-Daro. Roads were laid out in a grid pattern, and each city was dominated by a structure built on a hill, probably a fortress or temple. Enormous granaries stored crops that were grown in outlying villages. Houses, which were made of bricks, had plumbing with baths and chutes that led to sewers.

Most Indus Valley people were farmers. They were the first to grow cotton and weave it into cloth. Merchants traveled far, trading even with the cities of Sumer.

Aryan Invaders

Around 1750 B.C., for unknown reasons, Indus Valley civilization began to decline. Then, in about 1500 B.C., nomadic warriors called Aryans conquered the Indus Valley.

China

Geographic Setting

Chinese civilization grew up in the river valleys of the Huang He, or Yellow River, and the Yangzi. Geography—mountains, deserts, jungles, and an ocean—isolated Chinese culture more than it did many other early civilizations. Having little contact with other cultures, the early Chinese believed that their culture was the center of the Earth, so they called it the **Middle Kingdom.** Although China covers a huge area, until recent times most people lived only along the east coast or in the river valleys. Despite its isolation, China traded with other cultures. Chinese goods reached the Middle East and even beyond.

Government

About 1650 B.C., a Chinese people called the Shang gained control of part of northern China. Although there was a king in Shang China, clans—groups of families—controlled most of the land. In this way Shang China was more similar to the small kingdoms of Aryan India or Sumer's city-states than to the centralized government of Egypt. The Shang set up the first **dynasty,** or ruling family, in China.

Key Themes and Concepts

Governance
Hammurabi used law to unite his empire. Later empires, including the Byzantine and Muslim empires, also used systems of law as unifying forces.

Key Themes and Concepts

Political Systems
The well-planned cities of Harappa and Mohenjo-Daro suggest that these people must have had well-organized governments. Government officials probably planned these cities and made sure that there was a steady food supply.

Preparing for the Regents

1. Why did the Chinese call their culture the Middle Kingdom?
2. What were the main characteristics of the Shang government, society, and religion?

Key Themes and Concepts

Environment and Political Systems
The Huang He flooded when heavy rains swelled the river. The need to control the river through public works may have contributed to the rise of a strong central government in China.

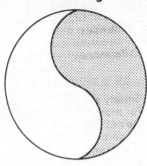

Yin-Yang

Vocabulary Builder

intercede—(in tur SEED) *v.*
to speak in support
of someone

Note Taking

Reading Skill:
Summarize
Make a chart like the one
below. Summarize the
information in Section 1.

Topic	Summary
Early Peoples	
Neolithic Revolution	
Rise of Civilization	
Egypt	
Mesopotamia	
Indus River Valley	
China	

Preparing for the Regents

• What were some
  important contributions
  of early river civilizations?
  How are these advances
  important today?

Social Structure

Shang society resembled that of other ancient cultures. A class of noble warriors owned the land. Merchants and craftspeople earned a living in cities. Most people, however, were peasants and lived in farming villages.

Religion

The Shang Chinese prayed to many gods and nature spirits. The Chinese looked to their dead ancestors to intercede with the gods to help the living, offering them sacrifices of food and other objects. The ancient Chinese also believed that the universe was held in a delicate balance between two forces, the yin and the yang. When these forces were in balance, peace and prosperity would result.

Contributions

One of the most important achievements of China was written Chinese, which developed about 4,000 years ago. The ancient Chinese used a system of writing that included both pictographs (drawings of objects) and ideographs (drawings of thoughts and ideas). Because the Chinese writing system consisted of tens of thousands of characters, only the upper classes had the time to learn to read and write.

Demographic Patterns and Migration

Demography is the study of human populations. Demographic patterns, or changes in populations over time, are often influenced by geographic features such as rivers. For example, ancient civilizations in Egypt, Mesopotamia, and India all developed in fertile river valleys. Rivers provided water for drinking and irrigation. Rivers also served as highways for the transport of people and goods.

Bantu Migrations

As populations grew, some groups began to migrate in search of new lands to settle. The Bantu migrations are an example of this movement. The Bantu peoples originally lived in West Africa. Then, as the Sahara region began to dry out, these skilled farmers and herders migrated south and east in search of fertile land. Between 500 B.C. and A.D. 1500, Bantu settlers spread their knowledge of farming and ironworking, as well as their language, across the continent. Today, about a third of all Africans speak a language in the Bantu family.

Summary

The earliest people were nomadic hunters and gatherers. When they learned how to grow food, they settled in villages. These changes led to the growth of civilizations. Early civilizations grew up in river valleys. Civilizations developed governments, economic systems, and social structures. Early civilizations also had complex systems of belief and made advances in technology, architecture, and legal systems. These advances were spread among early civilizations by migration, trade, and warfare.

Classical Civilizations

Section Overview

The classical civilizations of China, India, Greece, and Rome have had a strong impact on the world. Each of these civilizations was influenced by its particular geographic setting. Each had a strong, well-organized government and a prosperous economy that allowed it to thrive. Each civilization made important contributions in such areas as art, science, architecture, and law. The growth of global trade routes during this period allowed classical civilizations to share ideas and technology.

Key Themes and Concepts

As you review this section, take special note of the following key themes and concepts:

Geography How did geographic conditions influence the development of classical civilizations?

Government What features of government allowed the classical civilizations of India, China, Greece, and Rome to remain strong?

Culture and Intellectual Life What contributions have the classical civilizations of India, China, Greece, and Rome made to later civilizations?

Movement of People and Goods How did trade routes link civilizations and lead to cultural diffusion?

Key People and Terms

As you review this section, be sure you understand the significance of these key people and terms:

Mandate of Heaven	polis	plebeians
feudalism	aristocracy	Pax Romana
Qin	direct democracy	Laws of the
Han dynasty	Hellenistic	Twelve Tables
Maurya dynasty	republic	aqueducts
bureaucracy	Senate	Silk Road
Asoka	patricians	

China (c. 1027 B.C.–A.D. 220)

Geographic Setting

China was the most isolated of all ancient civilizations. China's culture developed separately from the civilizations of Egypt, the Middle East, and India. China was separated from these civilizations not only by long distances but by physical barriers. For example, high mountains existed to the west and southwest of China. Also, the Gobi Desert lay to the north and the Pacific Ocean to the east. After the Shang united the area around the Huang He and Yangzi rivers, civilization prospered there.

The
Big
Idea

The classical civilizations of India, China, Greece, and Rome:

• had strong governments.

• developed ideas and technology that were important contributions to later civilizations.

• developed trade networks that enriched their economies and allowed them to exchange goods and technology.

Key People and Terms

What do many of the key people and terms have in common? Explain.

Vocabulary Builder

barrier—(BA ree ur) *n.* a physical object that keeps two areas, people, etc. apart

---

Note Taking

Reading Skill:
Recognize Sequence
As you read Section 2, create a timeline of the classical civilizations. Write when the dynasties and rulers begin and end.

Preparing for the Regents

- Practice your chart reading skills by describing how a dynasty might lose the Mandate of Heaven.

Vocabulary Builder

yield—(yeeld) *n.* the amount of profits, crops, etc. that something produces

Key Themes and Concepts

Government
Shi Huangdi was able to attain power because of divisions in the feudal Zhou government. He moved quickly to centralize his own government through political, economic, and cultural means.

Zhou Dynasty (1027 B.C.–221 B.C.)

Between 1100 and 1000 B.C., the Zhou people overthrew the Shang and set up their own dynasty, which lasted nearly 800 years. The Zhou told the people that the gods had become angry at Shang cruelty and now had chosen the Zhou to rule. This right to rule was called the **Mandate of Heaven,** a divine approval to rule. From that time on, each new dynasty would claim the Mandate of Heaven. The Chinese later expanded this idea to explain the dynastic cycle, the rise and fall of dynasties.

The Mandate of Heaven

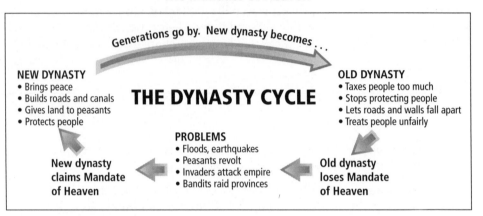

A Feudal Government   The Zhou kings granted control of large areas of land to their supporters. In a system called **feudalism,** local lords controlled their own regions but owed military service to the ruler. Over time, feudal lords came to hold the real power in China.

Economy   The economy grew under the Zhou. After the Chinese began using iron to make tools, they could produce more food. Irrigation projects also increased crop yields. Trade expanded along new roads and canals built by feudal lords. The Chinese began for the first time to use money, which spurred the development of trade.

Zhou Contributions   Under the Zhou, the Chinese made the first books. They also made progress in other areas. Astronomers studied planet movements and eclipses, developing an accurate calendar. The Chinese discovered how to make silk from the cocoons of the silkworm. Silk became a valuable Chinese export.

The Qin Dynasty (221 B.C.–206 B.C.)

By 221 B.C., a leader of the Qin people proclaimed himself Shi Huangdi, meaning "First Emperor."

Centralized Government   After conquering the Zhou empire, Shi Huangdi centralized his power.

- He abolished the old feudal states and divided the country into military districts, each ruled by an appointed official.
- He standardized measurements.
- He created national coins.
- He promoted uniformity in Chinese writing.
- He repaired canals and roads.

The Great Wall Shi Huangdi's greatest achievement was the Great Wall. The wall was built to keep out invaders. Thousands of workers worked for years to build the wall.

The Han Dynasty (206 B.C.–A.D. 220)

After Shi Huangdi's death in 210 B.C., the people revolted. A new dynasty, the Han, emerged. A peasant leader, Liu Bang, took control of China after Qin power collapsed. As emperor, he took the title Gao Zu. He reduced taxes and eased the harsh policies of the Qin. Gao Zu's policies allowed the dynasty he founded, the **Han dynasty,** to last for about 400 years.

Government and Economy The most famous Han emperor, Wudi, began his reign in 141 B.C. Wudi strengthened Chinese government by establishing a civil service system. Examinations based on the teachings of Confucius, not family influence, determined who would get government jobs. Wudi also strengthened the economy and improved canals and roads.

Han Society The civil service system had an impact on Han society and China for years to come. It established Confucian values in government and in daily life. Confucianism spelled out proper behavior for all parts of society. Men were thought to be superior to women. Because men were considered superior, women were excluded from taking civil service examinations and, thus, from holding positions in government. A few women, including religious recluses and noblewomen, did receive an education, however.

Han Contributions The Han period was a golden age in China.

- **Technology** The Chinese made technological advances such as learning how to make paper out of wood pulp. They also invented the wheelbarrow; the fishing reel; and the rudder, a device used to steer ships.

- **Science** In medicine the Han developed acupuncture, a technique in which needles are inserted under the skin to relieve pain or treat illness. The Chinese also experimented with herbal remedies and anesthesia. Furthermore, Han scholars wrote texts on chemistry, zoology, and botany.

- **Arts** Some craftsworkers created jade and ivory carvings. Other artisans worked in bronze, ceramics, and silk.

India (c. 1500 B.C.–185 B.C.)

Geographic Setting

The subcontinent of India juts out from the Asian continent. The Indian subcontinent includes three major geographic regions:

- The northern plain, fertile and well watered by the Indus and the Ganges
- The Deccan Plateau, dry and sparsely populated
- The coastal plains, flat land along the east and west coasts where farming, fishing, and trading can occur

This varied geography has made the subcontinent difficult to unite.

Mauryan Empire (321 B.C.–185 B.C.)

Many competing kingdoms were spread across the northern plains. Into this battleground of rival kingdoms came Chandragupta Maurya. Chandragupta first gained power in the Ganges Valley, but with his army he soon conquered much of northern India. His descendants moved southward, dominating the Deccan Plateau. From about 321 B.C. to 185 B.C., the **Maurya dynasty** ruled over the first united Indian empire.

Recognizing Effects

Make a concept web. As you read, fill it in with the effects of the rule of the Han Dynasty in China. Add circles if necessary.

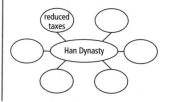

Vocabulary Builder

jut out—(jut owt) v. to stick out further than other things

Well-Organized Government The Maurya dynasty set up an efficient bureaucracy and a strong government with its capital at Pataliputra. A **bureaucracy** is a system of managing government through departments that are run by appointed officials. Officials collected taxes and oversaw the building of roads and harbors, which helped trade to flourish. Other officials managed government-owned factories and shipyards.

Maurya rule was harsh, however. Chandragupta was suspicious of his many enemies. A brutal secret police force reported on crime, corruption, and dissent within his empire.

Asoka and Reform Chandragupta's grandson Asoka ruled differently. Horrified by the brutality of a campaign to conquer the Deccan, Asoka rejected further conquest. He turned to Buddhism, hoping to rule by moral example rather than by violence. Asoka sent Buddhist missionaries across India. Despite his desire to promote Buddhism, he was tolerant of other beliefs.

Asoka's rule united his diverse people and brought peace and prosperity. After his death, however, the empire declined, and rival kingdoms once again competed for power.

Maurya Contributions The Maurya dynasty united much of India for the first time. Peace and prosperity resulted, and trade flourished. The capital at Pataliputra was one of the largest and richest cities of its time. The capital had schools and a library; learning was highly advanced. One of the most lasting contributions of the Maurya dynasty was the spreading of the Buddhist religion by means of missionary activity.

Greece (c. 1750 B.C.–133 B.C.)

The ancient Greeks adapted ideas from many earlier cultures, such as those of Mesopotamia and Egypt. However, they also developed their own ideas about the role of the individual and how society is best governed.

Geographic Setting

Greece, located in southeastern Europe, is made up of many mountains, isolated valleys, and small islands. This geography prevented the Greeks from building a large empire like that of Egypt or Mesopotamia. Instead the Greeks created many small city-states.

The Aegean and Mediterranean Seas were an important link to the rest of the world. The Greeks became skilled sea traders. They exchanged not only goods but ideas and technology as well. For example, the Greeks adapted the Phoenician alphabet for their own use.

The Rise of City-States

As you know, Greece is divided by mountains into isolated valleys. In addition, hundreds of scattered islands exist off its coast. As a result, Greece did not form a large, unified empire, but existed as a collection of small city-states. A city-state was also known as a **polis.**

A polis typically was made up of two parts. There was a hilltop acropolis, which included marble temples. On the flatter ground below was the main city, within a wall. This area included the marketplace, theater, other public areas, and homes.

Between 750 B.C. and 500 B.C., the Greek city-states had several different types of government. At first, kings ruled the city-states. Over time, landowning nobles gained power, creating an **aristocracy,** a government ruled by the landholding elite.

The two most powerful city-states were Sparta and Athens. Though they shared Greek culture, they developed different ways of life.

Militarism in Sparta

Sparta was a warrior society, and from an early age, boys trained for a lifetime in the military. At the age of seven, boys were moved into barracks, where they were toughened by a coarse diet, hard exercise, and rigid discipline. Girls were also trained to exercise rigorously and strengthen their bodies in order to give birth to healthy boys for the army. Although Sparta was an excellent military state, its power declined as a result of its rigid ways and its inability to change.

Limited Democracy in Athens

A wise leader named Pericles ruled Athens from 460 B.C. to 429 B.C. Under Pericles, Athens had a **direct democracy,** in which a large number of the male citizens actually took part in the day-to-day running of the government. Women, however, did not participate, since Athenians believed that women were inferior to men and needed male guidance. Another group that did not participate in the Athenian democracy were enslaved people. Enslaved people had neither political rights nor any personal freedom. Even so, Athens gave a greater number of people a voice in government than did any other culture of its time.

Key Themes and Concepts

Movement of People and Goods
All of the empires discussed in this section had trade ties with other cultures. Civilizations borrowed ideas and technology from trading partners and adapted them to their own use.

Preparing for the Regents

- How did the geography of Greece affect both its economic activity and its political divisions?

Recognize Cause

What was a cause of Sparta's decline in power?

Preparing for the Regents

- How were the roles of women in the Athenian and Han societies similar?

- What impact did classical Greece have on the development of modern political systems?

Athens prospered during this time and became the cultural center of Greece. Great buildings were built; many thinkers, writers, and artists came to Athens.

Athens and Sparta

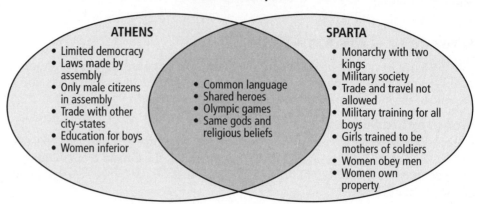

Preparing for the Regents

- In what ways were the city-states of Sparta and Athens similar? In what ways were they different?

ATHENS
- Limited democracy
- Laws made by assembly
- Only male citizens in assembly
- Trade with other city-states
- Education for boys
- Women inferior

- Common language
- Shared heroes
- Olympic games
- Same gods and religious beliefs

SPARTA
- Monarchy with two kings
- Military society
- Trade and travel not allowed
- Military training for all boys
- Girls trained to be mothers of soldiers
- Women obey men
- Women own property

Alexander the Great and the Hellenistic Age

Macedonia was a mountain kingdom north of Greece. In the 300s B.C., Philip of Macedonia conquered Greece, which had been weakened by years of civil war. His son, Alexander the Great, went on to build an empire that included the Nile Valley, Persia, and parts of India. Through his conquests Alexander spread Greek culture. A new Hellenistic culture arose that blended aspects of Greek, Persian, Egyptian, and Indian life. This culture gave more rights and opportunities to women, who even gained some political power. Although Alexander's empire fell apart soon after his death, Hellenistic culture had a lasting impact on the regions he had ruled.

Greek and Hellenistic Contributions

Ancient Greek and Hellenistic culture left an enduring legacy. In addition to their ideas about government, Greeks made contributions in philosophy, literature, science, and the arts.

Philosophy Greek thinkers tried to use observation and reason to understand why things happened. The Greeks called these thinkers philosophers, a word that means "lovers of wisdom." Three of the most famous Greek philosophers were Socrates, Plato, and Aristotle.

Key themes and Concepts

Culture

- **Socrates**
(c. 469 B.C.–399 B.C.) was born in Athens. He was a stonemason and a teacher.

- **Plato**
(c. 428 B.C.–347 B.C.) was a student of Socrates. He set up the Academy in Athens, the first known university in the Western world.

- **Aristotle**
(384 B.C.–322 B.C.) was Plato's student and Alexander the Great's teacher.

The Greek Philosophers

SOCRATES	PLATO	ARISTOTLE
Developed Socratic method: learning about beliefs and ideas by asking questions	Believed government should control lives of people	Believed one strong and good leader should rule
Government put him to death	Divided society into three classes: workers, philosophers, and soldiers	Believed people learned through reason

Vocabulary Builder

epic—(EP ik) *adj.* a book, poem, or film that tells a long story about brave actions and exciting events

Literature The first Greek plays developed from religious festivals. Stories of the gods usually served as the basis for plays. Aeschylus, Sophocles, and Euripides wrote tragedies, plays that told stories of human conflict. Other Greek playwrights wrote comedies. In addition, the Greek poet Homer wrote epic poems that inspired many later writers. Greeks applied observation and logic to their writing of history. The Greek historian Herodotus is often called the Father of History because of his careful historical writing.

Art and Architecture The Greeks believed in beauty, balance, and order in the universe. Greek art and architecture reflected those ideas. Greek paintings and statues were lifelike, but they also showed the human body in its most perfect form. The most famous Greek building was the Parthenon. Architects today still use ancient Greek ideas, such as Greek column styles, in their buildings.

Science The astronomer Aristarchus discovered that the earth rotates on its axis and moves around the sun. Archimedes explored the principles of the lever and pulley. Hippocrates, a Greek physician, studied the causes of illness and looked for cures.

Mathematics Greek and Hellenistic thinkers made great strides in mathematics. Pythagoras developed a formula to measure the sides of a right triangle; Euclid wrote a book that became the basis for modern geometry.

Rome (c. 509 B.C.–A.D. 476)

Geographic Setting

Rome is located near the center of Italy, a peninsula located in the Mediterranean. Unlike the geography of Greece, Italy's geography helped its people to unite. Low mountains presented fewer natural barriers. Fertile plains supported a growing population. In addition, the location of the Italian peninsula helped Romans to move easily through the lands of the Mediterranean.

The Roman Republic

The traditional date given for the founding of Rome is 509 B.C., when the Romans drove out the Etruscans who had ruled them. The Romans established a new form of government called a republic. In a **republic,** officials were chosen by the people. The most powerful governing body was the **Senate.** Senators were members of the landholding upper class, called **patricians.** These officials elected two consuls, who supervised the business of government and commanded the armies. The **plebeians**—farmers, merchants, artisans, and traders, who made up most of the population—had little power.

Under Roman law, the male head of the household had authority over his wife and family. During the late years of the republic and early years of the empire, however, women gained greater freedom. Roman women held prominent public roles and owned successful businesses.

The Roman Empire

By 270 B.C., Rome had conquered all of Italy. The Romans went on to conquer Carthage, Macedonia, Greece, and parts of Asia Minor. This expansion, however, led to a widening gap between rich and poor and also to increased corruption. Attempts at reform led to a series of civil wars. Out of this period of chaos, Julius Caesar came to power in 48 B.C. Caesar made new conquests as well as important reforms.

After Caesar was murdered, his grandnephew Octavian—later called Augustus—became ruler. Augustus ruled with absolute power, thus bringing the republic to an end. The age of the Roman empire had begun. The 200-year peace that began with Augustus is called the **Pax Romana,** or Roman peace. During this time, the Roman empire spread stability over a large area of the world, including parts of Europe, North Africa, and Southwest Asia.

Roman Contributions

Roman civilization spread to other lands. The Romans also absorbed the ideas of other cultures.

Key Themes and Concepts

Culture and Intellectual Life
Greek art portrayed individuals in perfect form, a reflection of the Greek belief in beauty, balance, and order in the universe.

Key Themes and Concepts

Geography
The location of Rome helped the Romans to carry on trade and build an empire around the Mediterranean Sea.

Preparing for the Regents

• What impact did Rome have on the development of later political systems?

Recognize Effects

Geography
List three effects of the Pax Romana.

Law A system of laws was Rome's greatest achievement. It applied to all people and created a stable Roman empire. Many of its basic principles—including equality under the law, the right of the accused to face one's accusers and mount a defense, and the idea of being considered innocent until proven guilty—are the basis for systems of justice to this day.

In 450 B.C., the plebeians demanded written laws, saying that they could not know what the laws were if they were not written down. These **Laws of the Twelve Tables,** inscribed on twelve tablets, were displayed in the marketplace. Later, plebeians won the right to elect their own officials and serve in all kinds of government jobs.

Art and Architecture The Romans borrowed many Greek concepts in the arts and architecture. They used Greek-style statues in their homes and public buildings. Roman buildings were mighty and grand, however, instead of simple and elegant. Roman writers used the Latin language, which united the empire, to write great poetic, historical, and philosophical works.

Engineering The Romans were very practical. They built excellent roads, bridges, harbors, and **aqueducts**—bridge-like stone structures that carried water from the hills to the cities. The Romans also improved the arch and the dome.

A Roman aqueduct in Segovia, Spain

The Growth of Global Trade Routes

The classical civilizations engaged in trade with one another. These exchanges of goods, technology, and culture expanded from the time of the first Indian empire to the time of the Romans.

Phoenician Trade

The Phoenicians were one of the earliest trading empires of the ancient Middle East. Phoenicia was made up of small city-states in the lands known today as Lebanon and Syria. Phoenicians made glass from sand, manufactured a purple dye from the sea snail, and created scrolls from Egyptian papyrus. Their ships carried valuable goods across the Mediterranean. As trade expanded, Phoenicia founded colonies throughout the region. The most important Phoenician contribution to history was the alphabet, developed to record business transactions. It is the basis of the alphabet we use today.

India's Role in Trade

Even during early Indus Valley civilization, trade had gone on between the peoples of the Indian coast and Mesopotamian civilizations such as Sumer. During the 300s B.C., when Alexander expanded his territory into India, he opened a trade corridor between India and the Mediterranean. By 100 B.C., Indian goods such as

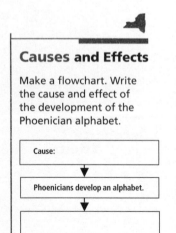

Cause:

↓

Phoenicians develop an alphabet.

↓

Mediterranean Trade Routes

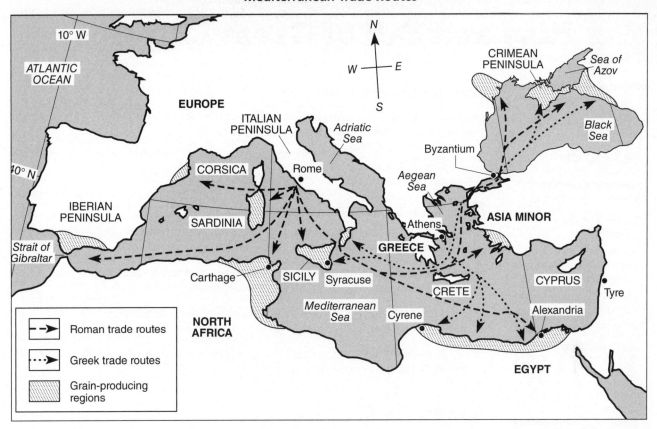

textiles, gems, and spices were in great demand. Some goods were sent overland into central Asia and China. Others went by ship to the Middle East, Egypt, East Africa, and Southeast Asia. Rome later became an eager market for Indian goods.

China and the Silk Road
The Han dynasty opened a trade route called the **Silk Road** that eventually linked China with lands as far west as Mesopotamia. Silk and other Chinese goods moved west, while products such as muslin, glass, and new foods flowed into China.

The Silk Road eventually stretched for 4,000 miles. Few merchants traveled the entire distance. Most goods were traded at various markets along the way. In the west, groups such as the Persians controlled the Silk Road.

Roman Trade
During the Pax Romana, trade flowed freely among the peoples of the Roman empire and other parts of the world. Egyptian farmers supplied grain; other Africans supplied ivory, gold, and even lions. Indians exported cotton and many spices to the Roman empire, and the Chinese supplied silk and other goods.

Summary

Great civilizations arose in India, China, Greece, and Rome from the 300s B.C. through about A.D. 500. Strong, centralized governments allowed these civilizations to rise and remain strong. Their cultural contributions in the arts and architecture, science and engineering, and law have lasted to the present day. As global trade began to develop, these civilizations shared ideas and technology.

Preparing for the Regents

• Practice your map skills by locating three grain-producing regions that were part of Mediterranean trade routes.

Preparing for the Regents

List three contributions of each of the classical civilizations listed below.

India:

China:

Greece:

Rome:

Rise and Fall of Great Empires

The **Big Idea**

The Han and Roman empires:

- grew through military expansion.

- were supported by strong government and thriving trade.

- fell as a result of internal weakness and invading forces.

Section Overview

The rise and fall of the Han dynasty and the Roman empire followed remarkably similar courses. Both empires gained power through conquest, strong central government, and profitable trade. Both eventually fell because of weak leadership, internal dissent, and aggressive invaders.

Key Themes and Concepts

As you review this section, take special note of the following key themes and concepts:

Political Systems What factors contributed to the rise of both the Han dynasty and the Roman empire?

Economic Systems What was the importance of trade to the Han and Roman empires?

Change What factors contributed to the decline of both the Han and Roman empires?

Key People and Terms

Key People and Terms

Put each of the key people and terms into these two categories: Han dynasty or Roman empire.

As you review this section, be sure you understand the significance of these key people and terms:

Wudi	Silk Road	Pax Romana
monopoly	Augustus	

Factors Leading to Growth

Both the Han and the Roman empires reached their height between 200 B.C. and A.D. 200. Both empires began by throwing off oppressive rulers: the Qin in China and the Etruscans in Rome. Although many elements contributed to the growth of these two empires, the most important factors that sustained them were strong government and profitable trade.

Key Themes and Concepts

Political Systems
Both the Han empire and the Roman empire instituted civil service systems. Working properly, such systems assured that officials were not just the most privileged or powerful people in the empire but instead were also skilled in government.

The Han Empire

Military Power The most famous of the Han emperors, **Wudi,** conducted many military campaigns to secure and expand China's borders. Many of the battles he fought were attempts to drive nomadic peoples beyond the Great Wall.

Government Wudi worked to strengthen the Chinese government. He removed many harsh laws. Also, the civil service system helped him to choose wise officials. He set up an imperial university to train scholars in Confucian teachings.

Economy and Trade Initially, Wudi improved the economy internally by adding canals and roads to ease the movement of goods. He also had storage areas for grain set up throughout his empire. When grain was plentiful, the government would buy and store it. Then, when it became scarce, the government could sell it.

Another source of government revenue was income from the sale of iron and salt. Wudi created a government monopoly on these items. A **monopoly** is the complete control of a product or business by one person or group—in this case, the Han government. Sales of iron and salt allowed the government to have a source of income besides taxes. Wudi and later emperors also developed the **Silk Road,** a caravan route stretching from the Chinese capital to the Mediterranean Sea.

The Roman Empire

Military Power The Romans were able to conquer partly because they had a strong, well-disciplined army. However, they also treated conquered peoples well, allowing them to keep their own governments and customs. In return, conquered lands were required to supply soldiers for the Roman army and pay taxes to Rome.

Government Emperor **Augustus,** who ruled the Roman empire from 31 B.C. to A.D. 14, stabilized the government. He, like the Han emperors, created a civil service system that ensured a supply of well-trained and well-educated government officials.

Both good and bad emperors followed Augustus. However, the 200-year period called the **Pax Romana,** or Roman peace, began with his reign. During this time, Roman rule brought order and prosperity to the empire. Roman legions maintained the road system and guarded the borders.

Economy and Trade Roman expansion allowed the empire to take over prosperous trade routes throughout the Mediterranean. The Mediterranean served as a natural highway for trade. In addition, the Romans built miles of fine roads that promoted trade and brought wealth into the empire. Grain from the Nile Valley, ivory and gold from Africa, spices and gems from India, and silk that came from China via the Silk Road flowed into the empire. Under Augustus the tax system was reformed, and new coins were issued to make trade easier.

The Roman Empire, 44 B.C.

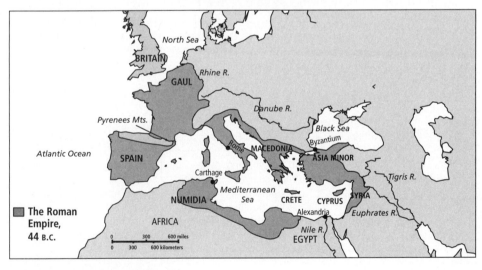

Geographic Setting

The Han and Roman empires arose on opposite sides of the Eurasian landmass. Both, however, expanded their borders over time.

Extent of the Han Empire

The Han empire was first located where the Qin had ruled: in eastern China. However, the empire expanded during Han times as Wudi secured and expanded China's borders. To the north, the Han moved into Manchuria and Korea. To the south, the empire moved into northern Vietnam. To the west, the Han gained territory in Tibet and central Asia.

Vocabulary Builder

caravan—(KA ruh van) *n.* a group of people with animals or vehicles who travel together for safety, especially through a desert

Key Themes and Concepts

Economic Systems
Trade was encouraged in both the Han and Roman empires by extensive road systems.

The Roman Empire
The Romans gained control of lands around the Mediterranean Sea through conquest and diplomacy.

Preparing for the Regents

• Name three lands that were part of the Roman empire in 44 B.C.

Extent of the Roman Empire

Rome also expanded from its initial location in central Italy. The powerful Roman military first took over the Italian peninsula. By about 44 B.C., Roman power extended throughout the Mediterranean, from Spain to parts of Asia Minor. To the north, the Roman empire spread to what is now France as well as into parts of Great Britain.

Causes of Decline

Both the Han and Roman empires grew weak as a result of internal problems and external pressures.

The Han Empire

Expansion helped to strengthen the Han empire but also led to its decline.

- **Political Causes** Rulers that followed Wudi were unable to control powerful warlords in outlying areas.
- **Economic Causes** Some rulers did not maintain the systems of canals and roads, which were vital routes of commerce. As a result, the economy suffered. High taxes oppressed the peasants and thus led to a revolt.
- **Military Causes** In A.D. 220, warlords overthrew the last Han emperor, and the empire was split into several kingdoms. Invaders overran the Great Wall and set up their own kingdoms.

The Roman Empire

Some of the same factors that led to the Han decline also led to the Roman decline. Overexpansion of the empire, high taxes, and foreign invasions all weakened the empire.

Roman emperor Diocletian divided the empire into two parts in a failed attempt to restore order. Although the decline of the Roman empire was a long, slow process, the year A.D. 476, when Germanic leader Odoacer ousted the emperor in Rome, is the date generally considered to mark its fall. The Eastern Roman empire survived, however, and became known as the Byzantine empire.

The Fall of the Roman Empire

Military causes	Economic causes	Political causes	Social causes
• Visigoths and other Germanic peoples invaded the empire. • Roman army lacked training and discipline. • Romans were forced to hire foreign soldiers to defend borders.	• Heavy taxes were necessary to support the government. • Farmers left land. • Middle class disappeared. • Romans used too much slave labor.	• Government became too strict. • People stopped supporting government. • Many officials were corrupt. • Divided empire became weak.	• Population declined because of disease and war. • People became selfish and lazy.

Summary

At opposite ends of the Eurasian landmass, two great empires thrived between 200 B.C. and A.D. 200. The Han empire in China and the Roman empire in the lands around the Mediterranean Sea shared many characteristics. Both grew through conquest and were supported for centuries by strong central governments. Far-flung trade thrived in both empires and led to prosperity. Eventually, however, internal weakness and external invasions brought about the decline of these two great empires.

Emergence and Spread of Belief Systems

Section Overview

Belief systems developed with the earliest humans, who saw the world as being full of spirits. With the rise of civilization, more complex belief systems developed. Hinduism and Buddhism emerged in India. In China, Confucianism and Taoism developed. In the Middle East, three great world religions—Judaism, Christianity, and Islam—grew. Each of these religions had its own beliefs and sacred texts, though all shared some concepts. Several of these religions spread and had an impact far beyond their places of origin.

Key Themes and Concepts

As you review this section, take special note of the following key themes and concepts:

Belief Systems What are the characteristics of the major religions? How are they similar and different?

Culture How did major religions affect cultures?

Movement of People and Goods How did belief systems spread over large areas?

Key People and Terms

As you review this section, be sure you understand the significance of these key people and terms:

animism	Buddha	hijra
brahman	nirvana	Qur'an
reincarnation	monotheistic	Sharia
karma	Torah	missionaries
dharma	Messiah	diaspora
Upanishads	Bible	

Major Belief Systems

Religious beliefs developed even in very early cultures. As civilizations arose in Africa, Europe, and Asia, more complex systems of belief developed.

Animism

The belief that every living and nonliving thing in nature has a spirit is called **animism.** Animism was a feature of the belief systems of many early people. Stone Age paintings on the walls of caves probably express these early beliefs.

Religions of some early civilizations combined animism with reverence for ancestors. People in Shang China and in some traditional African societies, for example, believed that the spirits of deceased ancestors could affect life in a positive or negative way. The prayers of ancestors were thought to be an important way to influence the gods. Therefore, people would offer food and other necessities to their ancestors' spirits.

The Big Idea

As civilizations developed and spread, so did belief systems and religions. These belief systems include:

- animism
- Hinduism
- Buddhism
- Confucianism
- Taoism
- Judaism
- Christianity
- Islam

Key People and Terms

List the terms that relate to sacred texts. Write a sentence explaining the significance of each of these terms.

Vocabulary Builder

reverence—(REV ur uns) *n.* great respect and admiration for someone or something

---

Preparing for the Regents

Understand Hinduism by answering the following questions.

1. What are the basic beliefs of Hinduism?

2. What system defines the social system of Hinduism? Explain.

Preparing for the Regents

Define each of the following terms:

1. brahman

2. reincarnation

3. karma

4. dharma

Hinduism

Hinduism is one of the oldest and most complex religions in the world. Unlike most major religions, Hinduism has no single founder. Hinduism developed and changed over 3,500 years, growing out of the diverse peoples who settled India. These groups include the original inhabitants of the Indus Valley as well as the nomadic Aryans who entered India in about 1500 B.C.

Universal Spirit Hindus believe in one unifying spirit, **brahman.** Because brahman is too complex for humans to understand, Hindus worship gods that give a more concrete form to brahman. The three most important Hindu gods are Brahma the Creator, Vishnu the Preserver, and Shiva the Destroyer. The goal of life is to achieve union with brahman.

Reincarnation Achieving union with brahman is said to occur as people free themselves from the selfish desires that separate them from the universal spirit. Most people cannot achieve this union in one lifetime. The concept of reincarnation, the rebirth of the soul in a new body, allows people to continue their journey toward union with brahman. People get closer to this union by being born into higher and higher levels of existence.

Karma and Dharma In each lifetime, a person can come closer to union with brahman by obeying the law of karma. Karma consists of all the deeds of a person's life that affect his or her existence in the next life. By living in a right way, a person will be reborn at a higher level. Evil deeds cause people to be reborn into a lower level. Good deeds involve following dharma, the moral and religious duties that are expected of an individual. A person's gender, class, age, and occupation all affect his or her dharma.

The Caste System

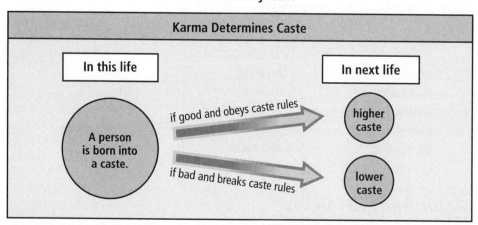

Karma Determines Caste

In this life — A person is born into a caste.

if good and obeys caste rules → higher caste

if bad and breaks caste rules → lower caste

In next life

Analyzing Documents

Use the text on castes and the chart to answer the following questions:

- What judgment would Hindus make about the past life of an Untouchable?

- What judgment would Hindus make about the past life of a Brahmin?

Castes The caste system is an important part of Hinduism. Castes are social groups into which people are born and out of which they cannot move during a lifetime. However, a person may be born into a higher caste in the next life by acquiring good karma. The three basic caste groups during Aryan times were priests (Brahmins), warriors (Kshatriyas), and a group that included herders, farmers, artisans, and merchants (Vaisyas). Later, a separate group was created for non-Aryans. This group (Sudras) included farm workers and servants. The lowest-ranked people, called Untouchables, were at the bottom of the social system.

Sacred Texts Over several thousand years, Hindu teachings were developed and recorded in a number of sacred texts. These include the Vedas, collections of prayers and sacred verses, and the **Upanishads,** philosophical dialogues about Hindu beliefs.

Buddhism

Buddhism also developed in India but later spread into other areas, such as China. Its founder, a prince named Siddhartha Gautama, was born a Hindu in the 500s B.C.

The Enlightened One Siddhartha Gautama left his wealthy home to search for the meaning of human suffering. While meditating under a sacred tree, he found the answer to his question, and he was thereafter referred to as the **Buddha,** or the Enlightened One.

The Four Noble Truths The central philosophy of Buddhism revolves around the Four Noble Truths.

1. All life is suffering.
2. Suffering is caused by desire for things that are illusions.
3. The way to eliminate suffering is to eliminate desire.
4. Following the Eightfold Path will help people overcome desire.

The Eightfold Path The Eightfold Path involves right views, right intentions, right speech, right conduct, right livelihood, right effort, right mindfulness, and right meditation. The ultimate goal is **nirvana,** union with the universe and release from the cycle of death and rebirth.

Comparison With Hinduism Buddhism accepts the Hindu concepts of karma, dharma, and reincarnation. However, Buddhism rejects the many Hindu gods as well as the rituals and priesthood of Hinduism. Buddhists do, however, accept the idea of religious communities that include monks and nuns. Buddhism also rejected the caste system.

Sacred Texts After the Buddha died, his teachings were collected into the *Tripitaka*, or "Three Baskets of Wisdom." This collection is made up of rules for Buddhist monks; sermons; and discussions of Buddhist beliefs. Later, other Buddhists added many more scriptures.

Two Philosophies of China

The late Zhou dynasty was a troubled time in China. There were many wars, and economic and social changes disrupted everyday life. Beginning in the 500s B.C., several major Chinese philosophies developed. Two of the most important were Confucianism and Taoism. These philosophies shared the common purpose of restoring harmony.

Confucianism Confucius, born in 551 B.C., was China's most influential thinker. Confucius's teachings, collected in *The Analects*, taught people to accept their given places in society. These individual places were expressed through five key relationships.

Confucius believed that, except for friendships, none of these relationships was equal. Older people were superior to younger, for example, and men were superior to women. Every person had duties and responsibilities that depended on his or her position.

Other ideas of Confucius include the following:

- People are naturally good.
- Education should be the road to advancement in society.
- To ensure social order, the individual must find and accept his or her proper place in society.

Recognize Effects

As you read the sections *Buddhism* and *Two Philosophies of China*, answer these questions.

1. What is the effect of following the Eightfold Path?

2. According to Confucius, what is the effect of following proper relationships in society?

Preparing for the Regents

List two similarities and two differences between the Hindu and Buddhist religions.

Similarities:

1.

2.

Differences:

1.

2.

Proper Relationships

Superior ruler, husband, father, elder brother

takes care of and sets good example for

owes loyalty and obedience to

Inferior subject, wife, son, younger brother

Vocabulary Builder

mystic—(MIS tik) *n.* someone who follows the religious practice in which people try to get knowledge of truth and to become united with God through prayer and meditation

Preparing for the Regents

• Make a chart comparing the basic ideas of Confucianism and Taoism.

Key Themes and Concepts

Belief Systems
Judaism influenced the development of two later monotheistic world religions: Islam and Christianity.

Judaism
Judaism is the Jewish religion. It evolved from ancient Hebrew beliefs.

Taoism Another influential Chinese philosophy was Taoism (often spelled *Daoism*). Taoism sought to help people to live in harmony with nature. Laozi, who founded Taoism, taught people to contemplate the Tao, or the "way" of the universe. Important virtues in Taoism are yielding and acceptance. Followers of Laozi rejected the world and human government and often withdrew to become hermits, mystics, or poets.

Taoists also believe in a balance between yin and yang. The yin stands for Earth, darkness, and female forces. The yang stands for Heaven, light, and male forces. The peace and well-being of the universe depend on harmony between yin and yang.

The beliefs of Taoism are collected in two works. Laozi is traditionally thought to be the author of the first, *The Way of Virtue*. A second text is the *Zhuang-zi*, written several centuries later. It contains fables, sayings, and dialogues.

Judaism

The Hebrews were one of the nomadic groups who lived in the Fertile Crescent. According to Hebrew tradition, the Hebrews became enslaved in Egypt, and God helped them escape this slavery. By about 1000 B.C., the Hebrews had set up the kingdom of Israel with Jerusalem as its capital. They believed that God had promised them this land. Over time, Hebrew beliefs evolved into the religion we today call Judaism. Several beliefs are very important to Judaism.

Belief in One God Judaism is **monotheistic,** teaching a belief in one God. Most other religions of the time worshiped many gods and goddesses. The Hebrews believed that God was their special protector and was all-knowing, all-powerful, and present everywhere.

Sacred Texts and Moral Teachings According to the sacred scriptures of the Hebrews, the **Torah,** God made a covenant, or a binding agreement, to be the God of the Hebrews. Jews also believe that God gave them the Ten Commandments through Moses. These are laws that describe how people should behave toward God and each other. The Old Testament of the Bible includes the Torah, which is made up of five books. The Torah also sets out many other laws that establish the moral basis for Judaism.

Hebrew sacred scriptures also include the writings of spiritual leaders called prophets, who urged Hebrews to act according to God's teachings. The prophets preached a strong code of ethics, or moral standards of behavior. Judaic thought had a strong influence on two other world religions: Christianity and Islam.

Judaism

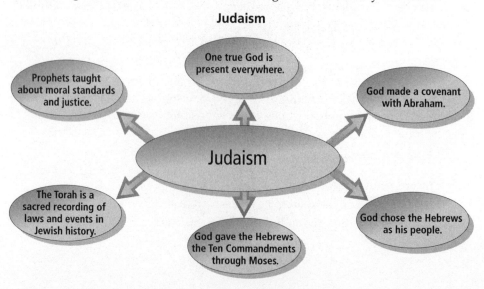

One true God is present everywhere.

Prophets taught about moral standards and justice.

God made a covenant with Abraham.

Judaism

The Torah is a sacred recording of laws and events in Jewish history.

God gave the Hebrews the Ten Commandments through Moses.

God chose the Hebrews as his people.

Christianity

Christianity began in Palestine with the teachings of a Jew named Jesus in about A.D. 30. Beginning with a small group of followers, Christianity grew and spread to become the official religion of the Roman empire by A.D. 392.

Life and Death of Jesus According to Christian tradition, Jesus' mother, Mary, had been told before his birth that he would be the Messiah. **Messiah** is the Jewish word, derived from Hebrew, for a savior sent by God. Jesus grew up worshiping God and following Jewish law. At about age 30, he began to travel through the countryside preaching and teaching new beliefs.

Many Jews and Romans worried that Jesus was dangerous. Around A.D. 29, the Romans arrested Jesus, tried him, and executed him by crucifixion. By this method a person was tied or nailed to a cross and left to die. After Jesus' death, many of his followers said that he had risen from the grave. His followers worked to spread his teachings. The Romans persecuted Christians, who set up an organized church. In A.D. 313, Roman Emperor Constantine ended the persecution of Christians. In A.D. 392, Christianity became the official religion of the Roman Empire.

Teachings of Jesus The teachings of Jesus were rooted in Jewish tradition. For example, Jesus accepted the Ten Commandments that God had given to the Jews through Moses. At the same time, he preached new ideas. According to his followers, he was the son of God and the savior that the Jews had been expecting. His mission was to bring salvation and eternal life to anyone who would follow his teachings. Jesus taught mercy and sympathy for the poor and helpless. Jesus also preached brotherhood and the equality of people before God.

Sacred Text The sacred text of Christianity is the Christian **Bible.** It has two parts. The Old Testament includes the Hebrew scriptures, books of law, history, prophetic writing, and poetry. The New Testament includes the Gospels (describing Jesus and his teachings) and other writings, mostly letters written by Christians that explain Christian doctrine.

Preparing for the Regents

- Prepare a timeline that shows events in the growth of Christianity as well as several other global events of the same period.

Compare and Contrast

Look at the concept webs for Judaism and Christianity. Compare and contrast the information. Write two similarities and two differences.

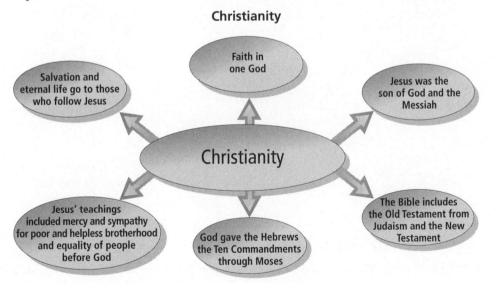

Christianity

- Faith in one God
- Salvation and eternal life go to those who follow Jesus
- Jesus was the son of God and the Messiah
- Jesus' teachings included mercy and sympathy for poor and helpless brotherhood and equality of people before God
- God gave the Hebrews the Ten Commandments through Moses
- The Bible includes the Old Testament from Judaism and the New Testament

Key Themes and Concepts

Belief Systems
Jews, Christians, and Muslims all believe in one God, and their holy writings share many themes and ethics. Despite these similarities, the three groups have often come into conflict, as they did during the Crusades in the 1000s. Even today, especially in the Middle East, these groups do not always coexist peacefully.

Islam

In A.D. 622, a new religion called Islam arose in Arabia. Like Christians and Jews, people who follow Islam believe in one God.

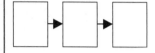

Recognize Sequence

Life of Muhammad In about 570, an Arab named Muhammad was born in Mecca. Muhammad became a caravan merchant, married, and had children. He was troubled, however, by the idol worship of the Arabs of the time. According to Muslim tradition, the angel Gabriel commanded Muhammad to spread the message of Islam.

Muhammad obeyed this command. Soon Meccan merchants sought to kill him. In 622, Muhammad and his followers left Mecca for Yathrib (later named Medina) on a journey known as the **hijra** (often spelled hegira). The hijra was a turning point for Islam. Muslim converts in Medina welcomed Muhammad, and the religion grew.

Muslim Beliefs The followers of Islam are called Muslims. All Muslims accept five basic duties, known as the Five Pillars. First, Muslims believe in one God, Allah, who is compassionate and all-powerful. Muhammad is God's greatest prophet. Second, Muslims are expected to pray five times daily. Third, Muslims are expected to give money to the poor. Fourth, Muslims are expected to fast from sunrise to sunset during the holy month of Ramadan. Fifth, Muslims are supposed to visit Mecca at least once in their lives.

Vocabulary Builder

compassionate—(kum PASH un it) *adj.* feeling sympathy for people who are suffering; kind and generous

Sacred Text The sacred scriptures of Islam are contained in the **Qur'an.** The Qur'an is the final authority on all matters and provides a guide to life for Muslims. Muslim scholars have also developed an immense body of laws, called the **Sharia,** that covers all aspects of life. Over time, this system of law acted as a means to unite Muslims of differing backgrounds.

The Five Duties of Islam

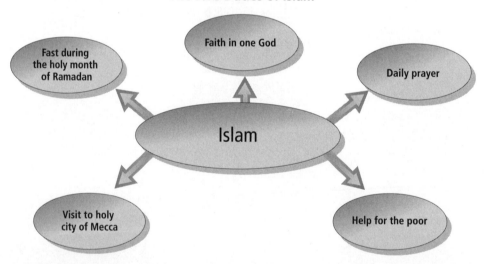

Faith in one God

Fast during the holy month of Ramadan

Daily prayer

Islam

Visit to holy city of Mecca

Help for the poor

Expansion of World Religions

Some of the religions discussed here, such as Confucianism and Taoism, remained within a fairly limited geographical area. Hinduism spread throughout India and into Southeast Asia. Other religions spread more widely.

Key Themes and Concepts

Movement of People and Goods
Three ways in which religions spread were through missionary activity, military conquest, and trade.

Spread of Buddhism

Over the centuries, the Buddha's teachings won wide acceptance. The Mauryan ruler Asoka converted to Buddhism and sent messengers to spread Buddhist beliefs. Over time, traders and **missionaries,** or people dedicated to spreading a religion, spread Buddhism far beyond India to many parts of Asia, including China, Japan, Korea, and Southeast Asia. In India, where Buddhism started, it eventually declined.

Spread of Judaism

Judaism spread in a unique way. The Romans expelled the Jews from Palestine in A.D. 135. This event became known as the **diaspora,** or scattering of people. Wherever Jews settled, they lived in close-knit communities and maintained their identity through the careful preservation of tradition.

Spread of Christianity

Christianity first spread through the work of Christian missionaries such as Paul. Even though Roman rulers persecuted Christians, the religion continued to spread throughout the Roman empire. This occurred for many reasons. The poor and oppressed found comfort in Jesus' message of love and a better life after death. Also, Christian missionaries often added Greek concepts to their teaching of the religion, appealing to educated Romans as well as others. In 313, Emperor Constantine allowed freedom of worship throughout the Roman empire. Later, Emperor Theodosius made Christianity the official religion of the empire.

After the fall of the western Roman empire, missionaries continued to spread Christianity throughout Europe. Trading networks also spread Christianity, especially as Europe began voyages of exploration and expansion in the 1400s. Europeans took Christianity with them when they established settlements in the Americas, Africa, and Asia.

Spread of Islam

In the 150 years after the death of Muhammad, Islam spread over three continents. Skillful Arab fighters spread Islam through military conquest. Because the Arabs treated conquered peoples in a fair way, many people converted to Islam willingly. The teaching of Islam appealed to many because it emphasized honesty, generosity, and social justice.

Trade had always been considered an honorable occupation for Muslims. Muslims built vast trading empires. Merchants established trading networks with Africa, China, and India. In India, Muslim traders were an important means of spreading Islam. At the other end of the Eurasian landmass, Islam spread from North Africa into Spain.

Summary

Many belief systems emerged over time in various parts of the world. In India, Hinduism and Buddhism developed. In China, Confucianism and Taoism were significant philosophies. In the Middle East, Judaism, Christianity, and Islam developed. All of these belief systems had important effects on the civilizations of their time as well as later on. Several belief systems spread widely through missionary effort, conquest, and trade.

Preparing for the Regents

Describe how each of these religions spread throughout the world:

• Buddhism:
• Judaism:
• Christianity:
• Islam:

Key Themes and Concepts

Movement of People and Goods
Although Christians were initially persecuted, Christianity spread throughout the Roman empire. Eventually, Christianity became the official religion of the empire.

Preparing for the Regents

Describe a major belief of each of the belief systems that follows.

Hinduism:

Buddhism:

Confucianism:

Taoism:

Judaism:

Christianity:

Islam:

Questions for Regents Practice

Multiple Choice

Directions: Review the Test-Taking Strategies section of this book. Then answer the following questions, drawn from actual Regents examinations. For each statement or question, choose the *number* of the word or expression that, of those given, best completes the statement or answers the question.

1 One result of the Neolithic Revolution was
 (1) an increase in the number of nomadic tribes
 (2) a reliance on hunting and gathering for food
 (3) the establishment of villages and the rise of governments
 (4) a decrease in trade between cultural groups

2 The ancient civilizations of Mesopotamia and Egypt were similar in that both cultures
 (1) established trade routes to China
 (2) used the ziggurat form for their temples
 (3) developed along rivers
 (4) used a hieroglyphic writing system

3 "If a seignior [noble] has knocked out the tooth of a seignior of his own rank, they shall knock out his tooth. But if he has knocked out a commoner's tooth, he shall pay one-third mina of silver."

 —Code of Hammurabi

 Which idea of Babylonian society does this portion of the Hammurabi code of law reflect?

 (1) All men were equal under the law.
 (2) Fines were preferable to corporal punishment.
 (3) Divisions existed between social classes.
 (4) Violence was always punished with violence.

4 The early civilizations of the Nile River valley, Mesopotamia, and the Huang He were similar because they were
 (1) dependent on fertile land
 (2) monotheistic
 (3) industrialized societies
 (4) dependent on each other for trade

5 All citizens in ancient Athens had the right to attend the assembly, where they could meet in the open to discuss and cast votes. This situation is an example of
 (1) direct democracy
 (2) totalitarianism
 (3) parliamentary democracy
 (4) absolutism

6 A major contribution of the Roman empire to western society was the development of
 (1) gunpowder
 (2) the principles of feudalism
 (3) monotheism
 (4) an effective legal system

7 A major impact of ancient Greece and Rome on western civilization was that

   (1) the Greeks and Romans achieved a classless society, which was later copied in Western Europe

   (2) Greek sculpture and Roman architecture were much admired and copied in Western Europe in later centuries

   (3) Greece and Rome transmitted Islamic philosophy to the areas they conquered

   (4) Greek and Latin are still widely spoken in universities throughout the West

8 In traditional India, the caste system and the Hindu beliefs in karma and dharma most directly resulted in

   (1) the establishment of a set of rules for each individual in society

   (2) the rapid industrialization of the economy

   (3) a strong emphasis on the acquisition of wealth

   (4) a strong belief in the importance of education

9 According to the teachings of Confucius, the key to the successful organization of society is that

   (1) the ruler should be chosen democratically

   (2) the evil in humans must be eliminated

   (3) ancestor worship should be discontinued

   (4) individuals should know and do what is expected of them

10 The Qu'ran, Mecca, and the hijra (hegira) are most closely associated with the practice of

   (1) Islam

   (2) Judaism

   (3) Christianity

   (4) Buddhism

11 One similarity between the Five Pillars of Islam and the Ten Commandments is that both

   (1) support a belief in reincarnation

   (2) promote learning as a means to salvation

   (3) encourage the use of statues to symbolize God

   (4) provide a guide to proper ethical and moral behavior

12 One way in which the Eightfold Path and the Five Pillars of Islam are similar is that these rules

   (1) represent codes of behavior

   (2) restrict social mobility

   (3) stress the spiritual being in all natural objects

   (4) suggest a deep respect for nature and reincarnation

13 Hammurabi's Code, the Ten Commandments, and the Twelve Tables were all significant to their societies because they established

   (1) democratic governments

   (2) official religions

   (3) rules of behavior

   (4) economic systems

14 What was one effect of Alexander the Great's conquests?

   (1) expansion of Hellenistic culture

   (2) formation of the Christian church

   (3) decreased importance of the Silk Roads

   (4) increased support of the Mayan leaders

Thematic Essay Question

In developing your answer, be sure to keep these general definitions in mind:

    (a) <u>describe</u> means "to illustrate something in words or tell about it"
    (b) <u>explain</u> means "to make plain or understandable; to give reasons for or causes of; to show the logical development or relationships of"

Directions: Write a well-organized essay that includes an introduction, several paragraphs addressing the task below, and a conclusion.

Theme: **Civilization**

> Throughout history, great civilizations have existed in various parts of the world. The cultural and intellectual achievements of these civilizations contributed to the advancement of humankind.

Tasks:

> - Define the term *civilization*
> - Describe some examples of cultural or intellectual achievements made by past civilizations
> - Identify each example with the particular civilization that made the contribution
> - Explain the lasting importance of each of these achievements or contributions to global history

    You may discuss any civilization from your study of global history, except the United States. Some civilizations you might wish to consider include ancient Egypt, classical Rome, the Gupta empire, classical China, or the Muslim golden age.

You are not limited to these suggestions.

Guidelines:

    In your essay, be sure to
- Develop all aspects of the task
- Support the theme with relevant facts, examples, and details
- Use a logical and clear plan of organization, including an introduction and a conclusion that are beyond a simple restatement of the theme

This question is based on the accompanying documents. The question is designed to test your ability to work with historical documents. Some of these documents have been edited for the purposes of this question. As you analyze the documents, take into account the source of each document and any point of view that may be presented in the document.

Historical Context:

> Throughout global history, people have established different systems of government. They have been based on different views of how people should be ruled.

Task: Using the information from the documents and your knowledge of global history, answer the questions that follow each document in Part A. Your answers to the questions will help you write the Part B essay in which you will be asked to

> - Evaluate different perspectives on government
> - Discuss the best kind of government

In developing your answers, be sure to keep these general definitions in mind:

> (a) <u>evaluate</u> means "to examine and judge the significance, worth, or condition of; to determine the value of"
>
> (b) <u>discuss</u> means "to make observations about something using facts, reasoning, and argument; to present in some detail"

Document-Based Question

Part A: Short Answer

Directions: Analyze the documents and answer the question or questions that follow each document, using the space provided.

Document #1

The Mandate of Heaven

Generations go by. New dynasty becomes . . .

NEW DYNASTY
- Brings peace
- Builds roads and canals
- Gives land to peasants
- Protects people

THE DYNASTY CYCLE

OLD DYNASTY
- Taxes people too much
- Stops protecting people
- Lets roads and walls fall apart
- Treats people unfairly

PROBLEMS
- Floods, earthquakes
- Peasants revolt
- Invaders attack empire
- Bandits raid provinces

New dynasty claims Mandate of Heaven

Old dynasty loses Mandate of Heaven

1. According to this chart, how did Chinese rulers lose power?

_____

_____

2. How did Chinese rulers show that they had the Mandate of Heaven?

_____

_____

Document #2

> *People become naturally spoiled by love, but are submissive to authority. . . . That being so, rewards should be rich and certain so that the people will be attracted to them; punishments should be severe and definite so that the people will fear them; and laws should be uniform and steadfast so that the people will be familiar with them.*
>
> **—Hanfeizi, 200s B.C.**

3. According to this philosophy, what is the best way to make sure that people will respect and obey government?

_____

_____

Document #3

> *We differ from other states in regarding the man who holds aloof from public life not as "quiet" but as useless; we decide or debate, carefully and in person, all matters of policy, holding, not that words and deeds go ill together, but that acts are foredoomed to failure when undertaken undiscussed.*
>
> **—Speech of Pericles (431 B.C.) in Thucydides, History of the Peloponnesian War**

4. According to Pericles of Athens, what was the best way for a government to make decisions?

_____

_____

Part B

Essay

Directions: Write a well-organized essay that includes an introduction, several paragraphs, and a conclusion. Use evidence from *at least two* of the documents in your essay. Support your response with relevant facts, examples, and details. Include additional outside information.

Historical Context:

Throughout global history, people have established different systems of government. They have been based on different views of how people should be ruled.

Task: Using the information from the documents and your knowledge of global history, write an essay in which you

- Evaluate different perspectives on government
- Discuss the best kind of government

Guidelines:

In your essay, be sure to

- Develop all aspects of the task
- Incorporate information from *at least two* of the documents
- Incorporate relevant outside information
- Support the theme with relevant facts, examples, and details
- Use a logical and clear plan of organization, including an introduction and a conclusion that are beyond a restatement of the theme

Expanding Zones of Exchange
(500–1200)

Unit Overview

During the period from about 500 to 1200, civilizations matured in various regions of the world. The Gupta dynasty united northern India. The Tang and Song dynasties each ruled a unified China. In southeastern Europe and the Middle East, the Byzantine empire carried on the traditions of Greece and Rome. The first Russian state was founded in Kiev. Islamic civilization flourished across several continents. In Europe, Christianity, feudalism, and the manor system dominated life.

As civilizations expanded, they often encountered one another. Sometimes the encounters were peaceful; at other times, violent. Always, however, encounters led to exchanges of people, goods, and ideas.

Using Good Social Studies Practices

Economics

Some of the many themes developed in Unit 2 are:

economic systems	diversity	interdependence
culture and intellectual life	power	political systems
movement of people and goods	belief systems	

Choose one of the themes listed above. As you review Unit 2, take notes about how your theme relates to the economic changes taking place between 500 and 1200. Write an essay using these details that includes major developments and key turning points having to do with your theme.

The Gupta Empire in India

The Big Idea

During Gupta rule, the people of India:

• experienced peace and prosperity under a strong government.

• were influenced greatly by Hindu ideas.

• produced many achievements in the arts and sciences.

Section Overview

The Gupta dynasty came to power in India in A.D. 320 and ruled until 550. The strong Gupta government, which gave power to local leaders, united much of the Indian subcontinent and ensured peace and prosperity. Hinduism had a very strong impact on Gupta society and cultural life. Gupta scientists and mathematicians made important discoveries and advances.

Key Themes and Concepts

As you review this section, take special note of the following key themes and concepts:

Political Systems What were some key characteristics of Gupta rule?

Belief Systems How did Hinduism influence Gupta society and culture?

Culture and Intellectual Life What advances did people of the Gupta empire make in the arts and sciences?

Key People and Terms

Place each of the key people and terms into these two categories: political system or culture/intellectual life.

As you review this section, be sure you understand the significance of these key people and terms:

Gupta dynasty	Untouchables	patriarchal	Arabic numerals
Pataliputra	joint families	decimal system	stupas

Note Taking

Reading Skill:
Identify Effects
Make a concept web. Fill in the impact of Hinduism on Gupta life. Add circles if necessary.

Impact of Hindusm on Gupta life

Geographic Setting

About 500 years after the rule of the Maurya dynasty in India, the **Gupta dynasty** came to power. The Mauryas and the Guptas were the only early Indian civilizations to be able to unite the subcontinent under their rule. Both arose in the north and spread southward. Geography benefited the northern empires in various ways. Mountains helped protect these civilizations from foreign invaders. In addition, the Indus and Ganges Rivers flowed through the northern region, providing water and fertile soil. The Gupta period was one of peace and prosperity for India.

The Influence of Hinduism

Hinduism had a strong impact on all areas of Gupta life. The Gupta dynasty adopted and actively promoted Hinduism. This set of beliefs affected the social life of Gupta villages through the caste system. Hinduism also had a strong effect on the flowering of cultural and intellectual achievements during the Gupta era.

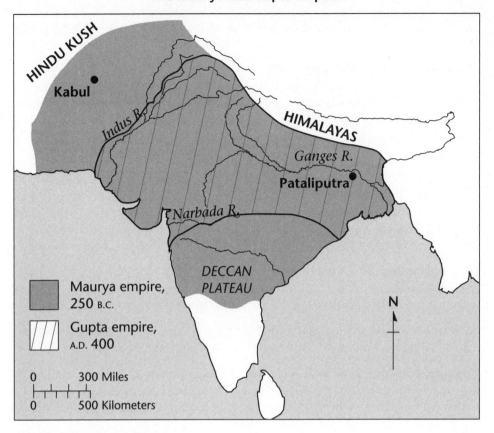

The Maurya and Gupta Empires

The Maurya and Gupta Empires
The Maurya and Gupta emperors united much of India under one rule. These empires included parts of present-day India, Pakistan, Afghanistan, Bangladesh, and Nepal.

Preparing for the Regents

- What geographic features of India were beneficial to both the Maurya and Gupta empires? Explain.

Gupta Government

Central Government

Gupta emperors ruled over a spectacular court at **Pataliputra**, the former Mauryan capital on the Ganges River. An efficient central government allowed farming and trade to prosper and provided a stable background for advances in learning and the arts.

Local Government

Although the Gupta rulers maintained a strong central government, they also gave great power to local leaders. These leaders were elected by merchants and artisans. In each village, a headman and council made decisions for the village. The most respected people of the village served on the council.

Role of Women

In earlier times, women were allowed to serve on the councils. Over time, however, Hindu law placed greater restrictions on women, excluding them from participation.

Hinduism and Gupta Society

Society came to be ordered by Hindu concepts during the Gupta period. Most Indian people lived in small villages, where Hindu ideas about caste and family regulated society.

The Caste System

Caste had originated in early Aryan times, and by the time of Gupta rule, the system had expanded from four basic castes to include many more groupings.

Key Themes and Concepts

Political Systems
Gupta emperors established a stable central government but also shared power with local leaders. The resulting peace and prosperity contributed to a golden age in India.

Key Themes and Concepts

Belief Systems
Hindu beliefs governed village life, creating a stable society.

Preparing for the Regents

- How did the Hindu caste system affect village and family life in Gupta India?

- Examine the role of women in Gupta life. How does it compare to the role of women in other civilizations and societies you have studied?

People believed that their karma, all the good and bad things they had done in life, determined their caste. People could not change their caste in one lifetime, but they could be born into a higher caste in the next life by fulfilling moral duties, or dharma.

Organization of Village Life

The village was the center of Indian life during Gupta times. A cluster of homes built of earth and stone was surrounded by fields, where farmers grew their crops. Villages ran their own affairs and faced little interference from the central government as long as they paid their taxes.

Village life was governed by caste rules and traditions. These strong traditions created a stable society. People in the higher castes had the strictest rules, which were designed to keep them from being contaminated by people from lower castes. The **Untouchables** were outcasts who lived harsh lives. They were given the jobs that were considered "impure," such as cleaning the streets or digging graves. Untouchables had to live apart from the other members of Gupta society.

Organization of Family Life

In villages, wealthier persons often lived in **joint families,** where parents, children, grandparents, uncles, and their children shared a common home.

Patriarchal Structure Indian families were patriarchal, with the father or oldest male heading the household. Heads of families had great authority.

Children and Marriage Indian children learned the family trade or worked in the fields and were taught what would be expected of them as adults. An important duty for parents was to arrange the marriage of their children. Hindu law required that people marry only within their own caste.

Role of Women Although the status of women varied throughout India, the role of women generally became more restricted over time because of the development of Hindu law. By the end of Gupta rule, upper-class women were largely restricted to their homes and had to cover themselves from head to foot when they went out. Lower-class women worked in the fields or did spinning and weaving.

Scientific and Artistic Contributions

An environment of peace and prosperity allowed scientific and artistic achievements to flourish during the Gupta dynasty. Education took place at religious institutions. At Hindu and Buddhist centers, students learned subjects such as mathematics, medicine, physics, and languages.

Mathematics

Zero and the Decimal System Indian mathematicians developed the concept of zero as well as the decimal system. The decimal system is the system we use, based on the number 10.

Arabic Numerals Gupta mathematicians developed the system of writing numerals that we use today. They are known as Arabic numerals because Arabs brought them from India to the Middle East and Europe.

Medicine

Gupta physicians began to use herbs and other remedies to treat illnesses. Surgeons were able to set bones and repair facial injuries with plastic surgery. Furthermore, Gupta physicians vaccinated people against smallpox approximately 1,000 years before this practice began in Europe.

Architecture

Architects built beautiful stone temples for Hindu worship. A typical shape was a square (symbolizing the Earth) within a circle (which stood for eternity). Hindu temples were filled with carvings of gods and goddesses, animals such as elephants and monkeys, and ordinary people.

Buddhist architects constructed **stupas,** large dome-shaped shrines that contained the remains of holy people. These Buddhist shrines were plain but included gateways with elaborate carvings that depicted the life of Buddha.

Literature

Extraordinary works of literature were created during the Gupta dynasty. Fables and folk tales in the Sanskrit language were collected and recorded. These stories were carried west to Persia, Egypt, and Greece.

End of Gupta Rule

After about 200 years, the Gupta empire declined because of weak rulers and foreign invasions. The invaders were the White Huns from central Asia, nomads who destroyed villages and disrupted trade in the Gupta empire.

Summary

The Gupta dynasty reigned successfully through a strong central government that also gave great power to local leaders. Gupta rule helped India to enjoy peace and prosperity for 200 years. The rules and rituals of Hinduism governed daily life. The Gupta era became known for its significant contributions to science, medicine, mathematics, architecture, art, and literature.

Key Themes and Concepts

Culture and Intellectual Life
Religion was a strong influence in Indian art and architecture. Gupta architects built beautiful temples for both the Buddhist and Hindu religions.

Causes

What were the causes of the decline of the Gupta empire?

Preparing for the Regents

Describe the achievements of the Gupta dynasty in each of the categories listed.

Mathematics:

Medicine:

Architecture:

Literature:

Tang and Song Dynasties in China

Section Overview

The Tang dynasty came to power in China in 618 and ruled until 907. This dynasty unified China and expanded the empire. The Song dynasty ruled China from 960 to 1279. Under the Tang and Song dynasties, government was efficient and society was well structured and stable. Farming and trade flourished. China produced great advances in literature, art, and architecture. During this period, Chinese culture spread to Japan.

Key Themes and Concepts

As you review this section, take special note of the following key themes and concepts:

Political Systems How did the Tang dynasty unite China and keep it strong?

Economic Systems How did Tang and Song rulers help the economy to flourish?

Culture and Intellectual Life What were the Tang and Song dynasties' contributions to the arts and architecture?

Movement of People and Goods How did Tang and Song China influence Japanese culture?

Key Terms

As you review this section, be sure you understand the significance of these key terms:

Tang dynasty	gentry	pagoda
tributary states	calligraphy	porcelain
Song dynasty		

The Rise and Fall of Dynasties

After the Han dynasty declined in the A.D. 200s, China was divided for nearly 400 years. Then, in the 600s, a young general came to power. He took the name Tang Taizong and established the **Tang dynasty,** a powerful dynasty that ruled China from 618 to 907.

The Tang dynasty built a vast empire with its capital at Xian (Changan). Tang rulers forced Vietnam, Korea, and Tibet to become **tributary states.** These states remained independent, but their rulers had to acknowledge China's greater power and send tribute, or regular payment. Japan sent missions to China to conduct trade and study Chinese culture.

Government corruption, drought, and rebellions all contributed to the collapse of the Tang dynasty in 907. Then, in 960, a scholarly general named Zhao Kuangyin reunited China under the **Song dynasty.** China prospered under Song rule, but the dynasty was weakened by invaders. The Song dynasty was finally conquered by the Mongols in 1279.

Government and Society

Confucianist beliefs guided both the nature of the government and the structure of the society. Confucian thought stressed social order based on duty, rank, and proper behavior.

Skillful Government

Tang rulers revived the civil service system that had first been developed during the Han dynasty. People who wanted to hold office had to pass difficult examinations that emphasized Confucian philosophy. Rulers set up schools that prepared male students to take these exams. This system gave Tang and Song China a highly educated ruling class.

Strict Social Order

China had a strict social structure under the Tang and Song dynasties. Chinese social structure consisted of three main classes: the gentry, the peasantry, and the merchants.

Key Themes and Concepts

Government
The Tang dynasty revived and improved the civil service system. As a result, both Tang and Song China had a highly educated ruling class.

Vocabulary Builder

revive—(rih VYV) *v.* to bring something back after it has not been used or has not existed for a period of time

The Tang and Song Dynasties, 618–1215

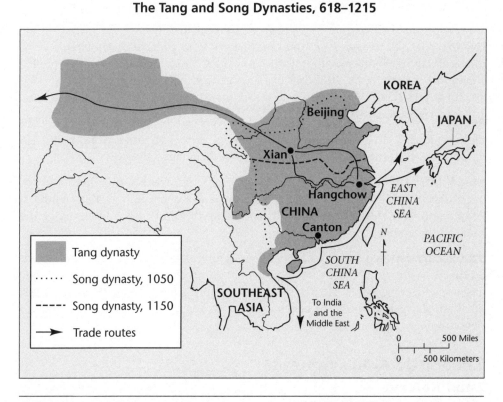

Tang dynasty
······ Song dynasty, 1050
----- Song dynasty, 1150
→ Trade routes

KOREA
Beijing
JAPAN
Xian
Hangchow
CHINA
Canton
EAST CHINA SEA
SOUTH CHINA SEA
PACIFIC OCEAN
N
SOUTHEAST ASIA
To India and the Middle East
0   500 Miles
0   500 Kilometers

Preparing for the Regents

• Use the map to explain how the extent of Song rule changed between 1050 and 1150.

The Tang and Song Dynasties Dynasties ruled China for most of its history until 1912. Under the Tang and Song Dynasties, China experienced a prosperous economy and rich culture.

GENTRY
- Were wealthy landowners
- Studied Confucian ideas
- Some became civil servants

PEASANTS
- Most Chinese were peasants
- Were farmers that worked the land
- Lived in small villages

MERCHANTS
- Some became very rich
- Were of lower status than peasants because their riches came from work done by other people
- Some bought land and educated a son so he could join the gentry

Vocabulary Builder

scholarship—(SKAHL ur ship) *n.* the knowledge, work, or methods involved in serious studying

Key Themes and Concepts

Economic Systems
Many aspects of Tang and Song rule benefited the economy. Land reform created more tax revenue. Improvements in farming increased productivity. The expansion of trade brought money into the empire from outside China. Better transportation improved economic efficiency.

Gentry The gentry were wealthy landowners who preferred scholarship over physical labor. Confucian thought was valued, and members of the gentry sometimes spent years studying it. The gentry had to pass a civil service examination to obtain honored positions in government.

Peasants Most Chinese were peasants. They worked the land and lived on what they produced. To supplement their income, they sometimes sold or traded handicrafts. Peasants lived in small villages that managed their own affairs.

Merchants Although some merchants acquired vast wealth, they held a lower social status than the peasants because their wealth came from the labor of others. As a result, some merchants bought land and educated their sons to enter the ranks of the gentry.

Status of Women Under the Tang and Song dynasties, many women held great authority. Within the home, women managed family finances, imposed discipline, and supervised servants. However, boys were still valued over girls. When a girl married, she was required to become a part of her husband's family and could never remarry.

Economic Achievements
Land Reform
During the Tang dynasty, a system of land reform redistributed land to peasants. Large landowners had less power, and peasants could contribute to government revenue by paying taxes.

Expanded Trade

Foreign trade expanded under both the Tang and Song dynasties. Chinese merchants traded with India, Persia, and the Middle East. The Chinese became expert shipbuilders and emerged as a naval power. To improve trade, the government issued paper money—the world's first.

Canals

Canals were built to encourage trade and improve transportation. The Grand Canal was the largest, linking the Huang He and the Yangzi. This canal allowed food from farms in southern China to be sent north.

Literature and Arts

The arts were important during the Tang and Song dynasties. Chinese writers wrote short stories and poetry. Chinese landscape painting became popular during the Song period, and **calligraphy**—fine handwriting—flourished. Chinese architects created the **pagoda,** a temple with a roof that curved up at the corners. The Chinese became experts at making **porcelain,** a hard, shiny pottery.

Chinese Influence on Japan

The Japanese first learned about Chinese culture through Korea. During the Tang dynasty, a Japanese prince sent nobles to China to study. Japanese nobles continued to bring Chinese ideas and technology back to Japan. By the 800s, as the Tang dynasty began to decline, the Japanese had begun to blend Chinese ideas with their own to create a unique culture.

Draw Conclusions

The Chinese influence over Japan changed from the 600s to the 1200s. Why?

Japan Adapts Chinese Ideas

600s–700s	800s	900s–1200s
• Japanese study Chinese civilization. • Emperor builds capital city modeled on Chinese capital. • Japanese nobles adopt Chinese language, food, and style of dress. • Japanese nobles adopt Chinese tea ceremony, music, dance, and gardens.	• Japanese stop traveling to China.	• Japanese keep some Chinese ways but build their own civilization. • Japanese artists develop their own styles. • Japanese change the Chinese system of writing.

Summary

Chinese civilization flourished under the Tang and Song. Efficient government was fueled by an educated ruling class, thanks to the revival of the civil service system. A fixed social structure added stability. Land reform, advances in farming, canals, and increased trade helped the empire economically. China made contributions in art, literature, and architecture. Chinese culture influenced other lands, including Japan.

Preparing for the Regents

List one achievement of the Tang or Song dynasty in each of the following categories.

Government:

Economy:

Art:

The Byzantine Empire and Russia

The Big Idea

The Byzantine empire:

• had a strong government and a uniform code of laws under Justinian.

• was closely tied to the Orthodox Christian Church.

• made contributions in architecture, engineering, and art.

• affected the later development of Russia and other nations of Eastern Europe.

Key People and Terms

Place each of the key people and terms into these three categories: government, religion, or art. Explain your choices.

Key Themes and Concepts

Culture
Constantinople was also known as New Rome. This name emphasized the role of the Byzantine empire as the bearer of the Roman heritage. The Byzantine empire blended ancient Greek, Roman, and Christian influences and spread them to the regions they conquered.

Section Overview

The Roman empire had been divided since the 200s. As the western half declined, the eastern half rose in importance. The emperor Constantine founded a capital on the site of Byzantium. Justinian, the greatest of the Byzantine emperors, ruled a vast empire with a centralized government and a codified set of laws. The Orthodox Christian Church became powerful as the official church of the Byzantine empire. The Byzantine empire blended Greek, Roman, and Christian influences and produced art and architecture that have lived on through the centuries. The empire also left a legacy in Russia. The Byzantines gave Russia a written language, and influenced Russian religion, government, art, and architecture.

Key Themes and Concepts

As you review this section, take special note of the following key themes and concepts:

Government How did Justinian organize his government and code of law?

Belief Systems What was the significance of the Orthodox Christian Church in the Byzantine empire and Russia?

Culture and Intellectual Life How was the Byzantine empire able to preserve and spread Greek and Roman knowledge and culture?

Movement of People and Goods What influence did the Byzantine empire have on Russia and other areas of Eastern Europe?

Key People and Terms

As you review this section, be sure you understand the significance of these key people and terms:

Justinian	icons	schism
autocrat	mosaics	Kiev
Justinian's Code	patriarch	czars

Geographic Setting

The Roman empire had been divided since the reign of Diocletian in the late A.D. 200s. As Germanic invaders weakened the western half, power shifted to the east. By 330, the emperor Constantine had built a splendid new capital in Constantinople, on the site of the Greek city of Byzantium. The Byzantine empire, as it came to be called, drew its name from this ancient city.

Greatest Extent

At its height, the Byzantine empire covered an area from Rome through southeastern Europe and Asia Minor, down to Egypt and across North Africa. Even a portion of southern Spain was once part of the empire.

Preserving and Spreading Culture

The city of Constantinople was on a peninsula overlooking the Bosporus, a strait connecting the Black Sea to the Mediterranean. The city possessed an outstanding harbor and was protected on three sides by water. From its central location Constantinople controlled key trade routes that linked Europe and Asia. Heir to Rome, the Byzantine empire blended Greek, Roman, and Christian influences and helped spread them to other regions of the world. In Russia, thriving trade with Constantinople helped Kiev become the center of the first Russian state.

The Byzantine Empire

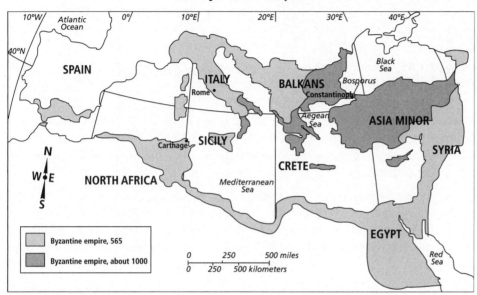

The Byzantine Empire
The Byzantine Empire reached its greatest size by the year 565. By 1000, it had lost much of its territory to invading armies.

Preparing for the Regents

• Practice your map skills by using the map to describe the extent of the Byzantine empire in 1000.

Achievements of the Byzantine Empire

The Byzantine empire reached its peak under the emperor **Justinian,** who reigned from 527 to 565. Like other Byzantine rulers, Justinian was an **autocrat,** a single ruler with complete authority. Justinian hoped to recover the western Roman provinces that invading tribes had seized. During his reign, Byzantine armies did reconquer parts of North Africa, Italy, and southern Spain. These conquests were expensive, however, and they were temporary. The achievements of the Byzantine empire were in other areas.

Preparing for the Regents

• How did Justinian go about reforming the law of the empire? What impact did Justinian's Code have on later legal systems?

Justinian's Code of Law

Emperor Justinian is probably best known for his code of law. Soon after he became emperor, he set up a team of scholars to gather and organize the ancient laws of Rome. His collection became the "body of civil law," known today as Justinian's Code. His code included Roman laws, legal writings, and even a student handbook. Later emperors continued to update the code. By the 1100s, it had reached Western Europe, where it became the basis of law for both the Roman Catholic Church and medieval rulers. Even today, international law is influenced by Justinian's Code.

Engineering and Architecture

The Byzantine empire extended Roman knowledge of engineering, especially in architecture. Justinian launched a building program designed to make Constantinople a dazzling city. The best known of his structures is the Church of Hagia Sophia, whose name means "Holy Wisdom." Byzantine architects blended Greek, Roman, Persian, and other Middle Eastern styles.

Preparing for the Regents

Describe how the Byzantine empire preserved and transmitted Greek and Roman knowledge and culture in the categories named.

Law:

Architecture:

Arabic calligraphy in Selimiye Mosque, Edirne, Turkey

Art

Byzantine artists made great contributions to religious art that influenced styles for many years. **Icons** were holy images of Jesus, the Virgin Mary, or saints of the Orthodox Christian Church. More than just paintings, they were supposed to create a sense that the sacred person was actually present. **Mosaics,** pictures or designs formed by inlaid pieces of stone or other materials, often showed biblical scenes. Beautiful mosaics adorned the interiors of churches, including the Hagia Sophia.

The Orthodox Christian Church

The art and architecture of Constantinople reflected the importance of the Orthodox Christian Church in Byzantine life. By the time of Justinian, divisions had grown between the Church in Rome and the Byzantine Church. The Orthodox Christian Church, also called the Eastern Orthodox Church, was the Christian Church of the Byzantine empire.

Imperial Authority Over the Church The Byzantine emperor controlled the business of the Church and appointed the **patriarch,** the highest church official, in Constantinople. The emperor was considered Jesus' co-ruler on earth. Byzantine Christians did not believe that the pope in Rome had supreme authority over them.

Differences With the West Other divisions widened over time between the Church in the East and the Roman Catholic Church. Byzantine priests could marry, while Roman Catholic priests could not. Also, Greek (instead of Latin) was the language of the Byzantine Church. A major disagreement arose over the use of icons. Some people believed that the importance placed on them by the Orthodox Christian Church bordered on idolatry.

Christian Schism In 1054, there was finally a permanent split, or schism, between the Orthodox Christian Church in the East and the Roman Catholic Church in the West.

Preservation of Greco-Roman Culture

The Byzantine empire remained a political and cultural force nearly 1,000 years after the fall of Rome. To Europe it was a symbol of the power and glory of Rome long after the Roman empire had faded. Justinian's Code preserved Roman law, and the accomplishments of Roman engineers were preserved and extended in Byzantine architecture.

Furthermore, Byzantine culture was strongly rooted in Greece. The Byzantine empire preserved Hellenistic (Greek) science, philosophy, arts, and literature. The empire even served to preserve some of the ancient texts of Greece, which were carried to the West as the Byzantine empire declined in the 1400s.

Decline and Fall of the Empire

The Byzantine empire had reached its height under Justinian. In the centuries after his reign, the empire lost much land to invading armies. It was also weakened by internal court struggles and constant warfare. During the Fourth Crusade in

Key Themes and Concepts

Political Systems
In the Byzantine empire, the power of both the state and the Church was centered in the emperor.

Key Themes and Concepts

Belief Systems
The Roman and Byzantine Churches shared many common beliefs, yet their differences became too difficult to overcome. Many world religions have experienced schisms over time.

Causes

What were the causes of the decline of the Byzantine empire?

the early 1200s, western Christians took Constantinople and ruled it for 50 years. The final blow to the empire was the taking of Constantinople by the Ottoman empire in 1453.

Russia and Eastern Europe

The first Russian state was established in the 800s. This early Russian state was centered in the city of **Kiev,** in present-day Ukraine. Kiev's location on the Dneiper River made the city easily accessible to Byzantine traders.

Around this time, states such as Poland, Hungary, and Serbia were established in Eastern Europe. Settlers arrived from Western Europe, Russia, and Asia, giving the region a wide variety of languages and cultural traditions. As in Russia, trade with the Byzantine empire helped bring Eastern Europe into the Byzantine sphere of influence. The Byzantines influenced both Russia and Eastern Europe in a variety of ways.

Written Language

The Byzantines gave Russia a written language. Two Byzantine missionaries adapted the Greek alphabet in order to translate the Bible into Slavic languages as early as the 800s. This alphabet, called the Cyrillic alphabet after Cyril, one of the monks, is still used in Russia and other countries of Eastern Europe today.

Orthodox Christianity

Byzantine missionaries carried Orthodox Christianity to Russia and other countries of Eastern Europe. The Orthodox Christian faith remains a powerful force through much of the region today. The close church-state relationship in the Byzantine empire also became a model for Russian government and religion. The Russian Orthodox Church became an important arm of state power.

Autocratic Government

One Byzantine tradition that continued was that of autocratic rule, which became the norm in Russian government. Autocratic rulers in Russia were known as **czars** (also, tsars). *Czar* is the Russian word for *Caesar*.

Art and Architecture

Russians adopted the religious art, music, and architecture of the Byzantine empire. Byzantine domes were transformed into the onion domes of Russian architecture.

Summary

As the Roman empire in the West declined, the Byzantine empire grew in power. The lasting heritage of the Byzantine empire lay in its preservation of classical culture, its traditions of law and government, and its spreading of Christian beliefs. The Orthodox Christian Church, a powerful force in the empire, developed its own practices and traditions and split from the Roman Catholic Church. The Byzantine empire provided Russia and other Eastern European lands with a written language, art and architecture, and an autocratic style of government.

Key Themes and Concepts

Change
The fall of Constantinople was a turning point in global history. It marked a change in power in the region from the Christian Byzantine empire to the great Muslim trading empire of the Ottomans.

Preparing for the Regents

Describe how the Byzantine empire affected Russia in the areas listed.

Language:

Religion:

Government:

Art and architecture:

St. Basil's Cathedral: a Russian Orthodox Church in Moscow, Russia

Islamic Civilization

The Big Idea

The Muslim world:

- included lands and peoples from parts of three continents.
- preserved, blended, and spread the cultures of classical Greece, Rome, India, and other civilizations.
- enjoyed a prosperous golden age with advances in art, literature, mathematics, and science.
- spread new learning to Christian Europe.

Key People and Terms

What do many of the key people and terms have in common?

Section Overview

In the years after the death of Muhammad, Islam spread across parts of three continents. Muslim empires ruled over vast areas of land that included parts of Europe, Africa, and Asia. The Muslim world was influenced by many cultures, including those of ancient Greece, Rome, and India. During the 700s and 800s, Islam experienced a golden age. A diverse society, an economy based on flourishing trade, and achievements in the arts and sciences characterized this era. The achievements of Islam's golden age reached Europe through Muslim Spain and Italy as well as through the Crusades.

Key Themes and Concepts

As you review this section, take special note of the following key themes and concepts:

Diversity What lands and peoples came under Muslim rule?

Economic Systems What was the importance of trade in the Muslim empires?

Culture and Intellectual Life What achievements did Muslim society produce in the arts and sciences?

Interdependence How did Islamic civilization interact with Christian Europe?

Key People and Terms

As you review this section, be sure you understand the significance of these key people and terms:

caliph	Shiite	Abbassid dynasty
Sharia	Umayyad dynasty	Averröes
Sunni		

The Spread of Islam

Islam arose in the Arabian peninsula in the early 600s. In 632, Muhammad, the founder of Islam, died. Abu Bakr was elected the first **caliph,** or successor to Muhammad. The period when Muslims were ruled by caliphs, from Muhammad's death until the 900s, was called the caliphate. The Muslim world expanded during the caliphate.

Diverse Lands and Peoples

In the years after Muhammad's death, Islam spread rapidly. Abu Bakr was successful in uniting Arabs in the Islam faith. His forces began an extraordinary military campaign that conquered parts of the Byzantine empire, the Persian empire, Egypt, and Spain. Their push into Europe was stopped only at Tours in 732. Over the following centuries, more and more people embraced Islam.

Middle East Arab armies took control of the Middle East in the early 600s. Syria and Palestine were quickly defeated by Arab forces. Persia and Egypt were conquered soon after.

North Africa Muslim armies carried Islam into North Africa in the mid- to late 600s. Muslim invaders initially fought African forces. Eventually, however, Muslims and North Africans joined forces to conquer Spain. Islam continued to spread to other parts of North and West Africa.

Spain and Sicily Muslim conquests included parts of southern and western Europe, especially Spain and the island of Sicily. Muslim Arabs and their North African allies attacked Spain in the early 700s. When Europe was weak, during the Middle Ages, the Muslims seized control of Sicily.

India In the early 700s, Muslim armies conquered the Indus Valley. For several hundred years, Islam did not spread beyond western India. In the 1000s and 1100s, however, Turkish converts to Islam conquered most of northern India. By the 1200s, the Turks had created a great Muslim empire on the subcontinent, with its capital at Delhi.

Southeast Asia After Muslims took control of northern India in the 1200s, Islam was carried into Southeast Asia. Islamic beliefs and civilization were spread mainly through trade. As Islam gradually spread to lands surrounding the Indian Ocean, thriving trade networks were established.

Reasons for Muslim Success

One reason for the spread of Islam was that the Arabs were strong fighters. Their cavalry, mounted on camels and horses, overwhelmed their opponents. The Muslims were also successful partly because the Byzantine and Persian empires were weak from fighting wars against each other. Another important factor was that the Muslims were united by their belief in Islam. In addition, Muslim rulers often treated conquered peoples fairly. People in defeated empires welcomed Muslim rule after years of living under harsh rulers. Many converted to Islam.

Islamic Law and Its Impact

As Islam spread, Islamic scholars developed a system of laws to help people interpret the Qur'an and apply it to everyday life. The **Sharia**—the Islamic system of law—regulated moral behavior, family life, business, government, and other areas of community life. The Sharia acted as a uniting force for Muslims. Unlike laws in the western world, the Sharia did not separate religious and worldly matters. It applied the Qur'an to all situations and aspects of life.

Divisions Within Islam

Several decades after the death of Muhammad, divisions grew among Muslims about who should be Muhammad's successor. Followers split into two groups: **Sunni** and **Shiite.** Sunnis believed that the caliph should be chosen by Muslim leaders. Sunni Muslims did not view the caliph as a religious authority. Shiites believed that only the descendants of the prophet Muhammad should be his successors. They believed that the descendants of the prophet were divinely inspired.

The split between Sunni and Shiite Muslims continues to this day. Like the differing branches of Christianity, these branches of Islam share many basic beliefs, such as devotion to the same God and reverence for the same scriptures.

Note Taking

Reading Skill:
Recognize Sequence
Make a flow chart. Show the sequence of the spread of Islam. Add boxes as necessary.

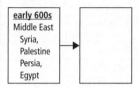

early 600s
Middle East
Syria,
Palestine
Persia,
Egypt

Vocabulary Builder

convert—(KAHN vurt) *n.* someone who has been persuaded to change their beliefs and accept a particular religion or opinion

Key Themes and Concepts

Justice
Islamic law was an important unifying element in the Muslim empires. Justinian had also unified his empire through a uniform code of law.

Preparing for the Regents

• Write a paragraph that describes several similarities and differences between the splits in the Christian Church and the division in Islam.

Vocabulary Builder

<u>seclude</u>—(sih KLOOD) *v.* to remove or separate from social contact and activity

Key Themes and Concepts

Diversity
The diversity of the Umayyad empire was one cause of its decline. The rich and the poor, Sunnis and Shiites, and Arabs and non-Arabs disagreed about important issues.

Social Patterns

Social Mobility

In some ways, Muslim society allowed more social mobility than did medieval European society. Under earlier dynasties, Arabs had considered themselves superior to non-Arabs, but this belief declined with later dynasties. It became possible to move up in the social order, especially through religious, scholarly, or military achievements.

Treatment of Conquered Peoples

Islamic leaders imposed a special tax on non-Muslims, but they allowed people to practice their own faiths. Christians and Jews often served as doctors, officials, and translators in Muslim communities.

Slavery

As in Greece and Rome, slavery was common in the Muslim world. Enslaved people from Spain, Greece, Africa, India, and central Asia were brought to Muslim cities. Most enslaved people worked as house servants, and some were skilled craftspeople. It was possible for enslaved people to buy their freedom. Also, if a slave converted to Islam, his or her children would be free.

Status of Women

Islam teaches the spiritual equality of men and women. The Qur'an protected women of the time in ways that some societies did not. For example, it prohibited the killing of daughters and protected the rights of widows. Women had inheritance rights, could be educated, and had to consent to marriage freely. Nevertheless, in Muslim society, the roles and rights of women differed from those of men. For example, a daughter's inheritance was less than a son's.

As Islam spread, Muslims adopted some beliefs of non-Arab people. In Byzantium and Persia, for example, Arabs veiled women and secluded them in separate parts of their homes. Restrictions on women varied by region and class in Muslim civilization. Upper-class women were more likely to be restricted. In rural areas, women continued to participate in the economy.

Muslim Empires

After the death of the fourth caliph in 661, many changes took place in the Muslim world. The **Umayyad dynasty** spread Islam to the Atlantic in the west and to the Indus Valley in the east. It was based in Damascus rather than Mecca. The expansion of Islam led to increased tensions between rich and poor, Sunnis and Shiites, and Arabs and non-Arabs. In 750, the **Abbassid dynasty** captured Damascus and moved the court to Baghdad, thus ending Arab domination of Islam. The Abbassid rulers enjoyed great wealth and power. Baghdad exceeded the size and wealth of Constantinople and ushered in a golden age for the Muslim world.

Political Divisions

Around 850, Abbassid rule of Islamic civilization began to decline. Independent dynasties began to rule separate Muslim states. In the 900s, the Seljuk Turks adopted Islam and built their own empire. They took control of the Arab capital, Baghdad. Then, in the 1200s, the Mongols destroyed Baghdad. Even so, the Muslim religion continued to link people over three continents.

Islam's Golden Age

At its height under the Abbassids, the Muslim world was composed of people from many cultures, including Arabs, Persians, Egyptians, and Europeans. Muslims absorbed and blended customs and traditions from many of the peoples they ruled. The glory of the empires was reflected in their emphasis on learning, achievements in the arts and sciences, and flourishing economies based on trade.

The Golden Age of Muslim Civilization

Art	Literature
• Used beautiful writing and patterns to decorate buildings and art • Adapted Byzantine domes and arches • Painted people and animals in nonreligious art	• Considered Qur'an most important piece of Arabic literature • Chanted oral poetry • Collected stories from other people

Muslim Civilization

Learning	Medicine
• Translated writings of Greek philosophers • Developed algebra • Observed Earth turning and measured its circumference	• Required doctors to pass difficult tests • Set up hospitals with emergency rooms • Studied diseases and wrote medical books

Preservation of Greco-Roman Culture

Muslim scholars translated the works of many of the Greek scholars. Muslim advances in mathematics, astronomy, and medicine were also based partly on their study of Greek and Indian knowledge.

Education

The prophet Muhammad taught a respect for learning that continued to characterize Muslim culture throughout the ages. The Muslim empires included dazzling centers of learning such as Baghdad, Cairo, and Cordoba. The vast libraries and universities of these cities attracted a large and diverse number of well-paid and highly respected scholars.

Art and Architecture

Mosques and Palaces Muslim architects were influenced by Byzantine domes and arches. The walls and ceilings of mosques and palaces were decorated with elaborate abstract and geometric patterns. Muslim religious leaders forbade artists to portray God or human figures in religious art.

Calligraphy Muslim artists were highly skilled in calligraphy, or artistic writing. Calligraphy decorated buildings and pieces of art. Often, Muslim calligraphers used verses from the Qur'an.

Drawings and Paintings In nonreligious art, some Muslim artists portrayed animal or human figures, although this was usually discouraged. Persian and Turkish artists adorned books with beautiful miniature paintings.

Mevlana Mosque, Turkey

Literature and Philosophy

Poetry A wide variety of themes dominated written Muslim poetry, from praise of important leaders to contemplation of the joys and sorrows of love. In addition, because the Qur'an was the most important piece of Muslim literature, many writers wrote poems based on this holy book.

Tales Muslim storytellers adapted stories from Greek, Indian, Jewish, and Egyptian culture, as well as others. The most famous collection of Muslim stories is *The Thousand and One Nights*, which includes fables, romances, and humorous anecdotes.

Philosophy Muslim scholars translated the philosophical works of Greek, Indian, and Chinese writers. In fact, the scholar Ibn Rushd, who was known in Europe as **Averröes,** strongly influenced medieval Christian scholars with his writings on Aristotle. The Jewish rabbi Maimonides influenced Christian scholars of the Middle Ages in much the same way.

Mathematics and Science

Algebra Muslims studied Indian and Greek mathematics before making their own contributions. Muslims pioneered the study of algebra. Eventually, the works of some Muslim mathematicians were translated into Latin and studied in Europe.

Astronomy Greek and Indian astronomical discoveries resulted in Muslim development of astronomical tables. Muslim astronomers also observed the Earth's rotation and calculated the circumference of the Earth within a few thousand feet.

Medicine Muslim medicine was remarkably advanced. Doctors were required to pass difficult tests before they could practice. Hospitals were set up. Physicians studied various diseases and wrote books that became standard texts in Europe.

Economic Achievements

The Muslim world developed a prosperous economy. Muslims had an extensive trade network and encouraged manufacturing. Agriculture also flourished.

Trade Merchants were honored in Muslim society. From 750 to 1350, Muslims established a large trade network across their empire. Traders not only exchanged goods but spread religious belief, culture, and technology as well.

Trading and a money economy allowed Muslims to take the lead in new business practices. They established partnerships, sold goods on credit, and formed banks to exchange different kinds of currency.

Manufacturing Guilds organized manufacturing in the Muslim world. Heads of guilds regulated prices, weights, and measurements, and they monitored product quality. Muslim craftworkers produced steel swords in Damascus, leather goods in Cordoba, and carpets in Persia.

Agriculture Muslim farmers grew crops such as sugarcane, cotton, medicinal herbs, fruits, and vegetables. These products were purchased and sold in many world markets.

Key Themes and Concepts

Culture and Intellectual Life Modern mathematics and science can trace many of their roots to the achievements of Islamic civilization.

Preparing for the Regents

List two Islamic achievements in each of the following areas.

Mathematics:

Art:

Literature:

Medicine:

Economics:

Vocabulary Builder

guild—(gild) *n.* an organization of people who do the same job or have the same interests

Christian Europe Enriched by Islamic Civilization

The advances of the Muslim world gradually reached Christian Europe through Spain and Sicily. The Crusades also encouraged cultural diffusion.

Muslim Spain

Spain became a magnificent Muslim cultural center. Muslim princes encouraged poetry, the arts, and learning. In Spain, the Muslims, who were called Moors, continued their policy of toleration, hiring Jewish officials and encouraging Christian students to study Greek thought.

Muslim Sicily

During the early Middle Ages, Arabs gained control of Sicily and other Mediterranean islands. The island of Sicily was soon regained by Europeans, but a Muslim presence remained. Muslim officials provided effective government, and Arab merchants and farmers helped the economy to grow. Muslim culture graced the courts of the Christian kings.

The Crusades

Crusaders came into contact with various Muslim peoples and cultures. Europeans were impressed with Muslim advancements in the arts and sciences as well as with their preservation of Greco-Roman culture. As a result, the advances of the Muslim world gradually influenced Christian Europe.

Summary

The Muslim world was richly diverse. It spread across an extensive area in Europe, Africa, and Asia. Muslim empires had flourishing economies supported by a vast trade network. At its height, the Muslim world made great advances in fields such as literature, mathematics, astronomy, and medicine. In these areas, Muslims were greatly influenced by other cultures, including those of classical Greece and India. In time, Islamic civilization had a great impact on Christian Europe.

Key Themes and Concepts

Interdependence
It was through Muslim Spain and Sicily, as well as through the Crusades and the Muslim trading network, that the achievements of Islam's golden age reached European society.

Key Themes and Concepts

Culture and Intellectual Life
By adapting ideas from other cultures, Muslims were able to expand their knowledge and develop new ideas.

Preparing for the Regents

Summarize how Christian Europe was enriched by Islamic civilization.

Medieval Europe

Section Overview

The Middle Ages, or **medieval** period, lasted from about 500 to the middle of the 1400s. The collapse of the Roman empire had left Western Europe with no unifying government. In response, political and social systems emerged, such as feudalism and manorialism, that were based on powerful local lords and their landholdings. A strict social hierarchy existed during the Middle Ages. The Christian Church emerged as a unifying force in Western Europe and had great influence over economic and social, as well as religious, life. Conditions gradually improved, allowing Europeans to build a new civilization based on Greco-Roman and Christian traditions.

Key Themes and Concepts

As you review this section, take special note of the following key themes and concepts:

Interdependence What duties and responsibilities guided people's lives in medieval Europe?

Political Systems What roles did individual citizens play in the medieval feudal systems?

Economic Systems How did manorialism provide for people's basic economic needs?

Belief Systems What roles did the Church play in medieval society?

Key People and Terms

As you review this section, be sure you understand the significance of these key people and terms:

medieval	serfs	monasteries
Charlemagne	secular	anti-Semitism
chivalry	excommunicated	Gothic
manorialism	Pope Innocent III	

Geographic Setting

The geography of Europe had a powerful effect on the development of the area. Europe's location and resources helped determine the groups of people who settled there and the people who would try to control it.

Location

Europe lay at the western end of the Eurasian landmass, which extends from present-day Portugal to China. Parts of Great Britain, Spain, France, Italy, Greece, and other areas of Eastern Europe had been within the Roman empire. Roman roads had allowed Roman and Christian customs to spread. As you have learned, Germanic tribes overran Europe from about 400 to 700, ending Roman rule.

Resources
Forests and Fertile Soil Europe had many natural resources. Dense forests, with valuable timber, covered much of northern Europe, and the area's fertile soil was well suited for raising crops. In addition, minerals such as iron and coal lay untapped beneath the Earth's surface.

Seas and Rivers The oceans and seas that surrounded much of Europe were also important resources. People on the coasts fished the waters and used them as a means of trade and transportation. Large rivers in Europe also provided food and a means of travel.

The Frankish Empire
The Germanic people who overran the Roman empire were warriors, farmers, and herders. Their culture differed greatly from that of the Romans they had conquered. Germanic tribes were governed by unwritten laws and customs and ruled by elected kings.

The Rise of the Franks
From about 400 to 700, warrior tribes divided Europe and fought for control of various territories. During this time, the Franks emerged as the most powerful and successful of the tribes in Gaul, or present-day France. In the late 400s, Clovis, a brilliant and ruthless leader, became king of the Franks. Clovis is probably best known for his conversion to Christianity, which gained him a powerful ally in the Christian Church.

Battle of Tours
As you have learned, Muslims had moved into Spain. They tried to advance into France. At the Battle of Tours in 732, the Franks defeated a Muslim army. Although Muslims continued to rule most of Spain, they advanced no farther in Western Europe.

Charlemagne
During the 800s, Charlemagne, a Frankish king, built an empire that stretched across modern-day France, Germany, and part of Italy.

Cooperation With the Church In 800, Pope Leo III, the head of the Christian Church of the time, called for help against rebellious nobles in Rome. Charlemagne answered the pope's call and defeated the Roman nobles in battle. To show his gratitude, Pope Leo III, on Christmas Day 800, crowned Charlemagne "Holy Roman Emperor." The crowning of Charlemagne helped revive the ideal of a united Christian Church and empire.

After being named emperor, Charlemagne strengthened his rule and attempted to create a united Christian Europe. Working closely with the Roman Catholic Church, he helped spread Christianity to the far reaches of his empire.

Government Charlemagne appointed nobles to rule local areas. He gave them land, expecting them in return to help with the defense of the empire. As a way to control these rulers, Charlemagne regularly sent out officials called *missi dominici* to check on conditions throughout the empire.

Learning Charlemagne also encouraged learning. He set up a school to ensure the education of government officials. He also established libraries where scholars copied ancient texts, including the Bible and science and history texts written in Latin.

Preparing for the Regents

• How did Europeans use natural resources to provide for basic economic needs?

Key Themes and Concepts

Change
Clovis, king of the Franks, converted to Christianity. By doing this, he gained the support of the leaders of the Christian Church.

Note Taking

Reading Skill:
Understand Effects
Make a chart. Record the effects of Charlemagne's rule.

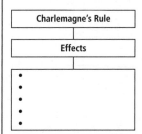

Charlemagne's Rule

Effects

•
•
•
•
•

Preparing for the Regents

• Describe several ways in which Charlemagne sought to restore order to medieval Europe.

Charlemagne's Empire
Charlemagne was able to rule a large empire because of his strong personality, his powerful centralized government, and his effective military strategy.

Preparing for the Regents

Practice your map skills by answering the following questions.

1. Name two groups that were part of Charlemagne's empire.

2. Name two modern-day countries that include areas once ruled by Charlemagne.

Charlemagne's Empire

End of Charlemagne's Reign
When Charlemagne died in 814, his empire quickly fell apart as his heirs battled for control. In 843, Charlemagne's grandsons signed the Treaty of Verdun, which divided Charlemagne's empire into three separate kingdoms, one for each grandson.

Charlemagne had a lasting influence, however. His strong government was a model for future medieval rulers. He also helped spread Christianity to northern Europe.

The Structure of Feudal Society

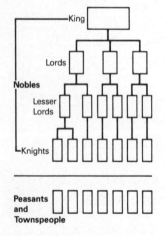

Feudalism and Manorialism

During the early part of the Middle Ages, kings were too weak to keep invaders out of their kingdoms. People began to leave towns and cities, banding together in the countryside for protection and survival.

Medieval Society
Everyone had a well-defined place in medieval society. People were born into their social positions, and there was little chance of moving beyond them. The nobility consisted of the kings and queens, greater lords, lesser lords, and knights. The elite class of nobles controlled the land and power. The lower class of peasants, who made up the bulk of the population, worked the land and served the nobles. The clergy was highly respected, due to the fact that the Christian Church dominated life during the Middle Ages.

Feudalism
Feudal Responsibilities Feudalism was a loosely structured political system in which powerful lords (nobles) owned large sections of land. They divided their land into estates called fiefs, which were given to lesser lords called vassals. Vassals pledged their loyalty and military support to their lords in return for this land.

Knighthood Because people in medieval Europe were often at war, many nobles trained to become knights, or mounted warriors. They practiced strict discipline and learned how to ride well and handle weapons skillfully. In addition, knights were bound by a code of conduct known as **chivalry.** This code charged them to be brave, loyal, and true to their word. The code also required knights to protect women.

Role of Noblewomen Women played an active role in feudal society. A "lady" was in charge of her husband's estate while he was away serving his lord in battle. She was responsible for all household affairs including the raising of children. In preparation for their adult role, girls received training in household arts such as spinning, weaving, and the management of servants. Women had limited inheritance rights, however, since most possessions went to the eldest son.

Manorialism

The basis for the medieval economy was **manorialism,** an economic system structured around a lord's manor, or estate. Manors often included one or more villages and the land surrounding them. Under the manorial system, each group in society had a place; each also had certain rights and responsibilities.

Peasants and Lords Most of the peasants who lived on the estate were **serfs**. Serfs were not enslaved, but they were bound to the land. They could not leave the estate without the lord's permission.

Mutual Responsibilities Serfs farmed the lord's land and did other work such as repairing roads and fences. In return for the service provided by peasants, the lord provided them with the use of several acres of land to farm. The lord was also supposed to protect them during times of war.

Harsh Life for Peasants For peasants, life on the manor was difficult and often harsh. Peasant men, women, and children worked long hours, and few peasants lived past the age of 35. In spite of such hardship, the lives of peasants were held together by the common thread of Christianity. Their celebrations—marriages, births, and holidays such as Christmas and Easter—were centered in the Christian Church.

The Church in Medieval Life

During the Middle Ages, two distinct Christian churches emerged: the Orthodox Christian Church in the east and the Roman Catholic Church in the west. (The two branches split permanently in 1054.) The Roman Catholic Church became the main stabilizing force in Western Europe. The Church provided religious leadership as well as **secular,** or worldly, leadership. It also played a key role in reviving and preserving learning.

Church Hierarchy

At the head of the Roman Catholic Church was the pope, whom followers believed to be the spiritual representative of Jesus on earth. Below the pope came archbishops, bishops, and local priests. For peasants and town dwellers, everyday life was closely tied to local priests and the village church.

Spiritual Role of the Church

The main responsibility of the Church was to serve the spiritual needs of medieval society. Local priests instructed peasants and townspeople in the faith and provided comfort to them in troubled times. The Church taught that all men and women were sinners but that Christians could achieve salvation, or eternal life in heaven, through faith in Jesus, good works, and participation in sacraments, or sacred spiritual rituals. To escape the punishment of hell, they needed to take part in the sacraments of the Church.

Key Themes and Concepts

Governance
Feudalism was based on personal agreements among individuals. This loose system of government differed greatly from the strong centralized government of Rome that existed before the Middle Ages.

Preparing for the Regents

• What was the most important economic resource in medieval Europe? Who controlled this resource? How did control of economic resources affect the power structure in medieval society?

Key Themes and Concepts

Interdependence
Feudalism and the manor system were both based on mutual responsibility. In feudalism, nobles owed duties to each other. In the manor system, nobles and peasants provided benefits to each other.

Belief Systems
Religion was an essential part of life for medieval people. The Roman Catholic Church spread the teachings of Jesus and administered the sacraments, including marriage and baptism.

Preparing for the Regents

Identify four ways in which the Roman Catholic Church affected economic or political affairs during the Middle Ages.

1.

2.

3.

4.

Vocabulary Builder

papal—(PAY pul) *adj.* relating to the pope

The Medieval Church
Religion shaped the everyday lives of Christian Europeans. The Church controlled the spiritual lives of Christians. It was also a powerful political force because it had authority over all rulers, such as kings and emperors.

Secular Role of the Church

Economic Power The Church filled many secular, or worldly, roles during the Middle Ages. As the largest landholder in Europe, the Church had significant economic power. The Church also gained wealth through the tithe, a tax Christians were required to pay that equaled ten percent of their income.

Political Power The Church had its own set of laws, called canon law, and its own courts of justice. The Church claimed authority over secular rulers, but monarchs did not always recognize this authority. As a result, there were frequent power struggles between the pope in Rome and various kings and emperors.

Popes believed that they had authority over kings. Popes sometimes **excommunicated,** or excluded from the Catholic Church, secular rulers who challenged or threatened papal power. For example, **Pope Innocent III** excommunicated King John of England in the 1200s during a dispute about appointing an archbishop.

The Medieval Church

Everyday Life
- Christians attended village churches.
- Some priests ran schools in village churches.
- All Christians paid taxes to Church.

Power of Church
- Pope led Roman Catholic Church.
- Church had its own laws and courts.
- Church excommunicated those who did not obey rules.

Nuns and Monks
- Some set up housing, hospitals, and schools for the sick and poor.
- Some became missionaries.
- Some preserved learning.

Reform
- Church became rich and powerful.
- Some clergy became corrupt.
- Reformers tried to make changes

Monastic Orders

Some men and women became monks or nuns, leaving worldly society and devoting their lives to God. They entered **monasteries,** communities where Christian men or women focused on spiritual goals. Monks and nuns took vows of chastity, or purity, and of obedience to the abbot, or head of the religious order. They also took an oath of poverty. Monks and nuns fulfilled many social needs, such as tending to the sick, helping the poor, and educating children.

Centers of Learning In monasteries and convents (religious communities of women), monks and nuns also preserved ancient writings by copying ancient texts. Some monks and nuns taught Latin and Greek classics; others produced their own literary works.

Missionary Work Not all monks and nuns remained in monasteries. Some became missionaries, risking their lives to spread the message of Christianity. The Church sometimes honored its missionaries by declaring them saints. St. Patrick was a missionary who set up the Church in Ireland. St. Augustine was sent as a missionary to the Angles and Saxons in England.

Women and the Church

The Church taught that women and men were equal in the sight of God. However, on earth, women were supposed to be subservient to men. There was some effort to protect women in medieval society. For example, the Church set a minimum age for women to marry. However, women were viewed in two opposing ways.

Preparing for the Regents

- What role did monks and nuns play in preserving Greco-Roman culture?

Preparing for the Regents

- Compare and contrast the roles of men and women in feudal society.

On one hand, the Church considered women weak, easily tempted into sin, and dependent on the guidance of men. On the other hand, women were seen as modest and pure in spirit, similar to Mary, the mother of Jesus.

Jews in Medieval Europe

Numerous Jewish communities existed throughout Europe during the Middle Ages. While Jews in Muslim Spain and northern areas of Europe were generally tolerated, most Christians persecuted Jews. Not only did the Church bar Jews from owning land or practicing many occupations; many Christians blamed Jews for the death of Jesus. As a result, the foundations for **anti-Semitism,** or prejudice against Jews, were laid. Gradually, Christians began blaming Jews for all kinds of misfortunes, from famines to disease. In time, Jews migrated to Eastern Europe, where they set up communities that survived until modern times.

Medieval Cultural Achievements

In early medieval times, life was very chaotic. People concentrated on protecting themselves from invasions and taking care of their own physical needs. Toward the end of the Middle Ages, however, European society became more stable and made cultural gains in the fields of literature, art, and architecture.

Literature

Although the language of scholars was Latin, new stories and writings began to appear in the everyday languages of the people. Medieval literature included stories of knights and feudal lords as well as tales about the common people. Authors such as Dante and Chaucer wrote stories about warrior heroes and ordinary people who showed courage, humor, and morality.

Architecture and Art

The architecture and art of the Middle Ages focused on glorifying God. Almost all of the artistic achievements of the time were a reflection of the power of the Church. With money from increased trade in the late Middle Ages, nobles and townspeople alike began contributing to great works of architecture and art.

Roman Influences Around the year 1000, towns began to build stone churches that reflected the influence of Rome. With thick supporting walls and towers and only small slits in the stone for windows, these structures were fortresslike and dimly lighted.

The Gothic Tradition The Gothic style of architecture first appeared in Europe in the early 1100s. These new buildings, unlike those in the Roman style, seemed to soar upward. The Gothic style was characterized by pointed arches and by flying buttresses, stone supports that stood outside the building. With this outside support, walls could be built higher, leaving space for huge stained-glass windows. These windows, along with sculptures and carvings inside the churches, often told biblical stories, serving to educate the illiterate people of medieval Europe.

Summary

The Middle Ages was a troubled period in European history. After the Germanic invasions, society began to come together under the strict political organization supplied by feudalism and the economic system of manorialism. The Christian Church helped to unify Western Europe and touched every aspect of medieval life. Monasteries and convents became centers of learning; monks and nuns preserved ancient writings by copying ancient texts. As conditions improved and life became more stable, medieval Europe began to develop its own unique culture.

Preparing for the Regents

• Describe the relationship between religion and art in both medieval Europe and Islamic civilization.

• What cultural contributions did medieval Europe make in literature? In architecture?

Notre Dame Cathedral in Paris

The Crusades

Key People and Terms

Choose one category for all of the key people and terms: political system, economic system, or belief system. Explain your choice.

Note Taking

Reading Skill:
Recognize Sequence
As you read, list the important dates for the Crusades. Record them in the order they occurred. Add boxes as needed.

Crusades	
Date	Event
1050	Seljuk Turks invade Byzantine empire
1095	

Section Overview

In the 1050s, Seljuk Turks, who were Muslims, invaded the Byzantine empire and conquered Palestine. The Christian Church called for a movement to drive the Muslims out of Palestine. For nearly 200 years, Christians fought a series of religious wars known as the **Crusades.** The wars failed to regain Palestine, and they left a legacy of ill will and distrust between Christians and Muslims. However, the Crusades had other effects as well. Trade increased, and the European economy expanded. Feudal monarchs gained more power, and Europeans learned of the existence of lands beyond their borders. Europeans also benefited from the learning and cultural achievements of Islam.

Key Themes and Concepts

As you review this section, take special note of the following key themes and concepts:

Imperialism Why did Christians and Muslims engage in the Crusades?

Change What effect did the Crusades have on the economy of Europe?

Power How did the Crusades affect the power of the Church and feudal lords?

Culture How did the Crusades expand Europeans' view of the world?

Key People and Terms

As you review this section, be sure you understand the significance of these key people and terms:

Crusades	Holy Land
Urban II	Saladin
Council of Clermont	Richard the Lion-Hearted

Beginning of the Crusades

In the 1050s, the Seljuk Turks invaded the Byzantine empire. Over the next four decades, they overran most Byzantine lands in Asia Minor as well as Palestine. In 1095, the Byzantine emperor asked the pope, **Urban II,** for help. Pope Urban agreed. At the **Council of Clermont,** Urban encouraged French and German bishops to recover Palestine, or the **Holy Land,** as it was called by Christians. Christians referred to this area as the Holy Land because it was where Jesus had lived and taught. Muslims and Jews also considered the land holy. Christians who answered the pope's call were known as crusaders. Men and women from all over Western Europe left their homes to reclaim the Holy Land. Many never returned.

Reasons for the Crusades

There were several other motives for the Crusades, some religious and some secular. These reasons included the following.

- Pope Urban believed that the Crusades would increase his power in Europe and possibly reunite the Eastern and Western churches.
- Christians believed that their sins would be forgiven if they participated in the Crusades.
- Nobles hoped to gain wealth and land by participating in the Crusades.
- Adventurers saw the Crusades as a chance for travel and excitement.
- Serfs hoped to escape feudal oppression by fighting in the Crusades.

An Initial Christian Victory

For 200 years, the fighting went on. Only the first of four Crusades, however, came close to achieving its goals. In 1099, Christians captured the city of Jerusalem. They followed the victory with a massacre of Muslim and Jewish inhabitants.

Crusaders divided their conquered lands into four small states called the crusader states. They divided these lands into feudal domains. Muslim leaders tried to regain these kingdoms, and this effort resulted in additional Crusades.

Saladin and Muslim Victory

A Respected Muslim Leader
During the late 1100s, Saladin united the Muslim world. Both Muslims and Christians admired and respected Saladin. However, when Saladin marched toward Jerusalem, the Christians were determined to stop him.

The Taking of Jerusalem
A Christian victory did not occur, however. The crusaders in Jerusalem surrendered. Saladin forbade his soldiers to kill, harm, or steal from the defeated crusaders.

Richard the Lion-Hearted became king of England in 1189. He was determined to retake Jerusalem from Saladin. During the Third Crusade, Richard won several victories. Richard's forces advanced to within a few miles of Jerusalem, but were unable to capture the city.

The End of the Crusades

Later Crusades also resulted in failure for the Christians. The Fourth Crusade was supposed to regain Jerusalem, but the knights were diverted. After helping Venetian merchants defeat their Byzantine trade rivals, the knights looted Constantinople itself. What had started as a war of Christians against Muslims ended in a battle between rival Christian factions.

In Palestine, Muslims overran the crusader states. They captured Acre, the last city to fall, in 1291. This time the Muslims massacred Christian inhabitants after their victory.

Impact of the Crusades

The crusaders failed to attain their main goal of retaking the Holy Land. Unfortunately, the Crusades left behind a legacy of religious hatred between

Christians and Muslims, since each group had committed terrible acts of violence against the other. Crusaders sometimes turned their hatred on Jews in Europe as they traveled to or from Palestine. At times crusaders destroyed entire Jewish communities.

The Crusades did, however, have some positive effects. Contact between Western Europeans and the Muslim world resulted in **cultural diffusion.** The European economy began to grow, and Europeans gained an expanded view of the world.

Causes and Effects of The Crusades

Use the Cause and Effect chart to answer the question: What were some of the benefits of the Crusades?

Causes

- People wanted to free the Holy Land from Seljuk control.
- Many people wanted to get rich and gain new land.
- Some people wanted to see new places

The Crusades

Effects

- Trade increased.
- People of different religions grew to hate each other.
- Popes became more powerful.
- Feudal kings became more powerful.
- Renting land helped to free serfs.
- Europeans became interested in traveling.
- People learned about other cultures.

Key Themes and Concepts

Economic Systems
The increase in trade that resulted from the Crusades had a significant impact on Europe. Desire for direct access to the riches of the East was one motive for the overseas explorations that began in the 1400s.

Increased Trade

Trade with the Byzantine empire before the time of the Crusades had sparked the interest of Europeans in goods from the east. The amount of trade increased during the time of the Crusades. Crusaders returning to Europe brought with them interesting new fabrics, spices, and perfumes.

Merchants from the Italian city of Venice had built ships to transport crusaders. After the conflicts, these ships were available to carry products to and from Palestine. After the fall of the Christian states, Italian traders helped keep the trade routes to Palestine open. Sugar, cotton, and rice were just a few of the goods traded. The economies of both the East and the West benefited from this commerce.

Encouragement of Learning

European interest in learning was stimulated as Europeans were introduced to Byzantine and Muslim culture. Europeans saw how the Byzantines and Muslims had preserved Greco-Roman learning and maintained great universities. Europeans were also exposed to advances these cultures had made in mathematics, science, literature, art, and geographical knowledge. Europeans gained a broader outlook and were introduced to many new ideas.

Changes in the Church

The Crusades temporarily increased the power of the pope. Papal conflicts with feudal monarchs in Europe eventually lessened this power, however. In addition, the rift between the eastern and western churches was not healed. In fact, it was widened after the crusaders' attack on Constantinople.

Changes in the Feudal System

The Crusades increased the power of monarchs, who had gained the right to increase taxes in order to support the fighting. Some feudal monarchs led crusaders into battle and thereby heightened their prestige.

At the same time, the institution of feudalism was weakening. Traditionally, lords had required grain or labor from their serfs. Now, needing money to finance the Crusades, they began to ask for payment of rent in money. Feudalism was weakened, and an economy based on money, not land, took hold.

Summary

The Crusades began in the 1000s for a variety of reasons. For 200 years, Christians and Muslims fought one another and committed terrible massacres. However, both sides also had admirable leaders. The Crusades had several effects on Europe. Trade began to increase, and a money economy emerged. The Church temporarily gained power. Although feudal monarchs were strengthened, feudalism itself was weakened. Christian Europe was influenced by various aspects of Byzantine and Muslim civilization as a result of the Crusades.

Vocabulary Builder

rift—(rift) *n.* a situation in which two people or groups have had a serious disagreement and begun to dislike and not trust each other

Preparing for the Regents

List two ways the Crusades were a turning point for each of the following aspects of Europe.

The economy:

1.

2.

Learning:

1.

2.

Political power:

1.

2.

Questions for Regents Practice

Multiple Choice

Directions: Review the Test-Taking Strategies section of this book. Then answer the following questions, drawn from actual Regents examinations. For each statement or question, choose the *number* of the word or expression that, of those given, best completes the statement or answers the question.

1 In traditional India, the caste system and the Hindu beliefs in karma and dharma most directly resulted in

(1) the establishment of a set of rules for each individual in the society

(2) the rapid industrialization of the economy

(3) a strong emphasis on the acquisition of wealth

(4) a strong belief in the importance of education

2 In traditional Chinese culture, which philosophy had the greatest influence on the development of social order and political organization?

(1) Taoism

(2) Shintoism

(3) Confucianism

(4) Marxism

3 After the fall of Rome, the eastern portion of the Roman empire became known as the

(1) Persian empire

(2) Byzantine empire

(3) Mongol empire

(4) Gupta empire

4 Which group had the greatest influence on early Russian culture?

(1) Franks

(2) Ottoman Turks

(3) Byzantine empire

(4) Roman Catholic Church

5 An important achievement of the Golden Age of Muslim culture was the

(1) preservation of ancient Greek and Roman ideas

(2) development of gunpowder

(3) establishment of trade with South America

(4) emergence of feudalism as a unifying force

6 Which factor helps explain the scientific and literary achievements of the Muslims during their golden age?

(1) expansion of transatlantic trade

(2) innovations introduced by the Europeans during the Renaissance

(3) cultural diversity accepted by many Islamic governments

(4) legal equality of all people in the Islamic empire

7 Which economic system existed in Europe during the early Middle Ages?

(1) free market

(2) socialism

(3) manorialism

(4) command

8 The growth of feudalism in Europe during the Middle Ages was primarily caused by the

(1) rivalry between the colonial empires

(2) suppression of internationalism

(3) decline of the Roman Catholic Church

(4) collapse of a strong central government

9 Which was a characteristic of feudalism?

(1) Land was exchanged for military service and obligations.

(2) Government was provided by a bureaucracy of civil servants.

(3) Power rested in the hands of a strong central government.

(4) Unified national court systems were developed.

10 "All things were under its domain. . . . Its power was such that no one could hope to escape its scrutiny."

Which European institution during the Middle Ages is best described by this statement?

(1) the guild

(2) the knighthood

(3) the Church

(4) the nation-state

11 The art, music, and philosophy of the medieval period in Europe generally dealt with

(1) human scientific achievements

(2) religious themes

(3) materialism

(4) classical Greek and Roman subjects

12 Buildings such as the Gothic cathedrals in Western Europe and the Parthenon in ancient Greece reflect each society's

(1) imperialist attitudes

(2) cultural values

(3) belief in democracy

(4) rigid social structure

13 As the Middle Ages ended, the rise of a middle class in Western Europe can be attributed partly to the

(1) economic policies of the Roman empire

(2) increase in trade that resulted from the Crusades

(3) strength of Christianity in medieval Europe

(4) self-sufficiency of the manor system

14 One major result of the Crusades was

(1) permanent occupation of the Holy Land by the Europeans

(2) long-term decrease in European trade

(3) conversion of most Muslims to Christianity

(4) spread of Middle Eastern culture and technology to Europe

15 In Europe, the Crusades resulted in

(1) a greater isolation of the region from the world

(2) an increased demand for goods from the Middle East and Asia

(3) the adoption of Islam as the official religion of many European nations

(4) the strengthening of the feudal system

Thematic Essay Question

In developing your answer, be sure to keep these general definitions in mind:

(a) <u>describe</u> means "to illustrate something in words or tell about it"
(b) <u>explain</u> means "to make observations about something using facts, reasoning, and argument; to present in some detail"

Directions: Write a well-organized essay that includes an introduction, several paragraphs addressing the task below, and a conclusion.

Theme: **Culture and Intellectual Life**

> Throughout global history, political conditions in some civilizations have produced "golden ages."

Task:

- Define the term *golden age*
- Describe a golden age in a specific civilization you have studied. Give specific examples that show why the time is considered such a memorable one in that civilization's history
- Explain the political, economic, and other conditions that help a golden age to occur

You may discuss any golden age you have studied. Some golden ages you may wish to consider include classical China, the Hellenistic Age, the Pax Romana, or the Muslim golden age.

You are *not* limited to these suggestions.
Do *not* use the United States in your response.

Guidelines:

In your essay, be sure to
- Develop all aspects of the task
- Support the theme with relevant facts, examples, and details
- Use a logical and clear plan of organization, including an introduction and a conclusion that are beyond a simple restatement of the theme

Document-Based Question

This question is based on the accompanying documents. The question is designed to test your ability to work with historical documents. Some of these documents have been edited for the purposes of this question. As you analyze the documents, take into account the source of each document and any point of view that may be presented in the document.

Historical Context:

> Throughout global history, interactions between people of different belief systems have had a variety of results. Sometimes the interactions have been peaceful. At other times conflict has occurred.

Task: Using the information from the documents and your knowledge of global history, answer the questions that follow each document in Part A. Your answers to the questions will help you write the Part B essay in which you will be asked to

> - Evaluate the effects of interaction between people of different belief systems
> - Discuss both positive and negative effects

In developing your answers, be sure to keep these general definitions in mind:

(a) <u>evaluate</u> means "to examine and judge the significance, worth, or condition of; to determine the value of "

(b) <u>discuss</u> means "to make observations about something using facts, reasoning, and argument; to present in some detail"

Document-Based Question

Part A: Short Answer

Directions: Analyze the documents and answer the question or questions that follow each document, using the space provided.

Document #1

> *Whoever honors his own [religion] and disparages another man's, whether from blind loyalty or with the intention of showing his own [religion] in a favorable light, does his own [religion] the greatest possible harm. Concord [peaceful harmony] is best, with each hearing and respecting the other's teachings. It is the wish of the [king] that members of all [religions] should be learned and should teach virtue.*
>
> **—Asoka, Edicts, about 270 B.C.**

1. Explain in your own words how Asoka felt people of one belief system should interact with followers of another belief system.

_____

_____

Document #2

The Spread of Islam

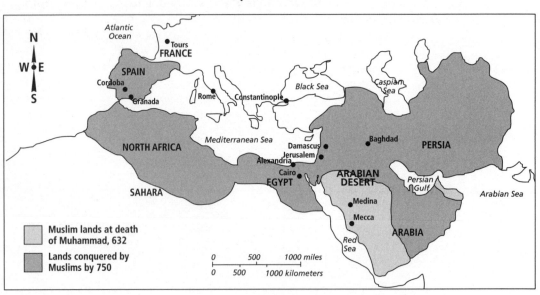

2. Over what areas did Muslim leaders exert control by A.D. 750?

_____

_____

Document #3

For your brethren who live in the east are in urgent need of your help, and you must hasten to give them the aid which has often been promised them. For . . . the Turks and Arabs have attacked them. . . . They have occupied more and more of the lands of those Christians, ... If you permit them to continue . . . the faithful of God will be much more widely attacked by them. On this account I, or rather the Lord, beseech you as Christ's heralds to publish this everywhere and to persuade all people of whatever rank, foot-soldiers and knights, poor and rich, to carry aid promptly to those Christians and to destroy that vile race from the lands of our friends. . . . Christ commands it.

—**Fulcher of Chartres,** *Gesta Francorum Jerusalem Expugnantium,* **1095**
[A contemporary account of Urban II's speech at the Council of Clermont]

3. What does the speaker want Christians to do in response to his words?

_____

_____

Part B

Essay

Directions: Write a well-organized essay that includes an introduction, several paragraphs, and a conclusion. Use evidence from *at least **two*** of the documents in your essay. Support your response with relevant facts, examples, and details. Include additional outside information.

Historical Context:

Throughout global history, interactions between people of different belief systems have had a variety of results. Sometimes the interactions have been peaceful. At other times conflict has occurred.

Task: Using the information from the documents and your knowledge of global history, write an essay in which you

- Evaluate the effects of interaction between people of different belief systems
- Discuss both positive and negative effects

Guidelines:

In your essay, be sure to

- Develop all aspects of the task
- Incorporate information from *at least **two*** of the documents
- Incorporate relevant outside information
- Support the theme with relevant facts, examples, and details
- Use a logical and clear plan of organization, including an introduction and a conclusion that are beyond a restatement of the theme

Global Interactions
(1200–1650)

Unit Overview

In the years from 1200 through 1650, groups from various parts of the world came into contact with one another. In East Asia, cultural exchange occurred among China, Korea, and Japan. The Mongols established a vast empire that stretched from China westward into Europe. Over time, overland and sea trade routes linked more and more of the world and encouraged diffusion between the East and the West. In Europe, global interactions led to a new type of economy, based on money, and a new middle class. New ways of thinking emerged, in which old authority was questioned. Nations began to take shape as individual rulers gained power. In Africa, commerce contributed to the rise of powerful trading empires and the spread of Islam.

Using Good Social Studies Practices
Geographic Reasoning

Some of the many themes developed in Unit 3 are:

interdependence	culture
movement of people and goods	change
nationalism	urbanization
economic systems	conflict

Choose one of the themes listed above. As you review Unit 3, create a chart which identifies relationships between your chosen theme and the people, places, regions, and environments discussed in this unit. Write a summary that includes any patterns you have discovered. Include major developments from 1200 to 1650 and key turning points relating to your theme.

Early Japan and Feudalism

The
**Big
Idea**

Early Japan:

• was strongly influenced
by geography.

• borrowed selectively
from Chinese culture.

• developed a feudal
system.

• experienced stability
and strong government
during later feudal
times.

Section Overview

Even though Japan was always an island nation, it was not completely isolated. It was influenced by Korea and China. Japan was ruled by an emperor since about A.D. 500, but fights between rival warlords led to the development of feudalism in the 1100s. For several hundred years, military rulers controlled Japan. The dynasty that took power in 1603 brought stability and prosperity to Japan but imposed a rigid political and social order.

Key Themes and Concepts

As you review this section, take special note of the following key themes and concepts:

Geography How did Japan's geographic setting contribute to its development?

Movement of People and Goods What influence did China and Korea have on Japan?

Political Systems How did the system of feudalism work in Japan?

Economic Systems and Culture In what ways did the economy and culture of Japan flourish during its later feudal age?

Key Terms

Key Terms

Place each of the key
terms into one of these
three categories: system of
belief, political system, or
cultural life.

As you review this section, be sure you understand the significance of these key terms:

Shinto	**samurai**
kami	**bushido**
Zen Buddhism	**kabuki**
shoguns	**haiku**
daimyo	

**Preparing for
the Regents**

Describe two effects of
geography on the
development of Japanese
culture.

1.

2.

Geographic Setting

Major Physical Features

Japan is made up of a chain of mountainous islands in the Pacific Ocean off the coast of mainland Asia. There are four main islands and more than 3,000 smaller islands. The Japanese islands are part of the Ring of Fire, a group of islands around the Pacific Ocean that are vulnerable to earthquakes and volcanoes. Underground earthquakes can cause deadly tidal waves to sweep over the islands, destroying everything in their path.

Impact on Japanese Life

Because the islands of Japan are mountainous, the land is difficult to farm. Most of the population has always lived in narrow river valleys or along the coast. The rugged terrain has sometimes acted as a barrier to political unity.

The Japanese learned to use the sea both as a source of food and as a means of transportation from one island to another. The sea sometimes isolated Japan from other cultures, but it also acted as protection from invasion.

In addition, the experience of living in an unsettled natural environment that could bring volcanoes, earthquakes, and tidal waves taught the Japanese a deep respect for the forces of nature.

Shintoism

The traditional Japanese religion is called **Shinto,** meaning "the way of the gods." Shinto is characterized by the worship of the **kami,** or divine spirits found in all living and nonliving things. Kami are thought to control the powerful forces of nature. Believers respect the kami and try to win their favor through prayer and offerings. The shared beliefs of the followers of Shinto eventually helped unite all of Japan. Shinto shrines still appear throughout Japan in places of unusual natural beauty or interest.

Diffusion From Korea and China

Japanese culture features a unique blend of its own original traditions and ideas borrowed from the nearby civilizations of Korea and China. Korea often acted as a bridge between China and Japan.

Contact between Korea and Japan occurred as a result of both warfare and trade. Koreans introduced the Japanese to various aspects of Chinese culture.

Great interest in Chinese civilization was sparked among the Japanese. Around 600, a Japanese ruler sent nobles to study in China. For over a century, during the Tang dynasty, the Japanese upper classes imported cultural traditions and ideas directly from China. Between the 700s and the 1100s, the Japanese blended the best of China with their own traditions to produce a distinctly Japanese civilization.

Chinese Influence on Writing
Around 500, the Koreans brought the Chinese system of writing to the Japanese. By the 800s, however, when Tang China began to decline, the Japanese adapted the Chinese system of writing to suit their own language and ideas.

Buddhism
Koreans also brought Buddhism from China. The religion spread quickly, and it flourished alongside traditional Japanese religions. During feudal times, a Chinese sect called **Zen Buddhism** spread throughout Japan. Zen Buddhists value peace, simple living, nature, and beauty.

Confucianism
The Japanese also were influenced by the Chinese philosophy of Confucianism, especially its ideas about proper behavior and social order. Although Buddhism took hold strongly in Japan, many Confucian ideas took root as well. These included ideas about family loyalty, honoring parents, and a respect for learning and the educated class.

Customs and the Arts
Japanese courts adopted such Chinese customs as tea drinking and the tea ceremony. Chinese music and dancing, as well as Chinese garden design, became popular. In addition, the Japanese built their Buddhist monasteries to resemble Chinese monasteries.

Key Themes and Concepts

Belief Systems
The Shinto belief system reflects the Japanese reverence for nature. Followers of Shintoism believe that all living and nonliving things possess divine spirits. This belief causes a strong respect for the natural world.

Key Themes and Concepts

Movement of People and Goods
The Japanese people borrowed ideas selectively from their mainland neighbors, Korea and China. Korea acted as a bridge between China and Japan.

Vocabulary Builder

sect—(sekt) *n.* a group of people with their own particular set of beliefs and practices, especially within or separated from a larger religious group

Preparing for the Regents

List three ways in which China influenced Japan.

1.

2.

3.

Feudal Society in Japan

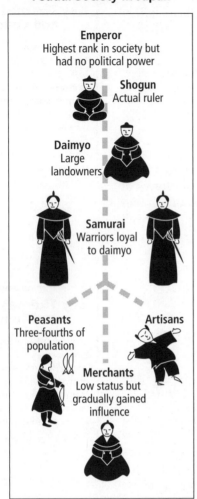

Emperor
Highest rank in society but had no political power

Shogun
Actual ruler

Daimyo
Large landowners

Samurai
Warriors loyal to daimyo

Peasants
Three-fourths of population

Artisans

Merchants
Low status but gradually gained influence

The Imperial Tradition

Early Japanese society was organized into clans with separate rulers and religious customs. Around A.D. 500, one clan, the Yamato, gained control over the largest island of Japan. They extended their rule and established themselves as the royal family of Japan, claiming to be direct descendants of the sun goddess. Between the 700s and 1100s, the emperor, who was revered as a god, presided over an elegant and sophisticated court. Although the Japanese emperor today no longer claims divinity, he still traces his roots to the Yamato clan.

Feudal Japan

In the 1100s, the central authority of the Japanese emperor declined. Local warlords fought one another. While armies battled for power, a feudal system developed. Feudal society had distinct levels. All members of society had a defined place.

Landowners and Warriors

Under the Japanese feudal system, the emperor still ruled in name, but powerful warrior nobles actually controlled the country. The Japanese warrior aristocracy consisted of the following groups.

Shoguns Under the feudal system, the real power lay in the hands of the shoguns, or top military commanders. Shoguns set up dynasties called shogunates.

Daimyo As in European feudalism, the shogun distributed land to vassal lords, called daimyo in Japan. The daimyo received land in exchange for a promise to support the shogun with their armies when needed.

Samurai The daimyo, in turn, granted land to lesser warriors called samurai, whose name means "those who serve." The samurai promised loyalty to the daimyo and lived by a strict code of conduct known as **bushido,** or "the way of the warrior." The samurai promised to be loyal, brave, and honorable. Honor was supremely important. A samurai who betrayed the code of bushido was expected to commit ritual suicide, an act called seppuku.

Other Classes and Groups

Peasants and Artisans Peasants farmed the land, and artisans made weapons for the samurai. For their services, peasants and artisans were granted the protection of the samurai.

Merchants Despite the fact that they might possess more wealth than members of the upper classes, merchants were the lowest social class in medieval Japan. Over time, however, merchants gained more influence.

Women Early in the feudal period, women sometimes became warriors or ran estates. The status of women declined, however. Japanese feudal codes did not place women in high esteem. As time passed, inheritance was passed on to sons only.

Preparing for the Regents

• How was the structure of Japanese feudalism similar to or different from European feudalism?

• Were the reasons for the development of feudalism in the two regions the same? Explain your answer.

The Tokugawa Shogunate

In 1603, the Tokugawa shogunate came to power, bringing peace and stability to Japan for nearly 300 years.

Centralized Feudal Government

The Tokugawa shoguns created a centralized feudal government. They halted the fighting among the powerful daimyo by at times forcing them to live at the capital of Edo (now Tokyo) instead of at their country estates. When the daimyo did leave the capital, their families were forced to stay under the shogun's careful watch.

Economic Prosperity

The stability of the Tokugawa shogunate resulted in economic gains. New seeds, tools, and techniques allowed farmers to grow more food. The population grew, and towns were linked by roads. Trade increased. In the cities, a wealthy class of merchants emerged.

In addition, Tokugawa shoguns became extremely hostile toward foreigners. By 1638, they had barred all Western merchants and prohibited Japanese from traveling abroad. During Japan's period of strict isolation, internal trade boomed. The economy prospered.

Cultural Advances

During the Tokugawa shogunate, many Japanese learned Zen Buddhist practices, such as the tea ceremony and landscape gardening. At the same time, the Japanese made advances in the arts and theater. In **kabuki** theater, actors wore colorful costumes and acted out stories about families or events in history. In literature, Japanese poets created a Chinese-influenced form of poetry called **haiku.**

Comparison With Europe

Japanese feudalism was similar to European feudalism. Both systems evolved in response to the basic desire for stability. In both Japan and Europe, emperors and kings were too weak to prevent invasions or halt internal wars. Feudalism provided a way for ruling classes to preserve law and order.

In the feudal systems of both Japan and Europe, everyone had a well-defined place in society. In both societies, power and wealth were concentrated in the hands of an elite land-owning class. As the class of respected warriors, Japanese samurai played a role similar to that of European knights. Peasants in both feudal systems worked the land and served the landowners in exchange for protection.

The position of women was different in Japan and Europe. In Japan, the status of women declined during feudal times. In Europe, the code of chivalry helped raise the status of women. Another difference was the role of religion. Leaders of the Catholic Church in Europe had more political power than Zen Buddhist monks in Japan.

Summary

Japan was strongly influenced by geographic conditions. It borrowed cultural elements from China but adapted them to develop its own unique culture. A decline in the power of the emperor led to the development of feudalism in the 1100s. In the early 1600s, the Tokugawa shogunate emerged, bringing stability and a flowering of culture but also strict government and a social structure consisting of unequal classes. Landowners and warriors dominated Japanese society.

Key Themes and Concepts

Political Systems
The Tokugawa shogunate brought stability to Japan by bringing the warring daimyo under central control.

Note Taking

Reading Skill:
Identify Supporting Details
Make a table. List at least two details for each main idea.

Tokugawa Shogunate	
Centralized Feudal Government	• •
Economic Prosperity	• •
Cultural Advances	• •

Comparisons

Compare and contrast Japanese feudalism and European feudalism.

List three similarities.

1.

2.

3.

List two differences.

1.

2.

Preparing for the Regents

• How was the position of women different in feudal Japan and medieval Europe?

The Mongols and Their Impact

Section Overview

Around 1200, the Mongols swept out of the grasslands of central Asia to build the largest empire in the world. Under leaders such as Genghis Khan and Kublai Khan, fierce Mongol fighters conquered an area from China to Persia, even entering Europe. Often, Mongol rulers provided stability, peace, and prosperity. This stability encouraged cultural exchange between the East and the West. Mongol power declined gradually because of the size and diversity of the area they ruled, poor administration, and internal revolt.

Key Themes and Concepts

As you review this section, take special note of the following key themes and concepts:

Diversity How did diversity both provide benefits and create problems for Mongol rulers?

Culture How did Mongol rule affect cultural development in the lands under their control?

Interdependence How did the exchange of goods and ideas throughout Eurasia increase with Mongol rule?

Key People and Terms

As you review this section, be sure you understand the significance of these key people and terms:

Genghis Khan	Yuan dynasty	Pax Mongolia
Golden Horde	Mughal dynasty	Marco Polo
Kublai Khan	Akbar the Great	Ibn Battuta

Rise of the Mongols

The Mongols of central Asia were nomadic herders who roamed the grasslands with their horses and sheep. The Mongols were skillful riders and fierce fighters and raiders. Under their leader Genghis Khan, the Mongols built the largest empire in the world.

Genghis Khan

Genghis Khan was born with the name Temujin in central Asia in the 1100s. After experiencing a difficult boyhood, Temujin became a courageous warrior and a skilled leader. As supreme ruler of the Mongol clans, he earned the title Genghis Khan, which meant "World Emperor."

With his organized and disciplined armies, Genghis Khan took most of Asia from Korea in the east to the Caspian Sea in the west. His armies advanced into Persia, India, and even northern China.

There were several reasons for these Mongol victories. The Mongols were skilled horsemen and bowmen. They also borrowed new military technology, such as cannons, from the Chinese and the Turks.

Expansion to the West

Eastern Europe During the time of Genghis Khan, the Mongols invaded Eastern Europe. They even came within reach of the Byzantine city of Constantinople. After the time of Genghis Khan, the Mongols attacked Russia, Hungary, and Poland.

One grandson of Genghis Khan, called Batu, led Mongol armies into Russia and other lands of Eastern Europe between 1236 and 1241. Known as the **Golden Horde** because of the color of their tents, this group conquered many Russian cities. They ruled from a capital on the Volga River for 240 years. Like other Mongols, the Golden Horde were fierce warriors but relatively tolerant rulers.

The Middle East In the late 1300s, Timur, also called Tamerlane, gathered Mongol groups together and conquered areas of Persia, Mesopotamia, Russia, and India. Eventually a descendent of Tamerlane established the Mughal dynasty in India.

A Mongol Dynasty in China

In 1279, **Kublai Khan,** another grandson of Genghis Khan, completed the job of conquering China by dominating the south. He ruled not only China but also Korea, Tibet, and parts of Vietnam.

Kublai Khan adopted a Chinese name for his dynasty, the **Yuan dynasty.** He did not want the Mongols to become absorbed into Chinese civilization, however. He gave the best government jobs to Mongol workers and allowed only Mongols to serve in the army, although Chinese officials still governed the provinces.

Mughal India

Babur, a descendent of Tamerlane, established India's **Mughal dynasty,** which ruled from 1526 to 1857. Babur's grandson **Akbar the Great** was the greatest Mughal ruler. Although he was a Muslim, Akbar won the support of Hindus because of his tolerant policies.

The Mongol Impact

Mongol power reached its greatest extent by about 1300. Mongol rule stretched throughout central Asia and China, into Russia and Europe, and into Southwest Asia and India.

Destruction and Conquest

Fierce Mongol warriors spread terror and destruction throughout the regions they conquered. For example, Mongols devastated the thriving province of Sichuan in China. In Russia, the Golden Horde looted and burned Kiev and other Russian cities, killing countless inhabitants.

Despite brutality in war, most Mongol leaders ruled with tolerance. Genghis Khan respected academics, artists, and artisans. He listened to the ideas of scholars of many religions. His heirs continued both his conquests and his tolerant policies. Conquered peoples were often allowed to live as before, as long as they paid tribute to the Mongols.

Lasting Effects on Russia

The Mongols ruled Russia for about 250 years. Mongol rule had a great long-term impact on Russia.

Absolutist Government The absolute power of the Mongol rulers served as a model for later Russian rulers who also expected to rule without interference from groups such as nobles or the Church.

Note Taking

Reading Skill:
Recognize Sequence
As you read, list the important dates or periods for the rise of the Mongols. Record them in the order they occurred. Add boxes as needed.

Rise of the Mongols	
Date	Event
1100s	Genghis Khan was born
1236–1241	

Preparing for the Regents

- Support this statement in a short paragraph: The Mongol empire in 1279 brought together many different groups and cultures.

Key Themes and Concepts

Political Systems
The Mongols were not oppressive rulers. They usually allowed people they conquered to live as they had before, as long as they paid to the Mongols the tribute they required.

Key Themes and Concepts

Global Interactions
Although Mongol rule brought varied peoples into contact, it cut off Russia from contact with Western Europe.

Isolation Mongol rule also cut Russia off from Western Europe. This isolation deprived Russia of many advances in the arts and sciences of the later Middle Ages and the Renaissance.

Prosperity and Discontent in China

The Yuan dynasty ruled China for 150 years. They established peace and order in their kingdom. Great cities flourished in China under Kublai Khan. His capital of Khanbalik (now Beijing) was a large, well-planned city into which riches flowed. The city of Hangzhou was described as ten times the size of Venice, one of Italy's richest city-states.

However, only Mongols could serve in the military and hold the best government jobs. Chinese resentment resulted, and uprisings occurred.

Preparing for the Regents

• Using the map, describe the extent of Mongol rule.

The Mongol Empire

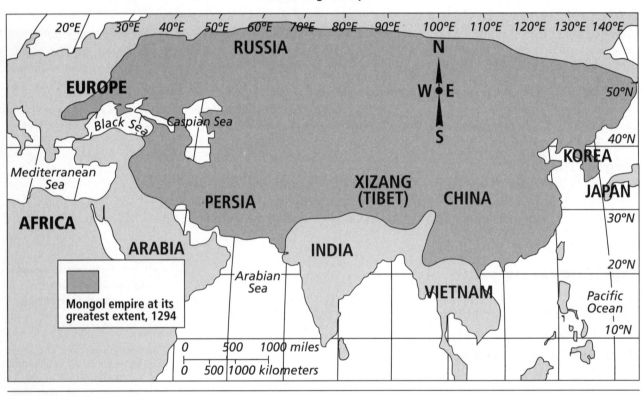

The Mongol Empire
In 1294, the Mongol Empire was the largest in the world up to that time.

Pax Mongolia and Global Trade

Political stability throughout much of Asia resulted from Mongol rule. This period of stability, known as the **Pax Mongolia,** allowed for an exchange of goods and ideas between the East and the West.

The Silk Road and Trade In the centuries before the rise of the Mongols, the Silk Road, the trade route that linked China to the Middle East, had become dangerous. Traders used it less. The Mongols, however, provided safe passage along the Silk Road; as a result, trade flourished. Products such as gunpowder and porcelain, as well as technology such as papermaking and the use of windmills, flowed west.

Marco Polo and Ibn Battuta Safer travel meant that people could explore other lands. Marco Polo, an Italian merchant, traveled to the court of Kublai Khan

Key Themes and Concepts

Urbanization
As China grew in importance as a center of trade and culture, European travelers such as Marco Polo wrote with awe of the cities of Kublai Khan.

in the late 1200s and remained for many years. His writings introduced Europeans to the beauty and riches of China.

Ibn Battuta, a scholar from Morocco, traveled at about the same time. He traveled first to Mecca and then through Asia Minor, Persia, India, Indonesia, and China. Later, he traveled to Spain. The record of his travels is of great interest to historians.

Decline of Mongol Power

Mongol power declined for several reasons. Mongol lands were too large and diverse for one power to govern effectively. Although the Mongols were excellent fighters, they had little experience in government. They often depended on other people to do this job. Sometimes the people they chose were incompetent or corrupt.

The death of strong leaders also hurt Mongol power. After the death of Kublai Khan, for example, the Yuan dynasty broke apart. In both China and Russia, there had long been resentment of Mongol rule. In both countries a desire for independence from foreign rule provoked leaders to overthrow the Mongols and establish new dynasties.

Summary

The Mongols conquered lands in Asia and Europe. Areas of Mongol rule included people of varied religions and nationalities, most of whom were allowed to continue their own ways of life. Mongol rule provided a period of stability and economic growth. Increased trade encouraged the movement of goods, ideas, and technology between the East and the West. As the pressures of such a diverse power grew, the Mongols declined.

Key Themes and Concepts

Interdependence
Marco Polo traveled from the West to the East and introduced Europeans to advanced Chinese culture. Ibn Battuta traveled from Africa throughout Southwest Asia and even to Spain. Both kept records of their travels. Their writings have been important to scholars all over the world.

Vocabulary Builder

resentment—(rih ZENT munt) *n.* a feeling of anger because something has happened that you think is unfair

Preparing for the Regents

List two causes of the decline of the Mongol empire.

1.

2.

Global Trade and Interactions

Section Overview

In the 1200s, global interactions increased. During the early Ming dynasty in China, trade thrived and cities grew. Goods continued to travel with Muslim traders by sea from China to Africa, where Venetian ships transported goods across the Mediterranean Sea to Europe. The population of Europe began to grow, leading to a revival of European trade and town life. Italian cities became flourishing centers of industry and trade. Also, the Hanseatic League gained control of trade in the Baltic and North Seas. In time, Portugal found a sea route to Asia, providing Europeans with easier access to the riches of the East. Trade and urbanization were slowed, however, by the coming of the bubonic plague in the 1300s. As a result, social, economic, and political upheaval occurred in Asia, Africa, and Europe.

Key Themes and Concepts

As you review this section, take special note of the following key themes and concepts:

Interdependence What factors led to increased global trade from the 1200s to the 1500s?

Movement of People and Goods What were some of the major trade centers and trade routes from the 1200s to the 1500s?

Urbanization Why did cities grow in importance?

Change How did the plague affect the world socially, economically, and politically?

Key People and Terms

As you review this section, be sure you understand the significance of these key people and terms:

Zheng He	Cairo	Hanseatic League
Canton	Venice	bubonic plague
Mogadishu	trade fairs	epidemic

Expansion of Chinese Trade

As you know, trade thrived in China under the Yuan dynasty in the 1200s. Goods traveled west along the Silk Road to Russia, Asia Minor, and lands beyond. Other goods, as well as travelers such as Marco Polo, traveled east.

The Ming dynasty took control of China in 1368, overthrowing the Mongols and driving them back behind the Great Wall. A time of economic prosperity and industrial growth followed. Population growth and expanded trade led to the growth of cities.

Ming rulers began a period of overseas expansion. In 1405, **Zheng He,** a Chinese admiral, set out with a fleet of ships. His goals were to promote Chinese trade and to collect tribute from less powerful lands.

The 1405 voyage was one of seven Zheng He would take between 1405 and 1433. During this time, he traveled through Southeast Asia, along the coast of India, around the Arabian Peninsula, and to the port cities of East Africa. He exchanged Chinese silks and porcelain for luxury items, including exotic animals for the imperial zoo. Along the way he convinced many people of the supremacy of Chinese culture.

The Chinese city of **Canton** became an important center for global trade. Canton, known today as Guangzhou, is located more than 90 miles inland from the South China Sea. In the 1500s, the Portuguese sent traders to Canton. In the 1600s, the Dutch and British followed. Europeans were allowed to trade with the Chinese in Canton, but only under strict limits.

Major Trade Routes

Important trade routes enabled people and goods to move across Asia, Africa, and Europe.

Across the Indian Ocean
Sea routes crossing the Indian Ocean and the Arabian Sea allowed easy trade between Asia and East Africa. Trading centers developed in eastern Africa. For example, **Mogadishu** and Great Zimbabwe thrived on trade across the Indian Ocean. European ships on their way to Asia often stopped at East African coastal cities.

Overland Between the East and the West
A variety of overland trade routes linked Asia with the Middle East, North Africa, and Europe. Trade from China followed the Silk Road and entered Europe through Russia or Constantinople. Goods also traveled between Constantinople and India.

Across the Mediterranean Sea
In the Middle East, Muslim traders brought goods to ports in Egypt, Syria, and Turkey. Major Egyptian ports included **Cairo** and Alexandria. In Egypt, goods could be transferred to Italian ships. Italian merchants carried the goods across the Mediterranean Sea to Europe.

Resurgence of European Trade

Europeans were more and more interested in trade with the East. Improved methods of agriculture during the later Middle Ages allowed the European population to grow, leading to an increase in trade. The Crusades had also had an impact.

Impact of the Crusades
As you have learned, one of the effects of the Crusades was increased European interest in the East. Returning crusaders brought back goods. Ships that had been used to carry crusaders back and forth to the Holy Land could now be used for trade. Even though the Muslims had captured the crusader states, trade continued between the Middle East and Europe through Italy.

Italian City-States
By the late 1300s, northern Italian cities had become flourishing centers of industry and trade. Venice, Genoa, and Florence had grown rich and powerful. Venice in particular took advantage of its location to control the valuable spice trade with Asia. Eventually **Venice,** in partnership with Egypt, came to dominate trade with the East. The Venetians and their Muslim counterparts prospered.

Discuss one reason for the growth of cities in each of the following areas.

China:

Italy:

Northern and Western Europe:

Key Themes and Concepts

Economic Systems
Weak central governments during the earlier Middle Ages led merchants to band together for protection. The Hanseatic League, an organization made up of German towns and commercial groups, developed for this reason.

Key Themes and Concepts

Movement of People and Goods
In the 1400s, Western Europeans were looking for ways to avoid the Muslim and Italian middlemen and obtain direct access to Asia's riches. This is why Portugal was looking for a new route to the East.

Key Themes and Concepts

Global Exchange
Increases in trade transmitted not only goods and ideas but diseases as well. The Black Death spread across Eurasia and Africa along the trade routes.

After goods arrived in Venice, traders took them over the Alps and up the Rhine River to Flanders. From there, other traders took the goods throughout Europe, as far as England and to areas along the Baltic Sea.

Trade Fairs and the Growth of Cities

Much trade within Europe went on at **trade fairs.** Trade fairs took place in towns where trade routes met, often on navigable rivers. These fairs contributed to the growth of European cities. Many traders came to settle in these areas, as did craftworkers and merchants. The population of towns increased. In time, some towns developed into large cities populated by thousands of people. The wealthiest cities were at either end of the trade routes: in Flanders in the north and in Italy in the south.

The Hanseatic League

In northern Germany, groups of traders and merchants began to join together in the 1100s. Because central governments were still weak in Europe at this time, merchants sometimes banded together to protect their interests. By the mid-1300s, Lübeck, Hamburg, and many other northern German towns were members of the **Hanseatic League.** Eventually the league monopolized trade in the Baltic and North Seas. The league worked to make navigation safer by controlling piracy, building lighthouses, and training sailors.

Portugal and the Spice Trade

Spices, such as pepper and cinnamon, were extremely valuable during the Middle Ages. Spices served many purposes. Not only were they used to preserve and flavor meats, but they were used in perfumes and medicines as well. The riches that spices could bring prompted many to risk their lives traveling to Asia to acquire them.

As the Ottoman empire expanded into Eastern Europe and the eastern Mediterranean, European trade routes were disrupted. As a result, Portugal, at the southwestern end of Europe, began to look for new routes. In the early 1400s, Portugal began to explore the coast of Africa. The goal was to find a direct sea route to the riches of the East. Before the end of the century, the Portugese found a route around the tip of Africa to the Indian Ocean. In the 1500s, the Portuguese established posts in Africa, India, Japan, and China. Trade brought great wealth to Portugal.

The Plague and Its Impact

The **bubonic plague,** also called the Black Death, was a highly contagious disease spread by the fleas that lived on rats. Shortly after being bitten by a flea, people developed swellings and black bruises on their skin. Within a few days, victims often died in agony. At the time, there was no cure for the plague, so many of those who became infected died.

Outbreak in China

Although the bubonic plague had previously broken out in parts of Europe, Asia, and North Africa, it had died out on its own without affecting a large area. However, in the early 1300s, the plague appeared in Chinese cities. Rats, common in the cities of the time, carried the disease through the crowded urban centers.

A Global Epidemic

The bubonic plague was a devastating **epidemic,** or outbreak that spreads quickly and affects a large number of people. The resurgence of trade that had been occurring since the 1100s had helped the plague to spread. Fleas from rats infested traders in the East, who then carried the plague to the Middle East. North Africa and Italy were hit next. By the mid-1300s, the plague had reached Spain and France. From there it swept across the rest of Europe.

Effects of the Plague

The plague brought terror and devastation to all the regions it struck. Because of the number of deaths, the plague devastated economies around the world.

Population Losses In the early 1300s, when the plague first began to spread in China, about 35 million Chinese died. At its peak, the plague killed about 7,000 people a day in Cairo. Other regions of Africa and the Middle East suffered similar fates. By the time the worst of the plague was over, about one-third of the European population had died.

Economic Decline In killing so many people, the plague devastated economies around the world. In Europe, farm and industrial production declined. The people who were left were in a position to demand higher wages, and prices rose. When landowners and merchants took action to stop this wage increase, peasant revolts occurred.

Because it devastated the economies of Eurasia and North Africa, the plague also disrupted trade. Some cities and provinces that had grown rich through trade struggled to survive.

Social and Political Change Economic changes had social results, as the strictly defined levels of society that had been in place before began to break down. Feudalism declined as peasant revolts weakened the power of landowners over peasants. The decline of feudalism led to the growth of new political systems. In England and France especially, monarchs gained power and began to build more powerful nations.

Confusion and Disorder The plague threw society into disorder. Some people questioned their faith and the Church, turning to magic and witchcraft to try to save themselves. Others blamed local Jews, whom they said had poisoned the wells. As a result, thousands of Jews were murdered.

Summary

Beginning in the 1200s, global trade and other interactions increased. China underwent a period of expanding overseas and overland trade. Trade between Asia, Africa, and Europe increased. The Crusades and a growing population helped European trade. Italian city-states transported goods across the Mediterranean Sea, becoming rich and powerful. Portugal found a direct sea route to the East. In the 1300s, however, the bubonic plague disrupted trade as well as social and political life in Europe, Asia, and parts of Africa.

Preparing for the Regents

Describe three ways in which the plague affected Europe, Asia, and North Africa during the 1300s.

1.

2.

3.

Key Themes and Concepts

Change and Political Systems
Many factors led to the decline of feudalism. One was that the social upheaval resulting from the plague led to the breakdown of Europe's strict social hierarchy.

The Resurgence of Europe

The
Big
Idea

In Europe at the end of the Middle Ages:

- the commercial revolution brought new ways of doing business.

- the Renaissance introduced new ways of thinking and a flowering of culture.

- religious reformers challenged the authority of the Roman Catholic Church.

- monarchs increased their power and formed nation-states.

- limits were placed on the power of monarchs in England.

Section Overview

From the 1300s through the 1700s, Europe underwent many changes. An increase in the importance of trade brought Europe not only an economy based on money but also a new middle class. The Renaissance brought new philosophies that emphasized the world and the individual. In art and literature, new styles and ideas emerged. Reformers challenged the power and authority of the Roman Catholic Church in a movement that divided the Church. Throughout this period, feudalism weakened. In England and France, nation-states were forming. In France, the monarchy gained power; in England, the monarch shared power with a representative body.

Key Themes and Concepts

As you review this section, take special note of the following key themes and concepts:

Economics What factors led to the commercial revolution?

Change What were the causes and impacts of the Reformation and Counter-Reformation?

Nationalism How did the governments of France and England differ as they moved toward a stronger sense of nationhood?

Key People and Terms

As you review this section, be sure you understand the significance of these key people and terms:

guild	Martin Luther
apprentices	95 Theses
capitalism	Protestant Reformation
commercial revolution	John Calvin
Renaissance	Ignatius Loyola
humanism	common law
Michelangelo	Magna Carta
Leonardo da Vinci	Parliament

Key People and Terms

Place each of the key people and terms into one of these four categories: system of thought or belief, culture, politics, or economics.

Key Themes and Concepts

Change
Feudalism and the manor economy were based on land. Those who had land held wealth and power. A money economy gave a larger number of people the ability to gain wealth and to rise in society.

The Commercial Revolution

With the expansion of trade and the growth of cities between about 1000 and 1300, new ways of doing business arose in Europe. Money grew in importance, and a new social class emerged.

Towns and the Middle Class

A growing population and an increase in trade led to the growth of towns and cities. Urban centers based on trade gave new power to a rising new class—a middle class of merchants, traders, and artisans. They were called the "middle" class because they ranked between the older feudal classes of nobles and peasants.

Importance of Guilds

Merchants and craftspeople formed guilds. A **guild** was a type of trade association. All of the people who worked in one craft, such as baking or weaving, would join together. Merchant guilds had great power. Typically, guilds did the following to protect the interests of their members:

- Made sure the quality of goods stayed high
- Provided social services for members, such as hospitals and aid to widows and children of members
- Regulated hours of work and prices of goods
- Ensured a supply of new artisans by training young people, called **apprentices,** in their crafts

Rise of Capitalism

As feudalism was declining all over Europe, a new system called capitalism was emerging. **Capitalism** is based on trade and capital, the name for money used for investment. When the demand for a product is great, prices rise, and traders therefore profit. However, traders can lose everything when the demand falls. Early capitalists devised new business methods to create wealth. This and other changes are known as the **commercial revolution,** or business revolution.

New Business Practices

The new middle class gathered together in various types of organizations. Business people were aided by banking and insurance services.

Partnerships and Joint Stock Companies Merchants sometimes joined together in partnerships. By pooling their capital, they could finance ventures that no single merchant could have afforded. In a partnership, a small group of merchants pooled their funds to finance a large-scale trading venture. A joint stock company allowed many merchants to pool their funds for business ventures. Joint stock companies invested in trading ventures around the world.

Banking Banking grew during this period. Individual merchants often did not have the capital they needed for an overseas trading venture. They borrowed from moneylenders, who developed systems of banking. Bankers also provided bills of exchange. These were needed because it was dangerous to travel over long distances with gold coins. Instead, a merchant deposited money with a banker in his hometown. The banker gave him a bill of exchange. The merchant could exchange this bill for cash in the city where he would be engaging in trade.

Insurance Insurance helped reduce business risks. For a small fee, a merchant's shipment was insured. If the merchant's goods were damaged or lost, the insurer paid the merchant most of the value of the shipment.

Social Changes

The commercial revolution reshaped medieval society. For example, the use of money undermined serfdom and led to the decline of feudalism. Because feudal lords needed money to buy goods, peasants sold their farm products and began paying their lords with money rather than labor.

The Renaissance and Humanism

The period from the 1300s to the 1500s was a time of great creativity and change in Europe. This period is called the Renaissance, which means "rebirth." It was a golden age in the arts, literature, and sciences.

Note Taking

Reading Skill:
Identify Effects
Make a concept web. Fill in the circles with the effects of guilds. Add more circles if needed.

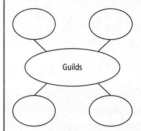

Guilds

Preparing for the Regents

- How does capitalism determine what goods and services are to be produced and in what quantities?

- Why were bankers important to the commercial revolution and the development of capitalism?

- What new business practices developed during the commercial revolution?

Key Themes and Concepts

Change
The Renaissance represented a widespread change in worldview. Instead of concentrating on spiritual things, people began to focus more on the world in which they lived.

The Renaissance began in Italy in the mid-1300s and then spread northward. The cities of Italy were thriving centers of trade and manufacturing. Merchants in these cities had great wealth and were willing to use it to promote art and education.

New Ways of Thinking

During the Renaissance, Europeans developed a new way of thinking called **humanism.** During the Middle Ages, philosophers and writers had wondered about life after death. Renaissance humanists, on the other hand, were more curious about life in the present. Another feature of this new way of thinking was an emphasis on the achievements of the individual. Instead of religious issues, humanists examined worldly subjects that the ancient Greeks and Romans had studied. They hoped to use ancient learning to increase knowledge about their own times.

Artistic Achievements

The Renaissance produced some of the greatest paintings, sculptures, and architecture in the history of the world. Renaissance architects rejected medieval forms of architecture. They returned to Greek and Roman styles for columns, arches, and domes. Artists were supported by merchants, popes, and princes.

The art of the time reflected humanist concerns. Many paintings still had religious subjects, but others portrayed important contemporary figures. Renaissance art was very realistic. Renaissance artists learned the rules of perspective—the technique used to give art a three-dimensional effect. These artists also studied human anatomy and often worked from live models, so they could portray the body in amazingly accurate detail. Two of the most famous artists of the Renaissance were Michelangelo and Leonardo da Vinci.

Key Themes and Concepts

Culture and Intellectual Life
Humanist thinkers used the Greeks and Romans as models. They also focused on individual achievement.

Preparing for the Regents

Name three Renaissance artists, and describe an achievement of each.

1.

2.

3.

Artists of the Italian Renaissance
The Renaissance began in Italy in the mid-1300s. Over the next hundred years it spread to the rest of Europe. Rich merchants, princes, and popes took a great interest in the arts and gave financial support to artists.

Artists of the Italian Renaissance

Leonardo da Vinci	Michelangelo
• Painter, sculptor, inventor, architect, musician, engineer • *Mona Lisa* (painting) • Sketches and plans for flying machines and submarines	• Sculptor, engineer, poet, painter, architect • *David* (statue) • Dome of St. Peter's Church in Rome
Raphael	**Sofonisba Anguissola**
• Painter • Student of Michelangelo and Leonardo da Vinci • Paintings of the madonna, mother of Jesus	• Female artist • *The Artist's Sisters Playing Cards* (painting) • Painter for King Philip II of Spain

Michelangelo Michelangelo was a sculptor, engineer, poet, painter, and architect. He is probably best known for his enormous mural on the ceiling of the Sistine Chapel in the Vatican. Michelangelo is also well known for his statue of the biblical character David.

Leonardo da Vinci The *Mona Lisa* is Leonardo da Vinci's most famous painting. Leonardo da Vinci was very much interested in human anatomy, and he dissected human corpses to see how muscles and bones worked. His sketches for flying machines and underwater boats were made centuries before the first airplane or submarine was actually built.

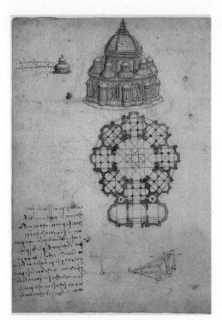

Northern Artists In the late 1400s, German artist Albrecht Dürer studied the techniques of Italian masters in Italy. When he returned to his homeland, he helped to spread Italian Renaissance ideas. Dürer's paintings, engravings, and prints portray the religious upheaval of his age. Flemish painters Jan and Hubert van Eyck developed oil paint in the 1400s. In the 1500s, Pieter Bruegel painted lively, vibrant scenes of daily life. Peter Paul Rubens, another Flemish painter, blended the realism of Bruegel with the classical themes and artistic freedom of the Italian Renaissance in the 1600s.

Literary Achievements

The humanist interest in this world was also expressed in the literature of the day. In the late Middle Ages, people had begun to write in the everyday language of ordinary people. Instead of scholarly Greek

Leonardo da Vinci's sketch of a domed building.

and Latin, they used vernacular languages such as Italian, French, English, and other languages.

Dante Dante Alighieri was an Italian writer who wrote in the years before the Renaissance took hold. Dante wrote about a journey through hell and heaven in his masterpiece *The Divine Comedy*. Because he wrote in the language of the Italian people, not in Latin, he is seen as a forerunner of the Renaissance.

Cervantes The work of Spanish writer Miguel de Cervantes shows the effects of the Renaissance as it moved westward. In the early 1600s, he wrote *Don Quixote*. Cervantes expressed Renaissance ideas by poking fun at the traditions of knighthood and chivalry. For example, Don Quixote, an old man who thinks he is a brave knight in battle with a giant, attacks a windmill.

Shakespeare William Shakespeare, writing in England around 1600, is another figure of the Renaissance. Shakespeare wrote extensively about human beings and the joys and sorrows of human life.

Machiavelli Niccolò Machiavelli wrote *The Prince* in the early 1500s. In this book he advises rulers on how to gain and maintain power. He tells rulers that they should use whatever methods are necessary to ensure their success. His work is seen today as a realistic picture of the politics of his time.

Impact of the Printing Press

By 1300, papermaking and printing technology had reached Europe from China. The invention of movable type in the 1400s led to Johann Gutenberg's printing of the Bible on his press in Germany in 1456.

The printing press was important for the Renaissance and later intellectual development for the following reasons:

- **Books became more available.** Books became cheaper and easier to make.
- **Literacy increased.** Because books were more readily available, more people learned to read and write.
- **Ideas spread rapidly.** People also had access to new knowledge about such subjects as medicine and geography. Printed bibles increased the spread of religious ideas.

Preparing for the Regents

- How did writing in the languages of ordinary people rather than Latin or Greek help Renaissance ideas to spread?

Key Themes and Concepts

Culture and Intellectual Life Machiavelli, in writing about court and politics, expressed the interest of the Renaissance in worldly rather than only spiritual things.

Preparing for the Regents

List three ways in which the printing press had an impact on European culture.

1.

2.

3.

Reformation and Counter-Reformation

In the 1500s, great changes occurred in European religious life: the Protestant Reformation and the Counter-Reformation.

Causes of the Reformation

The movement that resulted in the Reformation did not have a simple cause. A number of factors led to its emergence.

- **The Renaissance** Humanism led people to question Church authority. They placed increasing faith in human reason.
- **Strong Monarchs** Strong national monarchs were emerging. Sometimes they increased their own power by supporting reformers against the Church.
- **Problems in the Church** As ordinary people examined the Church, some felt that its leaders were acting more like kings, fighting for power and wealth, than like representatives of God. Others objected to the Church charging increased fees for marriages and baptisms and selling indulgences, or pardons for sins.

Protestant Reformers

Martin Luther By the 1500s, many Christians wanted to reform the Church. One such person was the German monk Martin Luther. Disgusted over the sale of indulgences, Martin Luther took action in 1517. He posted his famous **95 Theses,** which were 95 arguments against indulgences, on the door of a church in Wittenberg. This event sparked the **Protestant Reformation,** the period when Europeans broke away from the Catholic Church and formed new Christian churches.

Luther believed that people could reach heaven only through faith in God and that the pope could not grant a pardon for sins. He thought that the Bible was the only source of religious truth. Luther was excommunicated, or excluded from the Roman Catholic Church, for his radical views. The ideas of Luther, however, spread throughout northern Europe and Scandinavia, thanks in part to the printing press. Followers of Luther's beliefs were called Lutherans and— eventually—Protestants because they protested papal authority.

John Calvin John Calvin was another influential reformer. Born in France, Calvin was trained as a lawyer. Like Luther, Calvin believed that Christians could reach heaven only through faith in God. Calvin, however, had his own views on the power of God and the nature of human beings. He promoted the idea of predestination, the belief that God had determined before the beginning of time who would gain salvation. Calvin's followers lived strict, disciplined, and frugal lives. Calvinism spread to Germany, France, Scotland, and England.

Many other reformers also emerged. They included John Knox in Scotland and Huldrych Zwingli in Switzerland.

Note Taking

Reading Skill:
Identify Main Idea and Supporting Details
As you read Reformation and Counter-Reformation, complete an outline. Include the main ideas and supporting details. An outline has been started for you.

Reformation and Counter-Reformation
I. Causes of the Reformation
  A. Renaissance
    1.
    2.
  B.
  C.
II.

Preparing for the Regents

- How were Lutheranism and Calvinism different from Roman Catholicism?

Vocabulary Builder

frugal—(FROO gul) *adj.* careful to buy only what is necessary

Leaders of the Protestant Reformation

Martin Luther	John Calvin
• did not believe in the sale of indulgences • believed Christians reached heaven only through faith in God • did not believe that priests had special powers • had ideas that spread to northern Germany and Scandinavia • had followers that later called themselves Protestants	• believed Christians reached heaven only through faith in God • believed people are born sinners • preached predestination • had ideas that spread to Germany, France, Holland, England, and Scotland • led a community in Switzerland

The Counter-Reformation

As the Protestant Reformation continued to spread, a reform movement was also taking place within the Roman Catholic Church. That movement is called the Counter-Reformation, or the Catholic Reformation. The purpose of the Counter-Reformation was to strengthen the Catholic Church as well as to keep Catholics from converting to Protestantism.

The Council of Trent Pope Paul III called the Council of Trent in 1545 to guide the reform movement. The council, which met on and off for 20 years, reaffirmed traditional Catholic beliefs and worked to end abuses in the Church. It also ended the sale of indulgences and created the Index—a list of banned books.

Ignatius Loyola and the Jesuits Another strong force in the Counter-Reformation was Ignatius Loyola. Loyola founded the Society of Jesus, also called the Jesuits. The Jesuits are a religious order that emphasizes spiritual and moral discipline as well as strict obedience to Catholic authority. Early Jesuits saw themselves as the defenders of the Catholic faith throughout the world. Many Jesuits became advisors to Catholic rulers. Jesuit missionaries spread Catholicism to Asia, Africa, and the Americas.

The Inquisition The Church used a court made up of Church officials to root out heresy by force. Trials were held, often using torture, to find people suspected of having beliefs that differed from official Church teachings.

Key Themes and Concepts

Belief Systems
The Counter-Reformation was both an attempt to keep Catholics from leaving the Church and an effort to reform some aspects of the Church.

Vocabulary Builder

banned—(band) *adj.* not officially allowed to meet, exist, or be used

heresy—(HEHR uh see) *n.* a belief that disagrees with the official principles of a particular religion

The Protestant Reformation

Long-Term Causes
• Roman Catholic Church became more worldly
• Humanists urged return to simple religion
• Strong kings emerged and resented power of Church

Short-Term Causes
• Indulgences were sold in Germany
• Martin Luther wrote 95 Theses
• Luther translated the Bible into German
• Printing press helped spread ideas
• Reformers called for change

The Protestant Reformation

Long-Term Effects
• Loss of religious unity in Western Europe
• Religious wars broke out in Europe for more than 100 years
• Catholic Reformation took place
• Inquisition became stronger
• Many Jews forced into Eastern Europe

Short-Term Effects
• Peasants revolted
• Lutheran, Calvinist, Anglican, and other Protestant churches founded
• Holy Roman Emperor weakened

Effects of the Reformation

The Reformation had complex effects. Most obviously, it led to the formation of the Protestant churches. Other effects also occurred over time.

• **Religious and Political Divisions** The Reformation created a loss of religious unity in Western Europe. Political divisions resulted as well. Rulers often chose a religion for their nations. While some states remained Catholic, others became Protestant.

Preparing for the Regents

List and explain two causes and two impacts of the Reformation.

Causes

1.

2.

Impacts

1.

2.

- **Religious Conflicts** For more than 100 years after the Reformation, wars sparked in part by religion raged in Europe. In the 1500s, religious civil wars occurred in Germany and France, and Spanish Catholics battled English Protestants. The Thirty Years' War, involving many European states, occurred in the 1600s.

- **Anti-Semitism** The Reformation brought persecution to several groups, especially the Jews. Over time, restrictions placed on Jews by both Protestants and Catholics increased. For example, in some cities, Jews were forced to live in a separate neighborhood. Some Jews were expelled from their homes; others were murdered.

- **Witch Hunts** Religious fervor sometimes led people to accuse others of being witches, agents of the devil. Thousands of people, especially women, were put to death for this reason.

Rise of Nation-States

During the late Middle Ages, kings, nobles, and the Church struggled for power. Feudalism was on the decline. Kings slowly began to increase their power. This shift occurred first in England and France, taking a somewhat different path in each country. These changes marked the beginning of feelings of nationalism—pride and devotion to one's country.

Kings Increased Their Power

Kings in England
- Decided who could build castles and where
- Forced vassals to obey them
- Established common law so that all people were treated the same
- Collected records of who owned land

(overlap)
- Added to their lands
- Set up organized government
- Collected taxes
- Created a royal treasury
- Set up royal courts and royal law

Kings in France
- Made throne hereditary
- Became allies with the Church
- Organized army
- Took French lands from English king

Growth of Royal Power in France

When Hugh Capet became monarch in 987, feudal nobles did not perceive him as a threat to their power. However, Hugh and his heirs, known as the Capetians, slowly increased royal power. The Capetians made the throne hereditary. They also gained vast amounts of land by playing rival nobles against one another. They developed a system of tax collection as well.

The growth of royal power led in part to the Hundred Years' War, a conflict that occurred between England and France from the middle of the 1300s to the mid-1400s. When it looked as if the French would lose the war, a peasant woman named Joan of Arc managed to rally the French to victory. Killed by the English, she became an important focus of French national feeling.

Joan's efforts built up the power of the French monarchs. France's kings developed policies that weakened the power of the nobles and strengthened the power of the crown. The French representative body, the Estates General, did not limit the monarch's power during this period.

Make Inferences

Why was Joan of Arc a hero in France?

Nationhood and Limited Monarchy in England

When the Anglo-Saxon King Edward died in 1066, his brother-in-law was chosen to rule. However, Duke William of Normandy claimed the English throne as well. A battle for the throne began. William invaded England and won the throne. As king, William the Conquerer exerted firm control.

An English Legal System William's successors strengthened English finance and law. Under Henry II, **common law,** or law that was the same for all people, was established. Henry broadened the system of royal justice by sending out traveling justices to enforce laws. Henry also developed an early jury system. When justices visited an area, a jury, or group of men sworn to speak the truth, was gathered by local officials. The jury determined which cases should be brought to trial.

Magna Carta English rulers clashed with nobles and the Church over efforts to extend royal power. In 1215, the nobility rebelled against King John and forced him to sign the Magna Carta, a charter that placed limits on the king's power. The Magna Carta stated, for example, that the monarch must obey the law and that the monarch could not raise taxes without first consulting his Great Council of lords and clergy.

Parliament During the 1200s, this council evolved into the representative assembly known as Parliament. In order to finance their wars, English monarchs repeatedly had to ask Parliament for funds, thus strengthening the power of Parliament.

An English Church The final break between the English monarchy and the Catholic Church occurred under Henry VIII in the 1500s. Angered that the pope refused to grant him an annulment of his marriage, Henry consulted Parliament and had a series of laws passed. Under these laws, Henry gained control of the English church. He created the Anglican Church, or Church of England. In 1558, Henry's daughter, Elizabeth I, became queen and firmly established England as a Protestant nation.

Summary

A growing population and an increase in trade led to a commercial revolution in Europe and a rising middle class. At the same time, the Renaissance brought new ideas about the world and the place of people within it. Great works of art and literature emerged from this period. Inventions such as the printing press helped learning and new ideas to spread throughout Europe. There were also religious changes, as Protestant reformers challenged the authority of the Roman Catholic Church and founded new Christian churches. Throughout this period, feudalism weakened, while nations united under strong monarchs. In 1215, England instituted the Magna Carta, which placed limits on royal power. Under the Magna Carta, the English monarch shared power with Parliament, a representative body.

African Civilizations

The Big Idea

Prior to 1600, people in Africa:

• formed diverse societies in different geographical areas.

• built trading empires in Ghana, Mali, Songhai, and Axum.

• became part of the global trade network through West African and East African trading states.

• were introduced to the religion of Islam.

• maintained traditions around village, family, and religious belief.

Section Overview

Africa's varied climates and terrains contributed to the development of diverse societies on that continent. From about A.D. 800 to 1600, several civilizations rose and fell in Africa. West Africans built the powerful kingdoms of Mali and Songhai as they gained control over internal trade routes. In East Africa, the kingdom of Axum became a center of international trade. Africa played an important role in the global trading network. Trade with the people of Europe, the Middle East, and India encouraged an exchange of ideas between Africa and other lands. During this time, Islam became established in various parts of Africa. Still, traditional patterns of village, family, and religious life remained important through most of Africa.

Key Themes and Concepts

As you review this section, take special note of the following key themes and concepts:

Geography How did the geography of Africa encourage the development of diverse civilizations?

Power What factors contributed to the rise and fall of powerful kingdoms in Africa?

Movement of People and Goods What links did Africa have with global trade routes?

Culture How did traditional art and literary forms reflect the beliefs of African peoples?

Key People and Terms

Place each of the key people and terms into one of these categories: geography or power.

Key People and Terms

As you review this section, be sure you understand the significance of these key people and terms:

savanna	Ghana	Songhai
desert	Mali	Axum
rain forests	Mansa Musa	Swahili

Key Themes and Concepts

Geography
The geographic diversity and geographic barriers of Africa led to the development of many different cultures on the continent.

Africa's Varied Geography

As the second-largest continent in the world, Africa accounts for one-fifth of the land surface on the Earth. Africa includes varied climates and terrains. Much of Africa is made up of **savanna,** or grassy plains. Despite hot weather and occasional droughts, this area generally has good soil and enough rain to support farming. It is therefore the most densely populated climate region. A large part of Africa, however, is made up of **desert,** or dry, barren land. The Sahara in North Africa is the world's largest desert, with extremely hot temperatures during the day and little vegetation. Africa also has a small belt of **rain forests** along the Equator and small areas of Mediterranean climate along the coast of North Africa and at the southern tip of the continent. In these areas, there is fertile farmland.

Africa has few good natural harbors. Because much of the interior is a high plateau, the rivers that flow down to the coast cascade through a series of rapids. Barriers such as these sometimes made travel difficult for Africans.

Despite geographic barriers, early Africans traveled within and beyond their continent. Much of this movement was linked to trade. Africa's gold, salt, iron, copper, and other minerals were important goods in early trade networks.

Traditional Society and Culture

Village Government

In most traditional African communities, power was shared among members of the community rather than exercised by a single leader. Within a village, decisions were often made by a process known as consensus. Village members gathered together for open discussions. Elders and other respected people presented their arguments before a general agreement was reached.

Family Patterns

While the family was the basic unit of society in traditional Africa, patterns of family life varied in several ways. For example, the nuclear family was common in hunting and gathering societies. In a nuclear family, parents and children worked and lived together as a unit. In other communities, and more commonly, several generations lived in one household or near each other as an extended family.

Because traditional African social structures emphasized the group over the individual, extended families who descended from a common ancestor formed clans. Community values were greatly enhanced through identification with a particular clan.

Religious Beliefs

Across Africa, religious beliefs were varied. Like many other ancient peoples, early Africans identified the forces of nature with divine spirits and worshiped many gods and goddesses. Many Africans believed that the spirits of their departed ancestors were present on Earth. They would call on these spirits for help in times of trouble. Some people in these long-ago African societies believed in one supreme being who was the creator and ruler of the universe.

Rise and Fall of African Kingdoms

In Africa, towns soon became part of an important trade network. Gold and salt were the most important products that were traded. People needed salt in their diets to prevent dehydration, the dangerous loss of water from the body. There was plenty of salt in the Sahara, but there was little in the savanna. The people of the savanna traded the plentiful gold of their region to obtain salt from the Sahara.

Strong African rulers created powerful kingdoms by gaining control over the most profitable trade routes. Three trading kingdoms of West Africa were Ghana, Mali, and Songhai. The trading kingdom of Axum thrived in East Africa. Over time, Islam became an important social and religious force, particularly in North Africa and West Africa.

Ghana

Around A.D. 800, the rulers of many farming villages united to create the kingdom of Ghana. Ghana had a powerful king who ruled over a splendid court in his capital of Kumbi Saleh. Income from the gold trade allowed him to maintain a

Key Themes and Concepts

Movement of People and Goods
Throughout history, trade had a major impact on the societies of Africa. Trade brought new cultural influences to Africa, adding to its diversity.

Note Taking

Reading Skill:
Identify Main Ideas
Make a table. As you read, write the main ideas about traditional society and culture in Africa.

Government	Family	Religion
•	•	•
•	•	•

Preparing for the Regents

• As you read, take note of what forces contributed to the rise and fall of the kingdoms of Ghana, Mali, Songhai, and Axum.

large army of foot soldiers and cavalry. This army helped the king to control and expand his kingdom.

Muslim merchants brought their religion and ideas when they settled in the kingdom of Ghana. The king had Muslim officials and thus was influenced by Muslim military technology and ideas about government. Ghana also absorbed Muslim cultural influences, such as Arabic writing and Muslim styles of architecture. Most of the people of Ghana, however, kept their traditional religious beliefs. Women in Ghana had a high status and played an active role in the economic life of the empire.

Mali

Mali was also ruled by powerful kings, called mansas. Under **Mansa Musa,** the most powerful ruler, Mali extended its borders and dominated West Africa. Mansa Musa's large army kept order in the empire and protected it from attack. Although warriors were an elite class in Mali, most of its people were farmers and herders.

Mansa Musa ran an efficient government, appointing governors to rule particular areas. Mansa Musa converted to Islam, basing his system of justice on the Qur'an. He also made the city of Timbuktu a center of Muslim learning. The empire, however, declined in the 1400s, when the people could not agree on who should rule the kingdom.

Key Themes and Concepts

Belief Systems

After Mansa Musa converted to Islam, he traveled to Mecca. In making this trip, he fulfilled one of the Five Pillars of Islam. His pilgrimage had a cultural impact on Mali, since Mansa Musa brought home Muslim scholars and artists and forged new trading ties.

Kingdoms of West Africa
Trading centers developed over time throughout Africa. Powerful kingdoms took control of the prosperous cities and their trade.

Kingdoms of West Africa

Ghana (800–1000)	Mali (1200–1450)	Songhai (1450–1600)
• Controlled trade in gold and salt across West Africa	• Conquered kingdom of Ghana	• Grew into largest West African state
• Women worked in business and government	• Mansa Musa became a great emperor	• Controlled important trade routes
• King had Muslim advisors	• Mali controlled gold trade routes	• Emperor set up Muslim dynasty
	• Timbuktu became a great trading city and center of learning	

Songhai

Like Ghana and Mali, the **Songhai** empire depended on a strong army to control trade routes. The emperor Sonni Ali built Songhai into the largest state that had ever existed in West Africa, bringing the wealthy city of Timbuktu under his control. Songhai established an efficient bureaucracy to govern the kingdom. Its people also expanded trade to Europe and Asia. Songhai prospered until the late 1500s, when civil war broke out. At that time, invaders from the north defeated the disunited forces of Songhai and caused the downfall of the kingdom.

Axum

As in the kingdoms of West Africa, trade helped **Axum** become a powerful kingdom. Axum's location on the Red Sea helped Axumites command a thriving trade network linking Africa, India, and the Mediterranean world. Axum's population was descended from African farmers and from traders who had immigrated from Arabia. This merging of cultures introduced Jewish and Christian religious traditions to Axum. After being weakened by civil war and cut off from its harbors, Axum declined.

Key Themes and Concepts

Government

The West African kingdoms were ruled by powerful emperors. They had strong armies to maintain order and protect the kingdoms from attack.

Preparing for the Regents

• What influence did Islam have on the kingdoms of West Africa?

Africa's Role in Global Trade

African states in both the eastern and western parts of the continent played a significant role in global trade. The Mediterranean and Red Seas linked Africa to the Middle East and Europe. In addition, the Indian Ocean linked East Africa to India and other Asian lands. Products from the African interior were transported overland to the coast and then out of Africa.

African Kingdoms, 1000 B.C.–A.D. 1600

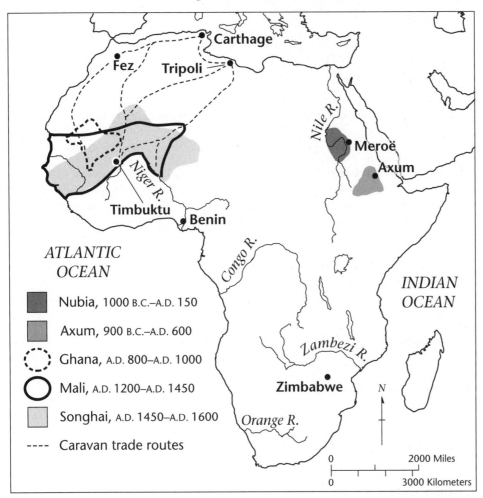

ATLANTIC OCEAN

Nubia, 1000 B.C.–A.D. 150

Axum, 900 B.C.–A.D. 600

Ghana, A.D. 800–A.D. 1000

Mali, A.D. 1200–A.D. 1450

Songhai, A.D. 1450–A.D. 1600

Caravan trade routes

INDIAN OCEAN

0 2000 Miles
0 3000 Kilometers

African Kingdoms
People of West Africa traded among themselves for many centuries. By about the 400s, this regional trade system had grown into an extensive trans-Saharan trade system connecting much of Africa. Over the centuries, different kingdoms controlled the routes.

Key Themes and Concepts

Geography
The bodies of water on Africa's east and west coasts were busy highways for trade with Europe and Asia. These contacts had an effect on Africa's history and culture.

Hausa

In the 1300s, the Hausa people built city-states in what became present-day Nigeria. The products of Hausa cotton weavers and leatherworkers from the city-states traveled on caravans across the Sahara and sometimes were transported as far as Europe. By the 1500s, the Hausa dominated Saharan trade routes.

Benin

In the rain forests on the Guinea coast, the Benin people traded ivory, pepper, and eventually enslaved people with their northern neighbors in the savanna. Benin traders also dealt with the Portuguese, who began arriving in growing numbers in the 1500s. The people of Benin learned how to cast bronze and brass. Benin bronze sculpture often portrays warriors and Benin rulers.

East African City-States

Around 600, trading cities rose along the coast of East Africa as Arab and Persian merchants established trading communities. By 1000, East African port cities such

Preparing for the Regents

Describe one positive and one negative effect of global trade on Africa.

Positive:

Negative:

as Mogadishu, Kilwa, and Sofala conducted a booming trade with India. Part of this commerce system included enslaved people, who were seized inland and then sold to Persian traders.

Trade led to a mixing of cultures in the city-states of East Africa. Over time, this blending of cultures resulted in the rise of a new language, **Swahili,** in which Arabic words were mixed with Bantu, an African language.

Contributions

The Arts

African art, most often created in ivory, wood, and bronze, was sometimes used for decorative purposes, such as jewelry. More often, however, art was closely tied to religion. Statues and masks, for example, were used in religious ceremonies and rituals.

African art also strengthened bonds within the community. Art linked people who created it with those who used it. Moreover, decorative patterns on an object often identified it as the work of a particular clan or as a possession of royalty.

Literary Traditions

Africans used both oral and written literature to preserve their culture. Arabic was a common written language used by people in parts of Africa that were influenced by Islam. Today, Arabic documents offer insight into the laws, religions, and history of African societies.

Most often, histories and folk tales were passed down in oral form from generation to generation. Histories praised the heroism of famous ancestors or kings. Folk tales, on the other hand, blended fantasy and humor to teach important moral lessons.

Education

In most African societies, it was the duty of the elders to teach boys and girls what their special roles would be in the community. The elders also passed down information about their clan's history and religious beliefs.

In the 1400s, Timbuktu in Mali had become a leading center of learning. Manuscripts were brought to Timbuktu to be sold at high prices. The university at Timbuktu, built by Mansa Musa, attracted students from all over the Muslim world.

Commerce

The development of commerce by African kingdoms did much to establish trade routes that would endure for centuries. Commerce also introduced Africa to crops and animals from other lands. In addition, a rich mix of cultures developed. An unfortunate result of commerce, however, was the rise of trading enslaved people.

Summary

Africa's geography encouraged the formation of separate kingdoms. After A.D. 800, powerful trading empires formed in western Africa. Through trade, Africans were introduced to Islam. During the same period, trading kingdoms on Africa's eastern coast were forming ties with India, the Middle East, and the Mediterranean. African societies were exposed to many new influences but retained the traditional importance of village, family, and religion.

Vocabulary Builder

manuscript—(MAN yoo skript) *n.* a book or document written by hand

Note Taking

Reading Skill:
Identify Main Ideas and Details
Make a concept web. Complete it with main ideas and details about the contributions of African societies. Add more circles if needed.

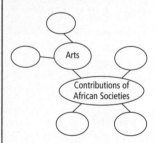

Arts

Contributions of African Societies

Multiple Choice

Directions: Review the Test-Taking Strategies section of this book. Then answer the following questions, drawn from actual Regents examinations. For each statement or question, choose the *number* of the word or expression that, of those given, best completes the statement or answers the question.

1   One similarity between the cultures of traditional China and traditional Japan was that

   (1) the educated class was held in high esteem
   (2) religion played a minor role in society
   (3) social mobility was encouraged
   (4) the people elected the political leaders

2   The code of bushido of the Japanese samurai is most similar to the

   (1) belief in reincarnation and karma of Hindus
   (2) practice of chivalry by European knights
   (3) teachings of Judaism
   (4) Enlightenment writers' theory of natural rights

3   When Russia was under Mongol domination, the effect on Russia was to

   (1) end feudalism
   (2) convert the Russian people to Hinduism
   (3) keep Russia isolated from Western Europe
   (4) reunite the Orthodox Christian Church with the Roman Catholic Church

4   Which was a major characteristic of the Renaissance?

   (1) conformity
   (2) humanism
   (3) mysticism
   (4) obedience

5   Which long-term effect did the Magna Carta and the establishment of Parliament have on England?

   (1) The system of mercantilism was strengthened.
   (2) The power of the monarchy was limited.
   (3) The new American form of government was adopted.
   (4) The influence of the middle class was reduced.

6   Which societal condition was basic to the development of Greek philosophy and Renaissance art?

   (1) rigid social classes
   (2) emphasis on individualism
   (3) religious uniformity
   (4) mass education

7   Which factor helped most to bring about the Protestant Reformation?

   (1) The Catholic clergy had lost faith in their religion.
   (2) Islam had attracted many converts in Western Europe.
   (3) Kings and princes in northern Europe resented the power of the Roman Catholic Church.
   (4) The exploration of the Americas led to the introduction of new religious ideas.

8   Which was a major result of the Reformation?

   (1) New Christian denominations emerged.

   (2) Religious teachings were no longer allowed
       in the universities.

   (3) The Crusades were organized.

   (4) The power of the pope was strengthened.

Base your answers to questions 9 and 10 on the map below and on your knowledge of social studies.

Trade Routes (13th – 15th centuries)

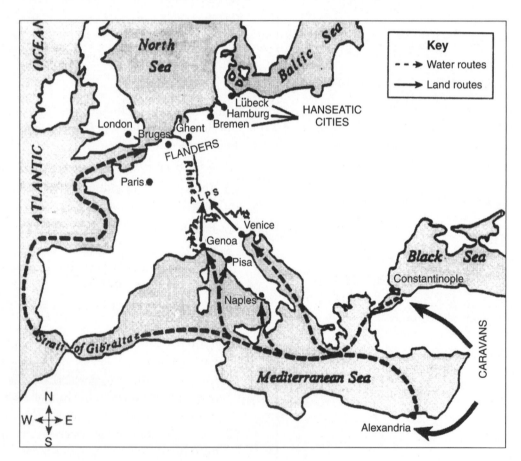

9 One reason Italian city-states were able to dominate the trade pattern shown on the map was that they were

   (1) centrally located on the Mediterranean Sea

   (2) situated north of the Alps

   (3) unified by the Hanseatic League

   (4) located on the trade routes of the North Sea

10 The development of trade along the routes shown on the map led to the

   (1) decline of the Greek city-states

   (2) start of the Renaissance in Italy

   (3) beginning of the Crusades to the Middle East

   (4) first religious wars in Europe

11 African kingdoms such as Ghana, Songhai, and Axum flourished mainly because they

   (1) controlled important trade routes

   (2) developed self-sufficient economies

   (3) became religious centers considered sacred by Africans

   (4) received support from European colonial governments

12 Mansa Musa's journey to Mecca in the 1300s is evidence that

   (1) the Crusades had a great influence on western Africa

   (2) most African leaders were educated in the Middle East

   (3) European culture was superior to the cultures of western Africa

   (4) Islam had a major influence on the Mali empire

Thematic Essay Question

In developing your answer, be sure to keep these general definitions in mind:

    (a) <u>describe</u> means "to illustrate something in words or tell about it"

    (b) <u>identify</u> means "to establish or indicate who or what someone (or something) is"

    (c) <u>explain</u> means "to make plain or understandable; to give reasons for or causes of; to show the logical development or relationships of"

Directions: Write a well-organized essay that includes an introduction, several paragraphs addressing the task below, and a conclusion.

Theme: **Change**

> Throughout global history, events and changes have occurred that historians have considered turning points.

Task:

- Describe what would make an event or a change a turning point in global history.
- Identify and describe two specific examples of turning points in global history.
- Explain why each of these events or changes is considered a turning point in global history. Provide specific examples of the impacts each had.

You may discuss any major changes or turning points from any period of global history you have studied. Some periods you might want to consider are prehistoric times or Europe in the 1400s.

You are not limited to these suggestions.

Do not use the United States in your answer.

Guidelines:

In your essay, be sure to
- Develop all aspects of the task
- Support the theme with relevant facts, examples, and details
- Use a logical and clear plan of organization, including an introduction and a conclusion that are beyond a simple restatement of the theme

Document-Based Question

This question is based on the accompanying documents. The question is designed to test your ability to work with historical documents. Some of these documents have been edited for the purposes of this question. As you analyze the documents, take into account the source of each document and any point of view that may be presented in the document.

Historical Context:

> Throughout global history, cultures and civilizations have held different viewpoints on diversity in society. Diversity has been seen as both positive and negative.

Task: Using the information from the documents and your knowledge of global history, answer the questions that follow each document in Part A. Your answers to the questions will help you write the Part B essay in which you will be asked to

- Evaluate the different viewpoints societies have held about diversity
- Discuss the positive and negative impacts that diversity may have on a society

In developing your answers, be sure to keep these general definitions in mind:

(a) <u>evaluate</u> means "to examine and judge the significance, worth, or condition of; to determine the value of"

(b) <u>discuss</u> means "to make observations about something using facts, reasoning, and argument; to present in some detail"

Part A: Short Answer

Directions: Analyze the documents and answer the question or questions that follow each document, using the space provided.

Document #1

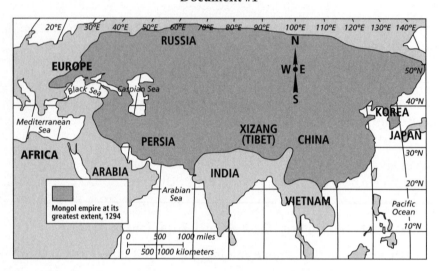

1. Use this map to support the statement that the Mongols ruled a diverse empire.

_____

_____

_____

Document #2

A nation is an association of those who are brought together by language, by given geographical conditions, or by the role assigned them by history, who acknowledge the same principles and who march together to the conquest of a single definite goal under the rule of a common body of law. . . . It is necessary that [a nation's] ideas be shown to other lands in their beauty and purity, free from any alien mixture.

—Giuseppe Mazzini, Italian nationalist leader, 1835

2. Did Giuseppe Mazzini believe that diversity of ideas within a nation was positive or negative? Explain your answer.

_____

_____

_____

Document #3

To make our dream of a united, democratic, non-racial, non-sexist South Africa real is an immense challenge. Yet we look forward to the future with confidence and hope because we know that the people of South Africa — every racial group, every faith, every ethnic and language community in our country — are possessed of many talents, skills, and an infinite resourcefulness.

—Nelson Mandela, President of South Africa, 1994

3. Does this document express a positive view of diversity? Explain your answer.

_____

_____

Document #4

India has not ever been an easy country to understand. Perhaps it is too deep, contradictory, and diverse.
—Indira Gandhi, Prime Minister of India, 1970s

4. What problems caused by diversity does Indira Gandhi refer to in this quotation?

_____

_____

Document-Based Question

Part B

Essay

Directions: Write a well-organized essay that includes an introduction, several paragraphs, and a conclusion. Use evidence from *at least **three*** of the documents in your essay. Support your response with relevant facts, examples, and details. Include additional outside information.

Historical Context:

Throughout global history, cultures and civilizations have held different viewpoints on diversity in society. Diversity has been seen as both positive and negative.

Task: Using the information from the documents and your knowledge of global history, write an essay in which you

- Evaluate the positive and negative impacts of diversity on a society
- Discuss whether you think diversity has a positive or negative influence today

Guidelines:

In your essay, be sure to
- Develop all aspects of the task
- Incorporate information from *at least **three*** of the documents
- Incorporate relevant outside information
- Support the theme with relevant facts, examples, and details
- Use a logical and clear plan of organization, including an introduction and a conclusion that are beyond a restatement of the theme

The First Global Age
(1450–1770)

Unit Overview

In the 1400s and 1500s, Europeans began exploring much of the world. These European explorers encountered rich and powerful civilizations in Africa, Asia, and the Americas. Thus began a period of increasing global interaction that continues to the present day. As interaction among civilizations increased, so did conquests and global exchanges. Around the world, these developments had significant impacts on the way people lived. One major result was that, by the 1600s and 1700s, Western European monarchs had increased their power within their own countries and around the world.

Using Good Social Studies Practices

Global Reasoning

Some of the many themes developed in Unit 4 are:

economic systems	government
belief systems	change
places and regions	culture
movement of people and goods	political systems

Choose one of the themes listed above. As you review Unit 4, create a timeline based on the theme you have chosen and the changing interactions between regions and places. Your timeline should stretch from 1450 to 1770 and include major developments and key turning points having to do with your theme.

Mesoamerican Civilizations

Section Overview

Tens of thousands of years ago, Paleolithic hunters migrated to North America from Asia. People learned to cultivate plants and to domesticate animals. These changes led to an increase in population. In the Americas, complex societies developed. The Olmecs and, later, the Mayas and Aztecs ruled great empires in Mexico. In South America, the Incas conquered a vast area along the western coast. The people in these empires were skilled farmers, were devoted to their religions, and possessed advanced knowledge in many areas.

Key Themes and Concepts

As you review this section, take special note of the following key themes and concepts:

Economic Systems Why was agriculture important to Mesoamerican civilizations?

Belief Systems What significance did religion have in the empires of the Americas?

Government What types of governments allowed Mesoamerican societies to rule large areas?

Culture and Intellectual Life What were the accomplishments and advances of the Mesoamerican empires?

Key People and Terms

As you review this section, be sure you understand the significance of these key people and terms:

pre-Columbian	Incas
Mayas	terraces
Aztecs	quipus

Geographic Setting

During the last ice age, large amounts of ocean water froze into thick ice sheets. A land bridge between Siberia and Alaska was created as the ocean levels dropped. Across this bridge, groups of Paleolithic hunters in Asia followed herds of bison and mammoths into North America. Over the following centuries, the nomadic hunter-gatherers in North America migrated eastward and southward. These first Americans settled in many different regions and had to adapt to a variety of climates and landforms, including woodlands, fertile plains, mountain ranges, and thick rain forests.

Slowly, between 8500 B.C. and 2000 B.C., important changes occurred. Groups of Americans learned to cultivate crops. They began to domesticate animals, perhaps in response to the disappearance of large mammals. Neolithic farmers in Mexico raised a variety of crops, including corn, beans, sweet potatoes, peppers, tomatoes,

The Big Idea

The Mayas, Aztecs, and Incas:

- developed agriculture that could support large populations.

- placed great importance on religion.

- formed governments that ruled large empires.

- had advanced knowledge in areas such as agriculture, engineering, and architecture.

Key People and Terms

For each of the key people and terms, write a sentence explaining its significance.

Key Themes and Concepts

Technology and Innovation The Agricultural Revolution occurred throughout the world during Neolithic times.

and squash. Farmers in South America domesticated llamas and other animals that were valued for their wool.

In the Americas, as in Africa and Eurasia, this agricultural revolution had a major impact on the population. Farmers settled into villages that sometimes developed into large religious centers, which could then grow into major cities. The first great American civilizations developed in Mesoamerica (also called Middle America), the region that includes Mexico and Central America.

Ancient Cultures of Mexico

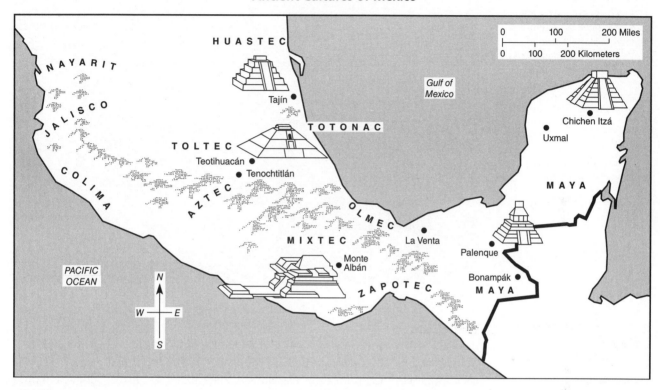

Ancient Cultures of Mexico
The descendants of the first Americans spread throughout the Americas. They established small settlements and large civilizations. Each society developed individual traits that set it apart. But they also shared some cultural elements, such as the architecture of the stepped pyramid.

Pre-Columbian Civilizations in the Americas

Civilizations that emerged in Mesoamerica are called pre-Columbian because they existed before the arrival of Christopher Columbus in 1492. The earliest of these major American civilizations was the Olmec Empire, which developed along the Gulf coast of Mexico and lasted from around 1400 B.C. to 500 B.C. The Olmecs built pyramid-shaped temples, invented a calendar and a system of writing, and were very religious. Through trade links, their influence extended over a large area, and characteristics of their civilization were common in later Mesoamerican civilizations.

The Mayas

One major civilization influenced by the Olmecs was that of the Mayas, who flourished from about A.D. 300 to 900. During this period, the Mayas developed a complex agricultural society. They established large city-states in southern Mexico and throughout much of Central America.

Farming and Trade

Farmers made up most of the Mayan population. Men usually cultivated the crops, which included maize (corn), beans, and squash. Women were in charge of turning these crops into food. Farmers paid taxes, in the form of food, to support the cities and their temples. The Mayas accumulated much wealth from a profitable trade system. Traders carried valuable honey, cocoa, and feathers across Central America along hard-packed dirt roads.

Mayan temple

Religion

Because of the significance of religion to the Mayas, priests occupied an exalted place in the social hierarchy. These religious leaders held such importance because they alone could conduct the elaborate rituals that the Mayas believed would ensure bountiful harvests and victories in battle.

Social Structure

Mayan civilization featured a distinct social hierarchy. Each Mayan city-state had its own ruling chief. Immediately below this chief were the nobles, who served as city officials and military leaders. Although those in the ruling class were usually men, women could occasionally obtain some degree of power. Most Mayas, however, were farmers.

Contributions

Architecture In their cities, the Mayas built giant pyramid temples and large palaces. Elaborate paintings and carvings on the walls depicted events from Mayan history.

Agriculture Despite the tropical environment, the Mayas grew enough food to support large city populations. Farmers made this possible by clearing out the dense rain forests and then building raised fields that were capable of holding and draining rainwater.

Learning and Science Perhaps the most impressive achievement of the Mayas was their advanced learning. Mayas developed a hieroglyphic (picture) system of writing and recorded much of their knowledge in books made of bark. Mayan priests developed a very accurate 365-day calendar. They also used a numbering system and understood the concept of zero before Europeans did.

Key Themes and Concepts

Belief Systems
The importance of religion to the Mayas may be judged from the size of their temples. Priests climbed these tall structures to perform rituals while the common people watched from far below.

Key Themes and Concepts

Economic Systems
The Mayas were advanced enough to modify their natural environment to increase their agricultural output. For example, they developed ways to drain excess water from fields.

Decline

Around A.D. 900, the Mayas abandoned their cities. Historians speculate that warfare or overpopulation may have caused agriculture to decline or that there were revolts by the lower classes. Remnants of this great culture remain, however. Today, millions of people in Guatemala and southern Mexico speak Mayan languages.

The Aztecs

In the late 1200s, a nomadic group migrated from the north into the Valley of Mexico. They settled in the area, establishing their capital at Tenochtitlán. The Aztecs, who developed from this group, were fierce warriors. In the 1400s, the Aztecs used conquests and alliances to build a huge empire. Their capital grew to become a magnificent city with temples, palaces, gardens, and zoos.

Aztec Expansion

The Aztecs founded Tenochtitlán in 1315. In the early 1400s, Aztec leaders began forming alliances with neighboring states. The Aztecs soon became the dominant power in what is now central Mexico. Then, through a series of military conquests over hundreds of smaller states, the Aztecs steadily expanded their empire. Each conquered state was given an Aztec governor. The Aztecs became wealthy from tribute, payment they took from conquered peoples. By the early 1500s, the Aztec empire covered most of Mexico and included about 30 million people.

Social Structure

Rulers, Nobles, and Priests Unlike the Mayas, the Aztecs were ruled by a single emperor, who was chosen by a council of nobles and priests. Below this ruler was the noble class, from which officials, judges, and provincial governors were drawn.

Warriors and Traders The warriors came next in the Aztec class structure. A warrior might rise into the noble class through superior performance on the battlefield. Traders formed another group in Aztec society. They carried goods over long distances to exchange for exotic products from peoples who lived beyond the empire. Traders also scouted distant lands to help plan future conquests.

Farmers and Slaves Most of the people in the empire were farmers. Slaves made up the lowest class in the social structure. Members of this group were mainly criminals or enemy soldiers who had been captured. Despite their lowly status, they still had certain rights guaranteed by Aztec law. Some slaves even owned land and eventually bought their freedom.

Religion

Religion was important to the Aztecs. As in Mayan society, priests gained significance because they led rituals that were believed to appease the gods, who would then prevent disasters. The Aztecs built a huge pyramid in the center of Tenochtitlán to honor their chief deity, the sun god.

To please their gods, Aztec priests offered many thousands of human sacrifices. Both the Olmecs and the Mayas had also practiced human sacrifice, but not on such a large scale. Aztec sacrificial victims were usually captured enemy soldiers.

Contributions

Learning and Science Aztec priests devised an accurate calendar. They also established schools and recorded historical events. Aztec medical practices were advanced enough that practitioners could set broken bones and treat dental cavities.

Preparing for the Regents

- Compare the achievements of the Mayas with those of one or more of the classical civilizations of Eurasia and Africa.

Vocabulary Builder

alliance—(uh LY uns) *n.* an arrangement in which two or more countries, groups, etc., agree to work together to try to change or achieve something

Key Themes and Concepts

Power
The Aztecs' ability to collect tribute from so many groups over such a large area illustrates their power in the region.

Comparisons

List two similarities and two differences between the Mayas and the Aztecs.

Similarities:

1.

2.

Differences:

1.

2.

Key Themes and Concepts

Innovation
The development of a calendar was an important feature of nearly every early civilization. Calendars were useful in agriculture because they told early peoples when to plant and when to prepare for floods.

Make Inferences

What are some advantages of building a city on an island in a lake? What are some disadvantages?

Architecture and Engineering The Aztec capital of Tenochtitlán was one of the great achievements of Mesoamerican civilization. Built on the site of present-day Mexico City, Tenochtitlán began as two small islands in Lake Texcoco. Engineers filled in parts of the lake and built wide stone causeways to connect Tenochtitlán to the mainland. Architects designed huge pyramid temples, an elaborate emperor's place, and busy outdoor markets. An estimated 200,000 people lived in Tenochtitlán in 1500, making it the largest and most densely populated settlement in Mesoamerica.

Agriculture As their population grew, the Aztecs found ingenious ways to create more farmland. They used a variety of fertilizers and converted swampy areas into productive farmland. They also built *chinampas*, artificial islands made of earth piled on reed mats that were anchored to the shallow bed of Lake Texcoco. On these "floating gardens" Aztec farmers raised corn, squash, and beans. The Aztecs' ability to produce an abundance of food was a major factor in the success of their empire.

The Incas

In the 1400s, the Incas emerged from the Andes Mountains and conquered a large area that extended over 2,500 miles down the Pacific coast. The Incas ruled an empire made up of many separate conquered peoples.

A Centralized Government

An emperor ruled the Incas. The first emperor was a warrior who led his armies through many successful campaigns of conquest. The emperor held absolute power and owned all of the people, land, herds, and mines. The emperor was also the chief religious leader and claimed divine status as the son of the sun.

Preparing for the Regents

• How was the Incan emperor similar to the pharaohs of ancient Egypt?

The emperor headed a strong central government from the mountain capital at Cuzco. Nobles ran the provinces along with local chieftains from the conquered people of each area. Other officials collected taxes, enforced laws, and performed routine government business. The Incan government strictly controlled the lives of the millions of people within its empire. Everyone had to speak the same language, Quechua, and practice the Incan religion.

An Empire Linked by Roads

The emperor could not have imposed this centralized rule over such a large area without a remarkable system of roads. Runners used these roads to carry news swiftly from far-off provinces to the emperor in the capital. This arrangement allowed him to keep a close watch on his empire. If necessary, Incan armies could move quickly over the roads to crush any rebellions that formed in distant corners of the empire.

Key Themes and Concepts

Government
The Incan government used military power, local rulers, and an excellent road system to impose a more centralized control over the empire.

Religion

Incan religion affected all parts of daily life. The people worshiped many gods related to forces of nature as well as guardian spirits in the home. The chief Incan deity was the sun god. A powerful class of priests conducted rituals and led monthly religious festivals that featured sports and games.

Contributions

Engineering and Architecture The Incan system of roads stands out as a major accomplishment of their civilization. It extended more than 12,000 miles, included hundreds of bridges, and even used tunnels and steps to pass through mountainous terrain.

Key Themes and Concepts

Culture and Intellectual Life
Like many other groups throughout history, the Incas built upon the work of earlier civilizations to achieve even greater progress.

The capital city of Cuzco was home to other Incan engineering feats. In the city center stood the giant Temple of the Sun, built with huge stone blocks and featuring inner walls lined with gold. The engineering of this temple was so advanced that the building was strong enough to withstand major earthquakes.

Agriculture Like the Aztecs, the Incas frequently borrowed and built upon ideas from other societies. Incan farmers used stone walls to improve upon **terraces** built by earlier peoples. The improved terraces of the Aztecs held strips of land in place on steep hillsides and prevented rain from washing away the soil. The terraces made it possible to farm effectively in places where flat land was scarce.

Communication Incan government officials kept records by means of a system of knotted, colored strings called **quipus.** Historians believe that quipus may have been used to record dates and events as well as population and crop statistics.

Science The Incas had a calendar but were not as advanced in astronomy as the Mayas had been. One area in which the Incas excelled was medicine. They performed successful surgery to treat head wounds. The Incas also had knowledge about diseases and medicines; they used herbs as antiseptics.

Vocabulary Builder

feat—(feet) *n.* something that is an impressive achievement, because it needs a lot of skill, strength, etc., to do

Achievements of Mesoamerican Civilizations

Mayans	Aztecs	Incas
• Built giant pyramid temples	• Built city of Tenochtitlán by filling in part of a lake	• Built system of roads, bridges, and tunnels to connect empire
• Cleared rain forest and built raised fields for farming	• Drained swamps, built artificial islands and floating gardens for farming	• Built temple that withstood earthquakes
• Developed hieroglyphic writing	• Established schools	• Used terraces to farm sides of mountains
• Developed 365-day calendar	• Developed a calendar	• Kept records using knotted strings called quipus
• Used numbering system	• Treated broken bones and dental cavities	• Performed surgery and used herbs as antiseptics

Note Taking

Reading Skill:
Recognize Causes
Make a chart. Show the causes of the success of the Incas. Add as many boxes as you need.

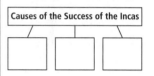

Summary

Complex civilizations grew in the Americas from about 1400 B.C. to A.D. 1500. The Olmecs had the first major American civilization, followed by the Mayas and Aztecs in Mexico and Central America and by the Incas in South America. For all these civilizations, agriculture was a primary economic activity that allowed populations to grow. Religion unified the empires. The later Mesoamerican civilizations developed complex government systems and trade networks. Mesoamerican societies made advances in agriculture, medicine, mathematics, engineering, and other areas.

Preparing for the Regents

List three ways in which the Incan and Roman empires were similar.

1.

2.

3.

The Ming Dynasty in China

The **Big Idea**

During the Ming Dynasty, the Chinese:

• restored Chinese rule and reaffirmed belief in Chinese superiority.

• achieved economic and cultural growth.

• after a brief period of exploration, sought to limit contact with most outsiders.

• continued to influence neighboring Asian countries culturally and intellectually.

Section Overview

In the mid-1300s, the Chinese overthrew foreign conquerors, the Mongols, and restored self-rule under the Ming dynasty. Ming China experienced an economic and cultural revival. In the early 1400s, China began voyages of exploration and came into contact with Europe. Later the empire turned inward, seeking to protect itself from outside influences. China did, however, greatly affect nearby Asian lands that fell into its zone of influence. Over time, Chinese culture exerted religious and cultural influence in Korea, Japan, and Southeast Asia.

Key Themes and Concepts

As you review this section, take special note of the following key themes and concepts:

Change How did Chinese government, industry, and trade change after China overthrew its Mongol rulers and established a restored Chinese empire?

Choice Why did China choose to isolate itself from foreign trade after 1433?

Culture What impact did China have on other societies in Asia?

Key People

As you review this section, be sure you understand the significance of these key people and terms:

Ming dynasty	**Zheng He**
Middle Kingdom	**Matteo Ricci**

Key People and Terms

For each of the key people and terms, write a sentence explaining its significance.

Key Themes and Concepts

Change
The Mongol Yuan dynasty, instituted by Kublai Khan, declined after his death. This decline, coupled with the fact that many Chinese hated their Mongol rulers, led to the uprisings that ended in the formation of the Ming dynasty.

Restoration of Chinese Rule

In 1368, about 90 years after Mongol leader Kublai Khan had established Mongol rule in China, Chinese rule was restored under the **Ming dynasty.** Although the Mongols had improved trade and transportation, many Chinese resented foreign rule. In 1368, a peasant-led rebellion successfully overthrew Mongol rule, leading to the establishment of the Ming dynasty.

The Middle Kingdom

Under the Ming, China was once again ruled by the Chinese. Ming leaders sought to restore the country's greatness and its supremacy in the region. China traditionally thought of itself as the Middle Kingdom, the center of the earth and the source of civilization.

Ming Government Reform

Ming rulers enacted reforms to improve the government. They brought back the civil service system. In this system, candidates had to pass a difficult exam. Confucian learning once again became important, because knowledge of Confucian classics was a key part of the exam. Ming leaders also established a board of censors to eliminate corruption in the bureaucracy.

Vocabulary Builder

censor—(SEN sur) *n.* a person who supervises the conduct and morals of others

Looking Outward and Turning Inward

During the first several decades of the 1400s, the Chinese admiral **Zheng He** established links with many distant commerce centers and brought exotic animals back to China as tribute to the emperor. They were housed in the imperial zoo. After Zheng He's death in 1433, the Ming emperor banned the building of large oceangoing ships, and China, as a result, suddenly halted its voyages. The reasons for this abrupt change in policy were both economic and cultural. Zheng's voyages had not brought profits to the empire, and his fleets were costly to maintain. Also, Confucian scholars taught that China had the most advanced civilization in the world. Limiting contact with foreign influences therefore seemed the best way to preserve ancient traditions.

Preparing for the Regents

- Why did China's attitude toward commercial contacts with foreign lands change after 1433?

Economic and Cultural Contributions

Agriculture

Advances in agriculture, such as better fertilization methods, made it possible for farmers on China's eastern plains to produce enough food to support a large population. In the 1500s, corn and sweet potatoes were introduced from the Americas, further improving food production by Chinese farmers.

Effects

What was the main effect of advances in agriculture in China?

Industry and Trade

The Chinese also made advances in industry during the Ming period. They utilized new technologies to increase manufacturing production. Industries such as the making of porcelain, tools, and paper thrived in Chinese cities. The Ming also repaired their neglected canal system to improve trade links across the country.

Arts and Literature

The arts flowered during the Ming dynasty. Artists developed new styles of landscape painting and created beautiful porcelain jars and vases. Chinese silks were much admired by Europeans.

Confucian scholars produced classical poetry; other writers wrote popular fiction. Dramatic artists developed new art forms that combined drama, music, and dance.

Preparing for the Regents

- What contributions did the Ming dynasty make to China and to the world?

Preparing for the Regents

• What attitudes did Europe and China hold regarding trade with one another?

China and the West

European Interest in China

When Portuguese and other European merchants reached East Asia in the 1500s, they were impressed by Chinese goods. European visitors to China wrote enthusiastically about the exquisite silks and porcelains they found there. Europeans were also fascinated with Chinese production of guns and gunpowder.

Chinese Indifference

Ming leaders severely restricted foreign trade, believing European goods to be inferior. However, they allowed limited trade at the coastal outpost of Macao, near present-day Guangzhou. Imperial officials supervised this trade strictly.

Some European scholars, such as the Jesuit priest **Matteo Ricci,** did gain acceptance among the Ming. In the 1580s, the Chinese welcomed Ricci, who shared with them his knowledge of European arts and sciences. Although the Chinese were open to learning about European technology, they had little interest in the religious beliefs that Ricci and the Jesuits sought to promote.

China's Impact Within Asia

Over time, Chinese civilization exerted a cultural influence over its neighbors in Asia. Korea, Japan, and Southeast Asia were affected by China's customs and values.

Korea

Throughout history, China's civilization has influenced its smaller neighbor, Korea. At times, China even took political control of Korea. China affected Korea in many ways.

Korea continued to maintain its own culture, however. Sometimes, as with the Chinese civil service system, Korea made adaptations that fit its own traditions. After learning to make porcelain from the Chinese, Koreans developed a distinctive blue-green glaze called celadon. Korea also developed its own system of writing. The Korean language is unrelated to Chinese.

Key Themes and Concepts

Culture
China's ancient concept of itself as the Middle Kingdom, with a supreme culture, often motivated it to influence other cultures. It also made China unwilling, throughout much of its history, to be influenced by other cultures.

Key Themes and Concepts

Nationalism and Identity
Because of its location on the Asian mainland, Korea was strongly influenced by China culturally and sometimes politically. Even so, Koreans developed their own culture and way of life.

China Influences Korea

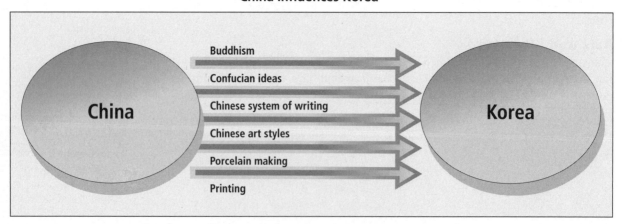

China → Korea
- Buddhism
- Confucian ideas
- Chinese system of writing
- Chinese art styles
- Porcelain making
- Printing

Japan

Korea served as a cultural bridge linking China with the Japanese islands. In the A.D. 500s, missionaries from Korea introduced Buddhism and other aspects of Chinese culture to Japan. In the centuries that followed, Japanese nobles studied in China, returning with Chinese ideas and technology. Later, however, the Japanese became less interested in China and began to blend Chinese ideas with their own.

Japanese paintings were often influenced by Chinese landscape techniques. Japanese artists developed their own styles, however, recreating historical events on magnificent scrolls. During Japan's feudal age, Japanese samurai increasingly adopted the beliefs of a Buddhist sect from China known in Japan as Zen. Zen Buddhism greatly influenced Japanese society, including its theater, literature, and art.

Southeast Asia

The diverse cultural region of Southeast Asia consisted of a mainland area and scattered islands. It was greatly influenced by traders from China and India, who often passed through Southeast Asian ports. Buddhism, Hinduism, and Islam all entered the region.

Indian influences prevailed in much of Southeast Asia. In Vietnam, however, China exerted a greater influence. China had conquered Vietnam by the first century B.C., and it ruled the region for 1,000 years. Vietnam absorbed the Confucian civil service system and established a bureaucracy that resembled China's. Even so, Vietnam retained a strong cultural identity of its own.

Summary

The Ming dynasty restored Chinese rule and remained in power for more than 250 years. During this period, China prospered economically and culturally. After 1433, however, the Chinese sought to limit contact with the outside world. Europeans established some trading posts in China, but the Chinese saw little value in products from the West. Chinese culture continued to exert a strong influence over Korea, Japan, and much of Southeast Asia, especially Vietnam.

Analyzing Documents

In what way did Korea influence Japan?

Preparing for the Regents

List two ways in which China influenced each of the following areas.

Korea:

1.

2.

Japan:

1.

2.

Southeast Asia:

1.

2.

The Ottoman Empire

The Ottoman Empire:

- expanded across a vast area in the 1400s and 1500s, from southeastern Europe through the Middle East and North Africa.

- extended Muslim influence.

- made contributions in the arts, architecture, and literature.

- forced Europeans to begin seeking new routes for trade with Asia.

Section Overview

In 1453, the Ottomans captured Constantinople and overthrew the Byzantine empire. Over the next 200 years, backed by military advances, the Ottomans built a large and powerful empire in Europe and the Middle East. During the reign of Suleiman, the Ottomans strengthened their government and military while spreading Islamic culture over a large area. Various religious beliefs, however, were tolerated within the empire. The Ottoman empire created impressive works of architecture, art, and literature. Ottoman expansion into Eastern Europe and the eastern Mediterranean disrupted European trade. As Europeans began to search for new trade routes in the 1400s, Ottoman domination was gradually weakened. This weakening, along with other factors, led to the decline of the empire.

Key Themes and Concepts

As you review this section, take special note of the following key themes and concepts:

Places and Regions What lands came under control of the Ottoman empire?

Belief Systems How did the Ottoman empire extend Muslim influence and permit freedom of worship for people of other religions?

Culture What contributions did the Ottomans make to the arts and literature?

Change Why did Europeans seek new trade routes to East Asia?

Key People and Terms

Put each of the key people and terms into these two categories: government or religion.

Key People and Terms

As you review this section, be sure you understand the significance of these key people and terms:

Constantinople	sultan	janissaries
Suleiman	millets	mosques

Key Themes and Concepts

Power
Many factors can contribute to a nation's power. At Constantinople, military technology helped the Ottomans bring about the final collapse of the Byzantine empire.

The Rise of the Ottoman Empire

By the 1400s, the once mighty Byzantine empire had been in decline for nearly two centuries. In the 1400s, it faced a growing threat from the Ottomans, a nomadic Turkish-speaking group that had migrated from central Asia into Asia Minor. In the previous century, the Ottomans had moved through Asia Minor and into the Balkans.

In 1453, Ottoman armies surrounded the Byzantine capital of **Constantinople.** During a two-month siege, Ottoman cannons pounded Constantinople's defensive walls, eventually allowing the attackers to break through and capture the city. The Ottomans changed the city's name to Istanbul and made this ancient Christian city the capital of their Muslim empire.

Geographic Expansion

The Ottoman empire greatly expanded its territory in the century that followed the fall of Constantinople. With its well-armed forces and effective military strategies, the Ottoman empire grew quickly. After 1453, the empire made spectacular gains, conquering lands south to Mecca as well as along the Nile River in Egypt. The Ottomans also expanded farther north into the Balkans and into Russia, capturing the Crimean peninsula. The Ottomans even laid siege to Vienna in 1529, causing great fear among Europeans. Ottoman forces failed to capture Vienna, however. Even so, by the 1500s, the Ottomans had built the largest, most powerful empire in the Middle East and Europe. At its peak, the Ottoman empire reached across three continents, from southeastern Europe through the Middle East and North Africa.

Reasons for Ottoman Success

The success of the Ottomans was due in large part to new military technology. In addition to the cannons that smashed Constantinople's defenses, the Ottoman army equipped its foot soldiers with muskets. This strategy increased the soldiers' battlefield effectiveness and reduced the importance of mounted soldiers. The new military technology allowed Ottoman leaders to consolidate their rule within the empire as well as to conquer new lands.

European Search for New Trade Routes

As the Ottoman empire expanded into Eastern Europe and the eastern Mediterranean, European trade routes were disrupted. For example, Ottoman control of the eastern Mediterranean interfered with Western Europe's trade with East Asia.

No longer able to depend on the old trade routes to Asia, Portuguese sailors sent explorers out over the oceans in search of new trade routes. They were followed later by other Europeans.

Ottoman Achievements and Lasting Impact

The Byzantine Heritage

The Ottoman empire absorbed many influences from the conquered Byzantine empire. As you know, the Byzantine heritage was itself a mingling of Greco-Roman and Middle Eastern influences. The Ottomans blended Byzantine culture with Muslim culture. Byzantine influences could be found in Ottoman government, social life, and architecture.

Suleiman's Golden Age

Suleiman, called Suleiman the Magnificent by westerners, ruled the Ottoman empire from 1520 to 1566. Suleiman was a **sultan,** the name Turks gave to their rulers. An effective military leader who further modernized the army, Suleiman continued to add new territories to the empire.

The years of Suleiman's rule are considered the golden age of Ottoman history. A wise leader, Suleiman strengthened the government and improved the system of justice in his empire. As a Muslim, he based his law on the Sharia, the Islamic system of law. In fact, he was known to his subjects as Suleiman the Lawgiver. Although Suleiman held absolute power, he did consult with an advisor and a council in governing the empire. He also chose able officials to run the large bureaucracy he needed to supervise everyday matters of government.

A Diverse Society

The Ottomans ruled a vast area that included many diverse peoples with many religions. Nevertheless, the Ottomans held their empire together successfully for hundreds of years, thus making Islam the dominant cultural force throughout the region.

Millets Non-Muslims in the Ottoman Empire were organized into religious communities called millets. Each millet was allowed to maintain its own religious traditions and educate its people—as long as it obeyed Ottoman law.

Janissaries Ottoman leaders furthered Muslim influence by recruiting military and government officers from conquered groups. Some Christian families in the Balkans were required to turn their young sons over to the government. The boys were converted to Islam and trained for service. The best soldiers became janissaries, members of an elite force in the Ottoman army.

Arts and Literature

Throughout the empire, Muslim architects built many palaces as well as Muslim houses of worship, or **mosques.** Muslim religious structures promoted the further spread of Muslim culture into the Christian areas of southeastern Europe.

Ottoman arts reflected Persian influences. Painters used Persian styles to create detailed miniatures and beautiful illuminated manuscripts. Ottoman writers and poets used Persian and Arab models to produce great works in the Turkish language.

The Decline of the Ottoman Empire

Although the Ottoman empire survived into the twentieth century, it began to decline much earlier than that. The reasons for this decline came from both within and outside the empire.

Internal Disorder

Problems developed within the Ottoman empire. Slowly, over time, nations were able to break free from foreign Ottoman rule. The empire also experienced government corruption and poor leadership in its later years.

European Advances

The rising power of European nations was the major external reason for the Ottoman decline. In 1571, Spain and its Italian allies defeated an Ottoman fleet at Lepanto. Even while the Ottomans were adding to their empire in the 1400s and 1500s, they were increasingly being cut out of global trade.

By the 1700s, European commercial and military technology had surpassed that of the Ottomans. Also, industrially based European economies became stronger than the Ottoman economy, which was still based on agriculture. The commercial revolution in Europe, therefore, was a strong factor in Ottoman decline.

Summary

During the 1400s and 1500s, the powerful Ottoman empire arose in Asia Minor. The empire expanded over time to cover a vast area, extending the influence of Islam. Ottoman architecture, literature, and other art forms flourished. The Ottoman empire dominated trade for many years, forcing European countries to begin seeking new routes to Asia. However, European advances in technology as well as internal disorder contributed to the fall of the empire.

Key Themes and Concepts

Diversity
The influence of the Ottoman millets can be seen in the many ethnic and religious groups that still exist in southeastern Europe. In the Balkans in particular, this diversity has sometimes led to conflict.

Key Themes and Concepts

Diversity
Although the Ottoman empire was ruled by Muslims, other religious beliefs were tolerated in the empire. For example, when restrictions on Jews in Europe became severe in the 1500s, many Jews fled to the Ottoman empire, where they were allowed to prosper.

Preparing for the Regents

• Describe at least one other example of a powerful empire that was weakened by internal rebellions, government corruption, or poor leadership.

Preparing for the Regents

• What factors contributed to the rise and fall of the Ottoman empire?

Explorations, Encounters, and Imperialism

Section Overview

In the 1400s, seeking a greater share of the rich Asian spice trade, Europeans began to make oceanic voyages of exploration. Benefiting from new technology, the Portuguese and the Spanish were the first to establish global trade empires in the 1500s. The Dutch, English, and French soon joined them, competing for colonies in Asia, the Americas, and Africa during the 1600s and 1700s. These interactions had a great global impact as food, people, plants, animals, technology, and diseases passed from continent to continent.

Key Themes and Concepts

As you review this section, take special note of the following key themes and concepts:

Movement of People and Goods How did global trade patterns change between the late 1400s and the 1700s?

Science and Technology What types of technology allowed Western Europeans to explore the oceans?

Interdependence What motives did Europeans have for establishing colonies between 1500 and 1700?

Change What major changes did the European expansion bring to peoples around the world?

Key People and Terms

As you review this section, be sure you understand the significance of these key people and terms:

Reconquista	imperialism	triangular trade
cartographers	Ferdinand Magellan	Middle Passage
astrolabe	sepoys	encomienda
Vasco da Gama	conquistadors	Columbian Exchange
Christopher Columbus	plantations	mercantilism

The Eve of Exploration

As Europeans were looking for new routes to the riches of Asia, two nations in Western Europe, Portugal and Spain, took the lead. Both of these nations had the technology, resources, and political unity to support sea travel. Both of these nations had also struggled with Muslim rule in their countries and had created Christian kingdoms.

Reconquista and Expulsions

The marriage of Ferdinand of Aragon to Isabella of Castile in 1469 brought together two powerful Spanish kingdoms. In 1492, Ferdinand and Isabella forced the Muslims from Granada, their last stronghold in Spain. This victory completed the Reconquista, a campaign begun by Christians in the 700s to recapture Spain

---

The **Big Idea**

Between the late 1400s and 1700s, Western Europeans:

- benefited from technology in mapmaking, navigation, shipbuilding, and weaponry.

- found new sea routes and dominated trade with Asia, Africa, and the Americas.

- competed with each other to establish profitable colonies.

- began global interactions that greatly affected people around the world.

Key People and Terms

Place each of the key people and terms into one of these categories: geography, economics, conflict.

Preparing for the Regents

- Why did Portugal and Spain pursue sea exploration?

from the Muslims. After achieving political unity in Spain, Isabella sought to establish religious unity. She launched a brutal crusade against the Moors (Muslims) and Jews who refused to convert to Christianity. Many people were killed, and about 150,000 were forced into exile.

Reasons for European Exploration

Although Europeans had long traded in Asian countries, travel to the east had been disrupted by Ottoman control of the eastern Mediterranean, a situation that interfered with Western Europe's trade with Asia. By the 1400s, seeking to gain access to the Asian spices so highly valued on their continent, Europeans looked to reopen global trade links. Italian and Muslim merchants, however, controlled the routes between Asia and Europe. Muslim traders brought goods to the Mediterranean, and Italian traders carried the goods to the rest of Europe. Each time the goods changed hands, they became more expensive. To gain direct access to Asian trade, Portugal and Spain looked for new oceanic routes.

Impact of Technology

Advances in technology greatly aided Europeans in their quest to explore the oceans.

The Printing Press In the mid-1400s, German printer Johann Gutenberg became the first person to use a printing press to print a book. Through the use of movable metal type, the printing press enabled people to make books quickly and cheaply. As a result, books became more readily available. Europeans were able to gain access to new ideas and information on a broad range of topics, including geography.

Gunpowder European explorers also benefited from advances in military technology. Since Arab traders had brought gunpowder to Europe in the 1200s, Europeans had been making advances in weaponry. By the late 1400s, the Portuguese were equipping their ships with sturdy cannons. Eventually, the use of cannons helped the Portuguese win control of the Indian Ocean trade network.

Naval Technology Mapmakers, or **cartographers,** created better maps and charts of the sea. Moreover, European sailors learned to use the magnetic compass to determine direction and the **astrolabe,** an instrument perfected by the Arabs, to figure out their latitude at sea. Europeans also built bigger and better ships. The Portuguese used caravels, ships whose sails, masts, and rudders allowed explorers to sail across or against the wind.

Early Explorations and Encounters

Around Africa to Asia

In 1415, Prince Henry, the son of the Portuguese king, carried out a plan to improve his country's navy. Known to later generations as Henry the Navigator, this prince gathered experts in science, mapmaking, and shipbuilding. Their work led to a fleet of ships that explored the coast of West Africa. In 1488, Bartholomeu Dias rounded the Cape of Good Hope at the southern tip of Africa.

About a decade later, **Vasco da Gama** followed Dias's route around Africa and traveled across the Indian Ocean to an Indian port. Although he lost half his ships, Da Gama returned home with Asian spices that he sold at a high profit. The Portuguese had established a successful all-water trade route to Asia and would soon expand their empire.

Summarize

In one sentence, summarize the reasons for European exploration.

Preparing for the Regents

- What technologies made European overseas expansion possible?

Key Themes and Concepts

Science and Technology This instrument to the right, the astrolabe, was used to calculate the exact latitude of a ship.

Note Taking

Reading Skill:
Recognize Sequence
Make a table. List the important dates or general times for the early explorations and encounters. Record them in the order they occurred. Add boxes as needed.

Early Explorations and Encounters	
Date	Event

Columbus Reaches the Americas

The success of the Portuguese inspired Ferdinand and Isabella of Spain to try to gain a share of the rich spice trade in the East. Furthermore, Isabella sought to spread Christianity.

In 1492, an ambitious Italian sailor from Genoa convinced the Spanish monarchs to finance his plan to reach Asia by sailing across the Atlantic Ocean. **Christopher Columbus** and his crew thus sailed west for India in three small ships, striking land after two months. Although he landed at an island in the Caribbean Sea, Columbus thought that he had reached islands off the coast of Asia. Later explorers realized that he had reached the Americas, a continent they had not known existed.

Spain and Portugal soon both claimed the islands that Columbus had explored in his voyages. In 1493, to settle the issue, Pope Alexander VI established the Line of Demarcation, which divided the non-European world into two zones. Spain could trade and explore west of the line; Portugal had the same rights east of the line. One year later, with the Treaty of Tordesillas, the two nations agreed to move the line.

Europeans Compete for Colonies

The domination by one country of the political and/or economic life of another country is called **imperialism.** Europe's activities in Asia, Africa, and the Americas from the 1500s through the 1700s foreshadowed the major era of European imperialism in the 1800s.

Imperialism in Africa

In the 1400s, the Portuguese explored the coasts of Africa, establishing a string of forts in the west and capturing several port cities in the east. The Portuguese, however, were unsuccessful in their attempts to push into the African interior. As a result, the Portuguese gained little profit from their victories.

In the mid-1600s, the Dutch arrived at the southwestern tip of Africa and established the Cape Town settlement. At Cape Town, Dutch sailors could repair their ships as they traveled to or from the East Indies. The Dutch farmers who settled in and around Cape Town were called Boers. The Boers ousted or enslaved many Africans, whom they considered their inferiors.

Imperialism in Asia

Soon after European powers had established direct trading links with Asia, they sought to gain more permanent control there. First Portugal and then other nations set up colonies in Asia, creating competition in the region.

European Trade in the East, 1700

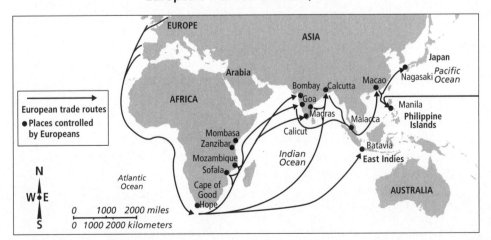

Note Taking

Reading Skill:
Identify Main Ideas and Supporting Details
As you read Europeans Compete for Colonies, complete an outline. Include the main ideas and supporting details. An outline has been started for you.

Europeans Compete for Colonies
I. Imperialism in Africa
  A. 1400s—Portuguese explore coasts of Africa
    1.
    2.
  B.
II.

Preparing for the Regents

Practice your map skills by listing three places controlled by Europeans in each of the following areas.

Africa:

India:

East Asia:

European Trade in the East, 1700 Merchants and traders established trading posts and ports throughout the Eastern Hemisphere. European ships carrying valuable goods criss-crossed the waters of Europe, Africa, and Asia.

Portugal In the early 1500s, the Portuguese took control of the Indian trade network from the Muslims. The Portuguese seized the port of Malacca on the Malay Peninsula in the Indian Ocean, the most important Arab trading city. They also conquered cities on the east coast of Africa and destroyed Arab ships at sea. For most of the 1500s, Portugal controlled the spice trade between Europe and Asia.

Although the Portuguese were powerful at sea, they were not able to conquer much territory on land. Also, they caused much resentment with their intolerant policies. Portuguese missionaries and traders destroyed Hindu temples, massacred Muslims, and sank pilgrim ships. By the late 1500s, Portuguese power in the Indian Ocean was declining.

Preparing for the Regents

• Describe differences between Portuguese and Dutch trading activity in Asia.

The Dutch The first Europeans to challenge Portuguese domination of the Asian spice trade were the Dutch. In the late 1500s, Dutch fleets had established their own trade links with Asia. Soon their sea power surpassed that of the Portuguese. A group of wealthy Dutch merchants formed the Dutch East India Company in the early 1600s. In 1641, the Dutch seized Malacca from Portugal and began trading with China. The Dutch established closer ties with local leaders and stirred less resentment among Asians than had the Portuguese. Soon they dominated the Asian spice trade. Their trading empire did not begin to decline until the 1700s.

Spain Spain also founded colonies in Southeast Asia in the 1500s. Spain financed the voyage of Portuguese noble **Ferdinand Magellan** that completed the first circumnavigation of the world. To circumnavigate something is to go completely around it. During this voyage Magellan claimed the island chain that today is called the Philippines for Spain in 1521. (The islands were named for the Spanish king, Philip II.) This island group gave Spain a base from which to trade with China and spread Catholic teachings to East Asia.

Identify Central Issues

How did England gain control over India?

England and France In the 1700s, England and France became competing forces in the Asian trade network, concentrating on India. The Mughal dynasty in India had been rich and powerful in the 1600s, but weak rulers and civil wars early in the next century weakened the kingdom. The British and French East India Companies made alliances with local rulers, and each company organized its own army of **sepoys,** or Indian troops. In the 1750s, the British East India Company and its sepoys pushed the French out of their trading posts. The British East India Company forced the Mughal emperor to allow it to collect taxes in northeast India. Before long, the company was the real power in the region.

Imperialism in the Americas

After Christopher Columbus landed in the West Indies, friendly relations existed between the Spanish and the Native Americans for a while. However, these friendly feelings did not last.

Cause and Effect

List two reasons why Spanish conquistadors came to the Americas.

1.

2.

Spanish Conquistadors Many Spanish conquistadors, or conquerors, traveled to the Americas in the years following Columbus's voyages. Some of these adventurers came in search of gold; others wanted to convert the inhabitants of the land to Christianity.

One of the earliest conquistadors, Hernan Cortés, landed in Mexico in 1519. Two years later, having formed alliances with discontented peoples within the Aztec empire, Cortés had conquered the empire. In 1532, another conquistador, Francisco Pizarro, destroyed the Incan empire in Peru.

Reasons for Spanish Success The Spanish were able to conquer these empires so quickly for several reasons.

- The Spanish used armor, horses, and powerful weapons that the Native Americans had never seen before.
- The Spanish found allies among Native American groups who hated being ruled by the Aztecs or Incas.
- Diseases brought by Europeans killed millions of native people, causing them to believe that their own gods had deserted them.

Battle for North America Spain's profitable American empire attracted the attention of other European powers. Dutch, English, and French explorers had long searched North America for a Northwest Passage to Asia. By the 1600s, these nations had planted permanent colonies on the continent.

In the 1600s, the French settled Canada. Naming their colony New France, the French sent over fur trappers and missionaries and established forts and trading posts from Quebec to Louisiana.

In 1607, the English established their first permanent colony in North America at Jamestown. Throughout the 1600s, large numbers of English settlers followed. Some came for profit, others hoped to own land, and still others, such as the Puritans, came seeking religious freedom. The English monarch asserted control over his 13 American colonies, but they still had more self-government than the French or Spanish in North America.

Spain, France, England, and the Netherlands frequently clashed over territory and trade in North America. In the mid-1700s, the British defeated the French in the French and Indian War. The French then had to give up Canada, leaving much of North America to England.

Triangular Trade and Slavery

Causes of the Slave Trade

In the 1500s, Europeans came to view enslaved Africans as the most valuable African trade goods. At that time, Europeans began buying large numbers of Africans to satisfy the labor shortage on American **plantations,** or large estates. The slave trade eventually grew into a huge and profitable business. The trade that involved Europe, Africa, and the Americas was sometimes referred to as **"triangular trade"** because the sea routes among these three continents formed vast triangles.

The Middle Passage

The voyage from Africa to the Americas on the slave ships was called the **Middle Passage**. Conditions were terrible on these ships. Hundreds of people were crammed onto a single ship. In fact, millions of Africans died on the way from disease, brutal mistreatment, or suicide. Those who survived were forced to work on plantations in the American colonies.

Effects of the Slave Trade

By the 1800s, when the slave trade ended, an estimated 11 million Africans had been sent to the Americas. The slave trade caused local wars to develop in Africa. As a result, traditional African political structures were undermined. Through slavery, many African societies were deprived of the talents of strong, intelligent people. West Africa especially lost many young men and women. Some societies and small states disappeared forever. Other states formed, some of them dependent on the slave trade.

Key Themes and Concepts

Science and Technology
One of the reasons for the relatively swift Spanish conquest of the Americas was the military technology of European powers.

Key Themes and Concepts

Government
English monarchs allowed their colonists more self-government than the French or the Spanish did. English political traditions of representative government and limited monarchy took root in the English colonies.

Note Taking

Reading Skill:
Identify Causes and Effects
Make a flowchart. Show the causes and effects of the slave trade.

Causes	The Slave Trade	Effects

Key Themes and Concepts

Human Rights
Slavery involved a complete disregard for human rights. Enslaved persons lost their freedom and could be bought and sold. In the Middle Passage, enslaved people endured disease, overcrowding, and brutal mistreatment.

The Spanish Empire

During the 1500s, the Spanish empire in the Americas stretched from California to South America and brought great wealth to the nation. In return, the Spanish brought their government, religion, economy, and culture to the Americas.

- **Government** Spain maintained a strict control over its distant empire. The king ran the colonial government through his representatives, or viceroys, who ruled the provinces.

- **Religion** The Catholic Church was very important in the colonies. Church leaders helped run the government and worked to convert thousands of Native Americans to Christianity.

- **Encomienda System** Spanish law allowed its colonies to trade only with Spain. Growing sugar cane on large plantations became an important business activity in the colonial empire. Because plantations needed so many workers, the Spanish created the encomienda system. A conquistador, under this system, was granted land along with permission to demand labor or tribute from Native Americans in the area. After many of the overworked Native Americans died, the Spanish brought enslaved Africans to do the work.

- **Culture** Over time, the people in the colonies developed a new culture that combined European, Native American, and African traditions. These people spoke Spanish but also used Native American and African words. The art, architecture, and daily life in the empire were influenced by all three cultures.

- **Social Classes** A social structure developed that placed people in a hierarchy. The Spanish-born people at the top of the class structure were known as *peninsulares*. Creoles was the name given to those of European descent who were born in the colonies. *Mestizos* were people of mixed Native American and European descent, and *mulattoes* was the term for those of mixed African and European descent.

Social Structure of the Spanish Colonies

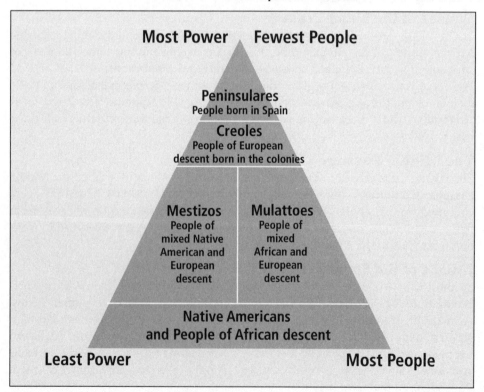

Note Taking

Reading Skill:
Identify Main Ideas and Details
Make a concept web. Complete it with main ideas and details about the Spanish empire. Add more circles as needed.

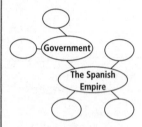

Key Themes and Concepts

Change
In the cultural blending described here, Europeans were influenced by Native American foods as well as African farming methods, music, cooking styles, and crops such as okra and palm oil.

Vocabulary Builder

descent—(dee SENT) *n.* your family origins, especially your nationality or relationship to someone important who lived a long time ago

Key Themes and Concepts

Movement of People and Goods
The introduction of American crops such as corn and potatoes to other continents contributed to population growth in Europe, Africa, and Asia in the 1700s.

The Columbian Exchange: Plants, Animals, People, and Diseases

A global exchange of people, plants, animals, ideas, and technology began during this time, leading to profound changes for people in Asia, the Americas, Africa, and Europe. Because it started with Columbus, it is called the Columbian Exchange.

Plants, including maize (corn) and potatoes, traveled to Europe, Africa, and Asia. Other plants, such as bananas and rice, traveled back to the Americas. From Africa and Asia, goats and chickens came to the Americas. Unfortunately, other exchanges occurred: diseases such as measles and typhus devastated populations in the Americas.

European Capitalism and Mercantilism

Increased trade with the colonies encouraged European capitalism, the investment of money to make a profit. Joint stock companies grew in significance, since they allowed Europeans to gather the capital necessary to finance overseas voyages. Moreover, European nations adopted a new policy of mercantilism. This policy involved building up national wealth by exporting more goods than the nation imported. Colonies supplied the parent nation with raw materials and served as a market for its exports.

The expansion of capitalism and mercantilism affected the lives of many Europeans. Nobles became less powerful because their wealth was based in the land they owned. On the other hand, many merchants, whose wealth was based in trade, grew richer. A middle class developed on the continent during this period. The lives of peasants did not change significantly in the 1500s and 1600s.

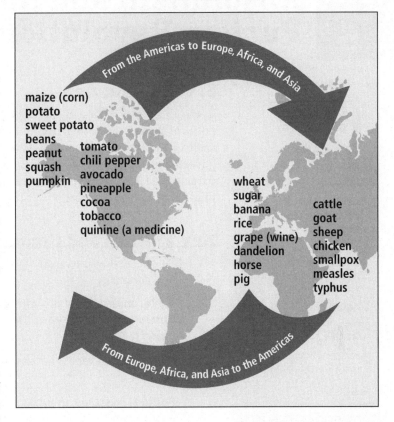

The Columbian Exchange

From the Americas to Europe, Africa, and Asia

maize (corn)
potato
sweet potato
beans
peanut
squash
pumpkin
tomato
chili pepper
avocado
pineapple
cocoa
tobacco
quinine (a medicine)

wheat
sugar
banana
rice
grape (wine)
dandelion
horse
pig

cattle
goat
sheep
chicken
smallpox
measles
typhus

From Europe, Africa, and Asia to the Americas

Preparing for the Regents

- Describe two positive and two negative aspects of the Columbian exchange.

Effects of European Imperialism

Slave trade and disruption of African political, economic, and social life	New economic policies of mercantilism and expansion of capitalism led to increased standard of living for Europeans	Increased cultural diffusion of people, plants, animals, ideas, and technology throughout the world

Summary

From 1500 to 1700, European nations set off on voyages of exploration, establishing empires and trade links around the world. Western European countries competed for colonies and trade in Asia, Africa, and the Americas. Slave trade between Africa and the Americas developed into a huge and profitable business. This European expansion had an enormous impact, resulting in many exchanges that altered the lives of people around the world.

Preparing for the Regents

- In what ways were the voyages of Columbus a major turning point in global history?

Absolutism and the Puritan Revolution

Section Overview

In the 1500s and 1600s, several rulers in Asia and Europe sought to centralize their political power. Claiming divine right, or authority from God, leaders such as Philip II in Spain and Louis XIV in France gained complete authority over their governments and their subjects. England resisted the establishment of absolutism. After a civil war, England's Parliament enacted a Bill of Rights that limited the English monarch's powers.

Key Themes and Concepts

As you review this section, take special note of the following key themes and concepts:

Government How did monarchs in India, Spain, France, and Russia work to increase their political power in the 1500s and 1600s?

Power What ideas did absolute monarchs use to justify their power?

Political Systems In what ways was England's experience of absolutism different from that of other European countries?

Choice What choices did Parliament make in England to assure a check on absolutism?

Key People and Terms

As you review this section, be sure you understand the significance of these key people and terms:

absolutism	Ivan the Terrible	Oliver Cromwell
Akbar the Great	Peter the Great	Glorious Revolution
Philip II	Puritans	English Bill of Rights
divine right	Thomas Hobbes	limited monarchy
Louis XIV	*The Leviathan*	
Jacques Bossuet	Puritan Revolution	

Global Absolutism

In the 1500s and 1600s, monarchs in Europe and Asia sought to centralize their power. This trend led to absolutism, in which autocratic rulers had complete authority over the government and the lives of the people in their nation.

Absolutism in Mughal India

One place where absolutism appeared in the 1500s was India. In the last half of the 1500s, **Akbar the Great** ruled the powerful Mughal empire in India. Akbar strengthened the central government and made his empire larger and stronger than any in Europe at the time. He modernized the army, encouraged trade, and introduced land reforms. Akbar solidified his reign by recognizing India's diversity and promoting religious tolerance. Akbar's successors were not as strong. Mughal rulers in the late 1600s were much less tolerant, and Mughal power declined, allowing France and England to spread their influence in the region.

Absolutism in Spain

In the 1500s, Spain became the most powerful nation in Europe. Wealth from its empire in the Americas helped Spain's power to grow.

Charles V From 1519 to 1556, Charles V, the grandson of Ferdinand and Isabella, was king of Spain as well as Holy Roman Emperor. Ruling such a large and diverse area in Europe took its toll on Charles, however. He faced military threats from the French, from German Protestant princes, and from the Ottoman empire under Suleiman. In 1556, an exhausted Charles gave up his titles and divided his empire. His brother Ferdinand became Holy Roman Emperor, and his son Philip ruled Spain, the Netherlands, and the vast Spanish overseas empire.

Philip II Ruling from 1556 to 1598, Philip II expanded his own power as well as the influence of the Catholic Church and the Spanish empire. Philip wanted to control all aspects of government, believing that he ruled by **divine right.** According to this way of thinking, the king is an agent of God, and his authority to rule comes directly from God. Philip was a hard-working ruler, and he did much to promote a golden age in Spain.

In the 1600s, however, Spanish power slowly declined as rulers spent too much money on wars overseas. The Spanish relied on gold and silver from their colonies and as a result neglected business at home. The middle class felt that they were being taxed too heavily and stopped supporting the government.

Absolutism in France

By the late 1600s, France had replaced Spain as the most powerful European nation. Over time, French kings had increased royal power by increasing the influence of the government and reducing the power of the nobles. During the reign of King Louis XIII and his chief minister, Richelieu, the two groups who did not bow to royal authority—the nobles and the Protestant Huguenots—were subdued or defeated. Additionally, the French army became the strongest in Europe.

The Sun King Inheriting the throne in 1643 as a five-year-old child, **Louis XIV** ruled France for 72 years. He continued to strengthen the monarchy, taking the sun as the symbol of his power and commanding complete loyalty from his subjects. Louis's claim to absolute power was strengthened by a court preacher, Bishop **Jacques Bossuet.** Bossuet argued that as God's representative on Earth, the king was entitled to unquestioning obedience. During his reign, Louis:

- expanded the bureaucracy, appointing officials to collect taxes, recruit soldiers, and carry out his rule in the provinces.
- built the lavish, immense Palace of Versailles outside of Paris.
- organized a highly disciplined army, the strongest in Europe.
- persecuted the Protestant Huguenots, depriving the nation of many of its most hard-working and prosperous citizens.

Louis's Legacy Under Louis XIV, France was a wealthy, powerful state with great cultural influence. However, Louis's extravagant parties at Versailles and his costly wars left France in debt, and there was social unrest among the starving peasants. The French monarchy would not survive even a century after Louis XIV's death in 1715.

Key Themes and Concepts

Power
Common features of absolute monarchies included strong armies, limited representative bodies, and high taxes.

Preparing for the Regents

According to the concept of divine right, the king was above the law and could rule as he saw fit.

- Compare divine right to the ancient Chinese Mandate of Heaven, another form of the divine right concept.

Key Themes and Concepts

Power
Armand Richelieu was a Roman Catholic cardinal. His role as advisor to the king—and virtual ruler of France—showed the power of the Catholic Church at that time.

Preparing for the Regents

- Why did Louis XIV consider himself the "Sun King"? How is that name an example of his belief in absolutism?

Absolutism in Russia

During the 1400s, the city of Moscow became the center of power in Russia. The driving force behind Moscow's rising power was Ivan III, known as Ivan the Great. Ruling from 1462 to 1505, Ivan the Great built the framework for absolute rule in Russia. Following Ivan the Great, a long series of absolute rulers dominated Russia.

Ivan the Terrible Czar Ivan IV centralized royal power and introduced Russia to extreme absolute power. His harsh ruling style and fits of violence earned him the title "Ivan the Terrible." To enforce his will, Ivan organized a personal police force. Dressed in black robes, these agents of terror slaughtered rebellious nobles and destroyed towns suspected of disloyalty.

Peter the Great Peter the Great ruled Russia as czar from 1682 to 1725. Peter worked to centralize royal power and bring all Russians under his authority. He reduced the power of the nobility and gained control of the Russian Orthodox Church.

Westernization Under Peter Peter wanted to modernize Russia. He traveled to Western European cities to study Western technology and brought back ideas on how to westernize Russia. For example, he copied European customs and dress, sent nobles to Europe to be educated, and developed mining and textiles. His capital at St. Petersburg served as his "Window on the West" to trade with Western Europe. However, Peter sometimes resorted to force and terror to achieve his goals.

Peter's Strong Foreign Policy Peter created the largest army in Europe in the late 1600s and used it to expand Russian territory and gain ports on the Baltic Sea. Russia also extended eastward, sending explorers across the Bering Strait into North America.

Peter failed at one of his goals, however: to gain a port that would not be closed due to freezing in winter. He fought the Ottoman Turks to gain a warm-water port on the Black Sea but did not succeed. However, Catherine the Great, another absolute ruler of Russia, would successfully acquire Black Sea ports in 1795.

Reaction to Absolutism in England

While other nations turned to absolutism in the 1500s and 1600s, England moved in a different direction. England's Parliament managed to resist successfully the consolidation of royal power.

The royal Tudor family ruled England from 1485 to 1603. These monarchs, who included Henry VIII and Elizabeth I, generally worked well with Parliament. Even though the Tudors believed in divine right, they saw great value in maintaining good relations with Parliament.

In 1603, however, the English throne passed to the Stuarts. Lacking the diplomatic skills of the Tudors, the Stuarts with their absolutist tendencies came into conflict with Parliament.

The Stuart Monarchs

The first Stuart king, James I, sought to increase his power, using divine right as his justification. Needing money for his wars and extravagant court life, he frequently clashed with Parliament over financial issues and foreign policy. Angering leaders in the House of Commons, James eventually dissolved

Note **Taking**

Reading Skill:
Compare and Contrast
Make a Venn diagram. Show the similarities and differences between absolutism in Spain, in France, and in Russia.

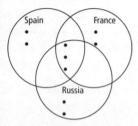

Statue of Peter the Great, St. Petersburg

Key Themes and Concepts

Political Systems
The tradition of sharing political power dates back to the Greek and Roman periods. In England, the Magna Carta of 1215 limited the ruler's power by protecting certain basic legal rights of English citizens and by forcing the monarch to consult an English council before raising taxes. To learn more about the Magna Carta, see Unit 3, Section 4.

Parliament and imposed his own taxes. The king also conflicted with **Puritans,** who were seeking to "purify" the church of England by eliminating Catholic practices.

The Stuart monarchs received support in their struggles with Parliament from the English thinker **Thomas Hobbes.** In *The Leviathan,* Hobbes wrote that people were by nature selfish and greedy and would fall into chaos unless ruled by a strong government that could suppress rebellion. Hobbes believed that an absolute monarchy—one that could command obedience—was needed to maintain order.

James's son Charles I inherited the throne in 1625. He continued his father's absolutist policies. Charles created problems during his reign by:

- putting his enemies in prison without trials.
- imposing very high taxes.
- angering the Puritans.
- dissolving Parliament.

Charles, however, had to summon Parliament back in 1640 to obtain funds to put down a Scottish rebellion. As a result, civil war broke out between Charles I and Parliament.

The English Civil War

The English Civil War, sometimes called the **Puritan Revolution,** pitted Charles's supporters, the Cavaliers, against Parliament's forces, the Roundheads. The Roundheads, a group consisting of Puritans, country landowners, and town-based manufacturers, were led by the skilled military commander **Oliver Cromwell.** Cromwell's disciplined army won several battles against the Cavaliers and captured the king in 1647. Parliament put Charles I on trial and beheaded him in 1649.

Charles I was the first king ever to be tried and executed by his own subjects. This event shocked other European monarchies and signified that absolutism would not prevail in England.

Cromwell and the Commonwealth

After Charles's execution, Parliament's House of Commons abolished the monarchy, the House of Lords, and the official Church of England. England became a republic, called the Commonwealth, with Oliver Cromwell as its leader. England's years as a republic were troubled, however. Supporters of Charles II, the uncrowned heir to the throne, attacked England from Ireland and Scotland. Cromwell led forces into Ireland to crush the uprising. In 1653, Cromwell took the title of Lord Protector and ruled through the army. By the time of his death in 1658, many people had become tired of Puritan rule.

The Restoration

In 1660, Parliament invited Charles II, son of Charles I, to become king of England. This marked the restoration of the Stuart monarchy. In 1685, his brother, James II, inherited the throne. James quickly became unpopular because of his Catholicism and his absolutist policies.

The Glorious Revolution

Parliament Overthrows James II Parliament, in 1688, fearing the return of Catholic dominance, took strong measures. Parliament asked James's daughter, Mary, and her Dutch husband, William, to take the English throne. William and

Vocabulary Builder

<u>suppress</u>—(suh PRES) *vt.* to stop people from opposing the government, especially by using force

Key Themes and Concepts

Change
The English Civil War was an important turning point in the history of constitutional government in England. The ideas of the Puritans also shaped the development of the colonies that became the United States in the 1700s.

Note Taking

Reading Skill:
Identify Causes and Effects
Make a flowchart. Write the causes and effects of the English Civil War.

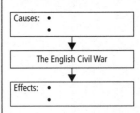

| Causes: • |
| • |

↓

| The English Civil War |

↓

| Effects: • |
| • |

Mary, both Protestants, arrived in England as James II fled to France, completing a bloodless transfer of power. This nonviolent overthrow is known as the **Glorious Revolution.**

Vocabulary Builder

ensure—(en SHOOR) v. to make certain that something will happen properly

English Bill of Rights Before they could take power, William and Mary were forced to accept the English Bill of Rights, a set of acts passed by Parliament to ensure its superiority over the monarchy. This Bill of Rights:

- stated that the king must work regularly with Parliament.
- stated that the king must give the House of Commons financial control.
- abolished excessive fines and cruel or unusual punishment.
- affirmed habeas corpus, meaning that no person could be held in jail without first being charged with a crime.

With this Bill of Rights, England became a **limited monarchy,** a government in which a legislative body limits the monarch's powers.

Key Themes and Concepts

Political Systems
Parliament imposed regulations that ensured its supremacy over the monarch with the English Bill of Rights.

Toleration Act The Toleration Act of 1689 granted Protestant dissenters, such as Puritans and Quakers, limited toleration. Catholics, however, were denied toleration.

Revolution in England

A.D.									
1600	1610	1620	1630	1640	1650	1660	1670	1680	1690

1649 English execute Charles I.

1688 During Glorious Revolution, William and Mary become king and queen.

1603 Stuart dynasty takes power in England.

1625 Charles I becomes king.

1642–49 English Civil War takes place.

1660 England restores the monarchy.

1685 James II becomes king.

Preparing for the Regents

- Outline the main points of the two competing political ideologies, absolutism and limited monarchy, described in this section.

Summary

Through the 1500s and 1600s, absolutism became dominant through much of Europe and parts of Asia. In India, Akbar the Great consolidated his power. In Spain, France, and Russia, absolutist monarchs claimed that they ruled by divine right and sought to extend their political power. While other nations accepted absolutism, England stood as a contrast to this trend. After the Puritan Revolution and the Glorious Revolution of the mid-1600s, the English Bill of Rights was passed, establishing England as a limited monarchy.

Multiple Choice

Directions: Review the Test-Taking Strategies section of this book. Then answer the following questions, drawn from actual Regents examinations. For each statement or question, choose the *number* of the word or expression that, of those given, best completes the statement or answers the question.

1   One way in which the civilizations of the Sumerians, the Phoenicians, and the Mayas were similar is that all

   (1) developed extensive writing systems

   (2) emphasized equality in education

   (3) established monotheistic religions

   (4) encouraged democratic participation in government

2   Inca terrace farming and Aztec floating gardens are examples of

   (1) the ability of civilizations to adapt to their region's physical geography

   (2) slash-and-burn farming techniques

   (3) Mesoamerican art forms symbolizing the importance of agriculture

   (4) colonial economic policies that harmed Latin American civilizations

3   "The challenges of the Andes helped the Incas develop a thriving civilization." Based on this statement, what does the author believe?

   (1) Language and religion are important to national unity.

   (2) Cultural diversity flourishes in areas of agricultural prosperity.

   (3) People can overcome the limitations of their environment.

   (4) Natural resources are necessary for economic independence.

4   The Incas, the Romans, and the Mongols were similar in that all

   (1) developed systems of writing

   (2) extended control over neighboring peoples

   (3) established industrial economies

   (4) adopted democratic political systems

5   One factor that accounted for Chinese influence on traditional Japanese culture was the

   (1) continuous warfare between the countries

   (2) geographical location of the countries

   (3) refusal of Western nations to trade with Japan

   (4) annexation of Japan into the Chinese empire

6   An observation that could be made about the Ottoman empire in the 1400s and 1500s is that the empire

   (1) originated in Hungary

   (2) had a strategic location between Europe and Asia

   (3) was totally landlocked

   (4) had control over most of Western Europe

7   Which was the characteristic of Western European nations that *most* enabled them to establish colonies in Asia and Africa?

   (1) rigid social class structures

   (2) self-sufficiency in natural resources

   (3) frequent political revolutions

   (4) advanced technology

8 One reason the Spanish conquistadors were able to conquer the Aztec and Inca empires rapidly is that

(1) these empires had no standing armies

(2) the Spanish had better weapons than the Aztecs and Incas did

(3) the Spanish greatly outnumbered the Aztecs and Incas

(4) the Aztecs and Incas joined together to fight the Spanish

9 In Latin America during the early period of Spanish colonialism, the deaths of large numbers of the native people led to

(1) a decline in Spanish immigration to the Americas

(2) the removal of most Spanish troops from the Americas

(3) the importation of slaves from Africa

(4) improved health care in the colonies

10 One major effect of the European slave trade on Africa was that the slave trade

(1) strengthened the traditional African economic systems

(2) led to a rapid decrease in tribal warfare

(3) hastened the decline of African kingdoms

(4) increased the number of trade routes across the Sahara

11 According to the theory of mercantilism, colonies should be

(1) acquired as markets and sources of raw materials

(2) considered an economic burden to the colonial power

(3) granted independence as soon as possible

(4) encouraged to develop their own industries

12 A major result of the European Age of Exploration was

(1) a long period of peace and prosperity for the nations of Western Europe

(2) extensive migration of people from the Western Hemisphere to Africa

(3) the fall of European national monarchies and the end of the power of the Catholic Church

(4) the end of regional isolation and the beginning of a period of European global domination

Base your answer to question 13 on the chart below and on your knowledge of world history.

Social Structure of the Spanish Colonies

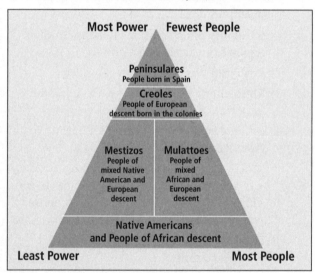

13 Based on the chart, which conclusion can be drawn about the social structure of the Spanish colonies?

(1) Power was evenly distributed among many people.

(2) Native Americans ruled over the Spanish.

(3) Native Spaniards dominated society.

(4) Creoles represented a majority of the population.

14 In English history, the Magna Carta (1215) and the Bill of Rights (1689) both reinforced the concept of

(1) a limited monarchy

(2) religious toleration

(3) a laissez-faire economy

(4) universal suffrage

15 During the Age of Absolutism (1600s and 1700s), European monarchies sought to

(1) increase human rights for their citizens

(2) centralize political power in their nations

(3) develop better relations with Muslim rulers

(4) encourage the growth of cooperative farms

Thematic Essay Question

In developing your answer, be sure to keep this general definition in mind:

> <u>discuss</u> means "to make observations about something using facts, reasoning, and argument; to present in some detail"

Directions: Write a well-organized essay that includes an introduction, several paragraphs addressing the task below, and a conclusion.

Theme: **Political Systems**

> Several empires and nations throughout global history have been ruled by strong leaders who have followed policies of absolutism.

Task:

> - Define the term *absolutism,* and identify the characteristics of absolutist rule.
> - Select a nation or empire you have studied that was ruled according to the principles of absolutism. Identify the specific characteristics of absolutist government that existed in this nation or empire.
> - Discuss the major positive and/or negative effects that absolutism had on this empire or nation.

You may discuss any nation or empire that you have studied. Some suggestions you may wish to consider are the Incan empire, the Byzantine empire, the Ming empire in China, the Ottoman empire of Suleiman the Great, Spain (Philip II), France (Louis XIV), or Russia (Peter the Great).

**You are *not* limited to these suggestions.
Do *not* use the United States in your answer.**

Guidelines:

In your essay, be sure to
- Develop all aspects of the task
- Support the theme with relevant facts, examples, and details
- Use a logical and clear plan of organization, including an introduction and a conclusion that are beyond a simple restatement of the theme

Document-Based Question

This question is based on the accompanying documents. The question is designed to test your ability to work with historical documents. Some of these documents have been edited for the purposes of this question. As you analyze the documents, take into account the source of each document and any point of view that may be presented in the document.

Historical Context:

Throughout history there has been widespread interaction among cultures. Sometimes the effects of this interaction have been positive, and at other times the effects have been negative.

Task: Using the information from the documents and your knowledge of global history, answer the questions that follow each document in Part A. Your answers to the questions will help you write the Part B essay in which you will be asked to

> - Evaluate the major effects that exchanges between cultures have had on the groups involved
> - Discuss both positive and negative effects

In developing your answers, be sure to keep these general definitions in mind:

(a) <u>evaluate</u> means "to examine and judge the significance, worth, or condition of; to determine the value of"

(b) <u>discuss</u> means "to make observations about something using facts, reasoning, and argument; to present in some detail"

Document-Based Question

Part A: Short Answer

Directions: Analyze the documents and answer the question or questions that follow each document, using the space provided.

Document #1

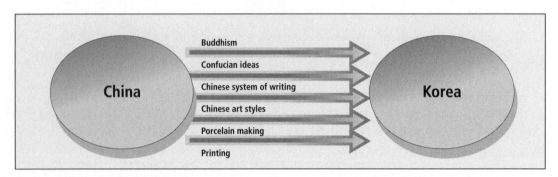

1. What were some of the effects of the interaction between China and Korea?

_____

_____

_____

Document #2

> *That which led the Spaniards to these terrible deeds was the desire for gold, to make themselves suddenly rich. . . . In a word their greed, their ambition gave occasion to their barbarism. For the Spaniards so little regarded the health of their souls that they allowed this great multitude to die without the least light of religion. The Indians never gave them the least cause to offer them violence until the excessive cruelties of the Spaniards, the torments and slaughters of their countrymen, moved them to take arms against the Spaniards.*
> —**Bartolomé de Las Casas,** *Brief Report on the Destruction of the Indians,* **1542**

2. Summarize the point of view of this writer concerning the interaction between Spaniards and Native Americans in the 1500s.

_____

_____

_____

_____

Document #3
Atlantic Trade Routes, 1750

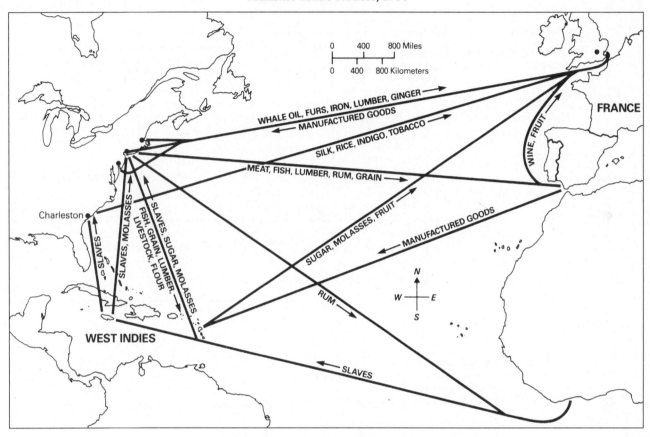

3. What negative effect did the Atlantic trade have on Africans? How did the Atlantic trade benefit Europeans?

_____

_____

Document-Based Question

Part B

Essay

Directions: Write a well-organized essay that includes an introduction, several paragraphs, and a conclusion. Use evidence from *at least two* of the documents in your essay. Support your response with relevant facts, examples, and details. Include additional outside information.

Historical Context:

Throughout history there has been widespread interaction among cultures. Sometimes the effects of this interaction have been positive, and at other times the effects have been negative.

Task: Using the information from the documents and your knowledge of global history, write an essay in which you

- Evaluate the major effects that exchanges between cultures have had on the groups involved
- Examine both positive and negative effects

Guidelines:

In your essay, be sure to

- Develop all aspects of the task
- Incorporate information from *at least two* of the documents
- Incorporate relevant outside information
- Support the theme with relevant facts, examples, and details
- Use a logical and clear plan of organization, including an introduction and a conclusion that are beyond a restatement of the theme

An Age of Revolutions (1750–1914)

Unit Overview

The years between 1750 and 1914 were years of enormous change. The Scientific Revolution and the Enlightenment brought a completely new way of looking at the world. Monarchies were overthrown, and representative forms of government emerged. In some areas, people tried to return to previous ways. In other areas, however, feelings of nationalism arose that led to the growth of nations. During this same time, enormous changes were occurring in Europe and Japan. The Industrial Revolution brought changes in social structure and created new ways of living and working. Industrialization also spurred nations to build empires in Africa and Asia, creating an economy that spanned the globe.

Using Good Social Studies Practices

Comparison and Contextualization

Some of the many themes developed in Unit 5 are:

change	political systems	science and technology
nationalism	conflict	culture and intellectual life
power	imperialism	

Choose one of the themes listed above. As you review Unit 5, identify, describe, and compare people's perspectives on historical developments, economic changes, and social movements having to do with your theme.

Scientific Revolution and Enlightenment

Section Overview

In the 1500s and 1600s, the Scientific Revolution changed the way Europeans looked at the world. People began to make conclusions based on experimentation and observation instead of merely accepting traditional ideas. During the 1600s and 1700s, belief in the power of reason grew. Writers of the time sought to reform government and bring about a more just society. Despite opposition from government and church leaders, Enlightenment ideas spread. Some absolute rulers used their power to reform society. Over time, concepts of democracy and of nationhood developed from Enlightenment ideas and contributed to revolutions.

Key Themes and Concepts

As you review this section, take special note of the following key themes and concepts:

Science and Technology How did the Scientific Revolution change the way Europeans looked at the world?

Culture and Intellectual Life How did the Scientific Revolution lead to the ideas of the Enlightenment?

Government What reforms did Enlightenment thinkers want to bring to government in the 1600s and 1700s?

Change What impact did the Enlightenment have on Europe?

Key People and Terms

Key People and Terms

- What do many of the key people and terms have in common? Explain.

As you review this section, be sure you understand the significance of these key people and terms:

Scientific Revolution	natural laws
Nicolaus Copernicus	John Locke
heliocentric	natural rights
Galileo Galilei	Baron de Montesquieu
Isaac Newton	Voltaire
scientific method	Jean-Jacques Rousseau
René Descartes	enlightened despots
Enlightenment	Joseph II

New Ideas About the Universe

Throughout the Middle Ages, European scholars believed that Earth was the center of the universe. This idea was based on Greco-Roman theories and the teachings of the Church. However, European scientists began to think differently in the 1500s. Influenced by the critical spirit of the Renaissance, they questioned the old ideas about the world. This period of change was called the **Scientific Revolution.**

Copernicus

In the mid-1500s, Polish scholar **Nicolaus Copernicus** challenged the belief that Earth was at the center of the universe. Using mathematical formulas, Copernicus suggested that the universe was **heliocentric,** or sun-centered. He said that the planets revolved around the sun. Most scholars rejected Copernicus's theory.

Galileo

In the early 1600s, an Italian astronomer, **Galileo Galilei,** provided further evidence to support the heliocentric theory. He did this by observing the skies with a telescope he had constructed. Galileo's conclusions caused an uproar because they contradicted Church teachings about the world. Church leaders put Galileo on trial. Threatened with death, Galileo was forced to take back his ideas publicly.

Newton

English scholar **Isaac Newton** built on the knowledge of Copernicus and Galileo. He used mathematics to prove the existence of a force that kept planets in their orbits around the sun. Newton called the force gravity, the same force that made objects fall toward Earth. Newton eventually theorized that nature follows uniform laws.

New Ways of Thinking

The Scientific Method

A new approach to science had emerged by the 1600s. It relied on experimentation and observation rather than on past authorities. This new way of thinking was called the **scientific method.**

The Scientific Method

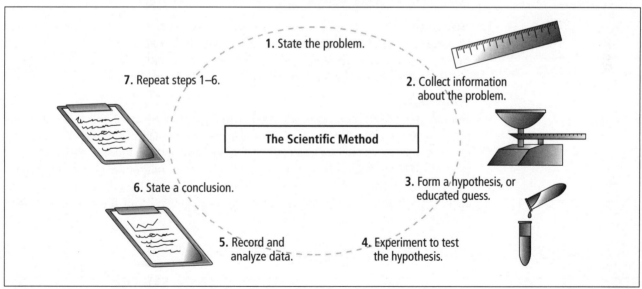

1. State the problem.
2. Collect information about the problem.
3. Form a hypothesis, or educated guess.
4. Experiment to test the hypothesis.
5. Record and analyze data.
6. State a conclusion.
7. Repeat steps 1–6.

The Scientific Method

Descartes and Human Reasoning

Frenchman **René Descartes** challenged the idea that new knowledge should be made to fit existing traditional ideas. Descartes emphasized the power of human reason. He believed that reason, rather than tradition, should be the way to discover truth. The ideas of Descartes and other thinkers of the Scientific Revolution paved the way for other changes that would occur in Europe in the 1700s.

Preparing for the Regents

- How did the Scientific Revolution prepare the way for the Enlightenment?

- Thomas Hobbes was an Enlightenment thinker, even though his philosophy favored absolutism. Contrast Locke's theory of natural rights with the thinking of Thomas Hobbes and the theory of divine right.

Science and the Enlightenment

During the Scientific Revolution, scientists used reason to explain why things happened in the physical universe. This success inspired great confidence in the power of reason. By the early 1700s, writers sought to use reason to discover **natural laws,** or laws that govern human behavior. By applying the scientific method of investigation and observation, scholars thought that they could solve the problems of society.

This way of thinking led to the Enlightenment, the period in the 1700s in which people rejected traditional ideas and supported a belief in human reason. The belief that logical thought can lead to truth is called rationalism. The Enlightenment introduced new ways of viewing authority, power, government, and law.

Leading Thinkers of the Enlightenment

Four of the most influential Enlightenment philosophers were John Locke, Baron de Montesquieu, Voltaire, and Jean-Jacques Rousseau.

Locke

John Locke, an English thinker of the late 1600s, believed that all people possess **natural rights.** These rights, he said, include the rights to life, liberty, and property. According to Locke, people form governments to protect their rights. If a government does not protect these rights, people have the right to overthrow it.

Key Themes and Concepts

Government
Locke's ideas about natural rights and the obligations of government later influenced both Thomas Jefferson's writing of the Declaration of Independence and the French revolutionaries.

Montesquieu

In the 1700s, French thinker **Baron de Montesquieu** wrote that the powers of government should be separated into three branches: legislative, executive, and judicial. This separation of powers would prevent tyranny by creating what is called a system of checks and balances. Each branch could keep the other two from gaining too much power.

Voltaire

Voltaire was a French thinker of the 1700s who believed in free speech. He used his sharp wit to criticize the French government and the Catholic Church for their failure to permit religious toleration and intellectual freedom.

Rousseau

Jean-Jacques Rousseau, another French philosopher of the 1700s, put forth his ideas in a book titled *The Social Contract.* He believed that people are naturally good but are corrupted by the evils of society, such as the unequal distribution of property. He felt that in agreeing to form a government, people choose to give up their own interests for the common good. Rousseau believed in the will of the majority, which he called the general will. He believed that the majority should always work for the common good.

Thinkers of the Enlightenment

Thomas Hobbes	John Locke
People are greedy and selfish. Only a powerful government can create a peaceful, orderly society.	People have natural rights. It is the job of government to protect these natural rights. If government does not protect these rights, the people have the right to overthrow it.
Baron de Montesquieu	**Jean-Jacques Rousseau**
The powers of government should be separated into three branches. Each branch will keep the other branches from becoming too powerful.	In a perfect society, people both make and obey the laws. What is good for everyone is more important than what is good for one person.

Impact of the Enlightenment

The ideas proposed by Enlightenment thinkers had a great impact throughout Europe in the 1700s. Greater numbers of people began to question established beliefs and customs. Enlightenment beliefs affected leaders and the development of nations.

Government Censorship

As Enlightenment ideas gained in popularity, government and Church leaders worked to defend the established systems. They started a campaign of censorship to suppress Enlightenment ideas. Many writers, including Voltaire, were thrown into prison, and their books were banned and burned.

Enlightened Despots

Some monarchs accepted Enlightenment ideas. They were known as **enlightened despots,** absolute rulers who used their power to reform society.

Maria Theresa Austrian ruler Maria Theresa implemented several reforms during her reign in the 1700s. She improved the tax system by forcing nobles and the clergy to pay taxes. This measure eased the tax burden on peasants. Maria Theresa also absorbed Enlightenment ideas on education and made primary education available to children in her kingdom.

Joseph II Maria Theresa's son, Joseph II, continued and expanded many of his mother's reforms. The most radical of the enlightened despots, Joseph modernized Austria's government, chose officials for their talents rather than because of their status, and implemented legal reforms. He also practiced religious toleration, ended censorship, and abolished serfdom. However, many of Joseph's reforms were later overturned.

Catherine the Great Catherine II, who became empress of Russia in 1762, read Enlightenment works and even corresponded with Voltaire and Montesquieu. As a result of her exposure to Enlightenment ideas, Catherine asked for the advice of nobles, free peasants, and townspeople. Never before had Russian citizens been allowed to advise the government. Catherine also built schools and hospitals, promoted the education of women, and extended religious tolerance. Unfortunately, many of Catherine's reforms were short-lived. Later in her reign, Catherine grew more repressive after a peasant uprising.

Democracy and Nationalism

Enlightenment ideas inspired a sense of individualism, a belief in personal freedom, and a sense of the basic equality of human beings. These concepts, along with challenges to traditional authority, became important in the growth of democracy. Nationalism also grew. As people in a country drew together to fight for a democratic government, strong feelings of nationalism arose. In the late 1700s, Enlightenment ideas would contribute to an age of revolution.

Summary

Beginning in the 1500s, the Scientific Revolution introduced a way of thinking based on observation and experimentation instead of acceptance of traditional authority. These changes inspired intellectuals to apply reason to the study not only of science but also of human society. The thinkers of the Enlightenment used this emphasis on reason to suggest reforms in government and society. Many Europeans, including several monarchs, were influenced by these ideas and sought to change the old order. These changes had an impact on all of Europe as democratic and nationalistic ideas grew and contributed to revolutions.

Vocabulary Builder

censorship—(SEN sur ship) *n.* the practice of examining books, films, letters, etc., to remove anything that is considered offensive, morally harmful, or politically dangerous, etc.

Key Themes and Concepts

Change
The term *enlightened despot* almost seems like a contradiction. These rulers believed in absolute power but also saw the value of reforms in government.

Nationalism
In both the American and French Revolutions, Enlightenment ideas contributed to democratic movements as well as strong nationalistic feelings. To learn more about the American and French Revolutions, see Section 2 of this unit.

Government
Enlightenment thinkers sought to use reason to improve government and society. Although they were able to influence only a few leaders of their day, they created a whole new set of assumptions about the proper use of power, who had authority, and what made up a good and lawful government.

Preparing for the Regents

- What policies did enlightened despots have in common?

Political Revolutions

Key People and Terms

• Place each of the key people and terms into these three categories: leader, government body, political document.

Section Overview

In the late 1700s and early 1800s, revolutions shook Europe and the Americas. In North America in 1776, Great Britain's 13 colonies, inspired by Enlightenment ideals, declared their independence. They then fought the American Revolution to throw off British rule. In France, economic misery and social discontent led to a revolt against the absolute monarchy in 1789. Periods of chaos and reform were followed by the rise of Napoleon Bonaparte. Napoleon built an empire that was short-lived, but his military victories fanned French nationalistic feelings and spread the revolution's ideals. Inspired by the American and French Revolutions, revolutionaries in Latin America threw off Spanish rule.

Key Themes and Concepts

As you review this section, take special note of the following key themes and concepts:

Culture and Intellectual Life What role did Enlightenment ideas play in the major revolutions of the late 1700s and early 1800s?

Conflict Why did the French people rebel against King Louis XVI?

Change What short-term and long-term effects did the revolutions of the late 1700s and early 1800s have on Europe and the Americas?

Key People and Terms

As you review this section, be sure you understand the significance of these key people and terms:

Declaration of Independence	Napoleon Bonaparte
Estates General	coup d'état
National Assembly	Napoleonic Code
Declaration of the Rights of Man and of the Citizen	Toussaint L'Ouverture
	Simón Bolívar
Maximilien Robespierre	José de San Martín

The American Revolution

By 1750, the British empire included 13 colonies along the eastern coast of North America. In 1776, the colonies declared their independence from Great Britain. Great Britain sent troops to crush the rebellion. However, with the aid of the French as well as the Dutch and Spanish, American forces defeated the British army and gained their independence. In their struggle, the colonists were inspired by Enlightenment ideals and by the traditions of British government. They established a new nation based on representative government and a guarantee of rights and freedoms.

Influence of British Traditions

Magna Carta and Parliament The Magna Carta had limited the power of English monarchs. For example, it stated that the king could not raise new taxes without consulting the body that would later become Parliament. The American colonists interpreted this idea to mean that any taxation without representation was unjust. Because colonists had no representative in Great Britain's Parliament, they felt that Parliament had no right to tax them. They protested by using the slogan "No taxation without representation."

English Bill of Rights The English Bill of Rights inspired colonists to fight for the creation of their own bill of rights.

Influence of the Enlightenment

The theories of thinkers such as Locke, Montesquieu, and Rousseau helped inspire the colonists' opposition to British policies after 1763.

Paine's Common Sense Influenced by Enlightenment ideas about a limited, representative government, Thomas Paine wrote in his pamphlet *Common Sense* that the colonists should no longer be the subjects of a distant monarch. Paine appealed to reason and natural law in his arguments for breaking away from Great Britain. His ideas were widely read in the colonies in 1776.

The Declaration of Independence Influenced by Locke and other Enlightenment thinkers, Thomas Jefferson drafted the Declaration of Independence. Jefferson wrote that governments rule only with the consent of the governed and that they should protect the unalienable rights of their citizens. The declaration also stated that people have a right to throw off governments that are unjust and that do not protect their citizens. After listing specific grievances against the British monarch, Jefferson wrote that the colonists were justified in forming their own government, independent of Great Britain.

The Constitution Like the Declaration of Independence, this document reflected the influence of Enlightenment ideas.

- **Social Contract** The Constitution of the United States set up a government by social contract. The government was established by the consent of the governed. The Constitution begins with these words: "We the People of the United States . . ."

- **Separation of Powers** Influenced by the ideas of Montesquieu, the Constitution created a republic in which power was to be divided between the federal government and the states. In addition, the writers of the Constitution established a government that divided powers among an executive, a legislative, and a judicial branch. Each branch could provide checks and balances on the other branches.

- **Protection of Rights** The Bill of Rights was added to the Constitution to protect the basic rights of American citizens, including freedom of speech and freedom of religion. The Constitution stated that it was the duty of the government to protect these rights.

Impact of the American Revolution

The American Revolution had a great impact around the world.

- The American republic stood as a symbol of freedom to both Europe and Latin America.

- The United States Constitution created the most liberal government of its time. Other nations would copy the ideas in this document.

- The success of the American Revolution would soon inspire major global changes as other peoples challenged the power of absolute monarchs.

Note Taking

Reading Skill:
Identify Main Ideas
As you read, fill in a table with main ideas about these political documents.

Common Sense	Declaration of Independence	Constitution

Key Themes and Concepts

Human Rights
The Declaration of Independence reflects many of Locke's Enlightenment ideas. These ideas include people's natural rights to life and liberty, the role of the government in protecting those rights, and the right of people to overthrow unjust governments.

Government and Change
The United States Constitution contributed to change in other parts of the world. It was a model for many other nations that formed new governments in the years that followed.

Preparing for the Regents

- Describe some Enlightenment ideas that inspired the American Revolution and influenced the founders of the United States of America.

- Why was the American Revolution an important turning point in global history?

Stages of Political Revolutions

```
  ┌──────────────────┐        ┌──────────────────┐
  │   Emergence       │        │  Injustices of the│
  │   of a Strong     │        │   Old Regime      │
  │   Leader          │        │                   │
  └──────────────────┘        └──────────────────┘

┌──────────────────┐                    ┌──────────────────┐
│   Return of       │                    │    Rule by        │
│   Moderates       │                    │   Moderate        │
│                   │                    │   Reformers       │
└──────────────────┘                    └──────────────────┘

          ┌──────────────────────┐
          │  Rule by Radical      │
          │  Revolutionaries      │
          └──────────────────────┘
```

The French Revolution

Soon after the American Revolution, a major revolution broke out in France. Starting in 1789, the French Revolution had a deep and lasting impact on France, Europe, and other areas of the world. The French Revolution followed a pattern common to many political revolutions. In this pattern, revolutions pass through different stages, caused by changes in leadership and shifts in power. Problems begin to appear in a country, and revolutionary groups form, hoping to correct the injustices. At the beginning of the revolution, moderate reformers come to power and as their compromise reforms fail, power passes to a more radical group of revolutionaries. The revolution grows more violent and extreme. A reaction to the violence follows, bringing moderates back to power. Often, at that point, there is a return to the old order as the people turn to a leader who promises order along with reform.

Causes of the Revolution

Many injustices existed in prerevolutionary France. Political, social, economic, and intellectual factors combined to bring about the French Revolution.

Absolute Monarchy On the eve of revolution, France was an absolute monarchy. Under absolutism, most people in France were denied basic rights and any say in government.

Social Inequality Since the Middle Ages, everyone in France had belonged to one of three social classes called estates. The clergy were the First Estate; the titled nobility composed the Second Estate. These two classes held enormous wealth, did not have to pay taxes, and enjoyed other special rights and privileges. The Third Estate made up most of French society and included a bourgeoisie (middle class), poor city workers, and rural peasants, the largest group. The Third Estate, which resented its heavy tax burden and lack of rights, grew increasingly discontented.

Population and Land Ownership in France, 1789

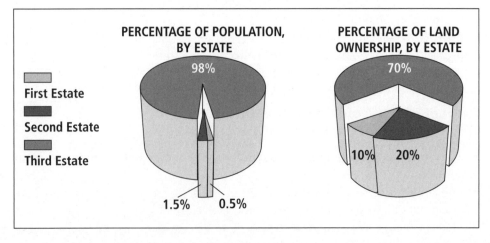

PERCENTAGE OF POPULATION, BY ESTATE

First Estate
Second Estate
Third Estate

98%

1.5%   0.5%

PERCENTAGE OF LAND OWNERSHIP, BY ESTATE

70%

10%   20%

Economic Injustices The situation in France became worse because of economic conditions in the late 1780s. The government, with its lavish court and expensive wars, spent more money than it earned. This debt added to the tax burden of the Third Estate. Bad harvests in 1789 caused food prices to rise. Peasants and city dwellers often did not have enough to eat and began to riot, demanding bread.

Enlightenment Through the 1600s and 1700s, Enlightenment thinkers were critical of France's absolute monarchy and called for democratic reforms. Enlightenment ideas led many French to question the traditional way of ordering society. It was not reasonable, they felt, for the First and Second Estates to have privileges at the expense of the Third Estate.

English and American Examples England's Glorious Revolution provided an example of how existing authority could be challenged. In addition, the French were inspired by the American colonies' successful fight for liberty and equality in the American Revolution.

Stages of the Revolution

The Revolution Begins As conditions grew worse in France, demands for reform increased. In 1789, King Louis XVI finally called the **Estates General,** a body made up of representatives of all three estates, into session. After this, change came swiftly.

- **National Assembly** The Third Estate, the only elected group in the Estates General, declared itself the National Assembly. The National Assembly vowed to write a new constitution for France.

- **Seizure of the Bastille** Working-class people, already rioting over the price of bread, stormed a prison called the Bastille on July 14, 1789. Fighting broke out through city and countryside. In a period known as the Great Fear, peasants attacked nobles and destroyed their homes.

- **Moderates in Power** The king, frightened by the increasing turmoil, agreed to allow the National Assembly to begin reforms.

- **Declaration of the Rights of Man and of the Citizen** The National Assembly abolished the privileges of the First and Second Estates and adopted the Declaration of the Rights of Man and of the Citizen. Based partly on the Declaration of Independence, it contained many Enlightenment ideas.

- **A Limited Monarchy** By 1791, the Assembly had written a constitution. The Constitution of 1791 defined the role and purpose of a new government.

  - It set up a limited monarchy and a representative assembly.

  - It declared that people had natural rights and that it was the job of the government to protect those rights.

  - It put the Church under state control.

News about the French Revolution quickly spread across Europe. Many European rulers and nobles feared that revolutionary ideas would spread to their own countries. They threatened to intervene—with military force, if necessary—to save the French monarchy. In 1792, to fight tyranny and spread the revolution, France declared war on Austria, Prussia, Great Britain, and several other states.

Preparing for the Regents

- List three factors that led to the French Revolution.

1.

2.

3.

Key Themes and Concepts

Individual Cultural Identity As you study the French Revolution, take note of the roles played by individual citizens. Members of the Third Estate formed the National Assembly. Working-class people stormed the Bastille, and peasants attacked the homes of nobles.

Preparing for the Regents

- What influences from the Enlightenment and the American Revolution can you see in the Declaration of the Rights of Man and the Citizen?

The French Declaration of Rights

DECLARATION OF THE RIGHTS OF MAN AND OF THE CITIZEN

- Written in 1789
- Uses American Declaration of Independence as model
- States that all men have natural rights
- Declares the job of government to protect the natural rights of the people
- Guarantees all male citizens equality under the law
- States that people are free to practice any religion they choose
- Promises to tax people according to how much they can afford

Key Themes and Concepts

Change
During the course of the revolution, the people in power changed, and ideas of those in power changed. At first, moderates were in power, and the constitution called for a limited monarchy. By 1793, the radicals were in control, and the king had been executed.

Radicals in Power The war with the other European nations went badly for France. In 1792, radicals took control of the Assembly, ended the monarchy, and declared France a republic. Their slogan was "Liberty, Equality, Fraternity." In 1793, the king was executed for treason. This event was followed by a period in France called the Reign of Terror, led in part by **Maximilien Robespierre,** a radical revolutionary. During this time, tens of thousands of people were executed. Thousands more were put into prison. Within a year, however, the violence turned back on itself. Robespierre himself was executed, and the Reign of Terror ended.

Moderates Return Beginning in 1795, a five-man "Directory" supported by a legislature held power in France. This government was weak and inefficient. Rising bread prices brought the threat of riots. Into this chaotic situation stepped an ambitious military leader, Napoleon Bonaparte.

Napoleon in Power

His Rise to Power When the revolution started, **Napoleon Bonaparte** was a low-level military officer with dreams of glory. Bonaparte rose in the ranks and won important victories against the British and Austrians. A popular general by 1799, Napoleon helped overthrow the weak Directory in a **coup d'état,** or revolt by military leaders to overthrow a government. He organized a new government and put himself in charge. Three years later, he took the title "Emperor of the French." Napoleon now had absolute power. The French people, hoping for stability, supported Napoleon at each step in his rise.

Napoleon in Europe, 1812

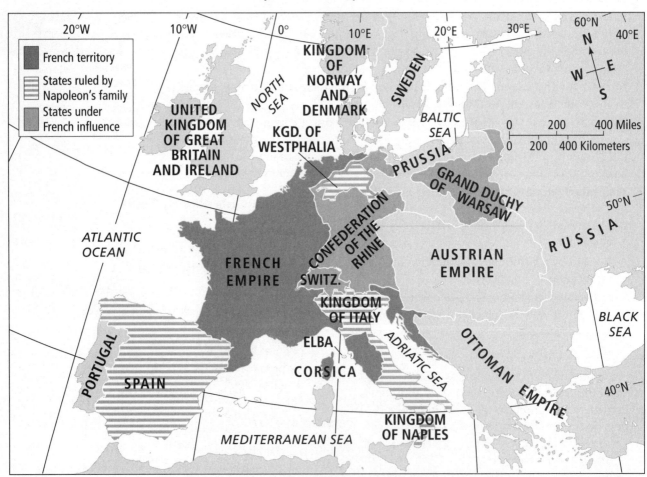

Napoleon's Empire Napoleon's empire was at its largest in 1812. Most of the countries in Europe today have different names and borders.

His Achievements Much of Napoleon's popularity came from his effective policies.

- **Economy** Napoleon controlled prices, supported new industry, and built roads and canals.
- **Education** Napoleon established a government-supervised public school system.
- **Napoleonic Code** The Napoleonic Code was a legal code that included many Enlightenment ideas, such as the legal equality of citizens and religious toleration.

Napoleon's Empire From 1804 to 1814, Napoleon ruled an empire. He conquered much of Europe. Napoleon often replaced the monarchs of defeated nations with his friends and relatives.

Of the European powers, only Great Britain and Russia remained beyond Napoleon's reach. Great Britain was shielded from French troops by a powerful navy and the English Channel.

Napoleon's Fall Napoleon's empire began to crumble for several reasons. First, most people in conquered states looked on Napoleon's armies as foreign oppressors. Inspired by nationalism, people across Europe revolted against French rule.

Another factor was Napoleon's invasion of Russia in 1812. As Napoleon's armies invaded from the west, the Russians retreated eastward. The "scorched earth" policy of the Russians, in which they burned crops and villages as they retreated, left the French troops hungry and cold. Most of Napoleon's army was lost during the long Russian winter.

The following year, an alliance of Russia, Great Britain, Austria, and Prussia defeated Napoleon, forcing him to step down in 1814. Napoleon returned to power in 1815, but the British and Prussians defeated him at the decisive Battle of Waterloo. This battle ended Napoleon's reign, and he lived the rest of his life in exile.

Key Themes and Concepts

Power
Despite Napoleon's reforms, order and authority were still higher priorities for him than individual rights. The Napoleonic Code included many Enlightenment ideas, such as the equality of citizens under the law. However, it also undid some reforms of the revolution, such as rights that had been granted to women.

Preparing for the Regents

- How did nationalism help Napoleon to build his empire? How did nationalism lead to Napoleon's defeat?

Preparing for the Regents

Practice interpreting political cartoons by answering these questions.

1. What does the large plum pudding represent? How do the slices represent Napoleon's quest for power?

2. Based on your knowledge of Napoleon's relationship with Great Britain, would this dinner be a cordial one? Explain.

British Prime Minister William Pitt and Napoleon carve a large plum pudding

Preparing for the Regents

- Create a chart that outlines the causes and lasting effects of the French Revolution.

- In what way was the French Revolution a turning point in global history?

Effects of the French Revolution

The French Revolution and the reign of Napoleon transformed both France and Europe in many ways.

Democratic Ideals Napoleon's conquests spread the ideals of democracy throughout Europe. Groups struggled to achieve the goals of the French republic: "Liberty, Equality, Fraternity." People wanted liberty from absolute monarchs and unjust governments. They pursued equality by opposing social inequality and injustice. They expressed fraternity, or brotherhood, by working together for a common cause.

Nationalism Among the French, the revolution and the conquests of Napoleon inspired feelings of national pride. This pride and sense of national identity replaced earlier loyalty to local authority and the person of the monarch.

The conquests of Napoleon also increased nationalistic feeling across Europe and around the world. His conquests had a part in the eventual unification of both Italy and Germany. His weakening of Spain led to the Latin American independence movements.

Key Themes and Concepts

Nationalism
Feelings of nationalism often develop when a group of people is under the control of a foreign power. List other examples of people embracing nationalism and working together to drive out foreign rulers.

Latin American Independence Movements

In the late 1700s, Enlightenment and revolutionary ideas spread from Europe and the United States to Latin America. Educated Latin Americans read works by Enlightenment writers. They debated about political and social reform. Thomas Jefferson's Declaration of Independence and the Constitution were eagerly read. The success of the American Revolution showed that foreign rule could be thrown off. Latin Americans also were inspired by what the French Revolution had accomplished. Beginning in the 1790s, they struggled to gain independence as well as other rights and freedoms.

Toussaint L'Ouverture

The French colony of Haiti was the first Latin American colony to revolt against European rule. In Haiti, French planters owned large sugar plantations. Here nearly half a million enslaved Africans lived and worked in terrible conditions. Moreover, the French gave few rights to free mulattoes (persons of mixed ancestry) living on the island.

Preparing for the Regents

- Explain the role of imperialism as a cause of the revolution in Haiti. Why would you expect other revolutions to occur in Latin America?

In 1791, a self-educated former slave named **Toussaint L'Ouverture** led a revolt. Toussaint was familiar with the works of the Enlightenment thinkers and wanted to lead his people to liberty. Toussaint proved to be an effective military leader and gained control of much of the island. Haitian slaves won their freedom in 1798.

In 1802, Napoleon sent an army to Haiti to reestablish French dominance. Toussaint led a guerrilla war to gain Haitian independence. The French captured Toussaint, but yellow fever took a heavy toll on their forces. In 1804, Haitians declared their independence. Napoleon then abandoned the island. Haiti became a republic in 1820.

Simón Bolívar

In South America in the early 1800s, an educated creole named **Simón Bolívar** led resistance movements against the Spanish. Bolívar had become an admirer of Enlightenment ideas and the French Revolution during a stay in Europe. He was also inspired by the American Revolution. He vowed to fight Spanish rule in South America. Called "the Liberator," Bolívar became one of the greatest Latin American nationalist leaders of this period.

Struggle For Independence In 1810, Bolívar started his long struggle against the Spanish. Over the next 12 years, he led a series of military campaigns that won independence for Venezuela, New Granada (present-day Colombia), Ecuador, Peru, and Bolivia. He then joined forces with **José de San Martín,** who had defeated the Spanish in Argentina and Chile in the 1810s.

Difficulties Ahead Despite his victories against the Spanish, Bolívar failed in his attempt to create a large, united Latin American state. Spain's former empire thus became divided into a number of separate independent states. These nations faced a long struggle to gain stability, achieve social equality, and eliminate poverty.

Summarize

- Who were the key revolutionaries for independence in Latin America?

- What were their accomplishments?

South America, 1790

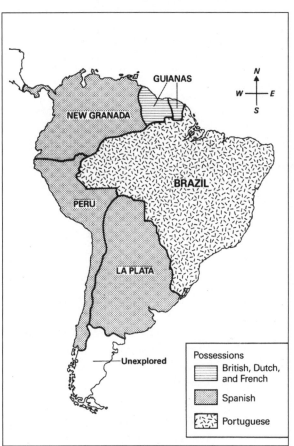

South America, 1828

Summary

Enlightenment ideas about natural rights and rejection of absolutist authority inspired major revolutions in the late 1700s and early 1800s. Colonists in America declared independence from Great Britain in 1776 and created a government based on the ideas of Locke and Montesquieu. Influenced by the American Revolution, revolutionaries in France overturned the monarchy and created a new social order. Napoleon helped spread revolutionary ideals across Europe. Both the American and French Revolutions contributed to revolutions in Latin America in the early 1800s. Leaders such as Toussaint L'Ouverture and Simón Bolívar led popular movements to overthrow European rule.

Key Themes and Concepts

Change
The revolutions of the late 1700s and early 1800s had several lasting effects. These included the creation of the United States, the spread of nationalism and democratic ideals, and the establishment of independent republics in Latin America.

Reaction Against Revolutionary Ideals

Section Overview

After the French Revolution, there was a reaction against revolutionary ideals. In 1815 at the Congress of Vienna, the leaders of the nations of Europe restored the old monarchies. In the following decades, conflicts between revolutionary ideals and the desire to maintain the old order would cause uprisings and repression. Although some reforms slowly took hold in Western Europe, absolutism remained strong in Russia. In Latin America, democratic reforms were slow to develop. In the early 1900s, however, Mexico experienced a political and social revolution accompanied by the growth of nationalistic feelings.

Key Themes and Concepts

As you review this section, take special note of the following key themes and concepts:

Power How did leaders react to revolutionary ideals in Europe after the French Revolution and the reign of Napoleon?

Political Systems What barriers to reform existed in Russia and Latin America in the 1800s?

Change What reforms occurred in Mexico in the early 1800s?

Key People and Terms

As you review this section, be sure you understand the significance of these key people and terms:

Congress of Vienna

Prince Clemens von Metternich

balance of power

conservatism

liberalism

nationalism

Russification

pogroms

oligarchy

caudillos

cash crop economy

Porfirio Díaz

Emiliano Zapata

Francisco "Pancho" Villa

The Congress of Vienna

After Napoleon's defeat, European diplomats met at the Congress of Vienna in 1815 to devise a peace settlement. The meeting was dominated by **Prince Clemens von Metternich** of Austria, who wanted to restore Europe to the way it was before the French Revolution. The decisions made at this meeting were designed to bring stability and order to Europe by repressing the feelings of nationalism and preventing liberal political change unleashed by the French Revolution and Napoleon.

The Congress of Vienna

GOAL	ACTION
To prevent France from going to war again	Strengthen countries around France • Add Belgium and Luxembourg to Holland to create the kingdom of the Netherlands • Give Prussia lands along the Rhine River • Allow Austria to take control of Italy again
To return Europe to the way it was in 1792, before Napoleon	Give power back to the monarchs of Europe
To protect the new system and maintain peace	Create the Concert of Europe, an organization to maintain peace in Europe

Balance of Power and Restored Monarchs

Despite their sometimes different goals, the leaders at the Congress of Vienna accomplished a great deal. Much of what the leaders did at the Congress of Vienna occurred for two reasons. First, they wanted to establish a **balance of power,** or a distribution of military and economic power that prevents any one nation from becoming too strong. They also wanted to restore power to monarchs. The Congress of Vienna was the first of many reactions in Europe against the revolutionary ideals of the 1700s and 1800s. It was also a victory for conservatives. **Conservatism** was a set of beliefs held by those who wanted to preserve traditional ways. As conservatism clashed with the ideals of the French Revolution, revolutions would occur throughout Europe and Latin America.

New Revolutions in Europe

The Vienna settlement helped to maintain peace among nations in Europe for almost 100 years. Revolutions did occur within nations, however. Revolutionaries were not happy with the results of the Congress of Vienna. They opposed the Congress's policy of trying to restore Europe to the way it had been before the French Revolution.

Causes

Revolts occurred in many places across Europe from the time of the Congress through about 1850. There were two main causes of these revolutions.

- **Liberalism** People opposed the power of monarchs and sought democratic reforms.
- **Nationalism** People wanted independent nation-states that were free from foreign rule.

Revolutions of 1830

In 1830, the French, alarmed by their monarch's attempt to restore absolutism, successfully revolted and created a constitutional monarchy. Attempts to gain independence in Greece and Belgium were successful while similar attempts in Italy, Germany, and Poland were defeated.

Revolutions of 1848

Additional revolutions occurred in 1848, led by the events in France.

- **France** King Louis Philippe's government was denounced as corrupt, prompting another revolution in 1848. Louis Philippe stepped down, and a republic was established. Within months of the uprising, upper- and middle-class interests gained control of the government and violently put down a

Preparing for the Regents

- Explain how the Congress of Vienna was a reaction against revolutionary ideals.

Vocabulary Builder

clash—(klash) *v.* if two people or groups clash, they argue because they have very different beliefs and opinions

Preparing for the Regents

- How do the events of 1848 reflect the long-term impact of the French Revolution?

Key Themes and Concepts

Civic Ideals
Note that nationalism has its roots in the Enlightenment and the French Revolution.

Key Themes and Concepts

Interdependence
As had occurred in 1789, a revolution in 1830 in France affected the other nations of Europe.

Revolutions in Europe, 1830 and 1848

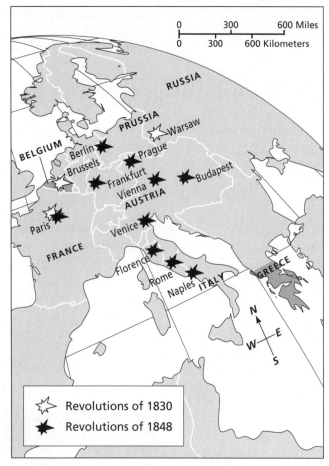

Legend:
☆ Revolutions of 1830
★ Revolutions of 1848

Revolutions in Europe In 1830 and 1848, revolutions in Europe took place in many cities and countries. Most failed. However, Europe was changed by reforms that resulted from the revolts.

workers' rebellion in Paris. The fighting left bitter feelings between the working class and the middle class.

- **Austrian Empire** When students revolted in Vienna in 1848, Metternich tried to suppress them. He resigned when workers rose up to support the students. As revolution quickly spread to other areas of the empire, the Austrian government agreed to certain reforms. However, the Austrian army soon regained control, and many revolutionaries were imprisoned, executed, or sent into exile.

- **Italy and Germany** Rebellions in Italy were successful just for short periods of time. In Germany, student protesters who were backed by peasants and workers demanded reforms. Although an assembly was formed, it was later dissolved as the revolutionaries turned on each other.

Impact of the Revolutions

The revolutions that occurred in 1830 and 1848 frightened many of Europe's rulers. As a result, some agreed to reforms. For the most part, however, the revolts of 1830 and 1848 failed. There were several reasons for these failures.

- Most revolutionaries did not have widespread support.
- Sometimes the revolutionaries themselves were divided.
- Powerful government forces often crushed the revolts.

Preparing for the Regents

- Use your map skills to tell which areas were the most affected by the revolutions between 1830 and 1850.

Absolutism in Czarist Russia

Impact of the French Revolution

While the countries of Western Europe were profoundly changed by the French Revolution, Russian czars strove to keep the ideals of the French Revolution—liberty, equality, and fraternity—from reaching their people. Unlike the countries of Western Europe, Russia changed very little throughout the 1800s.

Political Conditions

Russian czars resisted reforms, fearing that change would weaken their control. Czars refused to introduce elements of democracy into their societies, although democratic ideals were gaining strength in Western European countries at that time.

Social Conditions

A Feudal Society Russia had a rigid feudal social structure. Landowning nobles were powerful and resisted any change that would weaken their position. The middle class was too small to have any influence. Although serfdom had gradually disappeared in Western Europe by the 1700s, it had continued in Russia. Serfs were bound to the land, and the owner of the land had almost total power over the serfs who worked it.

Freeing of the Serfs Russia became involved in the Crimean War after trying to seize Ottoman lands along the Danube. Russia suffered a defeat in this war, making its leaders aware of the country's need to modernize and industrialize. Demands for reform, including freedom for the serfs, followed.

In 1861, during the reign of Alexander II, the serfs were freed. Freeing the serfs brought problems, however. Former serfs had to buy the land they had worked, and many were too poor to do so. Even those who could buy land often did not have enough to support their families. Discontent continued.

Many freed serfs moved off their land and into the cities, where they took jobs in industries. These freed serfs were sometimes part of the pressure for reform in Russia.

Russification Russia, as a vast empire, contained many ethnic minorities. The czars aimed to maintain tight control over these people as well as to encourage feelings of Russian unity. This policy of Russification was an attempt to make all groups think, act, and believe as Russians.

For example, Russian czar Alexander III persecuted non-Russians, including Poles, Ukrainians, and Armenians. He insisted on one language, Russian, and one church, the Russian Orthodox Church. Alexander also persecuted Jews, restricting the jobs they could have and even where they could live. These policies encouraged violent attacks on Jews, called **pogroms.** The authorities stood by and watched as the homes of Jews were burned and their businesses looted.

Imperialism in Asia

In the 1700s, Russia had expanded to the Baltic Sea, to the Black Sea, and into Eastern Europe, occupying much of Poland. The Russians also expanded eastward across Siberia and beyond the Bering Strait, into Alaska. During the early 1800s, the Russians began their practice of exiling convicts to Siberia.

Czars in the 1800s added lands in central Asia. This territory gave Russia the largest and most diverse empire in Europe and Asia. The construction of the Trans-Siberian Railway, begun in the 1890s, extended Russian economic and political control over the region.

Instability in Latin America

As you have learned, revolutionaries in Latin America had thrown off Spanish rule in the early 1800s. Life, however, did not improve for most people after they achieved independence. Revolts and civil wars broke out while poverty and prejudice continued. Many factors made it difficult for Latin American nations to benefit from the revolutions that had occurred.

Geographic Barriers

The Latin American nations that gained independence in the 1800s covered a vast area, from Mexico to the southern tip of South America. This area included numerous geographic barriers, such as the Andes Mountains, that hindered attempts at creating a unified Latin America. Fights between various leaders and nationalistic feelings within different groups also kept Latin Americans from uniting.

Social Injustice

Despite the establishment of Latin American republics with constitutions, democracy did not follow. One problem was that the colonial class structure remained largely intact. Creoles replaced peninsulares as the ruling class, and

Key Themes and Concepts

Change
Despite the problems faced by freed serfs, their emancipation in 1861 marked a major turning point in Russian history. A similar development occurred in the United States a few years later, when the enslaved African Americans were freed.

Diversity
Russian czars fought diversity in their nation. They tried to force minorities to abandon their own cultures and adopt Russian culture.

Preparing for the Regents

- How did conditions in Russia in the late 1800s contribute to the revolutions that occurred in the early 1900s?

Key Themes and Concepts

Political Systems
Three centuries of strong Spanish rule left most Latin Americans with little practical knowledge of how to establish a representative democracy.

land and wealth remained in their hands. This kind of system, in which ruling power belongs to a small, powerful elite, is known as an **oligarchy.** Mestizos, mulattoes, Indians, and Africans gained few rights and still faced racial prejudice. Most had to work as peasants on the large estates of the landowners.

Military Rulers

Because of the strong rule that colonial empires had exerted in Latin America, people of these countries had little experience with self-government. Local military strongmen called **caudillos** put together their own armies and challenged central governments. Some caudillos were strong enough to gain control of governments. These dictators were repressive, usually ignoring existing constitutions. Their policies usually favored the upper class.

Power of the Church

The Roman Catholic Church had acted as a stabilizing influence in Latin America. It also promoted education. But the Church had an interest in preserving the old order in Latin America. As in colonial days, the Church still owned large amounts of land. Liberals in Latin America hoped to end the Church's power over education and reduce its vast landholdings.

Economic Problems

Cash Crop Economies Under colonial rule, Latin American economies had become dependent on trade with Spain and Portugal. Latin Americans relied on a cash crop economy. The colonies sent raw materials such as sugar, cotton, and coffee to Europe and had to import manufactured goods. Dependence on just one crop or even a few crops makes a nation's economy very unstable. If a drought or crop failure occurs, or if prices for the products fall, the economy can be devastated.

Economic Imperialism In the mid-1800s, some Latin American economies began to grow. Foreign investment allowed them to develop mining and agriculture. Foreigners also invested in transportation improvement, such as the development of ports and the building of railroads. Even so, there were few benefits for the majority of Latin Americans. The rigid class structure limited economic gains to the few at the top of the social structure. In general, only the upper classes and the foreign investors profited.

The Mexican Revolution (1910–1930)

Causes

General **Porfirio Díaz** ruled Mexico as a dictator in the late 1800s and early 1900s. Díaz brought economic advances to Mexico. Railroads were built and industry grew. However, the wealth went to a small upper class as well as to foreign investors. The rule of Díaz, who brutally suppressed opposition, left most Mexicans uneducated, landless, and poor. In 1910, the discontent boiled over into a revolution that forced Díaz from power.

Key Figures

No one person led the revolution. Several local leaders gathered their own armies, destroying railroads and estates.

- **Emiliano Zapata,** an Indian, was one of the most famous leaders. He led a large peasant revolt in the south, calling for land reform.
- **Francisco "Pancho" Villa,** a rebel leader in the north, won the loyalty of a large number of peasants. When the United States supported the Mexican government against Villa, conflict erupted across the border between Villa and the United States government in 1916.

Preparing for the Regents

- In both Russia and Latin America, there were obstacles to reform. Which obstacles were shared by Russia and Latin America? Which obstacles were unique to Latin America?

- What economic problems can result from dependence on a cash crop economy?

Preparing for the Regents

- Compare the causes of the Mexican Revolution to those of the French Revolution.

- Venustiano Carranza was elected president of Mexico in 1917. He approved a new constitution that, with amendments, is still in force today.

Effects of the Revolution

The Constitution of 1917 The new constitution agreed to by Carranza in 1917 called for land reform, gave the government control of Church estates, and guaranteed more rights to workers and to women.

Social Reforms Reforms were eventually carried out in the 1920s, making Mexico the first Latin American nation to achieve social and economic reform for the majority of its people. For example, the government set up libraries and schools. Some Indian communities were given the opportunity to regain land that had been taken from them in the past.

Economic Nationalism Mexico, along with other countries of Latin America, experienced strong feelings of nationalism in the early 1900s. Much of the nationalistic spirit was aimed at ending economic dependence on industrial powers. Mexico became determined to develop its own economy. The Mexican government brought industries under government control or took over foreign-owned industries.

Cultural Nationalism In the 1920s and 1930s, nationalistic feeling caused writers in Mexico and other parts of Latin America to reject the influences of Europe. They began to take pride in Latin American culture, which displayed a mixture of Western European and Indian traditions. In Mexico, mural painting, which had been a common art form in the Aztec empire, was revived. Muralists such as Diego Rivera and José Clemente Orozco created works of great beauty. Many showed the struggles of the Mexican people for freedom.

Summary

After the defeat of Napoleon, conservative leaders sought to suppress the ideals of the French Revolution and restore monarchy. In 1830 and 1848, uprisings against the old order occurred all across Europe. Although these revolts were mostly unsuccessful, the ideals behind them continued to have an impact on Europe. In Russia and in Latin America, numerous barriers to reform existed. In Mexico, however, reforms took place that benefited the majority of the population.

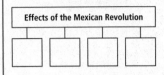

Note Taking

Reading Skill:
Identify Effects Make a chart. As you read, record the effects of the Mexican Revolution. Include the main idea and at least one supporting detail.

Effects of the Mexican Revolution

Key Themes and Concepts

Nationalism
In Mexico, nationalism had economic and cultural aspects. Mexicans wanted to end their economic dependence on foreign powers. They also wanted to show their pride in Latin American culture.

Preparing for the Regents

- Compare the reactions against revolutionary ideals in Europe, in Russia, and in Latin America in the 1800s.

Global Nationalism

Section Overview

During the French Revolution, people in France expressed great pride in their nation. Nationalism later spread to other peoples, inspiring uprisings across Europe and in Latin America. In the 1860s, nationalism led to the unification of Italy. By 1871, Germany had also united. Outside Europe, nationalist movements took root in India, Turkey, and elsewhere. Among Jews, a movement arose to create a separate Jewish state in Palestine. As the 1800s drew to a close, nationalistic forces created tensions in the Balkans that set the stage for a world war.

Key Themes and Concepts

As you review this section, take special note of the following key themes and concepts:

Nationalism How did nationalism cause revolutions?

Nation-State How did nationalism lead to the creation of nation-states in Italy and Germany?

Change How did nationalism affect Indians, Turks, and Jews?

Diversity How did nationalism cause conflict in the Balkans?

Key People and Terms

Key People and Terms

- Place each of the key people and terms into these two categories: person or movement/ political group.

As you review this section, be sure you understand the significance of these key people and terms:

Giuseppe Mazzini	Zionism
Count Camillo Cavour	Indian National Congress
Giuseppe Garibaldi	Muslim League
Otto von Bismarck	Young Turks
kaiser	Pan-Slavism

Key Themes and Concepts

Nationalism
Nationalism is a feeling of pride in and devotion to one's nation. It is a feeling that develops among people who may share a common language, history, set of traditions, or goal. Nationalism often causes people to join together to choose their own form of government, without outside interference.

Nationalism and Revolution

As you have learned, nationalism is a feeling of strong devotion to one's country. This feeling often develops among people who share a common language and heritage. Nationalism played an important role in political revolutions of the 1800s.

Revolution and war in the 1790s created a strong sense of national unity in France. This feeling inspired French armies to battlefield success as they sought to spread the ideals of their revolution. Napoleon also inspired nationalism among the nations he conquered. However, nationalistic feelings encouraged conquered peoples to rise up against Napoleon. In the years following the French Revolution, nationalism led to upheaval in Europe and elsewhere.

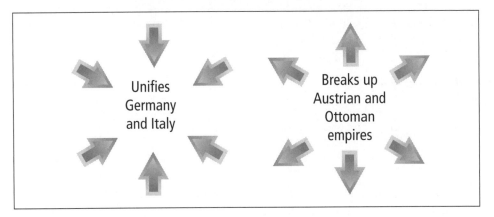

Unifying Germany and Italy
Before unification, the areas
that became Germany and
Italy were divided into small-
sized states.

Unification Movements in Europe

Nationalistic feeling became an increasingly significant force for self-determination and unification in Europe.

Italy

Ever since the Roman empire had fallen in the 400s, Italy had been divided into many small states. After Napoleon invaded Italy, he united some of the Italian states into the Kingdom of Italy. The Congress of Vienna, however, redivided Italy and put much of it under Austrian or Spanish control.

The three great leaders of Italian nationalism were Giuseppe Mazzini, Count Camillo Cavour, and Giuseppe Garibaldi.

- **Giuseppe Mazzini** formed the Young Italy national movement in 1831, but he was exiled for his views. His writings and speeches provided inspiration to the nationalist movement.
- **Count Camillo Cavour,** prime minister of the Italian state of Sardinia, shrewdly formed alliances with France and later with Prussia. He used diplomacy and war to drive Austrian power from Italy.
- **Giuseppe Garibaldi** was a soldier who led the forces that won control of southern Italy and helped it to unite with the north.

By 1861, Victor Emmanuel of Sardinia was crowned king of a united Italy. Rome and Venetia, at first not part of Italy, were included by 1870. With no tradition of unity, the new nation faced conflicts. The urban north quarreled with the rural south. Also, the Catholic Church resisted the new government. Despite economic growth, unrest grew in the late 1800s.

Germany

Another national unification movement occurred in Germany. In the early 1800s, most German-speaking people lived in small states, to which they felt loyalty. During Napoleon's conquests, feelings of nationalism stirred in those Germans who wanted to be free of French rule. After Napoleon's defeat in 1815, some nationalists called for a united Germany. Metternich, however, blocked this idea at the Congress of Vienna.

The Rise of Prussia In the 1830s, Prussia set up a trade union among German states called the Zollverein. This agreement ended trade barriers between the states and was a step toward unity. More important, it established Prussia as a leader among the states.

Key Themes and Concepts

Nationalism
In both Italy and Germany, the conquests of Napoleon inspired nationalism.

Preparing for the Regents

Explain one way in which each of the individuals listed here helped to unite Italy.

Mazzini:

Cavour:

Garibaldi:

Compare and Contrast

- What are the similarities and differences between unification in Italy and unification in Germany?

In 1862, **Otto von Bismarck** was appointed chancellor of Prussia. Over the next decade, Bismarck, a strong and practical leader, guided German unification. Bismarck was not driven by a feeling of German nationalism, however. His loyalty was to the Prussian king. Unification was merely a means for him to make the Prussian king the ruler of a strong and united German state.

"Blood and Iron" Bismarck believed that the only way to unify Germany was through a policy he called "blood and iron." Bismarck had no faith in speeches and representative government. He believed that the only way to unite the German states was through war. In seven years, Bismarck led Prussia into three wars. Each war increased Prussia's prestige and moved the German states closer to unity.

- **Danish War** In 1864, Prussia allied with Austria to seize land from Denmark.
- **Austro-Prussian War** In 1866, Prussia turned against Austria to gain more land. Prussia overwhelmed Austria in just seven weeks. Several German states were united with Prussia in the North German Confederation.
- **Franco-Prussian War** In 1870, Bismarck used nationalism and the bitter memories of Napoleon's conquests to stir up support for a war against France. Prussia and its German allies easily defeated France. During the war, southern German states agreed to unite with Prussia.

In 1871, the German states united under the Prussian king, William I. As their ruler, William called himself the **kaiser,** a title that was derived from the name *Caesar* and meant "emperor."

Zionism

The rise of nationalism in Europe had led to an intensification of anti-Semitism in the late 1800s. As citizens grew more patriotic about their own nations, they often grew more intolerant of those whom they saw as outsiders, including Jews. The pogroms that occurred in Eastern Europe and Russia are one example of this trend.

As anti-Semitism grew in Europe, some Jews moved to Palestine, the ancient Jewish homeland, buying land that they organized into farming communities. A Jewish journalist named Theodor Herzl became alarmed by the strong anti-Semitism he witnessed in France. In 1896, Herzl called for Jews to establish their own state. Herzl's writings helped to build Zionism, the movement devoted to building a Jewish state in Palestine. In 1897, he organized the first world congress of Zionists, which met in Switzerland. Herzl's dream of an independent Israel was realized a little more than 50 years later.

Nationalism in Asia

National movements were also at work outside of Europe.

India

Since the 1700s, the British had maintained control of the Indian subcontinent. Under British rule, nationalistic feelings began to stir among Indians, especially those who had been educated in the West. As Indian students learned about democracy and natural rights, they called increasingly for self-rule.

Indian National Congress In 1885, nationalist leaders in India formed the Indian National Congress, which became known as the Congress party. This group was made up mainly of Hindu professionals and business leaders. At first, the Congress party called merely for equal opportunity to serve in the government

Preparing for the Regents

- What role did Prussia and Bismarck play in German unification?

Vocabulary Builder

prestige—(prehs TEEZH) *n.* the respect and admiration that someone or something gets because of their success or important position

Preparing for the Regents

- The anti-Semitism that grew in Europe during the 1800s is an example of the negative effects of a group's nationalism on other peoples. Can you think of other examples of nationalism causing discrimination and violence against religious or ethnic minorities?

Key Themes and Concepts

Change
Western education introduced Indians to the ideals of democracy, nationalism, and basic human rights. This kind of thinking led eventually to self-rule for India. Western education brought change to other nations as well.

of India. They called for greater democracy and Western-style modernization, looking ahead to self-rule.

Muslim League Initially, Muslims and Hindus cooperated in their campaign for self-rule. However, Muslims grew distrustful of the Indian National Congress because the organization was mostly Hindu. The increasing strength of Hindu nationalism alarmed Muslims. In 1906, Muslim leaders formed the Muslim League to protect their own rights and interests. They even talked about setting up a separate Muslim state. After World War I, calls for Indian self-rule increased, followed by demands for independence. This goal would finally be achieved in 1947.

Turkey

In the 1800s, the multinational Ottoman empire faced challenges from the various ethnic groups in the empire.

Young Turks A group of liberals in the 1890s established a movement called the Young Turks. This group wanted to strengthen the Ottoman empire and end the threat of Western imperialism. In 1908, they overthrew the sultan and took control of the government.

The Armenian Massacre The Young Turks supported Turkish nationalism. They abandoned traditional Ottoman tolerance of diverse cultures and religions. Muslim Turks turned against Christian Armenians who were living in the Ottoman empire. Accusing the Armenians of plotting with Russia against the Ottoman empire, the Turks unleashed a massacre that resulted in the death of over a million Armenians over the next 25 years.

Nationalities in Eastern Europe Around 1870

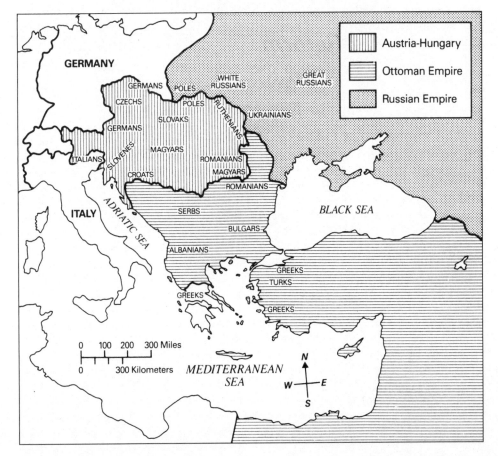

The Balkans The peninsula in southeastern Europe is called the Balkans. In the late 1800s, this area was a center of conflict. The various peoples and empires competed for power.

Preparing for the Regents

- How has nationalism been a force that divides as well as unifies? Give examples to support your answer.

- By the 1800s, the Ottoman empire was becoming weaker. How did European nations react to the decreasing power of the Ottomans?

- Choose one of the regions discussed in this section. Explain how nationalism remains a force in that region today.

Nationalism and Conflict in the Balkans

Nationalism was a source of conflict in the Balkan peninsula of southeastern Europe. In the 1800s, the Ottoman empire still ruled much of the area, which was home to many groups. Among these were Serbs, Greeks, Bulgarians, and Romanians. During the 1800s, nationalist groups in the Balkans rebelled against foreign rule. From 1829 to 1908, Greece, Montenegro, Serbia, Romania, and Bulgaria all gained their independence.

The nations of Europe viewed the Ottoman empire as "the sick man of Europe." They hoped to gain land from the Ottoman empire. Russia, Austria-Hungary, Great Britain, and France all entered into alliances and wars that were designed to gain territory from the Ottoman empire.

Russia sponsored a nationalistic movement called **Pan-Slavism,** based on the idea that all Slavic peoples shared a common nationality. Serbia had a large Slavic population and was supported by Russia. Austria-Hungary, however, feared Serbian nationalism and angered Serbia by taking control in 1908 of two provinces that would have given Serbia access to the Adriatic Sea.

In the early years of 1900, crisis after crisis broke out on the Balkan peninsula. By 1914, the Balkans were the "powder keg of Europe." Tensions soon exploded into a full-scale global conflict: World War I.

Note Taking

Reading Skill: **Summarize** Make a chart. Summarize the main ideas about nationalism in the three areas listed in the chart.

Nationalism	
Europe	•
	•
Asia	•
	•
Balkans	•
	•

Summary

Starting in the late 1700s, nationalism became a major force that helped inspire uprisings across Europe and Latin America. In the mid-1800s, nationalism led to the creation of two strong, united nations: Italy and Germany. Nationalistic sentiments also spread among Indians, Turks, Jews, and other peoples. Nationalism did not always draw people together, however. In the early 1900s, nationalism created conflicts in southeastern Europe that drove the continent to the brink of war.

Economic and Social Revolutions

Section Overview

Starting around 1750, Europe experienced a series of major changes. They began with improvements in farming that led to an increase in population. These changes contributed to the Industrial Revolution. With the Industrial Revolution, social classes, people's roles, working conditions, and city life changed greatly. When the new conditions led to problems, differing thinkers wanted to solve them in different ways. Some groups emphasized the rights of individuals. Socialists and others stressed the needs of society as a whole. A period of reforms followed. By the early 1900s, the world had changed even more: Global migration occurred and movement toward a global economy accelerated.

Key Themes and Concepts

As you review this section, take special note of the following key themes and concepts:

Change What changes occurred during the Agrarian Revolution?

Science and Technology What role did technology play in the Industrial Revolution?

Economic Systems What economic and social developments occurred as part of the Industrial Revolution?

Political Systems What parliamentary reforms came about as a result of the Industrial Revolution?

The Big Idea

In the 1700s and 1800s in Europe:

- the Agrarian Revolution led to population growth.
- the Industrial Revolution eventually transformed economic systems and social conditions around the world.
- people proposed different ways to deal with the problems created by industrialization.
- economic life became more global, and mass migrations of people occurred.

Key People and Terms

As you review this section, be sure you understand the significance of these key people and terms:

Agrarian Revolution	Adam Smith	Robert Owen
enclosure	capitalism	socialism
Industrial Revolution	supply and demand	Karl Marx
factories	Thomas Malthus	suffrage
laissez faire	Social Darwinism	

Key People and Terms

- Place each of the key people and terms into these three categories: science and technology, economic system, political system.

The Agrarian Revolution

In 1750, most people still lived in small villages and made their own clothing and tools. In the century that followed, dramatic changes took place in the ways people lived and worked.

Increased Food Production

The movement away from rural life began with the Agrarian Revolution, a change in methods of farming.

Technology The Dutch led the way by building dikes to protect their farmland from the sea and using fertilizer to improve the soil. The British discovered ways to produce more food. Jethro Tull invented the seed drill, which planted seeds in rows.

Enclosure Movement Landowners found a new purpose for enclosure, taking over and fencing off land that once had been shared by peasant farmers. The purpose of the enclosure movement was to replace the many small strip farms with larger fields. This practice made farming more efficient, improving agricultural production.

Population Explosion

The Agrarian Revolution led to rapid population growth. With a better diet, women had healthier and stronger babies. In addition, improved medical care and sanitation helped people live longer. During the 1700s, Europe's population increased from 120 million to about 190 million.

The Industrial Revolution

The Industrial Revolution was the period, beginning around 1750, in which the means of production of goods shifted from hand tools to complex machines and from human and animal power to steam power. During this period, technology developed rapidly and production increased. The Industrial Revolution brought great changes into people's lives.

Causes of the Industrial Revolution

Industrialization began in Great Britain. Belgium, France, Germany, the United States, and Japan would all industrialize by the end of the 1800s. In time, the Industrial Revolution would spread throughout the world. It happened first in Great Britain for several reasons.

The Industrial Revolution Begins in Great Britain

Geography	Population Growth and Change
Great Britain had plenty of iron ore and coal needed for industrialization. As an island, Great Britain had many natural harbors for trade and was protected from invasion. Rivers served both as a means of transportation and as sources of power for factories.	Growth in population due to the Agrarian Revolution led to more available workers. Because of the enclosure movement, fewer farm laborers were needed. People moved to the cities where they could work in factories.
Capital for Investment	**Energy and Technology**
The British overseas empire had made the economy strong. As a result, the middle class had the capital to invest in mines, railroads, and factories and the commercial and financial skills to manage investment.	Great Britain had experienced an energy revolution. In the 1700s, giant water wheels were used to power new machines. Soon coal was used to power steam engines, which would become an important power source for machines.

Factory System and Mass Production

The textile industry was the first to use the inventions of the Industrial Revolution. Before the Industrial Revolution, families spun cotton into thread and then wove cloth at home. By the 1700s, new machines were too large and expensive to be operated at home. Spinners and weavers began to work in long sheds that were owned by the manufacturers. These sheds, which brought workers and machines together in one place, became the first **factories.** At first, these factories were located near rapidly moving streams, which provided water power. Later, machines were powered by steam engines, fueled by coal. The factory system promoted mass production, meaning that goods were produced in huge quantities at lower cost.

Effects of the Industrial Revolution

The Industrial Revolution brought about many economic and social changes.

Laissez Faire Economics Before the Industrial Revolution, European nations had followed a policy of mercantilism, which called for government regulations, such as tariffs, to achieve a favorable balance of trade. However, during the Enlightenment, a theory called laissez faire emerged, which argued that businesses should be allowed to operate free of government regulation. In 1776, **Adam Smith** wrote *The Wealth of Nations* which promoted laissez-faire ideas. These ideas became the basis of the prevailing economic system during the Industrial Revolution. This system, known as **capitalism,** said that the economy should be governed by the natural forces of **supply and demand** and competition among businesses.

Rise of Big Business With new technology came the need for the investment of large amounts of money in businesses. To acquire this money, business owners sold stocks, or shares in their companies, to investors. Each stockholder therefore owned a part of the company. Stockholders allowed businesses to form corporations and expand into many areas.

New Class Structure In the Middle Ages, the two main classes in Europe had been nobles and peasants. During the 1600s, a middle class had emerged. The Industrial Revolution added more complexity.

- The upper class consisted of very rich industrial and business families. Members of these families often married into noble families.

- A growing upper middle class of business people and professionals—such as lawyers and doctors—emerged. Their standard of living was high. Below them a lower middle class of teachers, office workers, shopowners, and clerks existed.

- At the bottom of this social structure were factory workers and peasants. They benefited least from the Industrial Revolution. People in this class faced harsh living and working conditions in overcrowded cities.

Urbanization People moved from small villages to the towns and cities where factories were located. At first, conditions were very bad. Working-class people lived in crowded buildings. Without a sewage or sanitation system, garbage rotted in the streets. Disease spread.

Working Conditions Factory work hours were long. Men, women, and even children worked 12 to 16 hours a day. Mass production methods led to work that was boring. Many machines were dangerous.

Key Themes and Concepts

Time Continuity and Change
As you study current events, keep in mind that the Industrial Revolution is still occurring in the developing nations of the world.

Note Taking

Reading Skill:
Identify Effects
Make a chart. As you read, list the effects of the Industrial Revolution. Write details about each one. Add boxes as needed.

The Industrial Revolution	
Effects	Details
Laissez-Faire Economics	• •
	• •
	• •

Preparing for the Regents

- How did the Industrial Revolution lead to urbanization?

Preparing for the Regents

- How did the Industrial Revolution contribute to changing the roles of men and women?

Vocabulary Builder

dwelling—(DWEL ing) *n.* a house, apartment, etc., where people live

Note Taking

Reading Skill:
Identify Main Ideas and Supporting Details
As you read Competing Philosophies, complete an outline with the main ideas and supporting details. An outline has been started for you.

Competing Philosophies
I. Laissez-faire capitalism
  A. Adam Smith
    1. natural laws govern
      economic life
  B.
II.

Changing Social Roles The roles of men, women, and children changed in the new industrial society. Farming families had all worked the land together. Artisans had worked in their homes. Now the workplace became separated from the home.

The roles of middle-class men and women were redefined. Men worked in the public world of business and government. Women worked at home, where they were responsible for maintaining the dwelling and raising the children, including their moral instruction. Social class had an impact on family life. Middle-class children had a high standard of living and a better chance at education. Among the working class, on the other hand, children had to work long hours to help support their families. Working-class women also worked long hours, although they were paid less than men. Family life sometimes suffered as women worked 12 hours or more in a factory and then came home to care for their families.

Improved Transportation The growth of industry led to improvements in transportation.

- Roads and canals were built and improved.
- The steam locomotive was invented. Railroads grew.
- Steam engines powered ships at sea.

Rising Standards of Living Settlement patterns shifted over time. The rich lived in pleasant neighborhoods on the edges of the cities. The poor were crowded into slums in city centers, near factories. Over time, conditions in cities improved, however. In addition, people ate more varied diets and were healthier, thanks to advances in medicine.

Competing Philosophies

The hardships and changes brought by the Industrial Revolution inspired many varying solutions. Several different ways of thinking competed against each other.

Laissez-Faire Capitalism

Many economic thinkers supported Adam Smith's idea that natural laws governed economic life. **Thomas Malthus** published his *Essay on the Principle of Population* in 1798. He argued that because population tended to increase more rapidly than the food supply, the poor would continue to suffer. However, because he believed in laissez faire, he did not urge the government to step in to help the poor. He urged the poor to have fewer children.

Social Darwinism

Other new ideas of the 1800s challenged long-held beliefs. In 1859, British naturalist Charles Darwin caused an uproar by saying that humans had evolved over millions of years. This theory of evolution, as it was called, stirred conflicts between religion and science.

Part of Darwin's theory involved the idea of natural selection. Using the ideas of Thomas Malthus, Darwin said that species naturally produced more offspring than the food supply could support. Members of each species had to compete to survive. Thus, natural forces selected the most able members, producing an improved species.

Later thinkers used Darwin's ideas to develop a theory known as **Social Darwinism**. According to Social Darwinism, successful businesspeople were successful because they were naturally more "fit" to succeed than others. War allowed stronger nations to weed out weaker ones. Social Darwinism played a part in racism, the belief that one race is superior to another. It also contributed to the rise in imperialism.

Social Reformism

In contrast to laissez-faire philosophy, which advised governments to leave business alone, other theorists believed government should intervene to improve people's lives. Many different types of social reformism arose. Socialists hoped to replace the capitalist economic system. Reform movements attempted to correct the abuses of child labor. Labor unions attempted to improve the dangerous working conditions in the factories.

Socialism

Socialism concentrated less on the interests and rights of individuals and more on the interests of society. Industrial capitalism, the socialists claimed, had created a large gap between rich and poor. Under socialism, farms and businesses would belong to all the people, not to individuals. Different types of socialism emerged.

Utopian Socialism Early socialists, called Utopians, sought to create self-sufficient communities, where all property and work would be shared. Since all would have equal wealth, Utopians believed that fighting would end. In Scotland, **Robert Owen** set up a Utopian factory community.

Marxist Socialism German philosopher **Karl Marx** promoted a more radical theory, "scientific socialism." In 1848, Marx and German economist Friedrich Engels explained their ideas, listed here, in *The Communist Manifesto*.

- History was a class struggle between wealthy capitalists and the working class, or proletariat.
- In order to make profits, the capitalists took advantage of the proletariat.
- The proletariat would eventually rise up and overthrow the capitalist system, creating its own society.
- The proletariat society would take control of the means of production and establish a classless, communist society, in which wealth and power would be equally shared.

In the Soviet Union in the 1900s, Marx's ideas would lead to a communist dictatorship and a command economy, in which government officials made all economic decisions.

Labor Unions and Reform Legislation

Throughout the 1800s, reform movements sought to address the negative impact of the Industrial Revolution. The actions of workers and reformers forced governments to examine and reform many of the worst abuses.

Labor Unions By the 1800s, workers in the same occupation began to join together to form organizations to press for reforms. These unions engaged in collective bargaining with their employers, negotiating for higher pay and better working conditions. Workers would strike, or refuse to work, if employers refused their demands. From 1799 to 1824, labor unions were illegal in Great Britain. Eventually, however, labor unions contributed to improved wages, hours, and conditions for workers.

Preparing for the Regents

- Create a chart listing and briefly explaining the competing philosophies that emerged during and after the Industrial Revolution.

Vocabulary Builder

abuse—(uh BYOOS) *n.* the use of something in a way that it should not be used

Preparing for the Regents

- Compare and contrast Utopian socialism with Marxist socialism.

Note Taking

Reading Skill:
Identify Effects Complete a concept web with the effects of labor unions. Add more circles if needed.

British Reform Laws

British Reform Laws Throughout the 1800s, the British Parliament passed many important laws. These laws improved conditions for women, children, and the working class.

DIRECTION OF REFORM	LAWS ENACTED
Toward greater human rights	1884: Slavery is outlawed in all British colonies.
Toward more representative government	1832: Reform Act of 1832 gave representation to new industrial towns. 1858: Law ended property qualifications for members of Parliament. 1911: Law restricted powers of House of Lords; elected House of Commons became supreme.
Toward universal **suffrage** (the right to vote)	1829: Parliament gave Catholics the right to vote and to hold most public offices. 1867: Reform Act gave vote to many working-class men. 1884: Law extended voting rights to most farmers and other men. 1918: Women won the right to vote.
Toward more rights for workers	1825: Trade unions were legalized. 1840s to 1910s: Parliament passed laws • limiting child labor. • regulating work hours for women and children. • regulating safety conditions in factories and mines. • setting minimum wages. • providing for accident and unemployment insurance.
Toward improved education	1870: Education Act set up local elementary schools run by elected school boards. 1902: Law created a system of state-aided secondary schools. Industrial cities, such as London and Manchester, set up public universities.

Preparing for the Regents

1. Describe a reform law that helped women.
2. Describe a law that helped children.

Reform Legislation In the early 1830s, British lawmaker Michael Sadler persuaded Parliament to investigate the horrible conditions faced by child laborers in factories. **The Sadler Report** led to the Factories Regulations Act of 1833. This act prohibited children under the age of 9 from being employed in textile mills, and it limited the working hours of children under 18. This is just one of many types of reforms introduced in Great Britain in the 1800s. France and Germany enacted labor reforms as well.

Education and the Arts

Artists, musicians, and writers also took new directions during the Industrial Revolution.

Advances in Education

Governments had begun to set up public schools and require basic education for all children by the late 1800s. Schools not only taught subjects such as reading, writing, and mathematics but encouraged obedience to authority and punctuality as well.

Romanticism

From about 1750 to 1850, a movement known as romanticism thrived. The romantics appealed to emotion rather than to reason. In this way romanticism

Preparing for the Regents

• Discuss one important characteristic of each of these artistic movements.

Romanticism:

Realism:

Page 168   Unit 5: An Age of Revolutions (1750–1914)

was a rebellion against the ideas of the Enlightenment. It was also a reaction against the impersonal nature of industrial society.

Realism

The mid-1800s brought an artistic movement known as realism to the West. Realists sought to show the world as it was. They often looked at the harsh side of life, showing poverty and cruel working conditions. Many writers, such as Charles Dickens, were critical of the abuses of industrial society and hoped to contribute to ending them.

Global Impact of Industrialization

Global Migrations

A Wave of Migrations Improvements in transportation, population growth, and social and political conditions led to a wave of global migrations from about 1845 through the early 1900s.

- Polish nationalists fled Poland for Western Europe and the United States after the Russian army crushed the revolt of 1830.
- Several thousand Germans moved to cities in the United States after the failed revolutions of 1848.
- Russian Jews, escaping pogroms, left Eastern Europe.
- Italian farmers, seeing economic opportunity, also traveled to the Americas.

Mass Starvation in Ireland Another migration occurred from Ireland. Under British rule, the majority of Irish farmland had been used to grow crops, such as wheat and oats, which were sent to England. The Irish themselves used the potato as their main food crop. This system supported the Irish population until 1845, when a disease destroyed the potato crop. Other crops were not affected. Still, the British continued to ship the other products out of Ireland. Four years later, one million Irish had died of starvation or disease. Millions of others moved to the United States and Canada.

Movement Toward a Global Economy

By the mid-1800s, the Industrial Revolution had moved beyond Great Britain. New powers were emerging. As they became strong industrially, they competed for a share of the wealth in markets around the world. In addition, manufacturers traded with other countries for resources they needed. Steamships and railroads, and then automobiles and airplanes, made global trade easier and quicker. As markets expanded around the world and global trade increased, a new imperialism developed.

Summary

In the mid-1700s, the Agrarian Revolution in Europe contributed to an increase in population. The Agrarian Revolution led to the Industrial Revolution, which began in Great Britain and then spread to other countries. Economic and social conditions around the world changed dramatically as a result of the Industrial Revolution. Many new ideas about how to deal with the problems of industrialization developed, and reforms were enacted. Eventually, industrialization led to mass migration and increased global trade.

Preparing for the Regents

- How did British policy contribute to starvation in Ireland and mass migration from Ireland?

Note Taking

Reading Skill:
Recognize Sequence
List the important events of the Economic and Social Revolutions. Record them in the order they occurred. Add boxes as needed.

Date	Event

Preparing for the Regents

- Compare the ways in which the Neolithic Revolution, the Industrial Revolution, and the Computer Revolution changed human life.

Japan and the Meiji Restoration

The Big Idea

The Meiji Restoration brought great change to Japan in the last half of the 1800s.

- Japan ended its policy of isolation.
- Japan began a period of modernization and industrialization.
- Japan became a global imperial power.

Section Overview

In 1853, an American fleet sailed to Japan and ended over 200 years of isolation by opening Japan to trade. Soon afterward, Japan's ruling shogun was overthrown, and the Meiji Restoration began. During this period, Japan underwent a rapid period of modernization and industrialization. Changes took place within government, the economy, and social life. Within decades Japan became a modern industrial power and began to build an overseas empire.

Key Themes and Concepts

As you review this section, take special note of the following key themes and concepts:

Change What political, social, and economic changes occurred in Japan in the late 1800s?

Interdependence How did Japan use Western ideas to modernize and industrialize?

Power How did Japan become a global power by the early 1900s?

Key People and Terms

As you review this section, be sure you understand the significance of these key people and terms:

Matthew Perry	zaibatsu
Treaty of Kanagawa	Sino-Japanese War
Meiji Restoration	Russo-Japanese War

Key People and Terms

- For each of the key people and terms, write a sentence explaining its significance.

The Opening of Japan

In 1853, United States ships sailed into Edo (now Tokyo) Bay, ending more than 200 years of Japanese isolation. This contact led to changes that had a great impact on Japan.

Tokugawa Isolation

European traders had first arrived in Japan in the 1500s. In the 1600s, the Tokugawa shoguns had gained control of Japan. They brought stability to Japan but also banned almost all contact with the outside world. Limited trade was allowed only with the Dutch at Nagasaki.

Commodore Matthew Perry

In 1854, American warships commanded by Commodore **Matthew Perry** sailed to Japan. Perry presented a letter to the Japanese from the United States president, asking that Japan open its ports to trade. Europeans and Americans were not only offended by the Tokugawa isolation but resentful at not being able to use Japanese ports to resupply or repair their ships.

Key Themes and Concepts

Science and Technology Since the Tokugawa shoguns banned contact with the West, Japan was cut off from the advances of industrialization and fell behind Europe in science and technology.

Impressed by the American show of strength, the shogun agreed to the Treaty of Kanagawa, ending his country's long period of isolation. It was the first of many treaties Japan would sign with foreign powers.

The Treaty of Kanagawa

In the **Treaty of Kanagawa,** the shogun agreed to open two Japanese ports to American ships. The United States soon won other trading rights with Japan. In time, Great Britain, France, and Russia gained similar trading rights.

The Treaty of Kanagawa had a powerful impact on Japan.

- Some Japanese felt that the shogun had shown weakness in front of the foreigners by agreeing to the treaty.
- Some Japanese felt that Japan needed to modernize in order to compete with the industrialized West.
- A rebellion overthrew the shogun, restored the emperor to power, and launched Japan on the road to modernization and industrialization.

Preparing for the Regents

- What effects did the visit of Commodore Perry and the Treaty of Kanagawa have on Japan's development?

Modernization and Industrialization

In 1867, daimyo and samurai led a rebellion that removed the Tokugawa shogun from power. In 1868, the emperor was established as the leader of Japan. The period from 1868 to 1912 is known as the **Meiji Restoration.** *Meiji* means "enlightened rule." During this time, the emperor and his advisors implemented a series of reforms that changed Japan forever.

Borrowing From the West

The Meiji reformers were determined to strengthen Japan against the West. Members of the government traveled abroad to learn about Western government, economics, technology, and customs. In addition, foreign experts were invited to Japan.

Economic Development

The Meiji government used Western methods and machinery to develop an industrial economy in Japan. The government built factories and then sold them to wealthy families. These families became powerful in banking and industry and were known as **zaibatsu.**

The government supported the economy by developing a banking system and a postal system. It also built railroads and improved ports. By the 1890s, the economy was flourishing. The population grew, and peasants migrated to the cities in search of jobs.

Preparing for the Regents

- Why did the Industrial Revolution occur earlier in Japan than in African and other Asian nations?

Strong Central Government

Meiji reformers wanted to create a strong central government. They chose the government of Germany as their model. A constitution gave the emperor autocratic power and created a two-house legislature. Only one of the houses was elected, and suffrage was limited.

Military Power

By the 1890s, Japan had a modern army and a strong navy. No longer were the samurai the only warriors—all men had to enter military service. When Japan and China fought over Korea in 1894, Japan won easily. Later, Japanese troops defeated Russian troops in Manchuria. This victory marked the first time in modern history that an Asian power defeated a European nation.

Key Themes and Concepts

Choice
The reformers chose the German government as their model. Their choice influenced how Japan developed over the next 50 years.

Preparing for the Regents

- What changes were made in society during the Meiji Restoration? What group did not experience greater personal freedom?

- Practice your graph skills by answering the following questions.

1. During which five-year period did Japanese trade increase the most?

2. Why was Japanese trade increasing so much in the late 1800s?

Japanese Exports and Imports
Meiji leaders made the economy a major priority. Imports and exports grew at an amazing speed.

Key Themes and Concepts

Power
Industrialization contributed to Japan's strong military. In turn, a strong military contributed to the nation's imperialistic success.

Preparing for the Regents

- Japan, an island nation with few natural resources, had industrialized rapidly in the 1800s. How did geography affect Japan's decision to follow a policy of imperialism?

Social Change

Meiji reforms established a system of public education and set up universities with Western instructors to teach modern technology. Despite social reforms, however, class distinctions still existed. Also, Japanese women faced continuing inequality. Meiji reformers took away some political and legal rights that women had previously won.

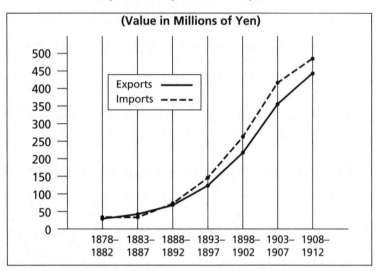

Japanese Exports and Imports

Japan as a Global Power

Soon, like Western powers, Japan used its industrial and military strength to begin a policy of imperialism. It sought colonies as sources of raw materials and as markets for finished products. Colonies were gained through war.

Sino-Japanese War

In 1894, Japan's territorial ambitions in Korea led to war with China. The conflict, which lasted from 1894 to 1895, was called the **Sino-Japanese War.** Japan quickly won, gaining Formosa (later Taiwan) and treaty ports in China from the Chinese. Japan later made Korea a Japanese protectorate.

Russo-Japanese War

From 1904 to 1905, Japan fought the **Russo-Japanese War** with Russia after the interests of the two nations conflicted in Korea. Japan's modern military defeated Russian troops and crushed Russia's navy. By 1910, Japan had complete control of Korea as well as parts of Manchuria.

Dependence on a World Market

Japan's industrialization drew it increasingly into the global market. Its economy therefore became dependent on trade. An island empire with few natural resources, Japan relied on raw materials from outside the country. It needed foreign markets for its manufactured products. In the years ahead, Japan would continue to compete with other industrialized nations. It would also continue its policy of imperialism.

Summary

In the mid-1800s, Japan ended its long policy of isolation. The Meiji government that took power in 1868 used Western ideas to begin a program of modernization that quickly turned Japan into a major industrial power. In the 1890s and 1900s, Japan used its modern military to become a global imperial power.

Imperialism

Section Overview

From the mid-1800s through the first decades of the 1900s, Western nations pursued an aggressive policy of expansion. European powers were motivated by economic, political, and social factors as well as by a strong sense of nationalism. During this time, Great Britain took control of India. In Africa, several European nations engaged in a scramble for colonies. Meanwhile, imperialistic nations forced unequal trade agreements on China. Imperialism had many immediate and long-term effects on the colonial nations and also had an impact on Europe and the rest of the world. Imperialism led to increased competition and conflict.

Key Themes and Concepts

As you review this section, take special note of the following key themes and concepts:

Imperialism What factors led to the new imperialism of the 1800s?

Power How did imperialistic countries gain power over the peoples of Africa and Asia?

Change What were the effects of imperialism?

Nationalism How did imperialism lead to nationalistic feelings in China and other nations of Asia and Africa?

Key People and Terms

As you review this section, be sure you understand the significance of these key people and terms:

imperialism	Opium War	Taiping Rebellion
"White Man's Burden"	Treaty of Nanjing	Boxer Rebellion
Sepoy Mutiny	spheres of influence	Sun Yixian
Boer War		

The New Imperialism

Imperialism is the domination by one country of the political, economic, or cultural life of another country. Historians often divide imperialism into two periods.

- **The Old Imperialism** Between about 1500 and 1800, European nations established colonies in the Americas, India, and Southeast Asia and gained territory on the coasts of Africa and China. Still, European power in these regions of the world was limited.

- **The New Imperialism** Between 1870 and 1914, nationalism had produced strong, centrally governed nation-states. The Industrial Revolution had made economies stronger as well. During this time, Japan, the United States, and the industrialized nations of Europe became more aggressive in expanding into other lands. The new imperialism was focused mainly on Asia and Africa, where declining empires and local wars left many states vulnerable. In Africa, many states had been weakened by the legacy of the slave trade.

The Big Idea

The imperialism that emerged in the mid-1800s had a lasting impact on the world.

- Powerful industrialized nations sought to gain power and economic might by building empires.

- Through economic and military power, Great Britain colonized and dominated India.

- European nations divided up the continent of Africa.

- Western powers and Japan established spheres of influence in China.

- Imperialism has had short-term and long-term effects on various regions of the world.

Key People and Terms

- What do most of the key people and terms have in common? Explain.

Key Themes and Concepts

Imperialism
The strong central governments and thriving economies of industrialized nations gave them the confidence to expand through imperialism.

Causes of Imperialism

Several important factors combined to lead to the development of the new imperialism.

Causes of the New Imperialism

Economy	Politics and the Military	Society	Science and Invention
• Need for natural resources • Need for new markets • Place for growing populations to settle • Place to invest profits	• Bases for trade and navy ships • Power and security of global empire • Spirit of nationalism	• Wish to spread Christianity • Wish to share Western civilization • Belief that Western ways are best	• New weapons • New medicines • Improved ships

The New Imperialism
From 1870 to 1914, European countries, the United States, and Japan gained control over much of the world.

Nationalism and Social Darwinism

A spirit of nationalism was one cause of the new imperialism. Because nationalism promotes the idea of national superiority, imperialists felt that they had a right to take control of countries they viewed as weaker. Social Darwinism also encouraged imperialism. This idea applied Darwin's theory of survival of the fittest to competition between nations. Social Darwinists argued that it was natural for stronger nations to dominate weaker ones.

Military Motives

Military motives were linked to nationalism, since military power was a way to promote a nation's goals. Colonies were important as bases for resupply of ships. A nation with many colonies had power and security.

Economic Motives

Imperialists needed raw materials to supply their factories. They needed foreign markets in which to sell their finished products. They needed places to invest their profits. Colonies could provide all these things.

"White Man's Burden"

Rudyard Kipling's poem **"White Man's Burden"** offered a justification for imperialism. Kipling expressed the idea that white imperialists had a moral duty to educate people in nations they considered less developed. Missionaries spread Western ideas, customs, and religions to people in Africa and Asia.

Preparing for the Regents

• How did the Industrial Revolution lead to imperialism?

British in India

British East India Company

The British East India Company had established trading rights in India in the early 1600s. By the mid-1800s, with the decline of the Mughal empire and the defeat of French rivals, this company controlled three fifths of India. The company employed Indian soldiers, called sepoys.

The Sepoy Mutiny

In 1857, tensions rose. The British had angered the sepoys by demanding that soldiers follow rules that were against their religious beliefs. The **Sepoy Mutiny,** or the Sepoy Rebellion, called for Hindus and Muslims to unite against the British. The British, however, crushed the revolt.

The Sepoy Mutiny left bitter feelings. It also caused the British to change their policies. In 1858, Parliament ended the rule of the East India Company. The British government took direct command of India.

The Effects of British Rule in India

GOOD EFFECTS
• New roads and railroads link parts of India.
• Telegraph and postal systems unite people.
• Irrigation systems improve farming.
• New laws mean justice for all classes.
• British schools offer education.
• Customs that threaten human rights are ended.

BAD EFFECTS
• Indian resources go to Great Britain.
• British-made goods replace local goods.
• Farms grow cash crops rather than food crops; Indians go hungry.
• Top jobs go to the British.
• Indians are treated as inferiors.
• Great Britain tries to replace Indian culture with Western ways.

Note Taking

Reading Skill: **Identify Causes and Effects**
Make a flowchart to show the causes and effects of British rule in India.

Causes	Event	Effects
• • •	British rule in Inida	• • •

The Scramble for Africa

d meg zzz

In the 1870s, King Leopold of Belgium sent a mission to the interior of Africa to establish trade agreements with leaders in the Congo River basin. The Belgian presence in the Congo set off a scramble among other European powers to establish their presence on the continent.

The Berlin Conference

In 1884, to avoid conflict among themselves, European leaders met in Berlin, Germany, to set up rules for colonizing Africa. European powers divided Africa with little regard for the people who lived there. The new imperialism affected Africa strongly. In 1850, most of Africa had been free. Seventy years later, most of the continent was under European rule.

Battle for Southern Africa

The Zulu Empire In the early 1800s in southern Africa, an African leader named Shaka organized Zulu warriors into a fighting force. He used his power against European slave traders and ivory hunters. Through conquest of other African groups, he united the Zulu nation.

Arrival of Europeans Dutch farmers, called Boers, had settled in southern Africa in the mid-1600s. They had built Cape Town as a supply station. In the 1700s, Dutch herders and ivory hunters began to move north. They fought African groups, such as the Zulus. In the early 1800s, the British acquired the Cape Colony from the Dutch.

Zulu Resistance Large numbers of Boers, resenting British rule, migrated north during the 1830s, coming into conflict with Zulus. Fighting between the Boers and the Zulus continued until late in the century.

The Zulus eventually came into conflict with the British as well. The Zulus experienced victory in 1879. Soon afterward, however, the superior weaponry of the British crushed the Zulu resistance. Others in Africa also resisted imperialism, including groups in Ethiopia and West Africa.

The Boer War Cecil Rhodes became prime minister of the Cape Colony in 1890. Under his leadership, Great Britain expanded its control of southern Africa.

In the late 1800s, Great Britain decided to annex the Boer republics. The Boers resisted and the Boer War began, lasting from 1899 to 1902. After heavy losses, the British won. In 1910, the British combined the Boer republics with the Cape Colony to form the Union of South Africa. The bitter struggles left a legacy of distrust and hatred.

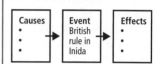

Draw Inferences

The European leaders did not invite the African leaders to the Berlin Conference. Why not?

Preparing for the Regents

• How did the Zulus display a nationalistic response to imperialism?

Vocabulary Builder

annex—(uh NEKS) *v.* to take control of a country or area next to your own, especially by using force

Anti-Slave Trade Legislation Most European powers had abolished the slave trade before the scramble for African colonies began. For example, Denmark passed anti-slave trade legislation in 1803, followed by Great Britain in 1807, and France in 1818. Illegal slave trading, however, continued throughout the 1800s.

The Scramble for Africa, 1880–1914

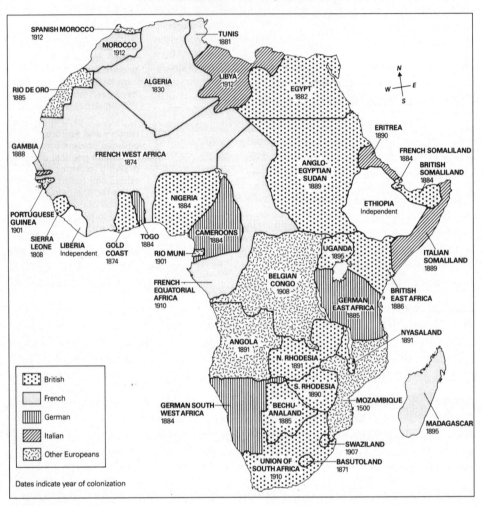

SPANISH MOROCCO 1912
TUNIS 1881
MOROCCO 1912
ALGERIA 1830
LIBYA 1912
EGYPT 1882
RIO DE ORO 1885
GAMBIA 1888
FRENCH WEST AFRICA 1874
ANGLO-EGYPTIAN SUDAN 1889
ERITREA 1890
FRENCH SOMALILAND 1884
BRITISH SOMALILAND 1884
NIGERIA 1884
ETHIOPIA Independent
PORTUGUESE GUINEA 1901
SIERRA LEONE 1808
LIBERIA Independent
GOLD COAST 1874
TOGO 1884
RIO MUNI 1901
CAMEROONS 1884
UGANDA 1895
ITALIAN SOMALILAND 1889
FRENCH EQUATORIAL AFRICA 1910
BELGIAN CONGO 1908
GERMAN EAST AFRICA 1885
BRITISH EAST AFRICA 1886
ANGOLA 1891
NYASALAND 1891
N. RHODESIA 1891
S. RHODESIA 1890
MOZAMBIQUE 1500
GERMAN SOUTH WEST AFRICA 1884
BECHU-ANALAND 1885
MADAGASCAR 1895
SWAZILAND 1907
UNION OF SOUTH AFRICA 1910
BASUTOLAND 1871

British
French
German
Italian
Other Europeans

Dates indicate year of colonization

Imperialism in China

Since 1644, rulers of the Qing dynasty had refused to adopt Western ways. As a result, the economic, political, and military strength of European imperialists was able to challenge China's Middle Kingdom.

The Opium War and the Treaty of Nanjing

British merchants began to trade opium in China in the late 1700s. China tried to halt imports of the addictive drug. In 1839, to keep trade open, the British fought with China in a conflict called the **Opium War.** Great Britain's superior military and industrial strength led to a quick victory.

In 1842, Great Britain forced China to agree to the harsh terms of the **Treaty of Nanjing.** China had to pay for Great Britain's war costs, open ports to British trade, and give Great Britain the island of Hong Kong. China also had to grant British citizens extraterritoriality, the right to live under their own laws and be tried in their own courts. In the years that followed, other Western powers forced China to sign unequal treaties. The Western powers carved out **spheres of influence,** areas in which an outside power claimed exclusive trade privileges.

Chinese Reactions to Imperialism

Foreign imperialism led to further clashes between the imperialist powers and China—and among the Chinese themselves.

The Taiping Rebellion From 1850 to 1864, Chinese peasants, angry at their poverty and at corrupt Qing officials, rose up in revolt. The Taiping Rebellion resulted in millions of Chinese deaths and weakened China.

The Boxer Rebellion In 1900, a group known to Westerners as the Boxers assaulted foreign communities across China in a conflict known as the Boxer Rebellion. Armies from Japan and the West, however, soon crushed the uprising and forced China to grant more concessions to foreign powers. After this defeat, greater numbers of Chinese called for Western-style reforms.

Sun Yixian and the Chinese Revolution In the first decade of the 1900s, Chinese nationalism blossomed. Many reformers called for a new government. Sun Yixian, also called Sun Yat-sen, led the movement to replace the Qing dynasty. He had three goals:

- To end foreign domination
- To form a representative government
- To create economic security for the Chinese people

Preparing for the Regents

- How did imperialism contribute to the rise of nationalistic feelings in China?

- Compare Japanese and Chinese responses to Western industrial power and Western imperialism.

Vocabulary Builder

concession—(kun SESH un) *n.* something that you allow someone to have in order to end an argument or a disagreement

Spheres of Influence in China Until 1914

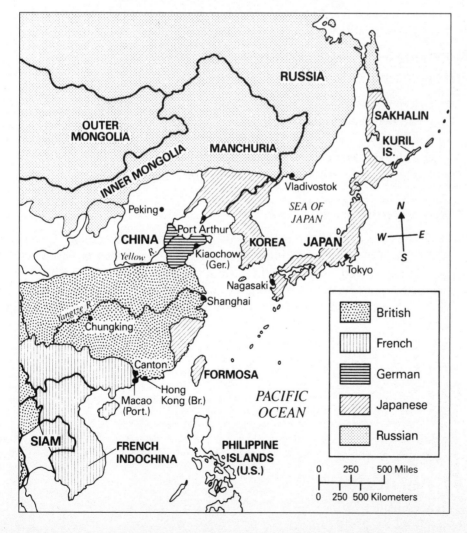

Preparing for the Regents

- Practice your map skills by describing Japan's sphere of influence in Asia in 1914. How do you think this influence benefited Japan?

Spheres of Influence in China The Western countries used diplomacy and war to gain power in China. They divided the country into special trade areas.

Preparing for the Regents

- List three arguments that were used by imperialist powers to justify imperialism.

1.

2.

3.

- List three motives people of Africa and Asia had to oppose imperialism.

1.

2.

3.

In 1911, workers, peasants, students, and warlords toppled the monarchy. Sun Yixian was named president of the Chinese Republic.

Impact of Imperialism: Multiple Perspectives

The new imperialism had a major impact on the European nations and on their colonies.

Effects on the Colonies

Imperialism had a number of short-term and long-term effects on the colonies themselves. Some were negative; others were positive.

Short-Term Effects Some effects were immediate.

- Large numbers of Asians and Africans came under foreign rule.
- Local economies became dependent on industrialized powers.
- Some nations introduced changes to meet imperialist challenges.
- Individuals and groups resisted European domination.
- Western culture spread to new regions.
- Traditional political units were disrupted or destroyed.
- Famines occurred in lands where farmers grew export crops for imperialist nations in place of food for local use.

Long-Term Effects Other effects took longer to emerge.

- Western culture continued to influence much of the world.
- Transportation, education, and medical care were improved.
- Resistance to imperial rule evolved into nationalist movements.
- Many economies became dependent on single cash crops grown for export.

Effects on Europe and the World

The West also changed because of imperialism.

- The West discovered new crops, foods, and other products.
- Westerners were introduced to new cultural influences.
- Competition for empires created and increased conflict between imperial powers. These conflicts sometimes led to war.
- The industrial nations controlled a new global economy.

Summary

In the 1800s, industrialized powers greatly expanded their empires. Great Britain took control of India, and European nations occupied much of Africa. Imperial powers also forced China to grant trading concessions. This led to the growth of nationalism in China. Other effects of imperialism included the emergence of a global economy, the spread of Western culture, and conflict between imperial powers.

Key Themes and Concepts

Nationalism
Nationalist movements in Asia and Africa often grew out of resistance to imperial rule.

Multiple Choice

Directions: Review the Test-Taking Strategies section of this book. Then answer the following questions, drawn from actual Regents examinations. For each statement or question, choose the *number* of the word or expression that, of those given, best completes the statement or answers the question.

1   John Locke and Jean-Jacques Rousseau would be most likely to support
   (1) a return to feudalism in Europe
   (2) a government ruled by a divine monarchy
   (3) a society ruled by the Catholic Church
   (4) the right of citizens to decide the best form of government

2   The writers and philosophers of the Enlightenment believed that government decisions should be based on
   (1) fundamental religious beliefs
   (2) the concept of the divine right of kings
   (3) laws of nature and reason
   (4) traditional values

3   A primary cause of the French Revolution in 1789 was the
   (1) increasing dissatisfaction of the Third Estate
   (2) rise to power of Napoleon Bonaparte
   (3) actions of Prince Metternich
   (4) execution of Louis XVI

4   In a number of European countries in the 1800s, which situation occurred as a result of the influence of the French Revolution?
   (1) increase in religious conflict
   (2) rise of nationalistic movements
   (3) decentralization of governmental power
   (4) economic depression

5   During the early 1800s, which was a major influence on the struggles for political independence in Latin America?
   (1) poor conditions in urban centers in Latin America
   (2) the American and French Revolutions
   (3) the desire of the Roman Catholic Church in Latin America to escape European control
   (4) demands by Latin American workers to own their own factories

6   Nationalism is most likely to develop in an area that has
   (1) land suited to agriculture
   (2) adequate industry to supply consumer demands
   (3) a moderate climate with rivers for irrigation
   (4) common customs, language, and history

7   Which statement about nationalism is most accurate?
   (1) It becomes a unifying force among a people.
   (2) It encourages diversity within nation-states.
   (3) It prevents the rise of militarism.
   (4) It eliminates the ethnic identities of different groups.

8   Which term refers to the Jewish movement to establish a homeland in Palestine?
   (1) Zionism
   (2) Marxism
   (3) animism
   (4) secularism

9 The theory of laissez-faire capitalism advocates

(1) government control of the economy

(2) noninvolvement of the government in the economy

(3) government regulation of big business

(4) government sponsorship of labor unions

10 An important result of the Industrial Revolution was the

(1) concentration of workers in urban areas

(2) increased desire of the wealthy class to share its power

(3) formation of powerful craft guilds

(4) control of agricultural production by governments

11 The arrival of Commodore Matthew Perry in Japan in 1853 signaled the end of Japanese

(1) cultural contacts with the West

(2) policies of isolationism

(3) militarism in Southeast Asia

(4) trade relations with the United States

12 In Japan, the period of the Meiji Restoration was primarily characterized by

(1) strict isolation

(2) feudal government

(3) religious revival

(4) reform and modernization

13 Russia in the 1700s and Japan in the 1800s were similar in that both countries

(1) began the process of modernization after a long period of isolation

(2) developed democratic governments after years under absolute monarchies

(3) refused to accept Western technological ideas

(4) adopted socialist economic systems after capitalism had failed

14 "All great nations . . . have desired to set their mark upon barbarian lands, and those who fail to participate in this great rivalry will play a pitiable role in time to come."

This quotation supports the concept of

(1) socialism

(2) human rights

(3) revolution

(4) imperialism

15 One way in which the Sepoy Rebellion in India and the Boxer Rebellion in China are similar is that both attempted to

(1) remove foreign influences

(2) restore democracy

(3) modernize their economy

(4) end religious conflict

16 The Boxer Rebellion of the early twentieth century was an attempt to

(1) eliminate poverty among Chinese peasants

(2) bring Western-style democracy to China

(3) restore trade between China and European nations

(4) remove foreign influences from China

In developing your answer, be sure to keep these general definitions in mind:

    (a) <u>describe</u> means "to illustrate something in words or tell about it"
    (b) <u>explain</u> means "to make plain or understandable; to give reasons for or causes of; to show the logical development or relationships of"

Directions: Write a well-organized essay that includes an introduction, several paragraphs addressing the task below, and a conclusion.

Theme: **Revolution**

> Throughout global history, there have been major political, economic, social, and cultural revolutions. These revolutions have had complex causes and left lasting impacts on people's lives.

Task:

> - Define the term *revolution.*
> - Select a specific revolution that you have studied, and describe three of the factors that helped to bring about that particular revolution.
> - Identify and explain at least one immediate effect and at least one long-term effect of this revolution on people's lives.

   You may discuss any revolution from your study of global history, except the American Revolution. Some suggestions you may wish to consider are the Commercial Revolution, the Reformation, the Enlightenment, the French Revolution, the Industrial Revolution, the Mexican Revolution, and the Russian Revolution.

You are *not* limited to these suggestions.
Do not use the United States in your answer.

Guidelines:

    In your essay, be sure to
- Develop all aspects of the task
- Support the theme with relevant facts, examples, and details
- Use a logical and clear plan of organization, including an introduction and a conclusion that are beyond a simple restatement of the theme

This question is based on the accompanying documents. The question is designed to test your ability to work with historical documents. Some of these documents have been edited for the purposes of this question. As you analyze the documents, take into account the source of each document and any point of view that may be presented in the document.

Historical Context:

Throughout history, imperialism has been interpreted from multiple perspectives. Some have seen it as a beneficial influence, while others have seen it as a harmful influence.

Task: Using the information from the documents and your knowledge of global history, answer the questions that follow each document in Part A. Your answers to the questions will help you write the Part B essay in which you will be asked to

> • Evaluate both the positive and the negative effects of imperialism

In developing your answers, be sure to keep this general definition in mind:

<u>evaluate</u> means "to examine and judge the significance, worth, or condition of; to determine the value of"

Part A: Short Answer

Directions: Analyze the documents and answer the question or questions that follow each document, using the space provided.

Document #1

Modern progressive nations lying in the temperate zone seek to control "garden spots" in the tropics, [mainly in Africa, Latin America, and Asia]. Under [the progressive nations'] direction, these places can yield tropical produce. In return, the progressive nations bring to the people of those garden spots the foodstuffs and manufactures they need. [Progressive nations] develop the territory by building roads, canals, railways, and telegraphs. They can establish schools and newspapers for the colonies [and] give these people the benefit of the blessings of civilization which they have not the means of creating themselves.

—O.P. Austin, "Does Colonization Pay?" *The Forum*, 1900

1. What nations does the author probably consider to be the "modern progressive nations"? Explain the reason for your answer.

_____

_____

Document #2

> *When the whites came to our country, we had the land and they had the Bible. Now we have the Bible and they have the land.*
>
> **—African proverb**

2. Does this proverb express a positive or negative viewpoint toward the white missionaries? Explain.

_____

_____

Document #3
"The Devilfish in Egyptian Waters"

3. What view of English imperialism is expressed in this cartoon? Explain.

_____

_____

Document #4

To begin with, there are the exporters and manufacturers of certain goods used in the colonies. The makers of cotton and iron goods have been very much interested in imperialism. Their business interests demand that colonial markets should be opened and developed and that foreign competitors should be shut out. Such aims require political control and imperialism.

Finally, the most powerful of all business groups are the bankers. Banks make loans to colonies and backward countries for building railways and steamship lines. They also make loans to colonial plantation owners, importers, and exporters.

—Parker T. Moon, *Imperialism and World Politics*, 1926

4. Based on this passage, explain two ways in which European businesspeople hoped to profit from imperialism.

_____

_____

Part B
Essay

Directions: Write a well-organized essay that includes an introduction, several paragraphs, and a conclusion. Use evidence from *at least **three*** of the documents in your essay. Support your response with relevant facts, examples, and details. Include additional outside information.

Historical Context:

Throughout history, imperialism has been interpreted from multiple perspectives. Some have seen it as a beneficial influence, while others have seen it as a harmful influence.

Task: Using the information from the documents and your knowledge of global history, write an essay in which you

> • Evaluate the positive and negative impacts of imperialism, developing a position either in favor of or against imperialism

Guidelines:

In your essay, be sure to
• Develop all aspects of the task
• Incorporate information from *at least **three*** documents
• Incorporate relevant outside information
• Support the theme with relevant facts, examples, and details
• Use a logical and clear plan of organization, including an introduction and a conclusion that are beyond a restatement of the theme

Crises and Achievements
(1900–1945)

Unit Overview

Science and technology brought many benefits to society in the late 1800s and early 1900s. In most industrialized countries, life expectancy increased and standards of living rose. People became hopeful, for they had experienced peace for many years. However, the forces of nationalism, militarism, and imperialism were moving the world toward war. By the time World War I was over, people understood how science and technology could change their lives in negative ways. The war caused new social and economic problems. In Russia, a communist revolution produced a totalitarian state. Perhaps worst of all, the problems that had led to World War I remained unresolved. A second global conflict erupted in 1939, resulting in even greater destruction than the first.

Using Good Social Studies Practices

Chronology and Causation

Some of the many themes developed in Unit 6 are:

change	nationalism	human rights
science and technology	political systems	economic systems
culture and intellectual life	power	

Choose one of the themes listed above. As you review Unit 6, create a timeline based on the theme you have chosen. Your timeline should emphasize your theme and stretch from 1900 to 1945. It should include major developments, key turning points, and their causes.

Scientific and Technological Achievements

Section Overview

In the late 1800s and early 1900s, advances in science and technology led to dramatic changes in daily life. Medical discoveries and better sanitation allowed people to live longer, contributing to a population explosion. New inventions revolutionized energy production, communications, and transportation. Scientific discoveries led to new knowledge about the universe and the workings of the human mind.

Key Themes and Concepts

As you review this section, take special note of the following key themes and concepts:

Change How did medical advances in the late 1800s affect life expectancy and population growth?

Science and Technology How did the scientific discoveries of the late 1800s and early 1900s change the way people lived?

Culture and Intellectual Life How did new theories affect the ways in which people thought about their world?

Key People and Terms

As you review this section, be sure you understand the significance of these key people and terms:

Louis Pasteur	dynamo	radioactivity
germ theory	Thomas Edison	Albert Einstein
antibiotics	Marie Curie	Sigmund Freud

Advances in Medicine

A series of discoveries revolutionized the field of medicine at the turn of the twentieth century. These medical advances greatly improved health care and increased human life expectancy.

The Germ Theory and Disease

Before the mid-1800s, the cause of disease was not clear, even to physicians. However, by the late 1800s, scientists were making great progress in this area.

Louis Pasteur In the 1600s, a Dutch scientist named Anton van Leeuwenhoek had discovered the existence of microbes, or germs, by using a microscope. He did not, however, recognize the role of these tiny organisms in causing disease.

In 1870, French scientist **Louis Pasteur** made two very important discoveries. He showed clearly the link between germs and disease. He also proved that killing certain germs stops the spread of certain diseases.

Robert Koch In the 1880s, the German physician Robert Koch discovered the bacteria that caused tuberculosis. His discovery started the long process of developing a cure for this deadly disease. The work of Pasteur and Koch established the **germ theory** of disease, the idea that many diseases are caused by the action of microorganisms. After people learned about the germ theory, they washed more often and made other lifestyle changes to limit the spread of disease.

Joseph Lister and Antiseptics

Before the mid-1800s, even a very minor surgical operation might be followed by infection and even death. An English surgeon named Joseph Lister became convinced that germs caused these infections. Lister insisted that doctors use antiseptics—substances that destroy or inhibit the growth of germs—on their hands, on their instruments, and on wounds. Lister's discoveries were a turning point in medicine, and they greatly reduced the number of deaths from infection in hospitals.

Antibiotics

In 1928, another turning point in medicine occurred. English scientist Alexander Fleming discovered that a mold called *Penicillium* killed germs. This discovery paved the way for the development of a class of drugs called **antibiotics** that attacked or weakened the bacteria that cause many diseases. Antibiotics were not widely developed and used, however, until the 1940s.

Improved Standard of Living

The advances of the late 1800s and early 1900s extended beyond the field of medicine. The standard of living of most Europeans began to rise.

Better Wages and Working Conditions

In the early years of the Industrial Revolution, workers had found it difficult to improve their harsh job conditions. By the late 1800s, however, labor unions became legal in many countries of Europe. Unions, reformers, and working-class voters pushed for better working conditions and higher wages. Over time, wages improved. People ate more varied diets and lived in cleaner, safer homes. Reform laws regulated working conditions and provided social benefits to the elderly and the unemployed.

Better Housing

Urban conditions were improving in the late 1800s and early 1900s. City governments paved their streets, making cities better places to live. Housing improved. Architects began to use steel to construct stronger, taller buildings.

Improved Sanitation

Underground sewage systems, introduced first in London and Paris, made cities healthier places to live. With underground systems, waste no longer ran through the streets, spreading disease and polluting sources of drinking water. A supply of clean water was necessary to combat diseases such as tuberculosis and cholera. Death rates were dramatically cut after the introduction of the new sewer systems.

Preparing for the Regents

Describe an effect on daily life of each of these inventions.

Electricity:

Telephone:

Radio:

Automobile:

Draw Conclusions

How did the new inventions help business and industry?

New Inventions

A tremendous number of new inventions appeared in the late 1800s and early 1900s. These inventions improved daily life in many ways.

Use of Electricity Early in the 1800s, Alessandro Volta and Michael Faraday had discovered how to produce small amounts of electricity. The later development of the **dynamo** enabled the generation of large amounts of electricity and made electricity a useful source of power. In 1879, an American inventor named **Thomas Edison** developed the first practical light bulb. Soon cities had electric street lights. By the 1890s, factories were powered by electricity. In homes, people used electricity to run appliances that made their lives more comfortable.

The Telephone In 1876, Alexander Graham Bell patented the telephone. His machine changed the human voice into electrical impulses, sent them through a wire, and then changed them back into sounds at the other end. The invention of the telephone transformed long-distance communication.

The Radio The telephone was an important means of communication, but it depended on wires. Guglielmo Marconi, in 1895, sent radio signals directly through the air. The first radios transmitted Morse code signals. The year 1906 marked the first voice broadcast over radio.

The Automobile Inventions also transformed transportation in the last half of the 1800s. In the 1870s, Nikolaus Otto developed a gasoline-powered internal combustion engine. In the 1880s, Gottlieb Daimler used Otto's engine to power the first automobile. By 1900, thousands of automobiles were on the roads of Europe and North America. Henry Ford's development of the assembly line for the mass production of automobiles made the United States a strong leader in the auto industry.

The Airplane The internal combustion engine also allowed humans to fly. In 1903, Orville and Wilbur Wright made the first powered flight.

Technology of the Industrial Age

INVENTOR OR DEVELOPER	NATION	INVENTION OR DEVELOPMENT	YEAR
Henry Bessemer	Great Britain	Process to turn iron ore into steel	1856
Alexander Graham Bell	United States	Telephone	1876
Thomas Edison	United States	Electric light bulb	1879
Gottlieb Daimler	Germany	Automobile	1887
Henry Ford	United States	Mass-produced automobile	1903
Orville & Wilbur Wright	United States	Airplane	1903

Population Explosion

In many ways, new technology made life healthier, safer, and easier. As a result, fewer children died, and the average life expectancy increased. In other words, people lived longer. Because of these changes, populations grew dramatically.

Western Populations in the Late 1800s

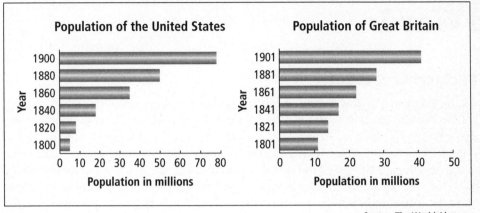

Population of the United States

Population of Great Britain

Source: *The World Almanac*

Preparing for the Regents

Practice your graph skills by answering the following questions.

1. About how many people lived in Great Britain in 1801?

2. What was the approximate population of Great Britain in 1901?

3. What developments could explain the population growth shown in these two graphs?

New Scientific Theories

While some scientists were developing knowledge and inventions that improved the quality of daily life, others were exploring the universe and the workings of the human mind.

The Curies and Radioactivity

Just before the turn of the century, French scientist **Marie Curie** was experimenting with **radioactivity,** a powerful form of energy released by certain substances. Working with her husband, Pierre, Marie Curie discovered two new radioactive elements that the Curies called radium and polonium. The discoveries of these scientists had enormous effects on fields such as energy production, medicine, and military technology.

Einstein and Relativity

In 1905, the German-born physicist **Albert Einstein** announced his theory of relativity. This theory revolutionized scientific thought. It proposed that space and time measurements are not absolute but are determined by many factors, some of which are not known. Einstein's work caused many people to question the common view of the universe as a machine that worked by easily understood laws.

Freud and the Human Mind

During the same period, an Austrian physician named **Sigmund Freud** was questioning basic ideas about the human mind. He believed that a part of the mind, which he called the unconscious, drives much of human behavior. Freud felt that the tension between the drives of the unconscious mind and the demands of civilized society caused psychological and physical illness. Freud pioneered psychoanalysis, a new way of thinking about and treating mental illness.

Summary

Scientific and technological advances brought many changes in the late 1800s and early 1900s. Improvements in medicine and sanitation led to a higher life expectancy, which caused an increase in population. People's lives were made easier by inventions such as electrical appliances, the telephone, and automobiles. In other areas of science, theories about the universe and the human mind shook ideas that had once been commonly accepted.

Vocabulary Builder

element—(EL uh munt) *n.* a simple chemical substance such as carbon or oxygen that consists of atoms of only one kind

Key Themes and Concepts

Science and Innovation The theories of both Einstein and Freud had an unsettling effect on many people of the time. The idea of a powerful unconscious mind or a universe without absolute laws disturbed many.

Preparing for the Regents

• What benefits have resulted from the use of radioactive elements? What problems have resulted?

• Write a short paragraph about whether you think that science and technology bring more problems or more benefits into people's lives.

World War I

The
Big
Idea

World War I:

- was caused by nationalism, militarism, imperialism, and alliance systems.

- was sparked in the Balkans and blossomed into a global war.

- was fought with highly destructive weapons, made possible by modern technology.

- resulted in enormous human and economic losses.

Section Overview

As the 1900s began, the people of Europe had enjoyed nearly a century of relative peace. At the same time, forces were pushing the continent toward war. Nationalistic feeling, a glorification of the military, imperial rivalries, and tangled alliances led to unrest. War was sparked in the Balkans, where the Ottoman empire had once maintained control. Soon all of Europe was at war. Industrialization and technology had allowed nations to develop more destructive weapons that resulted in millions of deaths. As Russia left the war and the United States entered, the Allies gained control and an armistice was signed. The costs of World War I were enormous.

Key Themes and Concepts

As you review this section, take special note of the following key themes and concepts:

Nationalism and Imperialism What role did nationalism and imperialism play in causing World War I?

Diversity How did ethnic diversity in the Balkans contribute to starting the war?

Science and Technology What impact did innovations in science and technology have on World War I?

Key People and Terms

What do three of the key people and terms have in common? Explain.

Key People and Terms

As you review this section, be sure you understand the significance of these key people and terms:

militarism	total war
Bosnia	propaganda
Archduke Francis Ferdinand	neutral
Central Powers	armistice
Allied Powers	reparations
trench warfare	

Causes

Although the world seemed at peace in the early 1900s, powerful forces were pushing Europe toward war. These forces included nationalism, militarism, imperial rivalries, alliance systems, and the decline of the Ottoman empire.

Nationalism

As you have learned, nationalism can bring people together. It can also, however, be a source of conflict. In Europe in the early 1900s, aggressive nationalism was a source of tension.

Germany and France Nationalism was strong in both Germany and France. Germany, now unified, was proud of its growing military and industrial strength. France, meanwhile, wanted to regain its position as a leading European power. It had lost the Franco-Prussian War in 1871. Besides having to pay money to Germany, France lost the provinces of Alsace and Lorraine. Many of the French people wanted revenge on Germany.

Pan-Slavism Russia had encouraged a form of nationalism in Eastern Europe called Pan-Slavism. The movement tried to draw together all Slavic peoples. Russia was the largest Slavic country, and it was ready to defend Serbia, a young Slavic nation in the Balkans. Throughout the Balkans, in fact, small Slavic populations looked to Russia for leadership in their desire for unity. The multinational empire of Austria-Hungary opposed Slavic national movements.

Militarism

During the late 1800s, **militarism,** the glorification of military power, arose in many nations of Europe. This development led to fear and suspicion as nations became more willing to use military force to attain their national goals. There was an arms race, in which the great powers competed with each other to expand their armies and navies. One of the fiercest rivalries was between Great Britain and Germany.

Imperialism and Economic Rivalry

Great Britain, France, Germany, and other nations competed for colonies and economic power. France and Germany competed especially for colonial gains in Africa. Great Britain and Germany competed industrially. Germany had industrialized rapidly, and the British felt threatened by this. Because of their mutual competition with Germany, Great Britain and France began to form close ties with each other.

Alliance Systems

Increased tensions and suspicions led nations to form alliances. Nations agreed to defend each other in case of attack. By 1914, there were several alliances. The two most important were the Triple Alliance and the Triple Entente. The triple Alliance consisted of Germany, Austria-Hungary, and Italy. The Triple Entente consisted of Great Britain, France, and Russia.

Decline of the Ottoman Empire

Other situations also set the stage for war. The Ottoman empire had become weak. British relations with the empire became strained after Great Britain signed an agreement with Russia. Germany, on the other hand, had taken an interest in establishing good relations with the Ottoman empire.

The Armenian Massacres Nationalistic feelings had caused periodic waves of violence against Armenians since the 1890s. New violence was a brutal result of the rivalry between Turkey, which ruled the Ottoman empire, and Russia. The Muslim Turks distrusted the Christian Armenians, believing that they supported Russia against the Ottoman empire. When Armenians protested oppressive Ottoman policies, the Turks unleashed a massacre on the Armenians. Additional massacres leading to the deaths of a million or more Armenians occurred over the next 25 years.

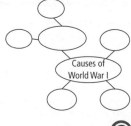

Causes of World War I

Vocabulary Builder

powder keg—(POW dur keg) *n.* a small container with gunpowder or explosives

Preparing for the Regents

Summarize how each of the following **main** causes contributed to World War I.

Militarism:

Alliance systems:

Imperialism:

Nationalism:

Key Themes and Concepts

Diversity
Serb nationalism led to the assassination of Archduke Francis Ferdinand. Slavic groups in the Ottoman empire hoped to unite and throw off the rule of Austria-Hungary.

Recognize Effects

How did Austria-Hungary react to the murder of the archduke?

The Balkan Powder Keg The Ottoman empire's control over the Balkans had weakened over time. Serbia declared its independence in 1878, hoping to build a Slavic state in alliance with Russia. Serbia wanted control of **Bosnia** and Herzegovina, two provinces that would give landlocked Serbia an outlet to the Adriatic Sea. These provinces, however, were Ottoman provinces administered by Austria-Hungary. Austria opposed Serbian ambitions, fearing that the same kind of nationalism would spread to its own multinational empire. Also, Austria-Hungary feared Russian expansion.

Tensions grew, and in 1912, Serbia and its allies attacked the Ottoman empire. The great European powers were all interested in gaining lands from the crumbling empire. By 1914, the Balkans were known as the "powder keg of Europe." Any small spark was likely to lead to an explosion.

The War Begins

The Balkan Crisis

Not surprisingly, World War I began in the Balkans. Although many Serbs lived in Bosnia, it was still ruled by Austria-Hungary. Serb nationalists felt that Bosnia belonged to Serbia.

Archduke Francis Ferdinand was the heir to the Austrian throne. On June 28, 1914, the duke and his wife were traveling through Sarajevo, the capital of Bosnia. Gavrilo Princip, a member of a radical Slavic nationalist group that opposed Austrian rule, shot and killed the archduke and his wife.

A Chain Reaction

After the assassination, the major nations of Europe responded. Each hostile action led to another hostile action.

The Outbreak of War

1.	Austria-Hungary blamed Serbia for the murders of the archduke and his wife and made harsh demands in Serbia.
2.	Serbia refused to comply with any of the demands.
3.	Austria-Hungary declared war on Serbia on July 28.
4.	Russia, a Slavic nation and a friend of Serbia, mobilized its forces in preparation for war.
5.	Germany, an ally of Austria-Hungary, declared war on Russia.
6.	Germany declared war on France, an ally of Russia.
7.	Germany invaded Belgium on August 3, 1914, so that German forces could enter France more easily.
8.	Great Britain declared war on Germany.

World War I: Who Was to Blame?

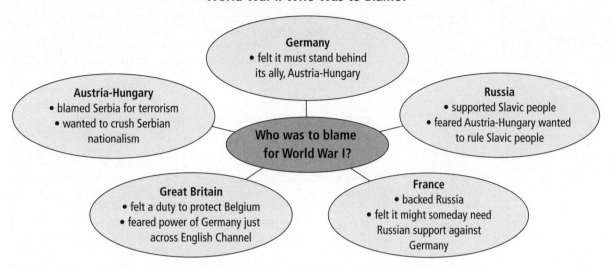

Germany
• felt it must stand behind its ally, Austria-Hungary

Austria-Hungary
• blamed Serbia for terrorism
• wanted to crush Serbian nationalism

Who was to blame for World War I?

Russia
• supported Slavic people
• feared Austria-Hungary wanted to rule Slavic people

Great Britain
• felt a duty to protect Belgium
• feared power of Germany just across English Channel

France
• backed Russia
• felt it might someday need Russian support against Germany

Central Powers and Allied Powers

The two opposing sides in World War I were the Central Powers and the Allied Powers. The **Central Powers** were Germany, Austria-Hungary, and the Ottoman empire (later joined by Bulgaria). On the other side were the **Allied Powers:** Great Britain, France, and Russia. Italy at first remained neutral, but it eventually joined the Allies. Other nations, including the United States, also joined the Allies later.

There were three major fronts in Europe where fighting occurred. The Western Front extended across Belgium and northeastern France to the border of Switzerland. The Eastern Front ran from the Baltic Sea to the Black Sea. The Southern Front ran between Italy and Austria-Hungary. Fighting also took place in Africa and the Middle East.

An Industrialized War

World War I was a war between groups of major industrial powers. New technology made this war an enormously destructive one. For example, Swedish chemist Alfred Nobel had invented dynamite in 1867. Used in mining and construction, it also became important in weaponry. Many of the other recent inventions of the time—the internal combustion engine, the airplane, and communications devices—were also put to military use.

Trench Warfare

Heavy fighting took place along the Western Front, a 600-mile stretch from the English Channel to Switzerland. The Germans hoped to win an early victory there, but French and British troops stopped them. For four years, neither side could make any significant gains.

Trench warfare began, so called because the troops dug trenches along the front. Very little ground was gained by either side in this way, and many soldiers were killed.

New Air and Sea Weapons

World War I was the first war to make full use of modern technology and machinery. Technology changed methods of warfare greatly.

Preparing for the Regents

• Study the graphic organizer and review the chain of events that occurred in 1914. Which nation or group do you think was to blame for World War I? Explain.

Preparing for the Regents

List the members of the Central Powers and the Allied Powers.

Central Powers:

Allied Powers:

Summarize

What made World War I extremely destructive? Explain.

Technology Changes Warfare

Preparing for the Regents

- What role did technology play in World War I?

Invention	Description	Use in World War I
Automatic machine gun	mounted gun that fires a rapid, continuous stream of bullets	made it possible for a few gunners to mow down waves of soldiers
Tank	armored vehicle that travels on a track and can cross many kinds of land	protected advancing troops as they broke through enemy defenses; Early tanks were slow and clumsy
Submarine	underwater ship that can launch torpedoes, or guided underwater bombs	used by Germany to destroy Allied ships; submarine attacks helped bring United States into war
Airplane	one- or two-seat propeller plane equipped with machine gun or bombs	at first, mainly used for observation; later, flying "aces" engaged in air combat
Poison gas; gas mask	gases that cause choking, blinding, or severe skin blisters; gas masks can protect soldiers from poison gas	lobbed into enemy trenches, killing or disabling troops; gas masks lessened the importance of poison gas

Vocabulary Builder

<u>draft</u>—(draft) *v.* to order someone to join the army, navy, etc., especially during a war

Civilian Life and Total War

The war was fought at home as well as on the battlefield. A war fought in this way is called a **total war.** In a total war, all of a nation's resources go into the war effort.

- Governments drafted men to fight in the war.
- Governments raised taxes and borrowed money to pay for the war.
- Governments rationed, or limited the supply of, goods at home so that the military could be provided for.
- Governments used the press to print **propaganda,** the spreading of ideas to promote a cause or to damage an opposing cause.
- Women at home took jobs that the soldiers had left behind. Some women joined the armed services. Other women went to the fronts as nurses.

Major Turning Points of the War

Several events that took place during World War I are seen as major turning points. They include the withdrawal of Russia from the war and the entry of the United States into the war.

Entry of the United States

Although the United States had allowed American ships to carry supplies to the Allies, the country had tried to remain **neutral** (not supporting either side) in the war. In 1917, however, Germany used unrestricted submarine warfare, meaning that it attacked any ships on the Atlantic, even if they were carrying American passengers. This policy brought the United States into the war in April 1917. The entry of the Americans helped the Allies win the war.

Preparing for the Regents

- Analyze how interdependence caused the United States to enter World War I.

- How was the entry of the United States a turning point?

Russian Withdrawal

In Russia, low morale contributed to a revolution in 1917. Early in 1918, Russia's new leader signed a treaty with Germany that took Russia out of the war.

Costs of the War

On November 11, 1918, an **armistice,** or an agreement to end the fighting, was declared. The costs of World War I were enormous. It would take many years for people and nations to recover.

Human Casualties

The costs of the war in terms of human lives were staggering.

- More than 8.5 million people had died.
- More than 17 million had been wounded.
- Famine threatened many regions.
- Disease was widespread in many regions.

Economic Losses

All over the world, there were also economic and political losses.

- Factories, farms, and homes had been destroyed.
- Nations had huge war debts to repay.
- The Allies, bitter at the destruction, insisted that the Central Powers make **reparations,** payments for war damage they had caused.

Percentage of Money Spent by Allies

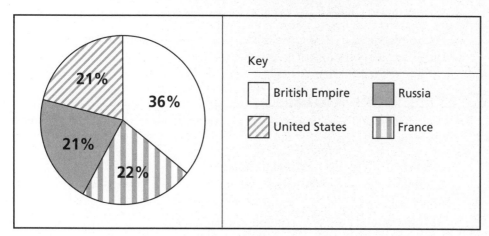

Key

British Empire   Russia

United States   France

Summary

Nationalism, militarism, imperialism, and political rivalries led to World War I. In the Balkans, what began as a local incident blossomed into a global war. Industrialization and new technology made the weapons of World War I much more destructive than any that had been used before. The war caused great human and economic losses.

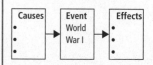
Money Spent by Allies
World War I cost an enormous amount of money. The Allies spent about 160 billion dollars.

Preparing for the Regents

- Based on the pie graph, which nation or groups of nations among the Allies spent the most money on World War I?

Preparing for the Regents

- In what way was World War I a turning point in global history?

Revolution in Russia: Causes and Impacts

Section Overview

Factors such as dissatisfaction with czarist rule, peasant unrest, and economic difficulties created long-term discontent in Russia. After a revolution in 1905, Czar Nicholas II agreed to reforms, but they failed to solve underlying problems. Hardships caused by World War I sparked a revolution that ended Nicholas's reign. Promises of peace, land, and bread allowed Vladimir Lenin and his Bolsheviks, later called Communists, to gain control of the country. After Lenin's death, Joseph Stalin created a communist dictatorship that controlled every aspect of people's lives. He brought the economy completely under government control. Stalin industrialized the country, focusing on heavy industry. Stalin also brought agriculture under state control, causing mass starvation in the process.

Key Themes and Concepts

As you review this section, take special note of the following key themes and concepts:

Change Why did the Russian people demand change in 1917?

Power How did the Bolsheviks take control of the Russian government from the czar?

Human Rights What was life like in Stalin's totalitarian state?

Economic System How did Stalin's command economy affect the Soviet Union's industry and agriculture?

Key People and Terms

As you review this section, be sure you understand the significance of these key people and terms:

soviets	Joseph Stalin	five-year plans
Vladimir Lenin	Great Purge	collectives
Bolsheviks	totalitarian state	
New Economic Policy	command economy	

Long-Term Causes of Revolution

A variety of factors had been leading up to revolution in Russia for a long time. Through the 1800s and early 1900s, discontent grew as Russian czars resisted needed reforms.

Czarist Rule

In the late 1800s, Alexander III and his son, Nicholas II, sought to industrialize the country and build Russia's economic strength. Although these czars wanted to import western industrialization, they hoped to block the ideals of the French Revolution. Still, Russian liberals called for a constitution and reforms that would eliminate corruption in government. Both Alexander and Nicholas used harsh tactics, such as the use of secret police, to suppress reform.

Peasant Unrest

A rigid system of social classes still existed in Russia at the beginning of World War I. Landowning nobles, priests, and an autocratic czar dominated society. A small middle class was prevented from gaining power.

Peasants faced many difficulties. Most were too poor to buy the land they worked. Even those who owned land often did not have enough to feed their families. Even though industrialization had proceeded slowly, it had angered some peasants. Some opposed it because they feared the changes it brought and preferred the old ways.

Problems of Urban Workers

Some peasants had moved to cities and found jobs in new industries. They worked long hours, and their pay was low. Most lived in slums that were nests of poverty and disease. It was among these workers that socialists spread ideas about revolution and reform.

Diversity and Nationalism

Russia ruled a vast and diverse empire. It included many ethnic minorities. The czars maintained strict control over these groups. Under the policy of Russification, czars attempted to make all people in their empire think, act, and believe as Russians. However, ethnic minorities did not want their native cultures destroyed. Pockets of nationalism remained.

Revolution of 1905

Russia's defeat in the Russo-Japanese War of 1904 triggered a crisis in Russia. On Sunday, January 22, 1905, peaceful marchers carrying a petition for reform were shot down by the czar's troops. "Bloody Sunday," as it was called, destroyed the people's faith and trust in the czar, and strikes and revolts exploded across the country.

In the face of this chaos, Nicholas made some changes. He agreed to reforms and promised to grant more rights, such as freedom of speech. He agreed to set up an elected national legislature, the Duma. However, the Duma had limited powers and did little to relieve peasant and worker discontent.

The Russian Revolution of 1905
The "Bloody Sunday" killings were a turning point for the Russian people. It destroyed their faith and trust in the czar.

The Russian Revolution of 1905

CAUSES
- low spirits after defeat in 1904 war with Japan
- poverty and bad working conditions
- corrupt government
- persecution of minority groups
- "Bloody Sunday" killings

Russian Revolution of 1905

RESULTS
- The "October Manifesto"– Czar Nicholas II announces reforms and new freedoms.
- Nicholas II sets up the Duma, which must approve all laws.
- Nicholas II dissolves the first Duma when its leaders criticize the government.
- Pogroms continue.
- New voting laws limit powers of later Dumas.

Note Taking

Reading Skill:
Recognize Sequence Make a timeline. As you read Section 3, record the sequence of important events in Russia's history.

Russia loses
Russo-Japanese
War

1905

World War I and the End of Czarist Rule

A Nation in Chaos

As you have learned, Russia was one of the Allied Powers in World War I. With little industry, however, Russia was not ready to fight a modern war. Russian soldiers lacked adequate weapons and supplies, and Russia suffered a series of battlefield defeats. Food was scarce. Many soldiers lost confidence in Russia's military leadership and deserted.

The March Revolution

In March 1917, military defeats and shortages of food, fuel, and housing in Russia sparked a revolt. In the capital city, St. Petersburg, rioters in the streets demanded bread. The czar's soldiers sympathized with the demonstrators and refused to fire on them. With no control over his troops and with the country nearing anarchy, Czar Nicholas II abdicated, or gave up his rule, in March 1917.

Failure of the Provisional Government

After the removal of the czar, Duma officials set up a provisional, or temporary, government. Middle-class liberals in the government planned to write a constitution and promised democratic reforms. However, the provisional government continued the war against Germany, an unpopular decision that drained away men and resources. The new government implemented only moderate reforms that did little to end unrest among peasants and workers.

The Bolshevik Revolution

The provisional government's slowness to bring about meaningful change led revolutionary socialists to plot further actions. They set up **soviets,** or councils of workers and soldiers, in Russian cities. At first, these soviets worked within the system set up by the government. Soon, however, they were taken over by a radical Socialist Party.

Lenin Gains Support

Following the March Revolution, an exiled Russian revolutionary named **Vladimir Lenin** returned home. Lenin and Leon Trotsky headed a revolutionary Socialist Party, the **Bolsheviks.** Lenin and Trotsky followed the ideas of Karl Marx, but they adapted them to the Russian situation. For example, Marx had said that the urban workers would rise on their own to overthrow the capitalist system. Russia, however, did not have a large urban working class. Lenin therefore suggested that an elite group of reformers—the Bolsheviks—would guide the revolution in Russia.

Lenin gained the support of many people by making promises of "Peace, Land, and Bread." The Bolsheviks promised an end to Russia's involvement in the war. They promised land reform and an end to food shortages.

Lenin Takes Over

The provisional government had lost the support of the people. In November 1917, the Bolsheviks led soldiers, sailors, and factory workers in an uprising that overthrew the government. The Bolsheviks, now called Communists, distributed land to the peasants and gave workers control of the factories and mines. The Communists, however, still faced a struggle to maintain control over Russia.

Lenin Rules Russia

Withdrawal From World War I

Lenin moved quickly to end Russian involvement in World War I. In March 1918, Russia signed the Treaty of Brest-Litovsk. The agreement was costly for Russia,

Key Themes and Concepts

Power
Lenin and the Bolsheviks gained power by promising "Peace, Land, and Bread." The people were tired of Russia's involvement in the world war. Peasants wanted land reform. Everyone wanted shortages of food and other goods to end.

Key Themes and Concepts

Economic Systems
The Communist revolution occurred in Russia, not in a fully industrialized nation as Marx had predicted. In industrialized countries, worker unrest had been eased by a higher standard of living. Also, representative governments in these countries allowed for some reforms. In Russia, however, rural poverty, limited industrialization, and autocratic rule led to revolution.

giving Germany a large amount of Russian territory. Lenin, however, believed that he needed to make peace with Germany at any price so that he could deal with his enemies at home.

Russia's Civil War

From 1918 to 1921, Lenin's Red Army battled against forces loyal to the czar, called the Whites. Nationalist groups in the Russian empire also rose up against the Red Army at this time, winning independence for Estonia, Latvia, Lithuania, and Poland.

Both sides used brutal tactics during the war. To eliminate a potential rallying symbol for the Whites, Communists executed Czar Nicholas II and his entire family.

Great Britain, France, and the United States sent troops to help the Whites. This foreign intervention, however, stirred Russian nationalism. An inspired Red Army, under Trotsky's leadership, defeated its enemies by 1921.

ТОВ. Ленин ОЧИЩАЕТ
ЗЕМЛЮ ОТ НЕЧИСТИ.

Vladimir Lenin
Lenin (1870–1924) believed that only revolution could bring needed changes to Russia.

Preparing for the Regents

• Lenin is the figure with the broom at the top of this poster. What is the point of the poster? Whom do the other figures represent?

Preparing for the Regents

How is a communist government different from a democratic government?

One-Party Government

Lenin's government had a constitution and an elected legislature. However, the Communist Party, not the people themselves, had the real power. The Communist Party was the only legal party, and only its members could run for office. The Party enforced its will through the military and a secret police force.

New Economic Policy

During Russia's civil war, Bolshevik leaders had taken over banks, mines, factories, and railroads. This takeover had resulted in economic disaster. In 1921, Lenin adopted the **New Economic Policy.** Under this plan, also called the NEP, the government still controlled banks, large industry, and foreign trade. Some privately owned businesses were allowed, however. These helped the economy to recover.

The Soviet Union

By 1922, Lenin and the Communists had gained control over much of the old Russian empire. The Communist government then created the Union of Soviet Socialist Republics, also called the Soviet Union. It was made up of diverse European and Asian peoples. Russia, the largest republic, controlled the other states in the Soviet Union.

Stalin and Communist Dictatorship

Lenin died in 1924, ending the reign of Russia's first Communist leader. A new Soviet leader, **Joseph Stalin,** emerged. Stalin ruled through terror and brutality. In the 1930s, for example, out of fear that other Communist Party members were plotting against him, Stalin launched the **Great Purge.** During the Great Purge,

Key Themes and Concepts

Economic Systems
The private ownership allowed by the New Economic Policy helped the Soviet economy to recover. Even in the early years, socialist economic policies met with limited success in the Soviet Union.

Vocabulary Builder

diverse—(duh VURS) *adj.* very different from each other

Preparing for the Regents

Describe five specific ways in which Stalin failed to respect the human rights of Russians and minority national groups in the Soviet Union.

1.

2.

3.

4.

5.

Summarize

Write a sentence explaining the term "Russification."

Stalin accused thousands of people of crimes against the government. Many of the accused were executed; others were exiled or sent to prison camps. For the next 20 years, he pursued ruthless policies that created a totalitarian state in the Soviet Union.

Totalitarian Rule

Stalin turned the Soviet Union into a **totalitarian state.** In this form of government, a one-party dictatorship attempts to regulate every aspect of the lives of its citizens.

Russification

Early in his rule, Stalin promoted individual local cultures. By the end of the 1920s, however, he had changed this policy. Stalin became a strong Russian nationalist. He began to create a Russian ruling elite throughout the Soviet Union. Like the czars before him, Stalin pursued a policy of Russification.

- He promoted Russian history, language, and culture, sometimes forbidding the cultural practices of native peoples.
- He appointed Russians to key posts in the government and secret police.
- He redrew the boundaries of many republics to ensure that non-Russians would not gain a majority.

Life in a Communist Totalitarian State

Economics	Politics	Arts	Religion	Society
• Growth of industry • Growth of military • Low standard of living • Shortage of foods and consumer goods	• One-party dictatorship • Total government control of citizens • Total government control of industry and agriculture • Use of propaganda to win government support	• Censorship of books, music, art • Purpose of all art to praise communism • Observation of artists, writers, and musicians by secret police	• Government war on religion • Takeover of houses of worship • Secret police control religious worship • Communist ideals replace religious ideals	• Fear of secret police • An upper class of Communist Party members • Free education and health care • Public transportation and recreation • Jobs for women

Key Themes and Concepts

Economic Systems
In a command economy, the state controls all factories and businesses and makes all economic decisions. In a capitalist economy, businesses are privately owned and operated for a profit. The free market controls economic decisions.

Power
When peasants resisted Stalin's plan of collectivization, he ruthlessly eliminated them through starvation.

A Command Economy

Stalin established a **command economy,** in which government officials made all basic economic decisions. Under Stalin, the government controlled all factories, businesses, and farms.

Industrialization One of Stalin's chief goals was to make the Soviet Union strong by turning it into a modern industrial power. In 1928, Stalin launched the first of a series of **five-year plans** to build industry and increase farm output. Emphasis was placed on heavy industry, while consumer goods were neglected. In the 1930s, Soviet production in oil, coal, steel, mining, and military goods increased. Across the nation, factories, hydroelectric power stations, and railroads were built.

Despite this progress, however, most Russians remained poor and endured a low standard of living. Soviet central planning created shortages in consumer goods. Also, to meet high production quotas, many factories mass-produced goods of low quality.

Collectivization Stalin forced peasants to give up their small farms and live on state-owned farms or on **collectives,** which were large farms owned and operated by peasants as a group. The collective owned all farm animals and equipment. The government controlled prices and farm supplies and set production quotas. Stalin's plan was for the collectives to grow enough grain for the workers in the cities and to produce surplus grain to sell abroad.

Many peasants resisted collectivization. They killed farm animals, destroyed tools, and burned crops. Stalin responded with a ruthless policy aimed at crushing all who opposed him. The government seized the land of those who resisted and sent the farmers to prison labor camps. There, many died from overwork or were executed.

Forced Famine The results of Stalin's policies were devastating. Some peasants continued to resist by growing just enough grain to feed themselves. The government then seized all the grain from some of those communities. Mass starvation resulted. In the Ukraine, where opposition to collectivization was especially strong, more than five million people died from starvation. Millions more died in other parts of the Soviet Union.

Vocabulary Builder

devastating—(DEV uh stayt ing) *adj.* badly damaging or destroying something

First Leaders of the Soviet Union

Lenin (Soviet leader 1917–1924)
• *Chief goal: to create a classless society with production in the hands of the people*
• Allowed some private business; let some peasants hold land
• Standard of living rose for many workers and peasants

(overlap)
• Spent time in Siberian exile before 1917 revolution
• Became Communist Party leader
• Used secret police to enforce Communist will
• Wanted to bring about a worldwide Communist revolution

Stalin (Soviet leader 1924–1953)
• *Chief goal: to make the Soviet Union into a modern industrial power with all production under government control*
• Created a command economy
• Brought all agriculture under government control; forced peasants to live on group farms
• Standard of living fell for most workers and peasants

Preparing for the Regents

Practice your chart-reading skills by answering the following questions.

1. What were two goals or practices that Lenin and Stalin held in common?

2. How did Stalin's chief goal differ from Lenin's?

Summary

In the late 1800s and early 1900s, autocratic rule and poor economic conditions caused many Russians to demand political and social reforms. In 1917, this discontent led to a revolution that ended czarist rule in Russia. Bolshevik leader Vladimir Lenin gained power by promising better economic conditions and an end to Russian involvement in World War I. He then set up a Communist government. After Lenin's death, Joseph Stalin took over and established a totalitarian state, in which every aspect of life was controlled. Stalin's five-year plans boosted industry but did little to improve the life of the average worker. His collectivization of agriculture angered peasants, whose resistance resulted in mass starvation.

Preparing for the Regents

• To what extent was the Russian Revolution a turning point in global history?

Between the Wars

Section Overview

After World War I, global problems remained. The Treaty of Versailles punished Germany. The League of Nations had little power. Old empires had collapsed, and new nations had come into being. Nationalism continued to cause conflict. World War I had disillusioned many, altered society, and prompted new forms of expression. In Europe and the United States, women struggled to gain the right to vote. Then, in 1929, the global economy crashed, leading to a worldwide depression. During this time, fascism, a new kind of dictatorship, rose in Italy and Germany. In Japan, aggressive military leaders gained power.

Key Themes and Concepts

As you review this section, take special note of the following key themes and concepts:

Interdependence How did the major powers try to resolve troublesome issues after World War I?

Nationalism What factors led to the nationalist movements of the 1920s and 1930s?

Human Rights What rights did women gain after World War I?

Economic Systems What were the causes and effects of the world economic crisis of the 1930s?

Political Systems What are the major characteristics of fascism?

Key People and Terms

As you review this section, be sure you understand the significance of these key people and terms:

Treaty of Versailles	**Pan-Arabism**	**fascism**
League of Nations	**Mohandas Gandhi**	**Benito Mussolini**
Kemal Atatürk	**civil disobedience**	**Adolf Hitler**
Reza Khan	**Kuomintang**	**Third Reich**
mandates	**Great Depression**	

Treaty of Versailles

World War I had a lasting impact on international politics. In January 1919, the victorious Allies gathered at the palace of Versailles, outside Paris, to work out the terms of peace. United States President Woodrow Wilson and Prime Minister David Lloyd George of Great Britain joined French leader Georges Clemenceau. They were known as the "Big Three" of the meeting that would be called the Paris Peace Conference. These men had differing goals. Wilson stressed self-determination, by which people would choose their own government.

He also hoped to create a world organization that would guarantee peace in the future. Great Britain and France wanted to punish Germany and be sure that it would never again become a threat.

Harsh Provisions for Germany

In the end, Great Britain's and France's ideas guided the **Treaty of Versailles.**

Territorial Losses Land was taken from Germany. Some of it was used to help create the new country of Poland. Alsace and Lorraine were returned to France. Germany also lost many of its overseas colonies.

Military Restrictions Germany's army and navy were limited. Germany had to remove its troops from the Rhineland, an industrial area along the French border.

War Guilt Germany had to accept full responsibility for the war and pay huge reparations, or large sums of money to help undo war damage. Accepting the blame and paying the reparations caused bitterness in Germany.

The League of Nations

The Treaty of Versailles also formed the **League of Nations,** a group of more than 40 countries that hoped to settle problems through negotiation, not war. The countries that joined the League of Nations promised to take cooperative economic and military action against any aggressor state. Although the league had been Woodrow Wilson's concept, the United States never joined. Many Americans were afraid that participation in it would drag the United States into future European wars. In refusing to join, the United States weakened the League of Nations.

Preparing for the Regents

- How did the League of Nations plan to deal with future international conflicts?

Preparing for the Regents

Practice your map skills by listing five nations that were created as a result of World War I.

1.

2.

3.

4.

5.

Europe After World War I
The peace treaties that ended World War I changed the map of Europe.

Europe After World War I

Collapse of Empires

World War I caused the collapse of the Austro-Hungarian and Ottoman empires. New nations were carved out of their former territories.

Breakup of Austria-Hungary

As a result of the war, the government in Austria-Hungary had collapsed. Several new nations were created out of the former empire. Austria and Hungary became independent nations. Czechoslovakia and Yugoslavia, two multinational states, were formed. Italy and Romania each gained land.

Breakup of the Ottoman Empire

The Ottoman empire, one of the defeated Central Powers, collapsed in 1918. Most of the Arab lands of the Ottoman empire were placed under the control of Great Britain and France. In theory these countries were being prepared for self-determination. In practice, however, the Allies added to their own overseas empires by creating a system of territories administered by western powers. The remainder of the empire became the country of Turkey.

Unfulfilled National Goals

Many nations were dissatisfied with the results of World War I. Various groups felt that their goals had not been achieved.

- Germany was horrified by the terms of the Treaty of Versailles.
- Italy had hoped to gain more land than it received. It had made a secret treaty with the Allies that was not fulfilled.
- Japan was angry because the Allies did not recognize its claims in China.
- China was angry that Japan had been given control over former German possessions in China.
- Russia was angry over the reestablishment of Poland and the creation of independent Estonia, Latvia, and Lithuania on lands that had been part of the Russian empire.

Nations and groups, however, waited and watched, hoping for a chance to change events in their favor.

National Movements

The spirit of nationalism continued after World War I. Nations in the Middle East, Africa, and Asia struggled for self-determination. In many cases, nationalists were influenced by western ideas. Even so, they were determined to throw off western rule.

Turkish Nationalism

Kemal Atatürk Mustafa Kemal was a general and a war hero in Turkey. After World War I, he led a Turkish nationalist movement. He overthrew the sultan, defeated western occupation forces, and declared Turkey a republic. Mustafa Kemal later called himself **Kemal Atatürk**. The name *Atatürk* meant "father of the Turks."

Westernization and Modernization Atatürk wanted to modernize and westernize Turkey. He believed that Turkey had to change to survive. In accomplishing his goals, he introduced great changes.

- Islamic law was replaced with a new law code, based on European models.
- The Muslim calendar was replaced with the western (Christian) one.

- People were required to wear western dress.
- State schools were set up. Arabic script was replaced with the western (Latin) alphabet.
- Women no longer had to wear veils and were allowed to vote. They could work outside their homes.
- Turkey was industrialized. Atatürk built roads, railroads, and factories.

Iranian Nationalism

Nationalists in Iran followed Turkey's lead. In Iran, the British and the Russians had carved out spheres of influence. In 1925, **Reza Khan,** an army officer, overthrew the ruler of Iran, called the shah. He set up his own dynasty and proclaimed himself shah. Reza Khan quickly tried to modernize and westernize Iran and make it fully independent. Factories, roads, and railroads were built. The army was strengthened. The western alphabet and western dress were adopted, and secular schools were set up. Islamic law was replaced by secular law, and women were encouraged to take part in public life. Reza Khan had the support of wealthy urban Iranians but not of Muslim religious leaders.

Arab Nationalism

During World War I, many Arabs had helped the Allies. In return they had been promised independence. After the war, however, Great Britain and France divided up the Ottoman lands between themselves. They set up **mandates,** territories administered by European powers. France had mandates in Syria and Lebanon. Great Britain had mandates in Palestine and Iraq.

In the 1920s and 1930s, Arab nationalists sought to be free of foreign control. Arab nationalism gave rise to **Pan-Arabism.** This movement sought a unity of all Arab peoples based on their shared heritage.

Zionism

Zionism, as you have learned, had arisen during the 1890s in Europe and the Middle East. Jewish people wanted to establish a Jewish state in Palestine. The situation was complex, however, since Arab peoples were already living there. The Allies had made conflicting promises during World War I. They had promised Arabs land that included Palestine. They had also pledged to set up a Jewish nation in the same region. As more Jews moved to Palestine to escape persecution in the 1930s, tensions grew.

Indian Nationalism

Nearly 1 million Indians had served the Allied cause in Europe during World War I, and many had died. At home, however, Indians had few rights. During World War I, Great Britain had promised India greater self-government. After the war was over, Great Britain failed to fulfill these promises.

The Amritsar Massacre A turning point came in 1919. There were riots and attacks on British citizens in the city of Amritsar. In response, public meetings were banned. When a large group of Indians assembled on April 13, British troops fired on them without warning, killing about 400 people and wounding about 1,200 more. The incident convinced many Indians that British rule must be ended.

Gandhi In the 1920s and 1930s, a leader named **Mohandas Gandhi** headed the Indian nationalist movement. He taught that nonviolent resistance and **civil disobedience** (the refusal to obey unjust laws), rather than bloodshed, were the way to win rights. He used tactics such as boycotting, or refusing to buy, British goods and peaceful demonstrations such as the "Salt March." Gandhi embraced

Vocabulary Builder

veil—(vayl) *n.* a thin piece of material that women wear to cover their faces at formal occasions or for religious reasons

Key Themes and Concepts

Change
In Iran—unlike Turkey—modernization eventually led, in 1979, to an Islamic revolution in which the government turned from secularism.

Preparing for the Regents

- What are the similarities among Pan-Slavism, Pan-Arabism, and Zionism? What are some differences?

Mohandas Gandhi
Gandhi's philosophy reflected Western and Indian influences. His ideas inspired Indians of all religious and ethnic backgrounds.

Preparing for the Regents

Write a brief statement about the historical importance of each of these figures.

Kemal Atatürk:

Reza Khan:

Mohandas Gandhi:

western ideas of democracy and nationalism. He rejected the caste system and urged equal rights for all, including women. India, however, did not achieve independence until 1947, one year before Gandhi's death.

Chinese Nationalism

Chinese civilization was in great disorder during and after World War I. After Sun Yixian (also known as Sun Yat-sen), founder of the Chinese Republic, stepped down, rival warlords fought for power. The economy collapsed, and peasants faced great economic hardship. During this time, foreign powers—especially Japan—increased their influence in China.

Rival Groups in China After the death of Sun Yixian in 1925, an army officer named Jiang Jieshi (also known as Chiang Kai-shek) took over the **Kuomintang**. Jiang's government, supported by middle class businessmen, did little to help the peasants. As a result the peasants were attracted to Mao Zedong and his Communist Party.

Civil War At first, the Nationalists and the Communists had worked together to unite China. Over time, however, Jiang Jieshi began to see the Communists as a threat. A civil war began between the Nationalists and the Communists that would last for 22 years.

Literature and Arts: The Lost Generation

World War I had produced disquiet in social as well as political arenas. The war had shaken many people's long-held beliefs. Scientific discoveries—such as those of the Curies, Einstein, and Freud—had brought new understanding, but they had also cast doubt on the ideas of the past.

The war itself had left scars on those who survived it. Writers, artists, and musicians throughout the 1920s and 1930s expressed a loss of hope, rejecting former rules and moral values. They became known as the "Lost Generation."

Preparing for the Regents

• How did World War I affect the literature and arts of the 1920s and 1930s?

Writers such as Ernest Hemingway expressed a loss of faith in western civilization. Poet T. S. Eliot portrayed the modern world as spiritually empty and barren. Some painters stopped trying to reproduce the real world. In an attempt to express their feelings of loss of meaning, they experimented with color and distorted shapes.

Women's Suffrage Movement

Key Themes and Concepts

Justice and Human Rights World War I brought great progress for women. Women kept the economy going at home by taking on jobs left vacant by men who became soldiers. Some joined the armed forces. This independence gave them a new sense of pride and confidence. After the war, women in various western democracies gained the right to vote.

In the mid-1800s in western democracies, women had begun to demand greater rights. These included property rights and suffrage, or the right to vote. The first country in which women won the right to vote was New Zealand in 1893. In Great Britain, Parliament finally granted women over 30 the right to vote in 1918. By 1928, Great Britain had granted suffrage to all women over the age of 21. In the United States, President Wilson proposed the Nineteenth Amendment in 1918. This amendment gave American citizens over the age of 21 the right to vote, regardless of gender. Congress adopted the amendment two years later in 1920. Women also gained the right to vote in Canada, Finland, Germany, and Sweden in the early 1900s.

Worldwide Depression

After World War I, economic problems emerged in Europe. Soldiers, returning from the war, needed jobs. Nations had war debts to pay and cities to rebuild. In the decade following the war, the economies of many European countries began a shaky recovery. Middle-class families enjoyed a rising standard of living.

The United States, on the other hand, experienced an economic boom after the war. It became the world's leading economic power and made investments in Europe to promote recovery. These came to an end, however, with the crash of the American stock market in 1929. This event triggered the **Great Depression** of the 1930s, a time of global economic collapse.

Causes of the Depression

Weaknesses in the economies of the United States and other nations around the world led to the Great Depression.

Impact of the Depression

The collapse of the American economy had a ripple effect around the world. American investors pulled their money out of Europe, and placed high tariffs on imported goods. Nations that depended on American loans and investments or on exporting their goods to the United States, saw their economies collapse. Unemployment soared in many countries.

As the Great Depression continued, some people lost faith in democracy and capitalism. Extreme ideas of many types arose. Communists celebrated what they saw as the failure of capitalism. Strong leaders supported intense nationalism, militarism, and a return to authoritarian rule.

The Rise of Fascism

Widespread economic despair paved the way for the rise of dictators. Strong leaders in Italy and Germany promised solutions.

The Fascist State

Common Ideals of Fascism

Fascism is the rule of a people by dictatorial government that is nationalistic and imperialistic. Fascist governments are also anticommunist. Fascism emerged in both Italy and Germany after World War I.

Mussolini in Italy

Italy was troubled after World War I. Treaties had given away land that the Italians had expected to control. In addition, many war veterans could not find jobs. Trade was slow and taxes were high. Furthermore, workers went on strike.

Benito Mussolini took advantage of the unrest, gathering a following of war veterans and other unhappy Italians. He called his group the Fascist Party and pledged to solve the nation's problems and strengthen Italy. Mussolini promised to end unemployment and gain more land for Italy. He also vowed to outlaw rebellion among workers and stamp out all threats of communism.

In 1922, the Fascists used force and terror to gain control of Italy. They ended free elections, free speech, and the free press. They killed or jailed their enemies. Grasping desperately for order, Italians put the goals of the state above their individual rights.

Hitler in Germany

The Weimar Republic After World War I, the kaiser stepped down. Germany was in chaos. The new democratic government, called the Weimar Republic, was blamed for agreeing to the harsh terms of the Versailles Treaty. Inflation created major economic problems. The troubles of the time led to the Nazi rise to power.

Adolf Hitler promised to provide jobs and rebuild German pride. He stated that the Germans were a superior race who were destined to build a new empire. In 1920, he headed the National Socialist German Workers, or Nazi, Party. His Party grew. In 1933, Hitler was appointed chancellor.

Hitler as Dictator Hitler's Germany, called the **Third Reich,** was a totalitarian state. He built a one-party government, ended civil rights, silenced his enemies with force, put businesses under government control, and employed many people in large public works programs. Germany's standard of living rose. Hitler rearmed Germany and rebuilt its military, which violated the Treaty of Versailles.

Preparing for the Regents

• Practice your graph skills by identifying the years during which the cost of living in Germany was the highest. What impact do you think this had on Hitler's rise to power?

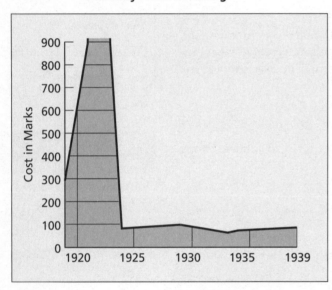

Germany: Cost of Living

Adolph Hitler and the Nazis
Adolph Hitler (1889–1945) and the Nazis wanted to create a new and powerful Germany. To achieve this goal, Hitler organized a brutal, totalitarian state.

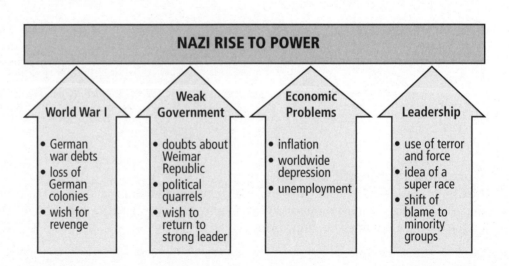

NAZI RISE TO POWER

World War I
• German war debts
• loss of German colonies
• wish for revenge

Weak Government
• doubts about Weimar Republic
• political quarrels
• wish to return to strong leader

Economic Problems
• inflation
• worldwide depression
• unemployment

Leadership
• use of terror and force
• idea of a super race
• shift of blame to minority groups

Hitler used the Jews as a scapegoat for Germany's problems. He instituted anti-Semitic policies. He used education and the arts as propaganda tools to push these policies. At first, Nazis organized boycotts of Jewish businesses, but by 1938 they were seizing the property and businesses of Jews and selling them to non-Jews. The Nuremberg Laws of 1935 took away the political rights and German citizenship of Jews. Few German citizens worried about Hitler's policies. Most were pleased at the growth of German pride and Germany's increased military and economic power.

Totalitarianism in Nazi Germany

Propaganda	Lack of Civil Liberties
The government controlled all sources of information—newspapers, radio, movies, and books. Schools taught Nazi ideas, and children joined the Hitler Youth. Forbidden books were burned.	Only the Nazi Party was allowed, and rival political parties were outlawed. The Gestapo (secret police) arrested and executed people without a trial.
Anti-Semitism	**Economic Controls**
Jews lost their property and citizenship. Their shops and synagogues were destroyed. They were forced to wear the yellow Star of David on their clothing. They were moved to ghettoes and concentration camps.	Agricultural and industrial production was controlled. Labor unions and strikes were outlawed. Germans were put to work building highways and weapons factories and drafted into the military.

Japan: Militarism and Expansion

Japan had moved toward greater democracy during the 1920s. However, there were underlying problems in Japanese society. The Great Depression that began in 1929 made these problems more apparent. Militarists and extreme nationalists gained power.

Japanese Militarists of the 1930s

CAUSES

- unhappiness over loss of traditions
- loss of foreign markets due to Great Depression
- unemployment
- poverty among peasants
- feelings of nationalism
- demand for expansion of Japanese empire

Rise of Militarists in Japan

EFFECTS

- 1931 attack on Chinese province of Manchuria
- withdrawal from League of Nations
- anti-western feelings
- end of many democratic freedoms
- renewed practice of traditions
- increased honor for emperor
- renewed expansion and efforts to control China

Summary

After World War I, conflict and turmoil continued. The Treaty of Versailles gave some nations self-determination, punished Germany severely, and created the League of Nations. New nations formed and old empires collapsed. Change occurred as nationalist groups struggled to overthrow foreign domination. Society and culture changed after the war, and people lost faith in old ideas. In 1929, the global economy plunged into a terrible depression. Fascism in Italy and Germany threatened the peace in Europe, while aggressive militarism by Japan caused tension in Asia.

Vocabulary Builder

scapegoat—(SKAYP goht) *n.* someone who is blamed for something bad that happens, even if it is not their fault

Preparing for the Regents

- How did war and economic depression lead to the rise of fascism?

Key Themes and Concepts

Power and Human Rights Both Mussolini in Italy and Hitler in Germany improved the economies of their nations and brought order. The price of order, however, was loss of personal freedoms and human rights.

Because of unrest in Japan in the 1930s, the government accepted military domination. It revived ancient warrior values.

Preparing for the Regents

The militarists in Japan were determined to restore Japan to greatness, rid themselves of western influence, and gain foreign territories.

1. What economic problems led to the rise of militarism in Japan?

2. What were the political effects of the rise of militarism in Japan?

World War II

Section Overview

During the 1930s, Italy, Germany, and Japan sought to build new empires. At first, the democratic powers did not stop them. When German aggression became impossible to ignore, in 1939, World War II began. With advanced technology, the war covered a larger area and was more destructive than any before. Civilians became involved on a larger scale as well. At first, the Axis powers—Germany, Italy, and Japan—won major victories. After the entry of the United States and the Soviet Union into the war on the Allied side, however, the tide began to turn. The war finally ended in 1945. It had many lasting effects. There were enormous losses of life and property. The United Nations was formed to try to maintain peace. Europe became divided, with communist governments in Eastern Europe and democratic governments in Western Europe.

Key Themes and Concepts

As you review this section, take special note of the following key themes and concepts:

Power What events led up to World War II?

Science and Technology How did new weapons technology affect the course of the war?

Citizenship How were the lives of individuals affected by the war?

Change What were the major turning points of the war that helped determine its outcome?

Key People and Terms

As you review this section, be sure you understand the significance of these key people and terms:

appeasement	D-Day	concentration camps
Munich Conference	Hiroshima	Holocaust
Franklin Roosevelt	blitz	Bataan Death March
Pearl Harbor	Winston Churchill	United Nations
Stalingrad	genocide	

The Road to War

In the 1930s, Italy, Germany, and Japan aggressively sought to build new empires. The League of Nations was weak. Western countries were recovering from the Great Depression and did not want any more war. As a result, acts of aggression occurred and were allowed to go unchecked.

Japan Invades China

The militaristic leaders of Japan wanted to build a Japanese empire. In 1931, Japan seized the Chinese territory of Manchuria. When the League of Nations condemned the action, Japan merely withdrew its membership from the League.

This incident strengthened militarism in Japan. In 1937, the Japanese army invaded the Chinese mainland. They established a puppet government in the former Chinese Nationalist capital of Nanjing. Their invasion of this city was so brutal that it became known as the "rape of Nanjing." Japan continued to gain territory during the period of war with China.

Italy Attacks Ethiopia

In 1935, the Italian army invaded the African country of Ethiopia. The Ethiopians resisted the attack, but their weapons were no match for the armored vehicles, aircraft, and poison gas of the Italians. The Ethiopian king appealed to the League of Nations. The league agreed to stop the sale of weapons and other war materials to Italy. However, the agreement was not honored by all nations.

German Aggression in Europe

Hitler glorified war as a means of restoring German national pride. This philosophy led to a policy of expansion.

- Hitler rebuilt the German army, in violation of the Treaty of Versailles.
- In 1936, Hitler sent troops into the Rhineland. This was an area located on Germany's border with France. The Treaty of Versailles had required that Germany remove its troops from this border region.
- In 1938, Hitler made Austria part of the German empire. In the same year, he also forced Czechoslovakia to give Germany a border area called the Sudetenland, where many Germans lived.

Appeasement

Western democracies adopted a policy of **appeasement.** Under this policy, nations gave in to aggressive demands to maintain peace. The western democracies responded weakly to German aggression. At the **Munich Conference** in 1938, western democracies agreed that Germany would seize control of the Sudetenland from Czechoslovakia.

Vocabulary Builder

puppet—(PUP ut) *n.* a person or organization that allows other people to control them and make their decisions

Key Themes and Concepts

Political Systems
Leaders of Great Britain, France, and the United States knew that their citizens were reluctant to get involved in another costly war. This factor and others kept them from responding immediately to the aggression of Germany, Italy, and Japan.

Military Aggression Leading to World War II

	1935 Italy attacks Ethiopia	1937 Japan invades China	1939 Germany invades Poland Germany takes Czechoslovakia
1930	1932	1934	1936	1938	1940
	1931 Japan invades Manchuria		1936 Germany occupies Rhineland	1938 Germany invades Austria Germany seizes Sudetenland	

Preparing for the Regents

List five acts of aggression that led to World War II.

1.

2.

3.

4.

5.

World War II Begins

In the face of this weakness, Japan, Italy, and Germany formed the Rome-Berlin-Tokyo Axis. These nations agreed to fight Soviet communism and not to stop each other from making foreign conquests.

It began to be clear that appeasement had failed. Several events led to a declaration of war. In March 1939, Hitler took over the rest of Czechoslovakia. In August 1939, he made a pact with Joseph Stalin, the leader of the Soviet Union. In the

Nazi-Soviet Pact, the two enemies agreed not to fight each other. In September 1939, Germany invaded Poland. Finally, Great Britain and France responded by declaring war on Germany. World War II had begun.

The Axis Powers Advance

The war was fought between the Axis powers (Germany, Italy, and Japan) and the Allied powers (France and Great Britain). The Allies were later joined by the Soviet Union, China, and the United States. At first, Germany and its allies prevailed. Nazi forces conquered Poland in a swift, massive attack known as blitzkrieg, or lightning warfare. In April 1940, Hitler overran Norway, Denmark, the Netherlands, and Belgium. By June 1940, the Germans had entered Paris. Charles de Gaulle formed a French government in exile, calling on French forces to continue fighting Germany. These "Free French" worked from England to liberate their homeland.

The Axis war machine extended across the world. It reached its height in Europe in 1942.

The World at War: World War II

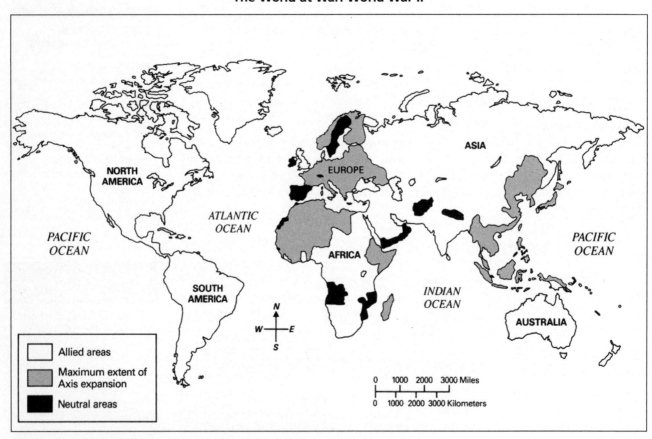

Preparing for the Regents

Describe the importance of each of the following turning points of the war.

Entry of the United States:

Battle of Stalingrad:

Invasion of Normandy:

Turning Points of the War

The Axis powers won quick victories in the first several years of the war. Several events after 1940, however, are seen as turning points for the Allies.

The Entry of the United States (1941)

Although the United States had declared its neutrality in the war, President **Franklin Roosevelt** met with England's prime minister, Winston Churchill, in August 1941, and they declared their common desire to end Nazi tyranny.

Roosevelt continued to supply arms to the Allies. To stop Japanese aggression, the United States banned the sale of war materials to Japan. Angered by the ban, Japan launched a surprise attack on American military bases at **Pearl Harbor,** Hawaii, on December 7, 1941. More than 2,400 people were killed, and many ships and planes were destroyed. In response, Franklin Roosevelt asked Congress to declare war on Japan. The entry of the United States into the war gave the Allies added strength.

Battle of Stalingrad (1942–1943)

The Germans invaded the Soviet Union in 1941. After steadily advancing, they became stalled outside Moscow and Leningrad. Hitler turned south in 1942 to try to take **Stalingrad.** Russian troops and a freezing winter caused the German invaders to surrender in 1943. The Red Army drove the Germans out of the Soviet Union. Soon Soviet troops were advancing toward Germany.

Invasion of Normandy (1944)

The Allies invaded France on June 6, 1944, also known as **D-Day**. Allied troops were ferried across the English Channel, landing on the beaches of Normandy. They broke through German defenses to advance toward Paris and freed France from German control. The Allies then moved from France into Germany.

The War Ends

The war in Europe ended on May 7, 1945, with the Germans' surrender. Fighting in the Pacific would continue until the Japanese surrendered in August 1945.

Yalta Conference

In February 1945, Roosevelt, Churchill, and Stalin met at a Soviet resort called Yalta. They knew then that the war was close to an end. The three leaders decided that at war's end, they would divide Germany temporarily. British, French, American, and Soviet forces would each control a zone of Germany. They agreed that Stalin would oversee the creation of new governments in Eastern Europe.

Victory in the Pacific

Japan was greatly weakened, and the United States took the offensive after two Japanese fleets were severely damaged by Americans in 1942. Gradually, American forces recaptured Japanese-held islands south of Japan and advanced north. By 1944, the Americans had begun to bomb Japanese cities. The Japanese, however, refused to surrender.

Hiroshima and Nagasaki

With no war in Europe, the Allies poured resources into the Pacific. By mid-1945, most of the Japanese navy and air force had been destroyed. Japan's army was still strong, however. On August 6, 1945, an American plane dropped an atomic bomb on the Japanese city of **Hiroshima.** The bomb flattened 4 square miles of the city and killed 70,000 people. They dropped another bomb on Nagasaki, killing 40,000 people. Some militarists wanted to hold out, but on August 10, Japanese emperor Hirohito forced his government to surrender. Japan signed a peace treaty on September 2, 1945.

Technology and World War II

Throughout the war, advanced technology led to more power, greater speed, and better communications. Technological innovation resulted in more widespread destruction than ever before.

Preparing for the Regents

Describe the significance of each of the following leaders.

Hitler:

Mussolini:

Stalin:

Churchill:

Roosevelt:

Identify Effects

Japan refused to surrender to the United States. What were the two main effects?

Preparing for the Regents

• How did World War II affect civilian life? How did civilians contribute to the war effort?

Civilian Life and Total War

Both the Allied powers and the Axis powers had engaged in total war. Cities became targets of bombing. In 1940, Germany began a **blitz,** or massive bombing, of London using warplanes. **Winston Churchill,** prime minister of Great Britain, rallied his people.

Democratic governments increased their power during the war. They ordered factories to produce war materials instead of civilian products. Prices and wages were fixed, and consumer goods were rationed.

Democratic governments sometimes limited the rights of individuals. In the United States and Canada, some people of Japanese descent were forced into internment camps. The British took similar action with those of German ancestry.

As men joined the war, women worked in the factories. They helped produce planes, ships, and ammunition. British and American women served in the armed forces by driving trucks and ambulances, decoding messages, and serving as nurses at field hospitals.

Key Themes and Concepts

Human Rights
The Holocaust as well as other atrocities committed during World War II were extreme violations of human rights.

The Holocaust

One of Hitler's goals was to create "living space" for Germans who he considered racially superior. He planned to destroy people he found inferior. Jews were the main target, but he also wanted to destroy or enslave others, including Slavs, Gypsies, and the mentally or physically disabled.

The attempt to destroy an entire ethnic or religious group is called **genocide.** Hitler committed genocide against the Jews. He began by limiting the rights and encouraging violence against Jews. On November 8, 1938, called Kristallnacht, organized violence began. Thousands of Jewish synagogues, businesses, cemeteries, schools, and homes were destroyed. The next day, 30,000 Jews were arrested for being Jewish and more restrictive laws on Jews and Jewish businesses began. Jews were forced to live in separate areas. Then, Hitler set up **concentration camps.** At death camps, like Auschwitz, Jews were starved, shot, or gassed to death. By 1945, more than six million Jews had died in what became known as the **Holocaust.**

Vocabulary Builder

atrocity—(uh TRAHS uh tee) *n.* an extremely cruel and violent action, especially during a war

Other Wartime Atrocities

The Holocaust stands as the starkest example of wartime inhumanity. Several other incidents, however, also stand out as especially brutal aspects of World War II.

• The Japanese invasion of Nanjing in 1937 involved mass shootings and terrible brutality. As many as 250,000 Chinese were killed.

• In the Philippines, Japanese soldiers forced American and Filipino prisoners of war on a march up the Bataan peninsula. Along the way, prisoners were beaten, stabbed, and shot. This event became known as the **Bataan Death March.**

• In Poland, Soviet troops subjected thousands of Poles to imprisonment, torture, and execution.

Impact of World War II

Human Losses

World War II had killed as many as 75 million people. In European countries alone, about 38 million people died. The Soviets, however, had suffered the heaviest losses, with more than 22 million dead. The Holocaust had inflicted death and misery on millions of Jews and others in the Nazi concentration camps.

Economic Losses

Throughout Europe and parts of Asia, cities were in ruins. Aerial bombardment had been very destructive. Coventry in England; Hamburg and Dresden in Germany; and Tokyo, Hiroshima, and Nagasaki in Japan were some of the hardest-hit cities. The European countryside was devastated as well. The economies of war-torn countries took many years to recover.

War Crime Trials

At meetings during the war, Allied leaders had agreed to punish those responsible for "crimes against humanity." Trials were held in Nuremberg, Germany, from November 1945 through September 1946. Hitler was already dead, but 22 surviving Nazi leaders were tried at the Nuremberg trials. Some received the death penalty; others were imprisoned. Additional trials were held in Italy and Japan. The trials demonstrated that leaders could be held accountable for their actions during war.

Occupied Nations

In order to prevent another world war and to promote democracy, western nations occupied West Germany and Japan. They built new governments with democratic constitutions, which protected individual rights and liberties.

However, Soviet forces occupied East Germany and most of Eastern Europe. They established communist governments in these nations, backed by the power of the Soviet Union. Thus, Europe was divided in two—between democracy in the West and communism in the East.

The United Nations

World War II resulted in the formation of a new international body. In April 1945, representatives from nations around the world met in San Francisco to establish the **United Nations.** The purpose of the United Nations is to provide a place to discuss world problems and develop solutions. The two main bodies of the United Nations are:

- the General Assembly, which includes representatives from all member nations; each representative has one vote.
- the Security Council, with 15 member nations, 5 of which are permanent: the United States, Russia, France, Great Britain, and China.

Summary

Germany, Italy, and Japan tried in the 1930s to build world empires. When Germany invaded Poland in 1939, World War II began, and the world faced the most devastating conflict in human history. During World War II, new weapons with massive power caused the loss of millions of lives. Civilians were greatly affected by the war, facing rationing, military attacks, and sometimes severe repression. The conflict continued until 1945. World War II resulted in millions of deaths, heavy economic losses, and brutality on a scale such as the world had not seen before. After 1945, the world became divided between communist and democratic forms of government.

Preparing for the Regents

List five effects of World War II.

1.

2.

3.

4.

5.

Compare and Contrast

Compare and contrast the United Nations and the League of Nations.

Questions for Regents Practice

Multiple Choice

Directions: Review the Test-Taking Strategies section of this book. Then answer the following questions, drawn from actual Regents examinations. For each statement or question, choose the *number* of the word or expression that, of those given, best completes the statement or answers the question.

Base your answer to question 1 on the graph below and on your knowledge of social studies.

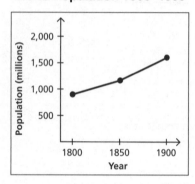

World Population 1800–1900

1 What factors would best account for the rise in population shown on this graph after 1850?

(1) lack of public sewer systems

(2) the end of World War I

(3) medical advances and improved diets

(4) the decline of feudalism

2 A major cause of World War I was

(1) a decline in the policy of imperialism

(2) the existence of opposing alliances

(3) an increase in acts of aggression by England

(4) the spread of communism throughout Europe

3 In Eastern Europe after World War I, the greatest obstacle to national unity in many nation-states was the

(1) great ethnic diversity found in the region

(2) economic dependence of Eastern Europe on Japan

(3) acceptance of democratic traditions by most Eastern Europeans

(4) expansion of United States influence in the region

4 The Russian peasants supported the Bolsheviks in the 1917 revolutions mainly because the Bolsheviks promised to

(1) establish collective farms

(2) maintain the agricultural price-support system

(3) bring modern technology to Russian farms

(4) redistribute the land owned by the nobility

5 The French Revolution of 1789, the Chinese Revolution of 1911, and the Bolshevik Revolution of 1917 were similar in that these revolutions

(1) were led by ruthless dictators

(2) were motivated by a desire to overthrow a monarch

(3) led directly to the establishment of communism

(4) established a higher standard of living for the middle class

6 Which statement best describes the political situation that existed in the Soviet Union immediately after the death of Lenin in 1924?

(1) The nation adopted a constitutional monarchy.

(2) Trotsky and his followers assumed full control of the Communist Party.

(3) Popular elections were held to choose a new general secretary.

(4) A power struggle developed among Communist Party leaders.

7 "... The organizations of the revolutionaries must consist first, foremost, and mainly of people who make revolutionary activity their profession. ... Such an organization must of necessity be not too extensive and as secret as possible. ..."

—V. I. Lenin, 1917

This quotation refers to Lenin's plan to

(1) defeat Germany in World War I

(2) establish representative democracy in Russia

(3) maintain Communist power in Western Europe

(4) overthrow the Russian government

8 Under Joseph Stalin, the Soviet Union emphasized centralized economic planning and five-year plans primarily to

(1) produce more consumer goods

(2) expand exports

(3) create an increased demand for high-quality imports

(4) develop heavy industry

9 A significant effect of Joseph Stalin's policy of collectivization on Soviet agriculture was

(1) a widespread food shortage

(2) an increase in the export of agricultural products

(3) a surplus of agricultural products

(4) the immediate creation of many small private farms

10 One similarity between Russia under the czars and the Soviet Union under Joseph Stalin is that in both types of government, these leaders

(1) tried to reduce their nation's influence in world affairs

(2) developed policies to limit industrial growth

(3) supported the creation of a national church

(4) established an authoritarian form of government

11 A study of the causes of the American, French, and Russian Revolutions indicates that revolutions usually occur because the

(1) society has become dependent on commerce and trade

(2) society has a lower standard of living than the societies around it

(3) existing government has been resistant to change

(4) lower classes have strong leaders

12 The harsh conditions imposed by the Treaty of Versailles after World War I helped lay the foundation for the

(1) rise of fascism in Germany

(2) uprisings during the French Revolution

(3) division of Korea along the 38th parallel

(4) Bolshevik Revolution in Russia

13 Mohandas Gandhi is best known for his

(1) use of passive resistance to achieve Indian independence

(2) desire to establish an Islamic nation

(3) opposition to Hindus holding public office

(4) encouragement of violence to end British rule

14 Which situation contributed to Adolf Hitler's rise to power in Germany after World War I?

(1) support of Hitler's radical policies by the Social Democrats in the Reichstag

(2) strong feelings of resentment and nationalism built up by economic and political crises

(3) refusal by the League of Nations to admit Germany as a member

(4) violence and terrorism promoted by Germany's former enemies

15 Which was characteristic of France under Napoleon's rule and Germany under Hitler's rule?

(1) Democratic ideas and diversity were encouraged.

(2) Authoritarian control and a strong sense of nationalism prevailed.

(3) Peaceful relations with neighboring countries were fostered.

(4) Artistic and literary freedom flourished.

16 Which policy best demonstrates appeasement?

(1) British policy toward Germany during the 1930s

(2) Japanese policy toward China in the 1930s

(3) Spanish policy toward Native Americans in the 1500s

(4) German policy toward the French during World War I

17 Which series of events is arranged in the correct chronological order?

(1) The Treaty of Versailles is signed. Adolf Hitler becomes chancellor of Germany. German troops invade Poland.

(2) German troops invade Poland. The Treaty of Versailles is signed. Adolf Hitler becomes chancellor of Germany.

(3) Adolf Hitler becomes chancellor of Germany. The Treaty of Versailles is signed. German troops invade Poland.

(4) The Treaty of Versailles is signed. German troops invade Poland. Adolf Hitler becomes chancellor of Germany.

18 The treatment of the Jews in Europe during World War II and of the Armenians in the Ottoman empire are examples of

(1) cultural diffusion

(2) fundamentalism

(3) modernization

(4) genocide

19 Which was a major result of the Nuremberg trials?

(1) National leaders were held personally responsible for war crimes against humanity.

(2) The State of Israel was created as a home for victims of the war.

(3) Soldiers were required to pay for the property damages they caused during the war.

(4) Prisoners from all countries were immediately released from captivity.

In developing your answer, be sure to keep these general definitions in mind:

    (a) <u>describe</u> means "to illustrate something in words or tell about it"

    (b) <u>explain</u> means "to make plain or understandable; to give reasons for or causes of; to show the logical development or relationships of"

Directions: Write a well-organized essay that includes an introduction, several paragraphs addressing the task below, and a conclusion.

Theme: **Nationalism**

> Throughout global history, nationalism has had positive and negative effects.

Tasks:

> - Define the term *nationalism*
> - Select one country or region you have studied
> - Describe two specific examples of nationalism within that country or region
> - Explain how each of the two examples had either a positive or negative impact on the future development of the country or region

You may use any nation or region from your study of global history, except the United States. Some suggestions you may wish to consider are: Latin America (1800s), Italy (1800s and 1900s), China (1900s), India (1900s), Kenya (post-World War II), and the Balkans (1900s).

You are *not* limited to these suggestions.
Do *not* use the United States in your answer.

Guidelines:

    In your essay, be sure to
- Develop all aspects of the task
- Support the theme with relevant facts, examples, and details
- Use a logical and clear plan of organization, including an introduction and a conclusion that are beyond a simple restatement of the theme

Document-Based Question

This question is based on the accompanying documents. The question is designed to test your ability to work with historical documents. Some of these documents have been edited for the purposes of this question. As you analyze the documents, take into account the source of each document and any point of view that may be presented in the document.

Historical Context:

Throughout history, leaders have viewed power in many different ways. There have been a variety of viewpoints on the acquisition and use of power.

Task: Using the information from the documents and your knowledge of global history, answer the questions that follow each document in Part A. Your answers to the questions will help you write the Part B essay in which you will be asked to

- Discuss several viewpoints on the attainment and use of power
- Evaluate positive and negative effects that the various viewpoints have had on people in different countries

In developing your answers, be sure to keep these general definitions in mind:

(a) <u>discuss</u> means "to make observations about something using facts, reasoning, and argument; to present in some detail"

(b) <u>evaluate</u> means "to examine and judge the significance, worth, or condition of; to determine the value of"

Part A: Short Answer

Directions: Analyze the documents and answer the question or questions that follow each document, using the space provided.

Document #1

> *Under the leadership of the working class and the Communist party, these classes [the working class, the peasantry, the petty bourgeoisie, and the national bourgeoisie] unite to create their own state . . . so as to enforce their . . . dictatorship over the henchmen of imperialism—the landlord class and bureaucratic capitalist class. . . . The people's government will suppress such persons.*
>
> **– Mao Zedong, speech on the anniversary of the founding of the Communist party, 1949**

1 According to Mao Zedong, do all classes share power in a communist state? Explain.

_____

_____

2 Describe one goal that Mao thought a communist government should strive to achieve.

_____

_____

Document #2
The Fascist State

3 According to this chart, what methods have fascist leaders used to acquire and maintain power?

_____

_____

Document #3

> *Passive resistance is a method of securing rights by personal suffering; it is the reverse of resistance by arms. When I refuse to do a thing that is repugnant to my conscience, I use soul-force.*
>
> **– Mohandas Gandhi,** *Hind Swaraj,* **1938**

4 What did Gandhi mean by the term *passive resistance*?

_____

_____

Document #4

> *The nation has placed its destiny in the hands and heads and hearts of its millions of free men and women; and its faith in freedom. . . . Freedom means the supremacy of human rights everywhere. Our support goes to those who struggle to gain those rights or keep them.*
>
> **– Franklin D. Roosevelt, address to Congress in January 1941**

5 According to President Roosevelt, who or what is the ultimate source of power in the United States?

_____

_____

6 For what purpose did Roosevelt promise to use the power of the United States?

_____

_____

Part B

Essay

Directions: Write a well-organized essay that includes an introduction, several paragraphs, and a conclusion. Use evidence from *at least three* documents in your essay. Support your response with relevant facts, examples, and details. Include additional outside information.

Historical Context:

Throughout history, leaders have viewed power in many different ways. There have been a variety of viewpoints on the acquisition and use of power.

Task: Using the information from the documents and your knowledge of global history, write an essay in which you

- Evaluate the differing views that leaders have had on the attainment and use of power
- Discuss how the views of at least two leaders have affected people of their own nations and people of other nations

Guidelines:

In your essay, be sure to
- Develop all aspects of the task
- Incorporate information from *at least three* documents
- Incorporate relevant outside information
- Support the theme with relevant facts, examples, and details
- Use a logical and clear plan of organization, including an introduction and a conclusion that are beyond a restatement of the theme

The Twentieth Century and Beyond (1945–The Present)

Unit Overview

After World War II, many nations participated in a struggle called the Cold War. On one side were communist states led by the Soviet Union and China. On the other side were noncommunist nations led by the United States. The Cold War finally ended in the 1980s with the collapse of the Soviet Union and the end of communism in Eastern Europe.

During the Cold War, imperialism ended and new nations were born. In the Middle East, there were many conflicts. Elsewhere, newly independent nations had to establish workable economic and political systems. In Latin America, there was political unrest.

Using Good Social Studies Practices
Civic Participation

Some of the many themes developed in Unit 7 are:

change	economic systems	diversity
political systems	conflict	belief systems
human rights	nationalism	

Choose one of the themes listed above. As you review Unit 7, identify how individuals participated in some way to initiate change locally, within their country, or on a global level. Include events from 1945 to the present, major developments, and key turning points having to do with your theme.

Cold War Balance of Power

The Big Idea

After World War II:

• West Germany and Japan developed democratic governments.

• the United States and the Soviet Union emerged as superpowers with differing political and economic systems.

• the Cold War developed, and the superpowers confronted one another throughout the world.

• the United Nations tried to maintain peace.

Section Overview

After World War II, Japan and West Germany adopted constitutions that built democratic governments. Two major powers emerged from the war: the United States and the Soviet Union. Political and economic differences between the two led to a division of Europe that would last more than 40 years. The conflict between democracy and communism also spread around the globe, resulting in a buildup of arms as well as a race to explore space. The United Nations experienced both failure and success in its quest to maintain peace in the years after 1945.

Key Themes and Concepts

As you review this section, take special note of the following key themes and concepts:

Change What impact did World War II have on the development of democracy in Germany and Japan?

Political Systems How did differing political systems help cause the Cold War between the United States and the Soviet Union?

Conflict How did the rivalry between the United States and the Soviet Union involve other nations around the world?

Justice and Human Rights What role does the United Nations play in the struggle for justice and human rights?

Key People and Terms

Place each of the key people and terms into one of these two categories: political or military.

Key People and Terms

As you review this section, be sure you understand the significance of these key people and terms:

iron curtain	Truman Doctrine	surrogate
asylum	containment	Fidel Castro
superpowers	Marshall Plan	Cuban Missile Crisis
Cold War	NATO	nonaligned nations
satellites	Warsaw Pact	

Preparing for the Regents

• How were conditions in Europe after World War II similar to the conditions that existed after World War I? How were the two postwar periods different?

A Divided Europe

After World War II, with help from the United States and Great Britain, democracy and free enterprise were restored to the nations of Western Europe. Eastern Europe, however, was occupied by armies of the Soviet Union. Joseph Stalin, the leader of the Soviet Union, wanted to spread communism throughout the area. He hoped to create a buffer zone of friendly governments to prevent possible attacks from Germany and other Western nations.

Although Stalin had promised free elections for Eastern Europe, he instead supported the establishment of procommunist governments throughout the region. Soon Europe was divided by an imaginary line known as the **iron curtain.** In the East were the Soviet-dominated communist countries. In the West were the Western democracies, led by the United States.

Germany and Japan Transformed

Both Germany and Japan had been physically and socially devastated by the war. The victorious Allied powers occupied the two countries.

Germany was divided into four zones of occupation. Great Britain, France, and the United States occupied the three zones in western Germany. The Soviet Union controlled eastern Germany. The United States alone occupied Japan.

Democracy in West Germany

Germany's armed forces were disbanded, and the Nazi party was outlawed. Nazi war criminals were tried in the Nuremberg trials, and some were executed. In western Germany, the Allies helped set up political parties. Germans wrote a federal constitution. This constitution set up a democratic government and was approved in 1949. In that year, West Germany also regained self-government as the Federal Republic of Germany.

Germany's constitution included an article that guaranteed political asylum for people who were persecuted for political reasons. **Asylum** is protection from arrest or from the possibility of being returned to a dangerous political situation. For many years, Germany's asylum policy was the most liberal in Europe. Germany's recognition of its role in the persecution of Jews and other groups probably led to this constitutional guarantee. In the late 1990s, Germany began to restrict this right after large numbers of asylum seekers came to Germany for economic rather than political reasons.

The Lessons of the Holocaust Germany was deeply shaken by the experience of the Holocaust. Germans wanted to be sure that such a thing could not happen again. Today, Germany's relationship with the nation of Israel is very friendly. Germany and Israel have strong diplomatic, economic, and cultural ties. There has also been an attempt to financially compensate some of the victims of the Holocaust.

Democracy in Japan

Like Germany, Japan was occupied after World War II by Allied troops, most of whom were American. Japan's armed forces were disbanded. Trials were held to punish people who had been responsible for wartime atrocities, and some of these people were executed. General Douglas MacArthur was the supreme commander of the American military government that ruled postwar Japan. The American government wanted to end militarism and ensure democratic government in Japan.

Japan's New Constitution In Germany, a German council had written the new constitution. Japan's constitution, on the other hand, was drafted by MacArthur and his advisors.

- It created a constitutional monarchy that limited the power of the emperor.
- It promised that Japan would not use war as a political weapon.
- It set up a democratic government. Representatives were elected to the Diet, the Japanese parliament.
- Women gained the right to vote.
- Basic rights, such as freedom of the press and of assembly, were guaranteed.

The Japanese government accepted this new constitution and signed a treaty that took away Japan's overseas empire. In 1952, the Allied occupation officially ended.

Vocabulary Builder

disband—(dis BAND) v.
to stop existing as an organization, or to make something do this

Preparing for the Regents

- Why do you think Germany developed one of Europe's most liberal asylum laws?

Key Themes and Concepts

Change
Germany's experiences in the Holocaust had many lasting effects on the nation's development.

Preparing for the Regents

- How were the political conditions in Germany and Japan similar after World War II? How were they different?

- How was the Japanese government after World War II different from the Japanese government that had existed before and during the war?

Two Superpowers

After World War II, several powerful nations of the past were in decline. Germany was defeated and divided. France and Britain were economically drained and needed to concentrate on rebuilding. The United States and the Soviet Union emerged from World War II as the two world superpowers. The word *superpower* has been used to describe each of the rivals that came to dominate global politics in the period after World War II. Many other states in the world came under the domination or influence of these powers.

Europe After World War II

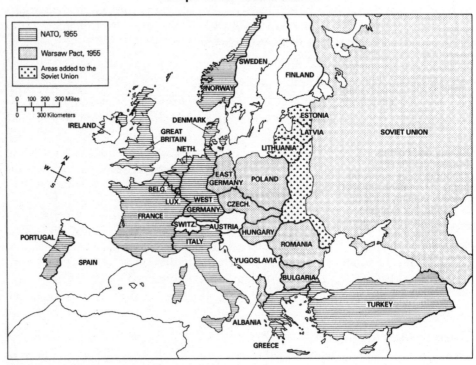

Europe After World War II
In 1949, the United States, Canada, and ten other countries formed the NATO military alliance. In 1955, the Soviet Union formed the Warsaw Pact military alliance with its seven satellites.

Preparing for the Regents

- Practice your map skills by listing the nations that were members of NATO and the nations that were members of the Warsaw Pact in 1955.

Key Themes and Concepts

Political and Economic Systems
The Cold War was much more than just a military rivalry. It was a struggle between two very different political and economic systems.

Preparing for the Regents

- What factors led to the breakup of the alliance between Britain, France, the United States, and the Soviet Union?

The Cold War Begins

The United States and the Soviet Union had cooperated to win World War II. Soon, however, conflicts in ways of thinking and mutual distrust led to the Cold War—a continuing state of tension and hostility between the superpowers. This tension was a result of differences in political and economic thinking between the democratic, capitalistic United States and the communist Soviet Union. It was a "cold" war because armed battle between the superpowers did not occur.

The Western powers feared the spread of communism. Stalin had forced pro-communist governments in Poland, Czechoslovakia, and elsewhere. These countries came to be known as **satellites** of the Soviet Union. When Stalin began to put pressure on Greece and Turkey, the United States took action.

The Truman Doctrine

In March of 1947, President Harry S. Truman established a policy known as the **Truman Doctrine.** This was an economic and military program designed to help other nations resist Soviet aggression. It was based on the theory of **containment,** which involved limiting communism to areas already under Soviet control. The United States pledged to resist Soviet expansion anywhere in the world. Truman sent military and economic aid to Greece and Turkey so that they could resist the threat of communism.

The Marshall Plan

The **Marshall Plan,** also proposed in 1947, was a massive economic aid package designed to strengthen democratic governments and lessen the appeal of communism. Billions of American dollars helped Western European countries recover from World War II. Although the United States also offered this aid to Eastern Europe, Stalin forbade these countries to accept it.

Crisis in Germany

The division of Germany into four zones after World War II was supposed to be temporary. Soon Great Britain, France, and the United States had combined their democratically ruled zones. Tension grew between democratic western Germany and Soviet-controlled eastern Germany. Germany became a major focus of Cold War tension. The Allies were trying to rebuild the German economy, but Stalin feared a strong, united Germany. Berlin, the divided capital, was located in East Germany.

The Berlin Airlift In 1948, Stalin hoped to force the Allies out of Berlin by closing all land routes for bringing essential supplies to West Berlin. In response to the crisis, the Western powers mounted a successful airlift. For almost a year, food and supplies were flown into West Berlin. Finally, the Soviets ended the blockade.

A Divided Germany This incident, however, led to the creation of the Federal Republic of Germany (West Germany) in 1949. Germany, like the rest of Europe, remained divided. In 1961, the East German government built a wall that separated East Berlin from West Berlin. East German soldiers shot anyone who tried to escape from East Germany.

Opposing Military Alliances

The NATO Alliance After the Berlin airlift and the division of West Germany from East Germany, Western European countries formed a military alliance. It was called the North Atlantic Treaty Organization, or NATO. Members of NATO pledged to support each other if any member nation was ever attacked.

The Warsaw Pact In 1955, the Soviet Union formed the Warsaw Pact. It included the Soviet Union and seven of its satellites in Eastern Europe. This was also a defensive alliance, promising mutual military cooperation.

The Cold War Heats Up

Repression in Eastern Europe

The Soviet Union kept a tight grip on its Eastern European satellites. Tensions arose in both East Germany and Poland in the 1950s. In East Germany, a revolt was put down with Soviet tanks. In Poland, some reforms were made, yet the country remained under the domination of the Soviet Union. Though Stalin died in 1953, his successors continued his policy of repression.

The Hungarian Revolt In 1956, a revolution began in Hungary. It was led by Imre Nagy, who was a Hungarian nationalist and communist. Nagy ended one-party rule, got rid of Soviet troops, and withdrew Hungary from the Warsaw Pact. In response, the Soviet Union quickly sent in troops and tanks. Thousands of Hungarians died, and the revolt against Soviet domination was suppressed.

The Invasion of Czechoslovakia Another rebellion against Soviet domination occurred in Czechoslovakia in the spring of 1968, when Alexander Dubçek called for liberal reforms and the easing of communist controls. The government of Czechoslovakia eased censorship and began to plan for a new constitution. The

Preparing for the Regents

- Briefly describe each of the terms listed below.

Truman Doctrine:

Marshall Plan:

NATO:

Warsaw Pact:

Berlin Airlift:

Preparing for the Regents

- Why were NATO and the Warsaw Pact formed?

Vocabulary Builder

repression—(rih PRESH un) *n.* cruel and severe control of a large group of people

Key Themes and Concepts

Conflict
The revolts and repression in Hungary and Czechoslovakia were signals to the West that the Soviet Union planned to use military force to ensure the survival of communism in Eastern Europe.

Soviet Union, however, sent troops to overturn the government and restore a communist dictatorship. Through these incidents, it became clear that the Soviet Union would use force whenever necessary to ensure the survival of communism and Soviet domination in Eastern Europe.

The Arms Race

Both the United States and the Soviet Union armed themselves, each preparing to withstand an attack from the other. The United States had developed the atomic bomb during World War II; Soviet scientists developed their own in 1949.

For 40 years, the two superpowers spent great amounts of money to develop more and more powerful weapons. The arms race raised the level of tension between the two superpowers. It also raised fears among many people that the superpowers might become involved in a conflict that would destroy the world.

The Space Race

The superpowers also competed in space. In 1957, the Soviet Union launched *Sputnik,* a satellite, into orbit around the Earth. Congress soon established NASA, the National Aeronautics and Space Administration, to improve American space technology.

The race was on. In 1958, the United States launched its own first satellite. In 1961, the Soviets sent the first man into space. Then, in 1969, the United States was the first nation to put a man on the moon. Both the Soviet Union and the United States explored the military use of space with spy satellites. Many people were concerned about the high cost of space exploration and the extension of the Cold War into space.

Conflicts Around the World

Although the United States and the Soviet Union did not engage in a war with each other, they did clash through **surrogate,** or representative, states. This meant that the United States and Soviet Union supported opposing forces in many nations throughout the world. These conflicts occurred in East Asia, the Middle East, Africa, and Latin America.

The Cold War in East Asia

Cold War tensions grew into bitter wars in Korea in the 1950s and in Vietnam in the 1960s. In each case, the superpowers supported opposing sides with economic aid, advisors, and troops.

Korean War (1950–1953) After World War II, Korea, like Germany, was divided into two parts. North Korea was occupied by Soviet forces and South Korea was occupied by American forces. North Korean forces, seeking to unify the country under communist rule, invaded South Korea in 1950. United Nations forces, commanded by General Douglas MacArthur, drove the North Koreans back, invaded North Korea, and approached the Chinese border. Chinese soldiers then entered the war and pushed the UN forces back into the south. In 1953 an armistice was signed, leaving Korea divided at the 38th parallel with a demilitarized zone between the two countries.

Vietnam War In 1954, Vietnam was temporarily divided into a northern half, ruled by communist leader Ho Chi Minh, and a southern half, headed by non-communist Ngo Dinh Diem. Large numbers of American forces were eventually sent to Vietnam to prevent Ho Chi Minh from uniting Vietnam under northern rule. American forces, however, were not able to defeat the communist forces in Vietnam. In 1973, President Richard Nixon ordered a cease-fire and began to pull

American forces out of Vietnam. In 1975, the North Vietnamese captured Saigon, reuniting Vietnam.

The Cold War in the Middle East

Arab States and Israel In the 1950s, Gamal Abdel Nasser emerged as a leader in the Arab state of Egypt. He was determined to end Western power in Egypt. In 1956, he nationalized the Suez Canal, ending British control. He received support from the Soviet Union and used Soviet money to build the Aswan High Dam. Egypt took part in two wars against the Jewish state of Israel. While the Soviet Union supported Egypt, the United States supported Israel.

Iran and Iraq Rivalries over oil resources fueled Cold War tensions in the Middle East. The United States and the Soviet Union both became interested in Iran after vast oil fields were discovered there. An Iranian nationalist leader who had communist support tried to nationalize the oil industry in the early 1950s. The United States helped to keep him from power. The United States then supported the repressive anticommunist shah of Iran with weapons and advisors. An Islamic revolution in 1979 toppled the shah's regime.

The Soviet Union meanwhile supported Iraq, which had become a socialist dictatorship in the 1960s and also had oil reserves. The Soviet Union eventually also supported governments in Syria and Libya.

The Cold War in Africa

Congo The Congo, a Belgian colony in Africa, became independent in 1960. The new premier asked for help in dealing with a revolt. The Soviet Union supported him against the rebels. Five years later, a strongly anti-communist dictator named Mobutu Sese Seko took control of the country, renaming it Zaire. Because of his anti-communist stance, he received the support of the West, allowing him to stay in power until the late 1990s.

Angola In southwestern Africa, the Portuguese colony of Angola gained independence in 1975, during a bloody civil war. After that, rival rebel groups continued their conflict with each other. One group, the MPLA, was supported by the Soviet Union and Cuba. The Soviet Union sent advisors and equipment; Cuba sent troops. The MPLA established a communist dictatorship in Angola, which the United States tried to undermine. South Africa supported the opposition, UNITA. This confrontation continued until 1991.

The Cold War in Latin America

Cuba Cuba had won independence from Spain in 1898. For 60 years, Cuba was strongly influenced by the United States. In 1952, Fulgencio Batista seized power. His government was repressive and corrupt. A young lawyer named **Fidel Castro** organized a guerrilla army and fought against Batista. He gained victory in 1959, and established a communist dictatorship in Cuba.

Castro turned to the Soviet Union for support. Cuba became involved in the rivalry between the United States and the Soviet Union. In 1961, the United States backed a plot by Cuban exiles to invade Cuba at the Bay of Pigs. However, the invading forces were quickly crushed.

Angered by American interference, Castro sought closer ties with the Soviet Union. Castro allowed the Soviets to build nuclear missile sites in Cuba, just 90 miles off the coast of Florida. In 1962, U.S. President Kennedy demanded the removal of these missiles from Cuba and ordered a naval blockade of Cuba. This incident, known as the **Cuban Missile Crisis,** ended when the Soviet leader, Nikita Khrushchev, agreed to remove the missiles in exchange for a pledge by Kennedy that the United

Key Themes and Concepts

Needs and Wants
The superpowers interfered in the governments of Iran and Iraq. One reason for their interest in these nations was the presence of oil reserves. Both superpowers needed oil to boost their economies.

Cause and Effect

For what reason did the Cold War superpowers support opposite sides in Africa?

Preparing for the Regents

• Describe one way in which the Cold War influenced conflicts or events in each of the following regions.

Asia:

Middle East:

Africa:

Latin America:

Note Taking

Reading Skill:
Recognize Sequence
List the important events of the Cold War in Cuba. Record them in the order they occurred. Add boxes as needed.

Date	Event
1898	

States would not invade Cuba. Since Cuba was heavily supported by the Soviet Union, the United States established a trade embargo and diplomatic isolation on Cuba. Cuba's economy suffered over the last 50 years. In 2014, US President Obama and Raul Castro announced they would restore diplomatic relations between the two countries. In 2016, President Obama visited Cuba and loosened the economic sanctions, although Congress has not ended them. Castro has made some reforms to Cuba's economic system and personal freedoms, but with the opening of Cuba, Castro's government is anxious about dissent within Cuba.

Causes and Impact of the Cuban Revolution

Causes of the Cuban Revolution	Impact of the Cuban Revolution
Political Conditions • Rule by a repressive dictatorship • Corruption and bribery among government officials	**Political Changes** • Creation of a communist dictatorship • Denial of basic political rights and freedoms
Economic Conditions • Control of Cuba's sugar plantations by the upper class • Unequal distribution of wealth • Foreign control of many businesses • High unemployment despite prosperity	**Economic Changes** • Establishment of collective farms, jointly operated under government supervision • Government control of business and industry • Seizure of foreign property with little or no compensation

The Nonaligned Nations

The nations that chose not to ally with either side in the Cold War were known as nonaligned nations. These nations remained neutral. India, Yugoslavia, and many African nations adopted a policy of nonalignment. Their goals were to make economic progress and to avoid involvement in the Cold War.

The Role of the United Nations

During the Cold War, the United Nations provided a forum for superpowers to air their differences peacefully. During much of the Cold War countries tended to vote in blocs, either as allies of the United States or as allies of the Soviet Union. This practice limited the United Nations' effectiveness.

After the end of the Cold War in 1991, the United Nations expanded several of its traditional roles. Today, it sends international peacekeeping forces to countries in conflict. It continues to provide health services to less developed countries. It also supports the struggle for human rights throughout the world.

Summary

After World War II, with the help of the United States, democratic governments were established in Japan and West Germany. The United States and the Soviet Union emerged as two rival superpowers with differing political and economic systems. Their rivalry threatened peace around the world in a struggle called the Cold War that went on for more than 45 years. The two superpowers engaged in the buildup of arms, competition in space, and surrogate conflicts in other parts of the world. Despite difficulties, the United Nations remained a force for stability and peace.

Key Themes and Concepts

Choice
Nonaligned nations did not side with either the Soviets or the United States during the Cold War.

Preparing for the Regents

• What role has the United Nations played in the Cold War and post–Cold War world?

Preparing for the Regents

• Write a brief essay discussing why the Cold War took place and what impacts it has had on the world.

Economic Issues

Section Overview

In the years after 1945, developing nations chose to develop either a market economy, a command economy, or a mixed economy. Countries in South Asia, Latin America, and Africa struggled to industrialize, improve agriculture, and curb population growth. In Western Europe and Japan, economies recovered and grew rapidly. West Germany and Japan became economic superpowers. The economies of the Pacific Rim, modeled on Japanese success, grew aggressively through trade and industrialization. After 1945, the economic interdependence of the world became clearer. When Middle Eastern oil suppliers limited oil in the 1970s, the economies of the West were hurt.

Key Themes and Concepts

As you review this section, take special note of the following key themes and concepts:

Economic Systems What are capitalism and communism?

Factors of Production How have developing nations combined human, natural, and capital resources to promote economic development?

Change Why did Western Europe and Japan experience great economic growth after 1945?

Needs and Wants How has the need for petroleum affected international relations?

Key People and Terms

As you review this section, be sure you understand the significance of these key terms:

developed nations	European Community	balance of trade
developing nations	European Union	Pacific Rim
mixed economy	euro	OPEC
Common Market	zaibatsu	

Market Economies and Command Economies

In the years after World War II, some nations were basing their economic development on the ideas of capitalism. Other countries were adopting command economies, such as that which existed under communism. The choices that countries made were often influenced by the Cold War. The United States and its allies supported market economies. The Soviet Union and its allies supported command economies.

The
Big
Idea

In the Cold War and post–Cold War eras:

- countries developed market economies, command economies, or mixed economies.

- developing nations struggled to strengthen their economies.

- Western Europe and Japan experienced rapid economic recovery.

- the nations of the world became increasingly interdependent.

Key People and Terms

- What do all of the key terms have in common? Explain.

Comparison of Market Economies and Command Economies

Market and Command Economies
After World War II, democratic countries had a market economy. Communist countries had a command economy.

	Market Economy	Command Economy
Ownership	All property, including the means of production, is privately owned.	The government owns the means of production, distribution, and exchange.
Economic decisions	Private businesses and individuals are free from public control so that they can make basic economic decisions, including what, where, how much, and at what prices goods will be produced.	Government officials make all basic economic decisions, such as what will be produced, when, and where.
Market controls	Prices are determined by supply and demand. Competition promotes high quality and low prices.	The government plans the economy. There is limited production of consumer goods and an emphasis on industrial growth.

Preparing for the Regents

- Compare and contrast market and command economies.

The Economies of Developing Nations

After World War II, the United States, the Soviet Union, Japan, and the countries of Western Europe came to be called **developed nations.** They had modern agriculture and industries, advanced technology, and strong educational systems. Nations with limited resources and without modern industrial economies were called **developing nations.**

Economic obstacles include overpopulation, natural disasters, and indebtedness. After World War II, many developing nations began to build their economies. Some were just emerging from imperialism. Many had to decide which of the two major economic systems they would follow. Some nations took elements of both.

The issues faced by developing nations were unique to each nation. However, several goals were common:

- Building industry
- Improving agriculture
- Controlling population

Case Study: India

After India became independent in 1947, it developed a **mixed economy** that combined elements of market and command economies. Heavy industry was brought under government control, and the nation worked with a series of five-year plans. These plans set economic goals and managed resources. Dams were built to produce hydroelectric power. The government poured resources into heavy industries such as steel production. In addition, crop output was increased with new types of seeds, chemical fertilizers, and improved irrigation.

However, India also faced obstacles. India lacked oil and natural gas, slowing growth. Many government-run businesses were ineffective. Agricultural output was not enough to keep up with population growth. In the 1990s, pressure from lenders forced India to institute reforms. Some industries were privatized, and foreign investment was made easier.

Case Study: Egypt

After Egypt became independent, Gamal Abdel Nasser installed a socialist government and economy. Nasser nationalized banks and businesses and instituted land reform. Peasant farmers were given land.

Key Themes and Concepts

Economic Systems
A mixed economy uses elements of both market and command economies. Developing nations, such as India and some nations of Africa, established mixed economies after 1945.

With the help of the Soviet Union, Egypt built the Aswan Dam. It controlled the flow of the Nile River and provided 2 million acres of additional farmland. However, it also increased the saltiness of the Nile and caused the soil of the Nile Delta to erode.

Nasser's successor, Anwar Sadat, encouraged foreign investment as well as free market practices. Sadat was assassinated in 1981. Sadat's successor, Hosni Mubarak, faced economic problems and a rising population. He also faced criticism from Islamic fundamentalists.

Case Study: Latin America

After World War II, many Latin American nations experienced unrest. Complex difficulties have sometimes hindered development.

Agricultural Reform Many Latin American nations have had to grow more staple crops, such as corn and wheat, in order to feed their growing populations. Because overdependence on any single cash crop is risky, these nations have sought to diversify their agriculture. Some, however, still rely on cash crops. A few countries, believing that uneven distribution of land leads to poverty, have also tried to institute land reform in order to get more land into the hands of a greater number of people.

Debt Crisis Often, Latin American nations had to borrow money to build industries. When a worldwide recession hit, demand for goods fell. However, these nations still had to make high interest payments. Money went toward paying off loans rather than building industry.

Free Market Reforms Some Latin American governments used free market reforms as a way to recover from their economic crises. Government spending was reduced, and private owners were allowed to buy out state-owned industries. Slowly, economic progress was made.

Population Explosion Many Latin Americans see the need to control population. Some cultural and religious beliefs, however, work against population control. As a result, populations are still growing rapidly, creating a severe economic burden.

Economic Recovery and Cooperation in Europe

After the end of World War II, the United States developed the Marshall Plan to encourage the economic development of Western Europe and to prevent the expansion of communism.

West German Economic Miracle

Capital from the Marshall Plan and the leadership of a democratic government helped West Germany to recover. West Germans rebuilt their cities and factories and developed a strong industrial economy. High-quality German exports were in great demand around the world. The recovery in Germany was so dramatic that it was referred to as an "economic miracle." After East and West Germany were reunited in 1990, difficulties emerged as East Germans made the transition to a market economy.

European Economic Unification

With aid from the Marshall Plan, other Western European countries also recovered quickly from World War II. The countries of Europe promoted their own prosperity through cooperation.

European Coal and Steel Community In 1952, France, West Germany, Belgium, Italy, the Netherlands, and Luxembourg set up the European Coal and Steel Community to regulate the coal and steel industries and spur economic growth.

Vocabulary Builder

fundamentalist—(fun duh MENT uh list) n. someone who follows religious laws very strictly

Preparing for the Regents

• Describe three economic problems that developing nations of Latin America face.

1.

2.

3.

Preparing for the Regents

• Why do you think West Germany's economy achieved much greater success than East Germany's?

Key Themes and Concepts

Interdependence
Many European countries prospered economically as a result of cooperation after World War II. Six Western European nations drew together in 1952 to form an economic community. Today, the European Union is made up of both Western and Eastern European nations.

The Common Market In 1957, these same six nations formed the **European Community** (EC), or Common Market. This organization expanded free trade by ending tariffs and allowing labor and capital to move freely across borders. Great Britain, Denmark, and Ireland later joined.

European Union In 1993, the EC expanded further and became the European Union with 12 members, although its membership has grown over the years. A new currency, the **euro,** was introduced in 1999 but not all EU members use the euro. The EU aims to bolster Europe's trade position and its political and economic power in the world.

Japan: An Economic Superpower

Economic Reforms

As you have learned, the United States occupation of Japan after World War II helped to establish democracy in that nation. The United States also brought economic reforms to Japan. Japanese workers were given the right to form unions. Land reform divided up large estates among tenant farmers. The United States tried to break up the **zaibatsu,** the powerful family-owned business concerns that dominated Japanese economic life, but the reform effort achieved only limited success.

Close Ties With the West

As the Cold War intensified, the United States and its allies viewed Japan less as a former enemy and more as a future ally. The outbreak of war in Korea in 1950 reinforced this view. Japan served as a staging area for operations in Korea. The American occupation of Japan ended in 1952. As Japanese industry prospered, the nation engaged in increased trade with the United States and other countries.

How the Japanese Economy Succeeded

Japan rebounded rapidly from the economic devastation that followed World War II. Japan sent many manufactured items to other countries, building a favorable balance of trade. A country that has a favorable **balance of trade** exports more goods than it imports. Why was Japan so successful?

- Japan adapted the latest Western technology to its own industries.
- Japan had a well-educated and highly skilled workforce.
- Japanese savings gave banks capital to invest in industry.
- The government, prohibited from spending money on defense, poured funds into the economy.
- The government imposed high tariffs and strict regulations to limit foreign competition.

How the Japanese Economy Faltered

In the late 1980s, Japan was hit by an economic recession which lasted many years. Banks staggered under a mountain of bad debt, companies went bankrupt, and unemployment rose. Japan's government seemed powerless to end the recession. However, in spite of these economic problems, Japan remained one of the world's largest economies with a strong favorable balance of trade. Its economy mostly held steady rather than growing.

Economic Development of the Pacific Rim

Southeast Asia and East Asia are part of a region known as the Pacific Rim, a group of nations in Asia and the Americas that border the Pacific Ocean. The Pacific began to be an important highway for trade in the 1500s. In the latter half of the 1900s, activity in this area increased dramatically. The size of the area's population makes it a huge market.

Four economies in the area have become known as the "Asian Tigers": Taiwan, Hong Kong, Singapore, and South Korea. The Asian Tigers are given this name because of their aggressive economic growth. These economies have followed the Japanese model. They experienced rapid industrialization that led to economic expansion and prosperity.

- **Taiwan** at first set up light industries, such as textile factories. In time, heavy industry developed and created a trade boom, the growth of industrial cities, and a higher standard of living.
- **Hong Kong** is a small island. Formerly a British colony, Hong Kong was returned to communist China in 1997 but was allowed to retain a capitalist economy. Hong Kong is a major financial center with many foreign banks and a busy stock market.
- **Singapore** is a city-state, located on a tiny island at the tip of the Malay Peninsula. Singapore includes one of the world's busiest harbors and is a center of trade.
- **South Korea** initially exported textiles and inexpensive goods. By the 1990s, South Korea was an economic powerhouse, exporting such higher-priced goods as automobiles.

Oil, OPEC, and Economic Interdependence

Oil became the most important energy resource after World War II. Global economic interdependence is shown in the crises that have developed over oil. Much of the world's oil comes from the Middle East.

The Formation of OPEC

In 1960, Iran, Iraq, Kuwait, Saudi Arabia, and Venezuela formed **OPEC,** whose initials stand for the Organization of Petroleum Exporting Countries. Other oil producers joined later and, in 2009, there were 12 members. OPEC's goal was to control the oil industry by setting production levels and prices.

OPEC and Oil Crises

In 1973, OPEC nations halted exports of oil to certain countries. Egypt and Israel were at war, and Arab countries declared the embargo against the United States and other countries that supported Israel. Prices skyrocketed, affecting Western economies by slowing growth. In the 1980s and 1990s, a surplus of oil allowed prices to fall.

Summary

In the years after 1945, some countries developed market economies, while others developed command economies. Developing nations struggled to build their economies. Western Europe and Japan, with the help of the United States, achieved economic success. Through international trade, the Pacific Rim became important to the global economy. Interdependence characterized the world economy. Oil crises in the Middle East, for example, slowed Western economic growth.

Key Themes and Concepts

Economic Systems
Taiwan, Hong Kong, Singapore, and South Korea are known as the Asian Tigers because of their aggressive economic growth.

Note Taking

Reading Skill:
Identify Main Ideas
Make a chart. Identify each economy's main source of economic prosperity.

Pacific Rim	
Economy	Source of Prosperity

Key Themes and Concepts

Needs and Wants
In the 1970s, OPEC nations took advantage of the fact that industrialized countries needed to import oil to keep their economies running. OPEC nations tried to use economic power to gain political power.

Preparing for the Regents

- How has the global economy changed since 1945?

Chinese Communist Revolution

Section Overview

The establishment of the People's Republic of China in 1949 began a new period in Chinese history. Communists had risen to power during the 1930s and 1940s by appealing to a large part of the population and by achieving military superiority. Under the communist dictatorship of Mao Zedong, however, programs such as the Great Leap Forward and the Cultural Revolution had negative economic results and restricted people's rights and freedoms. The next leader, Deng Xiaoping, made economic reforms but not political ones. The communist government continued to maintain strict control over people's lives.

Key Themes and Concepts

As you review this section, take special note of the following key themes and concepts:

Conflict How did the Communists come to power in China by 1949?

Human Rights In what ways did the communist government improve the status of women in China? How has the Chinese government violated people's rights?

Change What changes did Mao Zedong bring to China after 1949?

Economic Systems How did Deng Xiaoping reform the economy, and what were the results?

Key People and Terms

As you review this section, be sure you understand the significance of these key people and terms:

Mao Zedong	**communes**	**Deng Xiaoping**
Long March	**Cultural Revolution**	**Tiananmen Square**
Great Leap Forward	**Red Guards**	

Two Chinas

Today, China is the most populous nation in the world. There are two Chinas, however. The People's Republic of China is a communist state on the Asian mainland. It has a vast land area and many natural resources. Taiwan, also called the Republic of China, is a small island that today is one of the Asian Tigers. It has a noncommunist government. The People's Republic of China still considers Taiwan a part of China proper. Efforts to reunite the two Chinas have sometimes led to tension because Taiwan values its independence.

Communist Rise to Power

As you recall, Jiang Jieshi (also called Chiang Kai-shek) had taken over the Guomindang, or Nationalist Party, after the death of Sun Yixian. In the mid-1920s, Jiang began to strike at the Communist Party, which he saw as a threat to his leadership.

Mao Zedong emerged as the leader of the Communists in the 1930s. Along with 100,000 of his followers, Mao fled the Guomindang forces in 1934 in a retreat known as the **Long March.** After traveling more than 6,000 miles, Mao set up a base in northern China with about 20,000 survivors of the march. In the years that followed, the Communists, the Guomindang, and Japanese invaders battled for control of China. After World War II, civil war continued. Finally, in 1949, Mao's Communists were victorious. Jiang and his followers fled to the island of Taiwan.

Reasons for Communist Success

There were several reasons for the victory of Mao and the Communists over Jiang and the Guomindang.

- Mao won the support of the huge peasant population of China by promising to give land to peasants.
- Mao won the support of women by rejecting the inequalities of traditional Confucian society.
- Mao's army made good use of hit-and-run guerrilla warfare.
- Many people opposed the Nationalist government, which they saw as corrupt.
- Some people felt that the Nationalists had allowed foreigners to dominate China.

Communism Under Mao Zedong

The Communists set up the People's Republic of China (PRC) in 1949. They wanted to transform China from an agricultural society into a modern industrial nation. Under communism, literacy increased, old landlord and business classes were eliminated, and rural Chinese were provided with health care. However, Mao set up a one-party dictatorship that denied people basic rights and freedoms.

The Changing Role of Women

Traditionally, in China, women were treated as inferior to men. The only role for a woman recognized by the five Confucian relationships was that of wife. As a wife, a woman was considered inferior to her husband. The Nationalists did not change these policies greatly.

In Communist China, however, women gained some rights. Under the new Chinese constitution, women won equality under the law. They were now expected to work alongside men on farms and in factories.

Although Chinese women made progress, they did not have full equality with men. Only a few women had top jobs in government. Women were not always paid the same wages as men for doing the same work. Even so, the position of women improved under the Communists.

The Great Leap Forward

In 1958, Mao launched a program called the **Great Leap Forward.** He called on the people to increase agricultural and industrial output. To make farms more productive, he created **communes,** groups of people who live and work together and hold property in common. Communes had production quotas, which were set amounts of agricultural or industrial output that they were to produce.

Preparing for the Regents

- Describe three similarities between communism in China and communism in the Soviet Union.

1.

2.

3.

The Great Leap Forward failed. Commune-based industries turned out poorly made goods. At the same time, agricultural output declined. Bad weather added to the downturn, creating widespread famine.

The Cultural Revolution

In 1966, Mao launched the **Cultural Revolution** to renew people's loyalty to communism and establish a more equitable society. Mao feared that revolutionary peasants and workers were being replaced by intellectuals in running the country. He shut down schools and universities throughout China and urged Chinese students to experience the revolution for themselves. Students formed groups of fighters called the **Red Guards.** They attacked professors, government officials, and factory managers, many of whom were exiled or executed.

Programs of Mao Zedong

Program	The Great Leap Forward	The Cultural Revolution
Goals	• Increase farm and factory output	• Renew communist loyalties
Methods	• Communes • Production quotas	• Red Guards attack professors and other officials
Results	• Program fails • Two years of hunger and low production	• Economy slows • China closes to outside world • People fear arrest • Civil war threatened

Programs of Mao Zedong
Mao Zedong built a Communist totalitarian state. His government and programs tried to reshape the economy and society.

Vocabulary Builder

<u>rage</u>—(rayj) *v.* if something such as a battle, a disagreement, or a storm rages, it continues with great violence or strong emotions

United States Recognition

The Cold War was raging in 1949. Consequently, the United States had refused to recognize the People's Republic of China. In the Korean War, Communist China and the United States took opposing sides. By the 1970s, however, this situation was changing. China won admission to the United Nations in 1971, and President Richard Nixon visited Mao Zedong in Beijing in 1972. In 1979, the United States officially recognized the People's Republic of China.

Communism Under Deng Xiaoping

In 1976, Mao Zedong died. **Deng Xiaoping** took control. His leadership brought more economic freedom but little political change.

Economic Reforms: The Four Modernizations

To make China a more modern country, Deng promoted foreign trade and more contact with Western nations. He also introduced the Four Modernizations. These were concentrated in four areas.

- **Farming** methods were modernized and mechanized.
- **Industry** was upgraded and expanded.
- **Science and technology** were promoted and developed.
- **Defense** systems and military forces were improved.

Limited Privatization Deng got rid of Mao's unpopular communes. He allowed land to be leased to individual farmers. After delivering a certain amount of food to the government, farmers could grow anything they wished and sell it for profit. This system increased agricultural output. The government also allowed some private businesses to produce goods and offer services.

Foreign Investment Deng also welcomed foreign technology and capital. The government set up special enterprise zones where foreigners could own and operate businesses.

Preparing for the Regents

- Describe two ways in which Deng Xiaoping's methods differed from Mao Zedong's.

1.

2.

Results of Reforms Deng's policies had both positive and negative results. The economy grew, and some Chinese enjoyed a better standard of living. Foreign relations and trade improved. Crime and corruption grew, however, and the gap between rich and poor widened. Deng's economic changes caused some Chinese to demand greater political freedom.

Tiananmen Square

The government was willing to grant economic reforms but not political ones. In May 1989, demonstrators in Beijing occupied **Tiananmen Square,** demanding more rights and freedoms. When they refused to disperse as ordered, the government sent in troops and tanks. Thousands of Chinese were killed or wounded. The incident showed how important it was for China's communist leaders to maintain control. Order was more important than political freedom. During the 1990s, efforts were made to force China to end human rights violations. However, these efforts had limited effects.

Source: Henry Payne reprinted by permission of United Feature Syndicate, Inc.

Return of Hong Kong

In 1842, Great Britain had gained the island of Hong Kong, off the southern coast of China. During the years that Hong Kong was under British rule, it modernized and became wealthy.

In the 1980s, Britain and China decided that Hong Kong would return to Chinese rule in 1997. China agreed not to change Hong Kong's social or economic system for 50 years and to allow the island a degree of self-rule. The island was turned over to China on July 1, 1997.

Summary

The Communists, under Mao Zedong, rose to power in China after World War II. Their appeal to peasants and to women, their superior army, and lack of support for the Nationalists led to victory for the Communists. The communist government severely restricted the rights and freedoms of most Chinese. Later leaders, such as Deng Xiaoping, allowed free market reforms but little political freedom. Violations of human rights in China have often made relations between China and the United States difficult.

Collapse of European Imperialism

The Big Idea

After World War II, European imperialism ended, and nations faced difficult challenges as:

- India struggled with social, ethnic, and religious divisions.

- peoples of Asia and Africa used both peaceful and violent means to achieve independence.

- African nations struggled to overcome the legacy of colonial rule.

- Southeast Asia was ravaged by many years of war.

Key People and Terms

Place each of the key people and terms into these two categories: leader or conflict/cooperation.

Section Overview

The period after World War II marked the final collapse of European imperialism. India gained independence in 1947 but struggled with ethnic and religious conflicts. In Africa, independence was achieved both through peaceful efforts and through bloody conflicts. In South Africa, years of racial separation ended, and black South Africans gained a voice in government. In Southeast Asia, the struggle for independence came to an end only after many years of civil and international war.

Key Themes and Concepts

As you review this section, take special note of the following key themes and concepts:

Imperialism How did European imperialism collapse?

Nationalism How did nationalistic movements in Asia, Africa, and Southeast Asia result in independence?

Political and Economic Systems What kinds of political and economic systems developed in newly independent nations?

Key People and Terms

As you review this section, be sure you understand the significance of these key people and terms:

Mohandas Gandhi	African National Congress
Jawaharlal Nehru	Nelson Mandela
nonalignment	Desmond Tutu
Sikhism	F. W. de Klerk
Pan-Africanism	Ho Chi Minh
Kwame Nkrumah	Ngo Dinh Diem
Organization of African Unity	Khmer Rouge
Jomo Kenyatta	Pol Pot
tribalism	Aung San Suu Kyi
apartheid	

Indian Independence and Partition

Indian nationalists had been demanding independence since the 1800s. Indians were angered when, during World War II, the British put off granting them independence but expected them to support Great Britain in the war. **Mohandas Gandhi,** as you have read, played an important part in the independence movement with his policy of passive resistance. Over time, British control of India was weakened. Finally, in 1947, Britain granted independence to India. **Jawaharlal Nehru,** India's first prime minister, celebrated Independence Day with an impassioned speech, full of hope for India's future. Independence, however, brought some difficult problems.

Muslim and Hindu Conflicts

In India, Hindus were the majority, and Muslims were the minority. The Muslim League had been demanding a Muslim state. Also, there had been fighting between Muslims and Hindus. In 1947, British officials drew borders that created Hindu India and Muslim Pakistan. Pakistan was made up of West Pakistan and East Pakistan, two widely separated areas that had high Muslim populations. East Pakistan later became the nation of Bangladesh.

The partition, or division, of India did not bring peace. Independence set off mass migrations of Muslims fleeing India and Hindus fleeing Pakistan. Millions were killed crossing the borders. Mohandas Gandhi tried to bring peace, but a Hindu fanatic assassinated him.

Although the worst violence began to lessen after Gandhi's death, conflicts continued to occur. In the years ahead, Indian and Pakistani forces would clash repeatedly over border disputes. Tensions between Hindus and Muslims still exist and continue to erupt into violence today.

Indian Government and Foreign Policy

A Democratic Nation India is the world's largest democracy. It has a federal system of government, with powers divided between a strong central government and smaller local governments. For 40 years after independence, India was led by members of the Nehru family. Jawaharlal Nehru was the first prime minister.

Ethnic and religious conflicts have made democracy difficult for India. After Nehru's death, his daughter, **Indira Gandhi,** became prime minister in 1966. She was assassinated in 1984, and her son, Rajiv Gandhi, became prime minister. He too was assassinated, however, in 1991.

Nonalignment During the Cold War, India followed a policy of nonalignment. This policy, instituted by Jawaharlal Nehru, allowed India to accept help from both capitalist and socialist nations.

Obstacles to Progress in India

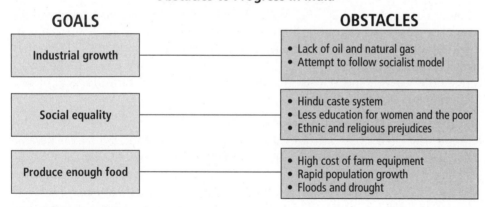

GOALS	OBSTACLES
Industrial growth	• Lack of oil and natural gas • Attempt to follow socialist model
Social equality	• Hindu caste system • Less education for women and the poor • Ethnic and religious prejudices
Produce enough food	• High cost of farm equipment • Rapid population growth • Floods and drought

Social Change in India

The Caste System The caste system, a system of social stratification, has been a part of Indian life for more than 2,000 years. In the 1900s, the system underwent change.

- Mohandas Gandhi campaigned to end the harsh treatment of the caste called Untouchables.
- The Indian constitution of 1950 banned discrimination against Untouchables.
- The government set aside jobs and places in universities for Untouchables.

Key Themes and Concepts

Nationalism
In India, nationalism resulted in freedom from colonial rule. Religious conflict led to the creation of two nations: India and Pakistan.

Note Taking

Reading Skill:
Categorize
Make a table. As you read, fill in the categories for India after independence.

India	
government	
foreign policy	
economy	
religion	
social system	

Key Themes and Concepts

Economic Systems
Nonalignment allowed developing nations to accept help from both communist and capitalist nations. India was a leader among nonaligned nations.

Preparing for the Regents

- How is the caste system that exists in India today different from the caste system of the past?

In spite of improvements in the legal status of Untouchables, discrimination still exists. Although there are movements for caste reform, the system is still a part of Indian society. It has a stronger effect in rural villages than in urban areas.

The Status of Women The Indian constitution of 1950 also granted rights to women. It gave women the right to vote and recognized their right to divorce and inherit property. Indira Gandhi, a woman, became prime minister in 1966. As with the caste system, traditional restrictions on women are more persistent in rural areas.

Sikh Separatism

Sikhism is a religion that began in India in the 1500s by blending elements of Islam and Hinduism. In the 1980s, there was an increased demand for self-rule by Sikhs in the state of Punjab. In the early 1980s, Sikh separatists occupied the Golden Temple in Amritsar to express their demands. Indira Gandhi, still prime minister at the time, sent troops. Many Sikhs died as a result. Not long after that, Gandhi herself was assassinated by two Sikhs who had served as her bodyguards. Continuing tension exists between Sikhs and Hindus.

Dispute Over Kashmir

India and Pakistan have disputed control of the state of Kashmir since the partition of the Indian subcontinent in 1947. Although governed by the secular government of India, the population of Kashmir is predominantly Muslim. The two nations fought wars over Kashmir in 1947–1948 and in 1965 and maintain a fragile truce today. In recent years there have been a number of terrorist attacks by Islamic separatists, which raise the fear of war between these two nuclear powers.

Independent Nations in Africa

A movement called Pan-Africanism had been nourishing nationalist movements in Africa since the 1920s. **Pan-Africanism** emphasized the unity of Africans and people of African descent all over the world.

Although a few African nations had achieved independence before 1945, most gained independence only after World War II. Many Africans had fought in the war. They resented returning home to second-class citizenship. Some Africans had migrated to cities during the war to work in defense industries. There they were exposed to nationalist ideas. In addition, the Atlantic Charter, signed by Franklin Roosevelt and Winston Churchill in 1941, had set forth the goal of self-determination for all nations.

Early Independence Movements

Ghana The Gold Coast was a British colony. American-educated leader **Kwame Nkrumah,** inspired by Pan-Africanism and by the writings of Mohandas Gandhi, organized a political party. Nkrumah used strikes and boycotts to battle the British. In 1957, the British granted the Gold Coast independence, and Nkrumah became its prime minister. Nkrumah renamed the country Ghana, a name that linked the new nation to its African past. In 1963, Nkrumah created the **Organization of African Unity,** or OAU. This group promoted Pan-Africanism and the end of colonialism in Africa.

Kenya In the British colony of Kenya, the independence struggle was led by **Jomo Kenyatta.** He was a spokesman for the Kikuyu people, who had been driven off their land by European settlers. When some Kikuyu turned to violent means to gain liberation, the British jailed Kenyatta. Later, however, Kenyatta was released. In 1963, he became the first prime minister of an independent Kenya.

Key Themes and Concepts

Diversity
India is a land of diverse peoples with differing religions and languages. The majority of the people is Hindu, but minorities hope to gain power; some even hope to create their own nations.

Vocabulary Builder

truce—(troos) *n.* an agreement between enemies to stop fighting or arguing

Preparing for the Regents

• List three ways in which World War II increased the desire for independence among Africans.

1.

2.

3.

Preparing for the Regents

• Describe how nationalism led to independence in Ghana.

Obstacles to Progress in Africa

Many of Africa's nations gained independence only after 1945, and more gained independence after 1959. The end of colonialism presented many challenges to the development of the countries of Africa.

Like other developing nations, African countries have focused on building industry and improving agriculture. Although industrial growth has sometimes been successful, many nations remain dependent on imports. Also, money borrowed to build industry created great debts. In some nations, such as Nigeria, people flocked to industrial centers. Food production fell, and rural poverty resulted. Cities could not keep up with population increases.

A continuing reliance on cash crops means that many African nations still need to import food to feed their growing populations. Cash crop economies also have other negative effects. For example, when oil prices fell, the economy of Nigeria—a nation rich in oil—nearly collapsed.

Obstacles to Progress in Africa

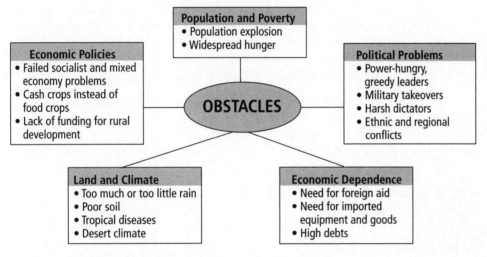

Even so, Africa shows great potential.

- Many African nations have moved from a socialist model to a free market economy, experiencing growth as a result.
- Other nations have expanded mining and manufacturing and built factories to process agricultural products.
- Some nations have improved transportation and communication.

Economic Links With Europe

Today, much of Africa suffers from trading patterns that were established during the age of imperialism. European nations had created colonial economies that depended on the export of raw materials and cash crops from Africa. Many African nations still rely on the export of just a few products. When the prices of these products fall, the nations' economies can be devastated. Many African countries also rely greatly on manufactured goods imported from Europe. As a result, these countries have trade deficits and rising debts.

Strong economic links have been maintained between many African nations and the colonial powers that once ruled them. Some former French colonies, for example, have adopted the French currency and many give preference to French products. This also occurs in countries that were once British colonies, especially those that are members of the Commonwealth, an association of former British colonies.

Ethnic Tensions and Nationalism

Most of the current national boundaries in Africa were established during the colonial period by Europeans. Unfortunately, the boundaries were made without consideration for the traditional territories of tribal and ethnic groups. As a result, some ethnic groups were separated into different nations. Other ethnic groups were united within nations. Today, therefore, the centuries-old loyalty to one's tribe is often stronger than loyalty to one's nation.

Nigeria is one of many nations where **tribalism** has led to civil war. More than 200 ethnic groups live in Nigeria. At independence, several of the larger groups fought for power. Among these groups were the Muslim Hausa and Fulani peoples in the north and the Christian Ibo and Yoruba peoples in the south.

In 1966, when a massacre of 20,000 Ibo took place, Hausa dominated the government. The next year, the Ibo declared their region independent, calling it Biafra. A war raged for several years. Nigeria blockaded Biafra and ended the war, but nearly a million people had been killed or died of starvation.

In Rwanda, ethnic conflict led to genocide. Before 1994, Rwanda was 85 percent Hutu and 14 percent Tutsi. In 1994, Hutu extremists, supported by government officials, launched a murderous campaign against the Tutsis. According to estimates, more than 500,000 people were killed in just a few months. The genocide was stopped when a Tutsi-led rebel army seized control of the government.

In 2002, 53 African countries formed a federation, the African Union (AU). Its goals include solving economic, social, political, and environmental problems in Africa. AU members deal with issues such as desertification, AIDS, and famine. The AU also works to control the conflicts between and within African countries. Eventually it plans to create an economic bloc.

End of Apartheid in South Africa

For nearly 350 years, Europeans ruled South Africa. Although South Africa won independence from Britain in 1910, its white citizens alone held political power. To control the nation's government and economy, whites in 1948 made official a system of **apartheid,** or separation of the races. Apartheid required black Africans and other nonwhites to live in certain zones, segregated public facilities and transportation, and forbade interracial marriage.

The Anti-apartheid Movement In 1912, a political party organized in South Africa. Later called the **African National Congress** (ANC), it used violence, boycotts, and nonviolent civil disobedience to oppose apartheid.

In 1960, the police killed 69 people and wounded 180 at a demonstration in Sharpeville. The South African government reacted by outlawing the ANC. In 1964, **Nelson Mandela,** an important ANC leader, was sentenced to life in prison. He became a powerful symbol of the struggle for freedom.

Desmond Tutu, a black Anglican bishop and civil rights leader, with other activists convinced foreign nations and businesses to limit trade and investment in segregated South Africa. These nonviolent protests had a strong effect.

F. W. de Klerk became president of South Africa in 1989. Knowing reform was necessary, he legalized the ANC, repealed segregation laws, and released Mandela in 1990. In 1994, an election in which people of all races could vote elected Mandela president. After ten years the ANC is still in power, but South Africa still suffers from economic inequality, land redistribution problems, and many HIV cases.

Preparing for the Regents

• How did the borders drawn by colonial powers eventually contribute to civil war in Africa?

Preparing for the Regents

• Use your knowledge of global history and recent current events to compare the genocide that occurred in Rwanda with another historical example of genocide.

Preparing for the Regents

• Describe the role of each of the following figures in the ending of apartheid.

Nelson Mandela:

Desmond Tutu:

F. W. de Klerk:

Truth and Reconciliation

The South African Truth and Reconciliation Commission (TRC) helped deal with the violence and human rights abuses under apartheid. It revealed past wrongdoing by the government, so to resolve past conflicts.

Difficult Struggles in Southeast Asia

After World War II, growing nationalist feeling spread through Indochina and other parts of Southeast Asia. Southeast Asians fought against foreign imperialist powers to gain their freedom. They also fought bloody civil wars.

Southeast Asia

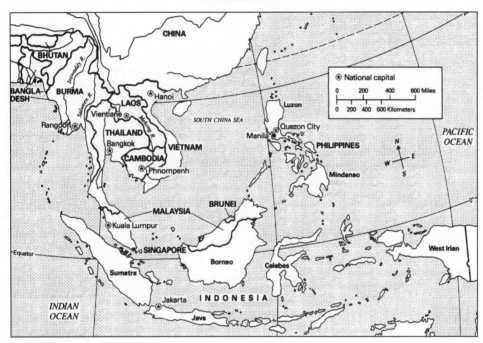

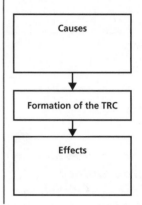

Note Taking

Reading Skill: Identify Causes and Effects
Make a flowchart. Show the causes and effects of the formation of the TRC.

Causes

↓

Formation of the TRC

↓

Effects

Southeast Asia
Southeast Asia includes part of the Asian mainland and thousands of islands. By World War II, European countries and the United States had colonized much of the area.

Vietnam

Vietnam had been ruled by the French since the mid-1800s. During World War II, the Vietminh, an alliance of nationalist and communist groups, fought the occupying Japanese. After the war, the French hoped to regain Vietnam. Instead, **Ho Chi Minh,** leader of the Vietminh, declared Vietnam free. Defeated by the Vietminh, the French abandoned Vietnam. A 1954 conference in Geneva led to the division of Vietnam into a communist north and a non-communist south.

The Vietnam War The American-supported South Vietnamese government of **Ngo Dinh Diem** refused to hold the 1956 elections to unite Vietnam because it feared that the Communists would win. Ho Chi Minh, leader of communist North Vietnam, supported the Vietcong, the communist rebels trying to overthrow Diem. The United States sent troops to support Diem's government. The Vietnam War lasted from 1959 to 1975, during which the United States sent hundreds of thousands troops and advisors to support Diem's government. Even with this help, South Vietnam could not defeat the communist forces. Antiwar sentiment in the United States forced President Nixon to withdraw American forces. In 1975, Saigon, the capital of the south, fell. The country was reunited under communist control.

Key Themes and Concepts

Conflict
In Vietnam, a local independence movement became a major Cold War battleground.

Note **Taking**

Reading Skill:
Summarize
Make a chart. Summarize the events connected to the struggles in Southeast Asia.

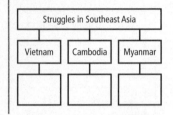

Vocabulary **Builder**

plague—(playg) *v.* to cause pain, suffering, or trouble, especially for a long period of time

Cambodia

During the Vietnam War, Cambodia was a supply route for the Vietcong and North Vietnamese forces. In 1969, American forces bombed and then invaded Cambodia to destroy that route. After the Americans left, Cambodian communist guerrillas, known as the **Khmer Rouge,** took control of the government. Under the leadership of **Pol Pot,** the Khmer Rouge began a reign of terror to remove all Western influence from Cambodia. More than a million Cambodians were slaughtered in what has become known as the "Killing Fields." In 1979, Vietnamese forces invaded and occupied Cambodia. In the early 1990s, the civil war ended. UN peacekeepers monitored elections, but some fighting continued.

Myanmar

Myanmar, formerly called Burma, was a British possession until it gained independence. It remained a very poor country, plagued by ethnic tensions and after 1962 was ruled by a repressive military.

An opposition party, lead by Nobel Peace Prize winner **Aung San Suu Kyi,** elected representatives in 1991, but the military junta repressed them. Suu Kyi spent 15 years in various forms of detention until 2010 when the government finally freed her. The military junta ended in 2011 and a steady move toward a more democratic government has occurred. This, along with economic reforms, allowed improved relations with various foreign countries. In 2015, Suu Kyi's opposition party won a landslide victory and established a new government by spring 2016. Suu Kyi, who cannot become president, created an expansive role for herself in this new government. However, economic problems, as well as ethnic and religious tensions, continue to affect many refugees who flee the country only to end up as economic slaves in countries such as Thailand.

Summary

European imperialism collapsed throughout the world in the years after World War II. In India, independence was accompanied by conflicts among various ethnic and religious groups. In Africa, nations suffered from the legacy left by colonial rule. Tribal conflicts brought civil war to many nations. In South Africa, the repressive system of apartheid was finally ended. In Southeast Asia, another war erupted between communist North Vietnam and noncommunist South Vietnam. Despite United States intervention, the communist forces were victorious. In Cambodia and Myanmar, hundreds of thousands died or fled their country due to political, military and cultural violence.

Conflicts and Change in the Middle East

Section Overview

Since 1945, the Middle East has been an area of tension and change. The state of Israel was created in 1948. After years of conflict between Israel and its Arab neighbors, the quest for peace began to achieve some success. In Lebanon, years of civil war ravaged the country. In Iran, an Islamic republic was born. Several international conflicts centered on Iraq, largely because of its dictator, Saddam Hussein. Throughout the Middle East, many Muslims have called for a return to a life based on Islamic law.

Key Themes and Concepts

As you review this section, take special note of the following key themes and concepts:

Diversity How has the diversity of the Middle East affected its recent history?

Conflict What efforts have been made to end conflict between Israel and its Arab neighbors?

Interdependence Why did the Persian Gulf War involve many nations from around the world?

Belief Systems How is Islamic fundamentalism affecting life in the Middle East today?

Key People and Terms

As you review this section, be sure you understand the significance of these key people and terms:

Palestine Liberation Organization (PLO)
Yasir Arafat
intifada
Camp David Accords
Yitzhak Rabin
King Hussein

Hamas
Ayatollah Khomeini
Islamic fundamentalism
Taliban
Saddam Hussein
Persian Gulf War
Kurds

The Impact of Geography

The Middle East has been a crossroads for people of Africa, Asia, and Europe since ancient times. This fact has led to an enormous diversity of peoples, belief systems, and cultures. These differences have sometimes led to conflict.

The discovery of oil in the region brought power to some Middle Eastern nations. Oil is a vital part of the global economy. Oil resources, however, are not evenly distributed across the region. As a result, Middle Eastern countries have gone to war over control of oil-rich lands. Dependence on oil is one reason why countries around the world take an active interest in conflicts in the Middle East.

The
Big Idea

In the Middle East, since 1945:

- the creation of Israel has led to conflicts between Jews and Arabs.

- the search for peace between Jews and Arabs has met with some success.

- a revolution in Iran has led to an Islamic republic.

- Iraq has been involved in several international conflicts.

- many Muslims have urged a return to Islamic government and law.

Key People and Terms

Place each of the key people and terms into these three categories: politics, conflict/cooperation, and belief system.

Preparing for the Regents

- What impact has geography had on the culture and history of the Middle East?

Forces Shaping the Middle East

Religious and Ethnic Differences	Natural Resources	Governments	Islamic Traditions
• Muslims, Christians, and Jews • Different sects within religions • More than 30 languages • Religious, racial, and cultural prejudices • Desire for a united Arab state	• Largest oil fields in the world • Oil-rich nations gain wealth and political and economic power • Limited water supply • Arguments over dams and water rights	• Democracy in Israel and Turkey • Rule by royal family in Jordan and Saudi Arabia • Single-party dictators in Iraq and Syria	• Laws of Islam influence government, society, and personal life • Antiwestern feelings • 1990s revival of Islamic traditions

A Jewish State Among Arab Nations

Large numbers of Jews had begun migrating to Palestine from Europe in the late 1800s as part of the Zionist movement. During World War I, the British made conflicting promises to the Jews and Palestinians about creating a Jewish homeland in the area. After World War II and the Holocaust, there was increased support for a Jewish state in Palestine. However, both Jews and Palestinian Arabs claimed a right to the land of Palestine. Jews claimed that they were entitled to return to a land they had once ruled 3,000 years ago. The Palestinian Arabs claimed they were entitled to the land they had been living in since Roman times. Many violent clashes between these two groups have occurred since 1947.

Creation of Israel

In 1947, the United Nations drew up a plan to divide Palestine, which was under British rule, into an Arab state and a Jewish state. Jews accepted the plan, but Arabs did not. In 1948, Great Britain withdrew, and Jews proclaimed the independent state of Israel, which was recognized by both the United States and the Soviet Union.

Israel developed rapidly. Between 1948 and the mid-1980s, nearly two million Jews migrated to Israel, some to escape persecution. The government built towns for settlers. A skilled workforce expanded the economy. American aid helped Israel as well.

Palestinians and Arab-Israeli Wars

When the state of Israel was created, Arab nations vowed to drive the Jews out and restore Palestine as an Arab nation. Since 1948, there have been four full-scale wars and several smaller conflicts between Israel and the Arab states.

War of Independence The first Arab-Israeli war occurred in 1948 when six Arab states—Egypt, Iraq, Jordan, Lebanon, Syria, and Saudi Arabia—invaded Israel. Israel defeated the invaders and gained control of land which doubled its size. Over 700,000 Arabs became refugees. Most were refused entry by neighboring Arab countries and were placed in temporary refugee camps, which became permanent over time. The poverty and discrimination experienced by these Palestinian Arabs fueled anger. Many dreamed of an Arab Palestinian state. Resistance to the state of Israel took many forms.

Palestine Liberation Organization (PLO) In 1964, the Palestine Liberation Organization (PLO) was formed to destroy Israel and win self-rule for the Palestinians. Led by **Yasir Arafat,** the PLO used terrorist tactics and fought a guerilla war against Israelis at home and abroad. Many Israeli civilians were killed by PLO terrorists.

Key Themes and Concepts

Movement of People and Goods
Since 1948, people have migrated to Israel from all over the world. As Eastern European communism and the Soviet Union collapsed, many Jews moved from Eastern Europe to Israel.

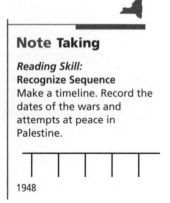

Note Taking

Reading Skill:
Recognize Sequence
Make a timeline. Record the dates of the wars and attempts at peace in Palestine.

1948

Further Wars Another war was fought over the Suez Canal in 1956. In 1967, during the Six-Day War, Israel overran the Sinai Peninsula, the Golan Heights on the Syrian border, and East Jerusalem. In 1973, Egypt and Syria launched a war against Israel on the Jewish high holy day of Yom Kippur. The Israelis won all of these wars.

Intifada In 1987, young Palestinians, who had grown up in the Israeli-occupied West Bank and Gaza, and who were frustrated with the lack of progress in gaining a Palestinian state, began widespread acts of civil disobedience called the intifada, or "uprising." Palestinians used boycotts, demonstrations, and attacks on Israeli soldiers by unarmed teenagers throwing rocks and bombs. The intifada continued into the 1990s. Crackdowns by the Israelis led to a wave of sympathy throughout the world for the Palestinians.

Israel's Changing Borders

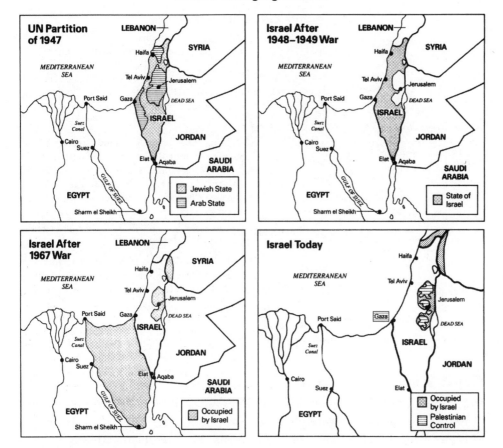

Israel's Changing Borders
Modern Israel was established in 1948. Israel and its Arab neighbors fought three wars—in 1956, 1967, and 1973. In these wars, Israel defeated Arab forces and gained more land.

Preparing for the Regents

- Practice your map skills by answering the following questions.

1. What countries border Israel?

2. What areas were gained by Israel after the 1967 war?

Attempts at Peace

Numerous attempts have been made to resolve the situation in Palestine. Limited progress has been made.

Camp David Accords In 1979, President Jimmy Carter invited President Anwar Sadat of Egypt and Prime Minister Menachem Begin of Israel to discuss terms of peace. The resulting treaty, the Camp David Accords, was based on the concept of "land for peace." Israel returned the Sinai Peninsula to Egypt in exchange for Egypt's recognition of Israel's right to exist. Sadat was later assassinated by a group of Muslim extremists angered by Egypt's peace with Israel.

Oslo Peace Accords In 1993, direct talks were held for the first time between Israel and the PLO. Arafat had renounced the use of terrorism, which opened the

Vocabulary Builder

renounce—(rih NOWNS) *v.* to reject; to publicly say or show that you no longer believe in something, or will no longer behave in a particular way door for Israeli Prime Minister **Yitzhak Rabin** to sign an agreement giving Palestinians in the Gaza Strip and West Bank limited self-rule. A year later, Jordan, led by **King Hussein,** also made a peace agreement with Israel. In 1995, Rabin was assassinated by right-wing Jewish extremists, opposed to making concessions to the Palestinians.

Israelis continues to build settlements in lands that Palestinians claim while Palestinian riots and suicide bombers began increasing. In 2002, Israeli military forces invaded Palestinian-ruled areas that were centers of terrorist activities. They arrested or assassinated PLO and other Palestinian leaders. Many Palestinian civilians also died. The United States, United Nations, European Union, and Russia outlined a roadmap of peace. This plan would establish a Palestinian state, but the PLO had to make democratic reforms and end the use of terrorism. Peace prospects improved when Palestinian leader Yasir Arafat died in 2004.

The Middle East and North Africa

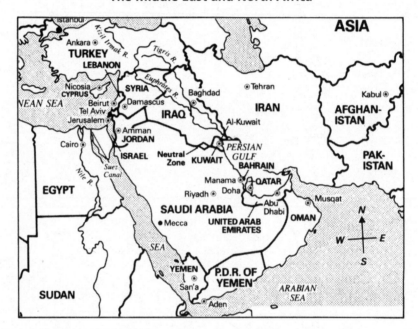

The Middle East and North Africa

The Middle East controls large oil resources and important waterways such as the Persian Gulf. Western nations have tried to prevent regional powers from interfering with the oil supply.

Key Themes and Concepts

Diversity
The diverse population of Lebanon, as well as outside political forces, led to civil war in Lebanon. Diversity has contributed to conflict throughout the Middle East.

Civil War in Lebanon

North of Israel, Lebanon had gained independence after World War II. It was a thriving commercial center with a diverse population. There, Christians and Muslims lived together peacefully. However, as Palestinian refugees entered Lebanon, especially after 1967, they created a Muslim majority. The PLO became powerful in Palestinian refugee camps.

A civil war between Christians and Muslims began in 1975. Israeli and Syrian forces participated in the conflict. By 1990, a degree of order had returned to Lebanon. In 2000, Israel withdrew its forces, and Syria followed reluctantly in 2005. In May 2005, Lebanon held its first legislative elections since the civil war. In 2006, Hezbollah, a radical Shi'a group, captured two Israeli soldiers, leading to a 34-day conflict with Israel.

Islamic Fundamentalism

Beginning in the 1970s, increasing numbers of Muslims opposed westernization. They wanted to apply Islamic principles to the problems in their nations. This movement for reform, called Islamic fundamentalism by many Westerners, has played a key role in the Middle East.

- **Libya** In 1969, Muammar al-Qaddafi established a government based on Islamic principles. He supported revolutionary organizations and activities in the Middle East and around the world. Qaddafi renounced terrorism in 1999.

- **Algeria** In 1992, the Algerian Islamic political party did well in elections. The ruling party feared that an Islamic revolution might occur. The military therefore seized power and took harsh measures against Islamic activists, resulting in the deaths of thousands of people. Since 2005, a newly elected government's offer of amnesty to terrorists who lay down their arms has not ended terrorist attacks by groups who want to return to strict Islamic rule.

- **Turkey** Throughout the 1900s, the government of Turkey based many of its policies on Western models. In the 1990s, however, Islamic political parties gained increasing support and influence. They hoped to restore traditional Islamic government to Turkey.

- **Afghanistan** From 1979 to 1989, Afghanistan fought a Soviet invasion whose goal was to strengthen the Afghan Communist government. Following the Soviet withdrawal, the country was torn by civil war. An Islamic group, the **Taliban**, seized power in 1996 and set up an Islamic government.

Preparing for the Regents

- Describe the influence of Islamic fundamentalism on the governments of the following countries.

Iran:

Algeria:

Afghanistan:

Turkey:

The Iranian Revolution

In 1953, Great Britain and the United States helped Muhammad Reza Pahlavi gain control of the Iranian government. He proclaimed himself the shah. He westernized and modernized the country; he also ruled as a dictator.

In the 1970s, opposition to the shah was led by the exiled **Ayatollah Khomeini.** *Ayatollah* is a title given to learned Shiite legal experts. With protests mounting, the shah fled Iran in 1979. Soon afterward, Khomeini returned, declaring Iran an Islamic republic based on Islamic fundamental beliefs. In 1989, Khomeini died, and more moderate leaders took control. Then, in 2005, elections put conservatives back in power. World concerns grew over Iran's nuclear program, which President Mahmoud Ahmadinejad refused to curb.

Note Taking

Reading Skill:
Identify Cause and Effects
Make a flowchart. Write the main cause of the 1979 Iranian revolution. Summarize the effects.

Impact of the Revolution
The Iranian revolution of 1979 had effects in Iran and beyond.

- The new Iranian government was extremely hostile to the West, especially to the United States. Western books, music, and movies were banned.

- The government required strict adherence to Islamic fundamental beliefs. There was no separation of religion and government.

- Many rights were taken away from women.

- Iranian militants seized the American embassy in Tehran and held a group of Americans hostage for more than a year.

- Iran encouraged Muslims in other countries to work to overthrow secular governments and establish Islamic republics.

Saddam Hussein and Iraq

Under the leadership of dictator **Saddam Hussein,** Iraq was involved in several conflicts in the Middle East.

Iran-Iraq War

In 1980, Hussein's forces seized control of a disputed border area between Iraq and Iran. War broke out between the two nations. When both sides attacked oil tankers in the Persian Gulf, the United States Navy began to protect shipping lanes in the region. The war continued until 1988 and created extreme hardship in both nations.

Persian Gulf War

In 1990, Iraq invaded Kuwait and seized its oil fields. The United States saw the Iraqi action as a threat to Saudi Arabia and to the flow of oil from the Middle East. The first response of the United States was to organize a trade embargo of Iraq. Peacekeeping troops from many Western and Middle Eastern countries were sent to Saudi Arabia. When Iraq refused to withdraw from Kuwait, the 1991 **Persian Gulf War** began. The United States and its allies quickly won the war, and Kuwait was liberated. The United States continued to view Iraqi dictator Saddam Hussein as a very dangerous force. They hoped that the war would topple his dictatorship. He remained in power, however.

Over the next 12 years, Saddam Hussein's rhetoric, tight military control, and human rights abuses alienated many countries. His actions, including allegedly stockpiling weapons of mass destruction, created fear in his own people as well as in Western countries.

Summary

The Middle East is an area of great diversity and economic importance. It is also an area of great conflict. The creation of the state of Israel in 1948, and the refusal of neighboring Arab nations to accept Israel, set off years of conflict between Arabs and Jews. A revolution occurred in Iran that created an Islamic republic. A growing influence in the area is that of Islamic fundamentalism, a movement to return to traditional Islamic ways. The aggressive actions of Iraqi leader Saddam Hussein led to a war that involved many countries of the world.

Key Themes and Concepts

Interdependence
Because the world economy depends so strongly on oil, the Iraqi takeover of Kuwaiti oil fields in 1990 provoked a reaction throughout the world.

Preparing for the Regents

- What factors have contributed to conflict in the Middle East?

Collapse of Communism and the Soviet Union

Section Overview

Eastern Europe underwent great change in the 1980s and 1990s. The Soviet invasion of Afghanistan heightened Cold War tensions and added to Soviet economic problems. Mikhail Gorbachev came to power in the Soviet Union and took steps to reform the economy and allow more openness. His policies contributed to the collapse of communism in Eastern Europe and the breakup of the Soviet Union. By 1989, Germany was reunited. The former Soviet Union and its satellites experienced varying degrees of difficulty as they tried to establish new political and economic systems in their countries. New nations emerged in Eastern Europe, sometimes accompanied by violent ethnic conflict.

Key Themes and Concepts

As you review this section, take special note of the following key themes and concepts:

Change What were the causes and impacts of the collapse of the Soviet Union?

Diversity and Conflict How has ethnic diversity contributed to conflict in Eastern Europe?

Political and Economic Systems What kinds of problems did Eastern European countries face in the transition to democracy and a market economy?

Key People and Terms

As you review this section, be sure you understand the significance of these key people and terms:

détente	**Vladimir Putin**
Mikhail Gorbachev	**Lech Walesa**
perestroika	**Solidarity**
glasnost	

Easing of Cold War Tensions

By the 1970s, the Cold War had been going on for more than 25 years. Both the United States and the Soviet Union realized that the tension could end in mutual destruction. Large amounts of money were spent by both powers on weapons. Under their leaders, Richard Nixon and Leonid Brezhnev, the United States and the Soviet Union promoted a period of **détente,** or lessening of tension. Détente involved:

- arms control talks and treaties
- cultural exchanges
- trade agreements

The Big Idea

Between 1970 and 1990, the Soviet Union broke up, and communist control of Eastern Europe ended. During this period:

- the invasion of Afghanistan weakened the Soviet Union.
- Gorbachev's reforms led to the end of the Soviet Union.
- communist governments fell in Eastern Europe.
- ethnic divisions led to civil wars and the creation of new nations.

Key People and Terms

For each of the key people and terms, write a sentence explaining its significance.

Soviet Invasion of Afghanistan

Détente came to a sudden end with the Soviet invasion of Afghanistan in 1979. The Soviet Union had invaded Afghanistan in order to keep a procommunist government in power there. This move convinced many in the West that the Soviet Union was still an aggressive force.

Relations between the two superpowers worsened. The United States increased defense spending to match the buildup of Soviet arms that had continued during the period of détente. In the Soviet Union, however, the war in Afghanistan was very unpopular.

Gorbachev in the Soviet Union

In 1985, **Mikhail Gorbachev** came to power in the Soviet Union. Gorbachev wanted to end Cold War tensions. He pulled troops out of Afghanistan. He also reformed the Soviet government and economy.

Perestroika

Gorbachev restructured the failing state-run command economy in a process called **perestroika.** The goals were to stimulate economic growth and to make industry more efficient. Gorbachev also backed free market reforms. Perestroika had some negative effects, however. Inflation increased, and there were shortages of food and medicine.

Glasnost

Gorbachev also called for **glasnost,** or openness. This policy ended censorship and encouraged people to discuss openly the problems in the Soviet Union. Gorbachev hoped to win support for his policies both among ordinary citizens and among members of the Communist Party.

Preparing for the Regents

- Define the following two terms, and tell how they affected the Soviet Union.

Perestroika:

Glasnost:

Effect on the Soviet Union:

The Fall of the Soviet Union
The Cold War between the United States and the Soviet Union lasted almost 50 years. In the years around 1990, the struggle finally ended with the fall of the Soviet Union. After 69 years, the Soviet Union ceased to exist.

Preparing for the Regents

- Choose two of the causes shown in this chart and explain briefly how they led to the fall of the Soviet Union.

The Fall of the Soviet Union

CAUSES
- Leadership of Mikhail Gorbachev
- Openness to democratic ideas (glasnost)
- Reshaping of economy and government (perestroika)
- Economic problems
- Freedom movement in Eastern Europe

Fall of the Soviet Union

EFFECTS
- Formation of the Commonwealth of Independent States
- Loss of role as world superpower
- End of the Cold War
- Economic hardships
- Conflicts between procommunist and prodemocratic groups
- Minority revolts and civil conflicts

Breakup of the Soviet Union

As Gorbachev eased political restrictions, people began to voice their nationalist sentiments. As you have learned, the Soviet Union was a multinational state. People in the non-Russian republics opposed Russian domination. In 1991, the Baltic republics of Estonia, Latvia, and Lithuania regained their independence. Soon, all the Soviet republics declared their independence. The Soviet Union ceased to exist.

In mid-1991, communist hardliners tried to overthrow Gorbachev and restore the previous order. Their attempt failed, but Gorbachev soon resigned. However, Gorbachev's reforms had helped to end communism throughout Eastern Europe. His policies also contributed to the breakup of the Soviet Union.

Vocabulary Builder

voice—(voys) *v.* to tell people your opinions or feelings about a particular subject

Preparing for the Regents

- Explain the meaning of the political cartoon on this page.

Source: Reprinted By Permission of Bob Englehart, The Hartford Courant

Difficult Challenges for Russia

Boris Yeltsin became the Russian president. Yeltsin struggled to make the transition from communism to democracy. One of the most difficult challenges was converting the state-run command economy to a market economy. Industries and farms were privatized. Still, economic problems grew worse. Food shortages increased and unemployment rose.

Yeltsin retired in 1999. To succeed him, voters chose **Vladimir Putin** and, in 2008, his chosen successor, Dmitry Medvedev. For the first time in Russian history, power passed peacefully from one elected leader to another. Putin curbed the power of regional leaders and exerted control over the Duma, Russia's legislature, and continued to wield power as Medvedev's prime minister. Although Putin's policies have led to economic growth, there are growing concerns about his suppression of dissents and the future of democracy in Russia. In 2002, Russia and the United States signed a nuclear arms reduction agreement and a new START Treaty in 2010, but tensions between Russia, Europe and the United States increased over the Ukraine and Russia's support of the Syrian government.

Note Taking

Reading Skill:
Summarize
Make a table. Summarize each leader's time in power.

Soviet Union/Russian Leaders	
Gorbachev	
Yeltsin	
Putin	
Medvedev	

Preparing for the Regents

- Identify and explain three key events in the fall of communism in Eastern Europe.

Cause and Effects

List the effects of the Solidarity union in Poland.

Eastern Europe Transformed

Throughout Eastern Europe, Gorbachev's reforms had sparked demands for democracy and national independence. Poland, East Germany, Romania, Bulgaria, and other countries of Eastern Europe broke away from Soviet control. Through much of the region, there were attempts to enact democratic reforms and make the transition from a command economy to a market economy.

Lech Walesa and Solidarity in Poland

In the 1980s in Poland, economic hardships caused labor unrest. Led by **Lech Walesa,** workers organized **Solidarity,** an independent trade union. With millions of members, Solidarity called for political change.

At first, the Soviet Union pressured the Polish government to suppress Solidarity. The government outlawed the union and arrested Walesa and other leaders. However, communism's power was weakening. International pressure as well as internal pressure led to reform. In 1989, the first free elections in 50 years were held, and Solidarity candidates won. Lech Walesa became president. Poland joined NATO in 1999 and the European Union in 2004.

East and West Germany United

Since World War II, Germany had been divided into a democratic western state and a communist eastern state. The Berlin Wall had been built in 1961 to keep East Germans from fleeing to the West.

The Fall of the Berlin Wall East Germans wanted to share the prosperity and freedom enjoyed by West Germans. By 1989, East German leaders could no longer count on support from the Soviet Union. A rising wave of protests forced the communist government from power. In November 1989, the Berlin Wall was torn down by joyous Germans.

The Fall of Communism in Eastern Europe

The Fall of Communism in Eastern Europe
Before 1990, the Soviet Union controlled Eastern Europe by force. As the Soviet Union weakened, Eastern Europeans demanded an end to Soviet domination.

Impact of Reunification The people of Germany welcomed reunification of their country, but there were problems. West Germans had to pay higher taxes to finance the rebuilding of impoverished East Germany. Unemployment rose in East Germany during the transition to a market economy. Social unrest followed, with some right-wing extremists trying to revive Nazi ideology. Foreign workers, many of whom came from Turkey, were attacked. However, by the beginning of the twenty-first century, Germany had regained its position as the dominant economy in Europe. It was a major player on the formation of the European Union and continues to be a dominant presence in that organization.

Ethnic Tensions Surface

Under communism, ethnic tensions in multinational states had been suppressed. With the fall of the Soviet Union, they resurfaced. Czechoslovakia split peacefully into two separate countries, the Czech Republic and Slovakia. Elsewhere, however, ethnic divisions often resulted in open warfare. In the early 1990s, for example, Armenia and neighboring Azerbaijan fought over a small area in Azerbaijan where many Armenians lived. Armenia eventually gained control of the area. In the Balkan peninsula, ethnic conflict ripped apart the country of Yugoslavia. The Chechen people, whose Muslim culture is very different from that of the Russians, have fought for independence from Russia for over 150 years. In 1991, when the Soviet Union collapsed, Russia refused to recognize Chechnya as an independent nation. A bitter war began between the Russian army and Chechen separatists. Russian troops and air attacks destroyed sections of Chechnya, while Chechen terrorists conducted deadly attacks on civilians across Russia, including in Moscow theaters. Although Chechnya continues to declare its independence and carry out terrorist attacks, Moscow refuses to recognize the area as an independent nation.

Summary

Cold War tensions eased in the 1970s, though they flared with the Soviet invasion of Afghanistan. During the 1980s, worker unrest in Poland led to the toppling of the communist government. During the same period, the reforms brought by Mikhail Gorbachev helped bring about the end of the Soviet Union and the collapse of communism throughout Eastern Europe. Germany reunited, and new nations were born. Sometimes these changes led to continuing ethnic conflict. Russia also experienced difficulty in its transition from a command economy to a market economy.

Key Themes and Concepts

Economic Systems
The reunification of Germany was a joyous moment for Germans, but restoring a market economy to East Germany created many problems.

Cause and Effect

- What are the causes of the Chechen fight for independence?
- What have been the effects?

Preparing for the Regents

- In what way was the collapse of communism and the Soviet Union a turning point in global history?

Political and Economic Change in Latin America

The
Big Idea

Many changes have occurred in Latin America as:

• social and political factors have led to unrest.

• nations have struggled to establish democracy and improve their economies.

• drug trafficking has continued to have an impact on the region.

Section Overview

Many of the nations of Latin America have experienced periods of unrest since 1945. In Argentina, a series of military regimes and repressive governments finally gave way to democracy in the last decades of the century. Guatemala endured a long civil war and has struggled to rebuild its society. Cuba underwent a revolution in 1959 that led to a communist dictatorship. In Nicaragua, years of strife between communists and counterrevolutionary groups gave way in the 1990s to a democratically elected government. Mexico has experienced more stability but has also had periods of revolt and unrest.

Key Themes and Concepts

As you review this section, take special note of the following key themes and concepts:

Conflict What factors led to continuing conflict in Latin America?

Change What types of political changes occurred in Latin American nations after 1945?

Political Systems What role does democracy play in Latin America today?

Key People and Terms

Key People and Terms

Place each of the key people and terms into these three categories: politics, economics, and cooperation.

As you review this section, be sure you understand the significance of these key people and terms:

Juan Perón	contras
import substitution	Organization of American States
dirty war	North American Free Trade
Mothers of the Plaza de Mayo	Agreement
indigenous	cartels
Sandinistas	

Sources of Unrest

Latin America is a diverse region with a great variety of peoples and cultures. Geographic barriers have discouraged unity, yet the nations of Latin America share similar problems. After World War II, political and social upheavals threatened stability in Latin America. Many Latin American nations looked to authoritarian leaders to provide solutions.

Argentina

By 1900, Argentina was the richest nation in Latin America. The Great Depression of the 1930s devastated the country, however. A military coup brought Juan Perón to power in 1946.

Juan Perón

Juan Perón was a former army colonel. He appealed to Argentine nationalism by limiting foreign-owned businesses and by promoting **import substitution,** in which local manufacturers produce goods at home to replace imported products.

Perón gained popularity by boosting wages, strengthening labor unions, and beginning social welfare programs. Perón's government was repressive, however, and his economic policies led to huge debts. In 1955, he lost power in a military coup.

Juan Perón

State Terrorism

Another military government took control in 1976. This government began a program of state terrorism against leftist guerrilla groups. In what came to be known as the **dirty war,** the military arrested, tortured, and killed thousands of people. As many as 20,000 people simply "disappeared."

Many of those who vanished were young people. Their mothers, organized as the **Mothers of the Plaza de Mayo,** marched silently every week in Buenos Aires for over thirty years, holding pictures of their missing children. Their protests demanding an accounting by the government of the whereabouts of their children won worldwide attention.

Democracy Restored

In 1983, Argentina held elections. Voters returned a democratic government to power. The new government worked to control the military and restore human rights. However, economic problems persisted. In 2001, an economic crisis rocked the nation. The hardships led to widespread protests and continued instability.

Guatemala

As you have learned, Cold War tensions caused the United States to view certain political movements in Latin America as threats. In Guatemala, the United States helped to overthrow Jacobo Arbenz in 1954, after his land reform program threatened United States business activities in Guatemala. Landowners and the military regained power.

A civil war soon began. The **indigenous** Indians, those who had lived there for thousands of years and who were in the majority, suffered. As many as 30,000 were killed in the fighting. Rebels finally laid down their arms in 1996, when a peace accord was reached. The accord brought hope for increased rights for all citizens of Guatemala, including its Indian population.

Nicaragua

From 1936 to 1979, the Somoza family had governed Nicaragua. The Somozas were repressive but had close ties to the United States because of their anti-communist stance. In 1979, the **Sandinistas,** a group that included both reform-minded nationalists and communists, overthrew the Somoza government.

Note Taking

Reading Skill:
Identify Main Ideas
Make a table. As you read, fill in the main ideas for each Latin American country in Section 7.

Change in Latin America		
Country	Political Change	Economic Change

Preparing for the Regents

- How did individual citizens make a difference in Argentina? What other examples of citizens making a difference can you think of in global history?

Key Themes and Concepts

Power
The United States has often intervened in the politics of Latin America. This intervention has caused resentment among many Latin Americans.

The Sandinistas in Power

The Sandinistas set up a government under the leadership of Daniel Ortega. Many in the government were Socialists or Communists. The new government introduced some reforms and socialized policies. At the same time, it grew closer to Cuba and other communist nations.

The Contras

In the 1980s, the Sandinistas faced armed opposition from the **contras,** a counterrevolutionary group. Fearing the spread of communism, the United States supported the contras in their fight against the Sandinistas. A civil war followed, leading to many deaths and weakening the Nicaraguan economy.

Other Central American countries helped reach a compromise. In 1990, the Sandinistas handed over power to a freely elected president, Violeta Chamorro. Nicaragua still had to struggle to rebuild its economy, however.

Mexico

Politics in Mexico

After the Mexican Revolution, one party, the Institutional Revolutionary Party (PRI), dominated Mexican politics for 71 years. Between 1960 and 2000, there were periods of upheaval.

- In 1968, police and the military brutally suppressed the student protests.
- In 1994, armed Indian Zapatista rebels in the southern state of Chiapas demanded social and economic reforms, but the group's goals were not achieved.
- Many groups called for election reforms. In 2000, the PRI lost Mexico's presidential election to the National Action Party. Then, in 2012, the PRI retook power, but promised not to return to being an authoritarian party.
- In 2006, a nationwide military crackdown on Mexican drug cartels began. Drug lords struck back with daily killings that threaten the stability of Mexico. Drug-related violence continues to be a major issue for Mexico.

Identify Central Issues

Why did the United States support the contras in Nicaragua in the 1980s?

Preparing for the Regents

- Briefly explain causes of unrest in Latin America in each of the categories listed below.

Gap between rich and poor:

Social classes:

Population and poverty:

Urban growth:

Causes of Unrest in Mexico

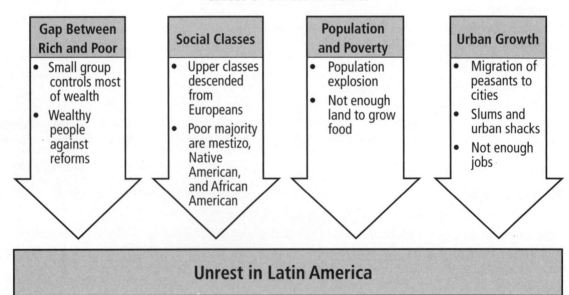

Gap Between Rich and Poor	Social Classes	Population and Poverty	Urban Growth
• Small group controls most of wealth • Wealthy people against reforms	• Upper classes descended from Europeans • Poor majority are mestizo, Native American, and African American	• Population explosion • Not enough land to grow food	• Migration of peasants to cities • Slums and urban shacks • Not enough jobs

Unrest in Latin America

Economic Links With the United States

In the 1950s, the **Organization of American States,** or the OAS, was formed to strengthen democracy, promote human rights, and confront shared problems such as poverty, terrorism, illegal drugs, and corruption. Thirty-five nations in the Western Hemisphere, including Canada and the United States, belong to the organization. The OAS expelled communist Cuba in 1962. Finally, in 2014, relations between Cuba and the United States began to move toward renewed economic and diplomatic relations.

In the 1990s, Mexico, the United States, and Canada signed the **North American Free Trade Agreement,** or NAFTA, a plan to allow free trade among the three nations. Many hoped that it would bring prosperity to Mexico by lowering trade barriers. Some business and investment did go to Mexico, but other manufacturers were hurt by competition from the United States.

Immigration provides another link between Mexico and the United States. Since the 1970s, millions of Mexicans have migrated to the United States, usually in search of better economic opportunities. The money they send back to Mexico is an important part of Mexico's economy.

Panama

In the late 1980s, United States officials suspected that the leader of Panama, Manuel Noriega, was helping criminal gangs called **cartels** smuggle drugs into the United States. United States troops invaded Panama in 1989 and arrested Noriega. Panama experienced greater stability in the 1990s.

The Panama Canal

The Panama Canal was constructed by the United States in the early 1900s. By connecting the Atlantic and Pacific oceans, the canal shortens voyages between the two oceans by thousands of miles. The United States had controlled the canal since it first opened in 1914. Then, in 1977, the United States and Panama signed a treaty designed to gradually turn over control of the canal to Panama. Panama assumed complete control of the Panama Canal on January 1, 2000.

The Role of Religion

The Catholic Church has played a major role in Latin American society since colonial times. Traditionally a conservative force, many church leaders became proponents of social reform during the late 1900s. Outspoken priests and nuns, for example, struggled against the oppressive military regimes that ruled many Latin American countries in the 1970s and 1980s. At the same time, evangelical Protestant groups have gained a growing following with the poor throughout Latin America.

Summary

Many of the nations of Latin America faced political unrest in the last decades of the twentieth century. Argentina suffered under military rule. Guatemala and Nicaragua experienced civil wars. Cuba was a Cold War battleground. Mexico also experienced unrest. Today, however, democracy is taking hold in the region. Still, some problems remain, including the presence and activity of international drug traffickers.

Draw Conclusions

• Why did the OAS expel Cuba in 1962?

Key Themes and Concepts

Political Systems
In Latin America and elsewhere around the world, drug trafficking causes political upheaval as well as social problems. Drug cartels put pressure on national governments and commit violent acts to gain their ends.

Vocabulary Builder

proponent—(pruh POH nunt) *n.* someone who supports something or persuades people to do something

Vocabulary Builder

evangelical—(ee van JEL ih kul) *adj.* evangelical Christians believe that they should persuade as many people as possible to become Christians

Multiple Choice

Directions: Review the Test-Taking Strategies section of this book. Then answer the following questions, drawn from actual Regents examinations. For each statement or question, choose the *number* of the word or expression that, of those given, best completes the statement or answers the question.

Base your answer to question 1 on the map below and on your knowledge of social studies.

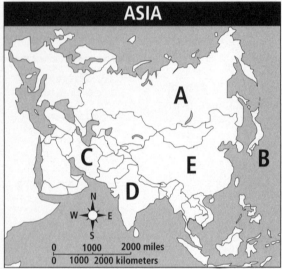

Source: *American History: Historical Outline Map Book With Lesson Ideas*, Prentice Hall, 1998 (adapted)

1 Which letter identifies the nation most closely associated with Mohandas Gandhi?

(1) A

(2) B

(3) C

(4) D

2 Border conflicts between India and Pakistan have most often occurred in

(1) Kashmir

(2) East Timor

(3) Tibet

(4) Afghanistan

3 The formation of the North Atlantic Treaty Organization (NATO), the division of Germany into East Germany and West Germany, and the Korean War were immediate reactions to

(1) Japanese military aggression in the 1930s

(2) the rise of German nationalism after World War I

(3) ethnic conflict and civil war in Africa in the 1950s

(4) communist expansion after World War II

4 Which headline concerning the Soviet Union refers to a Cold War event?

(1) **"Yeltsin Assumes Power"**

(2) **"Trotsky Forms Red Army"**

(3) **"Germany Invades Soviet Union"**

(4) **"Warsaw Pact Formed"**

5 "A group of planners makes all economic decisions. The group assigns natural, human, and capital resources to the production of those goods and services it wants. The group decides how to produce them and to whom to distribute them."

This description *best* applies to the

(1) manorial economy of feudal Europe

(2) mercantile economy of the 1700s in Europe

(3) command economy of the Soviet Union

(4) market economy of the United States

Source: Reprinted by permission of Bob Englehart,
The Hartford Courant

Base your answer to question 6 on the political cartoon above and on your knowledge of social studies.

6 What is the cartoonist saying about the impact of democracy on the Soviet Union?

(1) Democracy covered up hidden problems in the Soviet Union.

(2) Democracy led to the development of the Soviet Union.

(3) Democracy had no impact on the Soviet Union.

(4) Democracy led to the breakup of the Soviet Union.

7 The main reason the Chinese Communists gained control of mainland China in 1949 was that

(1) they were supported by many warlords and upper-class Chinese

(2) the United States had supported the Chinese Communist party during World War II

(3) Mao was a dynamic leader who had the support of the peasant class

(4) they had the support of the Nationalists and of Japan

8 The Tiananmen Square massacre in China was a reaction to

(1) Deng Xiaoping's plan to revive the Cultural Revolution

(2) demands for greater individual rights and freedom of expression

(3) China's decision to seek Western investors

(4) Britain's decision to return Hong Kong to China

9 Which statement best explains why India was partitioned in 1947?

(1) The British feared a united India.

(2) One region wanted to remain under British control.

(3) Religious differences led to a political division.

(4) Communist supporters wanted a separate state.

10 From the perspective of the North Vietnamese, the war in Vietnam in the 1960s was a battle between

(1) fascism and liberalism

(2) nationalism and imperialism

(3) republicanism and totalitarianism

(4) theocracy and monarchy

11 One similarity shared by the Meiji emperors of Japan, Peter the Great of Russia, and Shah Reza Pahlavi of Iran was that they all supported policies that

(1) increased the power of the aristocracy

(2) introduced new religious beliefs

(3) kept their nations from industrial expansion

(4) westernized their nations

12 A nation governed by Islamic fundamentalists would be most likely to

(1) allow many different interpretations of the Quran

(2) adopt the values and culture of the West

(3) emphasize the traditional beliefs and values of the religion

(4) promote active participation of women in government

13 "Cuba today is a puppet still dancing after the puppet master's death."

In this 1993 newspaper quotation, which nation is referred to as the "puppet master"?

(1) Haiti

(2) Soviet Union

(3) Spain

(4) United States

14 One similarity between Lenin's New Economic Policy and Gorbachev's policy of perestroika is that both policies

(1) supported collectivization of farms in the Soviet Union

(2) allowed some aspects of capitalism in the Soviet economy

(3) increased citizen participation in the Soviet government

(4) strengthened governmental control over the Soviet republics

15 "Take sides. Neutrality helps the oppressor, never the victim. Silence encourages the tormentor, never the tormented."

—*Elie Wiesel, Holocaust survivor*

According to this quotation, which situation would have most concerned Elie Wiesel?

(1) formation of the United Nations

(2) the world's initial reaction to ethnic cleansing in Bosnia

(3) Arab reaction to the creation of Israel in 1948

(4) dismantling of the Berlin Wall

Thematic Essay Question

In developing your answer, be sure to keep these general definitions in mind:

(a) <u>explain</u> means "to make plain or clear; render understandable or intelligible"
(b) <u>describe</u> means "to illustrate something in words or tell about it"
(c) <u>evaluate</u> means "to judge or determine the significance, worth, or quality of"

Directions: Write a well-organized essay that includes an introduction, several paragraphs addressing the task below, and a conclusion.

Theme: **Interdependence**

> Throughout global history, the world has been growing more and more interdependent. This process has accelerated in the twenty-first century.

Task:

> - Explain what is meant by *global interdependence*.
> - Describe two examples of interdependence.
> - Evaluate the positive and negative effects of the examples of interdependence you have chosen on individuals and nations.

You may discuss any nations or regions and any example of interdependence from your study of global history and geography. Some suggestions you may wish to consider are economic interdependence, political interdependence, military interdependence, cultural interdependence, and technological interdependence.

You are not limited to these suggestions.
Do not use the United States in your answer.

Guidelines:

In your essay, be sure to
- Develop all aspects of the task
- Support the theme with relevant facts, examples, and details
- Use a logical and clear plan of organization, including an introduction and a conclusion that are beyond a simple restatement of the theme

Document-Based Question

This question is based on the accompanying documents. The question is designed to test your ability to work with historical documents. Some of the documents have been edited for the purposes of the question. As you analyze the documents, take into account the source of each document and any point of view that may be presented in the document.

Historical Context:

After World War II, the world became divided by the Cold War. The Cold War policies of both superpowers affected nations around the world.

Task: Using the information from the documents and your knowledge of global history, answer the questions that follow each document in Part A. Your answers to the questions will help you write the Part B essay in which you will be asked to

> • Describe and evaluate the ways in which the Cold War affected nations around the world

In developing your answers, be sure to keep this general definition in mind:

> <u>discuss</u> means "to make observations about something using facts, reasoning, and argument; to present in some detail.

Part A: Short Answer

Directions: Analyze the documents and answer the question or questions that follow each document, using the space provided.

Document #1

A shadow has fallen upon the scenes so lately lighted by the Allied victories. . . . From Stettin in the Baltic to Trieste in the Adriatic, an iron curtain has descended across the Continent. Warsaw, Berlin, Prague, Vienna, Budapest, Belgrade, Bucharest, and Sofia, all these famous cities and populations around them lie in what I must call the Soviet sphere and all are subject to a very high and, in many cases, increasing measure of control from Moscow.

—Winston Churchill, from a speech given in Fulton, Missouri, 1946

1. What image does Churchill use to talk about the division of Europe? Why is this image appropriate?

_____

_____

Document #2

Europe After World War II

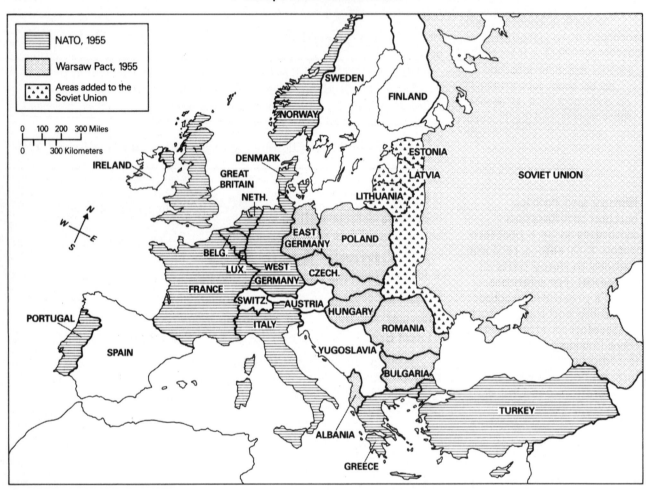

2. Name two European countries that were allies of the Soviet Union during the Cold War.

_____

_____

3. Name two European countries that were allies of the United States during the Cold War.

_____

_____

Document #3

The divisive force is international communism. . . . It strives to break the ties that unite the free. And it strives to capture—to exploit [use selfishly] for its own greater power—all forces of change in the world, especially the needs of the hungry and hopes of the oppressed. . . . To counter the threat of those who seek to rule by force, we must pay the costs of our own needed military strength, and help to build the security of others.

—Dwight D. Eisenhower, Second Inaugural Address, January 21, 1957

4. What did President Eisenhower promise to do in response to international communism? Why?

_____

_____

Document #4

United States Intervention in Latin America

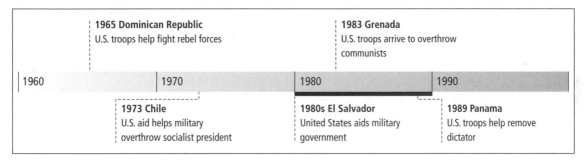

1965 Dominican Republic
U.S. troops help fight rebel forces

1983 Grenada
U.S. troops arrive to overthrow communists

1960   1970   1980   1990

1973 Chile
U.S. aid helps military overthrow socialist president

1980s El Salvador
United States aids military government

1989 Panama
U.S. troops help remove dictator

5. Explain how one event on this timeline was an effect of the Cold War.

_____

_____

Document-Based Question

Part B
Essay

Directions: Write a well-organized essay that includes an introduction, several paragraphs, and a conclusion. Use evidence from *at least* **three** documents in your essay. Support your response with relevant facts, examples, and details. Include additional outside information.

Historical Context:

After World War II, the world became divided by the Cold War. The Cold War policies of both superpowers affected nations around the world.

Task: Using information from the documents and your knowledge of United States history, write an essay in which you:

> - Describe and evaluate several effects of Cold War policies on nations around the world

Guidelines:

In your essay, be sure to
- Develop all aspects of the task
- Incorporate information from *at least* **three** of the documents
- Incorporate relevant outside information
- Support the theme with relevant facts, examples, and details
- Use a logical and clear plan of organization, including an introduction and a conclusion that are beyond a restatement of the theme

The World Today: Connections and Interactions
(1980–The Present)

Unit Overview

The years since 1980 have been a time of great change. Developing nations face challenges as they strive to progress economically despite rising populations and huge debt. There have been many regional conflicts, and international terrorism remains a great threat to world order. The United Nations addresses many of these issues.

As many nations look to the future, they struggle with the tension between modernization and traditional values. Changes come at a quick pace. Advances in computer technology, space exploration, and medicine have changed the way people live. Still, many problems remain, especially in the global environment. Whatever may be the long-term solutions to these problems, they depend on nations working together toward common goals.

Using Good Social Studies Practices

Context

Some of the many themes developed in Unit 8 are:

economic systems   urbanization
interdependence   science and technology
movement of people and goods   environment
change   power

Choose one of the themes listed above. As you review Unit 8, identify changes to the world that have occurred on the theme you have chosen. Focus on major developments and key turning points having to do with your theme. For each of those, identify the context in which it occurred.

Economic Trends

The Big Idea

In the final decades of the 1900s, global economic trends included the following:

- The world became divided economically between the relatively prosperous North and the developing South.

- Developing countries struggled to overcome problems such as poor geographical conditions, economic dependence, failed economic policies, and political unrest.

- Economic interdependence linked national economies around the world.

Key People and Terms

What do all of the key terms have in common? Explain.

Preparing for the Regents

- What are the differences between the prosperous countries of the global North and the developing countries of the global South?

Section Overview

There is an economic division between the more prosperous countries of the global North and the developing countries of the global South. Developing countries face many obstacles, such as rapid population growth, debt, and unrest. In today's world, however, the global North and South are interdependent. Cooperation among nations can lead to improvements for all. However, problems in one area of the world may have powerful effects on the global economy.

Key Themes and Concepts

As you review this section, take special note of the following key themes and concepts:

Places and Regions What global economic divisions exist today?

Economic Systems Why have some developing nations failed to achieve their goals?

Interdependence How has economic interdependence affected the world?

Key Terms

As you review this section, be sure you understand the significance of these key terms:

post-colonialism
emerging economies
trade deficit
refugees
globalization
World Trade Organization

International Monetary Fund
multinational corporations
Association of Southeast
  Asian Nations
North American Free Trade
  Association

North and South: Differences in Development

There is an economic division between the relatively rich nations of the global North and the relatively poor nations of the global South.

Wealthy Nations

The global North includes the nations of Western Europe and North America, along with Japan and Australia. These nations are highly industrialized and have high literacy rates and high standards of living.

Poor Nations

The global South includes developing economies in Asia, Africa, and Latin America. Many were once colonies and remain poor and industrially undeveloped, experiencing the problems of **post-colonialism.** Policies established during the age of imperialism continued after 1945. As a result, some nations have remained economically dependent on their former colonial rulers.

Nations with Emerging Economies

Countries with **emerging economies** are developing businesses and industries at a fast rate. Some were poor nations that are now richer, although they may have many poor and unemployed people.

Obstacles to Development

Geography

Several factors have hindered progress in developing countries. Uncertain rainfall, lack of fertile land, and geographic barriers are problems faced by many nations. Some countries are small and have few resources.

Natural disasters such as earthquakes and hurricanes can be devastating to struggling economies. For example, in September 1998, Hurricane Mitch struck Central America. Flooding and mudslides led to deaths and left many survivors homeless. It takes years to rebuild damaged economies.

Population Growth

High birthrates and better medical care in many nations of the global South have led to overpopulation. Also, specific religious and cultural beliefs, economic need, and a lack of reproductive information have led to increasing populations in certain countries. Overpopulation can cause a lack of food, as well as inadequate housing, jobs, and medical care. By 2012, the world's population reached the milestone of over 7 billion people. Many developing nations have tried to reduce population growth, but only China is willing to force people to limit family size. Even there, the policy is being challenged because of culture, an aging population, and a growing economy.

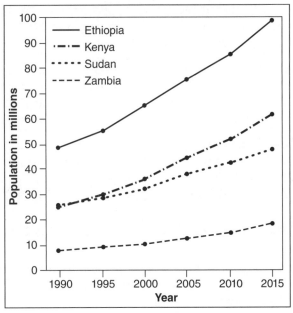

Population Projections for Selected Eastern and Southern African Nations

Source: The World Bank

Key Themes and Concepts

Geography
Natural disasters, such as the 2015 earthquake in Tibet, have a profound impact on the economy of a country. Industrial growth, tourism, and infrastructure are impacted and these countries, especially those with limited economies, need foreign aid until they recover.

Population Projections for Selected East and Southern African Nations
Because of population growth there may not be enough resources to meet people's basic needs. This can hurt efforts to improve living conditions.

Preparing for the Regents

- Practice your graph-reading skills by describing the general trend that this graph shows.

Past Economic Policies

After achieving independence, many new nations imposed socialist economic policies. Over time, socialism hindered economic growth. Beginning in the 1980s, some nations introduced market economies.

Economic Dependence, Trade Deficits, and Debt

For centuries, most people in Africa, Asia, and Latin America worked in agriculture. Today, much of the labor force in the global South is still engaged in agriculture and depends on developed nations for manufactured goods and technology while exporting cash crops or natural resources. These factors have led to trade deficits. A **trade deficit** is a situation in which a nation imports more than it exports.

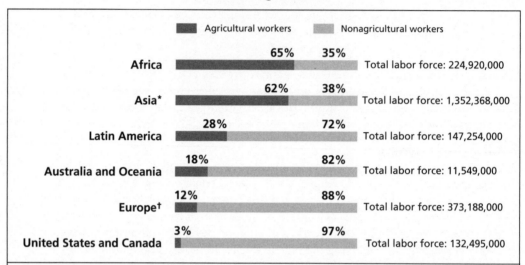

Labor in Agriculture

Agricultural workers | Nonagricultural workers

	Agricultural	Nonagricultural	Total labor force
Africa	65%	35%	224,920,000
Asia*	62%	38%	1,352,368,000
Latin America	28%	72%	147,254,000
Australia and Oceania	18%	82%	11,549,000
Europe†	12%	88%	373,188,000
United States and Canada	3%	97%	132,495,000

*Excluding Asian part of the former Soviet Union.
†Including Asian part of the former Soviet Union.

Source: FAO Production Yearbook, 1987, Food and Agricultural Organization of the United States. Figures are for 1987, prior to the breakup of the former Soviet Union.

Preparing for the Regents

• What evidence does this graph give of the economic division between the global North and the global South? How does having a large percentage of the population in agriculture affect a nation's economic progress?

Over the years, economic struggles and the desire to diversify their economies and develop quickly led to heavy borrowing from foreign banks. In the 1980s, interest rates rose, the global economy slowed, and resources were used to pay for high interest payments on these loans. This lowered productivity and increased debt.

Economic patterns are changing. Emerging economies, such as China, India, and Brazil, built factories and continue to develop advanced technology industries. They buy raw materials from poorer countries and build factories in some of the least developed countries. Poor countries no longer depend only on the richest countries.

Political Instability

In many developing nations, money is spent on warfare rather than on education or health care. People become **refugees** when they flee their homelands to seek safety elsewhere. This results in economic instability and a labor shortage.

Economic Development Case Studies

Congo

When, in 1960, Congo became independent from Belgium, it began years of civil war. People from some 200 different ethnic groups competed for power. In 1965, army general Mobutu Sese Seko seized control, renamed the country Zaire, and established a brutal dictatorship. Although it has vast natural resources, under Mobutu, Zaire's economy was ruined. Corrupt officials robbed the treasury. Roads were left to decay. Agriculture declined and mines closed. Finally in 1997, rebel forces removed Mobutu and the nation was renamed the Democratic Republic of Congo (DRC). Violence between rival groups continued and the DRC's government was tightly controlled. Millions have died because of violence between rebel groups, militias, ethnic groups, and the government. The International

Cycle of Poverty

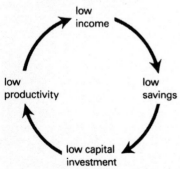

low income → low savings → low capital investment → low productivity → low income

Criminal Court convicted a powerful militia leader of using child soldiers. Today, DRC is among the poorest and hungriest countries in the world. Its violence and chaos has kept outside sources from investing in the country, and it is one of the least economically developed countries in the world.

China

In the past 30 years, political changes have allowed China to become a global economic superpower. It has the world's second-largest economy, but because it has so many poor people, its per capita income is not high. This economic inequality has caused unrest in both urban and rural regions. China's mixed economy focused on creating goods for export, and it is now the world's top exporter while the Chinese government is also encouraging the production and consumption of domestic goods, from steel to clothes. Multinational companies are successfully expanding into a growing Chinese market and Chinese companies are purchasing Western companies, partly because Chinese consumers trust Western products more than Chinese-made goods. Many Chinese consumers want Western products, like designer clothing and fast-food fried chicken. Internally, China has had problems with corruption, bribery, labor shortages, and labor strikes caused by poor working conditions. By 2015, China was experiencing a slowing of its economic growth. This was partly due to an industrial overcapacity of goods (such as ships and steel) and issues such as inefficiency and a heavy investment in manufacturing. Some Chinese companies have moved their operations to countries with lower wages, such as Cambodia. China is a major provider of aid to poor countries, especially in Southeast Asia and Africa.

Brazil

Military rulers controlled Brazil from the 1960s through the 1980s. Under their rule, Brazil experienced a boom due to foreign investment, exploitation of the Amazon rain forest, and reduction of oil imports (because they built hydroelectric plants). While the middle and upper classes of Brazil enjoyed prosperity, many workers remained in extreme poverty.

In the 1990s, democracy replaced military rule. Brazil faced serious economic troubles, but after 2000, its economy stabilized and it became an important emerging economic power. New reforms encouraged investment, economic growth, and judicial reform as well as reducing the deforestation of the Amazon. Brazil remains an economically divided society with high unemployment and a politically and economically unhappy middle class. After 2011, the worldwide recession began to affect Brazil's economy. This combined with low wages, concerns about public safety, and extensive government corruption has only intensified its economic problems. Increased problems flared as Brazil prepared for the 2014 World Cup and the 2016 Olympics. Protesters demonstrated against the eviction of people living in slums to make way for new sports venues and transportation systems. Continuing issues with unhealthy sanitation and unfinished projects continue to plague Brazil's cities and its political upheaval has limited the government's effectiveness in dealing with its problems.

Economic Interdependence

Globalization

Although people and countries in different parts of the world have been linked by trade for centuries, a global economy, the integration of national economies into an international economy, began to develop in the late 1800s. Advances in science and technology in the late twentieth century accelerated the pace of this **globalization.** Today, raw materials flow from one country to factories in another,

Note Taking

Reading Skill:
Understand Effects
Make a table. As you read, list benefits and challenges of a global economy. Add boxes as needed.

A Global Economy	
Benefits	Challenges

Preparing for the Regents

Explain the global relationships depicted in the cartoon and the consequences of these events on the global market.

Key Themes and Concepts

Global Connections
Russia and the United States have become major exporters of oil. This has changed global economic and political dynamics and the power of OPEC, and affected oil prices.

while the finished products are sold in both emerging and rich nations. In the garment industry, this flow is often hidden, or indirect, so foreign companies and consumers have no idea of the conditions under which the product is made. Factories in Bangladesh have low wages, poor working conditions, as well as minimal and poorly enforced regulations. Its limited infrastructure, such as erratic electricity and transportation, has led to production delays and dangerous working conditions. These conditions allow lower cost, higher production, and better profit margins. Recent industrial accidents have caused some companies to rethink using the cheapest suppliers, many of which are based in countries such as Bangladesh. They are putting pressure on governments and factories to improve working conditions, especially worker safety.

Dependence on Oil Oil prices affect economies everywhere. When oil supplies are high, prices fall, and many economies benefit. However, when oil supplies are limited, prices rise, and many economies suffer. Inflation caused by high oil prices has contributed to debt crises in developing nations, while falling oil prices can damage economies that depend heavily on oil sales. Regional issues, such as civil unrest in Iraq, Libya, and Syria, have disrupted oil production. A European embargo on Iranian oil was imposed to limit its nuclear program, and influenced oil production. Regional crises such as these raise the worldwide price of oil. In recent years, China has become the world's biggest oil importer. It purchases 50 percent of Iran's oil, partly because it is less concerned with price than Western oil companies that are profit-driven. It is presently trying to invest in oil fields rather than just purchase oil. This will increase its role in globalization.

New methods of oil extraction, such as hydraulic fracturing, have affected the global oil market. In mid-2014, the price of oil dropped until by December it was half what it had been in June. The drop hurt the economies of countries, such as Russia and Saudi Arabia, that depend on oil sales. Oil importing countries benefited from the lower prices. Some governments, such as India's, responded with positive economic actions.

Global Banking and Financial Markets Finances can immediately flow across international boundaries via the Internet and whatever happens in one country has an effect on other places. Many Western banks make loans to developing nations to be used for modernization. As interest rates rose in the 1980s, the world economy slowed and poor nations struggled to repay their loans. The **International Monetary Fund** (IMF) and **World Bank** stepped in to work out agreements that included lower interest rates, new payment schedules, and a move to free market policies. Because financial markets are also linked, changes in stock prices in one part of the world can affect other markets. So when many Asian countries faced economic problems in the 1990s, stock markets all over the world were shaken. Microfinancing has made smaller loans available to clients who do not meet the qualifications for a loan from a larger institution. Low-income individuals without collateral are able to obtain small loans to improve or start their often home-based businesses.

Multinational Corporations Businesses that operate in many countries are called multinational corporations. Many of these companies are based in the global North or in countries with emerging economies. They make investments in the global South and bring new employment opportunities, infrastructure improvements, and technology. Sometimes they compete with and may ruin local industries. Because these corporations are foreign-owned, they respond to the economies in their home country while creating social and economic changes in the countries in which they are operating.

Regional and Global Cooperation

Nations have created regional trade agreements with each other, like the successful European Union. Each works on increasing economic cooperation and free trade to spur economic development and reduce poverty.

EU The European Union began in the early 1950s by integrating its six members' coal and steel industries. It has grown until it it now a political as well as economic organization with an elected parliament and 28 member states. it carries out economic policies, including trade regulations and has its own currency (the euro). It also conducts peacekeeping missions.

ASEAN The **Association of Southeast Asian Nations** (ASEAN), formed in 1967, is made up of ten Southeast Asian countries. It coordinates policies among members in trade and agriculture and focuses on peace and stability in the region.

NAFTA In 1994, the **North American Free Trade Agreement** (NAFTA) was set up to eliminate tariffs and trade restrictions among Canada, the United States, and Mexico.

World Trade Organization The World Trade Organization (WTO) was established in 1995 as a global organization to deal with the rules of trade between nations. It has 153 members and negotiates agreements, handles trade disputes, and provides assistance to developing countries. At many WTO meetings major protests are held by those who believe its policies favor rich nations and harm the environment.

G-20 The Group of 20 (G-20) are the finance ministers and central bank governors of 20 countries—both industrial countries, such as Germany and the United States, and countries with emerging economies, such as China, India, and Brazil. They first met in 1999 and focus on international economic development, including ways to avoid and/or control financial crises.

International Drug Trade

The United States declared a "war on drugs" in the 1980s and pressured many Latin American, African, and Asian countries to move against drug cartels. There has been some international cooperation to eliminate illegal drug trade. Sometimes the United States has linked this cooperation to trade or aid agreements.

Draw Conclusions

Which countries benefit more from economic globalization—developed or developing countries? Explain.

Preparing for the Regents

- How has economic decision making become more global as national economies around the world become increasingly interdependent?

- How has that interdependence been tested by the global financial crisis?

Global Financial Crisis

In 2007, a financial crisis that began in the United States spread to many global financial institutions. Some were multinational companies, while others were affected because of investments or loans. In countries all over the world, unemployment rose as major financial institutions in the global North went out of business or had to seek governmental support. By 2008, trade had contracted because people in developed countries could afford fewer goods.

The G-20 and IMF worked with countries—developed, emerging, and poor—to create programs to limit the effects of the crisis. Although most countries were affected, by early 2010, emerging economies, such as China and India, were recovering. However, the decrease in demand for their goods and services in the United States and Europe meant a slow export market and long-term recovery.

In the more industrialized countries, like the United States and England, economic improvement moved much more slowly. Many developed countries cut government spending, as did private companies. Unemployment rose. The countries with the most critical financial problems, like Iceland and Greece, were not poor countries, but had large debts and deficits that grew worse during this crisis. The European Union helped its financially troubled members: Greece, Ireland, Portugal, Cyprus, and Spain. These countries made severe changes to their economies to get loans from the EU and international financial institutions. Ireland's economy is finally expanding, while others, like Greece and Cyprus, are recovering more slowly and continue to struggle with restrictions, taxes, high unemployment, and protests.

Preparing for the Regents

- Use this graph to identify which EU members are the slowest to recover from the recent global economic crisis.

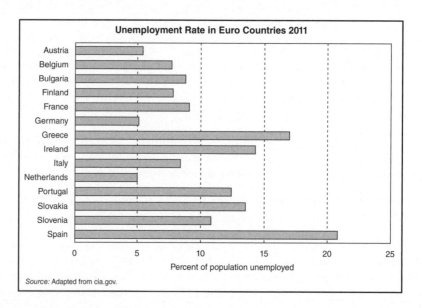

Unemployment Rate in Euro Countries 2011

Source: Adapted from cia.gov.

Europe's slow recovery has had a global impact. Less developed countries, like those in Eastern Europe and the Caribbean, worry that European companies will pull out of their country or go bankrupt. This would harm their fragile economies.

Changing Globalization

In 2012, European governments that seemed to be recovering, like the Netherlands, elected new leaders because austerity budgets were very unpopular. This crisis has showed that the world economic picture is rebalancing. Trade between emerging economies and poor nations improved more quickly than trade with more developed countries. China overtook Germany as the biggest exporter in

Vocabulary Builder

austerity—(au STAIR it e) *n.* harsh or severe economy

the world, although Chinese manufacturing has slowed. The countries that had been the biggest markets are not recovering quickly, so exporting countries have had to develop new markets. The continued fragile global economic recovery has been up-and-down for both high income and low income countries. Because of slow economic growth in most countries, including those that saw an initial spurt, multinational corporations are not making the profits they expected. The slow recovery, political issues, heavy fines, and taxes concern these corporations.

By 2016, many economists felt globalization was changing, but were cautious about predicting what future globalization would look like. They know there has been a steady drop in global trade and international investment. Some predictions include more trade barriers being enacted.

At the same time increased "digital globalization" is occurring. More multinational companies manage themselves digitally rather than open offices in many different countries. Consumers shop online buying goods from all over the world. Finally, social media, such as Facebook, is creating a new international conversation.

Summary

There is a great economic gulf between the global North and the global South, but this has been changing in recent years. Developing countries struggle with obstacles that hinder their growth. Meanwhile, the global interdependence in banking and trade helped spread a global economic crisis. While globalization has resulted in benefits to almost all nations, there is considerable debate about whether developed nations have benefited at the expense of poorer countries. In recent years, emerging economics are playing a more important role in the global economy and in helping the developing economies of poor nations. The financial crisis forced many developed countries to reassess their economies, their debts, and their loans to other countries as they struggle to recover from deep debt and high unemployment.

Preparing for the Regents

- Describe three policies that could help developing countries achieve greater economic prosperity.

Conflicts and Peace Efforts

Section Overview

In the last several decades, some nations and organizations have continued to use violence and terrorism to achieve political goals. In its peacekeeping role, the United Nations (UN) has intervened in many conflicts, with varying degrees of success. The UN also promotes human rights and helps with disaster relief throughout the world. In many areas of the world, ethnic and religious differences have sparked conflict. Even with the end of the Cold War superpower struggles, various areas of the world have become hot spots.

Key Themes and Concepts

As you review this section, take special note of the following key themes and concepts:

Power For what purposes have various groups used terrorist tactics?

Belief Systems How have religious and ethnic differences contributed to instability and conflict?

Interdependence How does global interdependence cause local conflicts to have potentially global consequences?

Conflict How has the United Nations tried to promote world peace and security?

Key People and Terms

As you review this section, be sure you understand the significance of these key people and terms:

terrorism	Saddam Hussein
al Qaeda	Kurds
Irish Republican Army	Darfur
ethnic cleansing	Universal Declaration of
Dalai Lama	Human Rights

The United Nations

Structure of the United Nations

The United Nations, or UN, was established in 1945. Its goals are to promote global peace and security as well as economic and social well-being. The UN has the power, through the votes of its more than 170 member nations, to take action against forces that threaten world peace.

The UN has five main bodies. The UN also has a number of specialized agencies. Some, such as the Food and Agriculture Organization (FAO) and the International Fund for Agricultural Development (IFAD), fight hunger through agricultural improvement. Others, such as the United Nations Children's Fund (UNICEF) and the World Health Organization (WHO), are concerned with health issues.

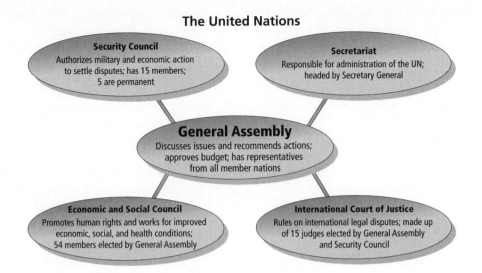

The United Nations

Security Council
Authorizes military and economic action to settle disputes; has 15 members; 5 are permanent

Secretariat
Responsible for administration of the UN; headed by Secretary General

General Assembly
Discusses issues and recommends actions; approves budget; has representatives from all member nations

Economic and Social Council
Promotes human rights and works for improved economic, social, and health conditions; 54 members elected by General Assembly

International Court of Justice
Rules on international legal disputes; made up of 15 judges elected by General Assembly and Security Council

Preparing for the Regents

Describe three different types of activities carried out by the United Nations.

1.

2.

3.

Social and Economic Programs

The UN also promotes social and economic programs.

Human Rights In 1948, the United Nations adopted the **Universal Declaration of Human Rights.** This document states that human beings are born free and equal with dignity and rights. It goes on to list basic rights and freedoms that all people should have. Nevertheless, human rights are in peril in many parts of the world, including China and the Balkans.

Disaster Relief The United Nations has responded over the years to famine and other disasters.

- In the late 1960s, the UN helped save millions in Biafra from starvation during the Nigerian civil war.
- In the early 1990s, UN forces brought food to Somalians who were caught up in a civil war.
- The UN provides relief and recovery aid after natural disasters, such as the 2004 tsunami in Indonesia and Pakistan's 2005 earthquake and 2011 floods.
- In 2010, Haiti, already the poorest country in the Western Hemisphere, had a devastating earthquake. Millions in aid was provided by the UN and individual countries for relief, reforms, and rebuilding. In 2011, the UN observers monitored a presidential election in which Haiti's voters elected a singer, Michel Martelly, president, in the hopes that a political outsider would guide the country into recovery and a prosperous future. However, in 2012, over 600,000 still lived in displacement camps, agriculture had not recovered, and a cholera epidemic raged on.

Peacekeeping Operations

The United Nations has taken action to maintain peace or restore order in places all over the world. The UN has had mixed success in keeping the peace. Although no worldwide conflicts have occurred, the sovereignty of individual nations often makes it difficult for the UN to enforce its wishes. As part of its Department of Political Affairs, the UN also advises and monitors milestone elections, such as in the Democratic Republic of Congo and in Nepal.

Iraq In August 1990, Iraqi troops invaded oil-rich Kuwait. The United Nations voted to impose economic sanctions on Iraq to force the troops to withdraw. When Iraq did not withdraw, the Security Council sent a multinational force that drove Iraq out of Kuwait. More recently, it monitored Iraqi elections.

Key Themes and Concepts

Needs and Wants
At its founding, the United Nations pledged to fight hunger, disease, and ignorance. Its programs to improve agriculture and promote health have accomplished these goals in many regions.

Vocabulary Builder

tsunami—(tsoo NAH mee) *n.* a very large wave, caused by extreme conditions such as an earthquake, that can cause a lot of damage when it reaches land

Note Taking

Reading Skill:
Identify Supporting Details
Make a chart. Record the details of the United Nations peacekeeping operations in the three countries.

```
          United Nations
       Peacekeeping Operations
      ┌──────────┬──────────┐
   ┌──────┐  ┌──────┐  ┌──────┐
   │ Iraq │  │ Haiti│  │Sudan │
   └──────┘  └──────┘  └──────┘
```

Preparing for the Regents

List three reasons why groups use terrorist tactics.

1.

2.

3.

Haiti From 1957 through 1986, Haiti was ruled by brutal dictators. In 1990, Haiti held free elections. However, Jean-Bertrand Aristide, the victor, was later ousted by a military coup. Several years later, UN forces helped restore Aristide to power and build a functioning democracy in Haiti.

Sudan Sudan has been torn by civil war for most of its 52 years. Its cultural diversity has been a factor in these wars. In 2003, government-supported Arabic militias attacked black villagers and rebel groups in the **Darfur** region. In 2007, forces from the African Union joined UN peacekeepers to try to end the violence. In 2011, South Sudan split away from Sudan, and although tensions eased enough for the countries to resume trade and oil production, the violence in South Sudan's Darfur region has remained intense. Sudan's government refused to cooperate with the UN while the violence here hinders and threatens the UN peacekeepers and humanitarian workers who are working to help Darfur's displaced people.

The Threat of Terrorism

Nature of Terrorism

Terrorism is the deliberate use of unpredictable violence, especially against civilians, to gain revenge or to achieve political goals. Terrorism is often used by groups that do not have their own military power. Terrorists use tactics such as bombings, kidnappings, assassinations, and hijackings. In recent years, new fears about nuclear terrorism, chemical terrorism, and cyberterrorism have developed. Terrorism spreads fear throughout the world.

At first terrorism was local, such as disputes between nationalist groups that both claimed the same homeland (such as the Palestinians and the Israelis) or that claimed the same land (such as both India and Pakistan claiming Kashmir).

Then terrorism became more global with a developed central leadership. Al Qaeda trained terrorists, raised money, and supported conflicts between traditionalist groups and modern Western societies. It encouraged extremist attacks on Western societies.

A newer trend involves local terrorists who are not part of al Qaeda. These independent groups in Syria, Algeria, Kenya, and Nigeria often target civilians in their own countries by attacking hospitals, religious pilgrims, even shopping malls. Although many have religious affiliations, it is often the local issues—religious, political, or cultural—that motivate their actions. These independent groups are harder for the global community to battle than a central network. Some terrorist groups raise money by ransoming the people they kidnap. Others raise it using secret donations or credit card fraud.

Ethnic and Religious Tensions

Religious beliefs and ethnic loyalties have united groups and sometimes led to the growth of nations. These forces have also divided peoples and led to persecution and violence. In every conflict, each group involved has its own point of view. In many instances, the violence is being renounced for more democratic, political methods of change.

Note Taking

Reading Skill:
Identify Causes
Make a chart. List the causes of each country/region's ethnic and religious tensions.

Ethnic and Religious Tensions	
Country/Region	**Causes**

Northern Ireland

Ireland won its independence from Britain in 1922. Britain, however, kept control of the six northern counties, which had a mostly Protestant population. The south was mostly Roman Catholic.

In Northern Ireland, violence increased in the 1970s because of extremists in both the Protestant and Roman Catholic communities. The **Irish Republican Army** (IRA) wanted Ireland to reunite and for British interference to end. They used violence to try and reach this goal. Protestant groups retaliated. Despite many attempts at peace, the violence and divisions continued until 2005, when the IRA ended its call for violence. In 2007, a new power-sharing government for Northern Ireland took control from the British government.

Spain and the Basques

A Basque separatist group had used violence, robbery, and terrorism since the 1950s to try to obtain a separate homeland for the Basques. In October, 2011, they ended their violent methods and vowed to work within Spain's democratic political system.

China and its Minorities

In 1951, the People's Republic of China invaded Tibet. The Chinese promised that Tibet would be an autonomous region of China. China's 1959 military crackdown on Tibetan rebels led to full-scale resistance. The **Dalai Lama,** the spiritual and political leader of Tibet, fled to India. China then began to impose Chinese culture on Tibet by creating land collectives and executing landlords. Protests against the Chinese flared again in 2008. The Chinese government reacted strongly, imposing curfews and strictly limiting access to Tibet. The Dalai Lama, in exile, accused the Chinese of cultural genocide and warned that Tibetan Buddhist culture was facing extinction. More recently, the Chinese government reacted to tensions with the Uyghur minority. These Muslims live in Western China but have conducted terrorist attacks across China. The government held huge show trials. In 2014, tens of thousands of pro-democracy demonstrators protested in Hong Kong. They wanted election reform and less control by the mainland communist government but police ended their protests.

South Asia and Southeast Asia

Ethnic and religious conflicts continue to produce violence on the Indian subcontinent.

- **Muslims, Hindus, and Sikhs** In India, both Muslims and Sikhs believe they are discriminated against by India's Hindu majority.
- **Indonesia** Indonesia's population is mostly Muslim, but in East Timor most people are Catholics. In 1999, East Timor demanded independence, and Indonesia's army responded with such force that less than a month later, international peacekeepers arrived. Despite free elections in 2007, newly independent Timor-Leste remains Asia's poorest country.
- **Sri Lanka** In 1976, the Tamil Tigers, a militant organization based in northern Sri Lanka, began a violent secessionist campaign to create an independent Tamil state. Approximately 80,000 people died by the time they were defeated in 2009.

Nationalism
Authoritarian communist
governments had kept
nationalism in check in the
years after World War II.
After the collapse of
communism, nationalism
revived and resulted in civil
wars.

The Balkans

Yugoslavia was a multicultural state created after World War I. Orthodox Christian Serbs, Roman Catholic Croats, Muslim Albanians, and other ethnic groups lived there. Some areas were home to predominately one ethnic group, while several groups shared other regions.

By 1991, several of Yugoslavia's regions had declared independence. Some, like Slovenia, had only brief fighting. In more ethnically mixed areas, tensions flared. In Bosnia and Herzegovina, Serbs practiced **ethnic cleansing,** which is the act of removing or killing people of a certain ethnic group.

*Ethnic Divisions in Yugoslavia
Before 1990*

*Before 1990, Yugoslavia
was made up of six republics,
similar to states in the United
States. Each republic had a
dominant ethnic group, but
they also had ethnic
minorities. Most people
spoke the same language,
Serbo-Croatian, but had
different religions. Others
spoke minority languages.*

Ethnic Divisions in Yugoslavia Before 1990

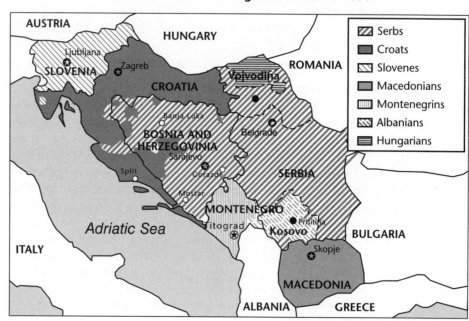

- Practice your map skills by explaining how this map supports the idea that diversity led to conflict in the Balkans.

In 1992, **Slobodan Milosevic,** the Serbian leader of the Yugoslavian government, encouraged or ordered brutal campaigns of ethnic cleansing against non-Serbians, such as ethnic Albanians in Kosovo. In order to restore peace, NATO and the UN took military action.

(adapted)

Copyright © 1994 by Jimmy Margulies, *The Record, Hackensack, NJ*

Preparing for the Regents

• How is the UN policy presented in this cartoon similar to the policy of appeasement practiced by the Western democracies in the 1930s?

In 2001, Milosevic was arrested and tried for war crimes and genocide by the UN's International Criminal Tribunal, but died before its verdict. After 2003, Yugoslavia changed its name to Serbia and Montenegro. By 2008, both Montenegro and Kosovo had gained their independence.

The Kurds

Most Kurds are Sunni Muslims but are not Arabs. Millions of Kurds live in Turkey, Iraq, Iran, Armenia, and Syria. Kurds have experienced harsh treatment and repression, especially in Turkey and Iraq. Since 1920 they have tried to create an independent Kurdish state, with land from all these countries. In 2005, the Kurds became participants in the new Iraqi government. In early 2008, Kurdish Iraq was invaded by the Turkish military in an attempt to stop Kurdish rebel attacks in Turkey. This is one conflict that continues to hinder Turkey's relationship with Iraq and the European Union. The Kurds' relationship with the United States is strong, as the Kurdish fighters are working with the United States military to fight ISIS in Syria and Iraq.

International Hot Spots

Throughout the world, continuing international tensions have the potential to cause local and global violence.

North Korea and South Korea

North Korea, is still ruled by a hard-line communist dictatorship that practices a foreign policy of brinksmanship, and it suffers from isolation and severe economic hardships including recurring famine. South Korea has a strong global economy but North Korea still hopes to unite the two Koreas under its rule and so still spends large sums of money on its military. It has one of the world's largest standing armies, although it is thought to be poorly trained and equipped. In 2006, North Korea became a nuclear power. Despite international warnings, sanctions, and unproductive disarmament talks, North Korea has conducted several more nuclear tests. Over the years, tensions have escalated between North

Note Taking

Reading Skill:
Summarize
Make a concept web. Summarize information about the international tensions described in this section. Add more circles if needed.

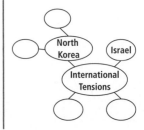

Preparing for the Regents

- Describe how isolation from the international economic community affects the people of North Korea.

and South Korea due to real or perceived hostile actions and verbal threats. When North Korea's longtime autocratic leader died, his son continued the militaristic government and policies of his father. He has made specific threats against South Korea and the United States, which has led to North Korea's continued political and economic isolation and the world's fear that it will take military, possibly nuclear, action. Since 2013, both military threats and new talks occurred between the two countries until North Korea once again violated UN agreements by test-firing medium-range missiles. Its actions sometimes affect the relationship between China and the United States. However, some analysts believe China is growing impatient with North Korea's erratic and embarrassing actions.

Israel and Its Neighbors

In 2005, when cease-fire talks began between Israel and the Palestinians, Israel began withdrawing settlers and soldiers from Gaza and parts of the West Bank. In a 2006 election, Palestinians elected **Hamas**, a party known for both its social services and its hard-line policies toward Israel. Hamas carried out its anti-Israeli policies using terrorists' methods, such as rockets and suicide bombings, to create chaos in Gaza before it assumed control.

To try to end Hamas's attacks, Israel and Egypt closed Gaza's borders. Economic sanctions destroyed the fragile Gaza economy, but a new economy developed using tunnels between Egypt and Gaza. In 2008, Israel launched a devastating attack on Hamas in Gaza. When it ended, much of Gaza was in ruins but Hamas remained in control. It reconciled with the less militant Fatah Party of the Palestinian Liberation Organization (PLO) to form a new joint Palestinian government for both Gaza and the West Bank. More recently individual young Palestinians with personal and financial problems have conducted uncoordinated attacks on Israeli citizens and security forces, especially in Jerusalem.

In 2011, the Palestinians asked the UN to give it full membership. Israel and its allies opposed this move, but in December 2012, the UN voted to give Palestine non-Member Observer State status. In 2015, Pope Francis recognized the Palestinian state.

Preparing for the Regents

Compare and contrast the factors affecting Israeli/Palestinian relations before 2005 with those affecting them more recently.

In recent years, Israel has lost support from its neighbors, such as Turkey. The downfall of President Mubarak of Egypt meant the loss of an ally. Because of the attacks on Gaza, which killed many women and children, Israel lost more international support. The war in Syria, one of Israel's most vocal enemies, leaves Israelis fearful of what will happen no matter who ends up in power. Israel fears a nuclear attack from Iran if its nuclear program is not stopped. Israel's isolation in the world has increased and peace talks have halted.

The Iraq War and its Aftermath

At the end of the Persian Gulf War, the United Nations required that Iraq destroy its nuclear, biological, and chemical weapons as well as its missiles. The UN sent inspection teams to ensure compliance until the late 1990s, when Iraq's leader, **Saddam Hussein,** refused to allow further inspections. In response, the United States and Britain staged air strikes against Iraq.

Saddam Hussein was a Sunni Muslim and his brutal dictatorship favored Sunnis while the majority of Iraqis are Shiite Muslims. These groups disagree on Iraq's culture, degree of westernization, and government.

In 2001, the United States accused Iraq of supporting terrorists, such as al Qaeda, and of hiding weapons of mass destruction. UN inspectors searched for these weapons, but found none. However, the grievances against Saddam Hussein included human rights abuses, such as the use of torture and poison gas against

Note Taking

Reading Skill:
Recognize Sequence
List the important events of the Iraq War. Record them in the order they occurred. Add boxes as needed.

Iraq War	
Date	Event

the Kurds. In March 2003, without UN support, the United States and its coalition forces invaded Iraq. Although the invasion led to a quick defeat of the Iraqi military, a violent insurgency developed against the coalition troops, the new Iraqi government, and workers repairing war damage. Saddam Hussein was captured in December 2003, convicted of crimes against humanity, and hanged.

In 2005, an Iraqi election took place amidst the violence. A new constitution was approved by voters and parliamentary elections were held. Sunnis, Shiites, and Kurds eventually agreed to a new government led by a compromise candidate, Nouri al-Maliki, as prime minister. In 2010, a second election with challenged results, more violence, and new alliances allowed Maliki to continue as prime minister. In 2011, the United States formally ended its military mission in Iraq. Subsequent elections did not bring factions together or provide the change necessary to make Iraq a safer place. Violence, including terrorism and battles sponsored by The Islamic State, combine with political divisions to leave this country torn by war and politics. Terrorist groups, such as those connected to Al Qaeda and the Islamic State, have a powerful presence in Iraq and deep ties to Syrian terrorists. Thousands of Iraqi civilians have died in car bombings and random killings in the unstable situation there.

Source: VIC HARVILLE/Stephens Media Group

Preparing for the Regents

• What political, religious, and social forces led the cartoonist to depict the Iraqi election in this way?

India and Pakistan

The long-standing hostility between India, with its Hindu majority, and Pakistan, with its Muslim majority, continued into the new century. Crises developed over control of Kashmir, a region divided between Pakistan and India; the 2001 Islamic terrorist attack on India's parliament; and the 2008 attacks on Mumbai by Pakistan-based terrorists. These crises raise fears of a nuclear conflict as both India and Pakistan have nuclear weapons. Relations between the two countries have improved and then disintegrated several times.

The Afghanistan War: Afghanistan and Pakistan

Soviet forces invaded Afghanistan in 1979 and supported a communist government there. More than three million Afghans fled, many to Pakistan. Afghan fighters resisted communist rule and finally forced the Soviets to withdraw. In the mid-1990s, the Taliban, a fundamentalist group, imposed an extreme form of Islam on Afghanistan. They also protected the terrorist group al Qaeda, which directed the 9/11 attacks on the United States in 2001.

Key Themes and Concepts

Belief systems
Some conflicts in Pakistan and Afghanistan are caused by differences in belief systems. Others are caused by a clash between modern and traditional values.

Vocabulary Builder

poppy—(PAHP ee) *n.* a plant that has brightly colored, usually red flowers and small black seeds

Key Themes and Concepts

Geography
The landscape of the region contributes to its cultural diversity and the continuing isolation of some cultural groups as well as limited communications and suffering due to frequent natural disasters.

In response to the 9/11 attacks, the United States launched an attack on Afghanistan that drove the Taliban from power. They sought al Qaeda's leaders, including Osama bin Laden. They were unsuccessful until 2011 when the Americans secretly located Osama bin Laden in Pakistan, and killed him. Because they did this without informing the Pakistani government, relations between the countries deteriorated.

In Afghanistan, the new remained weak and inconsistent, partly because of corruption, tribal loyalties, and the resentment of foreign intervention. Afghani's must also deal with a lack of modernization, land mines, thriving poppy fields that supply illegal opium, and a resurgence of the Taliban, al Qaeda and terrorists connected with the Islamic State.

Pakistan shares a mountainous border with Afghanistan. Violence, political problems, and tribal feuds are shared by both countries, and problems often spread back and forth between them. Neither country can control the border, and both countries resent United States' and NATOs military interference. The growing power and competition between terrorists in the region continues to create problems for both countries.

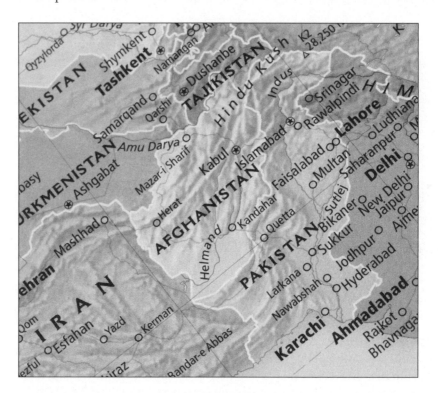

Since 2007, Pakistan's political stability has been shaky. Its former Prime Minister Benazir Bhutto returned from exile, only to be killed. It is suspected her death was planned by a Pakistani tribal leader with al Qaeda's help. The government failed to adequately respond to the devastating 2010 floods that displaced millions of Pakistanis. Aid from Islamic groups, such as the Taliban, and from the United States was necessary to rebuild the country's ruined infrastructure.

Terrorist bombings continue in both Pakistan and Afghanistan, but the goals of groups in these countries differ. In Afghanistan, the Taliban is trying to reassert its control over the government at the same time the Islamic State is terrorizing Afghani citizens in a Sunni against Shiite war. In Pakistan, terrorists focus on soft targets, such as hospitals and playgrounds. Many of these terrorists want to create a separate state in the northwest region of Pakistan. They are not after control of the whole country. Continuing attacks by the American military, especially by drones, on terrorist camps in Afghanistan and Pakistan along with the Pakistani government's reluctance to work against terrorists continues to weaken relations with the United States. Over the years, attacks by both terrorists and Americans have killed many Pakistani civilians, but many in the country depend on support and intervention by the United States.

President Obama changed the United States' military role in the region, several times. The use of unmanned drones has increased, as has the role of Afghani forces. Fewer countries provide military aid while the United States decided not to continue a full military withdrawal as it had planned. Peace talks between the Taliban and Afghan government have not yet lead to any positive outcomes.

Russia and Ukraine

Ukraine, located between Russia and Europe, has strong historic ties to Russia and was a republic in the Soviet Union Many Ukrainian residents considered themselves more Russian than Ukrainian. Most of these people live in eastern Ukraine and the Crimea. Ukraine leased its Crimean ports to Russia for its Black Sea fleet and gas pipelines run between Russia and Europe across Ukraine.

Key Themes and Concepts

Interdependence
Ukraine's conflict with Russia is causing economic consequences in Europe.

In 2013, Russia objected to a trade agreement between Ukraine and the EU. The agreement was never signed, but protests led to a government crackdown on protestors.

The conflict became more intense, protests more violent, and protestors took over government buildings. When the corrupt, pro-Russian president disappeared, Parliament stripped him of his powers and planned a presidential election. Then, Russia took over Ukraine's Crimean ports. Crimea declared its independence and voted to merge with Russia. Russia, eager to have total control of Crimea, immediately put Russian laws into effect.

The crisis continued to grow and pro-Russian separatists in eastern Ukraine took control of entire towns. Russia moved troops to the Ukraine border and vowed to protect ethnic Russians inside Ukraine. They challenged the Ukrainian military, which was smaller, weaker, and operating with older equipment.

Preparing for the Regents

Analyze how the Ukrainian crisis contains many issues similar to those causing conflict in other parts of the world: control of a region for economic or military advantage; people protesting poor and corrupt governments; economic control by a very rich few; overreliance on major powers; and language and ethnic divisions.

Other countries placed economic and travel sanctions on Russian and Ukrainian officials although EU countries worried that Russia would cut off their supply of natural gas. Ukrainian refugees fled to EU countries, such as Poland. NATO ended cooperative activities with Russia. Ukraine experienced violent protests and military actions. Its government remained corrupt and unsettled. In 2014, a passenger plane carrying 298 people was shot down over eastern Ukraine. Russia and NATO disagree about who fired the missile. A ceasefire was finally agreed upon and has held for several months. Changes to Ukraine's government encouraged its Western supporters, but Russian troops patrol the border and continue to control Crimea.

Sub-Saharan African Terrorism

Many sub-Saharan countries became independent in the 1960s, but their governments have continued to be corrupt, repressive, and unstable. Some countries divided into several or have continual turmoil because of the cultural, economic, or religious differences of their people. Many men from these regions join terrorist organizations because they are unhappy with the political instability, corruption, extremely high unemployment, and increasing problems due to urbanization and climate change. These issues and their local implications are critical factors for many terrorist groups.

In Northern Nigeria, Boko Haram began by wanting to create a region that followed strict Islamic law. Today, it kidnaps children, such as the 276 girls it kidnapped from a school in 2014. Victims like these are forced to become wives, suicide bombers, or to raid villages and kill the inhabitants. Because farmers flee the violence little is growing in the region. Terrorists must kidnap animals and steal grain to eat.

Like in Afghanistan, African terrorist groups like Boko Haram are hard to stop because they are not under the control of one leader. Individuals and local groups have their own methods, goals, and what they will accept to establish peace. The future of this region is troubled and unpredictable.

Efforts to Stop Terrorism

The attacks on New York and Washington, D.C., on September 11, 2001, alarmed government leaders everywhere. The attacks showed how terrorism affects the security and stability of all nations. At the same time, leaders recognized that defeating terrorism will require a lengthy effort. Some nations not accustomed to cooperating are working together, while a few still harbor or support terrorists. After the 2014 to 2016 terrorist attacks in Europe, Western governments realized they had to do more sharing of information. At the same time demonstrators across Europe joined together to show they were against terrorism as well as the loss of personal rights in that battle.

Summary

In many areas of the world, local conflicts threaten to become global struggles. The United Nations has intervened in various conflicts around the world to try to bring peace. It has also worked to promote human rights and bring relief to victims of famine and disaster. Terrorists use various tactics, such as bombings and kidnappings, to achieve their political goals. Terrorist activity creates a climate of fear and can lead to further violence. Ethnic and religious differences have sparked conflict in areas such as Northern Ireland and the Middle East. Terrorist attacks in one part of the world have led to long wars in other parts of the world, affecting neighboring countries and changing governments and alliances.

Key Themes and Concepts

Human Rights
Many countries have adopted anti-terrorism measures that sometimes violate the human rights of innocent citizens as well as terrorists.

Preparing for the Regents

Identify two causes of conflict in the world today.

1.

2.

Social Patterns and Political Change

Section Overview

Near the end of the twentieth century, modernization and industrialization created tensions. In some countries, these events have brought new opportunities to women; in others they have not. Excessive population growth is a problem facing many nations around the world today. Rapid urbanization is also a widespread change. Another trend is migration—people move to seek economic opportunity or political freedom.

Key Themes and Concepts

As you review this section, take special note of the following key themes and concepts:

Change What are the results of tension between tradition and modernization in societies today?

Culture What are the causes of overpopulation?

Urbanization What changes have resulted from the rapid urbanization that occurred in the late twentieth century?

Power How has modernization caused shifts in political power?

Movement of People and Goods How have changing patterns of migration created human rights issues?

Key Terms

As you review this section, be sure you understand the significance of these key terms:

westernization	urbanization	Arab Spring
overpopulation	shantytowns	human trafficking

Modernization and Tradition

In most societies, there is strain between the forces of modernization and those of tradition. This is especially true in non-Western societies. During the age of imperialism, modernization usually meant **westernization,** or the adoption of Western ways. Traditions were often weakened.

Many developing nations today work toward a balance between modernization and tradition. They want to embrace modern technology but preserve traditions and religious beliefs.

Japan

Japanese society has always been deeply traditional. The code of behavior that developed during feudal times gave each individual a very clear place in society. People had strictly defined duties toward each other. Families were patriarchal, or dominated by males. Individuals felt a strong sense of responsibility to their families or to a larger group. Personal desires mattered little. In modern Japan, many of these values survive, but create tensions with modern living.

The
Big Idea

In developing nations today, there are pressures for change.

- Strains between modernization and tradition have emerged.

- Overpopulation continues to be a difficult problem to solve.

- Urban areas have grown rapidly and produced social problems.

- People have migrated for better economic opportunities or more favorable political conditions.

Key People and Terms

For each of the key terms, write a sentence explaining its significance.

Key Themes and Concepts

Culture
Non-Western nations often want modern technology but do not want to lose completely their traditional culture and values.

Role of the Individual In the Japanese workplace, the sense of structure, duty, and individual sacrifice for the group remains strong. Japanese companies have always been based on teamwork. Although much was required of the worker, he or she had secure employment and was guaranteed advancement.

Recent economic difficulties, however, have weakened the Japanese economy and resulted in lost jobs. Devotion to the employer declined. At the same time, younger Japanese are less willing to sacrifice their personal lives for their jobs. Some Japanese are concerned about a weakening work ethic.

The Middle East

Muslim cultures of the Middle East are often traditional and place great importance on kinship ties and patriarchial families. Women are often subordinate to men and are expected to be modest and to remain secluded within their homes. In some conservative countries this includes the wearing of the **chador** in public, a kind of robe that completely covers the body and most of the face. Modernization and movement to cities have created tension regarding these traditions.

Great strains are clearly visible between the forces of westernization and tradition. Some Muslim countries, like Iran, have rejected Western values—though not Western technology. Some Muslims would like to abolish secular political systems and return to Islamic principles as a basis for government, including laws based on the Koran and Sharia.

Cultural strains in Saudi Arabia often stem from when many people moved to cities because of the oil industry. This weakened the traditional extended family structure. Some Saudi religious leaders worry about the influence of Western ideas, the place of women and their education in an Islamic society, and the effects of modern technology such as television and the Internet. Its conservative ruling family remains in control, but many Western ideas have taken hold in many areas. Because of global communications, Saudis are more aware of the freedoms available in other countries.

Urbanization

Urbanization, the movement of people to cities, is one of the most significant forces of social change, especially in the developing world.

Reasons for Urbanization

In developing countries, many people have moved to the cities to find jobs and escape the poverty of rural areas. Cities also offer other attractions, such as better health care, educational opportunities, stores, and modern conveniences.

Identify **Effects**

What are two effects of recent economic difficulties in Japan?

Vocabulary Builder

kinship—(KIN ship) *n.* a family relationship

Key Themes and Concepts

Change
Industrialization and urbanization are powerful agents of social change in developing nations. Traditional ways are often weakened in large industrial cities.

Percent of Population That Is Urban, 1950–2050

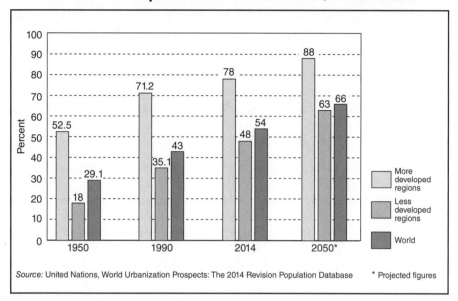

Source: United Nations, World Urbanization Prospects: The 2014 Revision Population Database   * Projected figures

Results of Urbanization
In the developing nations of Africa, South Asia, and Latin America, urbanization has had similar results.

Cultural Change In modern cities, people's traditional values and beliefs are often weakened. The caste system in India, for example, is not as strong in urban areas as in rural areas. Women have more opportunities in cities. Yet, some people feel cut off from their former communities and customs.

Poverty Those people who cannot afford to live in cities often settle nearby in **shantytowns,** areas of makeshift shacks that lack sewer systems, electricity, and other basic services. Their crowded conditions often lead to water pollution and other unhealthy effects. Lagos in Nigeria, Mumbai and Kolkata in India, and Mexico City in Mexico have been unable to cope with the waves of migration from rural areas.

Solving Urban Problems
Developing nations are trying to meet the needs that have resulted from urbanization. They sometimes rely on international relief organizations, such as the UN or the Roman Catholic Missionaries of Charity, founded by Mother Theresa in India. They must:

- Increase opportunities for education and better jobs

- Improve healthcare and working conditions

- Meet expanded demands on infrastructure: electricity, transportation, sewer and clean water

Human Rights
The global community has taken more notice of human rights abuses since World War II. The UN, various governments, and private nonprofit organizations work to ensure the rights of people all over the world. That hasn't stopped these abuses from happening.

Preparing for the Regents

Describe two problems that have resulted from urbanization in developing nations.

1.

2.

Key Themes and Concepts

Decision Making
Many social institutions, such as the family, religion, and education, change in developing nations in response to new urban problems.

Preparing for the Regents

- How do the background and political views of India's prime minister, Narendra Modi, reflect various urbanization and economic issues in India?

Note Taking

Reading Skill:
Identify Supporting Details
Make a chart. List details about the status of women before and after 1900 in various countries. What issues changed, and where? What issues didn't change, and where?

Status of Women		
Issue	What changed/ didn't change?	Where?

Vocabulary Builder

lucrative—(LOOK ruh tiv) *adj.* a job or activity that is lucrative lets you earn a lot of money

Status of Women

Women's status changed greatly in the 1900s in the West. Women gained the right to vote and entered the workforce in large numbers. Some developing countries have also expanded the role of women, while others have limited it.

In Japan, laws imposed after World War II ended some legal privileges given to Japanese males. Women gained many rights, including the right to vote. In the 1970s, they entered the workplace in great numbers. However, traditional views keep women in lower positions than men in the workplace. Few women have moved into higher-level jobs in business or government.

In the Middle East, the status of women varies greatly from country to country. Israel, for example, includes women in all facets of society, even as part of the military forces. Golda Meir was prime minister. The status of women in Muslim countries varies widely. In Turkey, Syria, and Egypt, many urban women gave up some traditional practices. In other countries, especially those with religious governments, such as Iran, women follow more traditional practices. In 2011, traditional Saudi Arabia granted women the right to vote and run for office in municipal elections but women are still unable to get a driver's license. However no matter what rights are granted to women, in some countries governments do not enforce them. The cultural attitudes toward women often remain traditional and sometimes repressive and abusive.

In most African and Southwest Asian nations, women won the right to vote when the countries gained independence, yet their social status often remains a subservient one. In rural areas, women traditionally work both at home and in the fields beside men. As men migrate to the cities to find work, women are left with more responsibilities. At the same time, women who go to the urban areas for jobs are both finding more freedom and are being attacked by men with traditional attitudes. In some societies, men who publicly gang rape, hang, or kidnap women are not seen as having committed a punishable crime. As these incidents become international news, international outrage grows and countries such as India and Pakistan are taking action.

Human Trafficking

One of the fastest-growing human rights issues in the world today is human trafficking. This is the recruiting and transporting of people for the purposes of slavery, forced labor, and servitude. Women are particularly at risk from sex trafficking. Criminals exploit the lack of opportunities these women have by promising them good jobs or opportunities to get an education. Then the victims are forced to become prostitutes. Thousands of children from Asia, Africa, and South America are sold into the global sex trade every year. Often they are kidnapped or orphaned, but sometimes they are actually sold by their own families to pay off debts or gain income. Other times they may be deceived about the prospects of training and a better life for their children. In West Africa, some trafficked children have lost one or both parents to the African AIDS crisis. Thousands of male (and sometimes female) children have been forced to be child soldiers. Trafficking is a fairly lucrative industry. In some areas, such as Russia, Eastern Europe, Hong Kong, Japan, and Colombia, trafficking is controlled by large criminal organizations.

Political Prisoners

Countries all over the world (developed, developing, and struggling) have been accused of human rights abuses in their treatment of political prisoners. Some prisoners were arrested for participating in protests. Others were accused of more serious crimes, like treason, even though they may only have joined an opposition party. In countries where the government tightly controls the media, such as in China and North Korea people do not have much freedom of speech. Once in prison, many of these people live in horrible conditions or solitary confinement, are used as forced labor, or undergo many hours of torturous questioning.

Arab Spring

Arab Spring is the period that began in Tunisia in December 2010, when a 26 year-old, college-educated street vendor set himself on fire to show his frustration with the government and police. This uprising's call for democratic changes spread across much of the Middle East via social media and the Internet.

- **Tunisia** This westernized North African country had a repressive government. Tunisian protests were photographed with cell phone cameras and sent around the world via the Internet. The protests spread quickly and the president fled the country. In October, 2011, Tunisia held its first free elections and elected a moderate Islamic party to run the country. Continuing tensions between ultraconservative Islamists and liberals have led to violent protests, a government crackdown on protestors, and a government promise for moderation. In 2014, after three years, the president lifted a "state of emergency" order.

- **Egypt** Social media played an important part in the revolution in Egypt, where more people use the Internet than in other Arab countries. Egyptians discussed their dissatisfaction with President Mubarak's government, and by 2011 videos and tweets calling for protest went viral. A Cairo protest was organized using Facebook®, Twitter®, and other social media, and spread quickly to other parts of the country. Within weeks, President Mubarak had resigned and the military had taken control of the government. This inspired people in other Middle Eastern countries to take action. In Egypt, demonstrations continued because many Egyptians feared the military would not relinquish power to elected officials. In 2012, Egyptians installed their first democratically elected parliament in 60 years, including many from the Muslim Brotherhood and ultraconservative Islamic parties. Mohamed Morsi of the Muslim Brotherhood was elected president. A year of popular protests centered on Egypt's poor economic conditions and political conflicts. These led to the Egyptian military forcing Morsi and the elected parliament out of office and making the Muslim Brotherhood illegal. The military arrested, tried, and convicted thousands of protesters, especially liberals and Islamists. A newly elected government is trying to control Egypt's economic and political instability.

- **Libya** Colonial Muammar Qaddafi led Libya for 40 years, the region's longest rule. Then, in February, 2011, protestors held a "Day of Rage" against his brutal regime. Qaddafi's violent reaction against protestors included the use of artillery, helicopter gunships, and antiaircraft missile launchers. A civil war erupted with rebels setting up a transitional government that won the support of the UN and many Western countries. When Qaddafi ignored the UN's call for an end to the violence against civilians, the Western alliance began bombing. They continued until Qaddafi fled and the transitional government took control. A few months later, a cell phone video went viral showing a humbled Qaddafi in the streets just before his death. But in 2016, rival governments, Islamic State terrorists, and battles within the city continued to plague the country. A UN-backed unity government has attempted to take control of the chaotic situation.

- **Yemen** Yemen, the poorest country in the Arab world, still has a strong traditional tribal culture. It was unified in 1990 but a violent struggle to create a separate South Yemen has created unrest. In 2011, new clashes, inspired by the

Preparing for the Regents

Compare and contrast the causes and events of Arab Spring in three different countries.

Vocabulary Builder

to go <u>viral</u>—(VAHY ruhl) *adj.* to spread an image or video very rapidly on the Internet or by e-mail

<u>secularist</u>—(SEK yoo lahr ist) *n.* someone who believes religion should not be part of government

Preparing for the Regents

- How do the events of Arab Spring show that modern technology is changing the culture in Middle Eastern countries?

Note Taking

Reading Skill:
Identify Supporting Details
List three ways social media helped create the events of Arab Spring.

Preparing for the Regents

• Compare and contrast the governments of these countries before Arab Spring. What was the relationship of each to their people?

events of Arab Spring, forced the resignation of the president of 33 years. Although deep divisions remain, many discussions are taking place between all sides. Since the 1990s, a branch of Al Qaeda in southern Yemen has been tied to terrorist attacks around the world. Yemen is working with the United States to combat the Al Qaeda threat and to train new government forces.

Country	Unique Elements to Arab Spring
Tunisia	• First uprising • Elected moderate Islamic government
Egypt	• Influential country, so uprising inspired others • Protests planned using Internet and social media • Competition for power between Islamists, secularists, and military
Libya	• Use of heavy military weapons against protestors led to bombing by Western countries • Leader Colonel Muammar Qaddafi killed by rebels
Syria	• Religious division between the majority of Syrians and those in power • Russia supports the government • Violence against demonstrators and towns where demonstrations were held • Refugees fleeing country and military shelling refugee camps in other countries • Becoming isolated from neighbors
Yemen	• Poorest Arab country • Division between north and south • South Yemen is home to a branch of Al Qaeda

Adapted from cia.gov

The events of Arab Spring touched other countries in the Middle East, as well. In some, divisions were exposed, refugees drained already shaky economies, or new political partnerships were formed. Some countries are becoming more isolated from their Arab neighbors and their traditional trade partners in the West. Arab Spring also revealed how much the world is changing due to modern communications technology.

Syria

Syria's civil war began as an incident during Arab Spring in March, 2011. It quickly turned violent when the repressive government responded to demonstrations and rebels with tanks, massacres and chemical weapons. Syria's religious divide adds a unique dimension. The government and well-armed military are controlled by Alawite Muslims, who compose only about 12 percent of the country's population. The opposition is a fragmented group that includes various Islamic conservatives, mostly members of Syria's Sunni majority. Some countries have recognized the opposition, but it is so splintered, its members cannot agree on a course of action against the government and its forces. The government forces are being supported and supplied by Russia, Iran, and Hezbollah (a powerful Lebanese Shiite military and political party). The UN has not been able to initiate lasting ceasefires or peace talks but the Syrian government finally did agree to turn over its chemical weapons to the UN for destruction. Tensions between Syria and its neighbors, Israel and Turkey, are very high. Heavy bombing of the opposition forces by the Russians to support government troops and Russian insistence that the government remain in power has made the civil war an international issue.

Key Themes and Concepts

Power
The Islamic State in Iraq and Syria (ISIS) is also called the Islamic State (IS) because its government is based only on Islamic law. It treats those who do not agree with them or who work against them with increasing violence and cruelty. Its power comes from the strength of its followers' beliefs and the fear it creates in anyone else.

The Islamic State and Terrorism

One opposition group in Syria, the Islamic State, has had many names including Islamic State in Iraq and Syria (ISIS). It broke away from al Qaeda because it was so violent and rigid. ISIS declared its own Islamic state incorporating parts of both Syria and Iraq but it has spread terrorism internationally. Its extreme tactics are often used against westerners, Shiites, and those of religions other than Islam. But their suicide bombings often target places where people gather and so kill without discrimination. Because its members are Sunni, they have support from Sunnis in many countries. However, Shiite governments and their Western allies, are joining forces to stop ISIS. Religion, rigid and competing traditional attitudes, and westernization are mixing in new ways in response to these latest threats.

The Islamic State has trained many terrorists who come to them from across the world. Their training camps in North Africa and Syria are targets for Western bombings. Terrorist acts in Africa, Libya, France, Belgium, and the United States have been caused by individuals or groups trained by the Islamic State, but not planned by a central organization. This makes them harder to investigate and prevent.

Patterns of Global Migration

Migration has grown due to economics, politics, and conflicts. There are always economic migrants, but a huge flood of migrants is arriving in Europe after fleeing war-torn and terrorized countries, like Mali, Afghanistan, Syria, and Iraq. Not since World War II has Europe had this many immigration and refugee issues.

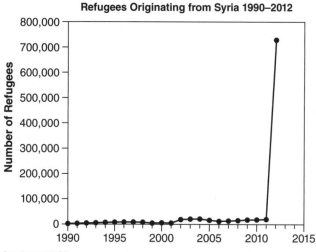

Refugees Originating from Syria 1990–2012

Data from: UNHCR

This huge wave of political and economic refugees and immigrants is surging toward Europe to escape the violence. They walk overland through the Balkans or pay human traffickers huge amounts to smuggle them across the Mediterranean into Greece or Italy. Thousands die when boats, loaded with many more people than they can safely hold, sink. Many end up in refugee camps, but most want to move on and resettle in Germany, France, or Sweden.

Europeans help the immigrants with food, housing and jobs, but some resent them. Some countries, like Hungary, have closed their borders. Others put a limit on how many people they will accept for resettlement. Many Europeans fear that trained terrorists will arrive among the starving women and children. Others fear the social, cultural, and economic changes that occur with the immigrants. Similar tensions are occurring in Southeast Asia and North America.

Summary

As nations in the developing world have modernized, tensions between modern and traditional ways of living and thinking have emerged. Dissatisfaction with the ruling political system has created violence and change. Women have gained new rights and roles in some nations, but they have been kept in traditional roles in others. Throughout the developing world, there has been an increased use of technology including the media. This has spread political and economic ideas faster than repressive governments can control them. Although urbanization has created more opportunities for some individuals, cities find it difficult to provide basic services for a quickly increasing population. People migrate to seek better economic opportunities and to try to escape violence and political repression. These migrations produce their own tension and violence.

Preparing for the Regents

- To what extent are current migrations similar to earlier migrations? How are they different?

Science and Technology

Section Overview

In the last half of the twentieth century, science and technology have brought great changes. These changes are continuing today. The Green Revolution increased the food supply in developing countries. Computers and advances in telecommunications have brought an explosion of information and, with it, a greater need for education. Technology has allowed exploration of space. Medical breakthroughs have brought better health and longer life.

Key Themes and Concepts

As you review this section, take special note of the following key themes and concepts:

Science and Technology How did science and technology change life in the last half of the twentieth century?

Change What social and economic changes are being produced by the Computer Revolution?

Interdependence In what ways is the world more interdependent than ever before?

Key Terms

As you review this section, be sure you understand the significance of these key terms:

Green Revolution	Information	genetic engineering
Computer Revolution	Revolution	clone
Internet	literacy	AIDS

The Green Revolution

Increasing the Food Supply

Throughout the 1900s, scientists applied technology in a number of ways to increase food production.

- **Irrigation** Farmers installed pumps to bring water from far below the surface of the earth and used other irrigation systems to distribute water.

- **Machinery** Farmers used machines, especially those powered by gasoline and diesel fuel, to increase yields from their land.

- **Fertilizer and Pesticides** Farmers enriched their soil with fertilizers and eliminated insect pests with pesticides.

- **New Varieties of Grains and Livestock** Scientists developed new, hardier grains and bred livestock that produced more meat or milk.

In the 1960s, farmers in developing countries applied some of these methods to increase their production of wheat and rice. Their efforts were so successful that the result was called the Green Revolution. In some countries, such as India and Indonesia, the Green Revolution doubled food output.

The Big Idea

Science and technology have brought great change as:

- new agricultural methods increase the food supply.

- people are able to obtain, process, and transmit information more quickly than ever before.

- nations are exploring space.

- medical breakthroughs are improving the quality of life.

Key People and Terms

Place each of the key terms into one of these categories: technology or medicine.

Preparing for the Regents

- What were the benefits and limitations of the Green Revolution?

Limits of the Green Revolution

The Green Revolution increased the food supply, but it did not solve the problems of world hunger and poverty. In some regions, population is still growing faster than food production. Also, technology has limitations. A region has to have enough water to start with to support new irrigation techniques. Also, irrigation systems, chemical fertilizers, and pesticides cost money that developing nations of the global South do not have. Poorer farmers usually cannot afford these innovations, and some have been forced off their land. Recently scientists have developed genetically modified food as another way to combat world hunger. Critics of this technology claim that malnutrition and hunger are often the result of politics that prevent food from reaching hungry people rather than lack of food. They say such foods are too expensive and that long-term effects of eating such foods are unknown.

The Information Age

The Computer Revolution

Probably the most revolutionary development since the mid-1900s is the computer. The first computers were enormous machines that filled a large room and worked slowly. After the invention of the silicon chip, computers were miniaturized. Computers have allowed people to obtain, process, and distribute information very quickly. Businesses today depend on computers for their accounting, word processing, ordering, and many other systems. This increase in the use of computers is often called the Computer Revolution. Today, access is more often on mobile devices, such as tablets and cell phones. New ways of providing access to the Internet for those who do not have it has become a priority.

The Information Revolution

The rapid spread of information, which began in the 1950s and increases with each passing year, is sometimes referred to as the **Information Revolution.** In the 1990s, the Internet began as a growing computer network that linked individuals, governments, and businesses all over the world. At first, people linked to the Internet through the telephone. Later, they connected by cable or with wireless devices, such as cell phones.

People use the Internet to communicate and do business more rapidly than ever before. The move to wireless and satellite technology has made the Internet available to people who previously were not able to be "connected."

At the same time access became easier, greater amounts of information became available. Facts, ideas, and opinions are openly discussed on websites, in emails, and on social media sites, such as Facebook®. Shopping, researching, gaming, and sharing are common activities. E-readers and tablets offer books that had been previously unavailable.

This access to information has had unexpected results. In 2010, many U.S. military and diplomatic files were published on the Internet by WikiLeaks. Disputes over the arrest or asylum of the WikiLeaks founder has created an international incident involving Great Britain, Ecuador, Sweden, and the United States. In 2009, many Iranians protested the results of their presidential election. Information and images from their protests and the government's violent response were sent all over the world via Internet-based sites such as Twitter® and YouTube®. Iranian authorities tried to limit Internet access, but the postings continued and soon contained ways to use social media to organize and take action. These events were duplicated during Arab Spring, as the protestors in one country learned about protests in other countries from the Internet and emails, and then organized their own demonstrations, often using Facebook and Twitter. Like Iran, most governments tried to control Internet access, but failed as protests continued and governments fell.

Daily Life

New technology is affecting many parts of our daily life. Besides easy access to the Internet, wireless communications allow safer driving and even self-drive cars.

3D printing is developing quickly. It will allow goods to be made closer to the consumer, changing manufacturing. It will also allow for much more customization of goods. It may revolutionize manufacturing, the global economy, and even some aspects of healthcare.

Literacy and Education

The Information Revolution has had a great impact on both education and the job market in the global North. In these nations, there has been a gradual decline in the number of jobs in industry and agriculture. New jobs are often based on information and communications services. Such jobs require more education and new types of learning, especially about technology.

Gains continue to be made throughout the world in **literacy,** the ability to read and write. Developing countries have recognized that economic and social progress depends in part on having a literate population. For this reason, most nations of the world provide—and, in fact, require—education through at least age 14. Some emerging economies, such as China and India, have encouraged technology-based businesses. Factories in China build computers and cell phones. Businesses in India provide technological support to technology users in more developed countries.

Preparing for the Regents

- Why is education so important to progress in today's world?

New Technology: Benefits and Limits

Technology	Benefits (+)	Limits (−)
The Computer and Information Revolutions	• Creates new jobs • Links people, businesses, and nations • Makes more information available	• Threatens some jobs • Available only to those who can afford equipment • Widens gap between those with power and those without
Medical breakthroughs	• Prevents illnesses • Wipes out diseases • Increases life span	• Available only to nations and people who can afford them • Presents new problems of quality of life and care of the aged
Revolution in agriculture (The Green Revolution)	• Increases food production • Develops new food products	• May succeed only where rainfall is regular • Requires costly chemicals • High cost may force out small farmers

Summarize

Write a summary statement about the benefits and limits of new technology.

The Space Age

Space Exploration

The space age began in the late 1950s with a space race between the United States and the Soviet Union. In recent years the United States and Russia have cooperated on joint space ventures. At the permanent International Space Station scientific experiments are done by astronauts from many countries who stay in space longer and longer. Humans have walked on the moon; space probes have sent back huge amounts of information from Mars and other planets. The United States' space shuttle program ended in 2011, but private companies and countries (such as China, India, and Japan) have established successful space programs.

Satellites

A satellite is an object that is launched into orbit around the Earth, usually for observation or telecommunications purposes. Satellites can be used to:

- map and forecast weather
- navigate in ships and aircraft
- monitor changes in the natural environment
- aid in rapid worldwide communications

Satellites are used to transmit television and telephone signals globally. Signals are transmitted from one point on Earth to the satellite. The satellite transmits the signals to another point on Earth. This technology allows rapid reporting of events happening anywhere in the world.

Medical Technology

Since 1945, medical science has achieved amazing successes. Throughout the world, people are living longer, infant mortality rates are lower, and people can enjoy a better quality of life.

Key Themes and Concepts

Science, Technology and Innovation
Ethics are values or moral standards. Scientific and technological innovations such as genetic engineering have caused ethical conflicts for some people. Many times these innovations must be reconciled with belief systems before they are accepted.

Important Advances

- **Antibiotics** Scientists have developed antibiotics to treat diseases.
- **Vaccines** Vaccines have wiped out diseases such as smallpox and prevented the spread of many other diseases. New vaccines are being researched and used.
- **Transplants** Surgeons developed and gradually improved procedures for the transplanting of organs to save lives.
- **Laser Surgery** Lasers, devices that make use of concentrated beams of light, have made surgery safer.
- **New Treatments** New ways to treat deadly problems, such as strokes, are being taught to doctors and hospitals. Sometimes these involve new machines or new medicines. Other times they involve new diagnostic procedures to correctly treat a patient.
- **New Medications** New medicines are being used to cure or slow the spread of many diseases and incurable ailments. Computers often help to design them.
- **New Diagnostic Procedures** New ways have been invented to identify what is wrong with someone use genes, blood, and other bodily samples.
- **New Medical Devices** New technological devices are being designed for people who have lost limbs or need help with some bodily function.

Difficult Challenges

- **Genetic Engineering** The process of genetic engineering, which involves changing the chemical codes carried by living things, holds promise for creating new drugs and curing disease. In 1997, the first **clone,** or exact genetic replica of an organism, was announced. Genetic engineering is controversial, however, because it has raised questions about how far science should go to change or create life.
- **New Epidemics** Challenges to medicine have arisen in recent decades. After the 1980s, the disease called **AIDS** (acquired immunodeficiency syndrome) resulted in millions of deaths. Scientists continue to search for a cure for it. Other epidemics include the pneumonic and bubonic plagues in southern India in 1994. Avian influenza (bird flu) spread from birds to humans across the world. Since the virus mutates easily, new outbreaks occur, as in China in 2013. In 2009, a flu virus created a pandemic by spreading throughout the world. Procedures to deal with a pandemic were tested. By mid-2010, over 18,000

Note Taking

Reading Skill:
Summarize
Make a concept web. Complete it with information about the challenges of medical technology. Add more circles if needed.

Challenges of Medical Technology

people were known to have died from this flu. This pandemic revealed problems: rich countries with a surplus of vaccine, and poor countries were without the necessary vaccine. A cholera epidemic in Haiti was the largest outbreak in the world, with hundreds of thousands sick and over 7,000 dead from the disease. A vaccine exists, but did not reach the people who needed it. The 2014 Ebola epidemic affected several countries in West Africa. The interconnectedness of modern life was highlighted when people outside these countries were also diagnosed with Ebola. They had been in the African countries or were healthcare workers and carried the disease with them to other countries. New methods for identifying and fighting an epidemic were in place, but these did not stop the disease before it caused many deaths and affected both international travel and healthcare in distant countries such as the United States.

- **Drug-Resistant Microbes** The widespread use of antibiotics has allowed some types of microbes to become resistant to drugs. Certain diseases that the medical community thought were under control, such as tuberculosis, are becoming a threat again.

- **Destruction of Tropical Rain Forests** The world's tropical rain forests are the source of many medicinal plants. As these forests are being destroyed, scientists worry that valuable drugs in use today, as well as new ones that might have been discovered later, will be lost.

Summary

Better food production, an explosion in information and communication, the exploration of space, and medical breakthroughs have changed the world. In many ways, science and technology have benefited people's lives. Many problems, however, remain to be solved.

The Environment

The Big Idea

Today, the world faces many important environmental issues and concerns. These include:

- pollution.
- deforestation.
- endangered species.
- desertification.
- nuclear safety.

Key People and Terms

What do four of the key terms have in common? Explain.

Preparing for the Regents

Describe the possible causes and impacts of the following environmental problems.

Acid rain:

Depletion of the ozone layer:

Global warming:

Section Overview

Many global environmental issues arose in the twentieth century. Pollution of water, land, and air threatens the health of all living things. Forests are being destroyed, species are disappearing, and deserts are growing. The safety of nuclear power plants and of nuclear waste disposal methods are additional environmental concerns.

Key Themes and Concepts

As you review this section, take special note of the following key themes and concepts:

Environment and Society What environmental problems exist today?

Interdependence How do these issues affect people globally?

Decision Making How are nations working together to make decisions that will solve environmental problems?

Key Terms

As you review this section, be sure you understand the significance of these key terms:

pollution	ozone layer	deforestation
acid rain	greenhouse effect	desertification
fossil fuels		

Pollution and Climate Change

Pollution is the contamination of the environment, including air, water, and soil. Pollution is harmful to humans as well as to plants and other animal life. It takes many forms. Factories and automobiles release gases and soot into the air. These substances can cause respiratory disease. They can even block sunlight, causing plants to grow more slowly. Water can become polluted by human wastes, fertilizers, pesticides, and toxic chemicals. These substances may lead to the development of cancers or even cause death. For this reason, many nations have set standards for both air and water quality.

In many developing countries, such as China and India, the rush to create a strong economy overrides pollution concerns. The impact of rapid industrialization and the accompanying urban growth often create a pollution crisis. Beijing and other cities in China are experiencing air pollution that is a thick, fog-like pollution. Thousands are dying from related respiratory diseases, plants are stunted, and tourism is suffering. The winds are blowing the pollution across the Pacific Ocean and it is affecting the western United States.

Air Pollution and Acid Rain

Acid rain occurs when rain falls through air that is polluted by the burning of fossil fuels. **Fossil fuels** include coal, oil, and natural gas. Factories, automobiles, and other sources release these chemicals. Acid rain damages forests, lakes, and farmland. Because of winds, air pollution in one part of the world can cause acid rain in another. International agreements have been signed to reduce emissions of the substances that cause acid rain.

Depletion of the Ozone Layer

Some scientists are concerned about depletion of the ozone layer, a layer of gases high in the atmosphere that protects the Earth from the dangerous ultraviolet rays of the sun. This layer is becoming thinner, perhaps because of the use of chlorofluorocarbons (CFCs) and other chemical pollutants. Depletion of the ozone layer could expose people to more solar radiation and result in increased skin cancer and eye disease. Ultraviolet rays might also damage crops and marine life. Many developed countries have agreed to eliminate production and use of CFCs and other harmful substances. In 2002, a scientific organization found that these limitations were helping reduce harmful pollutants.

Climate Change and Global Warming

Scientists are also concerned about a gradual rise in global temperatures. Since 1998, the world has experienced many of the warmest years on record. Many places around the world had their hottest temperatures ever measured. Abnormal cold was found in other places, such as Europe. Many scientists believe that this phenomenon is caused by the **greenhouse effect,** in which warm air becomes trapped in the lower atmosphere by CO_2, or carbon dioxide. The percentage of CO_2 in the air has been rapidly rising. Possible causes are the use of CFCs, the burning of fossil fuels, and the destruction of forests. This overall warming and related extreme weather events affect agriculture and cause coastal flooding as polar icecaps melt. In 2010, the arctic sea-ice was at the lowest level on record.

Climate change seems to be causing extreme events that affect people: destructive floods in Pakistan, Thailand, and Australia; droughts in the Amazon and Africa; and heat waves and record cold and snowfalls in Europe and Russia. Not only do these events kill people, but they destroy their ability to supply their basic needs. Rebuilding is often slow, especially in poor nations or those at war.

Since 1997, at UN meetings on global warming, attendees agreed to set limits on emissions that are thought to contribute to climate change. Those that emit the most, the United States and China, have not kept to limits. At the 2015 Climate Change Conference, almost 200 countries agreed to cooperate to limit climate change, preserve forests, and work to hold down unnecessary temperature increases.

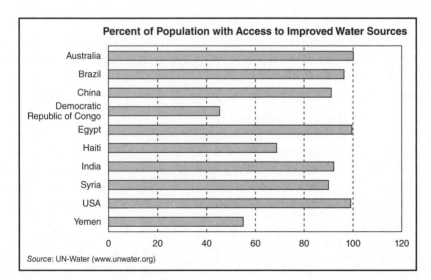

Source: UN-Water (www.unwater.org)

Identify Supporting Details

What role has the UN played in solving the problems of:

• climate change?

• clean water?

• deforestation?

Preparing for the Regents

• Describe how climate change has affected the availability of water for people to use.

• What parts of the world are presently most affected by climate change?

• Are these the same areas that are affected by water issues?

Scarcity of Clean Water

Approximately one billion people worldwide lack access to clean water, many because of population growth, pollution, and climate change. In developing countries, the lack of clean water is linked to diseases such as malaria. Where nations share lakes and rivers, such as in Israel and Jordan, disputes over pollution or water supplies could lead to war. The deadly cholera epidemic in Haiti that began in 2010 was traced directly to a river polluted with raw sewage. Private industry and organizations such as the United Nations are developing clean water technologies, improving water quality, and ensuring people's access to clean water.

Deforestation

Deforestation is the destruction of forests, especially tropical rain forests. Deforestation is usually caused by development as nations harvest lumber or clear land to raise crops, graze cattle, or build homes. Some estimate that the world is losing more than 50 million acres of tropical forest each year. Brazil, India, and Indonesia are the nations where forests are disappearing at the highest rate.

Effects of Deforestation

The effects of deforestation include changes in local weather patterns, a buildup of carbon dioxide in the atmosphere (which may lead to the greenhouse effect), soil erosion, and extinction of certain plants and animals.

Global Solutions

Many of the world's great forests are in developing nations. These nations need the income that would come from using deforested land for agriculture. Those who want to save the forests say that the economic needs of developing nations must be balanced against needs of the global population. Many nations debated these and other environmental problems at the 1992 UN-sponsored Earth Summit in Rio de Janeiro, Brazil. In 2008, the Brazilian government announced a new policy to reduce the rate of the deforestation of its rainforest.

Desertification

Causes and Effects

Desertification is the changeover from arable land (land that can be farmed) into desert. Desertification is caused mostly by human activity, especially the following:

- **Overgrazing** by livestock, such as sheep and cattle, eliminates the grasses that hold the soil together to prevent erosion.
- **Cutting down forests** robs the land of another barrier to soil erosion.

As grass and trees are eliminated, the soil loses its nutrients. Without plant roots to hold the soil, wind erosion removes the fertile topsoil. The land is then unable to sustain plant life. The Sahara in Africa, for example, is expanding at the rate of about 50 miles per year. The expansion of deserts is one cause of famine.

Controlling Desertification

Methods to control desertification include restricting livestock (to prevent overgrazing) and the planting of new trees to act as a barrier against erosion. These solutions are difficult to put into practice in developing countries, where farmers try to work as much land as possible. However, new farming methods, including improved irrigation, may help solve the problem.

Vocabulary Builder

erosion—(ee ROH zhun) *n.* the process by which something is gradually reduced or destroyed

Key Themes and Concepts

Needs and Wants
The economic progress of some developing countries conflicts with protecting the environment. Sometimes international pressure and economic support are used to help a developing country protect its environment and still continue to develop a strong economy.

Preparing for the Regents

- Why are cooperative solutions needed for international problems such as drug trafficking, deforestation, and the preservation of endangered species?

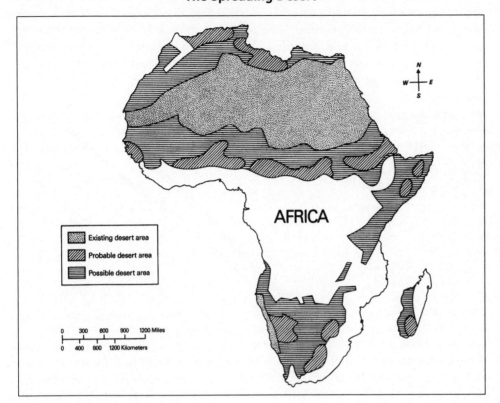

AFRICA

Existing desert area

Probable desert area

Possible desert area

0   300   600   900   1200 Miles

0   400   800   1200 Kilometers

The Spreading Desert
Desertification is a major problem in Africa, especially in the Sahel region just south of the Sahara Desert. Here, there has been a large loss of farmland and pastures.

Preparing for the Regents

Practice your map skills by answering these questions.

1. Where in Africa is the largest area of existing desert?

2. If desertification continues, what social conditions might result?

Endangered Species

Problems and Effects

A problem related to deforestation is the endangerment of various species of plants and animals. Various by-products of development—the clearing of land, the damming of waterways, and many types of pollution—all threaten to wipe out species of plants and animals.

If species are lost, the balance of the ecosystem of the world could be damaged severely. In addition, resources that people use for food and medicines may disappear.

Global Solutions

Several international agreements have attempted to address the topic of endangered species. Some agreements, for example, have banned the shipment and sale of endangered animals. Some people have suggested that these species can best be protected through preserving their habitats. The 1992 Earth Summit addressed this issue. Other agreements have been made about specific animals, such as whales and tuna, which have been endangered by commercial fishing and other economic practices.

Natural Disasters

Just as climate disasters affect people, so do natural disasters, such as volcanic activity. In 2010, a volcano in Iceland erupted and sent clouds of ash over Europe, stopping air traffic for weeks.

Earthquakes can cause untold disaster, no matter how prepared a country might be. Unprepared Haiti lost much of its capital city and much of the country's infrastructure in a 2010 earthquake. After several years, Haiti is still rebuilding,

Preparing for the Regents

• How do natural disasters affect governments, economies, and social structures?

hundreds of thousands still live in temporary camps, agriculture has not recovered, and a cholera epidemic has killed thousands. The much more prepared Japan had many earthquake-resistance standards in place, but was hit by one of the largest earthquakes ever recorded. The quake and resulting tidal wave swept away thousands of people, buildings, and farmland and caused one of the world's worst nuclear disasters.

Nuclear Proliferation

The use of nuclear energy and the proliferation, or spread, of nuclear weapons pose serious potential threats to the global environment.

Nuclear Accidents

In 1986, an accident at the Chernobyl nuclear power plant in the Soviet Union exposed people and crops to deadly radiation. Radiation was also blown across countries in Europe. This accident led to heightened concern about safe use of nuclear energy, but in spite of more regulations, another nuclear disaster happened.

Before 2011, one-third of Japan's electricity came from nuclear power plants. Then, a powerful earthquake sent a huge tsunami across part of Japan, including the Fukushima Daiichi Nuclear Power Station. Due to the water damage, the nuclear power plant experienced explosions, radiation leaks, contaminated water leaks, and partial meltdowns. Eventually, after a huge evacuation, most people were allowed to return home, if their home still remained standing. The reactor is so badly damaged and unstable that it will take many years before it can be completely sealed. Surprisingly, there was little immediate effect on people's health, but it did take a toll on the mental state of many. During the following year, Japan took almost all its nuclear reactors offline. By mid-2013, only two had been restarted.

Note Taking

Reading Skill:
Identify Supporting Details
Make a word web. List the dangers of nuclear energy. Add boxes as you need them.

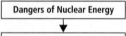

Key Themes and Ideas

Decision Making
Economics often play a role in a developing country's decision to build and maintain nuclear energy plants and nuclear weapons, and how they dispose of nuclear waste.

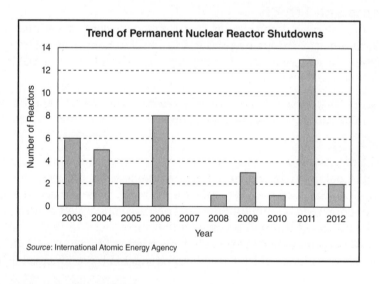

Trend of Permanent Nuclear Reactor Shutdowns

Source: International Atomic Energy Agency

Nuclear Waste Disposal

Dangers are also posed by nuclear waste that is created by nuclear weapons production facilities. Nuclear waste is radioactive and remains that way for many years. Exposure to high levels of radioactivity is very harmful to humans. Earlier methods of disposing of nuclear waste included dumping it at sea or burying it in deep wells. Both of these methods have been banned by the international community. Within nations and across the globe, solutions are being sought for the safe disposal of nuclear waste. Effective cleanup of nuclear waste is expensive, however. This expense makes other solutions more attractive for many nations.

Nuclear Weapons

As the 1900s ended, the United States and Russia controlled over 90 percent of the world's nuclear weapons. China, Britain, France, India, and Pakistan were also publicly declared nuclear powers. It was widely accepted that Israel had a small, undeclared nuclear arsenal.

Several nations gave up their nuclear weapons in the 1990s. South Africa dismantled its nuclear weapons. The nuclear missiles stationed in the former Soviet republics of Belarus, Kazakhstan, and Ukraine were returned to Russia.

While tensions between the major nuclear powers have eased since the end of the Cold War, a continuing concern is that regional conflicts, such as the dispute between India and Pakistan, could escalate into a nuclear exchange. North Korea continues to test nuclear bombs although it offers to restart talks under certain conditions at the same time it threatens to launch rockets at South Korea and the United States. It continues to be an unstable nuclear threat and to shroud its nuclear activities in secrecy.

Iran also had a nuclear program which it claims is for developing nuclear material to use to generate electricity and for medical uses. However, the Middle East is an unpredictable region and Iran has threatened countries like Israel and the United States. In 2012, the UN, the United States, and the EU placed sanctions on Iran for its continued nuclear activity. Iran, in turn, threatened to close the Strait of Hormuz, a critical shipping lane for oil exports. Israel threatened to bomb the Iranian nuclear facilities, as they see Iran's program as a major threat to its security. Then, in 2013, a new, more moderate Iranian government agreed to temporarily halt its nuclear program. In 2015, Iran signed an agreement to limit its nuclear research, rid itself of some uranium, and submit to inspections. In exchange, the severe economic sanctions will be lifted.

This brought an end to some nuclear tensions, but another dangerous possibility looms over the world. That threat is that a terrorist group could obtain nuclear weapons.

Summary

Nations are working together to resolve the environmental issues that face the global community. These issues include air and water pollution, global warming, deforestation, desertification, and nuclear safety. Weather, climate disasters, and natural disasters often affect human activity, and the world continually reacts to them. Sometimes making decisions involves balancing the protection of the environment with the needs of individual nations. Only with global cooperation, however, will these problems be solved.

Make Inferences

Why might the United States and Russia not want to give up their nuclear weapons? Why might less developed countries, like North Korea, want them?

Preparing for the Regents

Analyze the economic, military, and political factors that led to the nuclear treaty with Iran. Determine how a successful implementation would affect these factors. What do countries that did not sign the treaty think of it?

Preparing for the Regents

How do environmental issues—both problems and solutions—demonstrate the interdependence of the modern world?

Multiple Choice

Directions: Review the Test-Taking Strategies section of this book. Then answer the following questions, drawn from actual Regents examinations. For each statement or question, choose the *number* of the word or expression that, of those given, best completes the statement or answers the question.

Base your answer to question 1 on the graph below and on your knowledge of social studies.

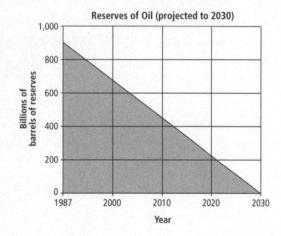

Reserves of Oil (projected to 2030)

1 Which action will help slow the trend indicated by the graph?

   (1) expanding Green Revolution technology
   (2) increasing industrialization in developing countries
   (3) using alternative energy sources
   (4) lowering worldwide oil prices

2 Bombings, kidnappings, and hijackings are tactics most often used by

   (1) imperialists
   (2) terrorists
   (3) nationalists
   (4) absolutists

3 Economic development in Latin American nations has been hindered most by

   (1) a scarcity of goods produced for trade and a lack of natural resources
   (2) governments that are primarily concerned with preserving the environment
   (3) problems of overpopulation, patterns of land distribution, and a lack of investment capital
   (4) corporations that are not interested in the use of modern technology

4 Which is the major reason that the United Nations has often been unsuccessful in solving international disputes?

   (1) The United Nations does not have sufficient funds to act.
   (2) The disputing nations are usually not members of the United Nations.
   (3) National sovereignty stands in the way of international cooperation.
   (4) The United Nations charter does not provide a means to settle disputes.

5 Since 1990, people in Timor, Kosovo, and Kurdish Iraq have all protested their lack of

   (1) membership in the European Union
   (2) economic stability
   (3) independent homelands
   (4) representation in the Arab League

6 In many developing nations, rising levels of pollution and continued housing shortages are a direct result of

   (1) increased urbanization
   (2) a reliance on single-crop economies
   (3) changing climatic conditions
   (4) increasing nationalism

7 In Middle Eastern societies, women have increasingly been at the center of a conflict between the forces of modernization and the

(1) values of traditional Islamic culture

(2) pressure for a Palestinian homeland

(3) shortage of capital for industrial development

(4) need to reduce the birthrate

8 The major goal of the Green Revolution has been to

(1) decrease the use of modern farm machinery

(2) decrease population growth

(3) increase agricultural output

(4) increase the number of traditional farms

9 A valid statement about the technology in the 1900s is that technology has

(1) eliminated famine and disease throughout the world

(2) delayed economic progress in developing countries

(3) led to the adoption of free trade policies

(4) accelerated the pace of cultural diffusion

10 A study of the accident at the Chernobyl nuclear power plant in the Soviet Union and of the severe air pollution in Mexico City would lead to the conclusion that

(1) technology can cause problems throughout the world

(2) international trade is more profitable than domestic commerce

(3) modern science cannot solve most political problems

(4) agricultural nations have caused major world environmental problems

11 A major environmental problem affecting Latin America, sub-Saharan Africa, and Southeast Asia has been

(1) air pollution

(2) deforestation

(3) disposal of nuclear waste

(4) acid rain

Thematic Essay Question

In developing your answer, be sure to keep these general definitions in mind:

    (a) <u>describe</u> means "to illustrate something in words or tell about it"

    (b) <u>evaluate</u> means "to judge or determine the significance, worth, or quality of"

Directions: Write a well-organized essay that includes an introduction, several paragraphs addressing the task below, and a conclusion.

Theme: **Science and Technology**

> Since 1945, technology has transformed human life. Advances have occurred in many different areas. These changes have had both positive and negative effects on human life.

Task:

- Describe one scientific or technological advance made since 1945 that has had a significant impact on global history.
- Give two examples of ways in which this advance has affected you or will have an effect on you in the future.
- Evaluate the positive and negative effects of that scientific or technological advance on the lives of human beings.

You may discuss any scientific or technological advance that has come about since 1945. Some types of advances that you may wish to consider are discovery of nuclear power, the widespread use of the computer or of Internet technology, and medical advances.

You are *not* limited to these suggestions.

Guidelines:

    In your essay, be sure to

- Develop all aspects of the task
- Support the theme with relevant facts, examples, and details
- Use a logical and clear plan of organization, including an introduction and a conclusion that are beyond a simple restatement of the theme

Document-Based Question

This question is based on the accompanying documents. The question is designed to test your ability to work with historical documents. Some of the documents have been edited for the purposes of this question. As you analyze the documents, take into account the source of each document and any point of view that may be presented in the document.

Historical Context:

> People have held differing views about human rights throughout history and in different cultures. In the 1900s, however, there have been movements all over the world to ensure basic human rights for all people.

Task: Using the information from the documents and your knowledge of global history, answer the questions that follow each document in Part A. Your answers to the questions will help you write the Part B essay in which you will be asked to

> • Describe and evaluate the progress of justice and human rights in the 1900s

In developing your answers, be sure to keep these general definitions in mind:

(a) <u>describe</u> means "to tell or depict in written or spoken words; give an account of"

(b) <u>evaluate</u> means "to examine and judge the significance, worth, or condition of; to determine the value of"

Document-Based Question

Part A: Short Answer

Directions: Analyze the documents and answer the question or questions that follow each document, using the space provided.

Document #1

> *Article 1 All human beings are born free and equal in dignity and rights. . . .*
> *Article 2 Everyone is entitled to all the rights and freedoms . . . without distinction of any kind. . . .*
> *Article 18 Everyone has the right to freedom of thought, conscience and religion. . . .*
> *Article 19 Everyone has the right to freedom of opinion and expression. . . .*
> *Article 25 Everyone has the right to a standard of living adequate for the health and well-being of himself and of his family, including food, clothing, housing and medical care. . . .*
> —**General Assembly of the United Nations,** *The Universal Declaration of Human Rights,*
> **adopted December 10, 1948**

1. Describe one economic right to which Document 1 says all people are entitled.

_____

_____

2. Which article or articles in Document 1 most closely support freedom of speech? Explain the reason for your choice.

_____

_____

Document #2

> *In many parts of the world the people are searching for a solution which would link the two basic values: peace and justice. The two are like bread and salt for mankind. Every nation and every community have the inalienable right to these values. No conflicts can be resolved without doing everything possible to follow that road…*
> —**Lech Walesa, Nobel Peace Prize Lecture, 1983**

3. What point was Walesa trying to make by comparing peace and justice to bread and salt?

_____

_____

Document #3

4. Explain why some people in this cartoon have been waiting for hours, while others have been waiting for years.

_____

_____

_____

_____

_____

Document-Based Question

Part B
Essay

Directions: Write a well-organized essay that includes an introduction, several paragraphs, and a conclusion. Use evidence from *at least two* documents in your essay. Support your response with relevant facts, examples, and details. Include additional outside information.

Historical Context:

People have held differing views about human rights throughout history and in different cultures. In the 1900s, however, there have been movements all over the world to ensure basic human rights for all.

Task:

Using information from the documents and your knowledge of global history and geography, write an essay in which you:

- Evaluate justice and human rights in the 1900s
- Describe advances in human rights as well as human rights violations
- Explain whether you think that the trend is toward greater human rights for all

Guidelines:

In your essay, be sure to
- Develop all aspects of the task
- Incorporate information from *at least two* documents
- Incorporate relevant outside information
- Support the theme with relevant facts, examples, and details
- Use a logical and clear plan of organization, including an introduction and a conclusion that are beyond a restatement of the theme

The Regents Examination takes a thematic approach to history. This section of the book will help you to review the themes that are mostly likely to be tested on the thematic essay and document-based parts of the exam. It is important to remember that the themes used in this course span the entire two-year course. The events you choose to write about in the thematic essay may be taken from either ninth or tenth grade or both.

Change

Change means basic alterations in things, events, and ideas. Throughout global history, major changes have had significant and lasting impacts on human development.

- **Neolithic Revolution** Some 11,000 years ago, people first developed farming methods and lived in permanent settlements. As a result, the first civilizations emerged.
- **Industrial Revolution** This change began in Europe in the 1700s and gradually spread throughout the world. Power-driven machinery in factories became the dominant means of production. The results of this change have included urbanization, a higher standard of living, and pollution of the environment.
- **Chinese Communist Revolution** In 1948, Mao Zedong established a Chinese Communist state. Since then, China has become a world economic power. Today, it works to control its growing population, as well as to adapt communism to modern needs.

Other examples of change are the Crusades, the spread of bubonic plague, the Renaissance, the Scientific Revolution, the Enlightenment, the Agrarian Revolution, the Reformation, African independence movements, and the emergence of Pacific Rim nations.

Turning Points

Turning points are times when decisive changes occur. Turning points often have political, social, and cultural impacts.

- **Fall of Constantinople** This event, which occurred in 1453, marked the end of the Christian Byzantine empire and the emergence of the powerful Ottoman empire, a Muslim power that dominated the region for centuries.
- **Voyages of Columbus** The voyages of Columbus began the European race to colonize the Americas. A far-reaching exchange of people, plants, animals, and ideas occurred between Europe, the Americas, and Africa.
- **French Revolution** The French Revolution of 1789 had a powerful influence well beyond France, spreading democratic ideals and a spirit of nationalism throughout Europe and around the globe.
- **Collapse of Communism in the Soviet Union** The collapse of communism in the Soviet Union initiated years of change in Eastern Europe and brought an end to the Cold War.

Other examples of turning points include the signing of the Magna Carta, the American Revolution, independence movements in Latin America, and the Russian Revolution.

Thematic Review

Belief Systems

Belief systems are the established, orderly ways in which groups or individuals look at religious faith or philosophical tenets.

- **Hinduism** A religion more than 3,000 years old, Hinduism has had an enormous effect on India, Southeast Asia, and the rest of the world.
- **Buddhism** A religion founded in the 500s B.C. in India, Buddhism spread throughout Asia.
- **Judaism** The first great monotheistic religion, Judaism has had an important effect on several other world religions.
- **Christianity** Greatly influenced by Judaism, Christianity is a monotheistic religion centered on the teachings of Jesus Christ.
- **Islam** Also greatly influenced by Judaism, Islam is a monotheistic religion and has followers all over the world, especially in the Middle East, Africa, and Asia.

Other examples of belief systems are animism, Confucianism, Taoism, Shintoism, and Sikhism.

Geography and the Environment

This theme has to do with relationships among people, places, and environments. Environment means the surroundings, including natural elements and elements created by humans.

- **Early River Civilizations** Early civilizations grew up around rivers. Rivers provided water for crops and for drinking, as well as a means of transportation.
- **Chinese Influence on Japan** Through the bridge of Korea, China had a strong influence on the culture of Japan.
- **Industrialization in Great Britain** Great Britain's natural resources, together with such geographical factors as rivers and natural harbors, allowed the Industrial Revolution to begin there.
- **Industrial Revolution: Impact on Environment** The Industrial Revolution had a lasting impact on the natural environment. For example, new sources of energy often created new types of pollution. Urbanization changed the landscape as cities and their suburbs grew.

Other examples of the impact of geography and the environment are the development of city-states in ancient Greece, the importance of the Middle East as a crossroads between three continents, and environmental problems such as desertification and the destruction of tropical forests.

Economic Systems

Economic systems include traditional, command, market, and mixed systems. Each must answer the three basic economic questions: What goods and services are to be produced and in what quantities? How shall these goods and services be produced? For whom shall these goods and services be produced?

- **Traditional Economy** An economic system based on farming, often subsistence farming, is a traditional economy.

- **Manorialism** The economic system of Western Europe in medieval times was called manorialism. It was based on the manor, an estate that often included one or more villages and the surrounding lands.

- **Mercantilism** The economic policy in which nations sought to export more than they imported is known as mercantilism. Overseas empires were central to mercantilism, which led to imperialism.

- **Capitalism (Market Economy)** Capitalism is an economic system in which the means of production are privately owned and operated for profit. It developed as an economic system in the 1500s.

- **Marxist Socialism (Command Economy)** Marxist socialism is the economic system found in communist states such as the former Soviet Union and its satellites. It is characterized by ownership of property and operation of businesses by the state rather than by private individuals.

Other examples of topics connected with economic systems are laissez-faire economics, the commercial revolution, cash crop economies, and imperialism.

Political Systems

Political systems, such as monarchies, dictatorships, and democracies, address certain basic questions of government such as: What should a government have the power to do? What should a government not have the power to do?

- **Monarchy** In monarchies, a king or queen exercises central power. Monarchies have been common since ancient times, and a few are still in existence today.

- **Feudalism** Feudalism was most prominent in medieval Europe and in Japan from about 1600 to the mid-1800s. It is a decentralized political system. In Europe, it declined with the growth of nation-states.

- **Democracy** Democracy, a system in which the people hold the ruling power—either directly or through elected representatives—had its roots in ancient Greece. It is a primary political system in the countries of the West today.

- **Totalitarianism** In a totalitarian system, a one-party dictatorship regulates every aspect of its citizens' lives. The Soviet Union under Stalin was a totalitarian state.

Other examples of political systems are the limited democracy of Athens, the militarism of Sparta and of Japan, absolutism, theocracy, communism, fascism, and apartheid.

Culture and Intellectual Life

Culture includes the patterns of human behavior (encompassing ideas, beliefs, values, artifacts, and ways of making a living) that a society transmits to succeeding generations to meet its fundamental needs. Intellectual life involves ways of thinking, studying, and reflecting on aspects of life.

- **Roman Civilization** Rome left a great cultural and intellectual legacy to the Western world, including a commitment to law and justice, the Latin language, and a body of great literature.

- **Gupta Golden Age** In India, from A.D. 320 through 550, lasting achievements in mathematics, medicine, arts, and architecture occurred, supported by the stable reign of the Gupta dynasty.

- **Islamic Golden Age** Between A.D. 750 and 1350, Islamic empires experienced a golden age. The roots of modern mathematics and science can be traced to this period.
- **African Civilizations** From the mid-1200s through the mid-1500s, Africa was the site of great activity in scholarship and art.
- **Renaissance Europe** The Renaissance in Europe, which began in the mid-1300s, was a time of great cultural and intellectual activity. Humanism—which recognized the importance of individual worth in a secular society—guided the Renaissance.

Other important eras of cultural and intellectual activity included early river civilizations, classical Chinese civilization, Mesoamerican civilizations, and the Enlightenment in Europe.

Nationalism

Nationalism is a feeling of pride in and devotion to one's country or the desire of a people to control their own government. It is sometimes a divisive force and sometimes a force that unifies. In many cases, it is a source of conflict.

- **German and Italian Unification** In the mid-1800s, both Germany and Italy experienced unification. In each case, many small states joined into one nation.
- **India** Ideals of Western democracy, as well as devotion to traditional Hindu and Muslim culture, sustained Indian nationalism through the first half of the 1900s, leading to independence in 1948.
- **Zionism** Since Roman times, Jews had dreamed of returning to Palestine. This dream grew into an international movement in the 1900s. By 1948, the nation of Israel had been created.
- **African Independence Movements** In 1945, just four European powers controlled nearly all of Africa. Less than 25 years later, a tide of nationalism had liberated many African peoples and set them on the road to self-determination.

Other historical situations in which nationalism had an impact are the development of the nation of Turkey, conflicts in the Balkans, the breakup of the Ottoman empire, Latin America in the 1800s and 1900s, Pan-Africanism, and Pan-Arabism.

Imperialism

Imperialism is the domination by one country of the political and economic life of another country or region. Imperialism has had both positive and negative effects on colonies.

- **British in India** The British controlled India by the late 1700s. Although railroads and the British educational system benefited some Indians, local industries and Indian culture suffered, and Indians were treated as inferiors. India gained its independence in 1948.
- **European Powers in Africa** European nations carved up the continent of Africa in the late 1880s. Africa was a continent made up mainly of colonies until after 1945, when African peoples began to demand independence. The legacy of imperialism still affects Africa today.

- **Japan** An imperialist power from the Meiji period, Japan ruled Korea from 1910 to the end of World War II. It also controlled areas in China and Southeast Asia. Japanese imperialism was a cause of World War II.

- **Imperial Rivalry** Competition between imperial powers was one of the causes of World War I. Germany and France, especially, clashed over territory in Africa. Imperial rivalry was also a cause of many smaller wars.

Other civilizations that practiced imperialism include the Chinese Han dynasty, the Romans, the Byzantines, and the Mongols. The collapse of European imperialism still affects many regions of the world today.

Diversity and Interdependence

Diversity involves understanding and respecting oneself and others, including differences in language, gender, socioeconomic class, religion, and other human characteristics and traits. It is closely related to interdependence, the reliance upon others in mutually beneficial interactions and exchanges. Sometimes the refusal to accept diversity leads to conflict.

- **Byzantine Empire** The Byzantine empire blended many diverse cultures. This diversity allowed it to preserve many differing traditions.

- **Balkans** This region of Eastern Europe has always been an area of great religious and ethnic diversity. Often this diversity has led to conflict.

- **Global Economy** In the 1900s, the world economy became more interdependent, a process that started during the age of imperialism. Today, the world's economy is truly global.

- **Environmental Issues** The global population shares the Earth, and what occurs in one part of the world often has an impact on many other areas. Increasingly, environmental decisions are reached by many nations working together for mutual benefit.

Other examples of diversity and interdependence include the links between the East and the West during the time of the Mongol empire, tensions that have arisen as a result of Islamic fundamentalism, and interactions among Muslims, Hindus, and Sikhs in India.

Justice and Human Rights

Justice is fair, equal, proportional, or appropriate treatment given to individuals in interpersonal, societal, or government interactions. Human rights are those basic political, economic, and social rights to which all human beings are entitled. At times throughout history, justice and human rights have been violated.

- **Code of Hammurabi** Because the Code of Hammurabi was carved on a pillar in Babylon (around 1800 B.C.), all people could see what the laws were. This was the first major collection of laws in history.

- **English Bill of Rights** The English Bill of Rights was an important document because it limited the power of the monarchy and returned traditional rights to English citizens.

- **Irish Potato Famine** A blight that affected the main food crop for the Irish people in the mid-1800s created widespread famine when the British, who ruled the island, continued to export crops that could have fed the Irish. At least a million Irish people died during the famine, also called the Great Hunger.

- **Tiananmen Square** When students in China demanded greater political freedom in the late 1980s, Chinese Communist authorities cracked down, wounding and killing many demonstrators.

Other examples of important developments in justice and human rights include the Laws of the Twelve Tables, Justinian's Code, the Sharia, and the Magna Carta. Violations of human rights include the Armenian massacres, the Holocaust, apartheid, the Khmer Rouge in Cambodia, and international terrorism.

Movement of People and Goods

Cultural diffusion is the constant exchange of people, ideas, products, technology, and institutions from one region or civilization to another. Cultural diffusion has occurred throughout history.

- **Muslim Influence on Africa** Muslim traders spread Islam across Africa. Their contacts with diverse cultures allowed them to spread a great number of other ideas and technologies along with the religion of Islam.
- **Silk Road** This 4,000-mile trade route stretched from western China to the Mediterranean. For centuries, from the A.D. 100s onward, goods, ideas, and technology flowed along this route from East to West and back again.
- **Crusades** From the late 1000s through the late 1200s, Christian and Muslim armies battled for control of Palestine. A great deal of cultural diffusion occurred during and after the Crusades, as Europe increased its interest in goods and ideas from the Middle East.
- **Modern Communication** In today's world, computers, the Internet, and satellite communications allow ideas to be passed in moments over great distances.

Other examples of movement of peoples, goods, and ideas include the spread of belief systems (such as Buddhism and Confucianism to Japan), the Muslim influence on Europe, and patterns of global migration.

Science and Technology

Science and technology means the tools and methods used by people to get what they need and want.

- **Neolithic Revolution** When people developed the knowledge and technology for farming and domesticating animals, permanent settlements grew.
- **Invention of the Printing Press** The printing press was a crucial breakthrough in technology, allowing ideas to spread.
- **Computer Revolution** Since the 1950s, our society has become increasingly dependent on computers and on digitized information.
- **Space Explorations** Humans have populated Earth and moved into the solar system. In recent years, space exploration has been a shared venture among major world powers.

Other examples of breakthroughs in science and technology are the improved standard of living that occurred in the 1800s, the Green Revolution, and advances in genetics.

Conflict

Conflict has occurred throughout history, and its costs have sometimes been very high. The causes of conflict may be political, social, or economic.

- **Religious Conflicts** Conflicts between peoples of differing belief systems began in ancient times and still exist today in places as widespread as Northern Ireland, India, and the Middle East.
- **Political Revolutions** Violent revolutions occurred within nations from the late 1700s through the 1800s as groups sought democratic reform, national independence, or both.
- **World War I** Sparked by several complex causes, World War I was the first modern, fully industrialized war and the first truly global conflict.
- **The Cold War** After 1945, the United States and its allies were engaged in a global competition with the Soviet Union and its allies. Surrogate conflicts occurred as the two superpowers—the United States and the Soviet Union— exerted their influence throughout the world.

Other examples of conflict include the Crusades, World War II, the Russian Revolution, ethnic disputes in the Balkans and Africa, and Arab-Israeli conflict in the Middle East.

Modern Global Connections and Interactions

Today's world is a web of connections and interactions. On every level, the people of the world meet, connect, interact, and sometimes collide. These interactions involve politics, economics, culture, or the environment.

- **Global Environmental Cooperation** Nations are becoming increasingly interdependent in their decisions about environmental issues, acknowledging that various peoples share one world.
- **Global Migrations** The last half of the 1900s was a time of great migration, especially from Africa, Asia, and Latin America to Europe and North America. Many people migrated to improve their economic conditions.
- **International Terrorism** Modern technology and transportation systems have allowed violent groups to express their frustration and anger globally through random acts of violence.
- **The United Nations** Created after World War II, the United Nations remains an organization through which nations can come together to seek peaceful solutions to global problems and conflicts.

Other examples of modern global connections and interactions include economic interdependence, nuclear proliferation, and the sharing of technology and ideas through the Internet.

Glossary

absolutism: political system in which autocratic rulers have complete authority over the government and the lives of people in their nations

acid rain: toxic mixture that is produced when rain falls through polluted air

African National Congress: group formed by opponents to apartheid in South Africa that encouraged political activism by blacks

Agrarian Revolution: change in farming methods in the 1600s that improved the quality and quantity of farm products

agribusiness: large commercial farm owned by multinational corporation

AIDS: acquired immunodeficiency syndrome

Allied Powers: World War I alliance of Great Britain, France, and Russia, later joined by Italy, the United States, and others

animism: the belief that every living and nonliving thing in nature has a spirit

antibiotic: drug that attacks or weakens the bacteria that cause many diseases

anti-Semitism: prejudice against Jews

apartheid: South African government policy calling for separation of the races

appeasement: policy of giving in to an aggressor's demands in order to keep the peace

apprentice: young person who is learning a trade from a master

aqueduct: bridgelike stone structure that brings water from hills to cities, first used by ancient Romans

Arabic numeral: type of numeral first developed in India and used by many Western countries today (1, 2, 3, etc.)

aristocracy: a government ruled by an upper class

armistice: agreement to end fighting

Association of Southeast Asian Nations: formed in 1967, group of nine Southeast Asian countries that coordinate policies among members in areas such as trade and agriculture

astrolabe: instrument used to determine latitude by measuring the position of the stars

asylum: protection from arrest or from being returned to a dangerous place from which one fled

artifact: an item made by humans that is used by archeologists to learn about past cultures

autocrat: a single ruler with complete authority

B

balance of power: distribution of political and economic power that prevents any one nation from becoming too strong

balance of trade: difference between how much a country imports and how much it exports

Bataan Death March: forced march of Allied prisoners by the Japanese during World War II

Bible: the sacred scriptures of Christianity

blitz: massive bombing

Boer War: war occurring from 1899 to 1902 between the British and the Boers, Dutch farmers; it began after the British tried to annex the Boer republics

Bolshevik: member of 1917 Russian revolutionary group

bourgeoisie: middle class in Marxism; it refers to capitalists

Boxer Rebellion: event in 1900 in which a group known as Boxers assaulted foreign communities across China

brahman: single unifying spirit of Hindu belief

bubonic plague: a contagious disease that devastated the world in the 1300s

bureaucracy: system of managing government through departments run by appointed officials

bushido: code of conduct for samurai during feudal period in Japan

C

caliph: successor to Muhammad as political and religious leader of the Muslims

calligraphy: fine handwriting

capitalism: economic system in which the means of production are privately owned and operated for profit

cartel: an association of businesspeople; used to refer to the criminal gangs that produce and smuggle drugs internationally

cartographer: mapmaker

cash crop economy: economy based on the raising and selling of one crop or a small number of crops

caudillo: military dictator in Latin America

Central Powers: World War I alliance of Germany, Austria-Hungary, and the Ottoman empire (later joined by Bulgaria)

chador: cloak worn by some Muslim women

chivalry: the code of conduct followed by knights during the Middle Ages

civil disobedience: the refusal to obey unjust laws

civilization: community characterized by elements such as a system of writing, development of social classes, and cities

clone: exact genetic replica

Cold War: continuing state of tension and hostility between the United States and the Soviet Union after 1945 because of differences in political and economic philosophies

collective: large farm owned and operated by workers as a group

Columbian exchange: global exchange of people, plants, animals, ideas, and technology that began in the late 1400s

command economy: economy in which government officials make all basic economic decisions

commercial revolution: the business revolution that occurred in Europe after the Middle Ages

common law: uniform system of justice, developed in England, based on court decisions that became accepted legal principles

Common Market: See *European Community*

commune: community of people who live and work together and hold property in common

Computer Revolution: great increase in the use of computers

concentration camp: detention centers instituted by Adolf Hitler where Jews and others were starved, shot, or gassed to death

Congress of Vienna: conference held in 1815 among European diplomats that had the purpose of restoring order and stability to Europe

conquistador: name, meaning "conqueror," for certain explorers of the 1500s and 1600s

conservatism: set of beliefs held by those who want to preserve traditional ways

Constitutional monarchy: a government in which the power of the king is limited by law

containment: Cold War policy that involved limiting communism to areas already under Soviet control

contras: counterrevolutionary group in Nicaragua that opposed the Sandinistas

Counter-Reformation: actions taken by the Catholic Church in the 1600s to oppose Protestantism

coup d'état: a revolt by a small group intended to overthrow a government

Crusades: series of religious wars fought between Christians and Muslims from the late 1000s to the mid-1200s

cultural diffusion: the exchange of ideas, customs, goods, and technologies among cultures

Cultural Revolution: program launched in 1966 by Mao Zedong to renew loyalty to communism and purge China of nonrevolutionary tendencies

cuneiform: wedge-shaped writing formed by pressing a penlike instrument into clay

czar: term for autocratic ruler of Russia; Russian word for *Caesar*

D

daimyo: in feudal Japan, warrior lords who held a place below the shogun

decimal system: number system based on 10

Declaration of Independence: document drafted by Thomas Jefferson that declared American independence from Great Britain

decolonization: the process by which European colonies in Africa and Asia became independent states

deforestation: destruction of forests, especially tropical rain forests

desaparecidos: word meaning "the disappeared ones," used to describe the thousands of people in Argentina who disappeared during the dirty war

desert: dry, barren land

desertification: the changeover of arable land into desert

despot: absolute ruler

détente: period in the 1970s during which there was an easing of tensions between the United States and the Soviet Union

developed nation: nation with established agriculture and industry, advanced technology, and a strong educational system

developing nation: nation with limited resources that faces obstacles in achieving modern industrial economies

dharma: in Hinduism, the moral and religious duties that are expected of an individual

diaspora: a scattering of people, as when the Jewish people were forced to leave their homeland in Palestine

direct democracy: system of government in which citizens participate directly rather than through elected representatives

Dirty War: period beginning in the late 1970s in Argentina during which the military arrested, tortured, and killed thousands of people

divine right: belief that a ruler's authority comes directly from God

Domino Theory: the belief that if one nation in Southeast Asia fell to Communism, the rest would soon follow

dynasty: ruling family

 E

empire: group of states or territories governed by one ruler

enclosure: process of taking over and fencing off land once shared by peasant farmers

encomienda: system created by Spanish government in the Americas allowing colonists to demand labor or tribute from Native Americans

English Bill of Rights: a set of acts passed by Parliament to ensure its superiority over the monarchy and guarantee certain rights to citizens

enlightened despot: absolute ruler who used royal power to reform society

Enlightenment: the period in the 1700s in which people rejected traditional ideas and supported a belief in human reason

epidemic: an outbreak of disease that spreads quickly and affects a large number of people

Estates General: a French legislative body made up of clergy, nobles, and common people, such as businesspeople and peasants

ethnic cleansing: policy of forcibly removing or killing people of a certain ethnic group

ethnocentrism: the belief in the superiority of one's own race, culture, or nation

euro: European currency introduced in 1999

European Community: group of nations established in 1957 to expand free trade in Europe; also called *Common Market*

European Union: expansion of the European Community in the 1980s and 1990s; sometimes abbreviated EU

excommunicate: to exclude from the Roman Catholic Church as a penalty for refusing to obey Church laws

 F

factory: place in which workers and machines are brought together to produce large quantities of goods

fascism: the rule of a people by a dictatorial government that is nationalistic and imperialistic

feudalism: system of government in which local lords control their own lands but owe military service and other support to a greater lord

five-year plan: one of a series of plans instituted by Joseph Stalin to build industry and increase farm output in the Soviet Union

fossil fuels: fuels such as coal, oil, and natural gas

 G

genetic engineering: process of changing the chemical codes carried by living things to produce cures for disease, better drugs, and so on

genocide: attempt to destroy an entire ethnic or religious group

gentry: wealthy landowning class

germ theory: medical theory stating that many diseases are caused by microorganisms

glasnost: period of openness called for in the mid-1980s by Mikhail Gorbachev in the Soviet Union

globalization: the growing integration of economies and societies around the world

Glorious Revolution: in Great Britain, nonviolent overthrow of the government of James II that resulted in the reign of William and Mary

Gothic: style of European church architecture characterized by pointed arches and flying buttresses

Great Depression: global economic downturn that began in 1929

Great Leap Forward: program begun by Mao Zedong in China in 1958 to increase agricultural and industrial output

Green Revolution: development of new varieties of plants and improved agricultural techniques that resulted in greatly increased crop yields

greenhouse effect: process in which excess carbon dioxide in the atmosphere traps heat and causes rising global temperatures

guild: a type of trade association of merchants or artisans that was active in the Middle Ages

Guomindang: Chinese nationalist party formed by Sun Yixian

H

haiku: form of Japanese poetry that expresses a feeling, thought, or idea in three lines

Hanseatic League: trade association of northern German towns in the mid-1300s

heliocentric: sun-centered

Hellenistic: type of culture, resulting from Alexander the Great's conquests, that blended Eastern and Western influences

hijra: Muhammad's flight from Mecca to Medina in 622; also spelled *hegira*

heresy: a religious belief that is opposed to the official teachings of a church

Holocaust: act of genocide by the Nazis during World War II in which more than six million Jews died

Holy Land: Palestine, a land holy to Jews, Christians, and Muslims

humanism: intellectual movement at the heart of the Renaissance that focused on worldly subjects rather than religious ones

I

icon: holy image of Jesus, the Virgin Mary, or a saint of the Orthodox Christian Church

imperialism: domination by one country of the political, economic, or cultural life of another country or region

Indian National Congress: group formed by Hindu nationalist leaders in India in the late 1800s to gain greater democracy and eventual self-rule

indigenous: native to a country or region

indulgence: a pardon (forgiveness) for sins that was sold by the Catholic Church

Industrial Revolution: period in which production of goods shifted from using hand tools to using power-driven machines and from human and animal power to steam power

Information Revolution: the rapid spread of information that began in the 1950s and increases with each passing year

International Monetary Fund: in the 1980s, group that stepped in to work out agreements to help debtor nations repay their loans

Internet: vast computer network that ties together millions of computers

Interpol: the International Criminal Police Network

intifada: uprising mounted in 1987 by Palestinians in territory held by Israel

iron curtain: the imaginary line through Europe that divided the democracies of the West from the communist countries of the East

Islamic fundamentalism: movement by Muslim reformers who oppose westernization and want to apply Islamic principles to problems in their nations

J

janissaries: members of an elite force in the army of the Ottoman empire

Justinian's Code: code of laws organized by the Byzantine emperor Justinian in the 500s

K

kabuki: form of Japanese drama developed in the 1600s

kaiser: German word meaning "emperor," used for German kings of the late 1800s and early 1900s

kami: according to Japanese tradition, the spirits in all living and nonliving things

karma: in Hinduism, all the deeds of a person's life that affect existence in the next life

Koran: holy book of Islam

L

laissez faire: policy allowing business to operate with little or no government interference

Laws of the Twelve Tables: laws of ancient Rome written on twelve tablets and displayed in the marketplace

League of Nations: group of more than 40 countries formed after World War I with the goal of settling problems through negotiation, not war

liberalism: way of thinking that supports personal freedom, democracy, and reform

limited monarchy: government in which a legislative body limits the monarch's powers

literacy: the ability to read and write

Long March: 1934 retreat by Mao Zedong and his followers from the Guomindang

Magna Carta: a charter signed by the English king John in 1215 that placed limits on the king's power

mandate: after World War I, a territory that was administered by a foreign power

Mandate of Heaven: according to Chinese tradition, the divine right to rule

manorialism: an economic system structured around a lord's manor, or estate

Marshall Plan: American aid package for Europe proposed in 1947 to strengthen democratic governments and lessen the appeal of communism

medieval: the name for the period of the Middle Ages, from about 500 to the middle of the 1400s

Meiji Restoration: period from 1868 to 1912 in Japan in which Japan industrialized and modernized

mercantilism: economic policy by which a nation sought to export more than it imported in order to build its national wealth

Messiah: Jewish word for a savior sent by God

mestizo: a person of mixed parentage in Latin America

Middle Kingdom: traditional name for Chinese civilization, so-called because the Chinese believed China was the center of the Earth

Middle Passage: the voyage from Africa to the Americas on slave ships

militarism: the glorification of military power

millet: within the Ottoman empire, a religious community of non-Muslims

missionary: person dedicated to spreading a religion

mixed economy: economic system with both private and state-run enterprises

monastery: community where men or women focus on spiritual goals

monopoly: complete control of a product or business by one person or group

monotheistic: believing in one god

mosaic: picture or design formed by inlaid pieces of stone or other materials

mosque: Muslim house of worship

multinational corporation: a business that operates in many countries

Munich Pact: 1938 agreement between Great Britain, France, Italy, and Germany that allowed Hitler to seize the Sudentenland

Muslim League: group formed by Muslims in India in the early 1900s to protect Muslim interests

Napoleonic Code: legal code of Napoleon that included many Enlightenment ideas

National Assembly: group formed mostly by the third estate in France in 1789 with the intention of writing a new constitution

nationalism: a feeling of pride in and devotion to one's country

NATO: acronym for the North Atlantic Treaty Organization, a pact between Western nations who pledged to support each other if any member nation was attacked

natural laws: according to some philosophers, rules that govern human nature

Neolithic: the period of human culture characterized by the development of a system of settled agriculture; also called the New Stone Age

neutral: not supporting either side in a conflict

New Economic Policy: plan instituted by Lenin in 1921 that privatized some industries

95 Theses: list of 95 arguments against indulgences, posted by Martin Luther on the door of a church in Wittenberg, Germany, in 1517

nirvana: in Buddhism, union with the universe and release from the cycle of death and rebirth

nomad: person who moves from place to place in search of food

nonalignment: policy of not supporting either side in a conflict, such as the Cold War

O

oligarchy: government in which ruling power belongs to a few people

OPEC: acronym for the Organization of Petroleum Exporting Countries, a trade group that attempts to set world oil prices by controlling oil production

Opium War: conflict between Great Britain and China in 1839 over the opium trade

Organization of African Unity (OAU): group founded in 1963 by Kwame Nkrumah to promote Pan-Africanism and the end of colonialism in Africa

overpopulation: overabundance of people in a region or country that lacks sufficient resources to adequately provide for them

ozone layer: layer of gases high in the atmosphere that protects the Earth from the dangerous ultraviolet rays of the sun

Pacific Rim: group of nations in Asia and the Americas that border the Pacific Ocean

pagoda: Buddhist temple with many levels and a roof that curves up at the corners

Palestine Liberation Organization (PLO): group formed in 1964 that represents many Palestinian nationalist groups

Pan-Africanism: movement emphasizing the unity of Africans and people of African descent all over the world

Pan-Arabism: movement emphasizing the unity of all peoples sharing a common Arab cultural heritage

Pan-Slavism: nationalistic movement that sought to unite Slavic peoples

Parliament: representative assembly of England

patriarch: the highest church official in the Orthodox Christian Church

patriarchal: family order in which the father or oldest male heads the household

patrician: member of the landholding upper class in ancient Rome

Pax Mongolia: period of stability through much of Asia created by Mongol rule from the late 1200s through the mid-1300s

Pax Romana: term meaning "Roman Peace" for a period covering about 200 years beginning with the reign of Augustus

peninsularies: European-born elite in Latin America

perestroika: restructuring of the government and the economy in the Soviet Union under Mikhail Gorbachev in the mid-1980s

Persian Gulf War: war in 1991 prompted by the Iraqi invasion of Kuwait in which a coalition of European and Arab powers drove Iraq out of Kuwait

pharaoh: ruler of ancient Egypt

philosophe: thinkers of the Enlightenment

plantation: large estate run by an owner or overseer

plebeian: member of the lower class in ancient Rome, which included farmers, merchants, artisans, and traders

PLO: (Palestine Liberation Organization) originally a terrorist group dedicated to the destruction of Israel;

later became an official organization representing Palestinians in negotiations with Israel

pogrom: violent attack on a Jewish community

polis: city-state in ancient Greece

pollution: contamination of the environment, including air, water, and soil

polytheistic: believing in many gods

porcelain: hard, shiny pottery

post-colonialism: term used to describe conditions shared by nations that were once colonies

propaganda: the spreading of ideas to promote a certain cause or to damage an opposing cause

Protestant Reformation: period when Europeans broke away from the Roman Catholic Church and formed new Christian churches

purge: the process of eliminating a nation of undesirable people

Puritans: group in England in the 1600s who sought to purify the church of England by eliminating Catholic practices

quipus: knotted strings used by Incan officials for keeping records

Quran: the sacred scriptures of Islam

R

radioactivity: powerful form of energy released by certain substances

Reconquista: a campaign begun by Christians in the 700s to recapture Spain from the Muslims

Red Guards: groups of radical students formed in China during the Cultural Revolution

refugee: person who flees his or her homeland to seek safety elsewhere

reincarnation: in Hinduism, the rebirth of the soul in a new body

Renaissance: period of great creativity and change in Europe from the 1300s through the 1600s; the word means "rebirth"

reparations: payment for war damages

republic: system of government in which officials are chosen by the people

Russification: attempt by Russian rulers to make all groups under Russian rule think, act, and believe as Russians

Russo-Japanese War: war occurring from 1904 to 1905 between Japan and Russia; won by Japan

S

samurai: member of the warrior class in Japanese feudal society

Sandinistas: group of revolutionaries that overthrew the Nicaraguan government in 1979

satellite: a smaller country that is economically or politically dependent on a more powerful country

savanna: grassy plain

schism: permanent split

scientific method: a method of discovering truth based on experimentation and observation rather than on past authorities

Scientific Revolution: period in the 1500s and 1600s in which scientific thinkers challenged traditional ideas and relied on observation and experimentation

secondary source: written information that is based on original or primary sources

secular: having to do with worldly rather than religious matters

Senate: the most powerful governing body of ancient Rome

sepoy: Indian soldier serving in the army set up by the British or French East India Companies

Sepoy Mutiny: rebellion fought by Hindu and Muslim sepoys against British rule in India in the mid-1800s

serf: in medieval Europe, peasant bound to the lord's land

shantytown: area of shacks that grows up around a city that is experiencing rapid growth

Sharia: the system of Islamic law

Shiite: one of the two main divisions of Islam

Shinto: traditional Japanese religion

shogun: in Japanese feudal society, top military commander

Silk Road: ancient trade route that linked China with lands to the west

Sino-Japanese War: war that lasted from 1894 to 1895 between Japan and China

socialism: system in which the people as a whole rather than private individuals own all property and operate all businesses

Solidarity: independent trade union formed in Poland in 1980

soviet: council of workers and soldiers set up by Russian revolutionaries in 1917

sphere of influence: area in which an outside power claims exclusive trade privileges

stupa: large dome-shaped Buddhist shrine

suffrage: the right to vote

sultan: Muslim ruler

Sunni: one of the two main divisions of Islam

superpower: name after 1945 for both the United States and the Soviet Union, the two nations that dominated global politics for more than four decades

surrogate: word for a representative state; used to describe smaller countries whose actions represented the interests of either the United States or the Soviet Union during the Cold War

Swahili: language that mixed Arabic words with Bantu, an African language

T

Taiping Rebellion: peasant rebellion in China occurring between 1850 and 1864

tariff: a tax on imports

technology: tools and skills people use to meet their basic needs

terrace: a flat area of land on a steep hillside

terrorism: deliberate use of unpredictable violence, especially against civilians, to gain revenge or achieve political goals

Torah: the most sacred scriptures of Judaism

totalitarian state: form of government in which a one-party dictatorship attempts to regulate every aspect of the lives of citizens

total war: the channeling of all of a nation's resources into a war effort

trade deficit: a situation in which a nation imports more than it exports

trade fair: site of regular trading activity in medieval Europe

trench warfare: type of warfare in which troops dig trenches and fight from them

tributary state: independent state that must acknowledge the supremacy of another state and pay tribute to its ruler

Truman Doctrine: an economic and military program of the United States designed in 1947 to help other countries resist Soviet aggression

U

United Nations: international group formed in 1945 to provide a place to discuss world problems and develop solutions

Universal Declaration of Human Rights: document adopted in 1948 by the United Nations that sets out the basic human rights of all individuals

Untouchables: within the ancient Indian caste system, outcasts who lived harsh lives

urbanization: movement of people to cities

utopian: a plan for creating a perfect social order

W

Warsaw Pact: defensive alliance among the Soviet Union and its satellites promising mutual military cooperation

westernization: process of adopting Western ways

Y

Young Turks: movement established by Turks in the late 1800s to reform the Ottoman Empire

Z

zaibatsu: Japanese families that became powerful in banking and industry

Zen Buddhism: sect of Buddhism that spread throughout Japan

Zionism: movement dedicated to building a Jewish state in Palestine

Index

Mughal empire, 126–127
multinational corporations, 277–278
Muslim League, 161
Muslims. *See* Islam/Muslims
Mussolini, Benito, 208
Myanmar, 248

N

Nagasaki, 213
Napoleon Bonaparte, 148–150
nationalism, 143, 150, 153, 157–162,
    173–174, 191, 197, 199, 205–206, 234,
    244–247, 257
nation-states, 90–91
Nehru, Jawaharlal, 242
Netherlands, the, 122–123, 212
Newton, Isaac, 141
Ngo Dinh Diem, 248
Nicaragua, 261–262
Nigeria, 246, 289
Nkrumah, Kwame, 244
North Africa, 49
North American Free Trade Agreement
    (NAFTA), 278
North Atlantic Treaty Organization
    (NATO), 229, 259, 280
Northern Ireland, 280
North Korea, 230, 283, 299
North Vietnam, 248
Norway, 212
nuclear proliferation, 299

O

oil, 249, 277
Olmecs, 107
Organization of African Unity (OAU), 244
Organization of Petroleum Exporting
    Countries (OPEC), 237
Orthodox Christian Church, 46–47, 57
Ottoman empire, 47, 116–118, 161,
    191–192, 204
overpopulation, 288

P

Pacific Rim, 236–237
pagoda, 43
Pakistan, 243, 283
Palestine, 49, 60, 61, 160, 205, 250–252
Palestinian Arabs, 250–252, 282, 287
Pan-Africanism, 244
Panama, 263
Pan-Arabism, 205
Pan-Slavism, 162, 191
Pax Mongolia, 78
Pax Romana, 15, 17, 19
Perestroika, 256

Perón, Juan, 261
Persia, 49, 77
Peru, 151
Philippines, the, 122, 215
Phoenicia, 16
plague, bubonic, 82–83
Poland, 77, 153, 199, 203, 212, 215,
    228–229, 258
political revolutions, 144–151, 153–154,
    156–158
pollution, 296–297
polytheism, 4–6
population growth, 164, 188–189, 235,
    262, 275
porcelain, 43
Portugal, 82, 120–121
Protestantism, 88–90, 127

R

Rabin, Yitzhak, 251–252
Reconquista, 119–120
red guards, 240
reformation, 88–90
religious conflicts, 90, 242–243, 280–283
Renaissance, 84–91, 140
revolutions, 139–143, 144–151, 152–157,
    158, 160, 162, 163–169, 173, 177, 185,
    187, 195–198, 201, 229, 231–232, 238,
    240, 253–254, 260, 262, 292–294
Roman Catholic Church, 46, 57, 84,
    88–91, 124, 127, 142, 156, 159, 263
Romania, 204, 258
Rome, ancient, 15–17, 18–20, 25, 27, 45
Roosevelt, Franklin Delano, 212–213, 244
Russia, 44–45, 47, 77–79, 80–81, 117, 128,
    130, 143, 149, 152, 154–155, 157,
    160–162, 171–172, 185, 190–195,
    196–201, 204–205, 213, 215, 252, 257.
    See also Soviet Union
Russification, 155, 197, 200
Russo-Japanese War, 172, 197
Rwanda, 246

S

Saladin, 61
samurai, 74–75, 115, 171
Saudi Arabia, 237, 250, 254, 287, 290
Scientific Revolution, 139–143
scientific theories, 189
Sepoy Mutiny, 174
Serbia, 162, 191–192, 280
Shang, 7–8, 9–10, 21
Sharia, 21, 26, 49
shintoism, 73
shogun, 74–75
Sicily, 49, 53
Sikhism/Sikhs, 244, 281

Singapore, 237
Sino-Japanese War, 172
slaves/slavery, 4–5, 13, 20, 24, 50, 95–96,
    109, 121, 124, 150, 214, 290. *See also*
    enslaved people
slave trade, 123, 125, 173, 175–176
Slovakia, 259
Slovenia, 280
Smith, Adam, 165–166
social classes, 3–4, 8, 41–42, 56, 74,
    84–85, 118, 124, 146, 165–166, 197, 262
social Darwinism, 166–167, 174
socialism, 167, 275
solidarity, 258
Songhai, 92–94
South Africa, 231, 242, 246–248, 299
South America, 106–107, 111, 150–151,
    155, 288, 290
Southeast Asia, 17, 26, 27, 49, 112, 115,
    122, 173, 236, 242, 247–248, 278, 281
South Korea, 230, 237, 283
South Vietnam, 248
Soviet Union, 167, 199–201, 210–213,
    215, 225–232, 233–235, 250, 255–259,
    294, 299
Spain, 20, 27, 49, 53, 55, 83, 118–120,
    121–124, 126–127, 150–151, 156, 231
spiritual beliefs, 3
Sri Lanka, 282, 285
Stalin, Joseph, 196, 199–201, 211, 213,
    226, 228–299
Sudan, 246, 275, 284
Sumer, 6, 7, 16
Suu Kyi, Aung San, 248
Sweden, 206
Syria, 16, 49, 205, 231, 250, 252, 283, 290

T

Taiwan (Republic of China), 172, 237–239
Taoism, 21, 23–24, 26–27
technology, 1, 3, 8, 9, 11, 13, 16, 17, 43,
    52, 76, 78, 87, 94, 113–115, 117–118,
    119–120, 123, 125, 128, 164–165,
    171–172, 185–186, 188–189, 190,
    193–195, 210, 213, 230, 273, 275,
    277–278, 286–287, 291, 292–295
terrorism, 251–253, 261, 263, 273,
    279–280
Tibet, 40, 77, 281
total war, 194, 214
trade, development of, 10, 12, 17, 27, 52,
    62, 84–86, 108, 113, 126
trade, European, 62, 81–82, 94, 114, 116,
    122, 125, 128, 159
trade, global, 16–17, 19, 43, 45, 47,
    78–82, 95–96, 118–123, 156, 169, 170,
    172, 176–177, 207, 234, 236–237,
    240–241, 245, 263, 277–278, 290

Acknowledgments

Staff Credits:
The people who make up the *Global History and Geography Brief Review team*—representing design, editorial, marketing, and production services—are listed below. Bold type denotes the core team members.

Jane Breen, Jennifer McQueeney Creane, Kerry Dunn, **Thomas Ferreira,** Rebecca Hall, **Linda D. Johnson,** Candi McDowell, Julie Orr, Rachel Youdelman

Additional Credits:
The Quarasan Group, Inc.: Chicago, IL

Lapiz Digital Services: Chennai, India
Lapiz, Inc.: Boston, MA

English Language Learning Consultant: Anita Raducanu

Independent Reviewers: Andrew Gardner, Linda K. Lapp

Photographs
Every effort has been made to secure permission and provide appropriate credit for photographic material. The publisher deeply regrets any omission and pledges to correct errors called to its attention in subsequent editions.

Unless otherwise acknowledged, all photographs are the property of Pearson Education, Inc.

Photo locators denoted as follows: Top (T), Center (C), Bottom (B), Left (L), Right (R), Background (Bkgd)

Cover ©JustASC/Shutterstock; **i** (C) ©JustASC/Shutterstock; **xxii** Rex Babin; **xxiii** Universal Press Syndicate; **1** (R) Gretchen Medeiros; **16** (C) ©emei/Shutterstock; **35** (R) Gretchen Medeiros; **46** (TL) ©Sufi/Shutterstock; **47** Leslie Deeb; **51** Eugene Gordan; **71** Library of Congress; **87** Art Resource, NY; **108** Library of Congress; **128** (L) Demetrio Carrasco/©DK Images; **139** Currier and Ives/Library of Congress; **149** Library of Congress; **183** ©The Granger Collection, NY; **185** Library of Congress; **199** Comrade Lenin Cleans the World of Filth (1920), lithograph. Viktor Nikolayevich Deni/©The Granger Collection, NY; **225** U. S. Air Force Photo; **241** United Media; **257** Bob Englehart/Hartford Courant; **261** Library of Congress; **265** Bob Englehart/Hartford Courant; **287** Stephens Media; **285** North Jersey Media; **288** zorani/Getty Images; **311** John Trever.

Regents Exams: January 2016 04 © Paula J. Becker, **11** General Photographic Agency/Getty Images, **18** AP Photo/File; **August 2015 04** Peter N. Stearns et al., World Civilizations: The Global Experience, Pearson Longman (adapted), **08** The University of Iowa, Special Collections and University Archives, **09** "Another type of fossil fuel." (May 7, 2008) by Glenn McCoy, Universal UClick, **18** Pig Iron and Cattle in the Soviet Union, 1920–1940 from A History of the Modern World by Palmer and Colton. Copyright (c) Alfred A Knopf, an imprint of Random House., **22** Source: Ben Kiernan, The Pol Pot Regime, Yale University Press, 1996 (adapted); **June 2015 05** The Granger Collection, New York, **17** Reprinted with permission from Compton's by Britannica, © 2010 by Encyclopædia Britannica, Inc.; **January 2015 03** World History: Connections to Today, Prentice Hall, **07** Cagle Cartoons, **12** Keen and Haynes, A History of Latin America, Houghton Mifflin Harcourt, **18** Excerpt from "Gandhi - Great Figures in History Series. Published by Young-Jin Singapore Pte Ltd. Copyright (c) 2007. Used by permission of Young-Jin Singapore, Pte. Ltd., **19** Associated Press; **August 2014 07** Leonard Raven-Hill, Punch, October 2, 1912, **08** Library of Congress, **09** © Martin Jones/CORBIS; **June 2014 08** Mike Keefe, **09** Christian Science Monitor, **10** Felipe Guaman Poma de Ayala, Nueva Coronica y Buen Gobierno, Biblioteca Ayacucho, **10** © The Granger Collection Ltd., **18** Edmund Valtman, Hartford Times, March 9, 1961, **22** Shutterstock, **22** German Trenches, ca. June 16, 1916, Library of Congress, Prints and Photographs online catalog.

Text
Grateful acknowledgment is made to the following for copyrighted material:

Regents Exams: January 2016 06 The Physical and Moral Condition of the Children and Young Persons employed in Mines and Manufactures, 1843/British Library, **07** The Communist Manifesto/Karl Mark & Friedrich Engels, **07** New York Times, **09** Lyrics from "East is Red," **14** From "Sources of the Japanese Tradition", © Columbia University Press. All Rights Reserved., **15** "Sankin Kotai and the Hostage System," from Nakasendo Way © Walk Japan, **16** A People's History of the World/©Verso Books, **17** From J. Noakes and G. Pridham, eds., Documents on Nazism, 1919–1945, The Viking Press, **17** From J. Noakes and G. Pridham, eds., Documents on Nazism, 1919–1945, The Viking Press, **18** The Jewish Victims of the Holocaust, © Enslow Publishers, **19** The Holocaust Chronicle, Publications International, © 2000, **20** Native Laws Amendment Act, Act No. 54 of 1952, Digital Innovation South Africa online, **20** "This is Apartheid", © Christian Action, London, **21** "Tell Freedom: Memories of Africa", © Alfred A. Knopf, **22** "South Africa", Children's Press, a division of Scholastic, Inc.; **August 2015 07** "A History of the World in 6 Glasses," Copyright © Walker Publishing Company, **09** From Iran Awakening: One Woman's Journey to Reclaim Her Life and Country, Copyright © Random House., **13** From

Acknowledgements

"Modern History; the Rise of a Democratic, Scientific, and Industrial Civilization" by Carl L. Becker. Copyright © Pearson Education., **16** From "Eyewitness: Russia," published by Dorling Kindersley, **17** Stalin: Russia's Man of Steel, © Puffin Books, a division of Penguin Random House, **18** From A History of the Modern World, Copyright © Alfred A. Knopf, **20** To Destroy You Is No Loss: The Odyssey of a Cambodian Family, Anchor Books, 1989, **20** "Memoir of a Child's Nightmare," Children of Cambodia's Killing Fields, Yale University Press, 1997, **22** The Pol Pot Regime, Yale University Press, 1996; **June 2015 02** Library of Congress, **02** National Geographic Traveler: India, 2007, **07** New York Times Company, **07** Worldpress.org, a division of All Media, Inc., **13** West, Louis C. "The Economic Collapse of the Roman Empire." The Classical Journal 28.2 (1932): 96-106. Web., **14** Steven Kreis, The History Guide: Lectures on Ancient and Medieval European History, Lecture 17, History Guide online, **15** "Ottoman Empire (1301–1922)," BBC online, 2009, **16** "European Imperialism and the Balkan Crisis," The Ottomans, World Cultures, **16** A History of the Middle East, Viking, **18** Indian Independence and the Question of Pakistan, Choices Program, Watson Institute for International Studies, Brown University, **19** Scholastic World Cultures: Western Europe, Scholastic, 1988; **January 2015 02** Library of Congress, **04** The Asian World: 600-1500, Oxford University Press, **05** Montesquieu, The Spirit of the Laws, **11** Charles Gibson, Spain in America, Harper Torchbooks, **12** "Bartolomé de Las Casas," History Channel, **13** Latin America: A Concise Interpretive History, Prentice Hall, **14** "Extracts from 'In Defence of the Committee of Public Safety and Against Briez,'" September 25, 1793, in Virtue and Terror, Verso, **15** Robespierre: The Force of Circumstance, St. Martin's Press, **15** Liberty, Equality, Fraternity: Exploring the French Revolution, online site, a collaboration of the Roy Rosenzweig Center for History and New Media and the American Social History Project, **16** Helen Williams and the French Revolution, Raintree Steck-Vaughn (adapted), **16** The French Revolution, Heinemann Library, **17** Gandhi, Indian Opinion, September 2, 1905, **19** "Mohandas Gandhi (1869–1948)," Time, December 31, 1999; **August 2014 02** Philip K. Hitti, Capital Cities of Arab Islam, **05** Abbe´ Sieye`s, 1789, **06** Voices from Twentieth-Century Africa: Griots and Towncriers, Chinweizu, **07** H. Trenchard, Marshal of the Royal Air Force, 1928, **07** Hashimoto Kingoro, 1939 Speech, **15** "Child Soldiers Edition," Rights Sites News, The Advocates for Human Rights, Spring 2008, in www.TheAdvocatesforHumanRights.org/spring_2008_child_soldiers_edition.html. Copyright (c) The Advocates for Human Rights. Used by permission., **18** "Bill Gates' war on disease, poverty is an uphill battle," Seattle Post-Intelligencer, March 21, 2001, **19** "A Lack of Medicine," Faces, March, 2005, **20** "Afghan Refugee Children and Adolescents in Pakistan's Cities Receive Minimal International Assistance" from Women's Refugee Commission, May 29, 2002. Copyright (c) Women's Refugee Commission. Used by permission., **22** "Celebration of the World Day Against Child Labour," The International Programme on the Elimination of Child Labour of the International Labour Organization, June 2006; **June 2014 02** Chris Hinton, 1998, **06** National Geographic, **09** Oberlander and Muller, Essentials of Physical Geography Today, Second Edition, Random House, 1987, **09** Oliver J. Thatcher and Edgar H. McNeal, eds. A Source Book for Medieval History (New York, 1905), pp. 364-5., **14** William H. McNeill, Plagues and Peoples, Quality Paperback Book Club (adapted), **15** "Plague," Decameron Web, Brown University, **16** "Plague," Decameron Web, Brown University, **17** "Treaty of Nanjing (Nanking), 1842," USC-UCLA Joint East Asian Studies Center, **20** "Causes of the First World War," A Web of English History online, **21** W. A. Dolph Owings et al., eds., The Sarajevo Trial, Volume I, Documentary Publications

Note: Every effort has been made to locate the copyright owner of material reproduced on this component. Omissions brought to our attention will be corrected in subsequent editions.

This section contains an actual Regents Examination in Global History and Geography that was given in New York State in January 2016.

Circle your answers to Part 1. Write your responses to the short-answer questions in the spaces provided. Write your thematic essay and document-based essay on separate sheets of paper. Be sure to refer to the test-taking strategies in the front of this book as you prepare to answer the test questions.

Part I

Answer all questions in this part.

Directions (1–50): For each statement or question, record on your separate answer sheet the *number* of the word or expression that, of those given, best completes the statement or answers the question.

1 Which social scientists focus their studies on scarcity, resources, and profit motives?

  (1) archaeologists   (3) economists

  (2) historians   (4) sociologists

2 A geographer attempts to understand and interpret patterns and processes primarily by

  (1) examining political theories

  (2) authenticating oral histories

  (3) studying supply and demand models

  (4) analyzing spatial data at different scales

3 In a parliamentary system with multiple political parties in which no single party gains a majority, elections usually result in

  (1) command economies

  (2) religious conflict

  (3) coalition governments

  (4) secessionist movements

4 Which factor most influenced the construction of semipermanent settlements during the Neolithic period?

  (1) production of surplus food

  (2) drawings on cave walls

  (3) ability to harness fire

  (4) introduction of fishing nets

5 Which geographic feature was central in helping the Romans unify their empire?

  (1) Alps   (3) Mediterranean Sea

  (2) Tiber River   (4) Great Rift Valley

6 Which region was the birthplace of Confucianism, Buddhism, and Hinduism?

  (1) Africa   (3) Europe

  (2) Asia   (4) South America

7 Which area served as a cultural bridge between early China and Japan?

  (1) Persia   (3) India

  (2) Russia   (4) Korea

8 The role of Muslim religious leaders in Africa was to

  (1) spread the Four Noble Truths

  (2) emphasize the importance of ancestor worship

  (3) promote the caste system

  (4) introduce the teachings of the Qur'an (Koran)

9 The Abbasid and Ummayad empires are most closely associated with

  (1) causing the fall of the western Roman Empire

  (2) creating an Islamic Golden Age

  (3) controlling trade in the Strait of Malacca

  (4) inventing the compass and gunpowder

10 The European system of manorialism is most closely associated with

  (1) promoting social mobility

  (2) reviving and preserving learning

  (3) serving the spiritual needs of society

  (4) maintaining economic self-sufficiency

Base your answers to questions 11 and 12 on the map below and on your knowledge of social studies.

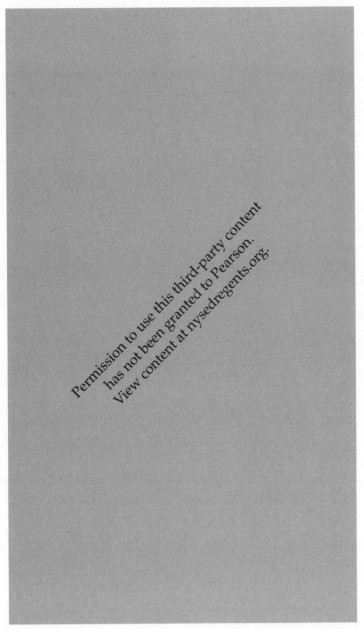

11 Based on this map, in which area did Europeans locate most of their trading bases?

(1) banks of the Ganges River   (3) coast of the Arabian Sea

(2) banks of the Indus River   (4) Bay of Bengal region

12 Which conclusion about the Indian economy during the Mughal period can best be supported using the information shown on this map?

(1) Cinnamon and pepper were the major products of Kashmir.

(2) Most textile-related goods were produced north of the Deccan Sultanate.

(3) Diamonds and gold were mined in the Bengal region.

(4) Many tropical products were raised near Delhi.

Base your answer to question 13 on the cartoon below and on your knowledge of social studies.

The Wittenberg Church

Source: Paula J. Becker (adapted)

13 Which period began as a result of the actions shown in this cartoon?

   (1) Italian Renaissance   (3) Scientific Revolution

   (2) Protestant Reformation   (4) Glorious Revolution

---

14 The kingdoms of Ghana and Mali became prosperous and powerful because of

   (1) their participation in the gold and salt trade

   (2) the military protection provided to them by the Egyptians

   (3) their dependence on legalism to enforce social control

   (4) the tax revenue they collected from Christian missionaries

15 The Chinese belief that China was the Middle Kingdom is an example of

   (1) extraterritoriality

   (2) ethnocentrism

   (3) filial piety

   (4) the Mandate of Heaven

Base your answer to question 16 on the graphic organizer below and on your knowledge of social studies.

Inca Civilization

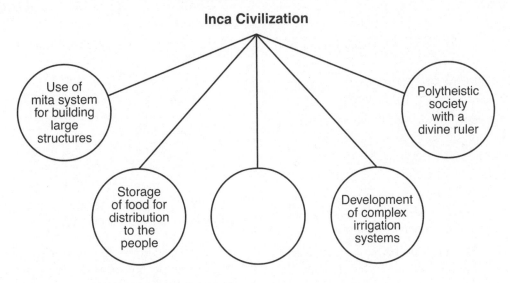

16 Which phrase best completes this graphic organizer?

(1) Building thousands of miles of roads
(2) Maintenance of a large naval fleet
(3) Establishment of a national library filled with hundreds of books
(4) Reliance on camel caravans

17 • Some Central Asian nomads made their living by fostering commerce along the Silk Road.
• Central Asian nomads invaded villages and cities when climate changes affected their food supply.
• Some Central Asian nomads adopted Islam and some embraced Islamic cultures.

Based on these statements, which generalization about Central Asian nomads can best be supported?

(1) They posed few challenges to settled societies.
(2) They allied with settled neighbors to repel common enemies.
(3) They interacted with settled societies.
(4) They contributed little to the culture of their settled neighbors.

18 The Ottoman Turks viewed Constantinople as being strategically important because it

(1) was the birthplace of the Prophet Muhammad
(2) would allow them to control the Vatican
(3) was a crossroads between Europe and Asia
(4) would provide them with access to the Persian Gulf

19 One way in which the voyages of Zheng He authorized by Emperor Yongle of China and the explorations funded by King Ferdinand and Queen Isabella of Spain are similar is that these voyages and explorations resulted in

(1) an increasing effort to preserve the status quo
(2) trade and cultural diffusion
(3) the creation of colonial empires
(4) naval wars between rival powers

20 Which country is located in the region known as Latin America?

(1) Portugal   (3) Vietnam
(2) Somalia   (4) Argentina

21 Which situation was an unintended consequence of Spain's colonization of the Americas?

(1) establishment of a favorable balance of trade
(2) introduction of the encomienda system
(3) transmission of communicable diseases
(4) exploitation of resources in new lands

22 One way in which Suleiman the Magnificent and Louis XIV are similar is that they both

(1) centralized political power
(2) introduced a new national religion
(3) strengthened the authority of the nobility
(4) freed peasants from feudal obligations

23 In the 16th and 17th centuries, the heliocentric theory became the centerpiece for debate between

(1) capitalism and communism
(2) science and religion
(3) colonialism and nationalism
(4) isolationism and globalism

24 In which way did the ideas of the Enlightenment influence the French Revolution?

(1) Superstition and ignorance were promoted.
(2) The principles of mercantilism were glorified.
(3) The divine right theory of kings was challenged.
(4) Punishments for criminal acts were rooted in vengeance.

25 In which way did the geographic diversity of Latin America affect newly independent countries?

(1) limiting the military power of Creoles
(2) forcing the Church to guarantee land reform
(3) making political unity difficult
(4) necessitating a reliance on Spain

26 Which statement best describes a consequence of Napoleon's failure to understand Russian geography?

(1) Rough waters in the Baltic Sea destroyed his fleet.
(2) A harsh winter cut off his army from needed supplies.
(3) His armies could not cross the high Ural Mountains.
(4) A long period of high temperatures and lack of water overcame his troops.

Base your answer to question 27 on the excerpt below and on your knowledge of social studies.

. . .That in some few instances the regular hours of work do not exceed ten, exclusive of the time allowed for meals; sometimes they are eleven, but more commonly twelve; and in great numbers of instances the employment is continued for fifteen, sixteen, and even eighteen hours consecutively.

That in almost every instance the Children work as long as the adults; being sometimes kept at work sixteen, and even eighteen hours, without any intermission. . . .

— *The Physical and Moral Condition of the Children and Young Persons Employed in Mines and Manufactures*, 1843

27 This type of evidence was used in the argument for

(1) modifying laissez-faire practices
(2) opposing the spread of communism
(3) restricting voting rights
(4) reforming the landholding system

Base your answer to question 28 on the passage below and on your knowledge of social studies.

. . .The bourgeoisie, by the rapid improvement of all instruments of production, by the immensely facilitated means of communication, draws all nations, even the most barbarian, into civilisation. The cheap prices of its commodities are the heavy artillery with which it batters down all Chinese walls, with which it forces the barbarians' intensely obstinate [persistent] hatred of foreigners to capitulate [give in]. It compels all nations, on pain of extinction, to adopt the bourgeois mode of production; it compels them to introduce what it calls civilisation into their midst, *i.e.*, to become bourgeois themselves. In a word, it creates a world after its own image. . . .
— Karl Marx and Friedrich Engels

28 Which statement supports the point of view expressed in this passage?

(1) The bourgeoisie needs to use military force to open markets.
(2) The bourgeoisie are backward compared to the barbarians.
(3) Foreigners and the bourgeoisie must work together to end the extinction of cultures.
(4) Cheap prices and industrial improvements are tools used by the bourgeoisie to impose its values.

29 • 1791—Declaration of the Rights of Women and the Female Citizen (France)
• 1829—Prohibition of sati (India)
• 1857, 1882—Married Women's Property Acts (Great Britain)

Which change in perception is suggested by these international developments regarding women?

(1) a decrease in political power for women
(2) a decline in the economic status of women
(3) a growing concern for the treatment of women
(4) an increase in the global exploitation of women

30 The Haitian Revolution and the Sepoy Rebellion happened in response to

(1) European colonial policies
(2) indigenous ethnic rivalries
(3) urban development
(4) religious divisions

Base your answer to question 31 on the notice below and on your knowledge of social studies.

> **NOTICE!**
> Travelers intending to embark on the Atlantic voyage are reminded that a state of war exists between Germany and her allies and Great Britain and her allies; that the zone of war includes the waters adjacent to the British Isles: that, in accordance with formal notice given by the Imperial German Government, vessels flying the flag of Great Britain, or any of her allies, are liable to destruction in those waters and that travelers sailing in the war zone on ships of Great Britain or her allies do so at their own risk.
> IMPERIAL GERMAN EMBASSY,
> Washington, D. C., April 22, 1915.

Source: *New York Times*, May 1, 1915 (adapted)

31 Which technological innovation of World War I is most closely associated with this German notice?

(1) tanks   (3) submarines
(2) airplanes   (4) machine guns

32 What was the main goal of Zionism?

(1) forming a representative government in China
(2) establishing a Jewish homeland in the region of Palestine
(3) improving the standard of living in developing countries
(4) creating an international peacekeeping organization to solve global conflicts

33 Which of these events that occurred in the Soviet Union was a direct cause of the other three?

(1) famine in Ukraine
(2) implementation of five-year plans
(3) establishment of collective farms
(4) development of heavy industry

Base your answer to question 34 on the map below and on your knowledge of social studies.

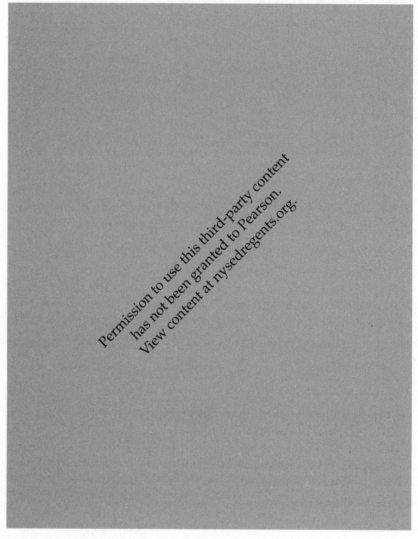

34 Based on this map, which region experienced the most severe drop in industrial production between 1929 and 1932?

(1) western Europe   (3) central Europe
(2) northern Europe   (4) southeastern Europe

35 Extreme nationalism, individuals existing for the good of the state, and unquestioning loyalty to the leader are the defining characteristics of

(1) fascism   (3) democracy
(2) liberalism   (4) theocracy

36 The Soviet Union's response to the formation of the North Atlantic Treaty Organization (NATO) was to create the

(1) Marshall Plan   (3) Truman Doctrine
(2) Warsaw Pact   (4) European Union

Base your answer to question 37 on the cartoon below and on your knowledge of social studies.

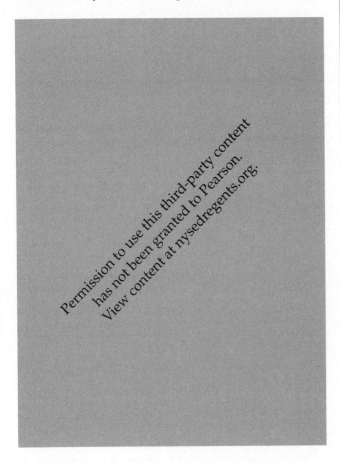

Permission to use this third-party content has not been granted to Pearson. View content at nysedregents.org;

37 Hitler's actions as expressed by this cartoon led Stalin to

(1) adopt a policy of appeasement
(2) take over Germany's industry
(3) join the Allies in the fight against Germany
(4) reduce the size of the Soviet army

38 Which statement about the impact of geography on the culture and history of the Middle East region in the 20th century is most accurate?

(1) Deserts have prevented military invasions.
(2) The uneven distribution of resources has led to conflict.
(3) The abundance of water has contributed to agricultural self-sufficiency.
(4) Mountains have halted cultural diffusion.

Base your answers to questions 39 and 40 on the song lyrics below and on your knowledge of social studies.

> **East is Red**
> The east is red, the sun is rising.
> China has brought forth a Mao Zedong.
> He amasses fortune for the people,
> Hurrah, he is the people's great savior.
>
> Chairman Mao loves the people,
> He is our guide,
> To build a new China,
> Hurrah, he leads us forward!
>
> The Communist Party is like the sun,
> Wherever it shines, it is bright.
> Wherever there is a Communist Party,
> Hurrah, there the people are liberated!

39 What is the main idea of this 1960s Chinese song?

(1) The Sun will never set on Chinese communism.
(2) Communist policies will liberate Mao Zedong.
(3) The Chinese people will become wealthy under communism.
(4) Mao Zedong will lead the Communist Party in building a new China.

40 This 1960s Chinese song would most likely have been sung during the

(1) return of Hong Kong
(2) Cultural Revolution
(3) Boxer Rebellion
(4) Tiananmen Square incident

41 During the Cold War, India's decision to support neither the United States nor the Soviet Union was based on its policy of

(1) nonalignment   (3) containment
(2) isolationism   (4) separatism

42 • Vietcong disappeared into jungle cover.
   • Sandstorms halted helicopter flights in Iraq.
   • Afghan mountain caves sheltered Osama bin Laden.

   Which generalization can best be applied to these situations?

   (1) Advanced technology ensures victory.
   (2) Religious tensions often promote disagreements.
   (3) Most military confrontations involve biological weapons.
   (4) Geography often has an influence on the course of a conflict.

43 A major obstacle to creating policies that address the issue of global warming is the conflict between

   (1) migrant labor and native workers
   (2) socialist governments and democratic governments
   (3) nations possessing nuclear weapons and those without
   (4) economic development and environmental protection

44 The practices of allowing animals to overgraze grasses and shrubs and of clearing trees to use for fuel have caused

   (1) coastal pollution   (3) acid rain
   (2) desertification   (4) desalination

45 In the late 1970s, the Chinese government created the one-child policy because its leaders realized that there is a direct relationship between population growth and

   (1) military strength
   (2) economic development
   (3) social mobility
   (4) political toleration

46 One way in which the Indian leaders Asoka and Akbar the Great are similar is that they are both best known for promoting

   (1) religious toleration
   (2) enslavement of prisoners
   (3) special taxes for Hindus
   (4) the spread of Buddhism

47 The Russian adoption of Orthodox Christianity and of the Cyrillic alphabet demonstrates the

   (1) impact of Ibn Battuta's travels
   (2) role of the printing press during the Reformation
   (3) leadership of Peter the Great
   (4) influence of the Byzantine Empire

48 Austria-Hungary's ultimatum to Serbia in 1914 and the United States military actions in Afghanistan beginning in 2001 are both reactions to acts of

   (1) imperialism   (3) communism
   (2) isolationism   (4) terrorism

49 Which leaders are most directly associated with the Cuban Revolution of 1959?

   (1) Emiliano Zapata and Francisco Villa
   (2) Juan Perón and Hugo Chávez
   (3) Fidel Castro and Che Guevara
   (4) Bernardo O'Higgins and Miguel Hidalgo

Base your answer to question 50 on the photographs below and on your knowledge of social studies.

Kemal Atatürk

Source: İlhan Akşit, Compiler,
Mustafa Kemal Atatürk, Akşit

Reza Pahlavi

Source: Iran Politics Club online,
Mohamad Reza Shah Pahlavi Photo Album

50 The style of clothing worn by Kemal Atatürk of Turkey and Reza Pahlavi of Iran in these photographs indicates these leaders' desire to

(1) westernize their nation

(2) support nationalist movements

(3) enforce fundamental Islamic principles

(4) adapt to the physical climate of their country

Answers to the essay questions are to be written in the separate essay booklet.

In developing your answer to Part II, be sure to keep this general definition in mind:

discuss means "to make observations about something using facts, reasoning, and argument; to present in some detail"

Part II

THEMATIC ESSAY QUESTION

Directions: Write a well-organized essay that includes an introduction, several paragraphs addressing the task below, and a conclusion.

Theme: Imperialism

> Since 1500, countries have pursued a policy of expansion known as imperialism for a variety of reasons. The effects of this policy can be viewed from different perspectives.

Task:

> Select *one* country that engaged in imperialism since 1500 and
> - Discuss the reasons this country engaged in imperialism
> - Discuss the effects of imperialism from the perspective of the people or society taken over *and/or* from the perspective of the conqueror

You may use any country that engaged in imperialism since 1500 from your study of global history and geography. Some suggestions you might wish to consider include Portugal, Spain, Great Britain, France, Italy, Belgium, and Japan.

You are *not* limited to these suggestions.

Do *not* use the United States as the focus of your response.

Guidelines:

In your essay, be sure to
- Develop all aspects of the task
- Support the theme with relevant facts, examples, and details
- Use a logical and clear plan of organization, including an introduction and a conclusion that are beyond a restatement of the theme

NAME _____ SCHOOL _____

Part III

DOCUMENT-BASED QUESTION

This question is based on the accompanying documents. The question is designed to test your ability to work with historical documents. Some of these documents have been edited for the purposes of this question. As you analyze the documents, take into account the source of each document and any point of view that may be presented in the document. Keep in mind that the language used in a document may reflect the historical context of the time in which it was written.

Historical Context:

> Throughout history, governments have developed and established laws and orders for a variety of reasons. The *laws for the warriors under the Tokugawa Shogunate, the Nazi orders and laws of the Third Reich*, and *the pass laws of the Republic of South Africa* had many impacts on societies, regions, and groups of people.

Task: Using the information from the documents and your knowledge of global history, answer the questions that follow each document in Part A. Your answers to the questions will help you write the Part B essay in which you will be asked to

> Select *two* sets of laws and/or orders mentioned in the historical context and for *each*
>
> - Explain what the government hoped to achieve by establishing these laws and/or orders
> - Discuss the impacts of these laws and/or orders on a specific society, region, or group of people

In developing your answers to Part III, be sure to keep these general definitions in mind:

- (a) <u>explain</u> means "to make plain or understandable; to give reasons for or causes of; to show the logical development or relationships of"
- (b) <u>discuss</u> means "to make observations about something using facts, reasoning, and argument; to present in some detail"

Part A
Short-Answer Questions

Directions: Analyze the documents and answer the short-answer questions that follow each document in the space provided.

Document 1

By 1603, Tokugawa Ieyasu had won the civil war and had become the supreme ruler of Japan, the Shogun. His successor, Shogun Hidetada, put forth laws for military households. These households included members of the warrior class: the daimyo, the greater samurai, and the lesser samurai.

Laws Governing Military Households (1615), Excerpts

. . . [4] Great lords (daimyō), the lesser lords, and officials should immediately expel from their domains any among their retainers [vassals] or henchmen who have been charged with treason or murder. . . .

[6] Whenever it is intended to make repairs on a castle of one of the feudal domains, the [shogunate] authorities should be notified. The construction of any new castles is to be halted and stringently [strictly] prohibited.

"Big castles are a danger to the state." Walls and moats are the cause of great disorders.

[7] Immediate report should be made of innovations which are being planned or of factional conspiracies [schemes by dissenting groups] being formed in neighboring domains. . . .

Source: Compiled by Ryusaku Tsunoda, et al., *Sources of the Japanese Tradition*,
Columbia University Press (adapted)

1 Based on this document, what is **one** way these laws limited the actions of the warrior class? [1]

_____

_____

Score ☐

Document 2

The sankin kotai or hostage system was included as part of the warrior class laws.

Alternate residence duty, or sankin kotai, was a system developed in the Warring States period and perfected by the Tokugawa shogunate. In essence, the system demanded simply that daimyo reside in the Tokugawa castle at Edo for periods of time, alternating with residence at the daimyo's own castle. When a daimyo was not residing in the Tokugawa castle, he was required to leave his family at his overlord's [shogun's] castle town. It was, at its simplest, a hostage system which required that either the daimyo or his family (including the very important heir) always be physically subject to the whim of the overlord. . . .

Source: "Sankin Kotai and the Hostage System," *Nakasendo Way*, Walk Japan

2 Based on this document, what is **one** way the daimyo were affected by the Tokugawa hostage system (alternate residence duty)? [1]

_____

_____

Score ☐

Document 3

. . . These measures [the hostage system, the isolation policy, and the banning of guns] succeeded in bringing the bloody wars of the previous period to an end. But the Shoguns could not stop the society beneath them continuing to change. The concentration of the lords and their families in Edo led to a growing trade in rice to feed them and their retainers, and to a proliferation [increase] of urban craftspeople and traders catering to their needs. Japan's cities grew to be some of the biggest in the world. The merchant class, although supposedly of very low standing, became increasingly important, and a new urban culture of popular poetry, plays and novels developed, different in many ways from the official culture of the state. A relaxation of the ban on western books after 1720 led to some intellectuals showing an interest in western ideas, and a 'School of Dutch learning' began to undertake studies in science, agronomy [agriculture] and Copernican astronomy. As money became increasingly important, many of the *samurai* became poor, forced to sell their weapons and to take up agriculture or crafts in order to pay their debts. Meanwhile repeated famines hit the peasantry—almost a million died in 1732 (out of a population of 26 million), 200,000 in 1775, and several hundred thousands in the 1780s—and there were a succession of local peasant uprisings. The Tokugawa political superstructure remained completely intact. But beneath it social forces were developing with some similarities to those in western Europe during the Renaissance period. . . .

Source: Chris Harman, *A People's History of the World*, Verso (adapted)

3 According to Chris Harman, what is **one** change that occurred in Japan as a consequence of the hostage system and isolationist policy? [1]

_____

_____

Score ☐

Document 4a

Excerpts of the [Nazi] Party Boycott Order, 28 March 1933

> . . . 3. The action committees must at once popularize the boycott by means of propaganda and enlightenment. The principle is: No German must any longer buy from a Jew or let him and his backers promote their goods. The boycott must be general. It must be supported by the whole German people and must hit Jewry in its most sensitive place. . . .
>
> 8. The boycott must be coordinated and set in motion everywhere at the same time, so that all preparations must be carried out immediately. Orders are being sent to the SA and SS so that from the moment of the boycott the population will be warned by guards not to enter Jewish shops. The start of the boycott is to be announced by posters, through the press and leaflets, etc. The boycott will commence on Saturday, 1 April on the stroke of 10 o'clock. It will be continued until an order comes from the Party leadership for it to stop. . . .

Source: J. Noakes and G. Pridham, eds., *Documents on Nazism, 1919–1945*, The Viking Press

4a In 1933, what is **one** action the Nazi Party wanted the German people to take against the Jews based on this excerpt? [1]

_____

_____

Score ☐

Document 4b

Decree Eliminating Jews from German Economic Life, 12 November 1938

> . . . *Article 1*
> 1. From 1 January 1939 the running of retail shops, mail order houses and the practice of independent trades are forbidden to Jews. . . .

Source: J. Noakes and G. Pridham, eds., *Documents on Nazism, 1919–1945*, The Viking Press

4b As a result of this Nazi decree, what is **one** specific economic situation faced by the Jewish people? [1]

_____

_____

Score ☐

Document 5a

"The Night of Broken Glass"

Source: Anne Frank Guide online

Document 5b

. . . The Nazis claimed that Kristallnacht was an uprising by ordinary Germans. Actually, it was carefully planned. The government ordered squads of Brownshirts into the streets. Their job was to destroy and terrorize. The Gestapo, or secret police, received orders not to stop the violence. Instead, they were to sweep through the burning neighborhoods, arresting Jews.

Kristallnacht was a turning point. The Nazis stepped up their efforts to "Aryanize" the German economy. Jews had been losing their property since Hitler came to power. Now, taking it from them became an official policy.

On November 12, the government levied a fine of one billion *reichmarks* on the German Jewish community. This was punishment for the act of one troubled teenager.* In addition to this, Jewish victims of Kristallnacht had to pay for the damage out of their own pockets. They could not collect insurance to cover their losses. . . .

Source: Linda J. Altman, *The Jewish Victims of the Holocaust*, Enslow Publishers (adapted)

*Herschel Grynszpan had killed a German at the German embassy in Paris out of anger over his parents' deportation. This act was used by the government to justify its actions on Kristallnacht.

5 Based on this photograph and passage, what are **two** impacts of the policy of Kristallnacht on the Jewish population in Germany? [2]

(1)_____

_____

Score ☐

(2)_____

_____

Score ☐

Document 6

- September 1996: A report by London's *Jewish Chronicle* claims that $4 billion ($65 billion in 1996 dollars*) looted by the Nazis from Jews and others during World War II was diverted to Swiss banks. The sum is about 20 times the amount previously acknowledged by the Swiss; . . .

- October 29, 1996: . . .Art, coins, and other items looted by Nazis from the homes of Austrian Jews are sold at a benefit auction in Vienna. It is the intent of the auction organizers to keep the items in the Jewish community. By day's end, the auction grosses $13.2 million, with proceeds going to aid Holocaust survivors and their heirs. . . .

- February 12, 1997: Switzerland, stung by allegations that the wartime government accepted and laundered [concealed the source of] funds from Nazi Germany that had been looted from Jews, agrees to create a $71 million fund for Holocaust survivors and their heirs.

Source: *The Holocaust Chronicle*, Publications International, 2000

*Four billion dollars during World War II had the approximate value of $65 billion in 1996.

6 Based on this information from the *The Holocaust Chronicle*, state **one** action taken in an attempt to compensate Holocaust survivors and their heirs many years after World War II ended.   [1]

_____

_____

Score ☐

Document 7a

Native Laws Amendment Act, Act No. 54 of 1952, Union of South Africa

> . . . 29 (1) Whenever any authorized officer has reason to believe that any native [black South African] within an urban area or an area proclaimed in terms of section *twenty-three*—
>
> (a) is an idle person in that—
>
>   (i) he is habitually unemployed and has no sufficient honest means of livelihood. . .
>
> he [authorized officer] may, without warrant arrest that native or cause him to be arrested and any European police officer or officer appointed under sub-section (1) of section *twenty-two* may thereupon bring such a native before a native commissioner or magistrate who shall require the native to give a good and satisfactory account of himself. . . .

Source: Native Laws Amendment Act, Act No. 54 of 1952, Digital Innovation South Africa online (adapted)

7a Under the Union of South Africa Act No. 54 of 1952, what could happen to a native person who was habitually unemployed? [1]

_____

Score ☐

Document 7b

Natives (Abolition of Passes and Coordination of Documents) Act, Act No. 67 of 1952, Union of South Africa

> . . . Any policeman may at any time call upon an African [black] who has attained the age of sixteen years to produce his reference [pass] book. If a reference book has been issued to him but he fails to produce it because it is not in his possession at the time, he commits a criminal offence and is liable to a fine not exceeding ten pounds or imprisonment for a period not exceeding one month. . . .

Source: Leslie Rubin and Neville Rubin, *This is Apartheid*, Christian Action, London (adapted)

7b Under the Union of South Africa Act No. 67 of 1952, what penalty could be given to a sixteen-year-old or older African black if he failed to produce his reference book? [1]

_____

Score ☐

Document 8

This excerpt is based on Peter Abrahams's memories and his conversation with his black South African boss, Jim.

> . . . When Jim left his Pedi village in the northern Transvaal he had to go to the nearest police station or Native Affairs Department. There he got a Trek Pass. This permitted him to make the journey to Johannesburg. On reaching the city he got an Identification Pass and a Six-Day Special Pass. He paid two shillings each month for the Identification Pass. The Six-Day Special was his protection while he looked for work. He did not find work during his first six days in the city. He did not go to the pass office to renew his Six-Day Special. He was picked up on the eighth day and spent two weeks in jail as a vagrant [person without residence or work]. That taught him to go to the pass office regularly. . . .

Source: Peter Abrahams, *Tell Freedom: Memories of Africa*, Alfred A. Knopf

8 According to Peter Abrahams, what was ***one*** way the pass laws affected his boss, Jim? [1]

_____

_____

Score ☐

Document 9

> Resistance to white domination was continuous but unsuccessful. The South African police and the army were called out every time blacks rose up against the apartheid laws that made their lives so miserable. On March 21, 1960, a group of unarmed blacks made their way to the police station in Sharpeville (a black township) to hold a peaceful protest against the passbook laws. No black in South Africa could travel, live, or work without a passbook. This hated document was the record of a person's life as defined by the white government. Thousands of demonstrators left their passbooks at home, expecting to be arrested. They thought this would show the government's policy could not continue if it had to arrest thousands. But the peaceful demonstration was met with gunfire. When it was over, sixty-nine blacks were dead, shot in the back by the police as they tried to flee when the shooting began. Their deaths sparked a nationwide protest.

Source: Blauer and Lauré, *South Africa*, Children's Press

9a Based on this document, what action did black South Africans take to oppose the pass laws? [1]

_____

_____

Score ☐

b Based on this document, what was the South African government's response to the situation in Sharpeville on March 21, 1960? [1]

_____

_____

Score ☐

Part B
Essay

Directions: Write a well-organized essay that includes an introduction, several paragraphs, and a conclusion. Use evidence from *at least four* documents in your essay. Support your response with relevant facts, examples, and details. Include additional outside information.

Historical Context:

> Throughout history, governments have developed and established laws and orders for a variety of reasons. The **laws for the warriors under the Tokugawa Shogunate, the Nazi orders and laws of the Third Reich,** and **the pass laws of the Republic of South Africa** had many impacts on societies, regions, and groups of people.

Task: Using the information from the documents and your knowledge of global history, write an essay in which you

> Select **two** sets of laws and/or orders mentioned in the historical context and for **each**
>
> - Explain what the government hoped to achieve by establishing these laws and/or orders
> - Discuss the impacts of these laws and/or orders on a specific society, region, or group of people

Guidelines:

In your essay, be sure to

- Develop all aspects of the task
- Incorporate information from *at least four* documents
- Incorporate relevant outside information
- Support the theme with relevant facts, examples, and details
- Use a logical and clear plan of organization, including an introduction and a conclusion that are beyond a restatement of the theme

This section contains an actual Regents Examination in Global History and Geography that was given in New York State in August 2015.

Circle your answers to Part 1. Write your responses to the short-answer questions in the spaces provided. Write your thematic essay and document-based essay on separate sheets of paper. Be sure to refer to the test-taking strategies in the front of this book as you prepare to answer the test questions.

Part I

Answer all questions in this part.

Directions (1–50): For each statement or question, record on your separate answer sheet the *number* of the word or expression that, of those given, best completes the statement or answers the question.

1 The Europeans referred to China as the *Far East*. The Chinese referred to China as the *Middle Kingdom*. What do these terms illustrate?

(1) The names of places refer to significant physical features.
(2) Most people do not understand geography.
(3) The point of view of people influences geographic labels.
(4) Place names sometimes commemorate important events.

2 In which economic system does the government make most major decisions about what to produce, how much to produce, and for whom the goods and services will be produced?

(1) traditional   (3) command
(2) mixed   (4) market

3 Throughout history, a basic purpose of government has been to provide

(1) equal rights for all people
(2) laws to maintain order
(3) representation for all social classes
(4) separate political and religious systems

4 The Neolithic Revolution is considered a turning point in global history because it led to

(1) increasing migrations of people in search of food
(2) increasing use of animal skins for clothing
(3) a belief in a spiritual world
(4) the development of civilization

5 The primary reason ancient peoples of the Nile River valley built levees, dikes, and reservoirs was to

(1) purify sacred waters
(2) create a shorter route to distant cities
(3) defend against invaders
(4) increase agricultural production

6 In the practice of religion, the Ten Commandments are to Christianity as the Eightfold Path is to

(1) Buddhism   (3) Islam
(2) Daoism   (4) Shinto

7 Mandate of Heaven, production of silk, and reverence for ancestors are all characteristics associated with civilizations in

(1) India   (3) Greece
(2) China   (4) West Africa

8 • Made advances in mathematics, science, and medicine
 • Preserved Greek and Roman learning
 • Influenced Spanish architecture and literature

These achievements are most closely associated with the

(1) Golden Age of Islam
(2) Maya Empire
(3) Gupta Empire
(4) Tang dynasty

9 Which country has acted as a cultural bridge between China and Japan?

(1) Philippines   (3) Korea
(2) Vietnam   (4) Bangladesh

10 After the fall of the Mongol Empire, which city emerged as the new political and cultural center of Russia?

(1) Moscow   (3) Novgorod
(2) Warsaw   (4) Kiev

Base your answer to question 11 on the chart below and on your knowledge of social studies.

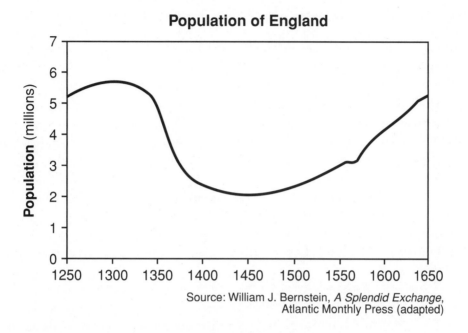

Population of England

Source: William J. Bernstein, *A Splendid Exchange*, Atlantic Monthly Press (adapted)

11 The population trend from 1350 to 1450 is most likely the result of the
  (1) development of trade with the Americas
  (2) raids by Vikings on coastal cities
  (3) defeat of the Spanish Armada by England
  (4) spread of the bubonic plague in England

12 Which characteristic was common to the cities of the Hanseatic League in Europe and the cities of the African kingdom of Ghana?

  (1) location on key trade routes
  (2) indirect control by the papacy
  (3) management of local gold mines
  (4) development as centers of woolen industry

13 Which leader started the Protestant Reformation by speaking out against papal abuses and the sale of indulgences in the Ninety-five Theses?
  (1) John Calvin   (3) John Wycliffe
  (2) Henry VIII   (4) Martin Luther

14 What was one important result of Mansa Musa's pilgrimage to Mecca?

  (1) creation of a large navy
  (2) translation of the Qur'an from Arabic to Swahili
  (3) establishment of diplomatic ties with other Muslim states
  (4) preservation of animistic traditions in the Arabian Peninsula

Base your answer to question 15 on the map below and on your knowledge of social studies.

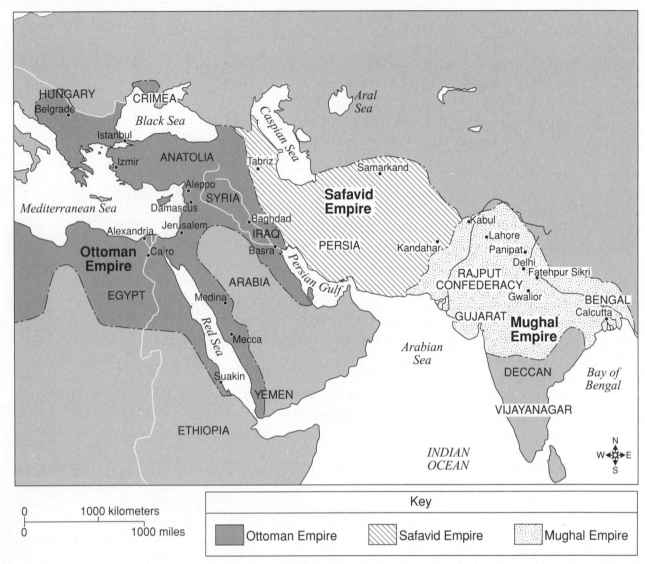

Source: Peter N. Stearns et al., *World Civilizations: The Global Experience*, Pearson Longman (adapted)

15 Which statement can best be supported by the information shown on this map?

(1) The Ottoman Empire included parts of northern Africa.

(2) The Safavid Empire controlled the entire Indian subcontinent.

(3) The Mughal Empire occupied territory adjacent to the Mediterranean Sea.

(4) The Ottoman Empire conquered less territory than either the Safavid or the Mughal Empire.

Base your answers to questions 16 and 17 on the speakers' statements below and on your knowledge of social studies.

Speaker A: It was a combination of the Protestant wind and the island nature of our nation that protected us. Surely, Philip must be upset at his defeat.

Speaker B: Our archipelago and divine winds have protected us once again. The Mongols may have taken China, but they cannot conquer us.

Speaker C: To support our growing population, we must find a suitable way to farm. With floating gardens on our lake, we should be able to grow enough to meet our demand.

Speaker D: We have connected highland and lowland areas by building networks of roads and bridges. We have also built terraces into our mountainsides to grow crops.

16 Which two speakers discuss how their society modified their environment?

(1) *A* and *B*   (3) *C* and *D*
(2) *B* and *C*   (4) *D* and *A*

17 Which speaker is most likely from 16th-century England?

(1) *A*   (3) *C*
(2) *B*   (4) *D*

18 Which statement best describes a key aspect of mercantilism?

(1) removing tariffs to increase free trade between empires
(2) acquiring colonies to provide a favorable balance of trade
(3) eliminating private ownership of the means of production
(4) encouraging subsistence agriculture

19 One way in which Suleiman the Magnificent and Peter the Great are similar is that they both

(1) modernized their military
(2) promoted free speech
(3) isolated their people from outside influences
(4) reduced taxes levied on their people

20 The Magna Carta and the English Bill of Rights both served to

(1) extend the voting privileges of commoners
(2) abolish the government's role in levying taxes
(3) limit the power of the monarchy
(4) support the theory of the divine right of kings

21 Which individual suggested the idea that if a government fails to protect its people's natural rights of life, liberty, and property, the people have the right to overthrow it?

(1) Karl Marx
(2) John Locke
(3) Thomas Hobbes
(4) Niccolò Machiavelli

22 One scientific belief held by both René Descartes and Isaac Newton is that

(1) reasoned thought is the way to discover truth
(2) new theories should be made to fit existing traditional ideas
(3) the method by which discoveries are made is unimportant
(4) difficult problems should be solved by reading religious texts

23 Simón Bolívar, Toussaint L'Ouverture, and José de San Martín are all associated with revolutions in

(1) Africa   (3) South Asia
(2) Europe   (4) Latin America

Base your answers to questions 24 and 25 on the maps below and on your knowledge of social studies.

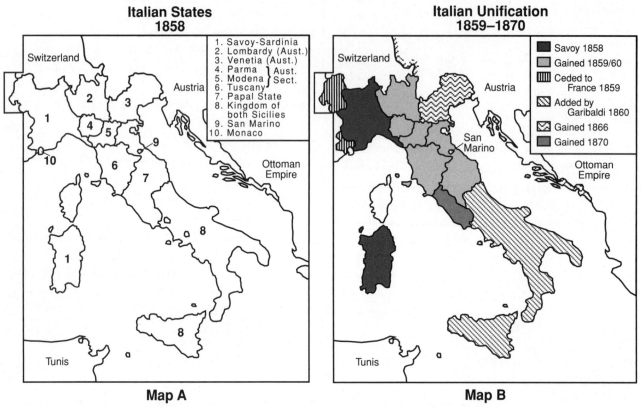

Map A

Map B

Source: Alexander Ganse, 2000 (adapted)

24 Which factor provided the motivation for the changes that took place between 1858 and 1870 as indicated on these maps?

   (1) exploration   (3) religion

   (2) appeasement   (4) nationalism

25 Which pair of individuals played a direct role in the changes that took place between Map A and Map B?

   (1) Otto Von Bismarck and Wilhelm II

   (2) Klemens von Metternich and Victor Emmanuel III

   (3) Camillo di Cavour and Guiseppe Mazzini

   (4) Alexander II and Frederick the Great

26 In the late 1700s, the Industrial Revolution developed in Britain because Britain

(1) possessed key factors of production
(2) excluded foreign investors
(3) suppressed the enclosure movement
(4) required a minimum wage be paid to workers

Base your answers to questions 27 and 28 on the passage below and on your knowledge of social studies.

… The Opium War of 1839–42 was short and one-sided, due to the superiority of European weapons, which came as a complete surprise to the Chinese. In the first skirmish alone, in July 1839, two British warships defeated twenty-nine Chinese ships. On land, the Chinese and their medieval weapons were no match for British troops armed with state-of-the-art muskets. By the middle of 1842 British troops had seized Hong Kong, taken control of the key river deltas, and occupied Shanghai and several other cities. The Chinese were forced to sign a peace treaty that granted Hong Kong to the British, opened five ports for the free trade of all goods, and required the payment of reparations to the British in silver, including compensation for the opium that had been destroyed by Commissioner Lin….

— Tom Standage

27 Which term best characterizes the events described in this passage?

(1) industrialization   (3) containment
(2) imperialism   (4) cultural diffusion

28 What was an immediate result of the Opium War described in this passage?

(1) signing the Treaty of Nanking
(2) forming the Guomindang
(3) beginning the Boxer Rebellion
(4) organizing the Taiping Rebellion

29 Which event sparked the outbreak of World War I?

(1) attack on Pearl Harbor by Japan
(2) Germany's invasion of Poland
(3) Bolshevik coup d'état in Russia
(4) assassination of the Austrian Archduke

30 Which agreement was labeled by the Nazis as unfair to Germany?

(1) Treaty of Versailles
(2) Soviet Nonaggression Pact
(3) Munich Pact
(4) Treaty of Brest-Litovsk

31 Japan expanded her empire in the 1930s and 1940s to include parts of

(1) eastern Europe and the Middle East
(2) China and Southeast Asia
(3) Turkey and the Soviet Union
(4) Australia and India

32 Which geographic factor enabled the German blitzkrieg to succeed?

(1) swift running rivers
(2) mountain ranges
(3) relatively flat terrain
(4) tropical climate

33 Which action is most closely associated with totalitarian governments?

(1) allowing public discussion of issues and building consensus
(2) accepting criticism and permitting dissent
(3) engaging in censorship and propaganda campaigns
(4) having open and transparent elections with multiple political parties

34 The purpose of Mohandas Gandhi's actions such as the Salt March and the textile boycott was to

(1) begin a cycle of armed revolution
(2) draw attention to critical issues
(3) increase the strength of the military
(4) resist the power of religious leaders

Base your answer to question 35 on the cartoon below and on your knowledge of social studies.

We Tried Everything but Dynamite

Source: J. N. "Ding" Darling, *Des Moines Register*, October 4, 1948 (adapted)

35 What is the main idea of this cartoon?

(1) The United Nations is usually successful in freeing nations from communist control.
(2) Western nations are frustrated by the strength of communist control in Eastern Europe.
(3) Nations of the West are willing to negotiate with the Soviet Union.
(4) The Soviet Union will usually cooperate with the United Nations.

36 The 38th parallel in Korea and the 17th parallel in Vietnam were used to mark

(1) boundaries created by mountain ranges
(2) demarcation lines instituted by papal authority
(3) territorial claims disputed between ethnic minorities
(4) political divisions established between communist and noncommunist territories

37 Prior to 1947, the Indian National Congress and the Muslim League worked together seeking to end

(1) nonviolence   (3) foreign rule
(2) religious diversity   (4) nonalignment

38 What was an immediate result of the Great Leap Forward (1958)?

(1) independence of Kenya from Great Britain
(2) the breakup of the Soviet Union
(3) the relocation of Bosnian refugees
(4) increased famine in China

Base your answer to question 39 on the passage below and on your knowledge of social studies.

… The grim statutes [laws] that I would spend the rest of my life fighting stared back at me from the page: the value of a woman's life was half that of a man (for instance, if a car hit both on the street, the cash compensation due to the woman's family was half that due the man's); a woman's testimony in court as a witness to a crime counted only half as much as a man's; a woman had to ask her husband's permission for divorce. The drafters of the penal code had apparently consulted the seventh century for legal advice. The laws, in short, turned the clock back fourteen hundred years, to the early days of Islam's spread, the days when stoning women for adultery and chopping off the hands of thieves were considered appropriate sentences.…

— Shirin Ebadi, *Iran Awakening*

39 Based on this passage, which statement is a valid conclusion about Iran following the revolution in 1979?

(1) Men were often penalized for their treatment of women.
(2) Laws were changed to reflect Western legal principles.
(3) The legal system discriminated against women.
(4) Legal decisions were based on economic values.

40 Which sequence of 20th-century Cold War events is in the correct chronological order?

(1) fall of the Berlin Wall → Cuban missile crisis → adoption of the Marshall Plan
(2) Cuban missile crisis → fall of the Berlin Wall → adoption of the Marshall Plan
(3) fall of the Berlin Wall → adoption of the Marshall Plan → Cuban missile crisis
(4) adoption of the Marshall Plan → Cuban missile crisis → fall of the Berlin Wall

Base your answer to question 41 on the cartoon below and on your knowledge of social studies.

Source: Glenn McCoy, Universal Press Syndicate, May, 2008
(adapted)

41 What is the main idea of this cartoon?

(1) Many people have died as a result of consuming ethanol.
(2) Ethanol is produced from fossils and plants.
(3) Biofuel production is contributing to the world hunger problem.
(4) Biofuel production is the source of deadly greenhouse gases.

42 **"Dalit [Untouchable] Families Forbidden to Use Public Water-Tap"**
"Nepal Bans Bias Against Untouchables in Move to End Hindu Caste System"

These headlines reflect a conflict between

(1) traditional customs and modern law
(2) child labor and industrialization
(3) national self-determination and ethnic diversity
(4) access to resources and forced migration

43 Which region is most closely associated with the expansion of the Sahel and overgrazing in the savanna regions?

(1) South America   (3) Africa
(2) China   (4) Southeast Asia

44 Feudalism and manorialism played an important role in western European society during the

(1) medieval period
(2) Pax Romana
(3) Enlightenment
(4) Age of Exploration

45 Pope Urban II, Saladin, and King Richard the Lion-Hearted are leaders associated with the

(1) Age of Charlemagne
(2) Crusades
(3) Glorious Revolution
(4) Counter Reformation

46 One way in which the travels of Marco Polo and the voyages of Zheng He are similar is that both

(1) established colonial territories
(2) stimulated trade
(3) encouraged mass migrations
(4) led to discoveries in Africa

47 Which civilization is credited with recording data with quipu, developing an elaborate road system, and constructing Machu Picchu?

(1) Roman
(2) Egyptian
(3) Mesopotamian
(4) Inca

Base your answer to question 48 on the outline below and on your knowledge of social studies.

I. _____

A. Rule of Porfirio Diaz
B. Peasant support for Francisco Pancho Villa
C. Constitution of 1917
D. Land reform

48 Which revolution best completes this partial outline?

(1) Mexican
(2) Chinese
(3) Cuban
(4) Iranian

49 Some of the ethnic strife in Africa today can be traced back to the European division of Africa resulting from the

(1) Treaty of Tordesillas
(2) Congress of Vienna
(3) Berlin Conference
(4) Yalta Conference

50 One way in which the Armenians in the Ottoman Empire (1915) and the Tutsis in Rwanda (1994) are similar is that both groups

(1) sought safe haven in the Soviet Union
(2) suffered human rights violations
(3) seceded to create an independent state
(4) fled to escape a severe flood

Answers to the essay questions are to be written in the separate essay booklet.

In developing your answer to Part II, be sure to keep these general definitions in mind:

(a) <u>explain</u> means "to make plain or understandable; to give reasons for or causes of; to show the logical development or relationships of"

(b) <u>discuss</u> means "to make observations about something using facts, reasoning, and argument; to present in some detail"

Part II

THEMATIC ESSAY QUESTION

Directions: Write a well-organized essay that includes an introduction, several paragraphs addressing the task below, and a conclusion.

Theme: Movement of People and Goods

> Goods and ideas have moved from one place to another for a variety of reasons. The changes that resulted from the movement of these goods and ideas to new places significantly influenced groups of people, societies, and regions.

Task:

> Select *two* goods and/or ideas that moved from one place to another and for *each*
> - Explain how this good or idea moved from one place to another
> - Discuss how the movement of this good or idea significantly influenced a group of people, a society, *and/or* a region

You may use any goods or ideas from your study of global history and geography. Some suggestions you might wish to consider include the *goods* silk, salt, sugar, gold, wheat, oil, horses, and gunpowder, and the *ideas* of Buddhism, Christianity, Islam, and the authority of government comes from the people.

You are *not* limited to these suggestions.

Do *not* make the United States the focus of your answer.

Guidelines:

In your essay, be sure to
- Develop all aspects of the task
- Support the theme with relevant facts, examples, and details
- Use a logical and clear plan of organization, including an introduction and a conclusion that are beyond a restatement of the theme

NAME _____   SCHOOL _____

Part III

DOCUMENT-BASED QUESTION

This question is based on the accompanying documents. The question is designed to test your ability to work with historical documents. Some of these documents have been edited for the purposes of this question. As you analyze the documents, take into account the source of each document and any point of view that may be presented in the document. Keep in mind that the language used in a document may reflect the historical context of the time in which it was written.

Historical Context:

> Throughout history, leaders and governments have taken actions to increase power and to control their people. Three such leaders include ***Louis XIV of France, Joseph Stalin of the Soviet Union,*** and ***Pol Pot of Cambodia.*** The actions taken by these leaders and governments had a significant impact on their people and their society.

Task: Using the information from the documents and your knowledge of global history, answer the questions that follow each document in Part A. Your answers to the questions will help you write the Part B essay in which you will be asked to

> Choose ***two*** leaders mentioned in the historical context and for ***each***
> - Describe actions taken by the leader and his government to increase his power ***and/or*** to control his people
> - Discuss an impact the actions had on his people *or* society

In developing your answers to Part III, be sure to keep these general definitions in mind:

(a) <u>describe</u> means "to illustrate something in words or tell about it"

(b) <u>discuss</u> means "to make observations about something using facts, reasoning, and argument; to present in some detail"

Part A
Short-Answer Questions

Directions: Analyze the documents and answer the short-answer questions that follow each document in the space provided.

Document 1

> **...How Louis obtained money enough to govern as he pleased.**
>
> The first need of a king who wished to rule as he pleased was money. Louis had little trouble in raising money, for the reason that he did not need to ask for it, as the English kings did. The institution in France which resembled the English Parliament was the Estates General. But this body had never met frequently, and it could scarcely be said to exist any more, since it had not been assembled for nearly fifty years. Louis was therefore free to collect taxes and use the money as he saw fit....

Source: Carl L. Becker, *Modern History*, Silver, Burdett and Company

1 According to Carl L. Becker, what was *one* way Louis XIV exercised power over the finances of France? [1]

_____

_____

Score ☐

Document 2

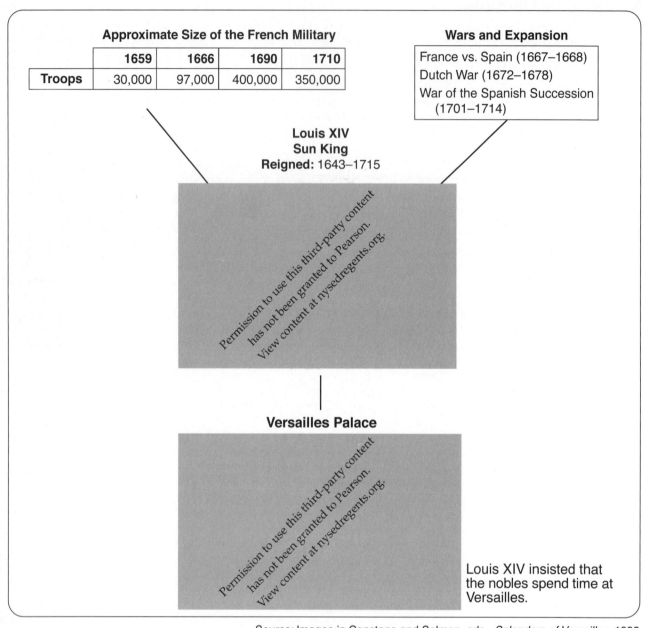

Approximate Size of the French Military

	1659	1666	1690	1710
Troops	30,000	97,000	400,000	350,000

Wars and Expansion

France vs. Spain (1667–1668)
Dutch War (1672–1678)
War of the Spanish Succession (1701–1714)

Louis XIV
Sun King
Reigned: 1643–1715

Permission to use this third-party content has not been granted to Pearson. View content at nysedregents.org.

Versailles Palace

Permission to use this third-party content has not been granted to Pearson. View content at nysedregents.org.

Louis XIV insisted that the nobles spend time at Versailles.

Source: Images in Constans and Salmon, eds., *Splendors of Versailles*, 1998

2 Based on the information in this graphic organizer, identify **one** way the rule of Louis XIV had an impact on France. [1]

Score

Document 3

Revocation [removal] of the Edict of Nantes

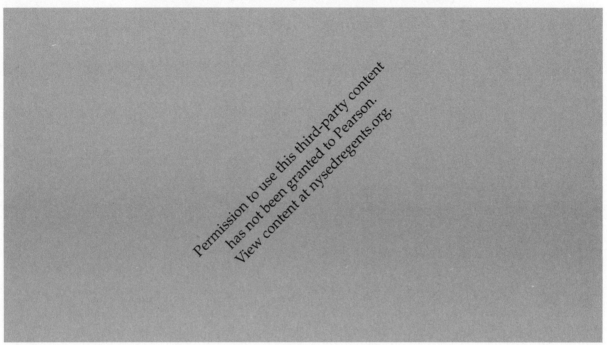

3 According to Martha Glaser, what is **one** impact the removal of the Edict of Nantes had on French society? [1]

_____

_____

Score ☐

Document 4a

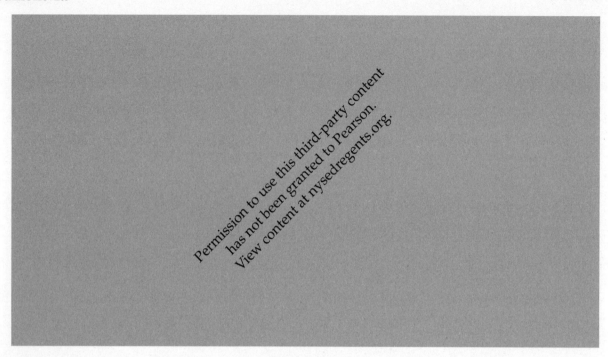

Permission to use this third-party content has not been granted to Pearson. View content at nysedregents.org.

Document 4b

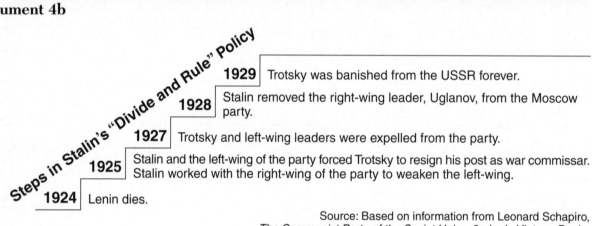

Steps in Stalin's "Divide and Rule" Policy

1929	Trotsky was banished from the USSR forever.
1928	Stalin removed the right-wing leader, Uglanov, from the Moscow party.
1927	Trotsky and left-wing leaders were expelled from the party.
1925	Stalin and the left-wing of the party forced Trotsky to resign his post as war commissar. Stalin worked with the right-wing of the party to weaken the left-wing.
1924	Lenin dies.

Source: Based on information from Leonard Schapiro,
The Communist Party of the Soviet Union, 2nd ed., Vintage Books

4 Based on these documents, identify *two* actions Stalin took to increase his power in the Soviet Union. [2]

(1) _____

_____

Score ☐

(2) _____

_____

Score ☐

Document 5

… The purge began its last, and deadliest, phase in the spring of 1937. Until then it had claimed thousands of victims from among the ruling classes. Now it began to claim millions of ordinary citizens who had nothing to do with politics.

Stalin knew that these people, let alone their families, hadn't committed treason and probably never would. He also knew the Russian proverb: "Fear has big eyes." He believed that arresting suspects for real crimes wasn't as useful as arresting the innocent. Arresting someone for a crime that could be proven would allow everyone else to feel safe. And safety bred confidence, and confidence drew people together. Fear, however, sowed suspicion. It built walls between people, preventing them from uniting against his tyranny. And the best way to create fear was to strike the innocent. Millions of innocent lives were, to Stalin, a small price to pay for safeguarding his power.

Creating fear was easy. The NKVD [Soviet secret police] had blanketed the country with informers. Like the secret police itself, informers were everywhere. An informer was stationed in every apartment house in every street in every Soviet town. Every office, shop, factory, and army barracks had its informers. He or she could be anyone: the janitor, the bank teller, the nice lady across the hall—or your best friend. Informers sat in the theaters, rode the trains, and strolled in the parks, eavesdropping on conversations. Although there is no way of checking, it was said that one person in five was a stool pigeon [informer]….

Source: Albert Marrin, *Stalin*, Puffin Books, 1988

5 According to Albert Marrin, what is **one** impact Stalin's policy had on the Soviet Union? [1]

_____

_____

Score ☐

Document 6a

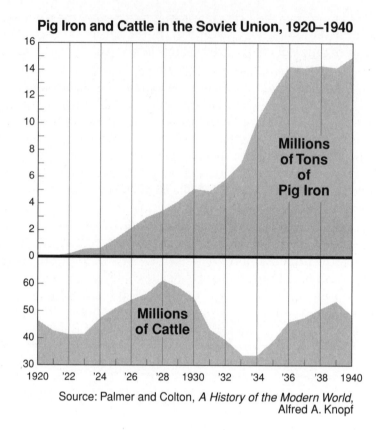

Pig Iron and Cattle in the Soviet Union, 1920–1940

Millions of Tons of Pig Iron

Millions of Cattle

Source: Palmer and Colton, *A History of the Modern World*, Alfred A. Knopf

Document 6b

PIG IRON AND CATTLE IN THE SOVIET UNION, 1920–1940

… If pig iron [cast iron] is taken as a measure of industrial activity and number of cattle as a similar indication for agriculture, the chart reveals clearly what happened in the twenty years after the Revolution—an enormous build-up of heavy industry at the expense of food supplies. Iron mines and forges, in the disorganization of the Revolution and civil war, were producing almost nothing in 1920. By the late 1920s, output of pig iron regained the pre-Revolutionary level, but the great upsurge came with the Second Five-Year Plan. By 1940 Russia produced more pig iron than Germany, and far more than Britain or France. Numbers of cattle grew in the 1920s, but fell catastrophically during the collectivization of agriculture after 1929, and by 1940 hardly exceeded the figure for 1920. Since 1940 the industrial development of the Soviet Union has been impressive, but agricultural production has continued to be a problem.…

Source: Palmer and Colton, *A History of the Modern World*, Alfred A. Knopf

6 According to Palmer and Colton, what was *one* impact of Stalin's control of the Soviet economy? [1]

_____

_____

Score ☐

Document 7

This passage recounts Teeda Butt Mam's experience in April, 1975 when Pol Pot and the Khmer Rouge took over Phnom Penh, the capital city of Cambodia.

> Khmer Rouge soldiers were on the streets when I awakened before dawn. Four- to six-man patrols moved through the avenues and alleys of Phnom Penh evicting everyone from homes, shops, and shelters. No delays were permitted. No requests allowed. Troublemakers were killed on the spot. Often, animals were slaughtered to intimidate owners.
>
> Already, on this second day of evacuation, orphanages and monasteries, hotels and hospitals, stood empty. Within hours of the takeover, people staying in these places had been driven from the city at gunpoint. Doctors and staff were killed if they resisted expulsion. Hospital patients too weak to walk were shot in their beds. Others, carrying still-attached plasma bottles, hobbled from the wards. Hospital beds, filled with the sick and dying, were pushed through the streets by relatives and friends....

Source: Criddle and Mam, *To Destroy You Is No Loss: The Odyssey of a Cambodian Family,* Anchor Books, 1989

7 According to Teeda Butt Mam, what was **one** action the Khmer Rouge took to control the people of Phnom Penh? [1]

_____

_____

Score ☐

Document 8a

Pol Pot's Khmer Rouge government, referred to as Angka, attempted to create an agrarian society. It established collective farms throughout Cambodia. This passage reflects the experiences of Sopheap K. Hang during this time period.

> … When the registration of the remaining people was over, a leader of Angka [Khmer Rouge] showed up. He stood before the people holding a microphone in one hand. He gathered the new people [primarily city people] to listen to his speech. "I am the new leader of Cambodia. From now on you have to address the new government as Angka. There are no homes for you to return to. You have to work as a group from now on. No one can own property. Everything you own belongs to Angka [the government]. No more city lifestyle. Everyone has to dress in black uniforms." My mother looked at my father with concern. "No one can question Angka," he said. "If you have courage to question Angka, you will be taken to the reeducation learning institution." That meant we would be executed. Everyone, including my parents, was numb. We could not think. Our bodies were shaking and our minds were paralyzed by the imposing speech of Angka.…

Source: Sopheap K. Hang, "Memoir of a Child's Nightmare," *Children of Cambodia's Killing Fields,* Yale University Press, 1997

8a According to Sopheap K. Hang, what was **one** action taken by Angka, Pol Pot's government, to control the Cambodian people? [1]

_____

_____

Score [ ]

Document 8b

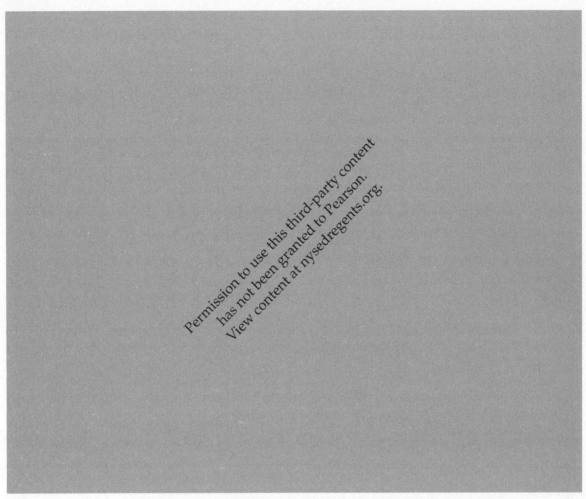

8b Based on this illustration by Sitha Sao, state **one** way the actions of Pol Pot's government affected the people. [1]

_____

_____

Score ☐

Document 9a

Approximate Death Tolls in Democratic Kampuchea [Cambodia], 1975–1979			
	1975 Population	Number who perished	Percent who perished
Total Cambodia	7,890,000	1,671,000	21

Source: Ben Kiernan, *The Pol Pot Regime,* Yale University Press, 1996 (adapted)

Document 9b

... I initially estimated the DK [Democratic Kampuchea] death toll at around 1.5 million people. This estimate was based on my own detailed interviews with 500 Cambodian survivors, including 100 refugees in France in 1979 and nearly 400 inside Cambodia in 1980. It was also supported by a survey carried out among a different sample, the refugees on the Thai-Cambodian border. In early 1980, Milton Osborne interviewed 100 Khmer refugees in eight different camps. This group included 59 refugees of non-elite background: 42 former farmers and fishermen and 17 former low-level urban workers. Twenty-seven of these people, and 13 of the other 41 interviewees, had had close family members executed in the Pol Pot period. The 100 refugees reported a total of 88 killings of their nuclear family members. 20 of the interviewees (14 of them from the non-elite group) also reported losing forty nuclear family members to starvation and disease during the Pol Pot period. This sample of 100 families (around 500 people) thus lost 128 members, or about 25 percent. Projected nationally, this points to a toll of around 1.5 million. The 39 farmers had lost 25 (of, say, 195) family members, suggesting a toll of 13 percent among the Cambodian peasantry....

Source: Ben Kiernan, *The Pol Pot Regime,* Yale University Press, 1996 (adapted)

9 According to Ben Kiernan, what was **one** way the actions of Pol Pot's government affected the people of Cambodia? [1]

_____

_____

Score ☐

Part B
Essay

Directions: Write a well-organized essay that includes an introduction, several paragraphs, and a conclusion. Use evidence from *at least four* documents in your essay. Support your response with relevant facts, examples, and details. Include additional outside information.

Historical Context:

Throughout history, leaders and governments have taken actions to increase power and to control their people. Three such leaders include *Louis XIV of France, Joseph Stalin of the Soviet Union,* and *Pol Pot of Cambodia.* The actions taken by these leaders and governments had a significant impact on their people and their society.

Task: Using the information from the documents and your knowledge of global history, write an essay in which you

> Choose *two* leaders mentioned in the historical context and for *each*
> - Describe actions taken by the leader and his government to increase his power *and/or* to control his people
> - Discuss an impact the actions had on his people *or* society

Guidelines:

In your essay, be sure to
- Develop all aspects of the task
- Incorporate information from *at least four* documents
- Incorporate relevant outside information
- Support the theme with relevant facts, examples, and details
- Use a logical and clear plan of organization, including an introduction and a conclusion that are beyond a restatement of the theme

This section contains an actual Regents Examination in Global History and Geography that was given in New York State in June 2015.

Circle your answers to Part 1. Write your responses to the short-answer questions in the spaces provided. Write your thematic essay and document-based essay on separate sheets of paper. Be sure to refer to the test-taking strategies in the front of this book as you prepare to answer the test questions.

Part I

Answer all questions in this part.

Directions (1–50): For each statement or question, record on your separate answer sheet the *number* of the word or expression that, of those given, best completes the statement or answers the question.

Base your answer to question 1 on the passage below and on your knowledge of social studies.

… Oral histories are as old as human beings. Before the invention of writing, information passed from generation to generation through the spoken word. Many people around the world continue to use oral traditions to pass along knowledge and wisdom. Interviews and recordings of community elders and witnesses to historical events provide exciting stories, anecdotes, and other information about the past….

—Library of Congress

1 Based on this passage, historians should treat oral histories and oral traditions as

(1) persuasive arguments
(2) statistical data
(3) unbiased sources
(4) cultural evidence

2 Which academic discipline focuses study on the roles and functions of government?

(1) political science   (3) geography
(2) anthropology   (4) economics

3 During the Neolithic Revolution, production of a food surplus led directly to

(1) a nomadic lifestyle
(2) a reliance on stone weaponry
(3) an increase in population
(4) a dependence on hunting and gathering

4 Discovery of streets arranged in a grid-like pattern and a system of pipes for moving water in Harappa and Mohenjo-Daro suggest that these ancient river valley cities in South Asia had

(1) organized governments
(2) subsistence-based economies
(3) polytheistic beliefs
(4) rigid social classes

Base your answer to question 5 on the passage below and on your knowledge of social studies.

… Monsoons are relied upon throughout the country to provide water for growing crops. Heavy monsoons, however, can bring floods that often have a high death toll. These floods have been exacerbated [made worse] by deforestation of the hills for industrial and agricultural purposes. It is a fine balance between having plenty of water to flood the rice fields and having too much so that crops, homes, and even lives are lost. The alternative to the floods may be famines. However, India's infrastructure can now deal successfully with these: When the monsoon fails in one area, the army is able to move supplies to the drought-stricken area. As a result of this organization, few lives were lost in the Maharashtra famines of 1965–66 and 1974–75, while more than two million people died in the Bengal famine of 1943.

—Louise Nicholson, *National Geographic Traveler: India*, 2007

5 Based on this passage, how have the negative effects of the monsoons been reduced in recent years?

(1) The army is building dams to hold back the floods.
(2) Farmers have begun to grow crops that require less water.
(3) Home construction in flood areas has been controlled by government regulations.
(4) An improved infrastructure makes it possible to bring supplies to areas in need of help.

6 The Egyptians used hieroglyphics in the same way as the Sumerians used

(1) ideographs   (3) cuneiform
(2) calligraphy   (4) letters

7 Which geographic feature served as a barrier to political unity and encouraged the rise of independent city-states in ancient Greece?

(1) broad plains
(3) navigable rivers
(2) mountain ranges
(4) numerous ports

8 The Tang dynasty contributed to the development of Chinese culture by

(1) creating a shogunate
(2) producing porcelain and block printing
(3) introducing Hinduism as a major philosophy
(4) devising a set of laws and carving them on rocks and pillars

9 A primary goal of European Crusaders fighting in the Middle East was to

(1) establish markets for Italian merchants
(2) rescue Pope Urban II from the Byzantines
(3) halt the advance of Mongol armies in the Asian steppes
(4) secure access to Christian holy sites in Jerusalem

10 Increases in trade and commerce that occurred during the late Middle Ages in Europe resulted in

(1) lower living standards for guild members
(2) the development of more towns and cities
(3) a decline in rivalries between kings
(4) an increase in the number of self-sufficient manors

11 The writings of both Marco Polo and Ibn Battuta inspired

(1) exploration and trade
(2) important military expeditions
(3) movements for political freedom
(4) the spread of Islam to Southeast Asia

12 Nanjing, Venice, and Mogadishu were powerful and influential cities in the 13th century because they all

(1) developed agrarian-based economies
(2) served as religious pilgrimage sites
(3) established democratic governments
(4) took advantage of the factors of location

13 The West African empires of Ghana, Mali, and Songhai were able to thrive because

(1) they controlled the gold-salt trade
(2) their herds of cattle were in demand
(3) their armies took control of much of Africa
(4) they adopted Christianity as their primary religion

14 What was an immediate result of the Black Death?

(1) labor shortages
(2) overseas exploration
(3) decrease in anti-Semitism
(4) improvements in medical science

15 Which statement best expresses the philosophy of humanism?

(1) God selects those to be saved.
(2) The pope expresses the ultimate word of God.
(3) People have potential and can improve themselves by learning.
(4) A person's life on Earth is merely preparation for the afterlife.

16 Which development is most closely associated with early Inca achievements?

(1) inventing the wheel as a transportation device
(2) improving iron weapons
(3) expanding global trade
(4) adapting a mountainous environment

17 What was a major effect of the Columbian exchange?

(1) economic collapse in Europe
(2) introduction of new food crops to Europe
(3) decrease in European population
(4) expansion of democratic rights throughout Europe

18 Which policy is a country using when it regulates its colonies' imports and exports to produce a favorable balance of trade?

(1) embargo
(3) mercantilism
(2) outsourcing
(4) transmigration

Base your answer to question 19 on the diagram below and on your knowledge of social studies.

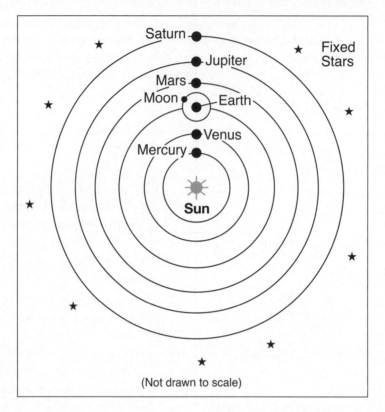

(Not drawn to scale)

19 Which scientist is most directly associated with formulating this view of the solar system?

(1) Ptolemy
(2) Descartes
(3) Copernicus
(4) Newton

20 Akbar the Great tried to unify the Mughal Empire and create peace between the different people of India by

(1) promoting a policy of religious toleration
(2) forcing all people to adopt modern dress
(3) building the Taj Mahal to inspire healing
(4) establishing Buddhism as the state religion

21 • Signing of the Magna Carta
• Signing of the Petition of Right
• Passage of the English Bill of Rights

In England, these events were instrumental in

(1) supporting a disarmament policy
(2) promoting government control of the economy
(3) justifying the acquisition of territory in foreign lands
(4) developing parliamentary democracy

22 Between 1500 and 1750, which commercial products were produced on Latin American plantations using enslaved laborers?

(1) corn and squash
(2) bananas and tea
(3) sugar and tobacco
(4) potatoes and wool

23 The ideas of Enlightenment philosophers were based on

(1) efforts to achieve salvation
(2) faith in human reason
(3) traditional practices
(4) the inevitability of poverty

24 Toussaint L'Ouverture and José de San Martín are leaders best known for

(1) leading independence movements
(2) supporting religious reforms
(3) promoting civil disobedience
(4) opposing democracy

Base your answer to question 25 on the poster below and on your knowledge of social studies.

**The Tsar, the Priest and the Rich Man
on the Shoulders of the Labouring People**

ЦАРЬ, ПОП И БОГАЧ
НА ПЛЕЧАХ У ТРУДОВОГО НАРОДА.

Source: A. Apsit, Coloured Lithograph, 1918 (adapted)

25 In early 20th-century Russia, which group may have gained support by circulating this poster?

(1) aristocracy   (3) monarchists

(2) Bolsheviks   (4) Orthodox clergy

26 Which course of action does the theory of laissez-faire suggest a government should follow?

(1) providing help for people in need
(2) establishing businesses to create jobs
(3) letting natural laws regulate the economy
(4) controlling the mineral resources of a country

27 One effect of the British landlord system in Ireland in the mid-1800s and in India in the early 1900s was that these landlord systems

(1) contributed to famine and suffering
(2) allowed local economies to prosper
(3) emphasized food crops over mining
(4) led to an agrarian revolution

28 Commodore Matthew Perry is best known for taking which action?

(1) leading the British East India Company
(2) rescuing Europeans during the Boxer Rebellion
(3) justifying European spheres of influence in China
(4) opening Japan to American and European influences

29 During World War I, developments in military technology led to

(1) an early victory by the Allied powers
(2) the establishment of industrial capitalism
(3) the use of poisonous gas and submarine attacks
(4) an increase in ethnic tension in western Europe

30 One major reason the League of Nations failed was that it

(1) was not included in the Versailles Treaty
(2) was controlled by communist Russia
(3) frightened many nations with its large military force
(4) lacked the support of many of the major world powers during crises

31 Which geographic characteristic of Japan most influenced its decision to engage in imperialism in the early to mid-20th century?

(1) mountainous terrain
(2) lack of natural resources
(3) abundance of rivers
(4) island location

32 Which condition was a result of Joseph Stalin's command economy?

(1) Peasants were encouraged to sell surplus grain for personal profit.
(2) The production of consumer goods increased.
(3) National revenue increased allowing for greater individual spending.
(4) The government controlled agriculture through collective farms.

33 After World War I, the rise of Benito Mussolini in Italy and the rise of Adolf Hitler in Germany are most closely associated with

(1) the development of fascism
(2) the desire for containment
(3) an emphasis on democratic traditions
(4) a return to conservative religious practices

34 What was a major reason the Soviet Union established satellite states in Eastern Europe after World War II?

(1) developing better trade relations with the West
(2) creating a buffer zone against future invasions
(3) participating in United Nations peacekeeping missions
(4) controlling the Organization of Petroleum Exporting Countries (OPEC)

Base your answer to question 35 on the excerpt below and on your knowledge of social studies.

… The achievement gap between black and white students in South Africa is enormous. In the province of Western Cape, only 2 out of 1,000 sixth-graders in predominantly black schools performed at grade level on a math test in 2005, compared with 2 out of 3 children in schools once reserved for whites that are now integrated, but generally in more affluent [wealthier] neighborhoods….

—Celia W. Dugger

35 Which underlying historical factor most significantly contributed to this achievement gap?

(1) inequalities existing between the races under apartheid
(2) economic sanctions placed on school communities
(3) lack of governmental support for white educational programs
(4) a period of political assassinations and civil war

36 **"India Partitioned at Independence"**
"Serbs Fuel Conflict in Kosovo"
"Grievances Divide Hutu and Tutsi"

Which conclusion do these headlines support?

(1) Cultural diversity leads to stable societies.
(2) Ethnic and religious differences have been sources of tension.
(3) Economic cooperation can overcome political issues.
(4) Gender differences are more powerful than differences in social status.

37 Many conflicts in the Middle East during the post–World War II period have directly resulted from

(1) the dissolution of the Arab League
(2) border clashes between Iran and China
(3) disputes related to Palestine
(4) the partition of Egypt

Base your answer to question 38 on the passage below and on your knowledge of social studies.

… More than 30 years after "Year Zero" and more than a decade after the "return to democracy," Cambodia remains in a league of its own — miserable, corrupt and compassionless. Only the toughest and the most unscrupulous can "make it" and get ahead. There is hardly any social net to speak of; the savage insanity of the Khmer Rouge has been replaced with savage capitalism, but often with the same people in charge….

— Andre Vitchek,
"A Tortured History and Unanswered Questions"

38 What does the author of this 2006 passage conclude?

(1) As democracy develops, circumstances will improve.
(2) Though governments change, circumstances often remain the same.
(3) New leadership is determined to replace the Khmer Rouge.
(4) Harsh living conditions have caused people to rely extensively on a social net.

39 Which action was taken by Deng Xiaoping to improve the economy of China?

(1) discouraging foreign investment
(2) encouraging some capitalist practices
(3) organizing the Red Guard
(4) practicing glasnost

40 Which revolution led to increases in global food production as a result of using genetically altered seeds and large amounts of chemical fertilizers and pesticides?

(1) Cultural   (3) Scientific
(2) Glorious   (4) Green

Base your answer to question 41 on the cartoon below and on your knowledge of social studies.

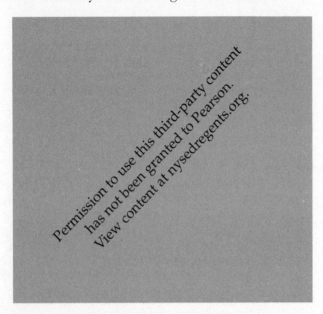

Permission to use this third-party content has not been granted to Pearson. View content at nysedregents.org.

41 What is the main idea of this 2010 cartoon?

(1) Pakistan plays a minor role in the affairs of Afghanistan.
(2) The United States and Pakistan will join forces to remove the Taliban.
(3) Disputes over water rights between Pakistan and Afghanistan continue to create challenges.
(4) The Taliban will pose a threat to Afghanistan when the United States leaves.

42 The World Trade Organization (WTO), North American Free Trade Agreement (NAFTA), and European Union (EU) all share the primary goal of

(1) promoting space exploration and maintaining satellites
(2) increasing economic aid to developing nations
(3) encouraging trade between countries and lowering trade barriers
(4) developing regulations to preserve the environment

43 The use of the decimal system, advancements in medicine, and construction of Hindu temples are most closely associated with the golden age of the

(1) Abbassid dynasty   (3) Gupta Empire
(2) Han dynasty   (4) Roman Empire

44 One reason the Justinian Code was significant was that it

(1) became the foundation of the modern legal systems of many Western countries
(2) established the basis for the development of the Code of Hammurabi
(3) incorporated laws from all over Asia and Europe
(4) led to the protection of inalienable rights in Roman territories

45 Which technological development contributed most directly to the success of the Protestant Reformation?

(1) astrolabe   (3) wheel
(2) compass   (4) printing press

46 "Liberty, Equality, Fraternity" and "Peace, Land, and Bread" are slogans used by revolutionaries to represent

(1) frameworks for economic stability
(2) political and economic ideals
(3) plans for maintaining the social hierarchy
(4) methods of political reform

47 One way in which Otto von Bismarck and Camillo Cavour are similar is that both leaders

(1) followed a policy of isolationism
(2) adopted papal policies
(3) led an African independence movement
(4) promoted unification to form a new nation-state

48 Which title best completes the partial outline below?

> I._____
>
> A. During the early 1800s, Napoleon Bonaparte's grand army sweeps across eastern Europe.
> B. During World War I, Germany invades France through Belgium.
> C. During World War II, Germans blitzkrieg western Europe.

(1) Importance of Rivers as Invasion Routes
(2) Stalemate of Trench Warfare
(3) Use of the Northern Plain for Conquest
(4) Role of Naval Blockades in Wars

49 One way in which the rule of Peter the Great in Russia and the rule of Emperor Meiji in Japan are similar is that both leaders

(1) emancipated serfs
(2) granted equality to women
(3) encouraged modernization
(4) ruled according to a constitution

50 One purpose of the Nuremberg Trials and of the Truth and Reconciliation Commission in South Africa was to

(1) address human rights abuses
(2) support the establishment of democratic governments
(3) establish free trade zones throughout the world
(4) provide encouragement to people behind the Iron Curtain

Answers to the essay questions are to be written in the separate essay booklet.

In developing your answer to Part II, be sure to keep this general definition in mind:

> **discuss means "to make observations about something using facts, reasoning, and argument; to present in some detail"**

Part II

THEMATIC ESSAY QUESTION

Directions: Write a well-organized essay that includes an introduction, several paragraphs addressing the task below, and a conclusion.

Theme: Belief Systems—Movements

> Belief systems are an established, orderly way that groups or individuals look at religious faith or philosophical principles. Some belief systems have spread outside their places of origin. The diffusion of these belief systems has affected other societies and regions in various ways.

Task:

> Select **two** belief systems that have spread outside their place of origin and for **each**
>
> - Discuss a central principle of this belief system
> - Discuss how this belief system spread to another region
> - Discuss an effect of the spread of this belief system on a society or region

You may use any belief system from your study of global history and geography. Some suggestions you might wish to consider include Buddhism, Confucianism, Judaism, Christianity, Islam, and communism.

You are *not* limited to these suggestions.

Do *not* use the United States as a region to which a belief system has spread.

Guidelines:

In your essay, be sure to
- Develop all aspects of the task
- Support the theme with relevant facts, examples, and details
- Use a logical and clear plan of organization, including an introduction and a conclusion that are beyond a restatement of the theme

NAME _____   SCHOOL _____

Part III

DOCUMENT-BASED QUESTION

This question is based on the accompanying documents. The question is designed to test your ability to work with historical documents. Some of these documents have been edited for the purposes of this question. As you analyze the documents, take into account the source of each document and any point of view that may be presented in the document. Keep in mind that the language used in a document may reflect the historical context of the time in which it was written.

Historical Context:

Throughout history, empires such as the **Roman**, the **Ottoman**, and the **British** have faced various problems that led to their decline. The decline of these empires has influenced changes in societies and regions.

Task: Using the information from the documents and your knowledge of global history, answer the questions that follow each document in Part A. Your answers to the questions will help you write the Part B essay in which you will be asked to

> Select **two** empires mentioned in the historical context and for **each**
> - Describe problems that led to this empire's decline
> - Discuss how this empire's decline influenced change in a society and/or a region

In developing your answers to Part III, be sure to keep these general definitions in mind:

(a) <u>describe</u> means "to illustrate something in words or tell about it"
(b) <u>discuss</u> means "to make observations about something using facts, reasoning, and argument; to present in some detail"

Part A
Short-Answer Questions

Directions: Analyze the documents and answer the short-answer questions that follow each document in the space provided.

Document 1

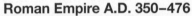

Roman Empire A.D. 350–476

1 Based on the information shown on this map, state *one* problem that helped bring about the decline of the Roman Empire. [1]

_____

_____

Score ☐

Document 2

... By the middle of the second century Italy [within the Roman Empire] was in a state of decline. By the time of Diocletian, at the opening of the fourth century, decay was apparent throughout the empire. Commerce had largely disappeared owing to the lack of customers, to piracy on the seas, and to insecurity of the roads on land. Generally speaking, purchasing power at that time was confined to the public officials, to the army officers, and to the great landowners. Trade in the everyday objects of daily use had all but disappeared, but trade in luxuries prospered. The cities in the west, omitting the places where government centered, were usually in decline; their commercial and industrial classes had disappeared, the old traders having been replaced by the traveling eastern merchant, of whom the Syrian was the most notorious. Foreign trade was sharply curtailed. At various times the government attempted to prohibit the export of various commodities, among them wine, oil, grain, salt, arms, iron, and gold. With this curbing of exports there was also an effort made to control certain imports such as is evidenced by the state monopoly in silk. These two movements hampered commercial contracts outside the empire and all but killed what was left of foreign trade....

Source: Louis C. West, "The Economic Collapse of the Roman Empire," *The Classical Journal*, November 1932

2 According to Louis C. West, what were **two** economic problems the Roman Empire faced during its period of decline? [2]

(1) _____

_____

Score ☐

(2) _____

_____

Score ☐

Document 3

> … As western Europe fell to the Germanic invasions, imperial power shifted to the Byzantine Empire, that is, the eastern part of the Roman Empire, with its capital at Constantinople. The eastern provinces of the former Roman Empire had always outnumbered those in the west. Its civilization was far older and it had larger cities, which were also more numerous than in the west.…

Source: Steven Kreis, *The History Guide: Lectures on Ancient and Medieval European History*, Lecture 17, History Guide online

3 According to Steven Kreis, what was **one** change that resulted from the fall of the western half of the Roman Empire? [1]

_____

_____

Score ☐

Document 4

> The power of the [Ottoman] Empire was waning [fading] by 1683 when the second and last attempt was made to conquer Vienna. It failed. Without the conquest of Europe and the acquisition of significant new wealth, the Empire lost momentum and went into a slow decline.
>
> Several other factors contributed to the [Ottoman] Empire's decline:
> - Competition from trade from the Americas
> - Competition from cheap products from India and the Far East
> - Development of other trade routes
> - Rising unemployment within the Empire
> - Ottoman Empire became less centralised, and central control weakened
> - Sultans being less severe in maintaining rigorous standards of integrity in the administration of the Empire
> - Sultans becoming less sensitive to public opinion

Source: "Ottoman Empire (1301–1922)," BBC online, 2009 (adapted)

4a According to the BBC, what was **one** *economic* problem that contributed to the decline of the Ottoman Empire? [1]

_____

_____

Score ☐

b According to the BBC, what was **one** *political* problem that contributed to the decline of the Ottoman Empire? [1]

_____

_____

Score ☐

Document 5

> ... In 1875, the Slavic peoples living in the Ottoman provinces of Bosnia and Herzegovina (currently the state of Bosnia-Herzegovina), led an uprising against the Ottomans in order to gain their freedom. The general weakness of the Ottomans led two independent, neighbor Slavic states, Montenegro and Serbia, to aid the rebellion. Within a year, the rebellion spread to the Ottoman province of Bulgaria. The rebellion was part of a larger political movement called the Pan-Slavic movement, which had as its goal the unification of all Slavic peoples— most of whom were under the control of Austria, Germany, and the Ottoman Empire—into a single political unity under the protection of Russia. Anxious also to conquer the Ottomans themselves and seize Istanbul, the Russians allied with the rebels, Serbia, and Montenegro and declared war against the Ottomans....

Source: Richard Hooker, "European Imperialism and the Balkan Crisis," *The Ottomans*, World Cultures

5 According to Richard Hooker, what was **one** problem faced by the Ottomans during the decline of their Empire? [1]

_____

_____

Score [ ]

Document 6

> ... Mustafa Kemal [Atatürk] was a secular nationalist who believed that all the inheritance of the Ottoman Empire should be abandoned and Turkey should be transformed into a modern European state. This involved less of a sudden break with the past than might appear. The *Tanzimat* reforms [between 1839 and 1876] had laid the foundations of a secular state, and the Young Turks, even while attempting to preserve the empire, had given a powerful impetus [motivation] to the cause of Turkish nationalism. During the war years [1914–1918], the secularization of education had proceeded and the universities and public positions had been opened to women. Certain of the law courts under the control of the religious authorities had been placed under the Ministry of Justice. A law in 1916 had reformed marriage and divorce....

Source: Peter Mansfield, *A History of the Middle East*, Viking

6 According to Peter Mansfield, what was **one** change that occurred as the Ottoman Empire declined and a new state of Turkey began to take shape? [1]

_____

_____

Score [ ]

Document 7

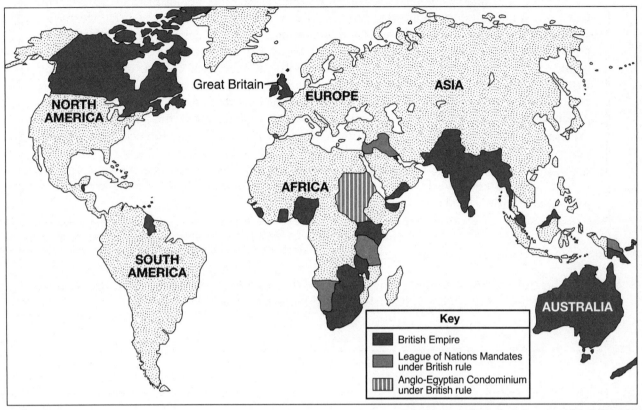

The British Empire and Mandates in the Early 1920s

Key

■	British Empire
▨	League of Nations Mandates under British rule
▥	Anglo-Egyptian Condominium under British rule

Source: Encyclopedia Britannica Kids (adapted)

7 Based on the information shown on this map, what was a problem the British faced that made it difficult to govern its empire? [1]

_____

_____

Score ☐

Document 8

… World War II greatly changed the British attitude toward the idea of India's freedom. The fear that an independent India would not pay its debt to Great Britain was no longer valid. Great Britain actually owed India over a billion pounds. Nor was the concern that there were not enough Indian military officers to take over the Indian army from the British. As a result of the war, more than fifteen thousand Indian officers were available. In addition, many British soldiers who returned home from serving in India realized how unpopular their government was among the Indian people. In Great Britain, the Labour Party under Clement Attlee defeated Winston Churchill's Conservatives and took charge of the government.…

The Labour Party, already sympathetic to the idea of India's independence, faced a great deal of unrest in India. The cold winter of 1945–46 made shortages of food and clothing even worse. Many nationalist leaders, recently released from prison, gave speeches encouraging violent actions to achieve freedom. In Calcutta, demonstrations led to riots in which over thirty people were killed and several hundred injured.…

Source: *Indian Independence and the Question of Pakistan*, Choices Program,
Watson Institute for International Studies, Brown University

8 Based on this excerpt from *Indian Independence and the Question of Pakistan*, what were **two** factors that made Great Britain more willing to grant India independence?   [2]

(1) _____

_____

Score ☐

(2) _____

_____

Score ☐

Document 9

> ... During the last 60 years [since 1928], the British Empire has broken apart. Most of the nations that were in the empire demanded and got their independence. With the empire gone, Britain lost a major source of wealth. At the same time, it lost industrial advantages it had enjoyed for many years....

Source: Clare McHugh, *Scholastic World Cultures: Western Europe*, Scholastic, 1988

9 According to Clare McHugh, what was *one* change Great Britain faced with the breakup of its empire? [1]

_____

_____

Score ☐

Part B
Essay

Directions: Write a well-organized essay that includes an introduction, several paragraphs, and a conclusion. Use evidence from *at least four* documents in your essay. Support your response with relevant facts, examples, and details. Include additional outside information.

Historical Context:

Throughout history, empires such as the **Roman**, the **Ottoman**, and the **British** have faced various problems that led to their decline. The decline of these empires has influenced changes in societies and regions.

Task: Using the information from the documents and your knowledge of global history, write an essay in which you

Select *two* empires mentioned in the historical context and for *each*
- Describe problems that led to this empire's decline
- Discuss how this empire's decline influenced change in a society and/or a region

Guidelines:

In your essay, be sure to
- Develop all aspects of the task
- Incorporate information from *at least four* documents
- Incorporate relevant outside information
- Support the theme with relevant facts, examples, and details
- Use a logical and clear plan of organization, including an introduction and a conclusion that are beyond a restatement of the theme

This section contains an actual Regents Examination in Global History and Geography that was given in New York State in January 2015.

Circle your answers to Part 1. Write your responses to the short-answer questions in the spaces provided. Write your thematic essay and document-based essay on separate sheets of paper. Be sure to refer to the test-taking strategies in the front of this book as you prepare to answer the test questions.

Part I

Answer all questions in this part.

Directions (1–50): For each statement or question, record on your separate answer sheet the *number* of the word or expression that, of those given, best completes the statement or answers the question.

Base your answer to question 1 on the map below and on your knowledge of social studies.

Source: www.worldatlas.com (adapted)

1 Which letter on this map represents an archipelago?

  (1) *A*   (3) *C*
  (2) *B*   (4) *D*

2 Historians follow rules to help them analyze primary sources. Some of the rules they use are:

- Every piece of evidence and every source must be read or viewed skeptically and critically.
- Each piece of evidence and source must be cross-checked and compared with related sources and pieces of evidence.

                    —Library of Congress

These rules are designed to help historians determine the

  (1) reliability of document information
  (2) popularity of a publication
  (3) differences in belief systems
  (4) laws of a civilization

3 Which type of economic system relies primarily on hunting, gathering, herding, and farming to maintain self-sufficiency?

  (1) traditional   (3) capitalism
  (2) command   (4) mixed

4 The creation of independent city-states in ancient Greece can be most directly attributed to the

  (1) diverse ethnic groups in the region
  (2) large number of different languages
  (3) rugged mountainous terrain
  (4) practice of oligarchy

5 Which term is most closely associated with Hellenism under Alexander the Great?

  (1) cultural diffusion   (3) theocracy
  (2) pacifism   (4) natural rights

6 Which river is most closely associated with Hinduism?

  (1) Nile   (3) Tigris
  (2) Yellow   (4) Ganges

7 Which individual developed an Asian philosophy associated with the five relationships, filial piety, and the Analects?

  (1) Laozi (Lao Tzu)
  (2) Confucius
  (3) Han Wudi
  (4) Siddhartha Gautama

8 In India, for which achievement is the Gupta Golden Age best known?

  (1) adoption of the printing press
  (2) invention of the iron foot stirrup
  (3) use of gunpowder
  (4) development of the concept of zero

Base your answer to question 9 on the chart below and on your knowledge of social studies.

Chinese Social Organization During the Tang and Song Dynasties

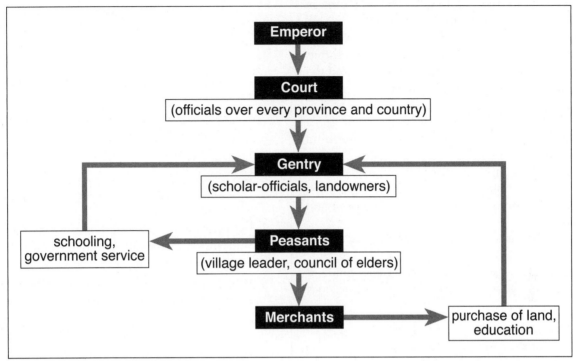

Source: *World History: Connections to Today*, Prentice Hall (adapted)

9 Based on the information in this chart, what is a valid conclusion about Chinese society during the Tang and Song dynasties?

(1) Most peasants in China were literate.

(2) The majority of Chinese people were merchants.

(3) Some people living in China had opportunities for social mobility.

(4) The social status of most Chinese people was determined by religious practices.

10 Around the 14th century, why were the cities of Nanjing, Calicut, Mogadishu, and Venice significant?

(1) Major centers of trading activity flourished there.

(2) The first democracies emerged there.

(3) Islamic religious centers developed there.

(4) The Portuguese established colonies there.

11 Which geographic factor best explains China's ability to influence the cultural development of Japan?

(1) tropical climate   (3) mountains

(2) location   (4) navigable rivers

Base your answer to question 12 on the passage below and on your knowledge of social studies.

... Trade along the Silk Road enriched China in many ways. The Chinese sent silk, herbal medicines, ceramics, and other local products westward by caravan, and received exotic things in return. From Persia (modern-day Iran) and the Middle East, they received new kinds of musical instruments, and musicians to play them, as well as gold and silver cups, bowls, and vases. From India they imported cotton cloth. From Byzantium (the eastern capital of the Roman Empire, today the city of Istanbul in Turkey) came glassware and jewelry. Chinese merchants also traded some of these imported goods eastward to Korea and Japan....

—Des Forges and Major, *The Asian World: 600-1500*

12 Based on this passage, the Silk Road made it possible for the Chinese to import cotton cloth from

(1) Persia   (3) Japan
(2) the Roman Empire   (4) India

13 The West African kingdom of Mali grew in wealth and power by controlling the trading of

(1) oil and coal   (3) gold and salt
(2) timber and fish   (4) sugar and ivory

14 Which term is defined as a Renaissance movement characterized by independent thought and a renewed interest in classical Greek and Roman culture?

(1) multiculturalism   (3) nationalism
(2) humanism   (4) monasticism

15 One major effect of the Protestant Reformation on western Europe was the

(1) decline in religious unity
(2) increased power of the Catholic pope
(3) reduction in religious wars
(4) increase in the sale of indulgences by the Catholic Church

16 Which statement best describes an effect of the westward expansion of the Ottoman Empire under Suleiman the Magnificent?

(1) Wealthy citizens adopted Russian dress.
(2) Islam became a major religion in the Balkans.
(3) Trade was disrupted throughout the Indian Ocean.
(4) Janissaries were stripped of their military power.

17 A key reason the Incas were able to control their large empire was that they

(1) outlawed human sacrifice
(2) formed a democratic government
(3) built a road system to connect distant areas and to move armies
(4) promoted literacy and mass education programs to teach loyalty to their subjects

18 Which key factor fueled competition between European countries for colonies in the Americas?

(1) a European shortage of pepper and nutmeg
(2) a mandate from the papacy
(3) the desire to control sources of gold and silver
(4) the need to secure laborers for factories in Europe

19 Which geographic feature is located in Latin America?

(1) rain forest of the Congo
(2) Himalaya Mountains
(3) plateau of Tibet
(4) Amazon River

20 What was an effect of the trans-Atlantic slave trade on Africa between 1500 and 1800?

(1) Power in West Africa shifted from kingdoms in the interior to coastal kingdoms.
(2) Malaria was introduced to the tropical regions of Africa.
(3) Islam became dominant in sub-Saharan regions.
(4) Plantation agriculture was developed in the Great Rift Valley.

21 The writing of the Magna Carta was a reaction to the

(1) economic restrictions under imperialism
(2) abuse of power by monarchs
(3) missionary work of clergy
(4) threats of revolution from colonial governors

22 Louis XIV strengthened the power of the monarchy in France by

(1) centralizing control
(2) granting democratic reforms
(3) practicing religious toleration
(4) reducing the size of the bureaucracy

23 • Copernicus' heliocentric model of the universe
• Newton's law of gravitation
• Descartes' belief in truth through reason

This set of ideas from the Scientific Revolution gave Europeans a new way to

(1) view humankind's place in the universe
(2) support the core beliefs of the church
(3) authenticate historical facts
(4) verify civil liberties

24 In the late 1700s, which situation in France is considered a cause of the other three?

(1) meeting of the Estates General
(2) unfair policies of taxation
(3) execution of the king
(4) storming of the Bastille

Base your answer to question 25 on the passage below and on your knowledge of social studies.

… Nor is there liberty if the power of judging is not separate from legislative power and from executive power. If it were joined to legislative power, the power over the life and liberty of the citizens would be arbitrary, for the judge would be the legislator. If it were joined to executive power, the judge could have the force of an oppressor.…

—Montesquieu, *The Spirit of the Laws*

25 In this passage, Montesquieu is making reference to

(1) an enlightened despotism
(2) a policy of mercantilism
(3) a separation of powers
(4) a social contract

26 The development of cash-crop economies promotes globalization by

(1) equalizing the standard of living for peasant populations
(2) establishing communities that are self-sufficient
(3) maintaining the diversity of indigenous agriculture
(4) meeting demands outside the region of production

27 During the late 19th century, Zionism focused on

(1) securing safe working conditions for urban factory workers
(2) acquiring a homeland for displaced Jewish people
(3) establishing colonies in southern Africa
(4) developing a strict set of laws based on equality

28 What was one reason the Industrial Revolution began in Great Britain?

(1) The government of Great Britain implemented a series of five-year plans.
(2) Great Britain had alliances with most European countries.
(3) Abundant natural resources were available in Great Britain.
(4) The practice of serfdom in Great Britain provided an abundance of laborers.

29 Adam Smith's laissez-faire theories are most closely associated with

(1) the separation of church and state
(2) minimal government regulation of the economy
(3) a command economy
(4) high tariffs to protect domestic businesses

30 The Berlin Conference is most closely associated with the colonialization of

(1) South Asia   (3) Latin America
(2) East Asia   (4) Africa

31 A major reason for Japan's foreign policy in Asia during the early 20th century was to

(1) promote democracy
(2) spread Shinto beliefs
(3) obtain natural resources
(4) reduce military expenses

Base your answer to question 32 on the speakers' statements below and on your knowledge of social studies.

Speaker A: A nation's strength is measured by the size of its armed forces. All resources must be mobilized into building a strong army and navy.

Speaker B: To maintain our international strength, we must look to our neighbors for alliances. They will help protect us if we face a threat.

Speaker C: To maintain our sovereignty, we need to be the strongest and most powerful.

32 Which concept is being described by *Speakers A* and *C*?

(1) collective security   (3) militarism
(2) self-determination   (4) isolationism

33 What was a major reason the Russian people engaged in the Revolution of 1905?

(1) dissatisfaction with czarist rule
(2) discontent with involvement in World War I
(3) irritation over the banning of the Orthodox church
(4) failure to emancipate the serfs

34 • Wearing of the fez outlawed (1925).
  • Turkish state declared secular (1928).
  • Women received the right to vote and hold office (1934).

Which idea was promoted by these actions taken in Turkey?

(1) industrialization   (3) ethnocentrism
(2) conservatism   (4) westernization

35 Which goal did Joseph Stalin establish for the Soviet Union?

(1) becoming an industrial power
(2) creating a golden age of culture
(3) instituting a parliamentary monarchy
(4) easing tensions using détente

36 What was a key cause for the rise of fascism in nations such as Italy and Germany?

(1) collectivization   (3) genocide
(2) economic hardship   (4) secret treaties

37 Which event caused the policy of appeasement to be viewed as a failure?

(1) creation of the League of Nations (1919)
(2) forced famine in Ukraine (1932)
(3) invasion of Czechoslovakia (1939)
(4) atomic bombing of Hiroshima (1945)

38 What was one concern associated with both the Korean War and the Vietnam War?

(1) Kim Jong Il and Ho Chi Minh possessed nuclear weapons.
(2) French colonial rule would continue to influence the region.
(3) Renewed Japanese imperialism would trigger another world war.
(4) Communism would spread through eastern and southeastern Asia.

39 One function of both the North American Free Trade Agreement (NAFTA) and the European Union (EU) is to

(1) oppose economic integration
(2) promote immigration
(3) reduce economic barriers
(4) eliminate unemployment

40 In 1989, the goal of the protest movement staged by Chinese students in Tiananmen Square was to

(1) bring about democratic reforms
(2) improve job opportunities in the military
(3) expand foreign investment in Hong Kong
(4) limit the amount of land designated for the "responsibility system"

41 Which country was the site of ethnic tensions and a civil war between the Hutu and Tutsi in the 1990s?

(1) Sudan   (3) Tanzania
(2) Kenya   (4) Rwanda

42 The government of Ayatollah Khomeini attempted to change Iranian society by

(1) implementing Islamic fundamentalist principles
(2) extending political equality to women
(3) allying with communist bloc countries
(4) adopting a western economic system

Base your answer to question 43 on the cartoon below and on your knowledge of social studies.

Source: Paresh Nath, *The National Herald*, India, 7/5/2007

43 What is the main idea of this cartoon?

(1) European rulers continue to exploit Africa.

(2) A strong, centralized authority is needed to govern Africa.

(3) African societies have flourished in spite of tough obstacles.

(4) Numerous problems have hindered Africa's development.

44 One way in which Aung San Suu Kyi, Lech Walesa, and Nelson Mandela are similar is that they all

(1) supported the use of violence to achieve goals

(2) inspired revolutions against autocratic monarchs

(3) led movements to end oppression of their people

(4) based their actions on the teachings of Karl Marx

45 Which action is a direct cause of desertification?

(1) contaminating fresh water supplies

(2) burning fossil fuels in factories

(3) damming rivers to produce hydroelectricity

(4) removing vegetation through overgrazing

46 • Mauryan Emperor Asoka incorporates Buddhist ideas into his laws.

• Constantine legalizes Christianity throughout his empire.

• Prince Vladimir forces Russians to become Eastern Orthodox Christians.

Which generalization can be made based on these statements?

(1) Religions have had little impact on the development of empires.

(2) Many political leaders discouraged religious toleration.

(3) Leaders are often influenced by cultural belief systems.

(4) Christianity has been a dominant force in Europe and India.

47 In the 14th century, the bubonic plague was primarily spread from Asia into Africa and Europe by

(1) sailors during Viking raids
(2) traders and pilgrims during Pax Mongolia
(3) enslaved Africans on the Middle Passage
(4) missionaries during the European Age of Exploration

48 One way in which apartheid in South Africa and the caste system in India are similar is that both systems

(1) allowed for educational opportunities
(2) determined roles based on gender
(3) revolved around central religious beliefs
(4) enforced different sets of rules for distinct groups of people

49 Which geographic circumstance affected the conduct of Russian foreign policy for centuries?

(1) frequent droughts
(2) deforestation of the tundra
(3) environmental damage caused by mining
(4) lack of warm-water ports

50 The treatment of Christian Armenians in Ottoman Turkey (1915) and the treatment of Bosnian Muslims in the former Yugoslavia (1990s) are examples of

(1) international relief efforts
(2) human rights violations
(3) expansion of voting rights
(4) government protection of minorities

Answers to the essay questions are to be written in the separate essay booklet.

In developing your answer to Part II, be sure to keep this general definition in mind:

discuss means "to make observations about something using facts, reasoning, and argument; to present in some detail"

Part II

THEMATIC ESSAY QUESTION

Directions: Write a well-organized essay that includes an introduction, several paragraphs addressing the task below, and a conclusion.

Theme: Human and Physical Geography

> Geographic features have influenced the political, economic, social, and historical development of countries and regions.

Task:

> Select *two* geographic features and for *each*
> - Discuss how this geographic feature influenced the political, economic, social, *and/or* historical developments in a country or region

You may use any geographic feature from your study of global history and geography. Some suggestions you might wish to consider include the influence of rivers in China, deserts in North Africa, climate in Russia, plains in Europe, islands of Japan, monsoons on India, mountains of South America, and natural resources in the Middle East.

You are *not* limited to these suggestions.

Do *not* write about the United States and its geographic features in your answer.

Guidelines:

In your essay, be sure to
- Develop all aspects of the task
- Support the theme with relevant facts, examples, and details
- Use a logical and clear plan of organization, including an introduction and a conclusion that are beyond a restatement of the theme

NAME _____ SCHOOL _____

Part III

DOCUMENT-BASED QUESTION

This question is based on the accompanying documents. The question is designed to test your ability to work with historical documents. Some of these documents have been edited for the purposes of this question. As you analyze the documents, take into account the source of each document and any point of view that may be presented in the document. Keep in mind that the language used in a document may reflect the historical context of the time in which it was written.

Historical Context:

> Throughout history, problems emerged that individuals wanted to address. Individuals such as *Bartolomé de Las Casas, Maximilien Robespierre,* and *Mohandas Gandhi* took different actions in their attempts to address problems. Their actions met with varying degrees of success.

Task: Using the information from the documents and your knowledge of global history, answer the questions that follow each document in Part A. Your answers to the questions will help you write the Part B essay in which you will be asked to

---

Select **two** individuals mentioned in the historical context and for **each**
- Describe a problem this individual addresses
- Describe how this individual attempted to address the problem
- Discuss whether this individual was successful or unsuccessful in solving the problem

---

In developing your answers to Part III, be sure to keep these general definitions in mind:

    (a) <u>describe</u> means "to illustrate something in words or tell about it"

    (b) <u>discuss</u> means "to make observations about something using facts, reasoning, and argument; to present in some detail"

Part A
Short-Answer Questions

Directions: Analyze the documents and answer the short-answer questions that follow each document in the space provided.

Document 1

> ... The West Indian experience from the time of Columbus' first voyage was one of Indian labor for Spanish masters. When this labor was not given "voluntarily" it was extracted by force. As Spaniards arrived in increasing numbers, the need for labor became more pressing, and the burden upon Indian manpower progressively more severe. Spaniards raided Indian communities, took captives, and, in order to prevent escape or to ensure the full measure of work, practiced large-scale enslavement. Columbus, at first, appears to have made some attempt to regulate this forced labor, but without appreciable [noticeable] success. In general the first Spanish contacts with the natives of America followed the precedent of European contact with the natives of Africa, and the practicality and legitimacy of enslavement were everywhere assumed....

Source: Charles Gibson, *Spain in America*, Harper Torchbooks (adapted)

1 According to Charles Gibson, what was **one** problem faced by the West Indian native population during Spanish colonization? [1]

_____

_____

Score ☐

Document 2a

Document 2b

Bartolomé de Las Casas

Source: Keen and Haynes, *A History of Latin America*,
Houghton Mifflin Harcourt

… Las Casas interrupted work on the book [*A History of the Indies*] only to send to the Council of the Indies in Madrid three long letters (in 1531, 1534, and 1535), in which he accused persons and institutions of the sin of oppressing the Indian, particularly through the *encomienda* system. After various adventures in Central America, where his ideas on the treatment of the natives invariably [regularly] brought him into conflict with the Spanish authorities, Las Casas wrote *De único modo* (1537; "Concerning the Only Way of Drawing All Peoples to the True Religion"), in which he set forth the doctrine of peaceful evangelization of the Indian. Together with the Dominicans, he then employed this new type of evangelization in a "land of war" (a territory of still-unconquered Indians) — Tuzutlan, near the Golfo Dulce (Sweet Gulf) in present-day Costa Rica. Encouraged by the favourable outcome of this experiment, Las Casas set out for Spain late in 1539, arriving there in 1540.…

Source: "Bartolomé de Las Casas,"
The History Channel website

2 Based on these documents, state **one** action Bartolomé de Las Casas took to address the problems faced by Native Americans. [1]

_____

_____

Score ⬚

Document 3

During the reigns of Charles V and his successors, the Spanish monarchy reacted to Bartolomé de Las Casas in different ways.

> … In response to both his fear and conscience, Charles promulgated [instituted] the New Laws in 1542. They forbade the enslavement of the Indians, their compulsory personal service, the granting of new encomiendas, and the inheritance of encomiendas. More positively they declared the Indians to be free persons, vassals of the crown, and possessed of their own free will. The colonists protested vehemently [passionately]. Rebellion threatened Mexico; in Peru encomenderos [holders of encomiendas] rose up to defy the law. Once again under extreme pressure, the monarch modified some of the laws and revoked others. Still, although the encomienda would continue for some time in parts of the sprawling American empire, the king had checked [limited] it. After the mid-sixteenth century the institution waned [faded away]. The state [Spanish monarchy] exerted even greater control over the declining Indian population.…

Source: E. Bradford Burns, *Latin America: A Concise Interpretive History*, Prentice Hall (adapted)

3a According to E. Bradford Burns, what was *one* way the New Laws addressed the problem Bartolomé de Las Casas had identified? [1]

_____

_____

Score [ ]

b According to E. Bradford Burns, what was a response of the Spanish monarch when the Spanish colonists protested against the New Laws? [1]

_____

_____

Score [ ]

Document 4

This is an excerpt from a speech given on September 25, 1793 by Maximilien Robespierre to the National Convention justifying measures taken by the Committee of Public Safety.

French Revolution: 1793

… Individuals are not at issue here; we are concerned with the homeland and principles. I tell you plainly: it is impossible, in this state of affairs, for the Committee to save the state; and if anyone disagrees, I will remind you just how treacherous and extensive is the scheme for bringing us down and dissolving us; how the foreigners and internal enemies have agents paid to execute it; I will remind you that faction is not dead; that it is conspiring from the depths of its dungeons; that the serpents of the Marais have not yet all been crushed.…

I know we cannot flatter ourselves that we have attained perfection; but holding up a Republic surrounded by enemies, fortifying reason in favour of liberty, destroying prejudice and nullifying individual efforts against the public interest, demand moral and physical strengths that nature has perhaps denied to those who denounce us and those we are fighting.…

Source: Maximilien Robespierre, "Extracts from 'In Defence of the Committee of Public Safety and Against Briez,'" September 25, 1793, in *Virtue and Terror*, Verso (adapted)

4 From Robespierre's perspective, what was **one** threat the government of France faced in 1793? [1]

_____

_____

Score ☐

Document 5a

... When he entered the Committee [of Public Safety], Maximilien [Robespierre] persuaded the other members to accept new procedures, to reorganize the clerical staff and to hold weekly meetings with the other Committee [of General Security]. The press, which, from intimate knowledge, the leader regarded as dangerous, was to be temporarily deprived of its freedom. Only when true democracy had been established would it be possible to allow journalists to have their say again! In all such decisions, the will and interests of the majority of citizens of France were both the pretext [alleged reason] and the inspiration. In other words: the government was to remain revolutionary until peace had been restored and all enemies put to flight....

Source: John Laurence Carr, *Robespierre: The Force of Circumstance,* St. Martin's Press

5a According to John Laurence Carr, what was **one** change Robespierre persuaded the government to make to address the threat to the revolution? [1]

_____

_____

Score ☐

Document 5b

The Law of Suspects

This law, passed on 17 September 1793 [by Robespierre and the National Convention], authorized the creation of revolutionary tribunals to try those suspected of treason against the Republic and to punish those convicted with death. This legislation in effect made the penal justice system into the enforcement arm of the revolutionary government, which would now set as its primary responsibility not only the maintenance of public order but also the much more difficult and controversial task of identifying internal enemies of the Republic—such as "profiteers" who violated the Maximum [decree to fix prices]—and then removing them from the citizenry, where they might subvert [sabotage] the general will....

Source: *Liberty, Equality, Fraternity: Exploring the French Revolution*, online site, a collaboration of the Roy Rosenzweig Center for History and New Media and the American Social History Project

5b According to this document, in what way did the Law of Suspects address the threats against the government? [1]

_____

_____

Score ☐

Document 6a

> **TIMETABLE, 1794**
>
> **... July 27:** The Convention ordered the arrest of Robespierre and his friends. They were taken to the Luxembourg. The jailer refused to lock them up. They left and went to the Town Hall to plan their next move. They could have beaten the Convention, but the Paris Commune did not help in time. They were declared to be outlaws and arrested again.
>
> **July 28 (early morning):** The Convention made Robespierre and his friends outlaws and arrested them at the Town Hall. Now either Robespierre was shot, or he shot himself. He was wounded.
>
> **July 28:** Robespierre and 21 friends went to the guillotine....

Source: Jane Shuter, ed., *Helen Williams and the French Revolution*, Raintree Steck-Vaughn (adapted)

6a According to Jane Shuter, what was *one* consequence Robespierre faced as a result of his actions? [1]

_____

_____

Score ☐

Document 6b

> ... By 1795, the Revolutionary armies had restored peace to the French borders, but, once again, turmoil threatened to sweep across France itself. The National Convention (now controlled by the moderate and conservative representatives, who had condemned Robespierre) could not prevent new outbreaks of radical demonstrations....

Source: Sean Connolly, *The French Revolution*, Heinemann Library

6b According to Sean Connolly, what was *one* issue France faced after Robespierre was removed from power? [1]

_____

_____

Score ☐

Document 7

... More and more as years go by a feeling of unrest is growing in India. More and more as the people understand their place in the Empire is a spirit of discontent prevading [spreading throughout] its three hundred millions of inhabitants. And more and more as they realise that amid the differences of creed and caste is one basic nationality, does agitation spread and take the form of definite demands for the fulfilment of the solemn assurances of the British Government that they should be given the ordinary rights of British subjects. It is impossible that national aspirations can be for ever repressed, and equally impossible for India to remain a "dependency" in an Empire to which it contributes more than half the population.... Is it then surprising that the teeming millions of India should be dissatisfied with being ruled by a number of too-often self-sufficient and unsympathetic aliens, ignorant of the genius of the people? Not even the "mild" Hindu can bear this for ever. Is it possible for the patriotic spirits of a people with the glorious traditions of India to be content with serfdom?....

Source: Gandhi, *Indian Opinion*, September 2, 1905

7 According to Gandhi, what is **one** issue India was facing in the early 1900s? [1]

_____

_____

Score ☐

Document 8

Source: Y. kids, *Great Figures in History: Gandhi,* YoungJin Singapore

8 Based on this excerpt from a graphic novel, state *one* action Gandhi suggests the Indian people take against the British. [1]

_____

_____

Score ☐

Document 9a

> ... By war's end, Britain was ready to let India go. But the moment of Gandhi's greatest triumph, on August 15, 1947, was also the hour of his defeat. India gained freedom but lost unity when Britain granted independence on the same day it created the new Muslim state of Pakistan. Partition dishonored Gandhi's sect-blind creed. "There is no message at all," he said that day and turned to fasting and prayer....

Source: Johanna McGeary, "Mohandas Gandhi (1869–1948)," *Time*, December 31, 1999

Document 9b

Muslim Refugees Fleeing India, 1947

Source: Mark A. Kishlansky, *Sources of World History: Readings For World Civilization, Volume II*, Wadsworth, Cengage Learning

9 Based on these documents, what was *one* reason Gandhi's greatest triumph was also seen as his defeat? [1]

_____

_____

Score ☐

Part B
Essay

Directions: Write a well-organized essay that includes an introduction, several paragraphs, and a conclusion. Use evidence from *at least four* documents in your essay. Support your response with relevant facts, examples, and details. Include additional outside information.

Historical Context:

> Throughout history, problems emerged that individuals wanted to address. Individuals such as **Bartolomé de Las Casas, Maximilien Robespierre,** and **Mohandas Gandhi** took different actions in their attempts to address problems. Their actions met with varying degrees of success.

Task: Using the information from the documents and your knowledge of global history, write an essay in which you

> Select *two* individuals mentioned in the historical context and for *each*
> - Describe a problem this individual addresses
> - Describe how this individual attempted to address the problem
> - Discuss whether this individual was successful or unsuccessful in solving the problem

Guidelines:

In your essay, be sure to
- Develop all aspects of the task
- Incorporate information from *at least four* documents
- Incorporate relevant outside information
- Support the theme with relevant facts, examples, and details
- Use a logical and clear plan of organization, including an introduction and a conclusion that are beyond a restatement of the theme

This section contains an actual Regents Examination in Global History and Geography that was given in New York State in August 2013.

Circle your answers to Part 1. Write your responses to the short-answer questions in the spaces provided. Write your thematic essay and document-based essay on separate sheets of paper. Be sure to refer to the test-taking strategies in the front of this book as you prepare to answer the test questions.

Part I

Answer all questions in this part.

Directions (1–50): For each statement or question, record on your separate answer sheet the *number* of the word or expression that, of those given, best completes the statement or answers the question.

1 Which feature is considered a natural barrier?

(1) Great Rift Valley
(2) Aswan Dam
(3) Panama Canal
(4) Great Wall of China

2 A library's holdings include the following title: *A Forgotten Kingdom, Being a Record of the results obtained from the excavation of two mounds, Atchana and Al Mina, in the Turkish Hatay.*

Which field of study would have been most responsible for conducting the excavation?

(1) economics   (3) archaeology
(2) sociology   (4) political science

3 Which practice is closely associated with most ancient river valley civilizations?

(1) recording events in cave paintings
(2) using irrigation systems
(3) developing democratic traditions
(4) spreading monotheistic religious customs

4 Which achievement played an important role in pre-Columbian Mesoamerican civilizations?

(1) use of gunpowder
(2) production of corn
(3) domestication of horses
(4) development of sugar plantations

5 One way in which filial piety in Confucian China and citizenship in ancient Athens are similar is that both

(1) emphasized duties and responsibilities in society
(2) encouraged the development of advanced technology
(3) promoted respect for the physical environment
(4) required that legalist principles be followed

Base your answers to questions 6 and 7 on the passage below and on your knowledge of social studies.

… It was during the Arab period, particularly under the Umayyads (756–1031), that Qurtubah [Cordova] enjoyed its prime and grandeur and took its place as the most civilized city in Western Europe. None of the other Spanish historic cities — Toledo, Seville, and Granada — approached it in material prosperity and intellectual attainments. When Christendom was deep in its Dark Ages, Moslem Cordova was rearing men, evolving ideas, writing books, erecting buildings, and producing works of art that constituted a unique civilization. In the West it had one peer in Constantinople and in the East another, Baghdad. At no time before or after did any Spanish city enjoy such distinction….

— Philip K. Hitti, *Capital Cities of Arab Islam*

6 Based on this passage, what is a major criterion used to measure the distinctive civilization found in Cordova?

(1) unique religious beliefs
(2) distance from Baghdad
(3) intellectual achievements
(4) depth of the Dark Ages

7 Which term is best illustrated using this passage?

(1) golden age
(2) divine right
(3) spheres of influence
(4) global interdependence

8 Which group used the stirrup, skilled horsemanship, and siege warfare techniques to conquer much of Asia and part of Europe in the 12th and 13th centuries?

(1) Japanese   (3) Persians
(2) Vikings   (4) Mongols

Base your answer to question 9 on the map below and on your knowledge of social studies.

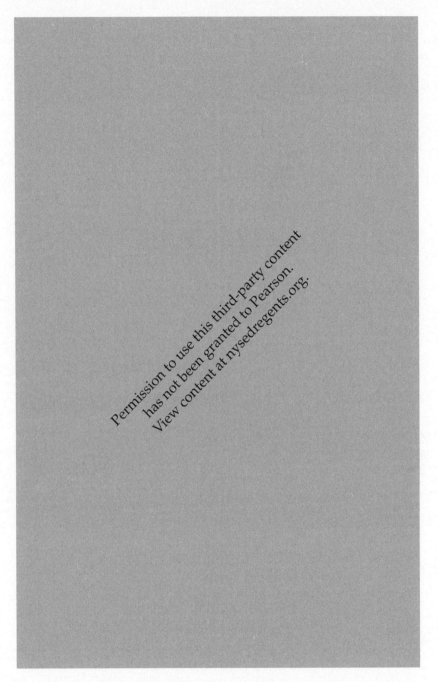

9 Which conclusion can best be inferred from the information on this map?

(1) The peoples of Europe and Southwest Asia were influenced by Eurasian nomads.
(2) Significant amounts of trade took place between Asia and Europe.
(3) African culture was shaped by Asian migration.
(4) The peoples of Southeast Asia migrated to South Asia.

Base your answer to question 10 on the map below and on your knowledge of social studies.

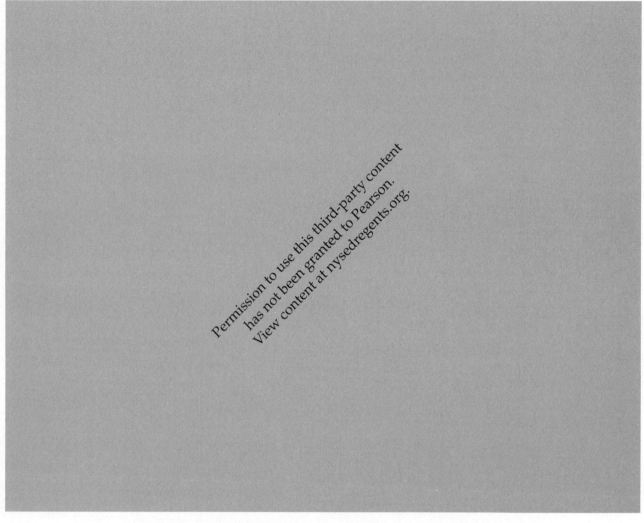

Permission to use this third-party content has not been granted to Pearson. View content at nysedregents.org.

10 Based on the information on this map, which statement is a valid conclusion?

(1) Indian Ocean trade existed before the European Age of Exploration.
(2) African cities were isolated from overseas trade.
(3) The Indian Ocean trade network ended in A.D. 1000.
(4) These trade routes united the Western Hemisphere.

11 Which statement concerning the influence of geography on Japan is most accurate?

(1) Widespread mineral deposits led Japan to industrialize before England.
(2) The lack of natural barriers made it easy to conquer Japan.
(3) Large tracts of arable land made Japan a leading agricultural exporter.
(4) Japan's location allowed selective borrowing from China.

12 Mansa Musa's pilgrimage to Mecca demonstrates that he practiced

(1) animism   (3) Islam
(2) Sikhism   (4) Buddhism

13 Which geographic region made up much of the Ottoman Empire?

(1) Scandinavia
(2) Iberian Peninsula
(3) Indian Subcontinent
(4) eastern Mediterranean Basin

14 During the rise of capitalism in Europe, merchants and bankers began to establish

(1) systems based on bartering
(2) rules that forbid loans to the wealthy
(3) quotas to control production
(4) insurance companies and joint stock companies

15 • Johannes Gutenberg
   • King Henry VIII
   • John Calvin

Which event in European history was most directly influenced by these individuals?

(1) Reconquista
(2) Glorious Revolution
(3) Protestant Reformation
(4) trans-Atlantic slave trade

16 Which situation came *first*?

(1) Spain introduced the encomienda system.
(2) Portugal claimed Brazil.
(3) Spain and Portugal competed for colonies in the Americas.
(4) Columbus arrived in the Caribbean region.

17 The term *mercantilism* is best described as

(1) an economic policy in which a colonial power controls trade
(2) an international policy of laissez-faire economics
(3) a network linking industrialized nations
(4) an exchange of land between nobles

18 Which characteristic is associated with the rule of both Akbar the Great and Suleiman the Magnificent?

(1) promoting equal rights for women
(2) expanding the role of legislative bodies
(3) forcing the conversion of citizens to Christianity
(4) practicing religious tolerance toward members of society

19 Historians frequently portray Louis XIV's construction of the palace of Versailles and Peter the Great's building of the city of Saint Petersburg as

(1) shrines to religious beliefs
(2) monuments to personal rule
(3) examples of colonial architectural influences
(4) efforts to isolate and protect the ruler

20 One way in which the Scientific Revolution and the Enlightenment are similar is that both

(1) led to increased power for royal families in Europe
(2) sought to reconcile Christian beliefs and science
(3) questioned traditional values and past practices
(4) promoted nationalistic revolutions in eastern Europe

Base your answer to question 21 on the passage below and on your knowledge of social studies.

> ... We must ask ourselves three questions.
> 1. What is the Third Estate? *Everything*.
> 2. What has it been until now in the political order? *Nothing*.
> 3. What does it want to be? *Something*. ...
>
> — Abbé Sieyès, 1789 (adapted)

21 Based on this passage, what did the Third Estate want?

(1) independence from France
(2) more influence in the political system
(3) removal of the monarchy
(4) freedom of religion in France

22 Adam Smith's *Wealth of Nations* stressed the importance of

(1) tradition
(2) supply and demand
(3) large corporations
(4) government ownership

23 Which social change occurred during the Industrial Revolution?

(1) growth of the working class
(2) development of the extended family
(3) expansion of privileges for the landed nobility
(4) increased status for religious leaders

24 During the 1800s, many Latin American countries were characterized by a

(1) reliance on cash crops
(2) transition to command economies
(3) redistribution of land to the peasants
(4) withdrawal from the world market

Base your answer to question 25 on the poem below and on your knowledge of social studies.

Colonizer's Logic

These natives are unintelligent —

We can't understand their language.

Chinweizu (Nigeria)
— *Voices from Twentieth-Century Africa*:
Griots and Towncriers

25 The "logic" of the colonizers described in this Nigerian poem reflects their

(1) utopian plan
(2) educational goals
(3) militaristic behavior
(4) ethnocentric attitude

26 Which description of trade patterns best represents the relationship between Africa and Europe during the late 19th century?

(1) Trans-Saharan trade caravans led by Europeans were the most profitable.
(2) South Africa was of no interest to European traders.
(3) Raw materials were shipped from Africa to European industries.
(4) Rivers were the key highways connecting Europeans to much of the African interior.

Base your answer to question 27 on the cartoon below and on your knowledge of social studies.

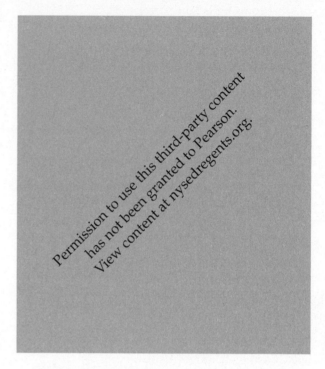

27 This cartoon suggests that political power is often acquired through

(1) the inheritance of land
(2) market demands
(3) religious conversion
(4) the use of technology

28 One way in which the government under Czar Nicholas II of Russia and the government under Benito Mussolini of Italy are similar is that both governments

(1) liberated the serfs and industrial workers
(2) reformed the executive branch by incorporating theocratic principles
(3) established policies of censorship and repression
(4) used televised propaganda to rally the masses

29 The movement to establish a Jewish homeland in Palestine is best known as

(1) Zionism   (3) Marxism
(2) multi-culturalism (4) militarism

Base your answer to question 30 on the cartoon below and on your knowledge of social studies.

THE BOILING POINT.

Source: Leonard Raven-Hill, *Punch*, October 2, 1912

30 This 1912 cartoon depicts

(1) efforts to contain the Boxer Rebellion
(2) tensions in pre–World War I Europe
(3) reactions to the Bolshevik Revolution
(4) responses to the rise of the Weimar Republic

31 A primary objective of the New Economic Policy (NEP) in the Soviet Union was to

(1) promote private ownership of heavy industry
(2) organize support for educational reforms to improve literacy
(3) coordinate efforts to end World War I
(4) gain stability by increasing production

32 Ho Chi Minh and Jomo Kenyatta were leaders of movements that were attempting to achieve

(1) nuclear disarmament (3) pan-Africanism
(2) self-determination   (4) collective security

Base your answer to question 33 on the passage below and on your knowledge of social studies.

… Whatever we may wish or hope, and whatever course of action we may decide, whatever be the views held as to the legality, or the humanity, or the military wisdom and expediency [advisability] of such operations, there is not the slightest doubt that in the next war both sides will send their aircraft out without scruple [hesitation] to bomb those objectives which they consider the most suitable.…

— H. Trenchard, Marshal of the Royal Air Force, 1928

33 This passage implies that the author is

(1) grateful for the availability of new weapons
(2) aware that new weapons have broadened the theater of war
(3) certain that there will be no future wars
(4) anxious about the legality of future military operations

Base your answer to question 34 on the excerpt below and on your knowledge of social studies.

… We have already said that there are only three ways left to Japan to escape from the pressure of surplus population. We are like a great crowd of people packed into a small and narrow room, and there are only three doors through which we might escape, namely, emigration, advance into world markets, and expansion of territory. The first door, emigration, has been barred to us by the anti-Japanese immigration policies of other countries. The second door, advance into world markets, is being pushed shut by tariff barriers and the abrogation [cancellation] of commercial treaties. What should Japan do when two of the three doors have been closed against her? It is quite natural that Japan should rush upon the last remaining door.…

— Hashimoto Kingorō, 1939 Speech

34 The author of this excerpt is presenting an argument for Japan to follow a policy of

(1) self-restraint
(2) isolation
(3) urbanization
(4) economic imperialism

Base your answers to questions 35 and 36 on the cartoon below and on your knowledge of social studies.

**'By Government Decree Every Member of the
Commune Is Entitled to a Private Lot'**

Source: Edmund Valtman, *Hartford Times,* March 9, 1961 (adapted)

35 The main purpose of this 1961 cartoon is to

    (1) criticize Chinese government policy   (3) reinforce Chinese government propaganda
    (2) praise Chinese government leaders   (4) question Chinese government spending

36 The Chinese communes referred to in this 1961 cartoon are most closely associated with the

    (1) Hundred Flowers Campaign   (3) Cultural Revolution
    (2) Great Leap Forward   (4) Four Modernizations

---

37 Which event was the primary reason the United Nations called for a Convention on the Prevention and Punishment of Genocide in 1948?

    (1) Bosnian massacres
    (2) killing fields in Cambodia
    (3) Holocaust
    (4) Hutu-Tutsi conflict

38 In the post–World War II period, which issue is most closely associated with the boundaries created for newly independent African countries?

    (1) expansion of urban centers
    (2) ethnic tensions
    (3) spread of AIDS
    (4) drought-related famine

Base your answer to question 39 on the photograph below and on your knowledge of social studies.

Telephone Kiosk, South Africa

Source: Bentley and Ziegler, *Traditions & Encounters: A Global Perspective on the Past*, McGraw-Hill, 2003 (adapted)

39 Which policy is represented in this photograph?

(1) perestroika   (3) détente
(2) apartheid   (4) extraterritoriality

40 Geopolitics play an important role in the Middle East today because of its

(1) fertile soil and favorable climate for cash crops
(2) navigable rivers and diamond mines
(3) effective natural barriers and high altitude
(4) strategic location and oil resources

41 • Over farming and overgrazing on marginal lands
• Extended droughts in the Sahel region
• Wind erosion of topsoil

These situations have all contributed to

(1) population growth in Southwest Asia
(2) deforestation in South America
(3) desertification in sub-Saharan Africa
(4) increased reliance on fossil fuels in Asia

42 **"Indira Gandhi Becomes Prime Minister of India" (1966)**

"Corazon Aquino Becomes First Elected Leader of Philippines" (1986)

"Benazir Bhutto Becomes Prime Minister of Pakistan" (1988)

These headlines indicate that women as leaders

(1) have gained some political power in traditionally patriarchal societies
(2) have attained key positions in a wide variety of industries
(3) were banned from political roles during the 20th century
(4) were limited to one term in office

43 Which description best fits the Neolithic Revolution?

(1) moving from urban centers to rural centers
(2) using petrochemical fertilizers and pesticides to increase production
(3) replacing human laborers with machines
(4) shifting from hunting and gathering to farming as a way of life

44 What was an important strategy used by both the Romans and the Incas to unify their empires?

(1) building a large network of roads and bridges
(2) using powerful navies to protect sea trade routes
(3) supporting free-market economies by minting silver coins
(4) granting citizenship and voting rights to conquered peoples

Base your answer to question 45 on the graphic organizer below and on your knowledge of social studies.

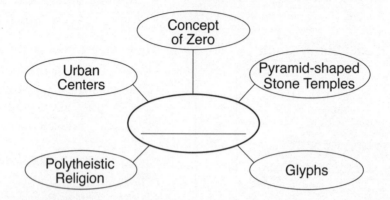

45 What is the best title for this graphic organizer?

(1) Features of Hellenistic Culture
(2) Achievements in Medieval Europe
(3) Developments in Czarist Russia
(4) Characteristics of Maya Civilization

46 A study of the Gupta Empire would include information about

(1) Egyptian conquests
(2) Muslim architectural influences
(3) medical and mathematical achievements
(4) the British East India Company's trading posts

47 • Zheng He's seven voyages are sponsored by the government.
• Corn and peanuts are introduced into the people's diet.
• The Forbidden City is built in Beijing.

Which time period is associated with these statements?

(1) Ming dynasty
(2) Tokugawa shogunate
(3) rule of Kublai Khan
(4) Japanese annexation of Korea

48 The 1453 conquest of Constantinople is an important turning point in global history because it

(1) ushered in Pax Romana
(2) began the Middle Ages
(3) contributed to the rise of the Ottoman Empire
(4) signified the end of the Napoleonic Wars

49 One way in which Karl Marx, Vladimir Lenin, and Fidel Castro are similar is that each believed in

(1) supporting a capitalist system
(2) preserving a rigid social system
(3) spreading the teachings of Christianity
(4) achieving change through revolution

Base your answer to question 50 on the map below and on your knowledge of social studies.

The World in 1930

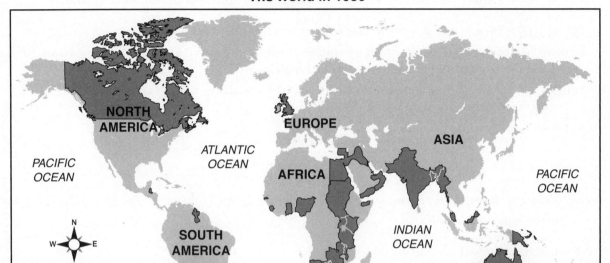

50 What do the *dark-gray* areas on this map represent?

   (1) the British Empire

   (2) countries attending the Congress of Vienna

   (3) newly independent French colonies

   (4) members of the Hanseatic League

Answers to the essay questions are to be written in the separate essay booklet.

In developing your answer to Part II, be sure to keep these general definitions in mind:

(a) **describe** means "to illustrate something in words or tell about it"

(b) **explain** means "to make plain or understandable; to give reasons for or causes of; to show the logical development or relationships of"

(c) **discuss** means "to make observations about something using facts, reasoning, and argument; to present in some detail"

Part II

THEMATIC ESSAY QUESTION

Directions: Write a well-organized essay that includes an introduction, several paragraphs addressing the task below, and a conclusion.

Theme: Change—Political Leaders

> Political leaders have come to power under a variety of circumstances. Once in power, these leaders implemented policies and practices that have affected people, societies, and regions in different ways.

Task:

> Select *two* political leaders and for *each*
> - Describe the historical circumstances that brought this political leader to power
> - Explain *one* policy or practice that was put into effect under this leader
> - Discuss how this policy or practice affected a specific group of people or society or region

You may use any political leader from your study of global history and geography. Some suggestions you may wish to consider include Shi Huangdi in China, William and Mary in England, Napoleon Bonaparte in France, Emperor Meiji in Japan, Vladimir Lenin in Russia, Jawaharlal Nehru in India, Fidel Castro in Cuba, Ayatollah Khomeini in Iran, and Nelson Mandela in South Africa.

You are *not* limited to these suggestions.

Do *not* use political leaders from the United States in your answer.

Guidelines:

In your essay, be sure to
- Develop all aspects of the task
- Support the theme with relevant facts, examples, and details
- Use a logical and clear plan of organization, including an introduction and a conclusion that are beyond a restatement of the theme

NAME _____   SCHOOL _____

Part III

DOCUMENT-BASED QUESTION

This question is based on the accompanying documents. The question is designed to test your ability to work with historical documents. Some of these documents have been edited for the purposes of this question. As you analyze the documents, take into account the source of each document and any point of view that may be presented in the document. Keep in mind that the language used in a document may reflect the historical context of the time in which it was written.

Historical Context:

> *Armed conflict*, *disease*, and *child labor* have affected children throughout the world. Governments, groups, and individuals have attempted to reduce the effects of these global issues on children.

Task: Using the information from the documents and your knowledge of global history, answer the questions that follow each document in Part A. Your answers to the questions will help you write the Part B essay in which you will be asked to

> Select *two* global issues mentioned in the historical context and for *each*
> - Describe the effects of the global issue on children
> - Discuss how governments, groups, and/or individuals have attempted to reduce the effects of this global issue on children

Do *not* make the United States the focus of your essay.

In developing your answers to Part III, be sure to keep these general definitions in mind:

(a) <u>describe</u> means "to illustrate something in words or tell about it"

(b) <u>discuss</u> means "to make observations about something using facts, reasoning, and argument; to present in some detail"

Part A
Short-Answer Questions

Directions: Analyze the documents and answer the short-answer questions that follow each document in the space provided.

Document 1

The Toll of War

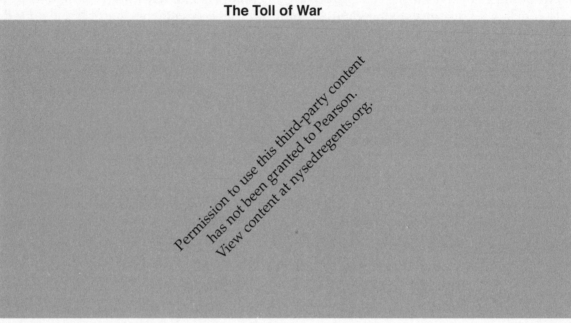

1 Based on the information in this chart, state **one** way a child's life may be changed as a result of armed conflicts. [1]

_____

_____

Score ☐

Document 2

Child Soldiers

To commemorate our 25th anniversary, The Advocates for Human Rights would like to dedicate this issue of Rights Sites News to the abolition of one of the worst forms of child labor, child soldiers. When armed conflict exists, children will almost inevitably become involved as soldiers. In over twenty countries around the world, children are direct participants in war. Denied a childhood and often subjected to horrific violence, an estimated 200,000 to 300,000 children are serving as soldiers for both rebel groups and government forces in current armed conflicts. These young combatants participate in all aspects of contemporary warfare. They wield AK-47s and M-16s on the front lines of combat, serve as human mine detectors, participate in suicide missions, carry supplies, and act as spies, messengers or lookouts.

Physically vulnerable and easily intimidated, children typically make obedient soldiers. Many are abducted or recruited by force, and often compelled to follow orders under threat of death. Others join armed groups out of desperation. As society breaks down during conflict, leaving children no access to school, driving them from their homes, or separating them from family members, many children perceive armed groups as their best chance for survival. Others seek escape from poverty or join military forces to avenge family members who have been killed….

Despite progress achieved over the last decade in the global campaign to end the recruitment and use of child soldiers, large numbers of children continue to be exploited in war and placed in the line of fire. The international treaty on child soldiers, the *Optional Protocol to the Convention on the Rights of the Child on the involvement of children in armed conflict*, entered into force on February 12, 2002. With over 100 countries signed on, this treaty is a milestone in the campaign, strengthening the legal protection of children and helping to prevent their use in armed conflict….

Source: "Child Soldiers Edition," *Rights Sites News*, The Advocates for Human Rights, Spring 2008

2a According to the Advocates for Human Rights, what is **one** problem faced by child soldiers? [1]

_____

_____

Score ☐

b According to the Advocates for Human Rights, what is **one** effort that has been made to keep children, or former child soldiers, from being used in armed conflict? [1]

_____

_____

Score ☐

Document 3

Permission to use this third-party content has not been granted to Pearson. View content at nysedregents.org.

3a What is **one** problem land mines or unexploded ordnance cause for children, according to UNICEF? [1]

_____

_____

Score ☐

b What is **one** effort being made to reduce the effects of land mines or unexploded ordnance, according to UNICEF? [1]

_____

_____

Score ☐

Document 4

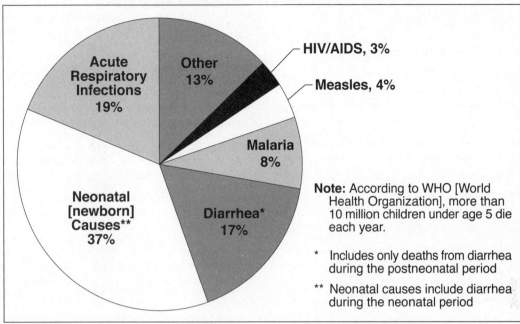

Deaths to Children Under 5, by Cause, 2000–2003

Source: *World Health Report*, World Health Organization, 2005 (adapted)

4 As shown in this World Health Organization chart of children who died under the age of five, identify *one* health issue that caused more than 15% of the deaths. [1]

_____

_____

Score ☐

Document 5

... Millions of children in developing nations die from diseases like pneumonia, measles and diarrhea that claim twice as many lives each year as AIDS. Vaccines prevent these basic illnesses. Bill Gates pledges billions of dollars to vaccinate the world's children. Problem solved. But it's not that easy.

Money alone won't rid dirty water of parasites that can blind and cripple. It won't fix bad roads that keep people from getting care. It won't end the political corruption and violent unrest that erase health advances. It won't stop a population explosion that contributes to poor health. It can't even prevent a rat from gnawing through the power cord of a refrigerator used to store vaccines in a remote West African clinic....

In late 1998, Gates donated $100 million to create a program dedicated to getting new and underused vaccines to children in the poorest countries. A year later, he gave a stunning $750 million to help launch a new superstructure for improving childhood vaccinations, the Global Alliance for Vaccines and Immunization (GAVI)—a coalition of international public health agencies, philanthropists and the pharmaceutical industry....

Gates knows that vaccines can't do it all, not when a regional hospital in Nigeria draws its water from an open pit in the ground. Or where a 6-year-old Ivory Coast boy with a leg twisted by polio faces a life of begging because his mother couldn't afford a trip to a clinic for vaccines. Or where a broken board on a bridge can halt the shipment of medicine for days....

Source: Tom Paulson, "Bill Gates' war on disease, poverty is an uphill battle,"
Seattle Post-Intelligencer, March 21, 2001

5*a* According to Tom Paulson, what is **one** situation that makes it difficult to reduce childhood diseases in developing nations? [1]

_____

_____

Score ☐

b According to Tom Paulson, what is **one** way money donated by Bill Gates has been used to help reduce childhood diseases in developing nations? [1]

_____

_____

Score ☐

Document 6

...Doctors Without Borders/Medecins Sans Frontieres (MSF) [a non-profit medical organization] has witnessed firsthand how a lack of medicine for treatable infectious disease destroys many lives in the developing world. In response, MSF has launched the Access to Essential Medicines Campaign. Introduced in November 1999, the MSF campaign has been working worldwide to find long-lasting solutions to this crisis. The campaign has four main goals: to increase access to certain medicines; to support high quality local manufacture and import of less expensive medicines; to implement and apply international trade rules regarding medicines; and to bring together governments, the pharmaceutical industry, and organizations to focus on investment in, research on, and development of essential medicines for neglected disease....

Source: Catherine Gevert, "A Lack of Medicine," *Faces*, March, 2005

6 What is **one** way Doctors Without Borders/MSF hopes to reduce the occurrence of infectious diseases in the developing world, according to Catherine Gevert? [1]

_____

_____

Score ☐

Document 7

... "Tens of thousands of refugees have fled to urban areas in Pakistan since September 11, [2001], but almost all international assistance and protection efforts are focused on refugees in camps, and the situation for young Afghans in the cities is deteriorating seriously," said Jane Lowicki, Senior Coordinator, Children and Adolescents Project, who visited Pakistan in January. "Many of these refugees and the communities that are struggling to support them are wondering why help promised by the U.S. and other countries has not reached them."

With few alternatives for earning a livelihood, many Afghan refugee parents in urban areas are forcing their children to work in high-risk industries to support the household. "Thousands are carpet weavers, others are street children working as garbage pickers, beggars, brick makers, house servants and, in some cases, drug sellers," Lowicki said. "These young workers are the poorest and most desperate among the Afghan community. Their work exposes them to disease, physical and sexual abuse, and few have access to health services, education or recreation. Their situation has become even more difficult since Sept. 11 because many new young refugees have entered the competition for work, and resources are scarce."

Afghan refugee adolescents and children, some as young as five years old, are working harder than ever for less money. The formerly lucrative carpet weaving industry, for example, which relies heavily on cheap Afghan child labor, bottomed out after Sept. 11; young refugees are now being paid less than half of what they were making to weave carpets for markets around the world.

In many cases, children and adolescents are the primary wage earners for their families, and all of the young Afghan refugees interviewed for the report said they urgently need food, shelter and medical care. They are also eager for a chance to go to school and to learn skills and trades to support themselves through less hazardous work....

Source: "Afghan Refugee Children and Adolescents in Pakistan's Cities Receive Minimal International Assistance," Women's Commission for Refugee Women and Children Press Release, May 30, 2002

7 According to the Women's Commission for Refugee Women and Children, what is **one** problem Afghan refugee children face in Pakistan? [1]

_____

_____

Score ☐

Document 8a

This is an excerpt from a Web-only interview conducted as part of *Enterprising Ideas*, a project of *NOW on PBS*.

RugMark USA

Ten years ago [in 1994], RugMark USA was established to eradicate child labor in the handwoven rug industry. Using a unique "certification" method, RugMark USA has created a model that generates income to finance its programs for children and raises awareness among consumers about the prevalence of child labor. Nina Smith, RugMark USA's executive director, believes the RugMark model could be applied to other industries, including Brazil's shoe industry, India's silk weaving and embroidery sectors and the cocoa industry in West Africa. We talked with Smith about why the RugMark model works and what big challenges the organization is facing....

NOW [host]: Describe RugMark's strategy to change the use of child labor in the industry.

Smith: Our goal is to change the market dynamics so that there is no longer a demand for child labor. If we can educate the marketplace—consumers, interior designers, architects, importers, retailers—about what they can do then ultimately the message is sent to the manufacturers that child labor won't be tolerated—in essence eliminating the demand.

The idea has three components: First, you have to raise awareness and educate people about the problem of child labor and to look for our independently certified child-labor-free rugs. On the ground in South Asia we have an inspection and monitoring system. Companies whose rugs receive the RugMark label agree to random, surprise inspections at their factories or village-based looms....

Source: "RugMark USA," *NOW on PBS: Enterprising Ideas,* July 26, 2007

8a According to Nina Smith, what is **one** way RugMark USA is attempting to end the use of and eliminate the demand for child labor? [1]

_____

_____

Score ☐

Document 8b

This is an advertisement RugMark used in its campaign to raise awareness about carpets and rugs made with child labor.

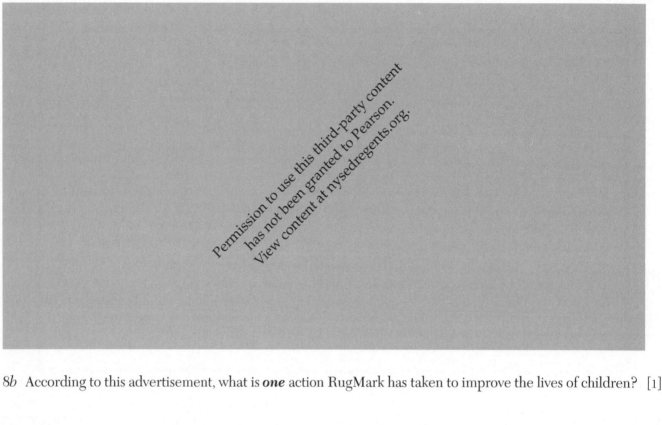

Permission to use this third-party content has not been granted to Pearson. View content at nysedregents.org.

8*b* According to this advertisement, what is ***one*** action RugMark has taken to improve the lives of children? [1]

_____

_____

Score ☐

Document 9

**Give a "Red Card* to Child Labour"
in celebration of the World Day Against Child Labour 2006!**

… The day, which is observed worldwide on the 12th of June, is intended to serve as a catalyst for the growing worldwide movement against child labour, as reflected in the 160 ratifications of Convention No. 182 on the worst forms of child labour and the 144 ratifications of Convention No. 138 on the minimum age for employment. The event on 12 June will be celebrated with the presence of football [soccer] stars that will "kick the ball" against child labour, in a match with girls from the Geneva International School and the Signal de Bernex Football Club. The idea behind the game is that girls and boys should be given the time to study and play, and that child labour and its worst forms symbolically get a "red card". This action is linked to the "Red card to child labour" campaign which since its inception in 2002 has reached thousands of people in all continents. The idea is that the values in football, such as, team spirit, youth empowerment, solidarity among countries, non-discrimination regarding religion, gender and race, are also shared by the ILO [International Labour Organization]. Using the symbol of the Red Card at International football competitions offers the opportunity to spread one simple, universal message over time and benefits from media coverage. Building this kind of strategic alliance is a very good way to reinforce the global movement against child labour.

Source: "Celebration of the World Day Against Child Labour," The International Programme on the Elimination of Child Labour of the International Labour Organization, June 2006

* A red card is issued to remove a player from a game for committing a serious violation.

9 Based on this excerpt from a brochure, what are **two** actions that have been taken to aid in the elimination of child labor? [2]

(1)_____

_____

Score ☐

(2)_____

_____

Score ☐

Part B
Essay

Directions: Write a well-organized essay that includes an introduction, several paragraphs, and a conclusion. Use evidence from *at least **four*** documents in your essay. Support your response with relevant facts, examples, and details. Include additional outside information.

Historical Context:

> ***Armed conflict***, ***disease***, and ***child labor*** have affected children throughout the world. Governments, groups, and individuals have attempted to reduce the effects of these global issues on children.

Task: Using the information from the documents and your knowledge of global history, write an essay in which you

> Select ***two*** global issues mentioned in the historical context and for ***each***
> - Describe the effects of the global issue on children
> - Discuss how governments, groups, and/or individuals have attempted to reduce the effects of this global issue on children

Do *not* make the United States the focus of your essay.

Guidelines:

In your essay, be sure to
- Develop all aspects of the task
- Incorporate information from *at least **four*** documents
- Incorporate relevant outside information
- Support the theme with relevant facts, examples, and details
- Use a logical and clear plan of organization, including an introduction and a conclusion that are beyond a restatement of the theme

This section contains an actual Regents Examination in Global History and Geography that was given in New York State in June 2014.

Circle your answers to Part 1. Write your responses to the short-answer questions in the spaces provided. Write your thematic essay and document-based essay on separate sheets of paper. Be sure to refer to the test-taking strategies in the front of this book as you prepare to answer the test questions.

Part I

Answer all questions in this part.

Directions (1–50): For each statement or question, record on your separate answer sheet the *number* of the word or expression that, of those given, best completes the statement or answers the question.

Base your answer to question 1 on the map below and on your knowledge of social studies.

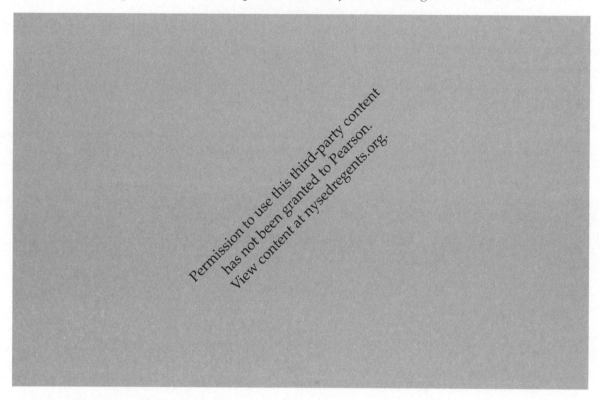

1 Based on the information provided by this map, where did Abraham's journey originate?

   (1) Sahara Desert   (3) Mesopotamia

   (2) Nile River valley   (4) Mediterranean Sea

2 People do not often create records for the benefit of historians. They produce them for other reasons....

             — Chris Hinton, 1998

Based on this statement, historical sources often contain

(1) evidence that can be biased

(2) facts that are completely balanced and reliable

(3) accounts that represent all points of view

(4) summaries that detail research about the distant past

3 Which concept is essential to the study of economic systems?

   (1) self-determination   (3) citizenship

   (2) factors of production (4) human rights

4 Which major geographic feature has hindered cultural diffusion between India and China?

   (1) Himalaya Mountains   (3) Gobi Desert

   (2) Deccan Plateau   (4) Great Rift Valley

5 Which statement about the Bantu migration is an opinion rather than a fact?

(1) The migration occurred gradually over a long period of time.

(2) Language and knowledge spread from northwestern to southern and eastern Africa.

(3) The lack of primary documents makes it difficult to determine the exact cause of the migration.

(4) Bantu civilization was superior to those civilizations that it displaced.

6 Historically, the Huang He has also been known as the "River of Sorrows" because

(1) frozen ports have made trade difficult

(2) cataracts have made transportation impossible

(3) floods have destroyed crops and villages

(4) burials have taken place at the sacred waters

7 Both the Han dynasty and the Roman Empire were known for

(1) developing decentralized political structures

(2) having governments dominated by a merchant class

(3) using examinations to select officials

(4) having long periods of stable government

8 Which belief system is considered monotheistic?

(1) Judaism (3) Confucianism

(2) Shinto (4) animism

9 The Golden Age of India's Gupta Empire is known for its

(1) development of gunpowder

(2) sea trade routes to Europe

(3) acceptance of Christianity as an official religion

(4) advancements in mathematics and medicine

10 Which geographic factor enabled the cities of Nanjing and Mogadishu to develop into powerful trading centers?

(1) location on waterways

(2) abundance of natural resources

(3) predictable rainfall from the monsoon cycle

(4) access to mountain passes

Base your answer to question 11 on the chart below and on your knowledge of social studies.

Objects Discovered off the Java Coast in the 10th-Century Cirebon Shipwreck

- Emerald green Islamic glass
- Chinese porcelain decorated with dragons and birds
- Jeweled gold-plated Arabian ceremonial daggers
- Bronze religious objects with Hindu and Buddhist symbols

11 What does this archaeological find indicate about Southeast Asia during the 10th century?

(1) Religious objects from China were a major import.

(2) Precious gems and metals were exported to Africa.

(3) Europeans dominated East Asian and Middle Eastern trade networks.

(4) The region served as a crossroads between Arab and Chinese traders.

12 Development and expansion of banking, insurance companies, and stock exchanges were essential to the system of

(1) feudalism (3) capitalism

(2) tribute (4) bartering

13 A key feature of European Renaissance culture was

(1) an outlook emphasizing classicism, secularism, and individualism

(2) a reliance on the Pope and his knights to maintain political stability

(3) a shift in production from the domestic system to the factory system

(4) a way of thinking stressing humility and Christian faith

14 Martin Luther, John Calvin, and Henry VIII all played a key role in the

(1) attempts made to reclaim the Holy Land
(2) fall of the Ottoman Empire
(3) end of religious unity in Europe
(4) establishment of parliamentary democracy in Britain

15 The practice of Islam throughout much of West Africa is evidence that

(1) Islam spread beyond the borders of the Arabian peninsula
(2) Chinese trade carried Islamic beliefs to West Africa
(3) Islam originated in West Africa and spread to the Middle East
(4) Europeans encouraged Islamic beliefs during the colonial period

16 Which statement is consistent with the ideas of Niccolò Machiavelli?

(1) Democratic principles should be followed faithfully.
(2) The law should be subject to the will of the leader.
(3) Human rights should be respected in all countries.
(4) Markets should operate with little governmental interference.

17 What was a major cause for the shift in European trade from the Mediterranean Sea to the Atlantic Ocean during the late 1400s?

(1) Ottoman Turks seized control of Constantinople.
(2) The Ming dynasty authorized Zheng He to make long-distance voyages.
(3) The Tokugawa shogunate adopted an isolationist policy.
(4) Christian crusaders captured Jerusalem.

18 The location of the Inca civilization of South America demonstrates the

(1) importance of trade with western Europe
(2) ability of humans to adapt the environment
(3) influence of cultural diversity
(4) complexity of indigenous belief systems

19 Why is Ferdinand Magellan's voyage considered a turning point in world history?

(1) Portugal's claims to southern Africa were established.
(2) His ship was the first to land in the Americas.
(3) One of his ships was the first to circumnavigate Earth.
(4) Britain's control of the seas ended.

20 In the 17th and 18th centuries, the primary goal of mercantilism as practiced by European countries was to

(1) glorify the power and aggressiveness of the military
(2) create laws which guaranteed individual freedoms
(3) teach the natives Christianity and offer them protection in exchange for labor
(4) increase their supply of gold and silver through a favorable balance of trade

21 The impact of the printing press, astrolabe, and caravel on 16th-century Europe demonstrates the ability of technology to

(1) limit which ideas can be transmitted
(2) redefine human understanding of the world
(3) reinforce established traditional beliefs
(4) exploit new sources of energy

22 One way in which Peter the Great, Louis XIV, and Philip II are similar is that each

(1) supported missionary efforts of the Roman Catholic Church
(2) sought to centralize power by limiting the power of the nobility
(3) fought to block the establishment of British colonies in the Western Hemisphere
(4) challenged feudal practices by emancipating serfs

23 New scientific knowledge and understandings that developed during the Scientific Revolution were most often based on

(1) observation and experimentation
(2) church law and faith
(3) superstition and ancient practices
(4) geometric formulas and astrology

24 Which pair correctly links the region where Enlightenment ideas first developed to a region to which those ideas spread?

(1) Asia → eastern Europe
(2) Africa → southeastern Asia
(3) western Europe → the Americas
(4) eastern Africa → India

25 Baron de Montesquieu believed that a separation of powers would

(1) prevent tyranny by acting as a check on power
(2) restore authority to the Roman Catholic Church
(3) increase corruption of political authority
(4) decrease the power of the middle class

26 Which mountains were an obstacle to Simón Bolívar's efforts to unify Gran Colombia?

(1) Alps   (3) Zagros
(2) Andes   (4) Urals

27 • Abundant coal resources
   • Development of steam power
   • Building of an extensive canal system

In the late 1700s, these conditions allowed the Industrial Revolution to begin in

(1) Japan   (3) Russia
(2) Germany   (4) England

28 Laissez-faire practices are most closely associated with a

(1) traditional economy
(2) market economy
(3) command economy
(4) mixed economy

29 As a result of the Russo-Japanese War, Japan came to be seen by Europeans as

(1) a likely area for colonization
(2) the strongest of the imperialist countries
(3) a leader in the movement for nonalignment
(4) an emerging global threat

Base your answer to question 30 on the speakers' statements below and on your knowledge of social studies.

Speaker A: The British East India Company does not respect my beliefs. I cannot follow dharma and remain their soldier. I will return to my family in a Tamil village.

Speaker B: My rebellious countrymen cannot accept my new religion and so they hate me and my "foreign devil" friends. The missionaries leave Beijing tomorrow for England. I must join them before the church compound is surrounded.

Speaker C: The czar's soldiers came again today, looted our village, drove off our livestock, and trampled anyone in their way. They even burned our synagogue. Our way of life is gone. It is time to emigrate to Palestine.

30 What is the primary focus of these speakers?

(1) civil war
(2) economic reforms
(3) religious persecution
(4) colonial oppression

31 Which condition is most closely associated with Mexico between 1910 and 1930?

(1) revolutions and political instability
(2) establishment of a state religion
(3) rapid industrialization by locally owned corporations
(4) widespread support for foreign intervention

32 The difficult, year-long journey made by Mao Zedong and his Communist followers in 1934 through China's mountains, marshes, and rivers was called the

(1) Cultural Revolution   (3) Boxer Rebellion
(2) Great Leap Forward   (4) Long March

Base your answer to question 33 on the map below and on your knowledge of social studies.

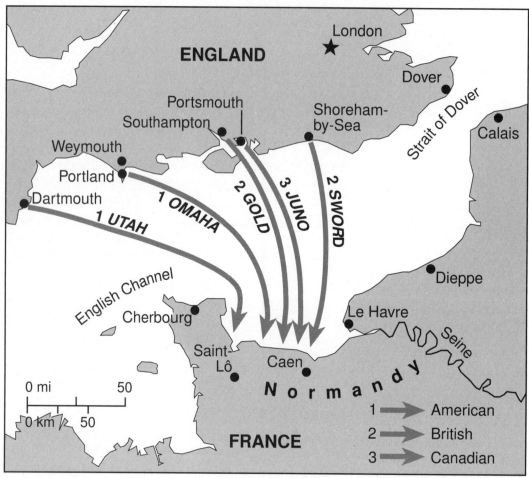

Source: National Geographic Magazine online, 2002 (adapted)

33 The World War II military action shown on this map was significant because it

(1) took the pressure off the war in the Pacific
(2) led directly to the war crimes trials in Nuremberg
(3) caused Germany to resort to unrestricted submarine warfare
(4) forced Germany to fight the Allies on eastern and western fronts

34 Which statement about the Soviet economy under Joseph Stalin is accurate?

(1) The Soviet Union increased its power by developing heavy industry.
(2) The government reduced its role in planning industrial production.
(3) Farmers were encouraged to compete in a free market economy.
(4) A large selection of consumer goods became available in the Soviet Union.

35 In the 1940s, the leadership of the Indian National Congress and the leadership of the Muslim League supported the goal of

(1) helping the British fight World War II
(2) removing British control from the subcontinent
(3) abolishing caste distinctions and discrimination
(4) establishing a unified government based on religious teachings

Base your answer to question 36 on the time line below and on your knowledge of social studies.

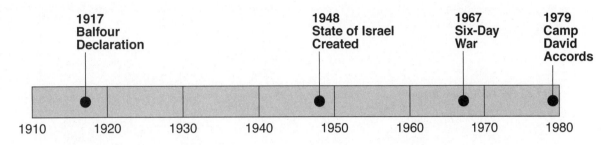

| 1917 Balfour Declaration | 1948 State of Israel Created | 1967 Six-Day War | 1979 Camp David Accords |

1910 1920 1930 1940 1950 1960 1970 1980

36 Which region is directly associated with the events shown on this time line?

(1) Latin America
(2) Middle East
(3) Central Africa
(4) Southeast Asia

Base your answer to question 37 on the cartoon below and on your knowledge of social studies.

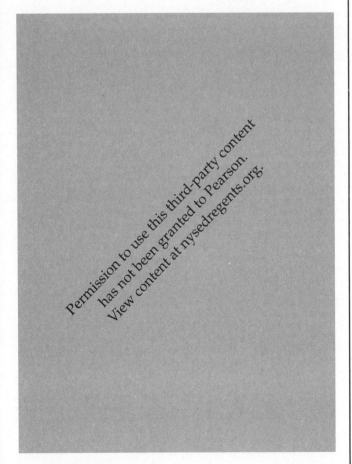

Permission to use this third-party content has not been granted to Pearson. View content at nysedregents.org.

37 Which type of political system is being depicted in this 1943 cartoon?

(1) direct democracy
(2) monarchy
(3) theocratic republic
(4) totalitarian

38 Immediately after World War II, which country exerted political and economic control over Poland, Hungary, and Romania?

(1) France
(2) United States
(3) Soviet Union
(4) Great Britain

39 The main reason oil-producing states formed the Organization of Petroleum Exporting Countries (OPEC) was to

(1) promote foreign ownership of oil fields
(2) lift economic sanctions and establish free trade
(3) improve trade relations with the West
(4) influence the price of oil and set production levels

40 What was a goal of the student protestors in Tiananmen Square in 1989?

(1) independence for Taiwan
(2) removal of troops from South Korea
(3) access to foreign products
(4) democratic reforms

41 What is one way post–World War II North Korea and post–World War II East Germany are similar?

(1) Monarchies were reestablished in both countries.
(2) Democratic principles flourished in both countries.
(3) Both communist governments faced economic stagnation.
(4) Both countries threatened to use chemical weapons against China.

Base your answer to question 42 on the cartoon below and on your knowledge of social studies.

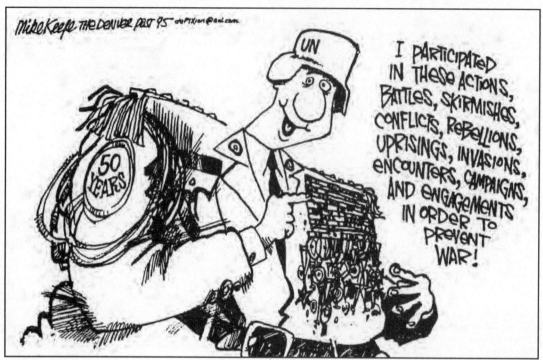

Source: Mike Keefe, *The Denver Post*, 1995

42 The cartoonist's point of view is best expressed in which statement about the United Nations?

(1) Its leadership celebrated its 50th successful military campaign.

(2) It engaged in acts of war as a method of peacekeeping.

(3) It succeeded in its diplomatic efforts.

(4) Its military forces received many awards for their actions.

43 • Tutsis and Hutus in Rwanda
  • Russians and Chechens in southwestern Russia
  • Tamils and Sinhalese in Sri Lanka

In the 1990s, which situation characterized the relationship of the peoples listed for each of these regions?

(1) cooperative political compromise

(2) development of a shared economy

(3) movement toward religious toleration

(4) brutal civil conflict

44 During the 20th century, in which area has deforestation been a significant environmental issue due to the expansion of industrial mining, the growth of corporate farms, and the development of new road networks?

(1) Sahara Desert   (3) Amazon Basin
(2) Tibetan Plateau   (4) Ukrainian Steppe

Base your answer to question 45 on the cartoon below and on your knowledge of social studies.

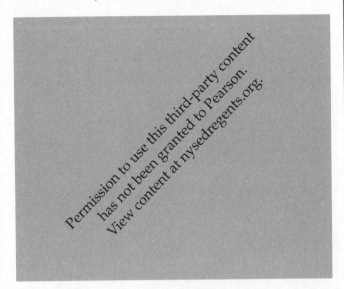

Permission to use this third-party content has not been granted to Pearson. View content at nysedregents.org.

45 The policies of which 20th-century leader helped to create the situation shown in this 2006 cartoon?

(1) Deng Xiaoping   (3) Aung San Suu Kyi
(2) Kim Jong Il   (4) Ho Chi Minh

Base your answer to question 46 on the passage below and on your knowledge of social studies.

...The deposits of fine sediment left by natural floods sustain the fertility of floodplain soils. The 5,000-year history of agriculture in the Nile Valley and delta of Egypt depended on the annual Nile River flood that left a veneer of new silt over the valley floor each year. Modern dams on the Nile — particularly the Aswan High Dam, which can store the entire annual flood — have destroyed the natural system of fertilization, necessitating huge imports of artificial fertilizers....

— Oberlander and Muller, *Essentials of Physical Geography Today, Second Edition*, Random House, 1987

46 Based on this passage, a valid conclusion would be that

(1) natural fertilizers are less effective than artificial fertilizers
(2) technological advances sometimes create unforeseen problems
(3) yearly flooding is harmful to Egyptian agriculture
(4) farmers in the Nile Valley operate at a subsistence level

Base your answer to question 47 on the passage below and on your knowledge of social studies.

... I, John of Toul, make known that I am the liege man of the lady Beatrice, countess of Troyes, and of her son, Theobald, count of Champagne, against every creature, living or dead, saving my allegiance to lord Enjorand of Coucy, lord John of Arcis, and the count of Grandpré. If it should happen that the count of Grandpré should be at war with the countess and count of Champagne on his own quarrel, I will aid the count of Grandpré in my own person, and will send to the count and the countess of Champagne the knights whose service I owe to them for the fief which I hold of them. But if the count of Grandpré shall make war on the countess and the count of Champagne on behalf of his friends and not in his own quarrel, I will aid in my own person the countess and count of Champagne, and will send one knight to the count of Grandpré for the service which I owe him for the fief which I hold of him, but I will not go myself into the territory of the count of Grandpré to make war on him....

47 In which period of western European history was the relationship described in this passage most common?

(1) Neolithic   (3) Medieval
(2) Classical   (4) Napoleonic

48 During the feudal period of Japanese history, the emperor had mainly symbolic authority. Which statement best explains the reason for this situation?

(1) Power had been granted to shoguns and daimyos.
(2) Communist guerillas had destabilized domestic political institutions.
(3) A democratic constitution prevented the emperor from centralizing authority.
(4) American occupation forces had undermined the belief in the emperor's divinity.

Base your answers to questions 49 and 50 on the images below and on your knowledge of social studies.

Image A: Inca

Image B: Ireland

Permission to use this third-party content has not been granted to Pearson. View content at nysedregents.org.

Source: John Reader,
Potato: A History of the Propitious Esculent,
Yale University Press

49 Which generalization is best supported by these images?

(1) Potatoes have been a key source of food for diverse populations at various times.
(2) The Inca produced more potatoes than any other civilization in history.
(3) The only crop Irish women and children produced was potatoes.
(4) Potatoes could only be grown in mountainous regions.

50 Which historical event connects the activity shown in Image *A* to the activity shown in Image *B*?

(1) opening of the Silk Road trade
(2) Columbian exchange
(3) formation of the Hanseatic League
(4) establishment of trans-Saharan trade

Answers to the essay questions are to be written in the separate essay booklet.

In developing your answer to Part II, be sure to keep these general definitions in mind:

    (a) <u>describe</u> means "to illustrate something in words or tell about it"

    (b) <u>discuss</u> means "to make observations about something using facts, reasoning, and argument; to present in some detail"

Part II

THEMATIC ESSAY QUESTION

Directions: Write a well-organized essay that includes an introduction, several paragraphs addressing the task below, and a conclusion.

Theme: Change—Challenges to Tradition or Authority

> Throughout history, individuals have challenged established traditions and authorities. Their efforts have inspired or influenced change and have met with varying degrees of success.

Task:

> Select *two* individuals who have challenged tradition or authority and for *each*
> - Describe the established tradition or authority as it existed before it was challenged by the individual
> - Discuss how the individual challenged established tradition or authority
> - Discuss the extent to which change was achieved as a result of this challenge

You may use any individual from your study of global history and geography. Some suggestions you might wish to consider include Martin Luther, Galileo Galilei, Mary Wollstonecraft, Toussaint L'Ouverture, Charles Darwin, Vladimir Lenin, Emiliano Zapata, Mohandas Gandhi, Ho Chi Minh, Nelson Mandela, Mikhail Gorbachev, Aung San Suu Kyi, and Wangari Mathaai.

You are *not* limited to these suggestions.

Do *not* choose an individual from the United States or Gavrilo Princip from the Balkan States for your answer.

Guidelines:

    In your essay, be sure to
    - Develop all aspects of the task
    - Support the theme with relevant facts, examples, and details
    - Use a logical and clear plan of organization, including an introduction and a conclusion that are beyond a restatement of the theme

NAME _____   **SCHOOL** _____

Part III

DOCUMENT-BASED QUESTION

This question is based on the accompanying documents. The question is designed to test your ability to work with historical documents. Some of these documents have been edited for the purposes of this question. As you analyze the documents, take into account the source of each document and any point of view that may be presented in the document. Keep in mind that the language used in a document may reflect the historical context of the time in which it was written.

Historical Context:

> Turning points are events that result in regional and worldwide change. Three turning points that transformed societies and regions were the ***outbreak of the bubonic plague,*** the ***signing of the Nanjing Treaty,*** and the ***assassination of Archduke Ferdinand.***

Task: Using the information from the documents and your knowledge of global history, answer the questions that follow each document in Part A. Your answers to the questions will help you write the Part B essay in which you will be asked to

> Select ***two*** turning points mentioned in the historical context and for ***each***
> - Describe the historical circumstances surrounding this turning point
> - Discuss changes that occurred within a society and/or region as a result of this turning point

In developing your answers to Part III, be sure to keep these general definitions in mind:

(a) <u>describe</u> means "to illustrate something in words or tell about it"

(b) <u>discuss</u> means "to make observations about something using facts, reasoning, and argument; to present in some detail"

Part A
Short-Answer Questions

Directions: Analyze the documents and answer the short-answer questions that follow each document in the space provided.

Document 1

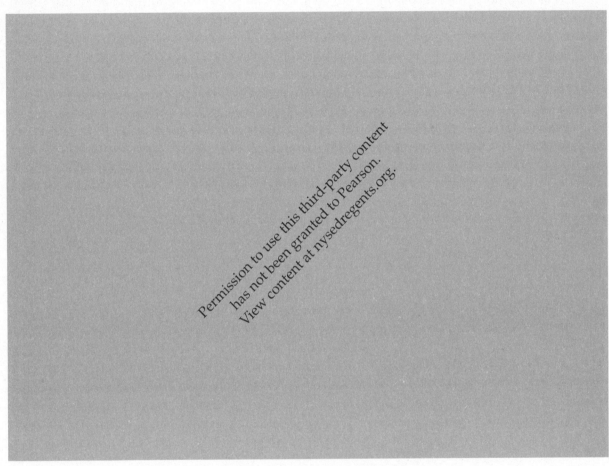

1 Based on the information on this map, what activity contributed to the spread of the Black Death? [1]

_____

_____

Score ☐

Document 2

In this excerpt, William H. McNeill discusses the interpretation of historical evidence to explain how the plague was spread. He suggests that available evidence makes it unlikely that the plague was found in China before 1331.

> ...By contrast, after 1331, and more particularly after 1353, China entered upon a disastrous period of its history. Plague coincided with civil war as a native Chinese reaction against the Mongol domination gathered headway, climaxing in the overthrow of the alien rulers and the establishment of a new Ming Dynasty in 1368. The combination of war and pestilence [disease] wreaked havoc on China's population. The best estimates show a decrease from 123 million [in] about 1200 (before the Mongol invasions began) to a mere 65 million in 1393, a generation after the final expulsion of the Mongols from China. Even Mongol ferocity cannot account for such a drastic decrease. Disease assuredly played a big part in cutting Chinese numbers in half; and bubonic plague, recurring after its initial ravages at relatively frequent intervals, just as in Europe, is by all odds the most likely candidate for such a role....

Source: William H. McNeill, *Plagues and Peoples,* Quality Paperback Book Club (adapted)

2 According to William H. McNeill, what was **one** way the plague affected China after 1331? [1]

_____

_____

Score ☐

Document 3

Social and Economic Effects of the Plague in Europe

The plague had large scale social and economic effects, many of which are recorded in the introduction of the *Decameron*. People abandoned their friends and family, fled cities, and shut themselves off from the world. Funeral rites became perfunctory [superficial] or stopped altogether, and work ceased being done. Some felt that the wrath of God was descending upon man, and so fought the plague with prayer. Some felt that they should obey the maxim [saying], "Eat, drink, and be merry, for tomorrow you may die." The society experienced an upheaval to an extent usually only seen in controlled circumstances such as carnival [festival]. Faith in religion decreased after the plague, both because of the death of so many of the clergy and because of the failure of prayer to prevent sickness and death....

Source: "Plague," *Decameron Web,* Brown University (adapted)

3 According to this article, what was **one** effect of the plague on European society? [1]

_____

_____

Score ☐

Document 4

> ...The Chinese had long been opposed to the opium trade. The drug had been introduced into China by Dutch traders during the seventeenth century. As early as 1729, there were imperial decrees forbidding the sale and smoking of this "destructive and ensnaring vice." In 1796, Jiaqing, the new emperor, placed a complete ban on its importation, but he was a weak administrator and soon pirates and opium merchants were bribing officials to look the other way. By 1816, the [British] East India Company had imported 3,000 chests of opium from its poppy fields in the north Indian state of Punjab. By 1820, this had risen to 5,000 and by 1825 to almost 10,000.
>
> As more and more Chinese became addicts, and silver flowed out of the economy to British coffers, the Chinese government moved toward confrontation. The emperor Daoguang, who came to the throne in 1821 was a reformer, and, supported by his advisor Lin Zexu (1785–1850), the emperor banned opium in 1836 and ordered the decapitation of "foreign barbarians" who concealed and traded the drug....

Source: Perry M. Rogers, ed., *Aspects of World Civilization: Problems and Sources in History, Volume II,* Prentice Hall
(adapted)

4a According to Perry Rogers, what was **one** reason the Chinese were unsuccessful in halting the opium trade? [1]

_____

_____

Score ☐

b According to Perry Rogers, what was **one** effort made by the Chinese to halt the European trade in opium? [1]

_____

_____

Score ☐

Document 5

The Treaty of Nanjing was signed by Great Britain and China following the Opium War (1839–1842).

An Excerpt from the Treaty of Nanjing

ARTICLE III.

It being obviously necessary and desirable, that British Subjects should have some Port whereat they may careen and refit their Ships, when required, and keep Stores for that purpose, His Majesty the Emperor of China cedes [gives] to Her Majesty the Queen of Great Britain, etc., the Island of Hongkong, to be possessed in perpetuity [forever] by Her Britannic Majesty, Her Heirs and Successors, and to be governed by such Laws and Regulations as Her Majesty the Queen of Great Britain, etc., shall see fit to direct.

Source: "Treaty of Nanjing (Nanking), 1842," USC-UCLA Joint East Asian Studies Center

5 What did the British gain as a result of the Treaty of Nanjing? [1]

_____

_____

Score ☐

Document 6a

THE REAL TROUBLE WILL COME WITH THE "WAKE."

Source: Joseph Keppler, *Puck*, August 15, 1900 (adapted)

Document 6b

6 Based on this 1900 Joseph Keppler cartoon and the information on this map, state **one** problem China faced after the Treaty of Nanjing took effect. [1]

_____

_____

Score ☐

Document 7a

The Eastern Question and the Balkans

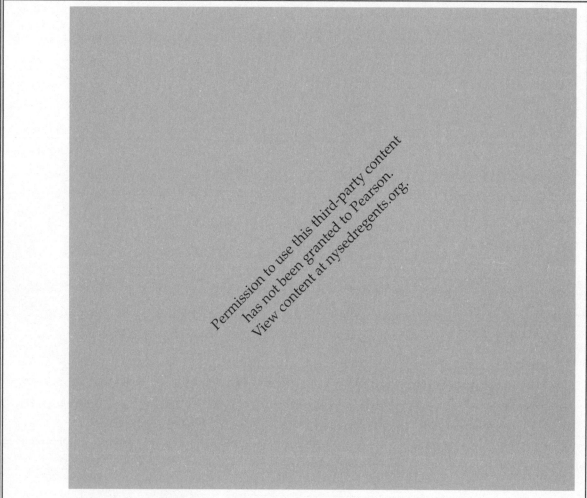

…As a result of the Balkan Wars (1912–1913) Serbia had doubled in size and there were growing demands for the union of south Slavs (Yugoslavism) under the leadership of Serbia. Austria had a large south Slav population in the provinces of Slovenia, Croatia, the Banat and Bosnia. Austria was very alarmed at the growing power of Serbia. She [Austria-Hungary] felt Serbia could weaken her [Austria-Hungary's] own Empire.

The Austrians decided that they would have to wage a preventative war against Serbia in order to destroy her growing power. They were waiting for the correct pretext (excuse). When Franz Ferdinand was shot, the Austrians saw this as the perfect opportunity to destroy Serbia. But when she [Austria-Hungary] attacked Serbia, Russia came to her [Serbia's] aid and the war spread.…

Source: Stephen Tonge, "Causes of the First World War," A Web of English History online (adapted)

7a According to Stephen Tonge, what was **one** cause for tension between Austria and Serbia? [1]

_____

_____

Score ☐

Document 7b

This is an excerpt of the testimony given by Gavrilo Princip reprinted in *The Sarajevo Trial*. He was accused of assassinating Archduke Ferdinand of Austria-Hungary and his wife in July 1914.

The Hearing of Gavrilo Princip
12 October 1914
In the Afternoon

> ...Pr. [Prosecutor]: — Call Gavrilo Princip. (He is brought in.) Do you consider yourself guilty?
>
> Acc. [Accused, Gavrilo Princip]: — I am not a criminal, because I destroyed that which was evil. I think that I am good....
>
> Pr.: — What kind of ideas did you have?
>
> Acc.: — I am a Yugoslav nationalist and I believe in the unification of all South Slavs in whatever form of state and that it be free of Austria.
>
> Pr.: — That was your aspiration. How did you think to realize [accomplish] it?
>
> Acc.: — By means of terror.
>
> Pr.: — What does that signify?
>
> Acc.: — That means in general to destroy from above, to do away with those who obstruct and do evil, who stand in the way of the idea of unification.
>
> Pr.: — How did you think that you might realize your objectives?
>
> Acc.: — Still another principal motive was revenge for all torments which Austria imposed upon the people....
>
> Pr.: — What was the feeling about Austria in your circles?
>
> Acc.: — It was the opinion that Austria behaved badly to our people, which is true, and certainly that she (Austria) is not necessary....

Source: W. A. Dolph Owings et al., eds., *The Sarajevo Trial, Volume I,* Documentary Publications

7b Based on this excerpt from *The Sarajevo Trial*, what was **one** goal of Gavrilo Princip?   [1]

_____

_____

Score ☐

Document 8a

British Training Poster

Source: W. G. Thayer, 1915,
Library of Congress,
Prints and Photographs online catalog

Document 8b

German Trenches, ca. June 16, 1916

Source: Library of Congress, Prints and Photographs online catalog

8 Using information from these images, state **one** impact Gavrilo Princip's assassination of Austria-Hungary's Archduke Ferdinand had on European countries. [1]

_____

_____

Score ☐

Document 9

Source: Abraham and Pfeffer, *Enjoying World History*, AMSCO
(adapted)

9 Based on these maps, what was **one** change to the political boundaries of Europe that occurred after World War I? [1]

_____

_____

Score [ ]

Part B
Essay

Directions: Write a well-organized essay that includes an introduction, several paragraphs, and a conclusion. Use evidence from *at least four* documents in your essay. Support your response with relevant facts, examples, and details. Include additional outside information.

Historical Context:

Turning points are events that result in regional and worldwide change. Three turning points that transformed societies and regions were the **outbreak of the bubonic plague,** the **signing of the Nanjing Treaty,** and the **assassination of Archduke Ferdinand.**

Task: Using the information from the documents and your knowledge of global history, write an essay in which you

Select **two** turning points mentioned in the historical context and for **each**
- Describe the historical circumstances surrounding this turning point
- Discuss changes that occurred within a society and/or region as a result of this turning point

Guidelines:

In your essay, be sure to

- Develop all aspects of the task
- Incorporate information from *at least four* documents
- Incorporate relevant outside information
- Support the theme with relevant facts, examples, and details
- Use a logical and clear plan of organization, including an introduction and a conclusion that are beyond a restatement of the theme